THE
LEGISLATIVE
PROCESS
IN THE
UNITED STATES

THE
LEGISLATIVE
PROCESS
IN THE
UNITED STATES

MALCOLM · E · JEWELL
University of Kentucky

&

SAMUEL · C · PATTERSON
University of Iowa

RANDOM HOUSE· New York

FIRST PRINTING

© *Copyright, 1966, by Random House, Inc.*

All rights reserved under International and Pan-American Copyright Conventions. Published in New York by Random House, Inc., and simultaneously in Toronto, Canada, by Random House of Canada Limited

Library of Congress Catalog Card Number: 66-12535

Manufactured in the United States of America by The Haddon Craftsmen, Scranton, Pennsylvania

DESIGN BY ANITA KARL

PREFACE

WE ARE living in an executive-centered world, a world of presidents and governors, prime ministers and premiers, kings and potentates. They dominate our political communication, our discourse, and our imagination. They are the prime foci of our electoral struggles; they are credited with the creation of the great public policies by which we live; they negotiate the questions of peace and war; to a very considerable extent, they set the policy agendas for legislatures, and, for that matter, for all public institutions.

This has not always been so. The seventeenth century produced the doctrine of legislative supremacy, and in parts of the Western world this doctrine was to be found in practice during the eighteenth and nineteenth centuries. The classical notion that legislatures have the task of making broad public policy, which the executive and the courts enforce, was a matter of common practice during the early decades of the American republic. But in the twentieth century the broad outlines of public policy tend to be formulated by executives. The policy-making process of the American national government now depends indispensably upon the President. He and the bureaucracy that is at least nominally under his command create the principal elements of public policy, and his program becomes the agenda for Congress. At the state level, the governor's program is usually, if not always, the central feature of the legislative process. The modern democratic legislature has become a response-oriented institution. It responds not only to the electorate organized into constituencies, but also to the executive, upon whom it necessarily depends.

The modern legislature may be more than ever subordinate to and dependent upon the executive, but it is nonetheless an important institution in a democratic political system. While the legislature is far less independent of the executive than it was in simpler times, legislative and executive activities are interdependent, and the legislature can check, frustrate, delay, reject, and modify the policy extensions and inventions of the executive. What is perhaps more important, the legislature provides a critical connecting link between the people and the bureaucracy. Explanation of this linkage, of the functions of legislative systems and their instrumental activities, is a fundamental part of political science.

Legislative analysis ought ultimately to accomplish at least three tasks of explanation: it ought to be descriptive of the structure and functions of a particular legislative system at a point in time; it ought to be developmental, explaining behavioral patterns over historical time; it ought to be comparative, testing explanations that are apparently adequate for one legislative system against those of others. Success in any one of these tasks of explanation depends upon success in the others. In this book we have sought to describe, develop, and compare a set of legislative systems for one society, the United States. We have taken as our universe of legislative systems those for which the national and state legislatures are the central nuclei. Every legislative body is, in a variety of ways, unique. A science of legislative systems utilizes structural-functional analysis, developmental analysis, and comparative analysis to identify uniformities in patterns of legislative behavior. Explanation of the unique can often be immensely important in the analysis of uniformities of behavior. The United States Congress is unique in many ways; it is, after all, the only national legislature in the country. There are fifty state legislative systems, with many variations among them that are important and deserve careful attention. Yet these legislative systems, embedded in a culture that is remarkably even across the land, exhibit far more similarities than differences, and comparative analysis makes it possible to investigate both. It would be foolhardy to assert that Congress is not significantly different from the state legislatures, or that the legislatures of California and New York are not different from those in Nevada and South Dakota, but this is no reason to neglect the marked advantages of comparative treatment.

If these comments are taken as prefacing a definitive analysis of American legislative systems, the reader will be disappointed. Our book is an exercise in taking stock of meager knowledge in the face of the overwhelming task of learning that lies ahead. We regard it as an interim report, not as an authority to provide absolutes for teaching. No one is more clearly aware of its flaws than we are. The research available about American legislatures is slim indeed, although it is rapidly growing. In some chapters we have had, of necessity, to rely principally upon data about Congress, while in others research about state legislatures is more fully developed. There is almost no theory about legislative behavior to provide limits to the number and variety of relevant variables for analysis. We have tried to be systematic where that has been possible, but we have often had to proceed by example when systematic analysis did not exist. Our book raises as many questions as it provides tentative answers, and urges new research as much as it uses old.

Yet we feel that there is much to be said for taking stock of legislative research now, however imperfect it is. A field of study can be improved by trying to organize it and beginning to theorize about it. We have adopted the general approach of structural-functional systems analysis as the principal mode of our analysis, and outlined it in the first two chapters. We have utilized this scheme as a peg on which to hang our analysis, but we have not attempted to select only those kinds of research that fit the scheme. Our paradigm calls for research that has not yet been done, and where our chart did not indicate our course, we have used dead reckoning. We proceed to describe and explain significant aspects of the process and product of legislative recruitment, dealing with geographical problems, the mechanism of election, and the attributes of those who are selected. We then move to the legislative institution itself, its organization, structures of leadership, bureaucracy, and procedures. We look at three sets of participants in legislative systems who are not legislators—lobbyists, executives, and constituents. We next examine the legislature as a normative system, describing legislative norms and roles. Then, we view the legislature as a system of action, examining the activities of roll call voting, committee work, and legislative oversight. Finally, we conclude with a brief exposition of reforms proposed for legislatures in America, and a prospectus for legislative behavior research.

We have synthesized a wide range of legislative research, adding some new analysis and reorganizing the old, and frequently relying upon fragmentary data or isolated studies with complete awareness of their limitations. This sort of synthesis thus constitutes a guideline and incentive for future research rather than an encyclopedia of established truths.

Our indebtedness to the many whose research we have used and to publishers who have given us permission to make use of quotations is evident in the footnotes. We wish to thank Hugh Douglas Price and Robert L. Peabody, who read the entire manuscript, and several persons who read and commented on specific chapters: Charles O. Jones, Warren Miller, Duncan MacRae, Jr., Thomas A. Flinn, Duane Lockard, Vernon Van Dyke, and Gerald Maryanov. Several persons have permitted us to read and utilize manuscripts not yet in print or have provided data beyond that included in published articles. The shortage of factual data on state legislatures led us to send questionnaires to one or more authorities—mostly political scientists—in many of the states. In collecting data on party organization, committee structure, procedures, and governors, we were heavily dependent on their generous contributions of time and knowledge. Anne Dyer Murphy provided editorial help and encouragement that are equally appreciated.

Our major indebtedness is intramural; the help from our wives
ranged from the tangibles of typing and proofreading to the intangibles
of encouragement and patience. Finally we note that this book is a joint
venture in its entirety; the authors are solely and equally responsible.

M. E. J.
S. C. P.

Lexington, Kentucky
Iowa City, Iowa

CONTENTS

FIGURES

TABLES

[Part I]

THE LEGISLATIVE SYSTEM

THERE ARE a number of ways in which we might conceptualize, analyze, or describe legislative institutions and the activities that surround and penetrate them. The traditional literature about legislatures shows an emphasis on the descriptive: legislative institutions were viewed largely as lawmaking machines, and described principally in terms of their constitutional powers and responsibilities, their organizations, and their procedures.

More recent analytical literature about legislative bodies has focused upon the policy process, adding to the mechanical emphasis of the older treatments an analysis of some of the "outside" forces impinging upon legislative decision making. The rediscovery of political interest groups in the immediate pre-World War II period marks the beginning of the development of case studies in legislative analysis with this kind of focus.

In the last few years, political scientists have adopted a more socio-logical perspective on legislative behavior, seeking to understand legisla-tive institutions in the context of a more inclusive legislative *system*—embedded in, reacting to, and affecting the wider political system. It is this general perspective that we adopt in this book. We cannot ignore legislative traditions, history, organization, and formal procedural rules, because these are important factors in the behavior of legislators. Nor can we ignore the importance of legislative policy-making processes. Legisla-tive enactments have important social, political, and economic con-sequences; therefore, we must seek to understand and explain the under-lying processes by which such enactments are made.

The conceptualization set forth in the two chapters that follow is not complete, or even entirely adequate. It does not include within its purview all the things we think it is important to say about legislative processes in the United States. It does constitute a step toward a more comprehensible conceptualization of American legislative behavior, and it does help both to synthesize the accumulated research on the legislative process and to make for a more systematic prospectus for further re-search and theory development. We present these chapters in a modest and tentative spirit: they display our point of view; they provide reference points for the substantive chapters in the remainder of the book, and independently, they constitute a kind of pretheory of legislative systems.

[I]

Legislative Functions

THE LEGISLATOR is a universal political leader in our political system, and his work is fundamental to any understanding of the processes of policy formation. Legislative systems and processes are familiar phenomena in the American polity. Legislative behavior takes place at all levels of government—national, state, county, municipal, school district. The focus of this volume is on the legislative process in Congress and in the fifty state legislatures. Local legislative bodies differ in many ways from those at the state and national level, and not enough research has been done on them to discover the uniformities that would make possible a comparative analysis of all levels of legislative activity.

This volume has a distinct institutional focus, because we believe that the behavior of legislators cannot be understood apart from the institutional or structural setting in which that behavior takes place. The legislature is a highly institutionalized human group, with timeworn traditions and practices that affect the attitudes and behavior of the men and women who enter its chambers. But the legislative system is more than a collection of formal rules, procedures, and organizational units. It is a social system, in which individuals interact in terms of normative expectations derived from both within and outside the legislature itself. The legislature is a group of individuals whose behavior as elected representatives is given both flexibility and restraint by the obligations and expectations imposed upon members by the system.

THE LEGISLATIVE SYSTEM

We have used the terms legislature, legislative system, and legislative process, and they require definition.[1] The *legislature* may be defined simply as those individuals who are elected as members of the formal legislative bodies prescribed by national and state constitutions. There are other political actors who have some part in the legislative process and who often interact with legislators. These others include lobbyists, constituents, the executive and his spokesmen, administrative agents, political party leaders, staffs and other expert groups, and so forth. When we refer to the legislative system, we are referring to these individuals

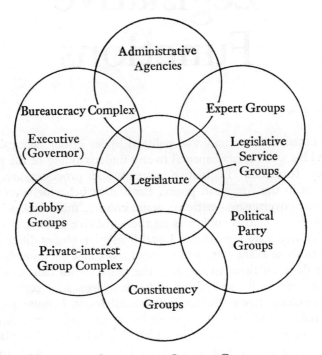

Figure 1.1. LEGISLATIVE SYSTEM CONFIGURATION

and groups outside the legislature as well as to the legislators themselves. The total legislative-system configuration is represented in Figure 1.1.

Although it is easy to understand why each of these actors might be described as part of the legislative system, it is also obvious that each of them engages in some activities that have no legislative significance. Political party leaders are not a part of the legislative system when they are running a campaign for county offices, nor is the Agriculture Department when it advises farmers on better methods for growing crops, nor is the lobbyist for an association of bicycle manufacturers when he is engaged in a promotional campaign aimed at the consumer. Most constituents are far too busy earning a living, killing their crabgrass, and watching television to be more than minimally engaged in the legislative system.

If we want to encompass the entire legislative system in our study, which of the activities of these outside actors must we include? To answer this, we must define our system more precisely. A *system* consists of a number of individuals who interact with each other in a situation that may lead to the achievement of some goal or set of goals defined in terms of culturally structured and shared symbols.[2] Thus Easton conceptualizes the political system in general as constituted by the multiplicity of social interactions involved in the policy-making process oriented toward the authoritative allocation of values for a society.[3] The keys to defining a system are the terms *interaction* and *goals*. Those who are outside the legislature enter the legislative system when they are interacting with legislators, sometimes when they are interacting with other outsiders—*and* when the purpose of this interaction is related to the legislative process. The lobbyist is a part of the legislative system when he calls on a congressman or when he writes to constituents in his organization urging them to write their congressman. The President is acting within the legislative system when he stresses at a cabinet meeting the necessity of clearing all patronage appointments with appropriate members of Congress. The county party chairman is an actor in the legislative system when he seeks a campaign contribution from a trucking official who wants legislation raising weight limits on the highways.

Most of these actors are also identifiable with other systems, such as the executive or bureaucratic, the electoral, and the judicial. In the strictest sense, all of these are subsystems of the general political system. It is obvious that they overlap and that for purposes of political analysis there may be various ways of defining and delineating these systems.[4] Moreover, the political system is not complete within itself but is a component in the general social system that we define as society. The problems of defining and distinguishing various systems may become quite technical and complex, but our purpose in defining the legislative system is quite simple. If the broad dimensions of the legislative system are recognized, it becomes clear that the range of our study must be much broader than the confines of the legislative chambers, that it must extend to all those with some interest in influencing what the legislature does.

A distinction must be made between the legislative system and the more common term, the *legislative process*. The legislative process refers to movement in the legislative system from one point in time and space to another. Although the notion of process is dynamic and has to do with the general process of social change, the legislative system may be viewed at one point in time in terms of its structure and functions. The term *legislative behavior* refers to the actions and the reciprocal expectations of the individuals in the legislative system. When we discuss legislative process or behavior, we do not mean to include lawmaking only in the sense in which it has been used in the traditional literature of political science.[5] Legislative groups perform a variety of activities that are not strictly lawmaking nor policy-making in character; at times, lawmaking may be only a subsidiary activity. But each of these activities can be expected to serve some purpose for the polity.

FUNCTIONS OF THE LEGISLATIVE SYSTEM
FOR THE POLITY

If you were to ask a number of legislators what the purpose of the legislature is, you might get a variety of answers: "Our job is to pass laws." "We have to represent the people." "It's all a matter of compromising the different interests." Each answer would be correct, but none would be complete. A very substantial part of legislative activity is directly related to the mechanical operation of enacting legislation. This is what the spectator sees from the galleries, what the lobbyist seeks to influence, and what is reported day by day in the press. The making of laws is of interest to the political scientist who wants to analyze the strategy of participants, the reasons for passage or failure of a bill, or the substantive content of legislation. A considerable portion of this book deals directly with the process of lawmaking. In the traditional division of power among the legislative, executive, and judicial branches of government, the task of lawmaking belongs to the legislature. Only in the most formal sense, however, is this a realistic way of distinguishing the work of the legislature from that of other parts of government. Administrative decisions, often formalized and published as orders and rules, constitute another part of the "law." The contribution of the judiciary to lawmaking includes common law, the interpretation of statutory law, and constitutional law. Moreover, if we define the legislature's task exclusively as lawmaking, how can we explain the fact that most bills are drafted by executive departments or by pressure groups?

We cannot adequately distinguish the legislative system from others, nor can we fully comprehend the purposes of the legislative system, if we focus our attention solely on lawmaking. We must try to "get behind" the manifest activity of legislative systems in order to understand their functional consequences for the polity. What functions does the legislative system perform that contribute to the maintenance of the political system?[6] We shall define the functions of the legislative system in broad terms as the *management of conflict* and the *integration of the polity.*[7] Defined as such, these are obviously functions performed by all components of government. As we define these functions more exactly, we can show how legislative systems perform them in practice, as distinct from the performance of these functions by other political systems.

Conflict Management. A legislative system is deeply involved in the problems of maintaining order, of attempting to assure a relatively high degree of stability in political relationships, and of creating and sustaining substantial equilibrium in the polity. In pluralistic societies, group conflicts are characteristic phenomena. Whenever human associations proliferate and people raise conflicting claims to scarce status, power, and resources, some techniques for resolving conflict are essential. In such cases, a primary task of government is to provide various arenas in which such conflicts can be resolved.

One of the major functional consequences of the legislative system is the management of political conflict. Other political subsystems—both the administrative and the judicial—share this function. In the legislative systems of this country, these conflicts are most characteristically resolved by some form of compromise. The technique of compromise is used by executives and even by judges; it is not unique to the legislature. But the legislative system may be distinguished by the extent to which compromise, as a mode of conflict resolution, is institutionalized in the system.

We speak of the legislative function as being the management of conflicts; it is not necessarily their resolution, because in a sense few political decisions are final. Boulding, for instance, has observed that

In one sense, in a successful political process all decisions are interim. We live in a perpetual state of unresolved conflict. A decision is a partial resolution of conflict. It should never be a complete resolution. The majority does not rule; a majority decision is simply a setting of the terms under which the minority continues the discussion—a discussion which presumably goes on forever or at least for the lifetime of the organization.[8]

There are at least four ways in which the legislative system contributes to the management of conflict: the *deliberative*, the *decisional*, the *adjudicative*, and the *cathartic*. Often the legislature deliberates without making a decision in the positive sense of taking action. But the process of deliberation itself, and the rules under which deliberation takes place, contribute to the reconciliation of divergent interests. When the legislature makes a decision, deliberation facilitates acceptance and thus holds conflict to a minimum. "The chief function of debates," according to Truman, "is as a part of the process of adjustment," and "formal debates facilitate acceptance of the final decisions, not necessarily by the immediate participants but by those on the periphery."[9]

Deliberation in the legislative system is not confined to formal de-

bate on the floor nor are the participants limited to members of the legislature. Deliberation may be carried on in the hearing rooms, the offices
of legislators, or in the lobbies and cloakrooms surrounding the chambers.
These informal modes of deliberation are sometimes the more important
ones, but the formal procedures for deliberation serve the purpose of
ensuring that there will be time and opportunity for a variety of interests
and viewpoints to be heard. The rules and procedures that permit hearings and extensive debate are among those that facilitate deliberation. It
is noteworthy that one of the most frequent criticisms of state legislatures
is that they do not permit adequate deliberation. Sessions are often brief,
hearings infrequent, debate sketchy, and the majority very strong in the
legislature. If the only purpose of the legislative system were lawmaking,
this kind of criticism would be pointless. It is symptomatic of the essential
part the legislative system plays in managing conflict that, if the legislature becomes a rubber stamp or a law factory, there may be no other
arena in which adequate deliberation is possible.

Legislative decisions are both tentative and likely to represent compromises that have been reached after deliberations among legislators and
other relevant participants in the legislative system. Latham has described
the process:

> Every statute tends to represent compromise because the process of
> accommodating conflicts of group interests is one of deliberation and consent.
> The legislative vote on any issue tends to represent the composition of
> strength, *i.e.*, the balance of power, among the contending groups at the
> moment of voting. What may be called public policy is the equilibrium
> reached in this struggle at any given moment, and it represents a balance
> which contending factions or groups constantly strive to weigh in their
> favor.[10]

Latham proceeds to point out, however, that in this process of the
resolution of conflict, "the legislature does not play the inert part of
cash register, ringing up the additions and withdrawals of strength, a
mindless balance pointing and marking the weight and distribution of
power among the contending groups," but that a legislature is itself a
group with an identity of its own, composed of members who themselves
have a multiplicity of group identifications.

Furthermore, both legislative deliberation and decision making are
likely, because of their functional place in the process of compromise, to
be diffuse and ambiguous. We are indebted to Truman for pointing out
that:

> The imperative of compromise among groups, between group demands
> and the "rules of the game," explains . . . the ambiguity of many legislative
> formulas. But ambiguity and verbal compromise may be the very heart of

a successful political formula, especially where the necessity for compromise is recognized but is difficult to achieve in explicit terms. Ambiguity may postpone or obviate the necessity for a showdown and as such has an important political function.[11]

In effect, the equivocal nature of much of what goes on in legislative systems tends to prevent the polarization of many issues; this equivocation therefore serves as a mechanism for resolving conflicts.

Frequently the decisional routines of American legislatures involve little else than the ratification, often by unanimous vote, of decisions effectively made by other structures in the legislative system. Interest group leaders or local officials, for example, may make agreements which they bring to the legislature for approval. In such cases, the legislative body merely ratifies or registers a reconciliation of conflicting interests made at an earlier stage in the decisional process, and perhaps arrived at entirely outside the legislature itself.

A variety of legislative structures facilitate the resolution of conflict in legislative systems. Dual partisanship in many legislative bodies provides the structure for contending forces; where two-party competition does not prevail, as is the case in many American states, bifactional or multifactional rivalry may be at least a partial substitute for partisanship in terms of providing structure for conflict and its resolution. We shall assess the partisan and factional structure of American legislatures in Chapter 8 and at the roll call voting stage in Chapter 17. Both within and without the legislature proper, political interest groups constitute divisive elements; we consider their representatives in detail in Chapter 12. As the conflicts confronting the legislature have become more complex, the executive has increasingly taken the initiative in proposing ways to resolve these conflicts, a process described in Chapter 13. In some legislative systems the vigor and effectiveness with which the executive has played this part have led to criticisms that the legislature has lost its share in decision making. But legislative authority to make decisions remains unquestioned. Specialization and division of labor in the legislative system facilitate the resolution of conflict. The committee structure of a legislature involves a specialization of tasks, and the tendency to accept the specialists' judgments contributes to conflict reduction. Legislative committees are dealt with in both Chapters 9 and 18. Finally, the rules of the legislature, both written and unwritten, are not neutral in the reconciliation of conflicting interests. Controversies over principles and issues are often converted into conflicts over means and thus more readily resolved. Truman has suggested how much of the conflict in legislatures focuses on struggles over procedures, technical rules of debate, the power to limit debate, committee assignments, calendars, timetables, and the like.[12] With reference to the use of the legislative calendar as a focal point for the resolution of intermediate conflicts, for instance, Bentley has observed that "most bills that become laws do so after a fight with other bills for space on the calendar, rather than after a fight with an opposition of a more direct kind."[13] Again, other rules of an unwritten kind, such as the seniority rule for the selection of committee chairmen, tend to remove areas of potential contention from the realm of conflict altogether.

Essentially adjudicative routines are frequently performed by American legislatures. Much of the private-bill process in the national Congress is largely adjudicative in nature, in the sense that individual grievances (conflicts between individuals and the authorities) are settled thereby. Similarly, the work of some legislative committees has been essentially adjudicative, as when hearings before investigating committees have in effect been trials, during the course of which sanctions have been applied.

A final mechanism for the facilitation of conflict resolution in the legislative system is the cathartic or safety-valve mechanism. This can be demonstrated with reference to a variety of legislative structures. The public hearing, for example, can be a cathartic mechanism—"a quasi-ritualistic means of adjusting group conflicts and relieving disturbances through a safety-valve."[14] In a public hearing the spokesmen for conflicting interests have an opportunity to "let off steam," and to get their complaints, arguments, and pleas "out of their system." And legislators, at a public hearing or during floor debate, may do the same. The legislature cannot accede to the demands of all interests, sometimes not even partially, but it can grant these interests a hearing—perhaps not obtainable elsewhere—and this hearing can be an important factor in the management of conflict. To discover the consequences of shutting off this safety valve, we have only to recall the demonstrations in the streets of Southern cities by Negroes who had been unable to obtain not only the policies they sought but even a hearing in state or local legislative systems.

Integration. The legislative system serves to integrate the polity by providing support for it. Any political system is subject to stress. Groups that are dissatisfied with the way in which conflicts have been resolved may become alienated from the system and unwilling to accept the political decisions emanating from it. Ultimately, this is the path to revolution. Unless ways can be found to provide support for the political system, the demands that are placed upon it can "not be satisfied or conflicts in goals composed."[15] The legislative system functions so as to engender a spirit of loyalty or patriotism, but it also provides support in a more immediate sense—as, for example, when interest group leaders endorse legislative programs and voters select legislators at the polls. An equally important contribution of the legislative system is to provide support to the executive and judicial systems, thereby contributing directly to the integration of the polity. We can distinguish three closely related ways in which the legislative system contributes to the integration of, and support for, the entire political system: *authorization, legitimation,* and *representation.*

One of the characteristics of a written constitution is the specific delegation of formal authority to various components of government. In American constitutions the legislative branch is given various kinds of authority over the executive branch. One of the most important of these is the budgetary process, through which the legislature authorizes the executive to collect taxes and expend funds. The earliest English parliaments were summoned by monarchs to authorize the collection of taxes because these monarchs were seeking support for their regimes. The battle cry of the American Revolution—"No taxation without representation"—was simply a negative statement of the principle that legislative authorization of taxation functions to provide support for a political system. In a variety of other ways the legislature authorizes the executive to act: to reorganize itself, to select its major officials, to regulate the economy. Authorization also involves legislative oversight of bureaucratic activity, which is discussed in Chapter 19. Lowi has contended that in this oversight the modern legislature engages in its most important activity—"as a place where the needs of the bureaucracy are continually being balanced against the prevailing special interests in the community."[16] If this is the most important task, it is one that is not being fully performed by many state legislatures, and this failure could contribute to the relatively low level of support accorded to some state governments by the public. Similarly, legislative systems in the United States confer authority upon the courts, authorizing them to assert jurisdiction, creating their organizational machinery, and qualifying their members.

The legislative system functions for the integration of the political system, not only by authorization but by legitimation. The constitutional and traditional base of the legislature, and the orderly procedures that it follows, make legislative action appear legitimate; it has the quality of rectitude. It is regarded by the public as right and proper. When the legislature gives other agents of government permission to act (that is, when others are authorized to exercise power), their exercise of authority is legitimized in the process (that is, they have the right as well as the power to act). The importance of this function can be illustrated by the consequences that follow when Congress questions the legitimacy of governmental actions. When congressmen question the right of the Supreme Court to adjudicate certain topics, such as legislative apportionment, or when a committee or one house of Congress approves legislation to withdraw a subject from the Court's jurisdiction, the result is to weaken popular support for the Court, even though its legal authority remains unchanged. In a similar sense the courts not only invalidate some legislative acts, but also strengthen the appearance of legitimacy, and consequently public support, for most pieces of legislation.

The legislative system contributes to the support of the polity by virtue of its representative character. Legislators are the spokesmen for, and are empowered to act for, constituencies as a result of the legitimacy of their selection as representatives. But the pervasiveness of the representative role goes beyond the legislative body itself. Other participants in the legislative system—the lobbyist, the administrative agency, the chief executive, the party leader—play representative roles. The legislative system is a system of interaction, in which individuals are expected to act for their clienteles. The legislator represents a geographically designated group of individuals, although he may act for wider interests as well. The lobbyist represents interests and associations, often economic, which may be nationwide. The executive represents the political forces that are at least temporarily dominant in the polity as a whole. The administrative agent represents a segment of the bureaucracy, and often its wider clientele as well. The party leader represents the controlling elements of the political organization at the electoral level. Representation provides the channels for and mediates the interaction among the many participants in the legislative system.[17] Legislative acts have authority and are regarded as legitimate in part because of the representative quality of the system. The nature of representation in the legislative system is explored in more detail in the next chapter.

Historically and traditionally it is the legislature that has provided support for the political system through representation. But as modern government has grown more complex, elaborate techniques for representing interests have been developed within the administrative agencies, and even in the courts. Compared with the administrative system, the legislative system has established more traditional methods of formal representation and a more elaborate network of informal representation, but the techniques are common to both because an urban, industrial society requires representation at many levels.

Some of the most severe criticisms of state legislatures and Congress pertain to the inadequacy of their representation, a problem described in Chapter 3. Although the techniques of apportionment affect only the formal aspects of representation, these have a critical effect on the access to the legislators of other participants in the legislative system. At both the state and national level, it has been argued by some, the executive and the judicial systems have provided more adequate representation than the legislative system has.[18] It is true that groups that have been denied effective representation in the legislative system, such as urban dwellers and Negroes, have turned to the executive and judicial systems, both of which have often been more accessible to them.

FUNCTIONAL MAINTENANCE OF THE LEGISLATIVE SYSTEM

We have described the functions of the legislative system for the polity—the contributions that it makes toward preserving the political systems in the nation and in the states. What are the requirements for maintaining it as a viable system that will support the entire political system? The legislative system in a democracy, like the democratic political system of which it is a part, does not live a charmed life; it is capable of collapse. There are many examples of legislative systems abroad that have collapsed, and in so doing have usually brought about the collapse of the entire political system. The legislative systems in the United States, though varying in effectiveness, have remained viable. Why? What characteristics have made this possible? In attempting to catalogue and analyze the functional requisites of a legislative system, we run some risks. More research and more theoretical analysis are necessary before it becomes clear what aspects of the system may properly be described as essential to its preservation. But this technique offers a useful, if incomplete and tentative, approach to the understanding of legislative life.

Recruitment. A legislative system, to develop and persist, must establish mechanisms for the recruitment and selection of personnel. Obviously, a legislative system cannot exist without members. The extensive knowledge available about the selection of legislators is summarized in Chapters 3, 4, and 5. The recruitment mechanisms for American legislators involve apportionment (allocation of seats), districting (territorial demarcation), and election. These mechanisms have nonrandom political effects, which are summarized in Chapter 5. Our analysis deals only with the legislators themselves. We cannot deal thoroughly with the recruitment of others involved in the legislative system (lobbyists, party leaders, executives, etc.), partly because for some almost nothing systematic is known about their selection, and partly because our analysis would then be unmanageable in size.

Communication. Channels of communication have to be available, if a legislative system is to be maintained. A communications network must exist. In the legislative system, such networks are highly complex and highly differentiated as to form. Our knowledge of the internal and external communications channels that characterize legislative systems is very limited, fragmentary, and unsystematic. Our analysis deals with communication obliquely in terms of structure, where the exposition is concerned with legislative organization and procedure in Part III, more directly in terms of strategy, where we discuss pressure groups and executive leadership in Chapters 12 and 13, and specifically, though impressionistically, where we deal with legislator-constituent and legislator-lobbyist communication in Chapters 14 and 12.

Normative Regulation. A legislative system must have enforceable, sanctioned standards of proper conduct by which participants are expected to abide. Legislative norms must exist which regulate the means of taking action and affective expression and control disruptive forms of behavior. The formal, written rules of procedure provide one set of norms, a set which must be known before legislative behavior can be understood. Legislators abide by the rules; they can be and are punished for violating them. The rules also have significant political effects, and are thus part of the strategy of political conflict. We deal specifically with the written rules in Chapter 11. The unwritten rules of the game, however, are frequently of equal importance to an interpretation of legislative life. They govern when the written rules can be violated in the pursuit of system-goals, and they prescribe, proscribe, and prohibit action in the legislative system beyond the formal rules. These unwritten but highly institutionalized rules are treated in Chapter 15.

Integration of Subsystems. A legislative system must integrate adequately its subsystems and the systems related tangentially to it. While the standards of adequacy are not fully known, it is clear that the parts must work together. The legislature is usually the central arena wherein the internal integration of the system is accomplished. It is very doubtful, for instance, whether the American legislature could operate adequately without minimal cooperation from lobbyists, the executive, party leaders, significant constituents, judges, and bureaucrats. Such individuals belong to the legislative system when they play roles related to legislative action. Similarly, the internal subsystems of the legislature itself, i.e., committee structure and party organization, must be minimally integrated. The practical and theoretical problems involved in an analysis of this function are great. We shall develop the present knowledge in this connection sporadically in the following pages, and shall particularly endeavor to demonstrate the meshing of forces from the point of view of the legislative product in Part VI.

Shared Goal Orientation. It does not seem likely that a legislative system could exist unless its participants shared a goal or set of goals. The goal orientation of the legislative system may be crucial to the distinction between it and other political subsystems. It may be said that the principal goal orientation of a legislative system is the resolution of group conflicts. As Bentley observed many years ago, "If we take these legislative bodies as they stand today, we shall find in all of them group oppositions which form the body and soul of their activity."[19] Other observers of the legislative system in action make similar comments. For instance, the whole orientation of Gross's study of the legislative system is around the concept of the legislative "struggle," and he refers to the legislative process as "combat on the legislative terrain."[20] The conflicts in legislative systems over differing instrumental goals provide the substantive content of legislative processes, but the resolution of conflict itself is characteristic of the legislative system. The sharing of goals among participants, e.g., the resolution of conflict, may be said to be functional for the maintenance of the system. The resolving of conflict itself has wider significance, and we shall deal with it momentarily.

Role Allocation. Allocation of roles is requisite for the maintenance of a legislative system. We shall develop the available knowledge on legislative role differentiation and assignment in Chapter 16. However, so fundamental to our whole analysis of American legislative systems is the role concept that it must be expanded at some length in this introductory chapter.

The term *role* first came into general usage in the social sciences as a result of the theoretical work of the anthropologist Ralph Linton.[21] In its simplest form the role concept is a theoretical analogy to the parts that actors play in a drama, although of course in a Shakespearean play the dramatic actors read fixed lines, whereas social roles are more flexible and less clearly defined. For the purpose of this analysis, a role is defined by the total pattern of expectations, including the person's own expectations, having to do with the "tasks, demeanors, attitudes, values and reciprocal relationships" that the actors have with respect to a position in the social structure.[22] A role "is defined by what others expect of the person filling it," as well as by what the individual expects he ought to do as the occupant of a position.[23]

A distinction must be made between role, which is defined by the expectations of individuals, and *role behavior*, which refers to the actual behavior or performance of specific individuals as they play their roles.[24] It is clear, for instance, that actors in a system may have certain expectations about the nature of proper behavior in particular positions in the structure of the system, and yet specific individuals may add to, subtract from, or otherwise transform the expected pattern of behavior in their actual role performance.

Roles are inexorably related to the social norms that prevail in particular social structures.[25] The norms of a social group, the "ought" behaviors that group members come to expect, are to a considerable extent organized around roles. Thus roles will consist of the expected rights, duties, and obligations of occupants of positions in the structure of a system.

Although it is difficult to discuss the role concept except in relation to positions in the social structure, it should not be assumed that each position has associated with it one and only one specific role. In complex social structures a particular position will involve a whole set of behaviors, which are more or less expected of individuals occupying that position. Thus, for instance, the father in a family has a given position in the family structure, but may behave differently in his role with respect to a teen-age daughter, an adult son, and the baby in the family.

Position is a static abstraction, which refers to "a place in a structure, recognized by members of the society and accorded by them to one or more individuals."[26] Obviously, an individual occupies positions in a variety of social structures; that is, he holds multiple positions.[27] A role, on the other hand, is dynamic. Linton first defined role as "the dynamic aspect of status."[28] It refers to the expected behavior of occupants of a position, though "not to all their behavior, as persons, but to what they do as occupants of the position."[29] In this way the concept of role provides the link between the individual personality and the social system of which he is a part.[30]

Roles have mutual and reciprocal implications. The majority floor leader and the rank-and-file member have similar—but not identical—perceptions of the leader's role. Moreover, the viewpoints of each concerning the leader's role affect their respective attitudes concerning the legislator's role as a member of the legislative party. We may define the pattern of expected role behavior in a social structure as a system, but this means neither that there is perfect harmony among all the participants in a system concerning their roles, nor that we can expect to comprehend fully or describe completely the entire pattern of roles.[31]

The participants in a system may differ in their role expectations concerning a legislator, a lobbyist, or some other occupant of a given position. There may be widespread agreement that certain kinds of behavior are prohibited by the norms in the system, or that other behavior is required. In still other cases, the expected behavior may simply be preferred. For example, in a legislative system, acceptance of a bribe from a lobbyist may be flatly prohibited by legislative norms (as well as by law), yet accepting certain favors from lobbyists may be frowned on by some legislators and tolerated by others. If there is too much difference in the viewpoints of participants concerning norms and roles, the resulting confusion and misunderstanding can be dysfunctional for the system.[32]

In an analysis of legislative behavior, role can be used as a basic unit of analysis. The role concept is also central to the problem of defining the boundaries of the legislative system, which may be said to be the limits of the legislative role system. Although it must be pointed out that political subsystem boundaries are likely to be vague, and will usually be a "shading off" rather than a clear-cut line of demarcation, the limits will tend to be defined between actors who play system roles and actors who do not.[33]

Actors in the legislative system are susceptible to *role conflict*. This "refers to the situation in which incompatible demands are placed upon an actor because of his role relationships with two or more groups."[34] A legislator may be a member of an organized interest group in his constituency, a political organization in his constituency or state, or a series of groups in the legislature, including the House, a party group in the House, legislative committees, voting blocs, or even a national party.[35] In each of the organized groups to which the legislator belongs, he may play a variety of roles. Groups with which the legislator identifies, but in which he does not actually have membership, may be *reference groups* for him. A reference group is a comparison group, a group to whose norms the actor refers for his behavior.[36] Either membership or nonmembership groups may be reference groups for the legislator, but "functioning in terms of a reference group that is different from the group in which one is participating physically is especially well-illustrated by the behavior of political representatives."[37]

The role expectations—the rights, duties and obligations associated with the roles—of a legislator in the variety of groups of which he is an interacting member, or the norms of groups that are reference groups for him, may be conflicting. It has been suggested that the resolution of political conflict in the legislative system is related to the extent of role conflict.[38]

A variety of institutional mechanisms may be employed by the legislator in an attempt to integrate or reduce role conflicts. He may invoke a hierarchy of role obligations, and avoid sanctions by employing an equally high or higher claim. He may assert that the conflict was an accident, that circumstances beyond his control prevented his playing the approved role. He may take refuge in the legislative rituals of etiquette, tact, or procedure, which will tend to reduce social frictions. He may employ a segregation of roles by repudiating his role in one group, playing off one group against another, stalling until pressures subside, redefining his role or roles, leading a double life, absenting himself from the field when conflict approaches, or, in some extreme cases, becoming physically or mentally ill.[39]

Again, the legislator may reduce role conflicts by compromise or bargaining.[40] Compromise appears to be a characteristic mechanism for role-conflict reduction by those who play the legislative role. The legislator, as a leader "whose control depends upon successful bargaining," tends, according to Dahl and Lindblom,

To have attitudes toward the control process substantially different from those of other American leaders, like those in business and administration, whose control depends upon a successful use of hierarchy. Probably the role both attracts and shapes the men who play it. . . . In any case the role calls for actions such as compromise, renunciation, face-saving of oneself. . . .[41]

Further, it seems likely that there are some norms shared by actors in the legislative system which "serve to rank the relative importance of various roles or spheres of behavior, thus serving to mitigate potential conflicts between inconsistent role definitions."[42] Such norms link the reference group behavior of legislators to their roles and role conflicts.

We have far from complete knowledge of legislative role systems, and can by no means fulfill the specifications for analysis suggested in these paragraphs. We have begun to accumulate specific data, however, and we shall see in Chapter 16 some of the concrete role allocations in several American legislative systems.

Socialization.   A legislative system must have formal or informal mechanisms, or both, for the socialization of members. Participants have to learn how they ought to behave, what are the written and unwritten rules of the game, and what are the potentialities and limitations of their roles. We shall deal only briefly with the socialization processes (Chapters 5 and 14), which political scientists and political sociologists are only beginning to investigate. The problem of socialization for the legislative system becomes most visible and acute with respect to the incorporation of new members into the legislative body, although socialization strains may be just as difficult for the initiate lobbyist, the new President or governor, or the bureaucrat.[43]

When the legislator enters the legislative system, he enters a new group, which has time-honored norms, and he faces the necessity of learning new roles. The new legislator must undergo a socialization process in order to learn the role system of which he is to be a part. In several state legislatures a formal training period is held prior to the legislative session so as to begin the socialization of new members.[44] It is true that "the tyro who reaches the capitol breathing fire after a vigorous campaign soon finds that he can accomplish nothing until he learns how to get along with his colleagues."[45]

Wilson, in his classic treatise on Congress, suggested that the socialization process for new legislators is very difficult for them. He contended:

The newly-elected member, entering its (the House) doors for the first time, and with no more knowledge of its rules and customs than the more intelligent of his constituents possess, always experiences great difficulty in adjusting his preconceived ideas of congressional life to the strange and unlooked-for conditions by which he finds himself surrounded after he has been sworn in and has become a part of the great legislative machine. No man, when chosen to the membership of a body possessing great powers and exalted prerogatives, likes to find his activity repressed, and himself suppressed, by imperative rules and precedents which seem to have been framed for the deliberate purpose of making usefulness unattainable by individual members. Yet such the new member finds the rules and precedents of the House to be. It matters not to him, because it is not apparent on the face of things, that those rules and precedents have grown, not out of set purpose to curtail the privileges of new members as such, but out of the plain necessities of business; it remains the fact that he suffers under their curb, and it is not until "custom hath made it in him a property of easiness" that he submits to them with anything like good grace.[46]

Shared Meanings. In order for a legislative system to operate and to maintain itself, the individuals who are involved must tend to "see things" in about the same way. More than a minimum level of knowledge is required; the participants must share meanings and have the capacity to understand one another in the legislative situation. For a variety of reasons, legislatures seem to be characterized by a high degree of shared cognition among a very high proportion of their participants, a characteristic that becomes clear when the high degree of *morale* is observed in legislative groups. "It is pleasurable," writes Gosnell, "to be with one's own kind," and so "legislators draw together in their misery of exposure to the populace."[47]

Because legislators, and others in the legislative system, tend to define situations in about the same ways, legislative bodies tend to develop "styles of life," characteristic climates or atmospheres.[48] Some legislative bodies, notably the United States Senate, are usually solemn, deliberate bodies. They function on the basis of traditionally established norms of decorum and etiquette. At the other extreme, perhaps, is the kind of atmosphere McKean found in the New Jersey legislature in the late 1930s. He describes the turmoil in the following way:

A visitor going to the State House in Trenton some Monday night to observe the legislature in session would be struck by the crowds of men in the corridors, most of them in small groups of five or six, talking earnestly and smoking furiously. On an average evening there are about two hundred of these men, and perhaps twenty-five women. Some of them are political hangers-on, some are public employees, some are politicians from different parts of the state, but the greater part of them is composed of representatives of various state associations. The visitor would notice that they congregate thickest near the doors of the Assembly and Senate chambers, where many of them seem to be trying to get inside. . . .

By the time the legislature convenes at eight-thirty o'clock the floor of the house is packed with people, all talking vigorously. The clamor is deafening. In the confusion each legislator who is present is surrounded by men and women, all trying to convince the man of the soundness of their views. Some thrust printed or mimeographed material into his hands or pile it on his desk.

When the Clerk begins to call the roll most of them have to leave the floor. A few manage to stay by having press passes, by being former members, or simply by avoiding the sergeant-at-arms until he has made his rounds.[49]

No doubt most legislative groups operate in an atmosphere of considerably more solemnity than that described by McKean. The architecture of the buildings, the floor plan and furnishings, and the other accoutrements of the situation tend to make the legislature a solemn body most of the time. Even so, legislative groups have their "off" days, when humor and horseplay break the monotony of a long session.

Another aspect of legislative atmosphere is that of morale. Generally speaking, legislators are more like each other than like their constituents in education, dress, age, social class, and so forth. The claims that are made on the new legislator by his other group memberships must be adjusted to those of the legislative group. This adjustment is at least partially strengthened and facilitated by the morale of the legislative body. "The morale of legislative groups is often marked," writes Truman, "even when mutual confidence of the members is not productive of the most widely approved results." In legislative groups,

Politicians of quite different opinions and of at least nominally opposed political party are likely nevertheless to understand and respect a colleague's fears and triumphs . . . they speak a language which the uninitiated can never quite understand: they have had roughly parallel experiences that set them a little apart from those whose struggles have been of a different order. These commonalities help to support the conforming influences of the legis-group. . . .[50]

Indeed, Routt observed that *"the esprit de corps* displayed by legislative bodies, especially the smaller ones, is probably not rivaled by any other formally organized self-governing body."[51]

The explanation for the cohesiveness of legislative groups, which may extend to the protection of group prerogatives by stubborn opposition to all the recommendations of the executive, or to rivalry and suspicion between houses of a bicameral legislature, is not clearly established by empirical evidence. But the phenomenon has been observed often, and discussed frequently by legislators themselves. It may have been stated in classic form by Speaker Champ Clark before the House of Representatives on March 4, 1915, after minority leader Mann of Illinois had introduced a resolution commending the Speaker for his long record of impartial service. Said Clark,

A man who has never been in the Army has no adequate concentration of and never can understand the feeling that soldiers who have fought shoulder to shoulder have for each other; but, next to that, men who fight together in this legislative body have a feeling approximating that of the soldiers' feeling for each other.[52]

And the morale of legislative bodies goes beyond mere affect to shared definitions of the situation.

The Function of Legislative Outputs

The functions of the legislative system for its maintenance and for the larger polity are highly related. The adequate performance of one set of functions facilitates the performance of the others. Thus, adequate conflict management facilitates integration for the political system, and the relationship is reciprocal. Similarly, the more effectively the legislative system maintains itself as a viable system of interaction among roles, the more effectively it functions for the polity as a whole. This interrelatedness is demonstrable in terms of the legislative outputs. The concrete outputs of a legislature are decisions, public policy, services, supervision, and information. Such outputs have functional consequences for the integration of the political system, in that "one of the major ways of strengthening the ties of the members to their system is through providing decisions that tend to satisfy the day-to-day demands of these members."[53] Legitimate, representative, authoritative legislative decisions facilitate the resolution of conflict among contending interests in the polity. Wahlke maintains that

The general legitimacy of the legislature as a decision-making system ultimately depends upon the character of its output. So does the assuasion or exacerbation of individual and group tensions or conflicts in society which potentially threaten to rupture the bonds of political community and destroy the basis of government itself. The degree of stability, or lack of it, and the potentiality of degeneration, solidification, or transformation of the total political system are also affected by the character and quality of legislative output.[54]

The consequences of legislative output for the general political system ultimately affect the legislature itself through "feedbacks" in such forms as electoral effects, communications to legislators, and so forth (see Figure 1.2).

Legislative outputs have direct consequences for the legislature as well. As Wahlke has said,

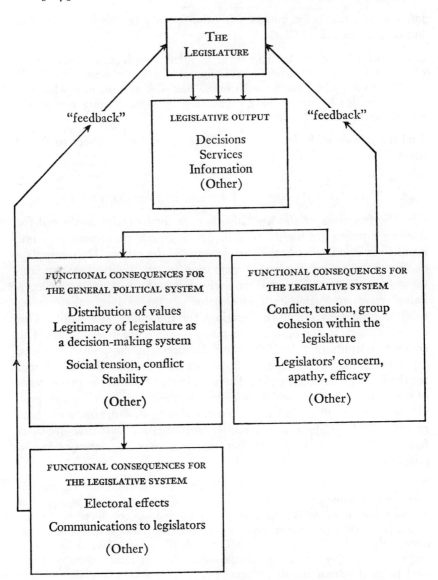

Figure 1.2. FUNCTIONAL CONSEQUENCES OF LEGISLATIVE OUTPUTS

SOURCE: J. C. Wahlke, et al., *The Legislative System* (New York: John Wiley and Sons, 1962), p. 27.

A given decision or decisions may so alienate one group of legislators as to affect drastically the course of all future deliberations and debate. That is, the state of conflict, tension, and group cohesion within the legislature itself is directly affected by its own output and its process of arriving at that output. In the same way, legislators' sense of concern, apathy or efficacy may be affected by prolonged stalemate or continuing dissatisfaction with the legislative product on the part of individual legislators.[55]

That is, there is a direct "feedback" from output to the legislature itself, which may be dysfunctional for the operation and maintenance of the legislative system. Output "feedback" can also have effects upon non-legislator components of the legislative system as well as upon the legislature itself. For instance, legislative outputs of certain kinds may intensify the lobbying demands of some groups, reduce those of others, or force interest groups to concentrate their attention on some other political subsystem.

This chapter does not constitute a functional theory of legislative systems. A great deal more empirical evidence than is now available is necessary to begin the process of specifying relationships among the significant variables suggested here. It is a convenient, if taxonomic, way of looking at legislative life. The chapters that follow are far more eclectic than this chapter may have suggested. We hope that this book will make a contribution toward a better theoretical understanding of legislative systems, but we recognize that the body of knowledge of legislative systems is only beginning to grow significantly, and is at present quite inadequate for a fully developed theoretical analysis. The present chapter attempts only to integrate and to make more meaningful what we shall say in those that follow.

NOTES

1. Much of the material in the next few pages relies heavily upon and quotes directly from Samuel C. Patterson, *Toward a Theory of Legislative Behavior* (Stillwater, Okla., 1962), pp. 16–37.

2. Talcott Parsons, *The Social System* (Glencoe, 1951), pp. 5–6; and *Essays in Sociological Theory* (Glencoe, 1954), p. 213.

3. David Easton, *The Political System* (New York, 1953), pp. 129–30. See also Samuel C. Patterson, "The Role of the Deviant in the State Legislative System," *Western Political Quarterly*, XIV (1961), 460–72; and William C. Mitchell, "The Polity and Society: A Structural-Functional Analysis," *Midwest Journal of Political Science*, II (1958), 403–20.

4. The problems of drawing lines around behavioral systems are many, and abstracting a subsystem makes its definition somewhat arbitrary. This point is discussed in A. R. Radcliffe-Brown, *A Natural Science of Society* (Glencoe, 1957), pp. 60–62.

5. Legislative activities are defined in more traditional terms by Roland

Young in Ernest S. Griffith (ed.), *Research in Political Science* (Chapel Hill, 1948), p. 45; and in the Council of State Governments' study, *Our State Legislatures* (Chicago, 1948), p. 1.

6. Our analysis of legislative functions relies upon the following: D. F. Aberle, A. K. Davis, M. J. Levy, Jr., and F. X. Sutton, "The Functional Prerequisites of a Society," *Ethics*, LX (1950), 100–11; Marion B. Levy, Jr., *The Structure of Society* (Princeton, 1952); Robert K. Merton, *Social Theory and Social Structure* (Glencoe, 1957), pp. 85–117; Talcott Parsons, *Structure and Process in Modern Societies* (Glencoe, 1960); David Easton, "An Approach to the Analysis of Political Systems," *World Politics*, IX (1957), 383–400; Mitchell, *op. cit.*, pp. 403–20; Gabriel A. Almond, "A Functional Approach to Comparative Politics," in G. A. Almond and J. S. Coleman (eds.), *The Politics of the Developing Areas* (Princeton, 1960), pp. 3–64; John C. Wahlke, Heinz Eulau, William Buchanan, and LeRoy C. Ferguson, *The Legislative System* (New York: John Wiley and Sons, 1962), pp. 3–28.

7. See Wahlke et al., *op. cit.*, chap. 1; Mitchell, *op. cit.*, pp. 403–20.

8. Kenneth E. Boulding, *The Image* (Ann Arbor, 1956), p. 103.

9. David B. Truman, *The Governmental Process* (New York, 1951), p. 394.

10. Earl Latham, *The Group Basis of Politics* (Ithaca, 1952), pp. 35–36.

11. Truman, *op. cit.*, p. 393.

12. *Ibid.*, pp. 322–32.

13. Arthur F. Bentley, *The Process of Government* (Bloomington, 1949), p. 493.

14. Truman, *op. cit.*, p. 372.

15. Easton, "An Approach to the Analysis of Political Systems," p. 390.

16. Theodore J. Lowi, *Legislative Politics U.S.A.* (Boston, 1962), p. xix.

17. For example, Herman Turk and Myron J. Lefcowitz, "Towards a Theory of Representation between Groups," *Social Forces*, XL (1962), 337–41.

18. Loren Beth, "The Supreme Court and State Civil Liberties," *Western Political Quarterly*, XIV (1961), 825–38.

19. Bentley, *op. cit.*, p. 363.

20. Bertram M. Gross, *The Legislative Struggle* (New York, 1953).

21. Ralph Linton, *The Study of Man* (New York, 1936), pp. 133–40, and *The Cultural Background of Personality* (New York, 1945), pp. 76–77.

22. Eugene L. and Ruth E. Hartley, *Fundamentals of Social Psychology* (New York, 1955), p. 486. Among a score of useful treatments of the role concept is the comprehensive analysis by Neal Gross, Ward S. Mason, and Alexander W. MacEachern, *Explorations in Role Analysis* (New York, 1958).

23. Hartley, *op. cit.*

24. *Ibid.*

25. We are here employing the familiar definition of "norm" of George C. Homans. "A norm . . . is an idea . . . that can be put in the form of a statement specifying what the members of other men should do, ought to do, are expected to do, under given circumstances," where "any departure or real behavior from the norm is followed by some punishment." See *The Human Group* (London, 1951), pp. 124–25.

26. Theodore M. Newcomb, *Social Psychology* (New York, 1950), p. 280.

27. Merton refers to the individual's occupancy of a number of positions as his "status-set." See *Social Theory and Social Structure*, pp. 369–70.

28. Linton, *The Study of Man*, p. 114.

29. Newcomb, *op. cit.*, p. 280.

30. Parsons, *Essays in Sociological Theory*, p. 230.

31. Newcomb, *op. cit.*, p. 286; S. F. Nadel, *The Theory of Social Structure* (Glencoe, 1957), pp. 59–60.

32. Hartley, *op. cit.*, p. 547; Parsons, *The Social System*, pp. 234–35.

33. Talcott Parsons and Edward A. Shils (eds.), *Toward a General Theory of Action* (Cambridge, 1954), p. 192.

34. John T. Gullahorn, "Measuring Role Conflict," *American Journal of Sociology*, LXI (1956), 299.

35. "Research in Political Behavior," *American Political Science Review*, XLVI (1952), 1028.

36. Merton, *op. cit.*, pp. 225–386.

37. Hartley, *op. cit.*, p. 465.

38. Samuel A. Stouffer suggested that "it may be the very existence of some flexibility or social slippage—but not too much—which makes behavior in groups possible." See "Analysis of Conflicting Social Norms," *American Sociological Review*, XIV (1949), 717.

39. These alternatives have been adapted from Jackson Toby, "Some Variables in Role Conflict Analysis," *Social Forces*, XXX (1952).

40. This is the emphasis of the analysis of Robert A. Dahl and Charles E. Lindblom, *Politics, Economics and Welfare* (New York, 1953), p. 329.

41. *Ibid.*, p. 334.

42. Merton, *op. cit.*, pp. 31–33.

43. For example, Bernard Schwartz, *The Professor and the Commissions* (New York, 1959).

44. For example, York Y. Willbern and Donald H. Clark, "Pre-Legislative Conferences in Indiana," *State Government*, XXXII (1959), 43–46.

45. Truman, *op. cit.*, p. 343.

46. Woodrow Wilson, *Congressional Government* (New York, 1956), pp. 59–60. First published in 1885.

47. Harold F. Gosnell, *Democracy, the Threshold of Freedom* (New York, 1948), p. 233.

48. See Hartley, *op. cit.*, pp. 396–400.

49. Dayton D. McKean, *Pressures on the Legislature of New Jersey* (New York: Columbia University Press, 1938), pp. 50–51.

50. Truman, *op. cit.*, p. 344.

51. Garland C. Routt, "Interpersonal Relationships and the Legislative Process," *Annals of the American Academy of Political and Social Science*, CXCV (1938), 130.

52. *Congressional Record*, 63rd Cong., 3rd Sess., p. 5520.

53. Easton, "An Approach to the Analysis of Political Systems," p. 395.

54. Wahlke et al., *op. cit.*, p. 26.

55. *Ibid.*, p. 27.

[2]

Legislative Representation

Representation is a very general characteristic of human behavior. In fact, it might be said that all forms of human interaction are representative in the sense that "every individual is the natural representative of his own person."[1] Social, political, and economic institutions, where interpersonal relationships have become organized, stable, and accepted, typically manifest representative characteristics. The managers and directors of corporations represent the stockholders, or some portion of them. Trade union leaders represent union members.[2] In intergroup relations of all kinds, social groups are "linked together by persons who act as representatives for these groups."[3] The father may represent the family, or the elder male may represent the family clan in relationships with other kinship associations.[4] The college administration may represent the faculty and students to the public or to the legislature, and the school teacher may be represented by the principal.[5] Representative roles are played by a wide variety of individuals in our society, and functional social interaction and accommodation would seem to be inconceivable without them.

Political representation, representation of the body politic by political leaders, has a similar generality. Political leaders are always representative in some sense, whether the political system in which they operate is closer to the authoritarian or the democratic end of the continuum of political control. It is difficult to imagine how any kind of political regime could long survive unless it represented the people in some way or another. Thus, it is not improbable to suppose that all political systems have representative qualities and that representation stretches back historically to the earliest modes of political control.

DIMENSIONS OF REPRESENTATION

In Chapter 1 we dealt with representation as a mechanism for political integration, but we have as yet left its precise definition unspecified. There is a great deal of ambiguity in the literature about its definition.[6] Without enveloping ourselves in the contradictions and obfuscations about this term, we should like to suggest that representation is a functional mechanism that is multidimensional. We can then identify three distinct dimensions of representation: the *authority* dimension, the *symbolic* dimension, and the *instrumental* dimension.[7]

The *authority* dimension of representation relates to the authorization of a person or persons to represent others. In the lawyer-client relationship, for instance, it is easy to see that the lawyer is a representative in the sense that he has been authorized by his client to represent him. The authorization of representation may be very formalistic and legalistic. The United States Congress and the American state legislatures are authorized representatives, and their authority can be found specifically granted in their respective constitutions and statutes. In the case of Congress, for example, legislative authority is specifically granted in Article I of the United States Constitution, and Section 8 of that article sets forth detailed authority for particular kinds of enactments.

Thomas Hobbes, the renowned seventeenth-century English political philosopher, thought of representation primarily in terms of formal authorization. He held to the view that, in the relationship between represented and representative, representatives "have authority from them so far-forth as is in their Commission, but no farther."[8] Later on in his great work, *Leviathan*, Hobbes spelled out in greater detail his notion of the strictly contractual relation between citizen and representative. He said:

But if the Representative be an Assembly; whatsoever that Assembly shall Decree, not warranted by their Letters, or the Lawes, is the act of the Assembly, or Body Politique, and the act of every one by whose Vote the Decree was made; but not the act of any man that being present Voted to the contrary; nor of man absent, unlesse he Voted it by procuration. It is the act of the Assembly, because Voted by the major part; and if it be a crime, the Assembly may be punished, as farre-forth as it is capable, as by dissolution, or forfeiture of their Letters, (which is to such artificiall, and fictitious Bodies, capitall,) or (if the Assembly have propriety,) by pecuniary Mulct. For from corporall penalties Nature hath exempted all Bodies Politique. But they that gave not their Vote, are therefore Innocent, because the Assembly cannot Represent any man in things unwarranted by their Letters, and consequently are not involved in their Votes.[9]

More modern writers have held closely to the Hobbesian view of representation.[10] When asked, "Who are the representatives?" these writers have replied, "Whoever are authorized in advance to act in behalf of their constituents and bind them by their decisions."

Analysis of the authority dimension of representation draws attention to the technique of election and its operation in a system of accountability.[11] Elections provide a way in which authorization can be given to representatives, who are, in some regimes, held accountable to the electorate for their stewardship by means of regular elections. We can give substantial attention to legislative elections in the United States as techniques for conferring authority because we are dealing with relatively democratic legislative systems. But elections provide only one means of conferring authority on representatives, and in less democratic regimes status, or merely the threat of physical force, may perform the same function. In addition, when we are dealing with the Congress and the state legislatures in the United States, we have under consideration conditions wherein authority to represent is formally conferred, but there is no theoretical reason why such conferral might not be tacit or even unconscious.

The *symbolic* dimension of representation has to do with the image of the representative or the legislative body as "standing for" the polity. In political mythology the representative body is sometimes seen as a microcosm of the nation, a kind of body politic writ small, a miniature of the society as a whole; the importance to political integration of such symbolism cannot be belittled.[12] Again, the legislator is a symbol for his constituents. He is expected to be the kind of person his constitutents want him to be. As de Grazia has said,

> The representative embodies the traits, the outlook, even the sins, of the larger group. Furthermore, if the larger group has anything to say about it, the representative *ought* to possess some large measure of identity of characteristics with the group qualities, or at least some large measure of agreement with the group norms. How familiar in many societies are terms like "foreigner," "hick," and "snob" directed at representatives who lack such qualities. In American society there are unacknowledged qualifications of name, nationality, occupation, and education for many offices; such prerequisites for acting as a representative are none the less effective for not being incorporated into the written laws. Electors often demand these qualifications and, therefore, they often exist.[13]

Representation may be defined in its symbolic dimension as a condition in which an individual is represented "when the characteristics and acts of a person in a position of power in the society are in accord with the desires, expressed and unexpressed, of the individual."[14]

Symbolic representation places emphasis upon the character of the representative, upon the recruitment process, and upon the manner in which the legislative membership is apportioned. To what extent are representatives similar to the larger group in their characteristics? In some democratic systems, constituents "have been known to select representatives *by reason* of their superior class position rather than to reject them because of it," because "the society's norms for representation may have demanded special differences rather than identity."[15] Such norms are often combined with expectations that maintain the political fictions of the "folksy" strategy because representatives are well aware of them. Senator Robert S. Kerr, an oil-millionaire Democrat from Oklahoma, used to board an airplane in Washington dressed like a New York banker and emerge in Tulsa in a baggy white suit and floppy hat. It is said that Huey Long, Louisiana's "Kingfish," wore silk pajamas to bed, but quickly put on an old-fashioned nightgown one night when newspaper photographers came to the executive mansion to photograph him signing a bill. Such symbolic identification has also been an important factor in the political appeal of dictators.

The symbolic dimension in representation also draws attention to the apportionment of legislatures. Apportionment and the drawing of legislative district boundary lines are important techniques of representation, and they have become especially controversial in the United States. No device of representation extends equally to all individuals, and none is politically neutral. "The process of apportionment," de Grazia reminds us, "is a point of entry for preferred social values. The existing system of apportionment, whether legal, illegal, or extra-legal, institutionalizes the values of some group in a society."[16]

The *instrumental* dimension in representation refers to the action of representatives. Representatives are expected by their constituents to act for them, to be their instruments for getting things done.[17] In these terms, representation may be defined as a kind of activity, a way of acting, or an expectation about how a representative ought to act in place of or in behalf of his constituents. The relationship between the represented and the representative provides the basis for controversy about how the representative ought to act, as well as for recent empirical investigations into the reciprocal role expectations and policy agreements between represented and representative, which we shall explore in detail in Chapter 16.

Political philosophers and legislators have differed diametrically over the question, "In what manner should the legislator act in representing his constituents?" The classic answer to this question is supplied by Edmund Burke's theory of representation. Burke, a member of the English Parliament, told the electors of Bristol in 1774 that:

To deliver an opinion is the right of all men; that of constituents is a weighty and respectable opinion, which a representative ought always to rejoice and hear, and which he ought always most seriously to consider. But *authoritative* instructions, *mandates* issued, which the member is bound blindly and implicitly to obey, to vote, and to argue for, though contrary to the clearest conviction of his judgment and conscience,—these are things utterly unknown to the laws of this land, and which arise from a fundamental mistake of the whole order and tenor of our Constitution.

Parliament is not a *congress* of ambassadors from different and hostile interests, which interests each must maintain, as an agent and advocate, against other agents and advocates; but Parliament is a *deliberative* assembly of *one* nation, with one interest, that of the whole—where not local purposes, not local prejudices, ought to guide, but the general good, resulting from the general reason of the whole. You choose a member, indeed; but when you have chosen him, he is not member of Bristol, but he is a member of *Parliament.* If the local constituent should have an interest or should form an hasty opinion evidently opposite to the real good of the rest of the community, the member for that place ought to be as far as any other from any endeavor to give it effect.[18]

The modern legislator faces similar problems in defining how he should represent his constituents. Consider the remarks made by Senator J. William Fulbright, Democrat of Arkansas, who made a speech at the University of Chicago in 1946 in which he said:

The average legislator early in his career discovers that there are certain interests, or prejudices, of his constituents which are dangerous to trifle with. Some of these prejudices may not be of fundamental importance to the welfare of the nation, in which case he is justified in humoring them, even though he may disapprove. The difficult case is where the prejudice concerns fundamental policy affecting the national welfare. A sound sense of values, the ability to discriminate between that which is of fundamental importance and that which is only superficial, is an indispensable qualification of a good legislator. As an example of what I mean, let us take the poll-tax issue and isolationism. Regardless of how persuasive my colleagues or the national press may be about the evils of the poll tax, I do not see its fundamental importance, and I shall follow the views of the people of my state. Although it may be symbolic of conditions which many deplore, it is exceedingly doubtful that its abolition will cure any of our major problems. On the other hand, regardless of how strongly opposed my constituents may prove to be to the creation of, and participation in, an ever stronger United Nations Organization, I could not follow such a policy in that field unless it becomes clearly hopeless. . . .[19]

These two statements illustrate competing conceptions about how the legislator ought to represent his constituents. They suggest "two possible foci of representation: local, necessarily hostile interests, on the one hand; and a national interest, on the other hand."[20] Burke rejected the local focus of representation, and advocated the latter. Senator Fulbright's comments suggest that legislators may often combine the two foci, depending upon the nature of the issue involved. Burke also linked a particular focus of representation with a certain representational "style." He held to the "free agent" conception of representation, believing that the representative ought to be guided by his own best judgment, rather than to the "delegate" notion of representation, in which the legislator is instructed by his constituents and ought to vote their instructions regardless of his own views.

Of course, modern legislative life is not as simple as these comments may suggest. For Senator Fulbright, it is the issue that counts—whether or not it is fundamental to the national welfare; if not, he will accept the mandate of his constituents *as he sees it*. Obviously, many referents may "constitute significant foci of orientation for the representative as he approaches his legislative task."[21] These foci may be geographical interests, such as the electoral district, the state, or the nation; or they may be political parties, political interest groups, or administrative agencies.

The development of the modern party systems of Western democracies has had significant ramifications for legislative representation. In some political systems, political parties are, in effect, intermediate representative agencies between the constituent and the legislature. The British parliamentary system is a polity in which, at least in the immediate post-World War II period, the member of the House of Commons was elected by his constituents to be a cog in the party machinery of the House. While party orientations are less pronounced in the United States than in Britain, continental European nations, and some Asian systems, the party representative is to be found in American legislative systems. Illustrations can be cited of the pressure-group oriented legislator: Senator Henry Jackson, Democrat of Washington, has, for instance, often been denominated the "Senator from Boeing" because of his active representation of the interests of the Boeing Aircraft Company, an important concern in his state. We are familiar with other shorthand descriptions of legislators in the United States: oil senators, wheat senators, cotton senators, and so forth. Again, examples abound of legislators whose representative orientation sometimes is in the direction of administrative agencies; Senator Stuart Symington, Democrat of Missouri, a former Secretary of the Air Force, has often been said to speak in defense matters from the point of view of the Air Force.

It is possible analytically to keep distinct the focal and stylistic character of representation and to emphasize that a variety of combinations are theoretically possible. "Burke's linkage of a particular areal focus of representation with a particular representational style constitutes only a special case on a generic series of empirically viable relationships between possible and different foci of representation and appropriate styles of representation."[22] And emphasis upon the foci and styles of representation permits empirical observation of the instrumental dimension of representation; that is, we are concerned here not with how decisions should be made, whether legislators are authorized to decide, or whether constituents acquiesce, but rather with how decisions are actually made.

THE DEVELOPMENT OF REPRESENTATION

We have defined representation in three dimensions, maintaining that representation may involve: (1) the authority of a person to represent others, (2) the symbolic reflection of constituents' expressed or unexpressed desires, and (3) the instrumental acts of the representative vis-a-vis his constituents. Obviously, these conditions may exist at the same time, and are not mutually exclusive. Historically, some of these dimensions have been more important than others. A brief excursion into the origin and development of representation will help us to understand it as a developmental process.

As a political function, representation may be found in any society. We began this chapter by alluding to the probable universality of representation. There is evidence of representative assemblies among primitive tribes of American Indians (the Iroquois Federal Republic) which clearly had no Greek or Roman origin.[23] Furthermore, it is probable that representative assemblies go back historically far beyond the Greek city-states.[24] Our central concern with legislatures in the United States permits us to concentrate upon the development of legislative assemblies in Western political systems.

In the Western political tradition, representative assemblies clearly date back to Greek and Roman antiquity.[25] Representative councils existed in the Greek city-states as early as the fifth century B.C. They both set the agendas for the larger popular assemblies and performed a variety of kinds of governmental supervision. During the fifth century the council of Athens consisted of five hundred members chosen by lot for a one-year term from among the ten tribes of the city-state. Representation was based upon population, and members of the council were, in part at least, chosen within the tribes from local subdivisions called *demes*. Similar, though smaller, representative bodies existed in other Greek city-states, notably Chios and Erythrae. More important, representative assemblies were utilized in the Greek confederacies, governmental agencies which developed within a geographical region when several cities grew up and, rather than becoming independent city-states, maintained political ties with each other. The best example of representative assemblies among these confederacies is the Boeotian Confederacy during the period 447–386 B.C. The federal council of the Boeotian Confederacy consisted of 660 members chosen on a population basis from among eleven districts. It met in the Cadmea, the acropolis of Thebes. Representative assemblies are known to have existed also in the Achaean and Lycian confederacies, to have been adopted by the Thessalian Confederacy after the Second Macedonian War (194 B.C.) and by the Macedonian republics in 167 B.C. Some of these representative assemblies lasted until well into the first century B.C.; some even survived in limited ways under Roman imperial control.

The Roman provincial assemblies, which exhibit borrowings from the Hellenistic tradition, contained both elected delegates and dignitaries appointed for life. These assemblies were particularly active and effective in Gaul, where the approximately sixty tribes were represented. In other provinces the unit of representation was the city. Although the early Roman provincial assemblies operated primarily as organs of local administration, they were an important link between the citizens and the central government. In the Late Empire the provincial assemblies were reorganized, and the election of delegates eliminated. By the late third or early fourth century A.D., these assemblies had become representative only of the landed aristocracy, often "more interested in securing and increasing their own wealth and power than in the welfare of the Empire."[26]

Whether representative assemblies survived from the fourth to the eleventh centuries is unclear. These were centuries of absolute monarchy. Some historians have maintained that representative government was kept alive in the municipal self-government of the cities of southern France and northern Spain.[27] The Roman Catholic Church, within which countless political controversies were fought during the medieval period, was probably "both the initiator and the carrier of political innovations in representative government."[28] Political philosophies of representation began to develop in the late Middle Ages, and the conciliar movement in the Roman Catholic Church involved proposals for democratic assemblies. Similarly, a doctrine of consent to public acts of political leaders, stemming from Roman law, became increasingly accepted in the late Middle Ages, particularly with regard to taxation.[29]

In southern France, especially in the provincial estates of Gascony, and in some provinces of northern Spain, representative assemblies date back to very early times, though their beginnings are not known. Popular representatives are known to have had a voice in the deliberations of the assemblies (Cortes) of Aragon as early as 1163, of Castile in 1169, and of Leon in 1188. In Castile two deputies were assigned to each town, and in 1315 ninety towns sent a total of 192 members to the Castilian Cortes.[30] Sometimes the delegates to the Cortes were elected by the town councils, sometimes directly by the citizens. The popular deputies represented the third estate (commoners); the clergy and nobility were also represented in the Cortes. It seems unlikely that those who innovated representative bodies in England in the thirteenth century were totally unfamiliar with practices on the continent. A substantial portion of France was a part of the dominions of the Angevin kings, and King John of England was probably familiar with local representative practices in Gascony when he summoned representatives of the shires in 1213. Further, knowledge of representative techniques may have been available to English political leaders partly as a result of intermarriages between them and French and Spanish nobility in the twelfth and thirteenth centuries, and it may be "safe to say that representative assemblies would have been a common subject of discussion at the English court."[31] Finally, in those same centuries representative government had developed in some of the monastic orders of the Roman Catholic Church. The Order of the Dominicans played an exceptionally important part in this regard, particularly after their entrance into England in 1221, and their practices were probably a part of public discussion in London and Oxford.[32]

Early in the twelfth century representative practices were extant in England; the county court system, of Norman and Frankish origin, embodied representative principles, and a popularly elected representative council was chosen in London at the beginning of John's reign.[33] In the early 1200s the knights of the shires were periodically summoned by the King to consult on affairs of the realm. The first parliament to which representatives of a large number of English boroughs were called was that convened under the influence of Simon de Montfort in 1265.[34] Histories of the British Parliament ordinarily begin with that date. The development of representative principles before that time had certainly been an uneven progression. Subsequent parliaments were not securely established, though by the time of Edward I it appeared that Parliament could not be dispensed with entirely. Early parliaments were called mainly to get support for taxation and military affairs, and knights and commoners alike brought mandates from their constituents. The history of England after 1265 is a story of the long, arduous, and even bloody struggle for parliamentary independence and supremacy. Parliament did not develop its modern position until the sixteenth century, when the House of Commons began to rival the House of Lords in influence. Although elections were held in the Elizabethan period, elections in the modern, popular sense of relatively wide suffrage did not develop until late in the sixteenth century. Modern partisanship did not begin to develop until late in the seventeenth century, when debate on the Exclusion Bill produced opposing sides, one side called the Whigs and the other Tories. The practice of ministerial responsibility was essentially an early eighteenth-century phenomenon.[35]

REPRESENTATIVE GOVERNMENT IN THE UNITED STATES

American colonial representative conceptions owed a great deal to English law and practice, but they also differed from seventeenth-century English practice. The differences largely reflected colonial populism, which was itself related to the ideology of direct democracy espoused by the Levellers and the English Radicals.[36] All but one of the colonial legislatures were bicameral in the eighteenth century. The upper houses were usually appointed by the Crown or proprietors on the recommendation of the governors. The lower houses were elective, but restrictions on the suffrage meant that they were largely representative of the prosperous middle-class farmers and merchants. The bicameralism of the colonial legislatures reflected both social and economic distinctions in the colonies and British parliamentary practice. The committee systems, rules of parliamentary procedure, and many ceremonial activities were borrowed directly from the Houses of Commons and Lords. While the committee structure of Parliament waned as cabinet government gained strength, in America the committee structure of the legislatures became increasingly important.[37] Finally, many of the privileges and prerogatives won by the Parliament in its struggle with kings were claimed by the colonial assemblies. The most important of these was the power over the public purse, and the successful assertion of this power "was of tremendous importance in the growth of colonial autonomy," and "contributed substantially to a gradual depletion of internal British authority in America."[38]

The most significant difference between the colonial legislatures of the eighteenth century and the British Parliament was in the instrumental conception of representation. In England, Burke's free-agency style of representation was widely accepted, while in the American colonies the delegate conception prevailed. The practice of instructing delegates was widespread, dating from the early seventeenth century in Virginia and Massachusetts.[39] While constituent instruction of delegates to colonial and state legislatures was commonplace in the early history of the United States, it operated most effectively and persisted longest where representatives were chosen by town meetings. For example, Massachusetts towns instructed their colonial assemblymen on the Stamp Act question; John Adams drafted the instructions for the town of Braintree in 1765. "I prepared a draught of instructions at home," Adams wrote in his diary, "and carried them with me. The cause of the meeting was explained at some length, and the state and danger of the country pointed out; a committee was appointed to prepare instructions, of which I was nominated as one. We retired to Mr. Niles's house, my draught was produced, and unanimously adopted without amendment, reported to the town, and accepted without a dissenting voice."[40] Again, by way of illustration, in 1776 the Massachusetts House of Representatives adopted a resolution calling on the towns to instruct their representatives whether or not they supported the Declaration of Independence.[41] Although the practice of instructions gradually fell into disuse owing to the difficulty of assembling constituents, it persisted in states like New Hampshire for many years.

In addition, by the early eighteenth century, legislation in most of the colonies required representatives to be residents of the district they represented, a practice quite the opposite of that developing in England at the same time. Nonresidence representation prevailed at one time or another in ten of the thirteen colonies, but by 1700 it was forbidden in six colonies and in three others it was apparently not very extensively practiced. But it was widely practiced in Rhode Island until 1783, in Connecticut until 1818, in South Carolina until 1865, and in Georgia between 1755 and 1777.[42]

The revolutionary struggle in America was framed in terms of representational theory—in the debate over the prerogatives of the colonial legislatures versus British officialdom, and in the controversy over the "virtual" representation of the colonists in the British Parliament. Parliamentary leaders like George Grenville argued that the colonies had "an equal share in the general representation of the Commons of Great Britain . . . whether they had or had not particular representatives there."[43] The colonial arguments centered upon representative authority; "No taxation without representation" was its battle cry.

What had been a controversy over the representative relationships between the individual colonies and the British Empire now turned into conflict over the "community of interests between the collectivity of the colonies and the individual colonies."[44] The Continental Congresses and the Congress under the Articles of Confederation represented each of the new states equally. When the Articles of Confederation were debated, the Continental Congress rejected proposals that the confederate Congress be based upon population representation or representation based upon tax-paying, and provided one vote for each state regardless of the size of its delegation. The Constitutional Convention of 1787 in effect reopened the whole question of representation in a national legislature, and provided the most significant political compromise at the Convention. The so-called Virginia Plan provided for a bicameral legislature with population representation in both houses; the New Jersey Plan provided a unicameral body with equal representation of the states. The great compromise of the Convention was the decision to create a bicameral congress, with a house of representatives based upon population and a senate upon equal state representation.[45]

The Founding Fathers thought in terms of the representation of interests and the balancing of them in the coalescence of nearly independent states. In defense of the Constitution, Madison argued in *Federalist* No. 10 that it provided a method for the amelioration of factions and interests. Hamilton's arguments in support of the constitutional provisions for the House of Representatives reflect a similar concern. Madison contended, for example, that if the legislator's constituency is too large, "you render the representative too little acquainted with all their local circumstances and lesser interests"; if it is too small, "you render him unduly attached to these, and too little fit to comprehend and pursue great and national objects."[46] Hamilton defended the House of Representatives against the charge that it would be too small "to possess a due knowledge of the interests of its constituents" by maintaining:

It is a sound and important principle, that the representative ought to be acquainted with the interests and circumstances of his constituents. But this principle can extend no further, than to those circumstances and interests to which the authority and care of the representative relate. An ignorance of a variety of minute and particular objects, which do not lie within the compass of legislation, is consistent with every attribute necessary to a due performance of the legislative trust. . . . Divide the largest State into ten or twelve districts, and it will be found that there will be no particular local interest in either, which will not be within the knowledge of the representative of the district.[47]

The equal representation of states in the United States Senate illustrates the practical application of the federal principle of the Constitution. Population representation in the House of Representatives reflects the centralizing ideology of the makers of the Constitution and their recognition of the democratic spirit.[48] There were still substantial restrictions on the suffrage by state law, and the Constitution left the qualifications of voting for congressmen to the states. The original Constitution provided for the election of senators by the state legislatures, and senators were chosen in this manner until the ratification of the Seventeenth Amendment in 1913.

After the adoption of the Constitution, the House of Representatives of the First Congress debated a proposed constitutional amendment that would have permitted a constituency to instruct, or issue mandates, to its representatives in Congress. When what was ultimately to become the First Amendment of the Bill of Rights was debated, Congressman Thomas T. Tucker of South Carolina proposed an amendment to the freedom of assembly clause which would have guaranteed the right of the people "to instruct their representatives." The House debate on April 15, 1789 provided an excellent juxtaposition of the free-agent and delegate styles of representation. Although most House members opposed the amendment, John Page of Virginia and Elbridge Gerry of Massachusetts supported it. The proposal failed to be adopted by a vote of 41-10, perhaps largely because of the opposition of James Madison.[49] But the practice of constituents' instructing congressmen and senators was commonplace in the nineteenth century, on an entirely informal and customary basis which stemmed from colonial and early state experience.[50] Until the Civil War period, state legislatures commonly instructed the United States Senators chosen by them, and this practice remains vestigially today in state legislatures' adopting resolutions memorializing Congress to take, or refrain from taking, some action.[51]

The adoption and permanence of the American Constitution is a significant benchmark in the history of the development of representative government. A modern analysis of representation must anatomize the complexity of relationships associated with the three dimensions of representation: authority, symbolic, and instrumental. These are the tasks of the chapters that follow.

NOTES

1. Ferdinand Tonnies, *Community and Association* (London, 1955), p. 203.

2. Avery Leiserson, "Problems of Representation in the Government of Private Groups," *Journal of Politics*, XI (1949), 566-77.

3. Herman Turk and Myron J. Lefcowitz, "Towards a Theory of Representation between Groups," *Social Forces*, XL (1962), 337-41.

4. Francis X. Sutton, "Representation and the Nature of Political Systems," *Comparative Studies in Society and History*, II (1959), 1-10.

5. R. Jean Hills, "The Representative Function: Neglected Dimensions of Leadership Behavior," *Administrative Science Quarterly*, VIII (1963), 83-101.

6. For an exhaustive discussion of many definitions extant, see John A. Fairlie, "The Nature of Political Representation," *American Political Science Review*, XXXIV (1940), 236-48, 456-66; and Charles E. Gilbert, "Operative Doctrines of Representation," *American Political Science Review*, LVII (1963), 604-18.

7. The best contemporary treatment of political representation can be found in Hanna F. Pitkin, "A Theory of Political Representation" (Unpublished Ph.D. dissertation, University of California at Los Angeles, 1961). These dimensions are expressed in somewhat different terms in A. H. Birch, *Representative and Responsible Government* (London, 1964), pp. 13-22.

8. Thomas Hobbes, *Leviathan* (London, 1953), p. 84. First published 1651.

9. *Ibid.*, p. 119. See Hanna Pitkin, "Hobbes's Concept of Representation," *American Political Science Review*, LVIII (1964), 328–40.

10. For example, Karl Loewenstein, *Political Power and the Governmental Process* (Chicago, 1957), pp. 38–39; Edward M. Sait, *Political Institutions: A Preface* (New York, 1938), pp. 476–78; and a discussion of a variety of philosophical positions in Harold F. Gosnell, *Democracy: The Threshold of Freedom* (New York, 1948), pp. 124–42.

11. For example, Henry J. Ford, *Representative Government* (New York, 1924), p. 157.

12. On symbolic images see Kenneth E. Boulding, *The Image* (Ann Arbor, 1956), pp. 109–10. Boulding points out that "political images include not only detailed images of role expectations. They also include what might be called symbolic or personalized images of institutions themselves. A symbolic image is a kind of rough summation or index of a vast complexity of images of roles and structures. These symbolic images are of great importance in political life. . . ."

13. Alfred de Grazia, *Public and Republic: Political Representation in America* (New York, 1951), p. 5.

14. Gosnell, *op. cit.*, p. 130.

15. de Grazia, *op. cit.*, p. 6.

16. Alfred de Grazia, "General Theory of Apportionment," *Law and Contemporary Problems*, XVII (1952), 256–67, at 257.

17. For example, Carl J. Friedrich, *Constitutional Government and Democracy* (Boston, 1941), p. 260.

18. Louis I. Bredvold and Ralph G. Ross, *The Philosophy of Edmund Burke* (Ann Arbor, 1960), pp. 147–48.

19. Center for the Study of Democratic Institutions, *The Elite and the Electorate* (New York, 1963), p. 6.

20. Heinz Eulau, John C. Wahlke, William Buchanan and LeRoy C. Ferguson, "The Role of the Representative: Some Empirical Observations on the Theory of Edmund Burke," *American Political Science Review*, LIII (1959), 742–56; quotation at 744.

21. *Ibid.*, p. 744.

22. *Ibid.*, p. 745.

23. Gosnell, *op. cit.*, pp. 151–52; Sutton, *op. cit.*

24. For example, Geoffrey Evans, "Ancient Mesopotamian Assemblies," *Journal of the American Oriental Society*, LXXVIII (1958), 1–11, 114–15.

25. What follows is based upon J. A. O. Larsen, *Representative Government in Greek and Roman History* (Berkeley and Los Angeles, 1955).

26. *Ibid.*, p. 157.

27. Sait, *op. cit.*, pp. 482–84.

28. Gosnell, *op. cit.*, p. 156.

29. Maude V. Clark, *Medieval Representation and Consent* (London, 1936), pp. 247–77.

30. Sait, *op. cit.*, pp. 484–85.

31. *Ibid.*, p. 495.

32. Gosnell, *op. cit.*, pp. 156–57.

33. Clark, *op. cit.*, pp. 285–89.

34. May McKisack, *The Parliamentary Representation of the English Boroughs during the Middle Ages* (London, 1932).

35. Roland Young, *The British Parliament* (London, 1962), pp. 40–44. See also Samuel H. Beer, "The Representation of Interests in British Government: Historical Background," *American Political Science Review*, LI (1957), 613–50.

36. de Grazia, *Public and Republic*, pp. 50–61.

37. Ralph V. Harlow, *The History of Legislative Methods in the Period before 1825* (New Haven, 1917), pp. 1–23.

38. Alfred H. Kelly and Winfred A. Harbison, *The American Constitution: Its Origins and Development* (New York, 1948), pp. 28–32, quotations at p. 31. See also Mary P. Clarke, *Parliamentary Privilege in the American Colonies* (New

Haven, 1943); and Thomas F. Moran, *The Rise and Development of the Bicameral System in America* (Baltimore, 1895).

39. Robert Luce, *Legislative Principles* (Boston, 1930), pp. 448–59.

40. In George A. Peek, Jr. (ed.), *The Political Writings of John Adams* (New York, 1954), pp. 22–25.

41. For example, "Instructions from the Town of Malden, Massachusetts, for a Declaration of Independence, May 27, 1776," in Henry S. Commager (ed.), *Documents of American History*, 5th edition (New York, 1949), pp. 96–98.

42. Hubert Phillips, *The Development of a Residential Qualification for Representatives in Colonial Legislatures* (Cincinnati, 1921), pp. 244–47.

43. de Grazia, *Public and Republic*, p. 15.

44. *Ibid.*, p. 80.

45. For an excellent analysis of the politics of this compromise, see John P. Roche, "The Founding Fathers: A Reform Caucus in Action," *American Political Science Review*, LV (1961), 799–816.

46. *Federalist*, No. 10.

47. *Federalist*, No. 56.

48. See George B. Galloway, *History of the House of Representatives* (New York, 1961), pp. 1–7; Lindsay Rogers, *The American Senate* (New York, 1926), pp. 9–21; Joseph P. Chamberlain, *Legislative Processes: National and State* (New York, 1936), pp. 32–37; Arthur N. Holcombe, *Our More Perfect Union* (Cambridge, 1950), pp. 149–235.

49. *Annals of Congress*, I, 760–76.

50. Luce, *op. cit.*, pp. 460–91.

51. William H. Riker, "The Senate and American Federalism," *American Political Science Review*, XLIX (1955), 452–69.

[Part II]
SELECTION OF LEGISLATORS

How are legislators selected? The answer to that question has three facets. The method of apportioning legislative seats and dividing political units into districts provides the framework for the selection process. The primary and general elections constitute the political factors, providing a link between the electoral and legislative systems. A less obvious aspect of the selection process is the socio-economic factors that distinguish those who win election to the legislature from the ordinary citizens.

No aspect of the legislative process is undergoing more rapid change than selection. Since 1962 the courts have been forcing revolutionary changes in the standards used for apportioning state legislatures and substantial changes in U.S. House districts. These changes are occurring so rapidly that the newspaper has become an essential supplement for any account of legislative apportionment, and their eventual scope is not yet clear. Meanwhile, the growth of competitive party systems in the states is raising the electoral hurdles that face prospective legislators. Research concerning legislative elections and the characteristics of legislators has provided enough data to raise further questions but has barely begun to suggest the answers. Political scientists, who have devoted much attention to describing and decrying malapportionment, have only recently made serious efforts to understand the nature and effects of various apportionment and districting techniques.

The most important and most difficult question about the selection process is its impact on the legislative process and its output. In many states the drastic changes in the balance of urban, rural, and suburban representation brought about by reapportionment will change the immediate or potential balance of partisan power in the legislature. In Congress the most important consequence may be a decrease in the proportion of safe districts. The effects on the substantive content of legislation at the state and national levels remain more obscure. Changes in the boundaries and in the competitive quality of districts are important also because they will probably affect the legislator's role. His attitudes toward constituent opinion and toward the demands of his legislative party and of the executive branch are all likely to be influenced by new dimensions in districts and elections that he encounters. It is obvious that many aspects of the legislative process are affected in some way by the social and economic characteristics of legislators—and it is equally certain that we will not be able to define this relationship until we can collect much more comprehensive data on legislators.

[3]

Legislative Apportionment and Districting

ON MARCH 26, 1962, in the now famous case of *Baker* v. *Carr*, a majority of the Supreme Court declared that the federal courts will hear cases in which citizens claim that their rights under the equal protection clause of the Fourteenth Amendment have been abridged by malapportionment of state legislatures.[1] Two years later, in much more specific terms, the Court held that "the Equal Protection Clause requires both houses of a state legislature to be apportioned on a population basis."[2] These two decisions, as implemented by lower federal and state courts, have had the effect in state after state of destroying the apportionment systems carefully designed or preserved by rural legislators to perpetuate their majority position. The Court decisions meant that the majority of the population in Florida, who lived in the six largest counties, should elect more than 6 out of the 38 senators, and similarly that the one-fourth of the population who lived in Connecticut's five largest cities should elect more than 10 out of 294 House members. The principle of population equality meant that the 38 citizens of Stratton were no longer entitled to a voice in the Vermont House equal to that of the 35,531 citizens of Burlington, and it meant that the 6 million residents of Los Angeles County deserved more representation in the California Senate than the 14,000 residents of a Sierra Nevada district which, like Los Angeles, had a single senator. Not every state has had such great inequalities in its legislature, but in most states the changes in the apportionment pattern that are being induced by judicial decisions are major ones, the full implications of which can be seen only dimly.

The impact of another 1964 decision, *Wesberry* v. *Sanders*, in which the Supreme Court applied the principle of population equality to congressional districts, is less dramatic.[3] The congressional districts used in the 1962 election varied in population by 2 to 1 or more in twenty-one states, but the range was over 3 to 1 in only five states, and the greatest variations—in Michigan and Texas—were less than 5 to 1. Since these variations have been smaller than in state legislatures, the effect of applying the principle of population equality will be less. The congressional power structure will not be toppled by a whole-sale revision in district boundaries, but it will be affected.

The United States Constitution provides that the "times, places, and manner of holding elections for Senators and Representatives" shall be regulated by the states, but that "Congress may at any time by law make or alter such regulations." The debates over ratification of the Constitution make it clear that the framers intended Congress to have authority to ensure that the congressional districts meet standards of population equality.[4] At various times in the past, beginning in 1842, Congress set certain standards for congressional districts, requiring that members be elected from single-member districts that were compact, contiguous, and as nearly equal in population as possible. The 1929 law, which is currently in force, includes none of these requirements. Congress failed to adopt a new apportionment following the 1920 census, and in 1929 it passed a law to assure automatic redistribution of seats among the states. The Bureau of the Census determines the number of seats for each state, using the mathematical technique of equal pro-portions, and the Clerk of the House of Representatives tells each gov-ernor how many seats have been allotted to the state.[5] The size of the House is fixed at 435 members, although Congress could change this total and came close to doing so in 1962.

Although Congress no longer requires single-member districts, they have been used almost exclusively by the states. Several states elected one member-at-large temporarily following the 1960 census, but New Mexico—with two members—is the only multimember state that has not made any use of congressional districts. The task of drawing con-gressional district boundaries is left entirely in the hands of state legislatures. There is not even a requirement that a legislature take any redistricting action following a census if the total number of seats to which that state is entitled remains stable. The Supreme Court's de-cision requiring that congressional districts be as nearly equal in popula-tion as is practicable has inspired efforts in Congress to pass implementing legislation that will specify standards for districting.

In the states, the standards and procedures for legislative apportionment are spelled out, more or less clearly, in their constitutions. In most states this is the responsibility of the legislature. Some state constitutions contain a formula for the apportionment of seats among counties that leaves little or no discretion to the legislature. Most constitutions require periodic reapportionment by the legislature, but in the past these requirements were often ignored, and until the *Baker* v. *Carr* decision state courts had not attempted to force legislative compliance with such requirements. State courts sometimes determined whether an apportionment law, newly passed, met constitutional standards, but they did not try to force the enactment of laws that would meet these standards. The notorious reluctance of legislatures to apply the surgeon's knife to their own apportionments led to the adoption of constitutional provisions in several states, prior to *Baker* v. *Carr*, which transferred some or all of this authority to other bodies. Six states assigned the responsibility of apportioning one or both houses to a state official, to a commission or, under a specific apportionment formula, to local units of government. Six other state constitutions provided that the responsibility for action would rest with a designated official or board if the legislature failed to apportion one or both houses by a certain date after the census.[6] Such provisions solved the problem of legislative paralysis, but in most of these states the standards set by the constitutions guaranteed inequalities in apportionment.

THE DEVELOPMENT OF MALAPPORTIONMENT

Conflicts over legislative apportionment in the states are as old as the states themselves. The colonies adopted the British practices of apportioning seats to localities with little regard to population and requiring property qualifications for voters. In Britain the effects of these practices were such that by 1793 it was estimated that 84 individual landowners controlled 157 seats in the House of Commons and a majority of the House could be chosen by fewer than 15,000 voters. Malapportionment and restrictions on the franchise did not have such drastic effects in colonial America, but during and immediately following the Revolution both issues were subjects of heated debate in the conventions that drew up new state constitutions. Thomas Jefferson criticized inequities in population in the Virginia legislature during the Revolution and proposed a model constitution with apportionment by population. Under the threat of armed revolt on the frontier, Pennsylvania in 1776 adopted a new constitution that provided for representation by population.

From the Revolution through the period of Jacksonian democracy the twin issues of suffrage and apportionment were debated in state after state. Often the conflict was between the new frontiersmen and the aristocracy in the cities and coastal areas. By the 1830s universal male white suffrage had been adopted by most of the states, and most of the property qualifications had been removed. There was still, however, no single pattern of apportionment. In most of the older states there were changes in the apportionment to give greater weight to population, although frequently each county (or in New England each town) retained at least one seat in one house. The new states that joined the Union were usually apportioned primarily on the basis of population. The Northwest Ordinance adopted by Congress in 1787 set the pattern by stipulating that "the inhabitants of said territory shall always be entitled to the benefits . . . of a proportionate representation of the people in the legislature." Similar requirements were found in congressional acts pertaining to territories and new states. There was frequently a provision for assuring representation to each county, but population remained the underlying principle of representation in new state constitutions.[7]

Throughout the latter part of the nineteenth century, one and usually both houses of the legislatures in most states were apportioned, in both theory and practice, primarily by population. Periodic reapportionments took place after each census. As long as there were not gross differences in the populations of most counties, there was no objection to giving each county some representation, nor was there any fear that reapportionment would lead to legislative domination by a few counties. It was the growth of modern cities and eventually metropolitan areas that made apportionment once again a controversial issue. When rural legislators began to realize that their legislative majorities were becoming precarious, they either refused to reapportion according to the mandate of state constitutions or they sought new constitutional provisions to block urban domination of the legislature. During the late nineteenth century in rural America there was often a deep suspicion of the city, which was heavily populated by immigrants and often dominated by political machines. In more recent years conservative rural interests feared the power of labor unions and ethnic minorities, whose strength was concentrated in the cities. The conflict was sharpest, and rural fears greatest, in states where a single metropolitan center constituted a majority or near majority of the state's population. By the middle of the twentieth century it was the exploding suburbs within the metropolitan areas that were most seriously underrepresented, and the urban-rural conflicts that had been the cause of malapportionment had become less meaningful factors in legislative politics. But the majority of legislators from nonmetropolitan areas, supported by powerful interests that preferred the status quo, showed no signs of surrendering their positions of power.

In a substantial number of states, one of the political parties has had a stake in preserving the existing apportionment. In the industrial states of the Northeast and Midwest, Republican strength is greatest in the small cities and rural areas. In states like New York, Connecticut, Ohio, Illinois, and Michigan apportionment systems weighted in favor of rural areas have enabled the Republican party to maintain its control over one or both houses of the state legislature during some or all the terms of Democratic governors. Governor Al Smith described the New York legislature as "constitutionally Republican," and his Democratic successors in Albany rarely had a Democratic majority in either house. In Connecticut, where there is frequent alternation in control of the governorship, the lower house has been Democratic only once since 1876. During a fourteen-year period of Democratic governorships in Michigan that ended in 1963, that party never had a majority in either house. Other factors, such as the concentration of party strength in a few counties, played a part, but to a large extent the apportionment systems of these states have been "constitutionally Republican" and consequently have been staunchly defended by the Republican party. The growth of Republican strength in the underrepresented suburbs has had little effect on the party's position because its legislative delegation has remained predominately rural and satisfied with the status quo. In other words, the apportionment system has affected the balance of power not only between parties but also within the Republican party.[8]

In some of the Border and Southwestern states the apportionment system has helped the Democratic party maintain control. In Maryland and Arizona, for example, the rural areas are traditionally Democratic, and Republican voters are concentrated in urban and particularly suburban areas. A similar situation is evolving in some of the Southern states, such as Florida and Texas, which have substantial voting strength in the metropolitan centers. An outdated apportionment system is more likely to have lasted in a particular state if it has served partisan interests, because these have usually been more salient in the legislative process than urban or rural interests.

Often a more important deterrent to reapportionment than rural or partisan interests has been the personal interests of legislators. It is easy to understand the reluctance of a legislator to vote for a reapportionment bill that would merge his district with another and force him to run against another incumbent or to run in counties where he is little known. Moreover, widely accepted legislative norms have discouraged legislators from supporting any reapportionment that would inflict political injury on other members. Personal interests and such legislative norms have sometimes overshadowed a legislator's loyalty to his party or to the constituency that would benefit from reapportionment. For example, the only legislator representing an urban county might be reluctant to support a bill that would provide additional representation for the county and thereby diminish his political influence. Although recent judicial decisions on reapportionment have forced state legislatures to pass measures despite their impact on members' careers, the interests of incumbents are not likely to be ignored in the process. An account of the 1955 reapportionment in Illinois illustrates the point:

> Influential members all agreed that there was no point in chipping out districts that satisfied the constitutional requirement but did not satisfy the members, if it was possible to satisfy both the members and the constitution. There were innumerable combinations that would satisfy the constitution, and the more practical approach was to try to satisfy the members first.[9]

Personal considerations have also played an important part in the reluctance of state legislatures to change congressional boundaries. A member of Congress, particularly one with considerable seniority, is likely to be a figure of some importance in state politics, with friends in the legislature and with a committee seat in Congress that enables him to serve state interests. Neither he nor his constituents want the district boundaries changed, even if the district has grown too large. During the 1961 districting controversy in Ohio, Representative Clarence Brown voiced a familiar complaint: "My district fits better as it is. I don't want to lose a county of my district. I'm opposed to it. My people have grown to trust me."[10] In addition, state legislatures have been naturally slow to upset outdated arrangements of congressional districts, if they were favorable to the rural and partisan interests dominating the legislature.

Following the 1960 census there were 25 states that neither gained nor lost congressional seats. Seven of these were small states which elected one or two members at large; in none of the remaining 18 states were any changes made in congressional districts prior to the 1962 election. In only 9 of the other 25 states was there a sweeping redistricting that affected every district. More often, the legislature made a few boundary adjustments to overcome some of the more glaring inequities and to disturb incumbents as little as possible. Four states that gained a congressman elected him at large and made no change in congressional districts prior to the 1962 election.[11] It is true that, when redistricting becomes unavoidable, the majority party in the legislature usually seeks to accomplish this in such a way as to gain partisan advantage. There were examples following the 1960 census, notably in New York and California, of legislative majorities that utilized the opportunity to carry out a thorough gerrymander, which affected a large proportion of seats. More often the legislative majority proceeds cautiously, seeking partisan advantage only where changes in district boundaries appear inescapable. In legislatures with divided partisan control, compromise is essential; it is more easily accomplished by making a minimum of changes. It often appears that the two parties, and particularly the incumbent congressmen, share a common interest in creating and maintaining as many districts as possible that will produce safe majorities for one party or the other.

THE TECHNIQUES OF MALAPPORTIONMENT

Three techniques have been used by rural majorities in maintaining their dominant position in state legislatures. The simplest technique was to do nothing, to avoid periodic reapportionment. The second approach was to add to the state constitution standards for apportionment that would protect rural interests. The third technique, one of compromise, was to adopt periodic reapportionments that gave the growing urban counties less than they were entitled to by standards of equality in state constitutions. Examples of the do-nothing technique are found in Tennessee and Alabama, in both of which the legislature was still being apportioned according to the 1900 census at the time of the *Baker* v. *Carr* decision. In Illinois, where there had been no apportionment since 1901, the deadlock was broken by a 1954 constitutional amendment to assure periodic reapportionment of the House and to guarantee that Cook County (Chicago) would not get a majority of seats in the Senate.

Constitutional standards for apportionment took many forms, prior to judicial intervention. In a few legislative bodies, such as the Senate in Arizona and South Carolina or the House in Vermont, every county (or in Vermont every inhabited town) was equally represented. Most state constitutions used a population base, but only about one-third of the legislative bodies were based solely on population. A most common limitation on the equal-population principle was the provision that every county have at least one member. In a state like Iowa, with 99 counties and only 108 members of the House, this provision made the population base barely visible. In some states the population principle was used but with some maximum limit on representation of the largest counties. No city in Rhode Island, for example, could have more than one-fourth of the House membership, and no county in Oklahoma could have more than seven House members. Similarly, in Florida no county could have more than one senator; the result was a population range of districts from 10,000 to 935,000. In some states, guarantees for the smallest counties and limitations on the largest ones were combined. Some states, ostensibly following the population principle, used a sliding scale that required a smaller population (or ratio of representation) for the first member assigned to a county and a larger number for subsequent ones.

The greatest inequalities in representation occurred in states where such provisions were written into the constitution. In most states legislative approval was a prerequisite to constitutional amendment, and such limitations, once placed in the constitution, were seldom liberalized. In states whose constitution placed few, if any, restrictions on apportionment by population there was more likelihood that the legislature would fail to act, but there was also the possibility that it would make some accommodations to satisfy growing urban populations. Prior to 1962, it would be difficult to find any state in which a constitution requiring a strict population base for apportionment in both houses was promptly and accurately implemented every ten years by the legislature.

THE IMPACT OF THE COURTS

In the last few decades legislatures in malapportioned areas have not responded fully to the needs of growing urban centers. Proponents of urban interests, seeking government action to deal with the problems peculiar to metropolitan life, found rural legislators unfamiliar with and often unsympathetic to these problems. Denied effective access to the state legislature, they turned to the governor, and the development of his role as a spokesman for the urban majority contributed to his increasing influence in the legislative process. Urban interests also turned to Washington, where their demands received more response from the Democratic majority in Congress and particularly from Democratic Presidents chosen under an electoral system that overrepresented urban interests. It was because of this situation that the federal government repeatedly took the initiative in developing programs to meet urban problems and that the states played a subordinate role and were sometimes even bypassed altogether when federal assistance was extended directly to cities.

Despite the increasing involvement of the national government, the state and local government expenditures since World War II have grown twice as rapidly as the federal and have become twice as large as the domestic expenditures of the national government. Urban interests faced the inescapable fact that rural-dominated state legislatures continued to make decisions and to appropriate funds that vitally affected the cities and suburbs. Though governors were often responsive to the demands of urban interests, they usually proved to be unwilling or unable to bring about changes in legislative apportionment. Urban citizens turned to the courts for help.

Prior to 1962, the record of state courts regarding apportionment had been a negative one. They were unwilling to take steps that might force reapportionment, and their occasional decisions invalidating apportionment laws that conflicted with state constitutions were often counterproductive, in that they led to the resurrection of previous, and less equitable, apportionments. The leading federal decision was *Colegrove* v. *Green* (1946), in which the Supreme Court refused to intervene in a controversy over congressional districts in Illinois. Justice Frankfurter's opinion, in which he argued "it is hostile to a democratic system to involve the judiciary in the politics of the people," was interpreted by most lower courts to mean that the federal courts could provide no relief for malapportioned legislatures.[12] Federal district courts in Hawaii and Minnesota, however, accepted jurisdiction over apportionment cases in the late 1950s. The Supreme Court, meanwhile, was giving increasing scrutiny to Negro voting rights, and in the 1960 case of *Gomillion* v. *Lightfoot* invalidated a change of municipal boundaries in Tuskegee, Alabama, because it was designed to disenfranchise Negro voters. Justice Frankfurter, who wrote the opinion, based it on the Fifteenth Amendment and was careful to distinguish this case from cases of nonracial gerrymandering. The stage was set for a new look by the Supreme Court at the Fourteenth Amendment's guarantee of equal protection of the laws and its pertinence to the problems of apportionment.[13]

The Tennessee legislature, the subject of the Supreme Court's scrutiny in the *Baker* case, was a prime example of an inequitable apportionment system. In the sixty years since the last apportionment, the uneven growth of population had led not only to the underrepresentation of metropolitan counties in both houses but also to major inequalities among rural counties. In each house one-half of the members represented districts with just over one-fourth of the population.[14] The pattern of apportionment could not be defended as part of any rational design for balancing interests; rather it was, in Justice Clark's words, "a crazy quilt without rational basis." Clark emphasized another factor that motivated judicial intervention in the Tennessee case. In the absence of the constitutional initiative and as a result of legislative unwillingness to act, the "majority of voters were caught up in a legislative strait jacket."[15]

The Court's decision in *Baker* v. *Carr* answered only a single question: the right to equal protection under apportionment laws is "within the reach of judicial protection under the Fourteenth Amendment."[16] The Court did not say how strictly the standard of population equality would be applied, what factors might justify exceptions to it, or whether the same standard should apply to both houses of a legislature. Despite Justice Clark's remarks about the initiative, the Court did not determine whether judicial intervention was justified where other avenues were available for bypassing the legislature, nor did it mention the problem posed when a popular majority approves an apportionment that leaves minorities underrepresented in the legislature. The limited content of the Court's decision left doubts about the fate of apportionments that were more rational or more justifiable than that in Tennessee.

The answers came from state and federal district courts with surprising speed but without unanimity. In some states suits had already been filed, and in many states hearings were held quickly because of the urgency imposed by impending elections. Although the views of state and federal judges were presumably of help to the Supreme Court in its 1964 decisions, they provided nothing that could be called a consensus. Judges were sharply divided on mathematical standards of equality and on the application of the population principle to one or both houses. Some courts deferred to decisions on apportionment made at the polls, while others scorned them as irrelevant. There was greater agreement, approaching consensus, on the method of enforcement. Most federal and state courts preferred first to give the legislatures time to reapportion and then to pass judgment on the results. The courts sometimes approved the results, sometimes accepted them as a temporary expedient until a subsequent legislature could do better, and occasionally rejected the legislative product and ordered an alternative plan put into effect. The courts generally avoided the remedy of statewide at-large elections (in the belief that such elections would create more problems than they solved) and preferred apportionment plans, however imperfect or temporary, drafted by legislatures or by the courts themselves.[17]

The first clear evidence of the Supreme Court's attitude toward apportionment standards came in March of 1963 when it invalidated the Georgia county unit system used in primary elections. Speaking for the Court, Justice Douglas said: "The conception of political equality from the Declaration of Independence, to Lincoln's Gettysburg address, to the Fifteenth, Seventeenth, and Nineteenth Amendments can mean only one thing—one person, one vote."[18] On June 15 and 22, 1964, the Supreme Court handed down decisions affecting apportionment in fifteen states. In every case the result of the Court's decision was to strike down apportionments that gave too little weight to population or to uphold judicially imposed apportionments that had been challenged by rural interests. The Court's views were articulated most fully in the Alabama case, *Reynolds* v. *Sims*.

Although the Supreme Court recognized that "mathematical exactness or precision is hardly a workable constitutional requirement," it set a clear goal for the state: It must "make an honest and good faith effort to construct districts, in both houses of its legislature, as nearly of equal population as is practicable." Explicitly rejecting the federal analogy as irrelevant, the Court declared that there was "no constitutional difference" between the two houses and both must be based on population. It upheld the principle of periodic reapportionment, approved the decennial period as a reasonable one, and indicated that it would look with suspicion on any plan for less frequent reapportionment.[19] The Court refused to give any weight to popular votes on apportionment: "A citizen's constitutional rights can hardly be infringed simply because a majority of the people choose to do so."[20] The Court also refused to establish any precise or mathematical tests for population equality, but suggested that circumstances might permit some differences in standards from state to state.

What circumstances would be pertinent? The Court recognized that political subdivisions (cities and counties) have been traditionally used as a base for legislative districts and approved this as a constitutionally valid practice, provided it did not result in a significant dilution of the equal-population principle. In particular, the Court noted that some state legislatures devote much of their time to the passage of local legislation, and for this purpose it is valuable to have each political subdivision (usually the county) represented in at least one house of the legislature. The Court warned, however, that in some states this practice would not be permissible because it would result in "total subversion of the equal-population principle," and in the Ohio case the Court struck down an apportionment that was based on population except for the granting of at least one House seat to each county. The Supreme Court's instruction to lower courts and legislatures is clear: There is room for variation in the details and methods of apportionment, but the principle of population equality in both houses must always have priority.[21]

Although the *Baker* v. *Carr* case pertained to state legislatures, the Court's decision that apportionment cases were justiciable led to suits in a number of district courts which challenged congressional districts. On February 17, 1964, in the case of *Wesberry* v. *Sanders* involving Georgia's congressional districts, the Supreme Court decided that "as nearly as is practicable one man's vote in a congressional election is to be worth as much as another's." The Court did not challenge the authority of Congress to set standards regarding districts, but it did deny that Congress had exclusive authority (as Justice Frankfurter had argued in the *Colegrove* case). In a decision that reviewed in some detail speeches made at the Constitutional Convention and in the debates over ratification, the Court based its conclusion on the intent of the framers that the House should be the branch of Congress in which the people were directly and equally represented. The Court acknowledged that "it may not be possible to draw congressional districts with mathematical precision," but insisted that "that is no excuse for ignoring our Constitution's plain objective" of equal representation in the House.[22] It is also clear from the Court's remarks in the subsequent Alabama legislative apportionment case that there is less room for flexibility and less excuse for adapting congressional districts to conform to the lines of cities and counties than is true in legislative apportionment.

LEGISLATIVE RESPONSE TO JUDICIAL INITIATIVE

The judicial decisions regarding reapportionment stirred up little response from an apathetic public. There was no evidence of the bitter public resentment that had greeted the decisions on desegregation or prayer in the public schools. In the urban areas there was strong support from the newspapers and other leaders of public opinion. In states where referendums were held on constitutional amendments involving apportionment, there was no consistent pattern of voting, and it appeared that many of the voters had little understanding of their stake in legislative representation.

State legislators were often critical of the judicial pressure for reapportionment, but they preferred to undertake the task themselves, rather than leave it to the courts. In the first two years after the *Baker* v. *Carr* decision, when there was considerable doubt about how the decision would be interpreted in specific terms, most state legislatures sought to discover the minimum amount of change in apportionment that would be acceptable to the courts. In a number of states the courts found it necessary to review apportionments that were better than the previous ones but still retained some obvious inequities in population standards. In several states the legislature either enacted or submitted to the voters "federal" plans that would have based one house largely or entirely on population, and would have given equal or nearly equal representation to each county in the other house. Until the Supreme Court decision in 1964 that rejected the federal analogy, the attitude of some district courts had encouraged rural interests in the states to use this technique.

The strongest reaction to judicial initiatives came in Congress, and it did not appear until after the Supreme Court's decisions specifying that both legislative houses must be apportioned by population. During the 1964 session of Congress the House passed a bill that would have withdrawn all jurisdiction from both the federal district courts and the Supreme Court over apportionment. A similar proposal was defeated in the Senate. For a month Northern liberal Democrats in the Senate waged a filibuster against an amendment (to the foreign aid bill) that would have directed the federal courts to delay implementation of the apportionment decisions in order to prevent disruption of state election machinery. Ultimately the Senate passed a nonbinding "sense of Congress" resolution—which died in conference committee—recommending that the federal courts give the legislatures more time to apportion themselves.

During the Eighty-ninth Congress the debate continued, with attention focused on a constitutional amendment proposed by Senator Dirksen that would permit states to use factors other than population in apportioning one house of the legislature. The debate in both sessions of Congress brought to the surface the deep and bitter resentment felt by many congressmen about a wide variety of Supreme Court decisions. It served the more constructive purpose of probing the implications of the judicial decisions on apportionment for partisan, racial, and other groups in the states. Congressional deliberations have also added an element of uncertainty concerning the future pattern of apportionment in the states and the extent to which the courts will shape that pattern.

THE EFFECT OF REDISTRICTING ON CONGRESS

Although it is not possible to predict exactly how much congressional districts will be changed as a result of judicial pressures, the Supreme Court's decision in *Wesberry* v. *Sanders* clearly indicates that districts must be as nearly equal in population as is practicable. The most direct and measurable impact will be on the balance of urban, suburban, and rural power in Congress. There is no satisfactory way of classifying congressional districts as urban, suburban, or rural; many contain substantial numbers of residents in two or even all three of these categories. A rough estimate of the dimensions of change is possible, however. During the decade of the 1950s most of the districts that were substantially smaller than the average in population were outside of metropolitan areas, and most could be described as rural. Most of the districts that were substantially larger than average were in metropolitan areas. After the 1960 census a greater proportion of these large metropolitan districts were predominantly suburban, and in a few states urban districts began to appear among those substantially below the average. Urban areas were overrepresented only in the East; the greatest distortions were found in the South, where both urban and suburban areas were underrepresented. Some improvements were made when changes in district boundaries were required by the reapportionment of seats among states following the 1960 census, but at the time of the *Wesberry* decision wide variations in the size of districts remained in most states. The *Congressional Quarterly* calculated in 1963 that in an "ideal" reapportionment there would be six more urban seats and ten more suburban seats; there would be twelve fewer rural districts and four fewer districts classified as mixed.[23]

It is more difficult to evaluate the effect of congressional redistricting on the balance of partisan strength in Congress, because the party majority in a district can change over a short period of time and in some states could be changed by small revisions in district boundaries. During the 1950s the South had the largest proportion of districts that varied substantially from the average, but these variations had little effect on party fortunes. The growth of Republican voting strength in Southern metropolitan areas, however, meant that equitable representation for metropolitan districts in the South would have a potentially significant effect on the Republican party. In such states as Florida and Texas, the partisan implications of redistricting have been clearly in the minds of legislators engaged in drawing district boundaries. Outside the South during the 1950s the variations in the size of districts helped and hurt both parties. The undersized rural districts were more likely to be Republican, while the small urban districts, though fewer in number, were usually Democratic. Outside the South it is foolhardy to predict which party will gain the net advantage, either in the short run or the long run, from a redistricting that is based on a policy of maximum equality in district population. What is clear is that both parties will lose some seats in their traditional areas of strength and that a larger number of districts are likely to be marginal in their partisan allegiance.[24]

Small districts, by their very nature, are likely to be more homogeneous and therefore more safely Democratic or Republican. Moreover, most of the areas of declining population have been one-party areas: Republican in the rural North and Democratic in the South as well as in the centers of Northern metropolitan areas. The areas of the country that are gaining representation under the new standard of population equality are metropolitan areas, largely or partly suburban, which are characterized by rapid population growth and often—particularly in the South—by changes in the political environment. The most significant partisan effect of congressional redistricting appears to be that of decreasing the number of safe districts and transferring political power to areas that are in political flux or are heterogeneous in their political makeup.

Both the decline in the number of safe districts and the comprehensive redrawing of district boundaries every ten years will probably undermine the security of congressional seats, the security that makes the seniority system such an important factor in the congressional power structure. Speaker Sam Rayburn was the best known of many congressional patriarchs whose constituent base was unusually small in population and unusually homogeneous in population characteristics and partisan loyalties. It can be expected that legislatures will continue to try to protect the political base of seniority leaders in Congress, but the requirements of population equality in districting will have the gradual effect of decreasing the proportion of congressmen who enjoy long-term political security.

The most important question concerning the new standards for congressional districting is the probable effect on policies. It is also the most difficult to answer. In a subsequent chapter (17), we will explore the problem of determining differences in the roll call voting of urban and rural congressmen. An increase in the representation of metropolitan areas will guarantee that a larger proportion of congressmen are familiar with the needs of metropolitan areas. It will not necessarily guarantee that a larger proportion are "liberal" or can be counted on to vote a certain way on any particular issue. The interests of metropolitan voters are varied and are becoming more varied with the growth of suburbia. The new standards for congressional districting should mean that the average congressman must represent a more complex variety of interests, which are making greater but not always consistent demands on the national government.

EMERGING PATTERNS AND PROBLEMS IN THE STATES

Some of the consequences of the Supreme Court's decisions on the pattern of state apportionment are already evident, although others are not likely to emerge for several years. The Supreme Court has been unwilling to establish any mathematical standards for acceptable variations in the size of state legislative districts. It has sugggested some of the factors, such as local political units, that should be taken into consideration in evaluating the constitutionality of an apportionment, but it has left the clear impression that burden of proof will always be on those who are trying to justify large variations in the population of districts.

Judicial decisions have invalidated not only specific apportionments but the apportionment provisions of many state constitutions. If state constitutional provisions are invalid, legislatures are not bound by these provisions and are able to pass apportionment legislation on their own authority. Most states will presumably want to revise their constitutions to incorporate guidelines on apportionment for future legislatures. New constitutional provisions, such as legislative acts, are subject to review by the courts and presumably would be rejected unless they gave overriding consideration to the principle of population equality. Should the voters reject a constitutional amendment on apportionment that gave priority to population, the legislature would retain its authority over apportionment, subject to judicial review, until the voters had approved an amendment that met judicial standards. Because the legislature's discretion has been so strictly limited by the courts, the reapportionment process in some states may appear to have become almost automatic. As a consequence, there may be greater reliance on commissions to perform the task. In states where reapportionment involves the creation of many intracounty or multi-county districts, the legislatures may retain jurisdiction because of the political factors involved in districting.

It is too early to tell how extensively the courts will be involved in the review of apportionment measures, once the guidelines have been fully clarified by the Supreme Court and district courts. Will the courts accept the responsibility for reviewing decennial apportionments almost automatically? If so, there is the risk that legislative consideration of apportionment will become a mere preliminary skirmish. Will the courts reject only blatant deviations from the principle of population equality, or will they insist on maximum compliance with that principle? In the latter case there is the risk that the courts will be bogged down in technical details and besieged by population experts. How will the courts determine which aspects of the apportionment process are essentially political and thus beyond the scope of the court's review? These and other uncertainties will remain for some time.

Although the exact dimensions of legislative apportionment in the future remain more obscure than in the case of congressional districting, the impact of the Supreme Court decisions is more drastic and consequently the implications for state legislatures can be better assessed. Reapportionment will alter the urban–rural balance and the party balance in the state legislature, it will affect the role of the legislator, and it will have an impact on policies.

The clearest technique for measuring the arithmetical adequacy of legislative apportionment is the value of the vote (based on a value of 100 for persons equitably represented), as calculated in 1961 by David and Eisenberg for every county in the United States on the basis of the 1960 census. Table 3.1 shows how much greater the arithmetic value of the vote was in smaller counties than in the larger metropolitan counties at that time. The figures for a few specific states indicate the dimensions of urban underrepresentation in some of the states where malapportionment was most serious. This same table can be viewed as a measurement of the extent to which numerical representation will be transferred from rural to metropolitan counties when the reapportionment process initiated by the courts has been completed. The study also showed that in two-thirds of the 27 largest standard metropolitan statistical areas the value of the vote in counties containing central cities was less than 90, but usually the value of the vote was less in the suburban counties included in the metropolitan areas. The suburban parts of metropolitan areas have been most consistently underrepresented and will gain most from reapportionment. The pattern in the counties containing the largest cities has varied greatly, partly because the boundaries of some now include growing suburbs. In 1960 the value of the vote was 93 in New York City and 98 in Philadelphia, but only 54 in Los Angeles, 33 in Houston, and 12 in Atlanta. The overrepre-

Table 3.1. RELATIVE VALUES OF POPULAR VOTE
FOR REPRESENTATIVES IN STATE LEGISLATURES, 1960

States	Category of County by Population			
	Under 25,000	25,000 to 99,999	100,000 to 499,999	500,000 and over
National average—50 states	171	123	81	76
Average—7 largest states	194	155	100	77
Average—8 next largest states	180	119	78	79
Average—35 smallest states	162	105	58	67
California	562	319	132	63
Florida	476	177	46	16
Maryland	445	185	37	83
Michigan	205	146	94	74
New Jersey	—	356	100	76
Tennessee	162	118	58	49
Ohio	242	123	79	87

SOURCE: Adapted from P. T. David and R. Eisenberg, *Devaluation of the Urban and Suburban Vote* (Charlottesville, Va.: University of Virginia, Institute of Government, 1961). By permission of the publisher.

sentation of small rural counties has shown a consistent pattern, but the extent of overrepresentation has varied widely from state to state.[25] Another way of measuring the dimensions of political change implicit in the Supreme Court decision is to calculate the minimum percentage of the population that can elect a majority of legislators. Although these are hypothetical, not actual, majorities such calculations do provide a basis for comparing states. On the eve of the *Baker* v. *Carr* decision, one-third of the electorate could choose a majority of over half the state senates and two-fifths of the lower houses, and there were 14 states in which one house or both could be elected by less than 20 percent of the electorate.[26]

We have already noted that in a number of states the old apportionments that overrepresented rural areas served the interests of one political party, and that these partisan interests were usually more meaningful in the legislative process than either urban or rural interests as such. It necessarily follows that drastic changes in apportionment will substantially affect the balance of party strength in the legislature.

In the Northeast and Midwest, Democratic strength is usually concentrated in metropolitan areas that will be gaining representatives, while most of the rural counties that will be losing legislative strength are Republican. The effect is most obvious in states like Connecticut and New Jersey, where the Democratic party has usually been able to win one house when it elected a governor, but unable to carry the house in which urban areas were more seriously underrepresented. The Democratic party should benefit substantially, at least in the short run, in such states as New York, Pennsylvania, Ohio, and Illinois. Most of the Democratic central cities of metropolitan areas, even those that are losing population, have been substantially underrepresented in at least one house of the legislature. In the longer run, as reapportionment begins to benefit the suburbs at the expense of the central cities, the partisan effects are less predictable, but Republican gains may begin to outweigh their losses in rural areas. In some states the distribution of voters may have unexpected effects on the legislative strength of parties. In Michigan, for example, the Democratic vote is heavily concentrated in Detroit but represents an ineffective minority in most of the rural and smaller urban counties. As a consequence, the Democratic party will have great difficulty in translating a majority of votes into a majority of legislative seats.[27] Reapportionment will have an impact on the balance of power *within* legislative parties as well. Republican parties will gradually become more suburban than rural, and Democratic parties will be less dominated by a single big-city political organization.

In Border and Southwestern states and in parts of the South it is the Republican party that will benefit, as legislative seats are shifted from the traditionally Democratic rural counties to the cities and suburbs. In many of these states, urban Democratic organizations are weak and a low proportion of urban Democrats go to the polls. As a consequence the higher-income, Republican suburbs are outstripping the Democratic sections of the metropolis in power at the polls. The partisan impact of reapportionment will be immediate in such states as Maryland, Tennessee, Florida, Texas, and Arizona; in some parts of the metropolitan South, the Republican potential has not yet begun to be realized in legislative races. Maryland, Florida, and North Carolina are among those states where the probable Republican advantage from reapportionment has been an obvious factor in recent legislative battles over the issue. The Republican stake in reapportionment can be vividly illustrated in Florida. Most of the Republican effort in legislative contests has been concentrated in seven urban counties. In a partial reapportionment in 1963 the number of House members from these seven counties was increased from 18 to 46; in a special election the Republicans contested 27 of the 28 races for new seats, won 11 of them, and thereby tripled their strength in the Florida House.

The partisan implications of reapportionment are least evident in those states, particularly in the West, where partisan allegiance is not significantly polarized along urban-rural lines. In California, where the gross underrepresentation of Los Angeles did not mean a comparable underrepresentation of Democrats, the party that has won the governorship in recent years has usually won a majority in both houses.

Reapportionment is likely to have an effect on gubernatorial-legislative relations in many states. In states where reapportionment will make a partisan division in control of the government less likely, the governor's chances of playing a partisan role in legislative leadership are enhanced. In one-party states of the South, reapportionment may mean that a governor who is elected as a result of urban majorities will be more successful in building an urban-based bloc of supporters in the legislature. In the longer run, in the South and in other states where a minority party is beginning to challenge the traditional majority party, reapportionment will make it more likely, but far from certain, that the minority party can capture the legislature if it elects a governor.

Fundamental changes in apportionment will affect the roles of many legislators. As fewer rural legislators come to represent a single county, it is possible that fewer of them will be district-oriented and concerned primarily with local legislation. To the extent that reapportionment decreases the number of politically secure districts, the legislator's perception of his relationship to constituents is likely to change. Changes in the use of at-large and single-member districts, discussed below, will also affect the legislator. In short, all the role perceptions of a legislator that pertain to his constituency may be affected by the sweeping changes in legislative apportionment patterns now under way.

As in the case of congressional districting, it is the impact of reapportionment on policy that is most difficult to evaluate. There is ample evidence (presented in Chapter 17) that urban or metropolitan legislators seldom vote as a bloc against rural or nonmetropolitan members. Metropolitan legislators represent constituents with conflicting interests on many issues, and there are few issues on which a cleavage of interest between urban and rural groups is clearly obvious. There is considerable speculation and some evidence to suggest that in some states a major reapportionment would lead to changes in legislative policies with regard to segregation, labor, and welfare issues. The most direct effect is likely to be on taxing and spending policies. Changes are likely both in the types of taxes levied and in the authority given to cities to levy taxes. More important and more certain changes can be anticipated in the formulas adopted for the distribution of state aid, so as to overcome the gross discrimination in favor of sparsely populated counties in some states. In most two-party states, the most significant consequence of reapportionment will be the change in the balance of power both between and within the legislative parties. Consequently the most significant effects on policy will be indirect, the results of these changes in partisan strength. In most states, partisan differences on policy are much more significant than urban-rural differences per se.[28]

AT-LARGE ELECTIONS AND THE PROBLEMS OF LEGISLATIVE DISTRICTING

One effect of increasing the proportion of legislators elected from metropolitan counties is to intensify the problems of intracounty districting and to focus greater attention on the hazards of gerrymandering. This is a problem that a number of states have avoided by electing legislators at large within multi-member counties, or have minimized by creating a few multi-member districts within the largest counties. A comprehensive survey in 1954 showed that 88 percent of the Senate seats were in single-member districts, and the rest were in districts with 2, 3, or 4 members; thirty-two states elected all senators from single-member districts. In the lower houses, 55 percent of the seats were in single-member districts; although most of the multi-member districts had from 2 to 4 seats, several states had districts containing more than 10 seats, and the largest district elected 17. There were twelve states that had only single-member districts.[29]

A study of the districts at the time of the *Baker* v. *Carr* decision (summarized in Table 3.2) shows that the proportion of single-member districts had dropped slightly, to 84 per cent in the senates and 54 percent in the lower houses. It is evident from Table 3.2 that in the upper chambers almost half of the multi-member districts include more than one county. The purpose of this technique is often to make apportionment more equitable while still adhering to county lines. (Two counties, for example, may constitute a district to elect three members.) In the lower chambers, the great majority of the multi-member districts coincide with county boundaries or are formed within a county. The initial effect of reapportionment measures following the *Baker* v. *Carr* decision was to increase the number of members from multi-member districts in some of the metropolitan counties, particularly in the South.

The Mathematics of Districting. The most accurate method of translating the voting strength of parties into legislative seats is proportional representation. Although this is common in Europe, the only

Table 3.2. STATE LEGISLATIVE DISTRICTS AND MEMBERS BY TYPE OF DISTRICT, ALL STATES, MARCH 1962

Size of District vs. Size of County	Number of Districts			Number of Members		
	Single-member	Multi-member	Total	Single-member	Multi-member	Total
Lower House, 49 States						
Smaller than county	1,411	451	1,862	1,411	1,129	2,540
Identical	1,480	468	1,948	1,480	1,436	2,916
Multi-county	288	53	341	288	139	427
Total	3,179	972	4,151	3,179	2,704	5,883
Percent	76.6	23.4	100	54.0	46.0	100
*Upper House, 50 States**						
Smaller than county	365	0	365	365	0	365
Identical	578	65	643	578	180	758
Multi-county	655	62	717	655	125	780
Total	1,598	127	1,725	1,598	305	1,903
Percent	92.6	7.4	100	84.0	16.0	100

* Includes Nebraska (unicameral).

SOURCE: Adapted from P. T. David and R. Eisenberg, *State Legislative Redistricting* (Chicago: Public Administration Service, 1962), p. 20. By permission of the publisher.

such plan at the state or national level in this country is in the lower house of the Illinois legislature, where it is called *cumulative voting.* Each House district in Illinois has three seats. Each voter has 3 votes; he may give all of them to one candidate, a vote and a half each to two, 2 to one and 1 to another, or 1 vote to each of three candidates. Under this method, in most districts the stronger party elects two members and the minority party is virtually guaranteed a member in each district. But, since neither party wants to waste votes, this method has encouraged each party to run only as many candidates as it expects to elect, and in some districts it has become a common practice for the two parties to nominate a total of only three candidates. In Illinois the price for greater minority representation has been a minimum of competition and of choice for the voter.[30]

Any districting technique other than proportional representation benefits the majority party in that it wastes the votes of minority parties. Minor parties (or third parties) are severely handicapped by districting, because they rarely have a plurality in any district and, lacking pluralities, cannot elect legislators. The minority party (or second party) is handicapped by a single-member district plan and is hurt more by multi-member districts, even without any attempt at gerrymandering by the majority party. If minority party strength were evenly distributed throughout a state, that party would be a minority in every legislative district and would be unrepresented in the legislature. In practice, the minority party has concentrations of strength that enable it to elect some legislators, but in single-member districts more of its votes are wasted than the majority party loses. In a large county, if several multi-member districts are used, minority pockets of strength will be swallowed up by the majority, and if all legislators are elected at-large, all of the minority's votes may be wasted.

A	B	C	D
7,000 Dem 3,000 Rep	7,000 Dem 3,000 Rep	6,000 Dem 4,000 Rep	4,000 Dem 6,000 Rep
E	**F**	**G**	**H**
7,000 Dem 3,000 Rep	6,000 Dem 4,000 Rep	6,000 Dem 4,000 Rep	4,000 Dem 6,000 Rep
I	**J**	**K**	**L**
7,000 Dem 3,000 Rep	6,000 Dem 4,000 Rep	6,000 Dem 4,000 Rep	4,000 Dem 6,000 Rep

Figure 3.1. DIVISION OF A HYPOTHETICAL COUNTY INTO TWELVE LEGISLATIVE DISTRICTS WITH 10,000 VOTERS EACH, INDICATING THE NUMBER OF DEMOCRATIC AND REPUBLICAN VOTERS

Figure 3.1 illustrates the effects of districting in a hypothetical metropolitan county containing 120,000 voters—70,000 Democrats and 50,000 Republicans. Under a proportional representation system, the county would elect seven Democratic and five Republican legislators.

If the voters in each party were unevenly distributed throughout the county and twelve districts were established, with no attempt at gerrymandering and exactly 10,000 voters in each, the result might be as shown in Figure 3.1. The Democrats would carry nine districts, and the Republicans would carry only three (D, H, and L). The Republicans would have wasted 32,000 votes in the nine districts they lost, but the Democrats would have wasted only 12,000 votes in their three losing districts. If the county were divided into three or four multi-member districts, the Democrats could win all the seats by incorporating each of the Republican areas (D, H, and L) into a larger Democratic district.

Political Implications of At-large Elections. Multi-member districts, particularly the larger ones, are likely to be found in metropolitan counties. In Northern states using such districts, the Democratic party has gained an advantage in metropolitan areas that has helped to offset the Republican advantage derived from overrepresentation of rural areas. In Ohio the countywide metropolitan districts have been a source of recent partisan controversy, and in Michigan the Republican-dominated constitutional convention eliminated the multi-member districts that had given the Democrats virtually a monopoly over the Wayne County (Detroit) legislative delegation. In border and Southern states, where at-large elections are common, the Republican party is also likely to be handicapped by this practice as long as it represents a substantial minority in metropolitan counties.

Single-member districts, and to a greater extent multi-member districts, also contribute to the homogeneity of party delegations in the legislature. If two-thirds of the urban voters are Democrats and two-thirds of the rural voters are Republicans, the Democratic legislators are likely to represent exclusively urban areas and the areas represented by Republican legislators are likely to be exclusively rural. The greater the concentration of a party's voters in one section of a state or in urban or rural counties, the more this homogeneity in the legislature will be exaggerated by the districting system.

The advantage that the majority party derives from a multi-member district is dependent on straight party voting by supporters of that party; this has proven to be the usual pattern. Only if there is a close balance between Democratic and Republican voters, or if one man on the minority party's slate is particularly popular, is there likely to be a partisan division in the legislative delegation from the district. This can be indicated by recent election returns in 4 two-party states. The Pennsylvania House has had 41 multi-member districts electing 97 members; in three elections in the 1950s there were only four cases of partisan division in a district. In all five elections to the Indiana House during the

1950s, the nine multi-member districts, which elected 34 members, had only two examples of divided delegations. In the five elections, 1954–62, there were no divided delegations elected in the seventeen Michigan House districts, which chose 41 members. In five elections from 1952 through 1960, the seventeen West Virginia counties, which elected 62 members, had only eight divided delegations.

The type of district used in a state has an effect on competition in legislative primaries and elections. Evidence from Tennessee and Indiana suggests that the effect of the use of an at-large method in multi-member counties is to increase the number of candidates running.[31] Available statistical evidence fails to show whether incumbents benefit more from the chance to build a secure base in a small district or from the advantage of being well known, an important requirement for victory in a large, multi-member district.[32] A variation of the at-large method used in some states provides that candidates must designate which "place" or "position" they are running for, although the voters throughout the district vote for candidates for all places. Under this method, the incumbents are likely to have a minimum of opposition, while candidates scramble for the positions that have no incumbent in the race.

The nature of the districts may also affect campaign techniques and even legislative behavior. Candidates running at-large in a metropolitan county must wage a more extensive and expensive campaign than would be necessary in a small district. The candidates of one party running at-large know that their fortunes are linked together; it is likely that they will all win or all lose. These factors frequently lead the candidates to campaign jointly, with common advertising and financing. One study of Colorado politics showed that the joint campaigns in Denver made the Democratic candidates dependent on the party organization, which gained unusual influence over primary nominations through preprimary conventions. Moreover, Denver Democrats tended to vote together as a bloc in the legislature, considerably enhancing their influence.[33] In Texas, the development of liberal and conservative slates in the Democratic primary in metropolitan counties is probably enhanced by the fact that candidates run at-large (which is expensive), and run for a designated place (which facilitates cooperation, since candidates are not all running against each other).

The Problem of Gerrymandering. Gerrymandering is defined broadly as drawing district lines in such a way as to give an unreasonable or unfair advantage to one party. We shall use the term here in a somewhat narrower sense, to describe a tactic of districting for the benefit of one party that does not rely primarily on discriminatory variations in the population size of districts. There is, of course, no "right" way to draw district lines within a county or a city. There are an almost infinite number of ways to draw the boundaries, and some of these would be more likely to benefit one party or the other. The term gerrymandering is most often applied when natural or traditional boundaries are ignored or when the resulting districts have strange shapes, which betray their lack of compactness. The congressional districting in New York City, undertaken in 1961 by the Republican majority in the legis-

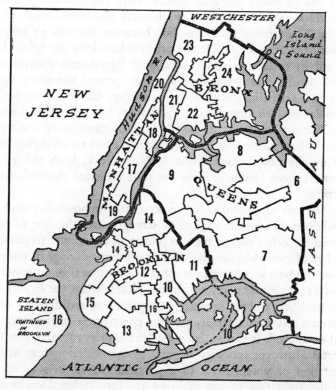

Figure 3.2. CONGRESSIONAL DISTRICTS IN NEW YORK CITY UNDER 1961 DISTRICTING

lature, is a classic example, illustrated in Figure 3.2. It is worth noting that none of the congressional districts in New York City varied by more than 16 percent from the state average and almost half of them varied by less than 10 percent.

We have noted that any single-member district system wastes votes, and that more votes are usually wasted by the minority party. The purpose of any gerrymander carried out by the majority party is to waste as many votes of the minority party as possible. This can be done in either of two ways. If the minority party is weak enough (or the majority party is bold enough), the areas of minority strength may be split up and attached to larger areas that are safe for the majority. The other alternative, practiced in areas where the minority strength is too great to be diffused, is to create one or more districts that can be carried overwhelmingly by the minority party, in order to waste minority votes and to assure majority control over the remaining districts.[34]

The map of New York City districts illustrates some of these techniques. The strange boundary line between districts 23 and 24 resulted from the transfer of Democratic pockets into the safely Democratic 23rd in order to ensure continued Republican control of the 24th. This is also the explanation for the unusual boundary between the 14th and 15th districts. The 15th district, like the noncontiguous 16th, was designed to unite Republican voters, however widely scattered their residences.[35] But gerrymandering is a hazardous sport, and the best-laid plans of the majority party are sometimes upset by changing political tides or mobile populations. Thus, in New York, both the 15th and 16th districts went Democratic in the 1962 elections that followed the redistricting.

The hazards of gerrymandering, its virtual impossibility under certain conditions of concentrated party strength, and the fear of retribution should the other party come to power all contribute to minimizing the number of more blatant examples of gerrymandering. In some states there may also be a legislative norm that discourages blatant or unreasonable efforts to maximize party advantage. Nevertheless, the larger number of urban members and the increasing frequency of redistricting required by the courts may now intensify partisan controversy over gerrymandering, real or alleged. Is this an issue that the aggrieved party can take to the courts? However seriously flagrant gerrymandering may affect the representation of voters loyal to a political party, the obstacles to a judicial determination of the question are formidable. Despite the reapportionment decisions, the Supreme Court is likely to continue its efforts to avoid issues that are strictly political, and this is a highly political issue in at least two senses. The question of gerrymandering is a partisan matter, directly involving the interests of party organizations. Moreover, it meets one of the tests of a political question as defined by the Court in *Baker* v. *Carr*, because there is "a lack of judicially discoverable and manageable standards for resolving it."[36] There is, as we have said, no "right" way to draw district lines, and there is no formula available for establishing districts in such a way as to minimize the votes wasted by either or both parties. Moreover, it is not always clear what kind of district best serves a party's interests, and there is an implicit contradiction between the party's interest in wasting as few votes as possible and a legislator's interest in being elected by a wide margin in a safe district.

Representation of Minority Groups. Districting affects not only parties but also minority groups. In the past the rate of speed at which members of various nationality groups won seats in the legislature was affected by the way in which district boundaries within cities were drawn. Today the minority most vitally concerned is the Negro. The growing size of the Negro vote in both Northern and Southern cities is bringing to the fore the question of Negro representation in state legislatures. In cities where Negro voters constitute a substantial minority, their interest in representation is similar, but not identical, to that of a minority party. It is possible, at least in theory, to design a "gerry-mander" that will minimize Negro representation, either by concentrating Negro voters in one district or by scattering them among a number of districts. If the Negro voters are highly concentrated geographically, however, it may be difficult to avoid their being concentrated in few districts; if their surplus votes are wasted, that is not necessarily a consequence of gerrymandering.

When boundary lines are being drawn, Negro political leaders often seek to create districts heavily enough Negro to ensure the election of Negro legislators, and they are not usually concerned with the votes that are wasted. It is understandable, at present, that their first concern is to elect Negroes. An alternative or supplementary strategy of the leadership might be, however, to create in a larger number of districts a minority Negro bloc substantial enough to influence elections; dispersion of Negro voting strength would not necessarily be as disadvantageous as dispersion of a minority party's strength. In short, the drawing of district lines will affect the ability of Negroes to translate their growing strength at the polls into legislative power, but the nature of the effect and the tactics of Negro leaders regarding districts may vary with circumstances.

The districting method that has the clearest effect on Negro representation is the at-large election. If Negro voters constituted a majority in a metropolitan county, they could dominate an at-large election; if they were a large enough minority, they might hold the balance of power. For the present, however, countywide at-large elections in a metropolitan county seem virtually certain to give Negroes less representation than nearly any other form of districting. At-large elections, and particularly those that use an entire county as the district, are more prevalent in the South than elsewhere. It is sometimes possible for Negroes to elect a member by "one-shot" voting, but in some states legislators must run for a particular position or place on the ballot and the "one-shot" technique is impossible. The "place" method has been discussed or adopted by some Southern counties in legislative or local elections to prevent such Negro tactics.[37]

The Supreme Court's decision, in the 1960 *Gomillion* case, that a redistricting of the municipal boundaries of Tuskegee to exclude Negro voters was invalid suggests that the Court might be more willing to review a gerrymandering case if it involved allegations of discrimination against Negroes, although the difficulties of determining judicial standards for districting are at least as great in racial cases as they would be in cases of partisan gerrymandering. Judicial intervention seems more likely in the case of multi-member at-large districts, which the Supreme Court has recognized might "operate to minimize or cancel out the voting strength of racial or political elements of the voting population."[38]

NOTES

1. 369 U.S. 186.
2. *Reynolds* v. *Sims*, 377 U.S. 533 at 576.
3. 376 U.S. 1.
4. Andrew Hacker, *Congressional Districting* (Washington, 1963), pp. 5–14.
5. *Ibid.*, pp. 41–42.
6. Gordon E. Baker, *State Constitutions: Reapportionment* (New York, 1960), p. 31.
7. Gordon E. Baker, *Rural Versus Urban Political Power* (New York, 1955), pp. 6–10.
8. For a more detailed analysis of the partisan implications of apportionment, see the articles by Gus Tyler and David I. Wells on New York and by Karl A. Lamb on Michigan in Malcolm E. Jewell (ed.), *The Politics of Reapportionment* (New York, 1962), chaps. 13 and 15.
9. Gilbert Y. Steiner and Samuel K. Gove, *Legislative Politics in Illinois* (Urbana, 1960), p. 97.
10. Jewell, *op. cit.*, p. 186.
11. Hacker, *op. cit.*, chap. 5.
12. 328 U.S. 549 at 553–54.
13. The cases leading up to *Baker* v. *Carr* are carefully analyzed in James E. Larson, *Reapportionment and the Courts* (University, Ala., 1962); and in Anthony Lewis, "Legislative Apportionment and the Federal Courts," *Harvard Law Review*, LXXI (1958), 1057–98.
14. For the background to the case, see the article by Wilder Crane in Jewell, *op. cit.*, chap. 17.
15. *Baker* v. *Carr*, 369 U.S. 186 at 254, 258–59.
16. *Ibid.*, at 237.
17. There are many studies analyzing the problems faced and decisions reached by lower courts between 1962 and 1964. See especially Paul T. David and Ralph Eisenberg, *State Legislative Redistricting* (Chicago, 1962); "The Problem of Mal-apportionment: A Symposium on *Baker* v. *Carr*," *Yale Law Journal*, LXXII (November 1962), 1–106; and Robert G. Dixon, Jr., "Apportionment Standards and Judicial Power," *Notre Dame Lawyer*, XXXVIII (1963), 367–400.
18. *Gray* v. *Sanders*, 372 U.S. 368 at 381.
19. *Reynolds* v. *Sims*, 377 U.S. 533 at 571–84.

20. *Lucas* v. *Colorado General Assembly,* 377 U.S. 713 at 736–37.
21. *Reynolds* v. *Sims,* 377 U.S. 533 at 578–81.
22. *Wesberry* v. *Sanders,* 376 U.S. 1 at 7–8, 18.
23. Hacker, *op. cit.,* chap. 4. *Congressional Quarterly Weekly Report,* XX (Feb. 2, 1962), 153–69; XX (Sept. 28, 1962), 1601–89; XXI (Sept. 20, 1963), 1642–44.
24. Hacker, *op. cit.,* chap. 4; Jewell, *op. cit.,* pp. 24–25.
25. Paul T. David and Ralph Eisenberg, *Devaluation of the Urban and Suburban Vote* (Charlottesville, Va., 1961), pp. 1–16.
26. *Compendium on Legislative Apportionment* (New York, 1962), pp. iii, iv.
27. Karl A. Lamb, William J. Pierce, and John P. White, *Apportionment and Representative Institutions: The Michigan Experience* (Washington, 1963), pp. 309–332.
28. For examples of the effect of malapportionment on policy, see Baker, *Rural Versus Urban Political Power,* pp. 27–39.
29. Maurice Klain, "A New Look at the Constituencies: The Need for a Recount and a Reappraisal," *American Political Science Review,* XLIX (1955), 1105–19.
30. George S. Blair, "Cumulative Voting: Patterns of Party Allegiance and Rational Choice in Illinois State Legislative Contests," *American Political Science Review,* LII (1958), 123–30.
31. Malcolm E. Jewell, "Competition and Factionalism in Southern Legislative Primaries and Elections" (Unpublished paper presented at the 1962 meeting of the American Political Science Association); William H. Standing and James A. Robinson, "Inter-party Competition and Primary Contesting: The Case of Indiana," *American Political Science Review,* LII (1958), 1066–77.
32. For an extensive analysis of this and other alleged consequences of multi-member districts, see Ruth C. Silva, "Compared Values of the Single- and Multi-member Legislative District," *Western Political Quarterly,* XVII (1964), 504–16.
33. William P. Irwin, "Colorado: A Matter of Balance," in Jewell, *The Politics of Reapportionment,* chap. 2.
34. A clear and well-illustrated analysis of gerrymandering and the wasting of votes is found in Hacker, *op. cit.,* chap. 3.
35. Jewell, *The Politics of Reapportionment,* pp. 225–29.
36. 369 U.S. 186 at 217.
37. See William E. Wright, *Memphis Politics: A Study in Racial Bloc Voting* (New York, 1962).
38. *Fortson* v. *Dorsey,* 85 Sup. Ct. 501 (1965).

[4]

Legislative Elections

CONGRESSMAN A comes from a district in the Deep South which consists of small towns and farm areas. It is below average in population, not having been affected by redistricting in forty years. Congressman A was first elected fourteen years ago, after a narrow victory in the Democratic primary following the retirement of the incumbent. In the next three primaries, he won by increasing margins. Since that time he has been unopposed in the primaries, and he has never had a Republican opponent. His personal popularity and the strength of his personal organization in the district seem to preclude effective opposition.

Senator B, a Democrat, was elected to his first term six years ago in a large Northern industrial state. He narrowly defeated a veteran Republican senator in a year when the Democrats were making electoral gains across the country. Since that time a popular Republican governor (who may run against him) has been elected, and there are other signs of Republican revival in his state. Senator B's prospects in the forthcoming election are precarious.

Legislator C is a Republican senator who represents a medium-sized city in the legislature of a Midwestern state. Long active in party organizational work, he agreed to run for senator four years ago in a normally Democratic district because the party was having difficulty filling that position on the slate. He was swept into office when his party's candidate for governor scored a surprisingly strong victory. Legislator C has no elaborate campaign plans because he believes that the outcome of his reelection contest depends largely on the coattails of the governor, who has promised to make several campaign appearances in his city.

No congressman or state legislator can be described as typical. These three examples illustrate the variety of situations that confront a legislator when he faces reelection. Districts vary enormously in size. United States Senators represent states which range in population from a quarter of a million to 18 million; in 1962 congressional districts ranged from less than 200,000 to nearly 1 million. It is even more difficult to describe a "typical" state legislative district. The single state senator from Los Angeles County once had 6 million constituents, but in several of the New England states there are legislators with fewer than 1,000 constituents. United States Senators face reelection every six years, and United States Representatives every two years. State senators serve four-year terms in 36 states and two-year terms in 14 states; representatives serve four-year terms in only four states, two-year terms in the rest. Legislative campaigns are affected by the nature of the districting system, the intensity of primary and two-party competition, and the candidate's dependence upon the party and its major candidates for assistance. We shall explore each of these factors to determine how it influences legislative elections.

An understanding of the factors affecting elections is important for several reasons. First, it helps to explain the recruitment of legislators and the variation among legislatures in turnover and personnel. The power structure in Congress and in some state legislatures is a product of variations in electoral districts; congressmen from safe districts with a minimum of competition have acquired the seniority essential for holding the positions of power. Above all, the electoral situation confronting a legislator affects his role. Congressman A, with his secure electoral base, has greater freedom to choose his role, and he is likely to respond to the demands of his congressional colleagues and the norms established in Congress and in his committees. Senator B has less freedom; if he can determine what his constituents want, he must give them priority in his resolution of the inevitable role conflicts that confront him. Legislator C, if he believes that the governor's coattails are essential to his political survival, may define his role in accordance with the expectations of the governor, and may thus contribute to a high level of party unity in the legislature.

TWO-PARTY COMPETITION

A congressman or state legislator faces two potential obstacles when he decides to run again: the primary and the general election. His role as a legislator and in the long run his power in the legislative body are affected by the frequency and strength of the opposition he encounters in hurdling these two obstacles. Several standards can be used to measure competition in the general election. A minimum level of competition requires that both parties run candidates. A higher level is attained when the election is close rather than one-sided. At the highest level of competition, there is some partisan turnover in a legislative seat over a period of years.

Congressional Seats. Senators face a possible challenge at the polls only one-third as often as representatives, but they represent constituencies that, with few exceptions, are larger and more heterogeneous. It it more difficult for a senator than for a representative to build a secure political base by assiduous attention to the needs of his constituents. There are vast differences, however, in the electoral problems faced by senators from various states. In some states, notably the larger industrial states and some of those in the West, even a strong senator with years of seniority is likely to face vigorous competition from the opposition party. In other states, reelection is assured for any incumbent, once the primary hurdle has been cleared. Out of almost 700 senatorial elections held from 1920 through 1962, nearly one-third were won by less than 55 percent of the two-party vote (almost evenly divided between Republican and Democratic victories). The Republicans won another one-fourth by larger margins (19 percent by a margin of 55 to 69 percent, and only 6 percent by 70 percent or more). The Democrats won 43 percent by larger margins (23 percent by a margin of 55 to 69 percent, and 20 percent by more than 70 percent, many of these in Southern states without any opposition).[1]

Table 4.1 summarizes the various levels of competition found in United States House districts during the 1952–1960 period. In over half of the districts, one party won every election by at least 55 percent of the vote. The 38 districts in which one party never had opposition were exclusively Democratic districts, located in nine of the Southern states. There were 113 districts in which one party always had at least 60 percent of the vote, and 70 other districts in which one party always had at least 55 percent of the vote. Districts in these two categories may also be classed as "one-party," because they never had turnover or close elections, they often had very one-sided elections, and (particularly in Democratic districts) there was frequently no opposition. Of the 116 Democratic districts of this kind, almost half (53) were in the South, and most of the rest were concentrated in urban and suburban districts of large industrial states. The 67 Republican districts included a majority of rural districts, but also a large minority of urban and suburban districts, both categories being concentrated in a few large industrial states. The proportion of congressional seats changing party control during a decade has declined from 30 percent (1932–1940) to 26 percent (1942–1950) to 22 percent in the 1952–1960 period.[2]

The South has by far the greatest concentration of one-party districts; 88 percent of the Southern districts were in that category from 1952 to 1960. The number of Republican candidates in the 106 congressional seats of the eleven Southern states grew gradually and unevenly from 31 in 1952 to 46 in 1960, and then increased more rapidly to 57 in 1962 and 75 in 1964. Republican efforts have focused on metropolitan areas; during the 1952–1960 period the party ran candidates in over half of the urban and suburban districts, but in just over one-fourth of the remaining Southern districts. In 1962 there were Republican candidates in all but 3 of the 25 urban and suburban districts.

Table 4.1. LEVEL OF TWO-PARTY COMPETITION IN CONGRESS: DEGREES OF COMPETITION IN FIVE ELECTIONS, 1952–1960

Level of Competition	Total	Southern	No. House Districts		
			Non-Southern		
			Rural	Urban	Suburban
ONE-PARTY	221	93	50	51	27
Democratic (unopposed)	38	38	0	0	0
Democratic (60% or more)	88	44	7	30	7
Democratic (55–59.9%)	28	9	7	8	4
Republican (60% or more)	25	0	16	2	7
Republican (55–59.9%)	42	2	20	11	9
COMPETITIVE	214	13	105	63	33
No partisan turnover	119	10	54	37	18
Partisan turnover	95	3	51	26	15
Total	435	106	155	114	60

SOURCE: Based on percentages compiled by the *Congressional Quarterly* and published in the *CQ Weekly Report*, XIX (March 10, 1961).

State Legislative Seats. Since state legislative districts are usually smaller than congressional districts, they are likely to have greater homogeneity, and we would expect to find a higher proportion of them consistently electing legislators of a single party. In states where one party is dominant, minority party strength is likely to be concentrated in a few districts of traditional support, and the number of competitive districts, as measured by party turnover, is likely to be small. This is the case for four states in Table 4.2: Kentucky, Tennessee, Oklahoma, and (with fewer safe Republican districts) North Carolina. Even in two-party states, each of the parties may have its strength so concentrated in different areas that relatively few seats change hands, as is the case for two other states in the table: Michigan and Rhode Island—both states where the Democratic party is overwhelmingly a metropolitan party. Party turnover in West Virginia and Indiana is considerably higher; both are states where party strength is less polarized along urban-rural lines.

The low proportion of districts with turnover in most states prompts us to use a lower standard of competition: the proportion of seats for which both parties run candidates. This varies in large part according to the strength of two-party competition at the state level. In most of the South two-party legislative contests are rare, except in a few large metropolitan counties. In such states as Tennessee, Kentucky, and North Carolina, from one-third to one-half the seats are contested. At the other extreme, there has been two-party competition in recent years for nearly every legislative seat in Michigan, Indiana, New York, Connecticut,

Table 4.2.   PARTY TURNOVER BY DISTRICT, LOWER HOUSES

State	No. of Elections	Years	Districts		Seats		
			Total	Party turn-over	Total	Party turnover	
						No.	%
SOUTH							
Kentucky	6	1947–57	100	13	100	13	13
North Carolina	5	1952–60	100	18	120	21	18
Oklahoma	7	1944–56	77	15	121	23	19
Tennessee	6	1950–60	82	15	99	17	17
NORTH							
Indiana	5	1950–58	75	44	100	64	64
Michigan	5	1954–62	86	10	110	11	10
Rhode Island	5	1950–58	100	22	100	22	22
West Virginia	5	1952–60	55	19	100	40	40

SOURCE: State yearbooks, appropriate years.

and Rhode Island. The degree of competition at the state level is not, however, the only factor affecting competition for legislative seats. Legislative contests are more prevalent where there are strong local party organizations, which carry at least part of the burden of recruiting candidates. A shortage of candidates indicates a breakdown of party responsibility. A party with a traditional minority status in a state is likely to have weak local organizations, but even a strong statewide party may have local weaknesses. New Hampshire and Kentucky are examples of states where the traditional majority party has failed to contest as many as 10 percent of the legislative seats in some recent elections.

What are the sources of strength or weakness in party organizations? V. O. Key has argued that the growth of the direct primary for nominations at both the state and local level has produced stagnation in local party organizations, which have been deprived of their responsibility for nominations.[3] Several of the states where most legislative elections are contested are ones in which the primary has been little used. Rhode Island and Connecticut were the last two states to adopt a primary, and in these states the legislative endorsements of local party organizations are seldom challenged in a primary. The continued use of the convention for statewide (although not local) nominations in Indiana and New York gives local party organizations there a continuing *raison d'être*. In some of the competitive two-party states where wide-open primary contests are frequent, a number of legislative races are uncontested; Massachusetts and California are examples of this.[4]

In the absence of a viable local party organization which receives support from the state party, the chances of candidates running for the legislature decline as the prospects of victory diminish in any given district. There are many counties across the country where local politics has been dominated for decades by a single party. Some are in one-party states and some are in competitive two-party states. These counties are likely to be rural ones. One-party domination of politics in a particular county is rooted in history: patterns of migration, the impact of the Civil War and Reconstruction, religious and ethnic characteristics of the population, or economic factors. The reason why a county is Republican or Democratic may be lost from the memory of inhabitants, but the tradition is a powerful one. Young voters inherit their party affiliation: they find only one set of candidates on the ballot in local elections, and grow accustomed to one-party government. Local politics may be insulated from the political trends that change the voting habits of some residents in national and even state elections. Legislative races are regarded as local, and the one-party monopoly over these is unlikely to be broken until two-party competition develops in other local elections.

Districts in metropolitan and other urban areas are more likely to be competitive than rural districts in some states, such as Ohio and Kentucky, where the contrasts are sharp.[5] Greater resources of finance and personnel are usually available to both party organizations, and the large numbers of votes at stake for national and state elections provide both parties with an incentive for presenting a full slate of local candidates to stimulate voting. Moreover, urban life is characterized by a greater population mobility, which upsets traditional voting habits. Again, larger cities have a variety of economic and social classes and consequently potential voting support for both parties. In some states other factors may offset this tendency. In some Northern metropolitan centers, such as Boston, Baltimore, Detroit, and Milwaukee, Democratic strength is so great in certain districts that the Republican party does not run candidates.

In a state where a party that is traditionally in the minority is making a serious statewide bid for power, it faces arduous organizational tasks at the local level if it hopes to produce a full legislative slate. Often a popular minority candidate wins the governorship while his party loses a large number of legislative races by default. The Michigan Democrats had only a handful of legislative seats and contested only one-fourth of them in the 1920s; even in the 1930s, when they won some governorship races and elected an occasional legislative majority, they left as many as one-fourth of the seats uncontested. Not until recent years did the party grow strong enough to contest nearly every seat.

In recent years the Republicans have begun to contest increasing numbers of legislative districts in the South. There are areas of traditional Republican strength in Virginia, North Carolina, Tennessee, and several of the Border states. But the increase in Republican candidacies, like that in congressional races, has been concentrated in metropolitan areas, where the party has organizational and financial strength and where it can solicit the support of the presidential Republicans found in the suburbs. This increase has been most marked in the most urbanized Southern states, Texas and Florida. The number of Republican legislative candidates in Texas rose from 5 in 1956 to 81 in 1964, out of a total of 166 seats. In both states the Republican candidates have been concentrated primarily in urban areas.

COMPETITION IN PRIMARIES

Congressional Seats. United States senators are nominated by direct primaries in most states. The convention system is used in Connecticut, New York, Delaware, Indiana, and Idaho, and by the Republican party in many Southern states. A tabulation of Democratic senatorial primaries from 1920 through 1954 showed that about 90 percent of all incumbent senators were successful when they sought renomination. The closest competition was in Southern Democratic primaries, where 42 percent of the elections involving incumbents were won by less than 60 percent of the vote; elsewhere, only 15 percent of the contests were that close. Among Democratic incumbents the chance of defeat was about 30 out of 100 in the South, and only 2 out of 100 in the rest of the country. In the absence of incumbents in the Democratic primary, Table 4.3 shows that competition increases as the likelihood of victory in the general election grows. V. O. Key reported a similar pattern in Republican senatorial primaries. The prospects for electoral victory are not the only factor affecting competition. In some cases, particularly in a closely competitive state, a strong party organization will succeed in designating the candidate and discouraging primary opposition; in competitive states, where party organizations are weaker, this is less likely.[6]

Table 4.3. COMPETITION IN DEMOCRATIC SENATORIAL PRIMARIES NOT INVOLVING INCUMBENTS, 1920–1960

Democratic % of General Election Vote	Percentage of Primaries by Percentage of Primary Vote to Nominee			Total No. Primaries
	Under 60	60–89	90–100	
10–39.9	20	12	68	76
40–59.9	44	25	31	197
60–100	51	35	14	43
Total	39	23	38	316
In South	60	31	9	35
Elsewhere	36	22	41	281

SOURCE: Adapted from V. O. Key, Jr., *Politics, Parties and Pressure Groups* (New York: Thomas Y. Crowell Co., 1964), p. 438. By permission of the publisher.

In House elections, Key found that with an incumbent running, the proportion of close primaries (those in which the winner has less than 60 percent of the vote) in the 1948, 1952, and 1954 elections ranged from 5 to 15 percent for both parties. When there was no incumbent, competition increased as electoral prospects rose: for hopeless, marginal, and safe districts the proportion of close Democratic primaries from 1952 through 1958 in a large selection of states was 21, 40, and 73 percent, respectively; the comparable proportions of close Republican primaries were 22, 44, and 58 percent.[7]

Congressmen in two-party districts are vulnerable to national political trends; the uncertainties of the general election and the need for party unity in a close district usually minimize the chances of primary opposition. In a one-party district the congressman is relatively immune from national trends; he is normally able to develop a reputation and cultivate support by careful attention to local needs, and consequently he is seldom challenged seriously and rarely defeated in the primary. After several terms in office, the congressman from either kind of district becomes nearly invulnerable to defeat in the primary.[8] Constituents become familiar with his name, recognize the value of the seniority he has acquired on committees, remember the favors he has done for them and their communities, and usually forget—if they ever knew—about votes that he has cast in conflict with their viewpoints. Candidates brash enough to challenge the incumbent in the primary are often scorned by party leaders, who consider their action almost a form of lèse majesté.

State Legislature Seats. Since the proportion of one-party districts is greater in many state legislatures than it is in Congress, it becomes even more important to inquire whether the primary serves as an adequate substitute for the general election in safe legislative districts. On the surface, this would seem to be true. Studies in a number of states, by V. O. Key and others, have shown that legislative primary competition increases with the prospects of victory in the general election.[9] When a party is virtually sure of victory, candidates have the greatest incentive to run in the primary. The prospect of a close election reduces the incentive and often leads to efforts by the party organization to preserve unity. When election prospects are dim, candidates may have to be drafted by party leaders, who are lucky if they can find one. As one writer points out, where electoral victory is unlikely, "the overriding criterion for the legislative candidate is simply the willingness to run as a sacrificial candidate. . . . To the politically ambitious, the race for the legislature appears the most nearly hopeless one in a one-party district."[10]

The contrast in primary competition between safe and marginal districts can be demonstrated most clearly in two-party states. Table 4.4 shows sharp contrasts in primary competition among safe, marginal, and hopeless districts in Indiana, Wisconsin, Pennsylvania, and Michigan. A breakdown among the safer districts in the first three states would show a slight decrease in primary competition in those districts that are safest, for reasons that may be related to incumbency or differing district characteristics. A similar pattern prevails in the border states of Kentucky and Tennessee, although the very low level of primary competition in hopeless districts results from the fact that in a number of these races the party runs no candidate at all. Although these figures show that primary competition in the majority party serves in a sense as a substitute for the election in areas dominated by one party, this is an imperfect substitute. In Wisconsin, from 1946 through 1956, 15 percent of the general elections were uncontested, and in nearly half of these the majority party had no contested primary. In the Kentucky House the number of members elected without primary or general-election opposition from 1947 through 1957 ranged from 13 to 24 and averaged 18 out of 100. The proportion is similar in Florida—20 percent in both houses in 1956.[11]

Table 4.4. PRIMARY COMPETITION AND ELECTORAL PROSPECTS

Legislative Body	Year	Contested Primaries by District, %		
		Safe*	Marginal*	Hopeless*
Indiana House	1948	84	65	33
Wisconsin Assembly	1954–56	52	43	14
Pennsylvania House	1958	53	36	9
Michigan, both houses	1958–62	72	60	40
Kentucky, both houses (Dem.)	1947–57	67	54	3
Tennessee, both houses (Dem.)	1950–60	68	46	1

* The definition of districts is based on the legislative election in the year specified for Indiana and Pennsylvania, and on the gubernatorial and legislative elections in Wisconsin in 1956. For Indiana and Pennsylvania, hopeless districts are under 40% and safe districts are 60% or over; for Wisconsin hopeless districts are under 45% and safe districts are 55% and over. For Michigan safe districts are those won consistently by one party from 1954 through 1962; marginal districts have some party turnover during that period. For Kentucky and Tennessee, safe districts are those won by a party in every election during the period or ones in which the minority party did not always run candidates; marginal districts are ones with turnover or in which both parties always ran candidates.

SOURCES: V. O. Key, Jr., *American State Politics* (New York: Alfred A. Knopf, Inc., 1956), p. 174 (Indiana); Leon D. Epstein, *Politics in Wisconsin* (Madison: University of Wisconsin Press, 1958), p. 201; Frank J. Sorauf, *Party and Representation* (New York: Atherton Press, 1963), p. 112 (Pennsylvania).

Other factors may affect the likelihood of primary competition. Key has suggested that in many rural areas less effort and fewer resources are necessary to monopolize party control than in large urban centers characterized by a multiplicity of power centers. Control by a small clique in a rural county may be easily preserved, if there are too few persons interested enough in politics to present an effective challenge. Studies have shown that legislative primary competition is greater in the urban than in the rural areas of some states, such as Wisconsin, Michigan, and Ohio, with the pattern consistent in both marginal and safe districts.[12]

Urban-rural differences are more easily discerned in those parts of the South that are under solid one-party control. In several Southern states, urban districts have more primary competition, although the contrasts with rural districts are moderate, and considerably less than the variations from state to state. The likelihood of contested primaries is slightly greater, and the prospects for more than two candidates considerably greater, in urban than in rural districts in the South. Several other factors complicate the picture. In at least two states, Alabama and Louisiana, there is substantially lower primary competition in "black belt" counties, rural areas with a large number of nonvoting Negroes, where white politicians have a greater incentive to minimize the competition and open controversy that might possibly lead to increased Negro registration and voting. In Southern states that use rotation agreements in rural, multi-county districts, the agreement affects competition by preventing incumbents from running.

Rotation agreements are best suited to one-party areas and are more widely prevalent in the South than elsewhere. They are agreements made by party committees in each county of a multi-county district, and provide for rotation of the legislative seat from county to county, with a member usually serving no more than two or four years. In Tennessee and North Carolina, the state law provides that ballots shall be cast in the primary only by voters in the county from which the candidate is selected; the other voters in the district are temporarily disenfranchised. A similar law in Georgia, which was invalidated by a federal court in 1962, differed by requiring rather than permitting such rotation agreements. Rotation agreements usually apply to the Senate, where multi-county districts are more common. They are used in nearly every multi-county Senate district in Alabama, where they have been common for sixty years. In Tennessee they are used in a smaller proportion of legislative seats, but those in effect in 1960 (prior to reapportionment) were virtually identical to those that had been used forty years earlier. In some other Southern states, such as Texas, for no obvious reason rotation agreements are not used. This institution appears to be a matter of custom and tradition, only occasionally reinforced by law.

Do incumbent state legislators develop the political strength to discourage primary competition, as we have seen congressmen do? In most states for which studies have been made, the evidence shows that competition drops when incumbents are running, but the drop is less pronounced than in congressional races. Incumbency has less effect on the proportion of contested primaries than on the proportion of those that are closely contested; one-sided races are more likely when an incumbent is running. There are sharp variations from state to state both in the proportion of incumbents who seek reelection and in the effect of incumbency on primary competition. In Texas there are incumbents in a high proportion of the races (80 percent), and their presence reduces by almost half the proportion of closely contested primaries (those won by less than 60 percent). In Ohio only two-thirds as many primaries occur when there are incumbents running.[13]

What are the chances of an incumbent losing in the primary? The few pieces of evidence available suggest that legislators in two-party states have a high survival rate in primaries, though it is not so high as that of congressmen. In three Michigan elections (1958–1962), only 5 percent of the legislators who sought renomination were defeated in the primary. In Wisconsin (over a period of six elections, beginning in 1940), 14 percent of the incumbents who ran in the primary lost, twice as many as those who lost in the election.[14] In Southern states that are dominated by a single party, the primary is a more serious obstacle, one that varies from state to state. The percentage of incumbents seeking renomination who lose primaries has averaged as follows in recent years: 35 to 45 percent in Louisiana and Alabama; 20 to 30 percent in Tennessee and Kentucky; 15 percent or less in Texas and North Carolina. In these Southern states the variation in losses by incumbents parallels the variation in other measurements of primary competition. In Texas the large proportion of incumbents seeking reelection may contribute to the low level of competition, and in Alabama the high involvement of legislators in local legislation may make them more vulnerable to attack in their districts. The high level of competition and the high rate of defeat for incumbents in Louisiana primaries are probably related to the unusually strong and persistent factions in the Democratic party of that state; in districts where these factions most often affect legislative candidates, the primary competition is more intense and the proportion of incumbents who lose is markedly higher.[15]

WHO'S GOT THE COATTAILS?

"The medieval query concerning the number of angels who can gambol on the point of a pin has at least one modern counterpart: How many congressmen can ride on the coattails of a president?"[16] This question introduces us to one of the most elusive problems in political research. Frequently there is some degree of correlation between a party's success in a presidential race and its showing in congressional elections. But the strength of this correlation varies widely from election to election, and its nature and causes are open to dispute. A presidential candidate who polls a larger proportion of the total vote than do his party's congressional candidates is presumably strong; one who lags behind is relatively weak. Politicians tend to assume that a strong presidential candidate will help the congressional ticket by providing the coattails to carry to victory some candidates who would otherwise lose.

This is presumably true in some cases, just as it is logical to expect that (to a lesser extent) a strong congressional candidate may win votes for a presidential candidate. The difficulty comes in trying to measure coattails. A strong presidential candidate is usually defined as one who runs ahead of his ticket, but Miller has pointed out that, paradoxically, the presidential candidate with perfect coattails would be one who could transfer all of his voting strength to the congressional ticket. In other words, a strong presidential candidate may not necessarily have strong coattails. He may, like President Eisenhower, appeal to independent and opposition party voters who will split their ticket in voting.[17]

In trying to clarify the concept of coattails, we can find evidence from two sources: election returns and survey research data. It is clear from a study of election returns that in nearly every year when congressional elections are held national trends are discernible which affect the likelihood of victory for candidates of either party. In presidential years these trends may result in greater or lesser part from the popularity of the two presidential candidates, but in nonpresidential years such trends are also evident. We know that in a number of states and a large proportion of congressional districts there is weak competition and little turnover. It is in the competitive areas that the impact of national trends is most evident.

Although senators are better known than representatives and should be better able to stand against hostile electoral winds, they are not immune to national trends. V. O. Key's compilation of statistics for presidential elections from 1920 through 1960 shows that the party that won the Presidency held 90 percent of its senatorial seats, 97 percent in states that the successful presidential candidate carried by at least 60 percent. Incumbent senators of the losing presidential party were in greatest danger in states where their party lost the presidential race. In Republican years one-third of the incumbent Democratic senators lost; in states carried by the Republican presidential candidate, half of the incumbent Democrats lost. In Democratic years, incumbent Republican senators were in greater jeopardy: over 40 percent of them lost; in states where their party lost the presidential race, two-thirds of them lost. In nonpresidential years there are similar trends favoring the party out of power. Except for the 1934 election (when the Democratic tide was still rising), the out party rarely lost a senatorial seat that it held during the 1922–1958 period.[18] In 1960 and 1962 the trends were much weaker, and contrary to the normal direction; the Republicans made slight senatorial gains in 1960 and the Democrats made modest gains in 1962. The Democrats gained a few seats in 1964.

There are many safe House districts, and we would expect national trends to be reflected in the limited number of competitive House districts. In most election years there is a trend favoring one party that is strong enough to prevent more than a very few incumbents of that party from losing. In recent years, this trend has been at least as strong in nonpresidential years. The Republicans lost only two seats in 1950; the Democrats lost five seats in 1954 and only one in 1958. In 1962, however (excluding seats affected by redistricting), the Democrats lost eight seats and the Republicans lost three; there was no clear, consistent trend.

In 1952 (excluding the effects of redistricting) the Republicans lost only two seats in the House, but in the next three presidential elections the pattern was more complex. In 1956, despite Eisenhower's sweeping victory, the Republicans gained only 9 House seats and lost 11. In 1960, despite Kennedy's win, the Democrats gained only 8 seats and lost 27. The Democratic congressional losses in 1960 can be understood only in the light of the 1958 election, in which Democrats won a number of normally Republican districts. Twenty-two of the 27 Democratic losses were seats that had been taken away from the Republicans in 1958. In 1964 a heavy Democratic trend led to the capture of 48 House seats, but at the same time the Democrats lost 10 seats. Seven of these were in deep Southern states which were carried by Goldwater; there the civil rights issue had a strong impact.

We can shed further light on the relationship between presidential and congressional voting by examining the states and districts in which a presidential candidate gains a larger or smaller percentage of the vote than does his congressional running mate (see Table 4.5). The winning party's congressional percentages are grouped by states for the first three elections and by districts for the last three; uncontested congressional elections are omitted, because they exaggerate the contrast with the presidential candidate's vote. The winning presidential candidate usually leads his ticket in districts where the congressional candidate is weak, and trails behind it where the congressional candidate is strong. Traditional voting patterns in districts dominated by one party appear to be stronger in congressional voting than in presidential voting. As Press points out, in safe districts "party identification is more often in conflict with issue or candidate orientations, with the result that more tickets were split."[19] A winning presidential candidate can make inroads into hostile territory where his congressional running mate makes little impact; the losing presidential candidate also appears able to win more votes where his party is weak than his congressional partner can. Table 4.5 also indicates that there is more straight-ticket voting in marginal districts; if a straight-ticket vote is a symptom of presidential coattails, they should be more effective in marginal districts.

Table 4.5 also provides us with more specific evidence of the differences in political strength of recent successful candidates for President. The figures for 1940, 1944, and 1948 run approximately parallel; Truman's strength in 1948 was actually considerably weaker because the table includes in the Democratic presidential total the votes cast for both Wallace and Thurmond. By comparison, Eisenhower in 1952 led his ticket by about as much where the Republicans were weak, but seldom trailed it where they were strong; in 1956 he was further ahead of his ticket than

Table 4.5. AVERAGE PERCENTAGE BY WHICH WINNING PRESIDENTIAL CANDIDATE LED OR TRAILED HIS CONGRESSIONAL TICKET, 1940–1960

Winning Party, Congressional %	1940*	1944*	1948*	1952	1956	1960
0.1–29.9	33.5	18.2	29.6	13.1	16.6	10.3
30.0–39.9	9.4	9.4	6.9	8.5	14.7	5.1
40.0–44.9	6.7	6.2	6.5	6.5	10.7	2.7
45.0–49.9	3.4	3.2	2.1	6.0	9.0	−2.3
50.0–54.9	0.3	1.8	1.4	3.8	7.4	−5.5
55.0–59.9	0.8	−2.5	−2.0	1.3	3.8	−5.9
60.0–69.9	−2.9	−5.6	−4.7	−0.1	2.5	−8.3
70.0–99.9	−9.6	−15.1	−8.1	−3.0	0.7	−14.9

* Figures for 1940, 1944, and 1948 are based on state rather than district averages. The Truman, Wallace, and Thurmond vote are combined for the 1948 Democratic presidential percentage.

SOURCE: Figures for 1940–1956 are from C. Press, "Voting Statistics and Presidential Coattails," *American Political Science Review*, LII (1958), 1044.

either Roosevelt or Truman, and never trailed in districts with two-party competition. By contrast, Kennedy in 1960 appears to be the weakest; he led his ticket only in districts where his congressional party had less than 45 percent of the vote. Comparable figures for the 1964 election show that Johnson led his ticket by margins comparable to those of Eisenhower in 1956. He also led the ticket by greater margins in weaker Democratic states (as measured by the congressional vote) and by smaller margins in strong Democratic states. Johnson trailed the ticket primarily in a few Southern states, where the civil rights issue appeared to have less impact on the congressional vote or where the Republican party had weak congressional candidates.

It is true that the chances of congressional victory are higher in a district where the party's presidential vote is high, but it is also true that party voting is more consistent in congressional than presidential elections. In fact, fewer congressional districts have changed hands in most recent elections and fewer have been won by narrow margins. In congressional districts where one party's congressional candidate is strong, the presidential candidate is likely to win a smaller percentage of the vote. The closest correlation between presidential and congressional voting percentages occurs in the marginal districts, and it is here that we should expect to find the most straight-ticket voting. Straight-ticket voting is a prerequisite for, but not a guarantee of, coattail voting. To measure the effect of coattails, we must look at the results of survey research.

Recent voting-behavior research has consistently stressed the importance of party affiliation as a motivating force. When party affiliation leads to a straight party vote, as is often the case, there are obviously no coattail effects. Voters appear likely to break away from party loyalties in voting for President more often than in voting for other offices. The voter who crosses party lines because of the personal appeal of a presidential candidate is not likely to vote for his congressional running mate. In some cases the potential coattail effect is probably reduced because (as in the South) a party runs no congressional candidate or runs such a weak candidate that the potential straight-ticket voter fails to vote that way in practice. Research on voting behavior also suggests that during a campaign there is an increase in the partisan consistency of voting intentions, which is not necessarily caused by the coattails of a major candidate.[20]

We can also gain insight into the fluctuations in congressional voting between presidential and nonpresidential years from survey research studies. We know that some voters are highly motivated, interested in politics, consistent in their appearance at the polls, and—usually—loyal to one party. At the other extreme are the casual, inconsistent, weakly motivated voters, usually with few party loyalties. Many voters, of course, fit somewhere between these two categories. The weakly motivated voter, seldom interested in most elections, is sometimes aroused by a presidential campaign and is likely to vote for a strong presidential candidate (Roosevelt in 1932 and 1936, Eisenhower in 1952 and 1956). If he bothers to vote in the congressional race, he may vote a straight ticket (particularly where the ballot form makes this simple). In the succeeding congressional election he is unlikely to vote, and the President loses some or all of his congressional majority.[21]

A study of the 1956 and 1958 elections by the Michigan Survey Research Center sheds further light on the characteristics of voters in presidential and nonpresidential years. Table 4.6 shows that the likelihood of voting is more closely related to the strength of party identification in congressional than in presidential election years. Consequently, the voters strongly identified with a party constituted a larger proportion of the electorate for congressional races in 1958 than they did in 1956.

A panel study identifying those who voted in 1956 but stayed home in the 1958 election similarly shows that these included a smaller proportion of strong partisans than did those who voted both times. Party identification is likely to have a greater impact on congressional voting in non-presidential years, both because there is no presidential candidate running with a possible coattail effect and because a higher proportion of the voters are strong party identifiers.[22]

Table 4.6.   RELATIONSHIP BETWEEN STRENGTH OF PARTY IDENTIFICATION AND LIKELIHOOD OF VOTING

Strength of Party Identification	Percentage Each Category of Voters Who Voted for Congressman		Percentage All Votes Cast for Congressman, Each Category	
	1956	1958	1956	1958
Strong D or R	74	67	40	47
Weak D or R	64	50	36	37
Independent D or R	65	50	15	11
Independent	64	37	9	5

SOURCE: Unpublished data from Michigan Survey Research Center.

The congressional vote in nonpresidential years is usually consistent with party loyalties, but it is seldom a vote of confidence or no confidence in the record or program of either party. In 1958, only 7 percent of the voters gave an explanation for their vote that included any reference to issues; furthermore, the proportions of these politically literate and issue-oriented voters were no higher among those who crossed party lines than among those who voted according to party loyalty. The only explanation that the poll-takers found for deviation from party loyalty involved the voters' knowledge of candidates. This, however, did not mean knowledge of their record or their position on issues. Only about 3 percent of the voters who expressed some knowledge or viewpoint about the incumbent congressman referred, even vaguely to legislative issues. Knowledge about the candidate simply means some scrap of information. It is a relatively scarce commodity: in 1958, nearly half the voters had read or heard nothing about either candidate. However superficial it may be, information about the candidates affects voting decisions. Less than one-fifth of the voters who knew about both candidates, and less than one-tenth of those who knew about neither, crossed party lines, but 40 percent of the relatively few voters who knew only about the other party's candidate voted for him.[23]

In many states the large proportion of one-party counties reduces the potential importance of a governor's coattails. Traditional voting habits often determine the voting for local and legislative candidates, and may determine whether there is any competition at all. In these counties a popular gubernatorial candidate of the minority party who attracts votes is not likely to have strong coattails. In Michigan, in three elections (1958–1962), 97 percent of the candidates who won House seats (outside Wayne County) were in districts that were carried by their party's candidate for governor; this was probably the result less of coattails than of the polarized stability of the vote in that state at both the gubernatorial and legislative level. In closely competitive counties, a governor's coattails might be stronger than a President's, because individual legislators usually have less stature and a weaker hold over their district than congressmen do. (It is possible, of course, that a President's coattails will sometimes be long enough to reach a legislator.) In Indiana, where an unusually high proportion of counties are competitive, in three elections (1948, 1952, and 1956) 88 percent of the counties cast a majority vote for gubernatorial and legislative candidates of the same party. In two-party states, this link between a governor and legislators of his party from competitive districts contributes to party loyalty in the legislature, although there is little evidence to show how important a factor this is.

In one-party states, neither the legislative election nor the primary provides the incentive for legislators to link their fortunes with the governor and support his program. Legislators recognize that their election is not dependent on any gubernatorial candidate's success, that there are no coattails available. Legislative candidates in one-party states usually campaign on purely local issues, generalities, and the strength of their own personalities. The exceptions are rare. In Louisiana, slating arrangements between gubernatorial and legislative candidates (as part of a broader pattern of slating) have been common in some parts of the state, particularly when the conflict between the Long and anti-Long forces was at its height. There has been occasional but not consistent evidence that such endorsements by successful gubernatorial candidates have influenced the outcome of legislative primaries. In other Southern states, the occasional ties between gubernatorial and legislative candidates in the primary have been so shadowy as to obscure any signs of coattail effects.

THE CAMPAIGN

Recruitment. The single clearest impression we get from looking at the wide variety of legislative campaigns is that most candidates—

whether incumbents or not—are on their own. This impression is even stronger for most—though not all—candidates for the state legislature. Congressional candidates may be persuaded to run by representatives of interest groups or by party leaders at the local, state, or occasionally national level. Party leaders are most likely to take an interest when a district is marginal, or when the retirement of an incumbent in the opposition party increases the chances of victory. Many congressional candidates and a larger proportion of state legislators appear to be self-recruited. From the viewpoint of most local party organizations, legislative seats are relatively unimportant and attract less attention from the slate-makers than do other local offices. One poll of legislative candidates in Pennsylvania showed that only about one-fourth were asked to run, usually by party leaders, in their first candidacy; in Wisconsin, the proportion was slightly lower.[24]

The study of Pennsylvania by Sorauf, the best recent analysis of state legislative recruitment and campaigns, emphasizes the contrasting practices of strong metropolitan organizations and other local parties. The contrasts are confirmed by less extensive studies in several other states. The strong, active party organizations, found particularly in metropolitan areas,

. . . present an impressive picture as they sort out the petitions of their many willing candidates. . . . Screening activities in these majority parties begin well in advance of the primary filing date. Although the party leadership may initiate its own recruitment and screening chores, party committeemen and other worthies carry to the leadership the cases for their favored candidates. . . . Eventually the party insiders, usually an executive committee, meet to fashion a slate which reflects a balanced appeal to all the interests and localities in the constituency.

The party is concerned with finding a winning candidate, but where it is well enough entrenched to assure victory, the legislative nomination becomes a pawn in the adjustment of claims by party groupings and a reward for faithful party workers. Potential candidates who fail to get the party's support may be expected to bow out of the race and wait for another opportunity. In both Pennsylvania and Wisconsin, legislators (particularly Democrats) from the metropolitan centers are more likely to be recruited by party leaders than are their rural colleagues.[25]

Outside the metropolitan areas, the recruitment process is often a haphazard one. Where the party is dominant, recruitment is unnecessary; as one Kentucky county chairman said, "We never have a scarcity of candidates." The leadership seldom sees any need to interfere unless the self-starting candidates are inept, or the candidacies have threatened to provoke serious divisions in the party. Polls of county chairmen in both

Kentucky and the Plains States have shown that most county chairmen occasionally find it necessary to encourage a candidate to run in the primary against someone who has already filed, presumably for reasons such as these. Where the party is weak, the situation is very different. In many states, like Pennsylvania, "in the hard-core minority parties, recruitment often involves little more than the harried efforts by the chairman and a few henchmen to fill a party ticket." A poll in the Plains States showed that most party leaders tried to find candidates to complete the ticket; for many leaders in one-party areas the pessimistic appraisal by a Kentucky Republican leader is appropriate: "I think most have lost heart, having failed so many times." Efforts by statewide party organizations to encourage more candidates are occasionally found, and sometimes have dramatic results, as recently in the Texas Republican party.[26]

In some states the contrast between strong, metropolitan party organizations and others applies to the practice of open endorsement in the primaries. Sorauf found in Pennsylvania that there were open, publicized endorsements by the organizations in more than half the legislative primaries of each party and covert endorsements in many others. The practice of endorsements was most common in the same kinds of organizations that followed systematic recruitment policies: the strong (and particularly Democratic) metropolitan parties. In Pennsylvania, a party organization that makes a preliminary choice and encourages a candidate to run cannot afford to abandon him in the primary, nor can it avoid recruiting in a district where it has developed the practice of primary endorsements. Once a candidate has been elected to the legislature, however, he can usually depend on the support of a strong organization and perhaps can count on its help in discouraging competition. Non-endorsement of the candidate is used—but only occasionally—as a disciplinary device in Pennsylvania. Here, as in states like New York or Massachusetts, where such "purges" appear to be more frequent, the reason may be a legislator's voting record, but it is just as likely to be a local conflict over patronage. Open endorsement of candidates in the primary by metropolitan party organizations is probably more common in the large industrial states. It is a standard practice of both parties in Louisville, Kentucky, but it is rare in both urban and rural areas of Wisconsin and the Plains States.[27]

Independent Campaigning. Most candidates for Congress or state legislatures organize their campaigns independently of other candidates who are running for statewide or local office. They maintain separate headquarters, recruit their own workers, and determine their own tactics for the campaign. The long-established legislator and the nonincumbent underdog may devote little effort to their campaigns; it is the candidate in a closely competitive situation who is most likely to wage an intensive campaign. Legislative candidates rely heavily on personal appearances. Congressmen consider it important to be seen frequently throughout their districts and to talk to as many groups as possible. State legislative candidates may find it possible and profitable to conduct personal door-to-door campaigns in a close race. More elaborate campaign techniques may be too expensive; television is not only expensive but often inefficient if a particular station covers a viewing area much larger than a legislator's district.

Legislative candidates sometimes run independently by their own choice, but usually it is because they receive little help from national, state, or local party organizations. Presidential and statewide campaigns absorb the attention and resources of national and state party organizations. The local party is likely to be more interested in county or city offices; as one congressman said, "The sheriff in my county has seventy or eighty jobs to pass out, and everyone is interested in who is sheriff. No one cares about us."[28] Legislative candidates discover that they are operating in a political vacuum, and must rely on their own resources. One congressman remarked, "If we depended on the party organization to get elected, none of us would be here."[29] Only in urban areas with a powerful and active party organization can the congressional or state legislative candidate ride along on a campaign organized by the party.

This does not mean that legislative campaigns are completely isolated from the electoral mainstream. The legislative candidate recruits his own workers, and sometimes develops a corps of supporters that can be relied on year after year, but he usually draws them initially from the reservoir of experienced party workers. He receives little money from national or state headquarters, but increasingly he is offered advisers, literature, campaign kits, ghost-written speeches, and other election paraphernalia. Even the local party headquarters may provide him with some assistance. Some state legislative candidates, particularly in at-large districts, organize and campaign jointly in order to reduce the costs and burdens of running individually. Perhaps more important, legislative candidates often depend on the personal campaigning of the presidential or gubernatorial candidate of their party in the district to provide a boost for their candidacy. This is likely to be the highlight of the local campaign.

Most candidates for legislative office are acutely aware of the fact that, when it comes to financing the campaign, they are on their own. Seldom does the party organization have funds to spare for legislative candidates, although some of the services that they provide may reduce the cost of campaigning. Legislative candidates may rely on associates to do the actual work of fund-raising, but often they must make the key decisions about the methods and sources for raising money. State legislative candidates and even congressmen—particularly nonincumbents—often have to contribute a substantial proportion of the costs from their own pockets. Candidates for Congress, particularly incumbents, may receive financial help from one of their party's congressional campaign committees, but this usually amounts to a small fraction of campaign costs.[30] In 1956, senatorial candidates received an average of $12,000 from their party's senatorial campaign committee in Washington. Less than half of the House candidates received such help; they averaged $2,000 for Republicans and $900 for Democrats.[31] The cost of a senatorial campaign may be several hundred thousand dollars in a large state. A recent survey of a group of United States House members showed that estimates of their campaign expenses varied from $1,200 to $60,000. This wide range results from variations not only in the closeness of a race but in the type of district. Campaigns in metropolitan districts are likely to be most expensive.[32]

The financial independence of legislative candidates is one reason why they can be independent in their voting record. Congressmen are neither dependent on nor indebted to the national party for financial help. State and local party leaders neither provide financing for, nor take an interest in, congressional campaigns; as a consequence, they rarely try to influence a congressman's vote on an issue. State legislators are also financially independent of the state party and (except for a few urban organizations) the local party. There are two recent examples of state legislative leaders who have served as brokers for campaign contributions and consequently accumulated political debts from legislators: Speaker Unruh of the California House and former President Powers of the Massachusetts Senate. Though the financial obligations of campaigning rarely make legislators indebted to a party organization, often they find it necessary to accept contributions from interest groups that tend to limit their freedom in voting. The problem of a conscientious legislator may not be simply one of raising money for a campaign, but of raising it from a large enough variety of sources to avoid being obligated to a few interests.

Less direct forms of assistance from the party may, however, place an obligation on the legislative candidate. When he accepts help from party headquarters, the party gets an opportunity to influence the theme of his campaign through the materials and advice it provides. If a legislator believes that his victory is dependent on the coattails of a presidential or gubernatorial candidate (whether or not this is precisely true), he may tailor his campaign to the issues being emphasized by that candidate. During the 1952 and 1956 campaigns President Eisenhower demonstrated that a popular presidential candidate could have an impact on congressional campaigns, as congressmen with isolationist voting records sought to convince the voters that they were in step with Eisenhower's record. When a President campaigns actively during a mid-term election, as both Eisenhower and Kennedy did, he has an opportunity to set the theme for the campaign, and congressional candidates may follow his lead. There are probably fewer congressional candidates, though still a number, who echo the spirit of Senator Robert Taft's remark in the 1942 election: "I see no reason why each senator should not run on his own foreign policy." We would make a mistake, however, to assume that most congressional campaigns are dominated by issues.

Issues and Images. Most legislators recognize that the average voter knows little or nothing about political issues or about the legislator's voting record, as is indicated by survey research data. The mail they receive—and the absence of it on some issues—and their personal contacts with constituents substantiate this judgment. Although the legislator may use the campaign as a means for trying to educate the voter about issues, he is likely to grow disillusioned about the effectiveness of his efforts. It is difficult for the congressman, and even more difficult for the state legislator, to attract enough public attention to persuade a substantial number of voters that his views and his record on issues are correct.

If the campaign does not deal with issues, what is its purpose? Many legislators would share this congressional view:

The people back home don't know what's going on. Issues are not most important so far as the average voter is concerned. The image of the candidate plays a much greater role. If voters feel the candidate is conscientious and is trying hard to serve them, then that man has a good chance of coming back.[33]

The image of the candidate is more likely to make an impression on the voter than issues; however superficial the image may be, voters are more likely to vote for a candidate about whom they know something, as shown by the polls referred to earlier in the chapter. What image does the legislator try to project? First, he must make his name known. Beyond that, most legislators try to project an image of a capable, conscientious, knowledgeable man, zealous on behalf of the district's obvious interests and able to use his judgment in determining how to vote.

If campaigns are conducted with more attention to image than to issues, it is unlikely that the outcome of an election will provide the legislator with a mandate to pursue particular policies. At the most, the legislator is likely to view his successful reelection as a vote of confidence by the electorate in his judgment, and perhaps in his general record (or image) as a liberal or conservative. He may be bound by the organized groups whose votes or financial aid he solicits, but he is seldom bound by promises or commitments made on specific issues. The nature of the district he represents, the coalition of interests that elect him, and his own public record are all factors that may limit his freedom in legislative voting, but it is rare for a campaign to be so focused on issues that the campaign in itself has an impact on the legislator's voting behavior.[34]

NOTES

1. V. O. Key, Jr., *Politics, Parties, and Pressure Groups* (New York, 1964), p. 548.

2. An analysis that emphasizes historical trends in competition is found in Charles O. Jones, "Inter-party Competition for Congressional Seats," *Western Political Quarterly*, XVII (1964), 461–76.

3. V. O. Key, Jr., *American State Politics* (New York, 1956), chap. 6.

4. Robert Pitchell, "The Electoral System and Voting Behavior: The Case of California's Cross-filing," *Western Political Quarterly*, XII (1959), 459–84.

5. Heinz Eulau, "The Ecological Basis of Party Systems: The Case of Ohio," *Midwest Journal of Political Science*, I (1957), 125–35; Malcolm E. Jewell, "Competition and Factionalism in Southern Legislative Primaries and Elections" (Unpublished paper presented at the 1962 meeting of the American Political Science Association).

6. Key, *Politics, Parties, and Pressure Groups*, pp. 438–41.

7. *Ibid.*, pp. 447–50.

8. Julius Turner, "Primary Elections as the Alternatives to Party Competition in 'Safe Districts,'" *Journal of Politics*, XV (1953), 197–210.

9. Key, *American State Politics*, pp. 171–81; Jewell, *op. cit.*, pp. 8–10; Leon D. Epstein, *Politics in Wisconsin* (Madison, 1958), p. 201.

10. Frank J. Sorauf, *Party and Representation* (New York: Atherton Press, 1963), pp. 107–08.

11. Key, *American State Politics*, p. 174; Epstein, *op. cit.*, pp. 199, 201. Sorauf, *op. cit.*, p. 112; Jewell, *op. cit.*, p. 10; William C. Havard and Loren P. Beth, *The Politics of Mis-representation* (Baton Rouge, 1962), p. 88.

12. Key, *American State Politics*, pp. 175–78; Epstein, *op. cit.*, p. 133.

13. Key, *American State Politics*, p. 177. In Pennsylvania, there are more contestants when there is an incumbent running; contests are closer among Republicans and more one-sided among Democrats with an incumbent running. Sorauf, *op. cit.*, p. 115.

14. Epstein, *op. cit.*, p. 198.

15. Jewell, *op. cit.*, pp. 10–13.

16. Warren E. Miller, "Presidential Coattails: A Study in Political Myth and Methodology," *Public Opinion Quarterly*, XIX (1955–56), 353.

17. *Ibid.*, pp. 353–68.

18. Key, *Politics, Parties, and Pressure Groups*, pp. 548–55.

19. Charles Press, "Voting Statistics and Presidential Coattails," *American Political Science Review*, LII (1958), 1041–50 at 1043.

20. John W. Meyer, "A Reformulation of the 'Coattails' Problem," in William M. McPhee and William A. Glaser (eds.), *Public Opinion and Congressional Elections* (New York, 1962), pp. 52–64.

21. William A. Glaser, "Fluctuations in Turnout," in *ibid.*, pp. 19–51.

22. Angus Campbell, "Surge and Decline: A Study of Electoral Change," *Public Opinion Quarterly*, XXIV (1960), 397–418.

23. Donald E. Stokes and Warren E. Miller, "Party Government and the Salience of Congress," *Public Opinion Quarterly*, XXVI (1962), 531–46.

24. Sorauf, *op. cit.*, p. 99; Epstein, *op. cit.*, p. 205.

25. Sorauf, *op. cit.*, pp. 55–58; Epstein, *loc. cit.*

26. Sorauf, *op. cit.*, pp. 56–57; Marvin Harder and Thomas Ungs, "Notes Toward a Functional Analysis of Local Party Organizations" (Unpublished paper presented at the 1963 meeting of the Midwest Conference of Political Scientists), p. 18; Everett Cunningham, "The Contemporary Republican Party in Kentucky" (Unpublished Ph.D. dissertation, University of Kentucky, 1964), p. 159.

27. Sorauf, *op. cit.*, pp. 52–58; Epstein, *op. cit.*, pp. 138–39; Harder and Ungs, *loc. cit.*

28. Charles L. Clapp, *The Congressman: His Work as He Sees It* (Washington: The Brookings Institution, 1963), p. 344.

29. *Ibid.*, p. 351.

30. *Ibid.*, pp. 333–51.

31. Alexander Heard, *The Costs of Democracy* (Chapel Hill, 1960), pp. 291–93.

32. Clapp, *loc. cit.*

33. *Ibid.*, p. 373.

34. For a fuller discussion of issues and images, see Charles O. Jones, "The Role of the Campaign in Congressional Politics," in Harmon Zeigler and Kent Jennings (eds.), *The Electoral Process* (Englewood Cliffs, N.J., 1966).

[5]

The Legislators

O NE OF the most persistent popular beliefs in our political culture is the belief in the openness of the political system. The "log cabin" image, the notion that "anybody can become President," and the unpopularity of class interpretations of politics are indicative of the egalitarian orientation of many Americans. While the American political system is relatively open to participation and activism by a wide range of citizenry, it is also a rather highly selective system in which recruitment to public office emphasizes certain well-defined strata of the population.

The American legislature is not a representative body in the sense that all elements of the population are included as legislators in direct proportion to their relative size. Partly as a result of the selection processes described in the two previous chapters, and partly as a result of more diffuse factors in the political system, American legislators tend to be distinctly different in their social origins and political experiences from the population at large.

ECOLOGICAL ORIGINS

One of the bases upon which to differentiate American legislators from the general population of the country is in terms of ecological origin. Typically, the American legislator has grown up in rural or small-town areas. The malapportionment of many state legislatures and the advantages given to rural areas of the country in the drawing of congressional district boundaries are factors that contribute to the recruitment of legislators who are essentially "small-town boys." With the exception of the New Jersey legislators, less than half the members of the legislatures shown in Table 5.1 grew up in a city, and about one-quarter of them (one-third in Tennessee) were raised on a farm. At the national level, an even higher proportion of legislators appear to have had rural and small-town origins. Sixty-four percent of the members of the United States Senate in 1959 had grown up in rural or small-town environments, while only 17 percent had been raised in a medium-sized city and 19 percent in a metropolitan center.[1]

Matthews has shown that, in the period from 1947 to 1957, more than two-thirds of the United States Senators were born in rural areas or small towns, and that "the most consistently overrepresented birthplaces ranged in size from 2,500 to 5,000 inhabitants." The small towns

Table 5.1. WHERE STATE LEGISLATORS GREW UP, 1957
(In percentages)

Grew Up	Cali-fornia	New Jersey	Ohio	Ten-nessee	Wis-consin
In a city	45	62	45	22	40
In a small town	23	32	28	34	29
On a farm	21	5	24	33	25
Combination of above	11	1	3	11	6
Total	100	99	100	100	100
Numbers	110	78	162	119	89

SOURCES: J. C. Wahlke et al., *The Legislative System* (New York: John Wiley and Sons, 1962), p. 489, for California, New Jersey, Ohio, and Tennessee legislatures. Data for the 1957 Wisconsin Assembly in this and subsequent tables come from unpublished material collected by Patterson.

of this size "produced twice as many Democrats and four times as many Republicans as one might expect on the basis of chance."[2] And, more than is the case for their populations in general, the legislators of these states tend to be born in the state rather than in some other state. Except for a few states like California with substantial in-migrant populations, the vast majority of state legislators have been born in the states in which they serve as legislators. In many states, including California, a higher proportion of legislators have been born in the state than is the case for the states' populations generally. The same pattern holds for Congress: 71 percent of the members of the United States House of Representatives for the Seventy-seventh Congress had been born in their states, while 24 percent had been born in another state and 5 percent were foreign-born.[3] Thus, the American legislator tends not only to have had a rural or small-town upbringing, but also to have been born in the state in or from which he serves.

The legislator also tends to have deep roots in his district. While aspirants to the legislature in the United States are not universally required by law to be residents of the districts they represent, this is invariably the case. New York is the only state without a legal residency requirement for state legislators, and there is no requirement that United States congressmen be legal residents of their states and districts.* The process of recruitment of legislators tends to place great weight upon extended residence in the district. This tendency is reflected clearly at the state level where, in the five states shown in Table 5.2, well over half of the members of each state's legislature shall have lived in their

Table 5.2. LENGTH OF RESIDENCE IN DISTRICT,
STATE LEGISLATORS, 1957
(In percentages)

Length of Residence	California	New Jersey	Ohio	Tennessee	Wisconsin
All their lives	14	60	65	53	39
80% of lives, or over 30 yr	42	23	23	23	30
20–29 yr	15	7	7	11	10
10–19 yr	19	10	3	9	12
Less than 10 yr	10	—	2	4	9
Total	100	100	100	100	100
Numbers	118	79	162	119	89

SOURCE: J. C. Wahlke et al., *The Legislative System* (New York: John Wiley and Sons, 1962), p. 488.

districts at least 80 percent of their lives or more than 30 years. To illustrate further, more than 73 percent of the members of the 1958 session of the Pennsylvania legislature had been born in the county from which they were elected (nearly 69 percent had lived all their lives in the county of their birth); 55 percent of both houses of the 1957 Georgia legislature were born and had lived all their lives in the districts they represented.[4] The American legislator is usually a "local boy," and legislative careers in the United States are generally closed to newcomers in the community. A small town or rural heritage and long residence in the community tend to confer representative legitimacy upon aspirants to legislative office in this country.

---

* The federal Constitution, in Article I, Section 2, requires only that a representative shall, "when elected, be an Inhabitant of that State in which he shall be chosen."

FAMILY BACKGROUND

The political recruitment process in the United States gives very disproportionate weight to those who have middle-class and upper-middle class family backgrounds. The extent to which political leaders are drawn from such families increases from the lower political levels to the higher ones, and is most marked among legislators who serve in the United States Congress. There, commonly more than half the members come from families in which the father had a professional or business occupation, in contrast to the occupational distribution of the fathers of people in the general population. Table 5.3 shows the father's occupations of legislators in several states and in the United States Senate, and the occupational distribution of the labor force in 1900. About

Table 5.3. OCCUPATIONS OF FATHERS OF AMERICAN LEGISLATORS
(In percentages)

Occupation	Calif., N.J., Ohio, Tenn. (1957)	Wisconsin (1957)	Pennsylvania (1957)	U.S. Senators (1947–57)	Labor Force (1900)
Professional	18	17	12	24	6
Proprietor, official	29	14	30	35	7
Farmer, farm manager	31	25	16	32	22
Other	28	38	42	9	66
Total	100	100	100	100	100
Numbers	504	100	106	180	—

SOURCE: J. C. Wahlke et al., *The Legislative System* (New York: John Wiley and Sons, 1962), p. 489; F. J. Sorauf, *Party and Representation* (New York: Atherton Press, 1963), p. 78; D. R. Matthews, "United States Senators: A Collective Portrait," *International Social Science Journal*, XIII (1961), 623.

60 percent of the members of the Senate came from families in which the father was a professional or a businessman. The sons of farmers most accurately represented the labor force in 1900, but the higher proportion of farmers' sons in the Senate reinforces the image of legislators as largely rural in background.

At the state level, a smaller (as compared to Congress) but still substantial proportion of legislators are drawn from families where the father's principal occupation was a profession or business, and a higher proportion come from families in which the father was a skilled or unskilled worker. Table 5.3 shows the combined percentages in each occupational category of legislators' fathers for six states. Less than half of the fathers of legislators in the first four states engaged in professional and business occupations, and only 31 percent were farmers or farm managers. An even smaller proportion of Wisconsin legislators' fathers were business and professional men, and a higher percentage were skilled workers. In Pennsylvania, a higher percentage were professional men and workers, and a smaller percentage were farmers. But even for state legislators, middle-class and upper-middle class occupational heritages are considerably overrepresented when legislators are compared with the labor force generally.

POLITICAL SOCIALIZATION

The family environment provides an arena for the politicization of the individual. While some legislators develop their interest in politics as adults, and some perhaps only after they have been elected to office, most begin to develop political interests at a time when they are greatly influenced by their families. Unfortunately, we know relatively little about the development of political interest among legislators, particularly members of the Congress. More is known about state legislators in a few states.

In their interviews with legislators in California, New Jersey, Ohio, and Tennessee, Wahlke, Eulau, Buchanan, and Ferguson found that a high proportion of the members of each legislative body (from 41 percent in N.J. to 59 percent in Ohio and Tennessee) had relatives in politics, and they concluded that "state legislators tend to come from families which are much more involved in politics than the average American family."[5] From one-third to nearly half of the legislators in these states indicated as agents in their political socialization their primary group associations, principally family members and relatives. The comments of one state legislator will illustrate the importance of the family in the socialization process:

My first recollection of politics was when I was four years old and my father was a member of the House of Representatives. I played here in this room when I was a little boy. . . . Then, too, I experienced a brief congressional campaign when my father was a candidate. He was defeated, but the whole thing left a deep impression on me. I met lots of people in politics through my father.[6]

Political socialization is very largely a matter of the inheritance of family political traditions. But other influences stimulate political interests as well, and the state legislators interviewed by Wahlke and his associates indicated other sources of stimuli for political activism. For some, activities in school politics or in the study of politics in school were recalled in adulthood as sources of political interest. Others became interested in legislative service through involvement in politics at the level of party or campaign work, lobbying, or civic activity. Others recalled the impact of great events—impressive presidential elections, war, or the Depression—as factors that had interested them in legislative careers. One legislator told the interviewers:

> During the Bryan–McKinley campaign I hanged a picture of McKinley on my bedroom wall. My father took it off and I hanged it up again. He took it off and took me to the woodshed. I've been a Republican ever since.[7]

A variety of factors, then, are likely to draw individuals into the orbit of the politically conscious and active, but it is in his early experiences with family, relatives, and friends that the legislator is likely to begin to develop political interests.

OCCUPATIONAL STATUS

The occupational composition of the American legislative bodies is such that those in some occupations have a better chance of legislative service than others. American legislators tend to have been in highly prestigious occupations prior to their election to the legislature. By and large, those in the professional and business occupations dominate the legislative halls in the United States, both at state and national levels (see Table 5.4). Some occupations, often represented among legislators, are "dispensable" for politics in the sense that those engaged in such occupations can take time out from their professional or occupational activity for politics with a minimum of sacrifice.[8] Legal, real estate, insurance, farming, and many business occupations are such that those involved can, without seriously endangering their livelihood, be away from their businesses for short periods of time to serve in the state legislature or run for Congress.

With the exception of the 1951 Minnesota House of Representatives, more than 60 percent of the members of the legislatures shown in Table 5.4 were professional or technical specialists, proprietors, managers, or officials. There is some variation among states, with a higher proportion of business and professional people in the legislatures of the more highly urbanized states of California, New Jersey, Ohio, and Pennsylvania, and a smaller proportion in the other less urbanized states. When one goes from the state to the national level, the preponderance of professional and business occupations greatly increases, with more than two-thirds of the members of Congress in the professional–technical category.

The proportion of farmers in the state legislatures varies in terms of the urbanization of the states, from as few as 2 percent in New Jersey in 1957 to as many as 39 percent in the 1951 session of the Minnesota House of Representatives. Furthermore, the number of farmer–legislators seems to have declined in some states and remained relatively stable in others. In Iowa, where the proportion of farmers is probably higher than in any other state legislature, 50 percent of the members of the 1961 session were farmers, a ratio which remains virtually the same as it was before World War II. Thirty-nine percent of the members of the Minnesota House in 1951 were farmers, compared to 37 percent in the period from 1925 to 1935. In the same ten-year, prewar period, 24 percent of the members of the Indiana House, and 28 percent of the Washington House were farmers, compared to 21 percent in both bodies in recent sessions.[9] The proportion of farmers in the houses of Congress is comparatively small.

Lawyers constitute an occupational category among legislators which deserves special attention. Attorneys have played a prominent role in the American political system since the early days of the Republic. Twenty-five of the 52 signers of the Declaration of Independence, and 31 of the 55 members of the Continental Congress, were lawyers. The legal profession provided 70 percent of the Presidents, Vice-Presidents, and cabinet officers between 1877 and 1934, 50 percent of the United States Senators from 1947 to 1957, 56 percent of the members of the United States House of Representatives in 1949–1951, nearly half of the state governors between 1870 and 1950, and about a quarter of the members of the state legislatures since 1900.[10] The overrepresentation of lawyers as an occupational group in the legislature is particularly marked, since lawyers have never constituted more than two-tenths of 1 percent of the labor force, and now account for about one-tenth of 1 percent of the work force of the country.

The proportion of lawyers in the houses of Congress has remained stable at well over half the membership in recent years. And in state legislatures the overall proportion of attorneys has not varied much: Hyneman found that 28 percent of the members of 13 lower and 12 upper houses of state legislatures between 1925 and 1935 were attorneys, and Zeller found that 22 percent of the members of 48 state legislatures were lawyers in 1949.[11]

Senates in the United States tend to contain a higher proportion of lawyer-legislators than do houses of representatives. In the Eighty-fifth Congress, for example, 65 percent of the members of the Senate were attorneys, while 55 percent of the members of the House of Representatives were in that category.[12]

There exists a very considerable amount of variation in the numbers

Table 5.4. OCCUPATIONS OF AMERICAN LEGISLATORS
(In percentages)

Occupation	Calif. (1957)	N.J. (1957)	Ohio (1957)	Tenn. (1957)	Wis. (1957)	Minn. (1951)	Ind. (1961)	Wash. (1951)	Pa. (1958)	U.S. Senate (1947–1957)	U.S. House (1949–1951)
Professional, technical	39	60	52	38	37	14	30	32	34	64	69
Proprietor, manager, official	44	23	31	41	26	19	31	34	35	29	22
Farmer, farm manager	13	2	10	13	18	39	21	21	7	7	4
Craftsman, foreman, operative	1	1	2	2	13	—	6	5	12	—	—
Clerical, sales	3	9	5	5	5	28	5	—	9	—	1
Unskilled labor, servant, farm labor	—	—	—	—	1	—	—	—	1	—	2
Other, not known	—	5	—	1	—	—	7	9	2	—	2
Total	100	100	100	100	100	100	100	101	100	100	100
Numbers	120	79	173	132	100	n.a.	99	145	106	180	435

SOURCES: J. C. Wahlke et al., *The Legislative System* (New York: John Wiley and Sons, 1962), p. 490; W. P. Tucker, "Characteristics of State Legislators," *Social Science*, XXX (1955), 94; K. Janda et al., *Legislative Politics in Indiana* (Bloomington, Ind.: Indiana University Press, 1961), p. 3; P. Beckett and C. Sunderland, "Washington State's Lawmakers: Some Personnel Factors in the Washington Legislature," *Western Political Quarterly*, X (1957), 195; D. R. Matthews, *The Social Background of Political Decision-Makers* (New York: Random House, 1954), p. 30; D. R. Matthews, "United States Senators: A Collective Portrait," *International Social Science Journal*, XIII (1961), 628; F. J. Sorauf, *Party and Representation* (New York: Atherton Press, 1963), p. 71.

of lawyer-legislators from state to state. In some states legal training
appears to be more congenial to a legislative career than in others. Furthermore, the lawyer composition of a state's legislature may vary over
time. For example, the number of lawyers in the Illinois Senate has
increased substantially, if the pre-1935 and post-1935 periods are compared. In the pre-1935 period, a third of the senators in Illinois were
lawyers, but in the twenty-year period thereafter the average proportion of lawyers was over 40 percent. Accurate information about the
occupational characteristics of state legislators over time has never been
gathered for all states, and thus systematic state-by-state comparisons
are not possible. But in some state legislatures changes similar to that
in Wisconsin may have occurred. In that state there was a marked increase in the proportion of lawyers in the Assembly (lower house)
between 1925 and 1957 (see Table 5.5). The percentage of farmer-
legislators declined, and their places were taken largely by an increasing
number of lawyers and skilled workers. Such a pattern may be par-

Table 5.5. OCCUPATIONAL TRENDS IN COMPOSITION OF WISCONSIN
ASSEMBLY, 1925–1957
(In percentages)

Occupation	Year				
	1925	1935	1945	1955	1957
Lawyer	11	12	11	25	30
Farmer	45	31	20	16	14
Laborer	1	4	6	13	11
Commercial	22	41	53	36	30
Other	21	12	10	10	15
Total	100	100	100	100	100

SOURCE: Wisconsin Legislative Reference Library, *The Profile of a Legislature*
(1956), p. 14.

ticularly characteristic of states that experienced fairly rapid urbanization and industrialization during these years, and represents in part the
increasing success of the Democratic party in what had been a traditionally Republican state. Further, the ratio of lawyers to farmers in
two Midwestern state legislatures has been shown to vary closely with
fluctuations in farm prices, the proportion of farmers increasing in
periods of depression and that of lawyers in times of prosperity.[13] But
the numerousness of lawyers in the American legislature is likely to be
related to factors other than urbanization, industrialization, and eco-

nomic prosperity, and interstate variations in the proportions of lawyer-legislators are not easy to explain from the available data.

Lawyer-legislators differ from nonlawyers in the legislature in a variety of ways. They are somewhat less occupationally mobile than nonlawyers, in the sense of the number of different types of occupations held prior to legislative service.[14] They tend to come from higher-status family backgrounds in terms of their fathers' occupations. Lawyers tend to have had more prelegislative political experience, and to be more highly involved in politics, more self-motivated for a political career, and more "professional" politically in viewing legislative service as only a step to other political offices. In their legal-professional ability, legislator-lawyers do not appear to differ significantly from lawyers in the general population. Furthermore, where evidence is available, it appears that lawyers are distributed about equally between the Republican and Democratic parties, and between rural and urban parts of the states.[15]

It is often argued that the lawyer brings a special kind of skill to politics. The nature of legal training itself may tend to prepare its recipients for representative roles. The lawyer's occupation is the representation of clients. He makes no great change when he moves from representing clients in his private practice to representing constituents as a legislator. In general, lawyers may find legislative service more congenial to their previous training and occupational experience than those who come to the legislature from other occupations. The occupational role strains associated with a legislative status may be reduced among lawyers; they may be more receptive to the "bargainer" or "negotiator" role so commonly played in the American legislature.

But the professional skills developed by lawyers cannot by themselves explain the dominance of lawyers in the legislature. "In a highly competitive society," asks Matthews, "who can, with the least danger, leave their jobs for the tremendous risks of a political career?"

Among the high-prestige occupations it seems to be the lawyers. Certainly, other professional men find the neglect of their careers for political activity extremely hazardous. To those in professions where the subject matter is rapidly changing, a few years of neglect of their vocations and their skills would be either lost or outmoded. The active businessman, be he an individual entrepreneur or a member of a corporate bureaucracy, would find the neglect of his vocation for politics no asset to his primary occupational interest. These barriers to political participation either do not exist or are decreased in significance for the lawyer. The law changes relatively slowly. The lawyer, as Max Weber argued, is "dispensable," he can most easily combine his occupation, on a part-time basis, with political activity. Moreover, this activity can be a positive advantage to his occupational advancement— free and professionally legitimate advertising, contacts, opportunities to meet important lawyers of his region result from his political activities. Finally, lawyers possess a monopoly of public offices relating to the administration of law and the court system. Since in America "every political question tends to become a legal question," the offices of judge and prosecuting attorney provide lawyers (and lawyers alone) relatively easy entry into the political world and important springboards to higher offices.[16]

American legislatures are thus dominated by professional men, especially lawyers, businessmen and farmers. Other occupational groups, and in particular those in the skilled labor or manual worker categories, are very markedly underrepresented among legislators. The recruitment of legislators is very selective in terms of occupational status; while the legislative system is by no means closed, legislators clearly tend to be drawn predominantly from high-status occupations.

Occupational Mobility. The American legislator not only tends to enter politics from a high-status occupation, but he also tends to be characterized by a high degree of occupational mobility. While a great deal more evidence about the intergenerational and intragenerational occupational movement of legislators is needed, the data available indicate that legislators are more "upward-mobile" than the population in general. It might be said that the legislator is "on the make" occupationally; he tends to have a higher-status occupation than his father, and he tends to exhibit more changes in his own occupational career than the ordinary jobholder.

Data for state legislators in California, New Jersey, Ohio, and Tennessee, as well as for Wisconsin, indicate the substantial intergenerational mobility of legislators. Eulau and Koff found that, of 325 legislators from the 1957 sessions of the legislatures in the first four states named above, 32 percent could be classified as occupational "mobiles" vis-a-vis their fathers' occupations.[17] These legislators had moved substantially ahead of their fathers in terms of occupational status. Using a somewhat different basis of classification, it was found that 46 percent of the members of the 1957 session of the Wisconsin Assembly could be seen as occupationally mobile in comparison with their fathers' occupational status.

If one views the occupational mobility of the legislator in intragenerational terms, there is evidence to suggest that American legislators are highly mobile in their own career experiences. There is, for instance, evidence that the variety of occupational experiences of American congressmen increased uniformly from the early nineteenth century until after World War I.[18] More recent findings about United States Senators in the period from 1947 to 1957 show enough of the presenatorial occupational career pattern to indicate their increasing movement into high-status occupations. Table 5.6 indicates the occupational categories into which occupations of senators in this period fell at the levels of their first occupations, their principal occupations before senatorial service, and their occupations at the time of their entry into the Senate. The table reiterates the extent to which United States Senators are recruited from high-status occupations no matter where in their career one looks. Even so, the prelegislative occupations of senators are clearly characterized by increasing movement into professional and business occupations from lower-status work.

Table 5.6. OCCUPATIONS OF U.S. SENATORS, 1947–1957
(In percentages)

Occupation	First Occupation after School	Principal Occupation	Occupation, Time of Entry into Senate
Professional	68	64	82
Proprietor, official	13	29	15
Farmer	4	7	2
Low-salaried worker	8	—	—
Industrial wage earner	6	—	1
Servant, farm laborer	1	—	—
Total	100	100	100
Numbers	180	180	180

SOURCE: D. R. Matthews, "United States Senators: A Collective Portrait," *International Social Science Journal*, XIII (1961), 628.

RELIGION AND ETHNIC ORIGIN

Protestant Anglo-Saxons are substantially overrepresented among American legislators, and Negroes, Jews, and foreign-born Americans are significantly underrepresented in their legislatures. The religious composition of most state legislatures and both houses of the Congress is predominantly Protestant. The national Senate is more Protestant than the House, and there is considerable interstate variation in the proportion of Protestant legislators in state legislatures. The 1957 Tennessee legislature, for instance, was almost entirely Protestant in composition, while more than 40 percent of the 1957 New Jersey legislators were Catholic or Jewish.

The relationship between the proportions of Catholics in the population and in the legislature may vary a good deal. Certainly it seems unlikely that the Catholic population is overrepresented in an American legislature, but in some states the proportions are similar. In the 1957 Wisconsin Assembly, for example, 32 percent of the members were Catholic, and 32 percent of the state's population had Catholic religious affiliation. At the level of the United States Senate, the country's Catholic population is underrepresented. Only 11 percent of the senators serving from 1947 to 1957 were Catholic, while 21 percent of a sample of the population in 1952 identified themselves as Catholic and the claimed Church membership reaches 34 percent of the population.[19] The Jewish representation in every American legislative body is small and underrepresentative in every known case; the same is true of the Negro population.

In addition, American legislators are overwhelmingly born in the United States, and are heavily Anglo-Saxon in ethnic origin. Very few members of the United States Congress have been foreign-born. Of 9,618 people who served in the Congress from 1789 to 1949, only 374 (4 percent) were born outside the United States. During the Eightieth Congress, to take a recent session, only 2 percent of the members were foreign-born. Those who are born outside the United States tend to come from Northwestern European countries: 82 percent of all of the foreign-born Congressmen up to 1949 had been born in Canada, England, Germany, Ireland, and Scotland. Furthermore, 75 percent of the *second-generation* United States Senators who served from 1949 to 1957 were from Northwestern European ancestry.[20]

EDUCATIONAL LEVEL

No characteristic of the American legislator is better documented than the fact that legislators are among the most educated occupational groups in the United States. Table 5.7 shows the levels of educational attainment of members of nine state legislatures and the U. S. Congress. More than half the members of these state legislatures had attended college, and a third or more of them were college graduates. Pennsylvania provides the illustration of a relatively poorly educated legislature, where nearly half the members of the 1958 session had no more than a high school education; New Jersey is an illustration of a well-educated legislature, where 87 percent of the members of the 1957 session had attended college. Almost 85 percent of the United States Senators from 1947 to 1957 and over 90 percent of the members of the United States House (Seventy-seventh Congress) attended college. As the table indicates, the legislators in each case were proportionately much better educated than the populations they represented.

The relatively high educational level of American legislators can be accounted for, in part, by their relatively high class origins. But, at least for United States Senators, more attended college than other members of the white adult population of the country, regardless of their class origins. While the middle-class and upper-middle-class parent in the United States is better able to assure a college education for his children, the educational system is sufficiently open to all so that, at the level of the Senate, legislators achieve a high educational level almost regardless of status differences.

AGES OF LEGISLATORS

The legislative recruitment process in the United States tends to select the middle-aged—men in their forties and fifties—for legislative careers. In general, the median ages of members of the senates are higher than for members of the lower houses, although in some states, like New Jersey in 1957, the age differences between the two houses are not great. Also, members of the national houses tend to be older in terms of median ages than members of the comparable state bodies.

The age of the candidate for legislative office may be independently significant in the selection process. The legislative candidate in his fifties may have an advantage over one in his forties in terms of his capacity to project a politically desirable image of wisdom and experience. It has been demonstrated with age data for one congressional election (1958) that winning candidates for the United States House of Representatives had higher average ages than losers, and age fluctuations occurred between "safe" and "marginal" congressional districts, such that younger men tended to be elected from the more politically competitive areas. The available evidence is consistent with the hypothesis that "middle-agedness is part of the electorate's image of a Congressman." A similar phenomenon may occur at the state level.[21]

THE LEGISLATOR'S POLITICAL CAREER

It is possible to conceive of the political system as a multiplicity of career patterns or in terms of lines of career development for politicians. Political career patterns exhibit some of the characteristics of an escalator, in that a political career can be entered at various points in a chain of interrelated political statuses. For some legislators, service in a legislative body is an *entrée* into politics, for others it is but an intermediate status, and for still others it is terminal. While we can by no means cover the whole range of the legislative career here, we can enter the career structure at several points to examine its salient characteristics.

Table 5.7. Educational Level of American Legislators
(In percentages)

Education	Calif. (1957)	N.J. (1957)	Ohio (1957)	Tenn. (1957)	Wis. (1957)	Minn. (1951)	Ind. (1961)	Pa. (1958)	Ga. (1961)	U.S. House (1941–43)	U.S. Senate (1947–57)
Elementary only	—(33)	—(47)	4(43)	4(60)	8(52)	(50)	7(46)	10(42)	12(50)	*	1(48)
Some high school	15(45)	13(38)	19(42)	22(29)	24(34)	(34) ⎱ 23	20(41)	39(45)	16(37)	9	14(38)
Some college	31(11)	24(6)	19(7)	28(6)	23(7)	23(9) ⎰	26(6)	15(6)	32(7)	3	⎱ 84(14)
College graduate	54(8)	63(7)	58(6)	46(4)	45(5)	54(6)	47(5)	36(6)	40(6)	88	⎰
Total	100	100	100	100	100	100	100	100	100	100	99
Numbers	120	79	162	120	n.a.	n.a.	99	106	259	431	180

NOTE: Numbers in parentheses indicate proportions of the total relevant populations in each category.

* Less than 1%.

SOURCES: J. C. Wahlke et al., *The Legislative System* (New York: John Wiley and Sons, 1962), p. 489; W. P. Tucker, "Characteristics of State Legislators," *Social Science*, XXX (1955), 94–98; K. Janda et al., *Legislative Politics in Indiana* (Bloomington, Ind: Indiana University Press, 1961), p. 3; M. M. McKinney, "The Personnel of the Seventy-seventh Congress," *American Political Science Review*, XXXVI (1942), 70; D. R. Matthews, "United States Senators: A Collective Portrait," *International Social Science Journal*, XIII (1961), 625; F. J. Sorauf, *Party and Representation* (New York: Atherton Press, 1963), p. 69; H. M. Thomason, "The Legislative Process in Georgia" (Unpublished Ph.D. dissertation, Emory University, 1961), pp. 82–83.

The state legislatures provide a convenient starting point. To a very marked degree, state legislative service is the first political office for legislators. As before, data are available for only a few states (shown in Table 5.8), and significant interstate variations are apparent. Even so,

Table 5.8. PRELEGISLATIVE PUBLIC AND PARTY OFFICEHOLDING,
STATE LEGISLATORS
(In percentages)

Legislature	No Other Public Office	No Previous Party Office	Number
California (1957)	51	52	113
New Jersey (1957)	34	41	79
Ohio (1957)	43	62	162
Tennessee (1957)	51	66	120
Wisconsin (1957)	48	—	111
Minnesota House (1951)	40	—	n.a.
Pennsylvania (1958)	63	31	106

SOURCES: J. C. Wahlke et al., *The Legislative System* (New York: John Wiley and Sons, 1962), pp. 95–97; L. D. Epstein, *Politics in Wisconsin* (Madison: University of Wisconsin Press, 1958), p. 191; W. P. Tucker, "Characteristics of State Legislators," *Social Science*, XXX (1955), pp. 94–98; F. J. Sorauf, *Party and Representation* (New York: Atherton Press, 1963), p. 83.

the proportion of state legislators who have not held public office prior to entry into the legislature is considerable, ranging in size from about one-third in New Jersey to more than half the members in California and Tennessee and almost two-thirds in Pennsylvania. Equally clear from Table 5.8 is the fact that legislators are not likely to have had party experience in substantial proportions.

While the previous table indicates the extent to which state legislators have not had experience in public office before their election to the legislature, it must be noted that more than half the members in New Jersey, Ohio, Wisconsin, and Minnesota, and nearly half in California and Tennessee, had served in some public office prior to their election to the legislature. Among those legislators with previous experience, the predominant kind of experience was service on local legislative or quasi-legislative bodies. Forty-eight percent of the New Jersey legislators, and approximately a third of the members of the California, Ohio, and Tennessee legislatures and of the Wisconsin Assembly who had prior political experience had served on city councils, county boards, and school boards.[22] Finally, Pennsylvania obviously diverges considerably from the pattern of other states. There political experience is much more likely than in the other states noted to come out of political party office rather than public elective office.

Generally, local political office predominantly of a legislative sort provides the *entrée* to a political career for about half or more of the members of state legislatures, and state legislative service is the *entrée* for the remainder, in most states. Once elected to the state legislature, members tend to aspire to reelection. In 1957, for example, over three-fourths of the New Jersey legislators and about 90 percent of the Wisconsin Assemblymen indicated plans or expectations to run for their legislative seats again. In some less politically competitive states the level of aspiration for reelection is lower but, in the states for which there is evidence, the proportion of members who clearly intend to withdraw from the legislature rises above one-fifth only in Tennessee.[23]

Some legislators who intend to run for reelection have that intention primarily because legislative service provides an interesting avocation to occupy the unemployed, the elderly, and the retired. "You might say that I'm sort of unemployed now," one legislator said, "and am here for lack of a better job."[24] Others view state legislative experience as a steppingstone to more advanced, and perhaps more professionalized, public office. Some of those who do not plan to run for reelection to the state legislature aspire to run for higher political office.

The level of aspiration for higher public office in state legislatures seems fairly high. Wahlke and his associates found that approximately one-third of the legislators in four states aspired to hold other political offices. Generally speaking, aspiration for service in the upper chamber or in a federal legislative post predominated in these four states, although executive and judicial offices were also stressed heavily by legislators in some states.[25]

In seeking or aspiring to other public offices, state legislators compete with those who enter politics from other channels. Still, it is important to take note, at least by way of illustration, of the extent to which state legislators migrate to other key offices. Schlesinger, for instance, studied the career patterns of state governors from 1870 to 1950; he found the state legislature an important, if declining, recruiting ground for the governorships. Between 1940 and 1950, 41 percent of the governors had had legislative experience, although only 13 percent had served in the state legislature immediately prior to election as governor.[26] Epstein found for Wisconsin that "between 1925 and 1955, almost one-third of the U. S. Senators, governors, other state constitutional officers, and U. S. Representatives . . . were former state legislators."[27] Over one-fourth of the members of the United States House of Representatives for the Seventy-seventh Congress had state legislative experience, and 21 percent of the United States Senators serving from 1947 to 1957 had served as state legislators in their first public office.[28]

Other kinds of political life seem less accessible to those for whom state legislative experience is a part of their political apprenticeship. Judicial offices seem unlikely to be generally sought and acquired by those whose experience is primarily legislative. Epstein has commented, for example, that "a district attorney, among partisan office-holders, may be in a better position than a legislator to be elected judge."[29] In addition, while it is commonly assumed to be otherwise, few state legislators appear to move from legislative to lobbyist roles.[30]

Election to the Congress is by no means terminal in terms of the legislative career. Service in the United States House of Representatives fairly frequently leads to other public office. In Ohio, for example, 42 percent of the governors who served from 1870 to 1950 came directly from Congress.[31] Twenty-eight percent of the United States Senators who served from 1947 to 1957 had previously served in the House of Representatives.[32] Senators have always been contenders for the Presidency.

Members of the United States House of Representatives have varied backgrounds of political experience. For instance, of those who served in the Seventy-seventh Congress, the largest proportion had served in a state legislature, but other kinds of experience seem significant as well. When all the law enforcement officers were taken together (prosecuting attorneys, judges, attorneys-general), they constituted an even larger segment in terms of prior experience. Further, a significant number of Congressmen had local political experience as a part of their political careers. About one-fourth of the members of the House serving in this session had not held public office prior to their election.

Matthews' study of United States Senators is particularly illuminating in helping to fill in our description of the legislative career. His comparison of senators' first public office with their last office before being elected to the Senate demonstrates the "escalator" character of the legislative career in the United States. Only 9 percent of the senators serving between 1947 and 1957 had had no previous experience in public office. About a fifth began their public careers in state legislatures, and about a fourth in law enforcement offices (see Table 5.9). When senators' first and last offices are compared, there is a clear shift from lower to higher positions—from local, law enforcement, or state legislative offices to state governorships and experience in the national House.

LEGISLATIVE TURNOVER

The state legislature tends to recruit new members at a relatively high rate. It is an amateur political body in a variety of ways, and one of the indicators of its amateurism is its high turnover rate. The turnover of members of the more professionalized national Congress is much lower than is the case in most state legislatures. It can be said in general about legislative turnover that (1) there are substantial interstate variations and, while they are not entirely explained, turnover tends roughly to be lower in the urban-industrial states and highest in the rural states; (2) turnover of membership is generally higher in houses of representa-

Table 5.9. POLITICAL EXPERIENCES OF U.S. SENATORS, 1947–1957
(In percentages)

Political Experience	First Public Office	Last Public Office before Senate
United States senator	9	—
State governor	2	22
U.S. House of Representatives	4	28
State legislator	21	10
Statewide elective official	4	2
Local elective official	14	6
Law enforcement	28	15
Administrative	14	17
Congressional staff	3	1
Total	100	100
Numbers	180	164

SOURCE: D. R. Matthews, "United States Senators: A Collective Portrait," *International Social Science Journal*, XIII (1961), 630.

tives than in senates; (3) turnover is generally much higher in most state legislatures than in the Congress. In his study of tenure and turnover among legislators in ten states in the prewar period between 1925 and 1935, Hyneman found that 40 percent of the members of lower chambers and 20 percent of the state senators were serving their first terms.[33] It seems likely that state legislative turnover has declined in the postwar period. Data are not available for a large enough number of states to make generalization safe, but for the states where comparisons over time can be made—these are shown in Table 5.10—a decrease in turnover can be noted. Only for Indiana is there evidence for stable turnover at more than half the membership of both houses of the legislature; at least for 1950, the turnover was higher than the pre-1935 average. The generally reduced state legislative turnover in the postwar years may be indicative of relatively greater political stability, although it may indicate as well the extent to which state legislative service is the end of the political career for many. Of course, an increase in turnover in the next few years may result from massive state legislative redistricting. And the substantial proportion of experienced members in every legislature, along with the extended experience of a few, should not be over-

Table 5.10.   STATE LEGISLATORS SERVING FIRST TERM

(In percentages)

State	1925-35	1950	Recent Session
California	32	23	18 (1957)
Georgia	—	41 (1951)	33 (1961)
Illinois	26	19	28 (1961)
Indiana	50	54	—
Iowa	40	24	20 (1963)
Kentucky	—	—	44 (1964)
Maine	49	43	—
Minnesota	27	18	11 (1961)
New Jersey	32	—	24 (1957)
New York	16	5	14 (1961)
Ohio	—	39	20 (1957)
Pennsylvania	36	25	18 (1958)
Tennessee	—	52	42 (1957)
Texas	—	38	33 (1961)
Washington	41	36	20 (1951)

SOURCES: C. S. Hyneman, "Tenure and Turnover of Legislative Personnel," *Annals of the American Academy of Political and Social Science*, CXC (1938), 23; B. Zeller (ed.), *American State Legislatures* (New York: Thomas Y. Crowell Co., 1954), pp. 66–67; J. C. Wahlke et al., *The Legislative System* (New York: John Wiley and Sons, 1962), p. 491; P. Beckett and C. Sunderland, "Washington State's Lawmakers: Some Personnel Factors in the Washington Legislature," *Western Political Quarterly*, X (1957), 183; F. J. Sorauf, *Party and Representation* (New York: Atherton Press, 1963), p. 82; H. M. Thomason, "The Legislative Process in Georgia" (Unpublished Ph.D. dissertation, Emory University, 1961), pp. 102–03; William E. Oden, "Tenure and Turnover in Recent Texas Legislatures" (Unpublished manuscript, 1964).

looked in assessing the capacity of the state legislature to perform its tasks. Most state legislatures contain at least a few members with very considerable legislative experience. To provide but three illustrations, 15 percent of the Wisconsin lower house in 1957 had served more than ten years, as had 17 percent of the 1961 Georgia House and 16 percent of the 1964 Kentucky Senate. Of course, the proportion of members with long experience is much higher in the Congress than is typically the case for state legislative bodies.

The small number of new members in each new Congress of the United States, underscored by Table 5.11, which shows the percentage of new members in the Eighty-fifth through the Eighty-eighth Congresses, indicates the relatively greater degree of previous experience in

Table 5.11.   NEW MEMBERS, U.S. CONGRESS

(In percentages)

Session	Senate	House
85th Congress	10	10
86th Congress	18	19
87th Congress	9	14
88th Congress	11	13

SOURCE: *Congressional Quarterly Almanac*, relevant years.

the legislative body on the part of legislators at the national level. However, some urban states like New York, Illinois, and California have turnover levels similar to that in Congress. Differences between houses of Congress are not great with regard to the proportions of new members, even though only a third of the senators stand for reelection at any one time. In addition, seniority has far greater significance at the national levels than at state levels toward the acquiring of prestige, influence, and perquisites for legislators. Finally, congressional turnover is higher in the urban-industrial two-party states of Michigan, Ohio, and Illinois, and lowest in the Republican Midwest and the Democratic South. Thus, the important fact about legislative turnover at the national level is not that it is in general minimal, but rather that the virtual absence of turnover in some states and regions gives a great advantage to members from certain states that is not available to members from others.

Tenure in office in Congress has increased very dramatically over the last century. Of the members of the Forty-second Congress (in 1871) about half of the House members and a third of the senators had been elected more than once to their houses. By the immediate pre-World War I period, three-fourths of the representatives and nearly half the senators had been returned at least once before. In 1961, 87 percent of the members of the House and two-thirds of the senators had served previous terms.[34]

CONCLUSION

In this chapter we have tried to summarize the salient social and political background characteristics of American legislators. Much more could be said of them, and much more should be known about them. Statistical summaries omit much of the color and individuality of legislative life; we hope to make amends for that omission in later chapters. And later we will treat in some detail legislators' attitudes, images, and ideological orientations. What is least known about legislators (and about political leaders generally) and where new knowledge is most required, concerns their personality characteristics. We have some reason to believe that legislators may be less neurotic than the general adult population, more self-sufficient, more extroverted, and only slightly more dominant.[35] But the data are very meager, and comparative generalizations cannot be made.

Direct inferences from knowledge about the social origins and political career patterns of legislators to their actions, their behavior, and their decision-making involvement would certainly be simplistic. Only the crudest biographical theory of the political process would assert a direct connection between social and political background factors and decision making. There is no reason at all why an upper-middle class, Protestant, old American male with a political career studded with service in legislative councils from municipal to national levels cannot fully and adequately represent a working-class district with a low level of political participation. But knowing something about the composition of American legislatures helps to understand the recruitment of legislative politicians in our political system and to map the structure of the political careers of legislators. Besides, as we shall see when we give detailed treatment to the voting behavior of legislators, at least some of the social and political background characteristics of legislators can be shown to have a significant bearing upon legislative behavior.

NOTES

1. Andrew Hacker, "The Elected and the Anointed: Two American Elites," *American Political Science Review*, LV (1961), 541.

2. Donald R. Matthews, "United States Senators: A Collective Portrait," *International Social Science Journal*, XIII (1961), 622.

3. Madge M. McKinney, "The Personnel of the Seventy-seventh Congress," *American Political Science Review*, XXXVI (1942), 68.

4. Frank J. Sorauf, *Party and Representation* (New York, 1963), p. 74; and Hugh M. Thomason, "The Legislative Process in Georgia" (Unpublished Ph.D. dissertation, Emory University, 1961), p. 74.

5. John C. Wahlke, Heinz Eulau, William Buchanan, and LeRoy C. Ferguson, *The Legislative Sytem* (New York: John Wiley and Sons, 1962), p. 82.

6. *Ibid.*, p. 83.

7. *Ibid.*, p. 89.

8. See H. H. Gerth and C. Wright Mills (eds.), *From Max Weber: Essays in Sociology* (London, 1948), p. 85.

9. Charles S. Hyneman, "Who Makes Our Laws?" *Political Science Quarterly*, LV (1940), 560–61.

10. See Donald R. Matthews, *The Social Backgrounds of Political Decision-Makers* (New York, 1954), p. 30, and "United States Senators: A Collective Portrait," p. 628; Joseph A. Schlesinger, "Lawyers and American Politics: A Clarified View," *Midwest Journal of Political Science*, I (1957), 28.

11. Hyneman, *op. cit.*, p. 557; Belle Zeller (ed.), *American State Legislatures* (New York, 1954), p. 71.

12. *Congressional Quarterly Student Guide* (Washington, D.C., 1957), p. 8.

13. David Gold, "Lawyers in Politics: An Empirical Exploration of Biographical Data on State Legislators," *Pacific Sociological Review*, IV (1961), 85.

14. Mapheus Smith and Marian L. Brockway, "Mobility of American Congressmen," *Sociology and Social Research*, XXIV (1940), 519–20.

15. David R. Derge, "The Lawyer as Decision-Maker in the American State Legislature," *Journal of Politics*, XXI (1959), 408–33, and "The Lawyer in the Indiana General Assembly," *Midwest Journal of Political Science*, VI (1962), 19–53; Heinz Eulau and John D. Sprague, *Lawyers in Politics: A Study in Professional Convergence* (Indianapolis, 1964).

16. Matthews, "United States Senators: A Collective Portrait," p. 629.

17. Heinz Eulau and David Koff, "Occupational Mobility and Political Career," *Western Political Quarterly*, XV (1962), 511.

18. Smith and Brockway, *op. cit.*, p. 514.

19. Matthews, "United States Senators: A Collective Portrait," p. 625.

20. Murray G. Lawson, "The Foreign-born in Congress, 1789–1949: A Statistical Summary," *American Political Science Review*, LI (1957), 1183–89; Matthews, "United States Senators: A Collective Portrait," p. 624.

21. David B. Walker, "The Age Factor in the 1958 Congressional Elections," *Midwest Journal of Political Science*, IV (1960), 1–26. See also Sorauf, *op. cit.*, p. 66.

22. Wahlke et al., *op. cit.*, p. 96.

23. *Ibid.*, p. 122.

24. *Ibid.*, p. 124.

25. *Ibid.*, pp. 129–30.

26. Joseph A. Schlesinger, *How They Became Governor* (East Lansing, Mich., 1957), p. 51.

27. Leon D. Epstein, *Politics in Wisconsin* (Madison, Wis., 1958), p. 117.

28. McKinney, *op. cit.*, p. 71; Matthews, "United States Senators: A Collective Portrait," p. 630.

29. Epstein, *loc. cit.*

30. Samuel C. Patterson, "The Role of the Lobbyist: The Case of Oklahoma," *Journal of Politics*, XXV (1963), 76–77; Lester W. Milbrath, "The Political Party Activity of Washington Lobbyists," *Journal of Politics*, XX (1958), 346.

31. Schlesinger, *How They Became Governor*, p. 18.

32. Matthews, "United States Senators: A Collective Portrait," p. 630.

33. Charles S. Hyneman, "Tenure and Turnover of Legislative Personnel," *Annals of the American Academy of Political and Social Science*, CXCV (1938), 23.

34. Samuel P. Huntington, "Congressional Responses to the Twentieth Century," in David B. Truman (ed.), *The Congress and America's Future* (Englewood Cliffs, N.J., 1965), p. 9.

35. John B. McConaughy, "Certain Personality Factors of State Legislators in South Carolina," *American Political Science Review*, XLIV (1950), 897–903.

[Part III]

LEGISLATIVE ORGANIZATION AND PROCEDURE

[Part III]

A T THE CENTER of the legislative system is the legislature itself, an institution with certain constitutional powers and traditional procedures, operating with an established structure of subsystems (such as committees) within a particular political environment. The patterns of behavior that are rooted in these characteristics of the legislature seldom permit a quick response to pressures for change that arise outside the legislature. An understanding of the legislative system and the way in which the roles therein are shaped, or an analysis of the legislative process and its output, requires knowledge about the structure of the legislature. The outline of this structure on paper is less useful for this purpose than a description of its operation in practice. Legislative structure varies tremendously in practice, more so than is apparent from a summary of rules or a list of leaders and committees in the various legislatures. It is neither possible nor desirable to describe in detail the structure and operations of 101 legislative bodies, but we can indicate the most common patterns of activity, provide examples from specific legislatures, and—most important—explain why certain structural patterns develop and how these affect the legislative process.

A starting point is the framework of the national or state constitution, which defines legislative structure and powers. There are few constitutional restrictions on Congress, but most state constitutions severely restrict both the substantive jurisdiction and the structural flexibility of the legislature. Few of these constitutional restrictions have been removed in recent years, but other structural changes have been made to improve the ability of both Congress and the state legislatures to cope with the growing demands made on them. The most important of these changes has been the development of larger and better trained staffs, particularly in Congress and in some of the larger states.

The legislative system cannot be considered in isolation from the entire political system in the state or nation of which it forms a part. The nature of party competition affects not only the selection of legislators, which we have discussed above, but also the structure of the legislature. In a two-party state, the legislature is organized along party lines. If the parties are well organized and cohesive at the state level, there are more likely to be tightly organized party organs in the legislature. The fractures evident in the congressional parties are in part a consequence of the decentralized national party system. If legislative parties are insignificant, the political vacuum in the legislature may be filled by the governor or by some factional leadership group.

Legislative organization is the apparatus of leadership. Leadership is personal, and in smaller legislative bodies it often appears that the nature of leadership can be defined exclusively in terms of personality —the style and skills of one or a few men. But leadership is also affected by the political environment. The Speaker's role is defined largely by the expectations of the group that selected him, whether that be a party caucus, a small clique of senior legislators, or a large coalition of personally recruited legislators. The floor leader's role is sometimes an ambivalent one, because of the demands made on him by both the Administration and the legislative party. A floor leader's power is derived both from his own skills and from the degree of cohesion that characterizes the party or faction. Similarly, the use of leadership committees and caucuses depends both on the preferences of the leaders and on the existence of sufficient unity in the party to make these devices workable.

Every legislative body has leadership, but it is not necessarily centralized in the presiding officers and the party or factional leaders. If there is a decentralized structure, the other loci of power are the committees. Every legislature uses standing committees; they make possible a division of the work load and specialization in the study of legislation. An analysis of committee structure and of the process by which members are chosen for committees is perhaps the best method available for determining the sources of leadership and the distribution of power in the legislature. Committees in some legislatures are little more than organs of the majority party; in others, they are just as tightly controlled by a clique or faction. In Congress the seniority principal is so important in the selection process that committees have developed an unusual degree of independent authority. Even the placing of bills on the calendar for floor consideration, a leadership responsibility in most states, in the House is vested in a Rules Committee not firmly controlled by the majority leadership.

Legislative rules and procedures are among the components of the legislative structure that must be known in order to understand the legislative process. Some can be defined and described in terms of their functional utility for the majority party or faction, for the minority, or for the protection of committee authority. Others serve the interests of the legislature as a whole.

[6]

Organization and Powers of Legislative Bodies

THE NEWLY elected member of a legislative body is comparable to the freshman who has met rigid entrance requirements and outlasted strong competitors in order to enter a university. Like the freshman, the legislator discovers that the institution has a history, regulations, and traditions—often long established—that define the limits of his authority and set the pattern for his behavior. The individual legislator, if he remains long enough and particularly if he attains leadership status, may be able to have some impact on the system or make some change in the rules. But in his day-to-day operations the legislator must conform to an environment that is the product of history and constitutional law as well as of political tradition. There are common elements in the fifty-one state and national legislatures of this country, but there are also significant variations in legislative environment.

CONGRESS

Constitutional Framework. One constitutional authority has written that "every provision of the federal constitution can be accounted for in American experience between 1776 and 1787."[1] The delegates to the Philadelphia convention of 1787 were able to draw upon their experience with the Continental Congress and the Congress under the Articles of Confederation as well as the experience of state legislatures. These in turn were modeled in part on the British Parliament and the colonial legislatures. One of the earliest and least disputed decisions of the Philadelphia convention was to approve the principle of bicameralism, which had been contained in the Virginia Plan. Most state legislatures had preserved the colonial practice of bicameralism, which had made possible representation of the colonies in one house and the mother country in the other. As the convention progressed, the agreement on bicameralism facilitated compromises between the proponents of large or small states and between the advocates of greater or lesser popular representation. It also gave more substance to the principle of checks and balances. The bicameral system established at Philadelphia, like those in the states but unlike those in many other countries, is a system in which substantially equal power is given to the Senate and the House. The Senate approves treaties and executive appointments, but the approval of both branches is required for all other legislation and appropriations, with the House initiating revenue bills.[2]

The relationship of Congress to the executive branch was a perplexing problem for the Founding Fathers. We know that many of them were influenced by the views of Locke and Montesquieu and believed that the separation of powers was an essential defense against tyranny. At the same time they recognized the dangers of a weak executive, like that under the Articles of Confederation and in the new state governments. Yet the early proposals at Philadelphia provided for election of the President by the Congress, and, in reviewing the debates, Burns notes how "one watches suspensefully as the Framers again and again come to the brink of letting Congress choose the President and then teeter off in the reverse direction."[3] The Framers finally decided on the awkward mechanism of the electoral college, with Congress given the authority to settle deadlocks; it was only the subsequent growth of the two-party system that avoided deadlocks and guaranteed the President electoral independence of Congress.

In the opening words of Article I, the Constitution provided: "All legislative powers herein granted shall be vested in a Congress. . . ." The President, however, was authorized to play both a positive and a negative role in the legislative process. He could recommend for the consideration of Congress "such measures as he shall judge necessary and expedient." He could veto legislation, subject to the authority of Congress to override his veto by a two-thirds vote of both houses. The Framers did not foresee the powerful role that the President plays today in the legislative process, but they provided the constitutional framework that makes it possible. In short, the Constitution established a presidential-congressional system in which the two branches are guaranteed independence of each other and both play an essential role in the legislative process. This is the most important constitutional fact determining how Congress functions.

Power and Functions. Since the Constitution vests "all legislative powers" in Congress, it is logical that the list of delegated powers of the national government should follow the heading: "The Congress shall have the power. . . ." There are also a few specific limitations on the scope of legislative power in the original Constitution and in the Bill of Rights. Congressional authority is broad, in contrast to legislative authority in most states, because the grants of power are broadly described and have been broadly interpreted by the courts, at least in recent years. The substantive scope of congressional authority has grown with the evolutionary changes in the federal system, and today there are relatively few areas in which legislation can be seriously proposed but congressional action is inhibited by the Constitution.

Formally, the functions of Congress may be divided into several categories. First, Congress is a lawmaking body, as the Constitution makes explicit by its vesting of legislative power. Closely related are the powers of Congress to levy taxes and to make appropriations, also made explicit in the Constitution. There have been no significant limits on these powers since the Sixteenth Amendment was passed, legalizing the progressive income tax. Closely related is the power of the Senate to give or withhold its consent to treaties by a two-thirds vote. The development of bipartisanship as a tactic of presidential leadership has minimized senatorial obstructionism but it has not eliminated senatorial power in treaty-making. Congress, by a two-thirds vote in each house, may recommend constitutional amendments; at the request of two-thirds of the states, Congress "shall call a convention for proposing amendments," although congressional discretion in complying with this latter provision has never been tested.

Congress has authority to supervise the administration of government. This is not explicitly granted in the Constitution, but it can be implied from the impeachment authority, senatorial approval of nominations to executive office, the appropriations power, and the need to investigate the implementation of legislation. Congress has, in fact, regarded this as one of its most important responsibilities, and has used its powers—particularly those with regard to appropriations and investigations—with skill and determination to carry out this function. Congress also has responsibility over the judiciary: the Senate must approve judicial appointments, and Congress must establish federal courts (other than the Supreme Court) and prescribe their jurisdiction (except for the original jurisdiction of the Supreme Court). The House has the responsibility for electing a President if no candidate receives a majority of the electoral vote, although it has not exercised this authority since 1824; it would vote by states, with each state casting one vote. The Senate would choose a Vice-President if no candidate had a majority of the electoral vote. Congress also provides for succession to the President below the level of Vice-President, an issue that has stirred renewed interest in recent years. Congress may regulate the holding of congressional elections (time, place, and manner), and each house is the judge of the election returns and qualifications of its own members. It also passes legislation regarding apportionment of the House.

The House. The casual visitor to Capitol Hill cannot help noticing one of the most important differences between the House and the Senate: the House is a much larger body. One consequence of this is that the House follows more rigid rules regarding debate and the conduct of business. It is too large to be a deliberative body, to give any substantial proportion of the members a chance to speak on issues; as a result, the House does not try to be a deliberative body, seldom devotes itself seriously to "debate," and rarely tries to rewrite the committee's version of a bill on the floor of the House. Sometimes there are drastic limits on the amendments that can be considered on the floor. Because of its greater size, and the absence of mechanical voting devices, the House has fewer roll calls than the Senate, and more of its decisions on important questions are unrecorded. Much of its decision making with regard to amendments is carried on in the Committee of the Whole, where the quorum requirement is small (100 members instead of a majority), with the result that important decisions are often not only unrecorded but also made by a small minority of representatives. The greater size of the House also leads to some less obvious consequences for the member. The workload is more specialized, and, with few exceptions, the individual member has little chance to become influential except with regard to a single narrow area related to his committee responsibilities.

The House of Representatives was intended by the delegates in Philadelphia to be the major representative body in the government; its members were the only ones directly chosen by the people. The political party system first developed in the House. After a period of presidential domination under Jefferson, the House emerged as the strongest branch of government under the speakership of Henry Clay. It is impossible to trace with precision the ups and downs of this branch's prestige and influence; the evaluation must be a subjective one. In the decades before the Civil War, however, the prestige of the House appears to have declined as the conflict over slavery and the weakness of Clay's successors in the speakership led to fragmentation of power and deadlock in the House. Webster, Clay, Calhoun, and other congressmen of stature transferred their talents to the Senate. The period from the end of the Civil War through the first decade of the twentieth century was, with few exceptions, one of congressional supremacy and growing influence of the House. A series of strong

Speakers, by enhancing their own power, made it possible for a majority of the House members to conduct business efficiently. The Senate's prestige declined because its members—still elected by state legislatures —came increasingly to be regarded as agents of powerful business interests and unrepresentative of the public.[4]

In the last half-century, however, the House has declined in prestige, as compared with the Senate. Effective political leadership in the House was weakened and diversified when the Speaker's powers were curbed in the revolt of 1910–1911. The Senate, on the other hand, became a more important body because its members were popularly elected after the adoption of the Seventeenth Amendment in 1913 and because foreign affairs became increasingly important in American life. In recent years the House has been a more conservative body, more often delaying or opposing programs initiated by the President and passed by the Senate; as a consequence, the House has become the target of criticism by liberal commentators. One additional factor may have contributed to its decline. In an age of increasing attention to public opinion and the public image, senators have been not only more "visible" to the public but also more successful in creating a favorable image.

The Senate. When students hear the Senate described as a "deliberative body," they sometimes envision it as the scene of repeated filibusters. The use of the filibuster today is unusual, though the possibility of a filibuster is an ever-present factor in legislative maneuvering. When we speak of the Senate as a deliberative body, we mean that, unlike the House, it gives extended and careful attention to the legislation that is reported from committees. The fact that bills are often debated at length on the floor does not mean that mere oratory changes many votes. It means that bills are sometimes substantially changed by the discussion and bargaining that occurs, on the floor and off, between the time the bill emerges from committee and the time when it passes.

The Senate was originally intended to be a conservative political institution, vaguely like the House of Lords in Britain today, restraining and moderating the rash impulses of the House of Representatives. The system of election by state legislators was viewed by the Framers as a method of assuring that senators would be men of the highest caliber, sensitive to the interests of the individual states.[5] In the half-century following the Civil War, however, this electoral system produced a Senate that was under Republican and conservative control and not responsive to changes in viewpoint or party preference on the part of the voters. The often used label, "millionaires' club," if not perfectly descriptive of the membership as a whole, was an apt description of the Senate majority.

The popular election of senators created, in time, a new Senate and a new breed of senators. The system of equal representation for each state has, at various times in the past, given disproportionate power to such groups as the silver bloc and the farm bloc. A combination of factors, but particularly the seniority system, has given the South particular influence in the Senate. William S. White's colorful description of the Senate as "the South's unending revenge upon the North for Gettysburg"[6] overstates the case, but there is evidence to support his contention that Southerners have played a dominant part in establishing the customs and norms of the Senate through their seniority and their membership in the inner circle or Senate "club." In addition they have used seniority and senatorial procedures to maintain a veto, of gradually declining effectiveness, over certain kinds of legislation, particularly in the field of civil rights. But the portrayal of a monolithic congressional delegation from the South is becoming less and less accurate. Today it is more accurate to describe the Senate as an urban institution than as a Southern institution. Senators, by the nature of their constituencies, represent a greater variety of interests than do members of the House. The growing number of states in which metropolitan areas play a major or a dominating role has produced the paradox that the Senate, where Montana is represented equally with New York, is more responsive to urban interests than is the House.

The senator as an individual differs significantly from the representative. He is usually more of a generalist, or at least a specialist in a larger range of subject matter. He is usually a more important political figure in his state, and far more likely to be an important figure on the Washington political scene. (In recent years nearly a dozen senators, and no representatives, have made serious efforts to secure a presidential nomination.) The senator has a much larger staff, receives more mail, and in general operates on a much larger scale in his day-to-day work. As we have seen, he is less able than the average representative to succeed in carving out a completely safe constituency for himself. It is worth noting that approximately one-third of the senators have previously been representatives.

The Senate differs from the House in its concern with foreign policy. The increasing importance of foreign aid and the reciprocal trade program has given the House a larger legislative role in foreign affairs than previously, but the Senate alone remains responsible for approving treaties. This treaty-making power and the Senate's tradition as a deliberative body have made the Senate throughout history the locus for the "great debates" over foreign policy. The Foreign Relations Committee remains more prestigious and more influential than its counterpart in the House.

Organizational Change. In 1946 Congress passed the Legislative

Reorganization Act, which, among other things, streamlined committees and provided for more adequate staffing. In one respect, however, the act reflected nostalgia rather than foresight; it provided that, except in time of war or national emergency, Congress should adjourn annually not later than the end of July. Only twice since then has Congress finished its business that early; usually the sessions have dragged on into late summer or into the fall, and even in election years congressional business has sometimes interfered with the campaign.[7] Perhaps the year-long session in 1963 was a portent of the future; on December 24th of that year, representatives trudged through the snow to cast their votes on the foreign aid bill at a session of the House which convened at 7 in the morning, and senators interrupted their brief holiday vacation to return for a final vote on the same bill on the 30th of December.

Congress has become not only a year-round operation, but a large and expensive one. The appropriation for operating Congress is about $100,000,000, a total which would have financed the entire government in any year prior to the Civil War. The legislative offices are now housed in two Senate office buildings and three House office buildings, in addition to the Capitol.

Political Setting. Congress is one of the best examples of a two-party legislative system in this country. Two political factions can be distinguished as early as the First Congress in 1789. Although there were several Congresses prior to the Civil War in which three parties were strongly represented, the two-party pattern predominated. Since 1873 minority party members have never constituted more than 5 percent of the House or 8 members of the Senate; the median number of minority party members has been 3 in the House and 1 in the Senate. There has been a remarkable balance of major party strength in Congress. Since 1873 the second party has consistently had at least one-fourth of the membership of the Senate and House, with two exceptions in each branch during the New Deal. There have been only seven other occasions in the House and only six other occasions in the Senate when the second party has had less than one-third of the membership. The normal pattern has been one in which nearly all congressmen belonged to one of the two major parties, and the second party had at least one-third—and very often almost half—of the congressional seats. Since the Civil War there have been eight Congresses in which the Senate was under Republican control and the House was under Democratic control, but this has occurred only twice in this century (the Sixty-second and Seventy-second Congress, at the start of Wilson's Administration and at the end of Hoover's).[8]

The strength of two-party competition may also be measured by the frequency of turnover in majority control; in this respect congressional party competition ranks lower. Since the Civil War there have been thirteen changes in majority control in the House and eleven changes in the Senate. From 1865 to 1895 party control was almost equally divided, with frequent alternations in control in the House, but the Republicans controlled the Senate—often by the narrowest of margins—for all but four years. From 1895 to 1931 the Republicans controlled the House except from 1911 to 1919 and the Senate except from 1913 to 1919. The Democrats won House control narrowly in 1931 and Senate control in 1933, and have held majorities in each ever since except for the Eightieth Congress (1947–1948) and the Eighty-third (1953–1954), when the Republicans had majorities in both branches. Since 1895 Congress has operated with one majority party and one usually strong minority party, but with little alternation between the two. A major factor in the political environment of Congress today is that the Democratic party has been the majority party, with only two brief interruptions, for one-third of a century.

The persistence of the two-party system in Congress has implications that may be obvious but should be stressed because they present a contrast with the practices in many state legislatures. Congress is organized along party lines. The Speaker of the House is the choice of the majority party and serves as a party leader. Responsibility for leadership on the floor of both houses rests with the majority leader. Committee membership is apportioned among Democrats and Republicans according to the proportions of each in the House and Senate. Party loyalties are highly significant in roll call voting, and party is a significant factor in determining social contacts and friendship groups in Congress. The frequent weakness of party cohesion and the occasional sharp splits within parties should not obscure the central fact that, in contrast to some state legislatures, Congress is oriented along party lines.

STATE LEGISLATURES

Constitutional Framework. The bicameral principle found in most early state constitutions was a continuation of the practice in the colonies, where one house was elected and the other represented the interests of the Crown and the colonial aristocracy. There were experiments with unicameralism in several of the early states, Vermont being the last to abandon it, in 1836. The Nebraska experiment with a single house was adopted in 1934 and has proved successful in the eyes of most observers, but in other states there has been little serious interest in following Nebraska's example.[9] In the early state constitutions the upper house continued to represent the landed interests as a result of higher property qualifications for both electors and members; it was regarded as a necessary check on the popularly elected house by those who feared that the latter would be radical. After property qualifications were abandoned, the principle of bicameralism remained popular because it accorded with the American belief in checks and balances and limitations on majoritarian government. More specifically, bicameralism facilitated the overrepresentation of the minority party or rural interests. It also provided a larger number of points of access for interest groups and particularly suited those groups that usually benefitted from obstacles to the passage of legislation. In most states, where there was no constitutional initiative, a constitutional amendment to abolish one house would require legislative approval; in the last analysis, it is the instinct for legislative self-preservation that has maintained bicameralism as the prevailing system.

The powers of a state legislature do not depend on constitutional delegation. As the authors of one comprehensive study point out: "The state legislature is a repository of the residual powers of the people. Unless restricted by provisions in the state constitution itself, it can do anything that has not been delegated to the national government or expressly or implicitly denied to the states by the federal Constitution."[10] The early state constitutions were usually relatively brief and contained few restrictions on the legislature, other than a bill of rights; colonial experience had led the Framers to put their trust in the legislature rather than in the governor, who in the past had represented the King. Lockard says that the early constitutions "establish in many instances virtual legislative supremacy while simultaneously proclaiming the doctrine of separation of powers."[11] As constitutions were rewritten and amended, more and more provisions were added that placed restrictions on the legislature, restrictions that often resulted from disillusionment with it. Particularly during the late nineteenth and early twentieth centuries, the public developed an impression—too often accurate—of the legislators as inept, corrupt puppets manipulated by powerful interests. Constitutional revisions were designed to minimize the amount of damage that these men could do. Since that time the quality of legislatures has improved, but with little resulting change in constitutional provisions.

These restrictions on the legislature take many forms. Every constitutional provision that specifies what shall and shall not be done concerning any area of public policy constitutes a limit on legislative power. Many constitutions rigidly dictate the organizational structure of both state and local governments, limit the taxing power or allocate tax revenue to specific purposes, and provide outdated or inflexible solutions for a great variety of problems. The Louisiana constitution devotes forty pages to the administration and financing of the highway program, complete with instructions for the location of bridges and highways.

The New York constitution had to be amended twice to permit the cutting of ski trails through the forests. And the California constitutional provisions on taxation exempt fruit- and nut-bearing trees under four years old.[12] The list of constitutional details could be extended for pages; each provision serves as a limit on legislative power. In large part as a result of the detailed nature of constitutional provisions, state courts have interpreted these provisions far more rigidly than the Supreme Court has with regard to the federal Constitution.

Another kind of dilution of legislative power is represented by the referendum and initiative, which were adopted, particularly in Western states, during the first two decades of the twentieth century as a result of efforts by the progressive movement. In 22 states, laws enacted by the legislature may be subject to a popular referendum, if a petition is signed by a substantial number of voters. All but two of these same states permit the statutory initiative: citizens, by signing a petition, may initiate a bill and place it on the ballot, either immediately or—in some states—if the legislature fails to pass it within a given time.[13]

There are many constitutional restrictions placed on the operation of the legislature itself. The effect of apportionment provisions has already been discussed in Chapter 3; in some states these contribute to creating a deadlock between the two branches. One of the most serious limitations, and one which reflects the greatest distrust of legislatures, is the restriction on the frequency and length of legislative sessions. Although special sessions are becoming increasingly frequent, only 19 states—including many of the most populous ones—have regular annual sessions; the rest meet biennially. The constitution limits the length of the legislative session directly in 23 states; in 10 other states a limit on the number of days for which legislators can be paid is just as effective. The limitation is most frequently 60 days, occasionally less, and rarely over 90 days.[14] Such limitations, often quite reasonable when they were adopted, limit severely not only the legislature's opportunities for deliberation but the effectiveness of its committees and the ability of less senior members to develop experience and to become acquainted with legislative norms. No single factor has a greater effect on the legislative environment than the constitutional restriction on the length of sessions.[15]

There are many other constitutional provisions that affect legislative structure; some are important, some trivial, and some ignored or evaded in practice. For example, the requirement of more than a simple majority vote for passage of a tax bill, found in at least 6 states, has a profound effect on legislative–executive relations. Limitations on legislative salaries probably affect the quality of legislators, and presumably increase turnover; the legislatures attract men who either have independent incomes or can be expected to devote most of their time and effort to non-

legislative business. In 34 states using a salary base, the median salary
for a two-year term is $4,000; only 7 states pay over $10,000, and the
lowest figure is $200, in New Hampshire. The remaining states have
a per diem salary, the median being $15, usually with a limit on the
length of the session. Most states grant expense allowances, but these
are seldom very large.[16] An example of trivial constitutional provisions
is one in Kentucky which specifies the number of clerks, janitors, and
doorkeepers that the legislature may employ. Since both chambers in
that state now have more than one door (and since patronage is involved), both houses employ more than the single doorkeeper provided
for in the constitution. Frequently constitutional provisions concerning
legislative procedure were designed to guarantee careful, publicized
consideration of bills, but these laudable objectives are often evaded,
usually because they are unwieldy in practice. A number of state constitutions require that a bill be read in full one or more times before
passage, and compliance often takes the form of having the clerk read
excerpts from the bill at a breath-taking pace, which makes the reading
incomprehensible. In more than half the states, a roll call is required
on final passage of all bills, but where there are no voting machines,
this has often meant that on noncontroversial bills all those who do not
object are simply recorded as voting in the majority.

State constitutions specify either the exact size or the maximum
size of the legislatures; this rigidity is one of the factors that lead to
inequalities when the legislature is reapportioned. The size of the legislature is obviously an important aspect of the environment, and it is a
varied one. The size of state senates varies from 17 in Nevada to 67 in
Minnesota, but 39 of them are between 25 and 50 in size. The lower
houses vary more widely: there are only 3 with fewer than 50 members, 38 with 50 to 150 members, and 9 with over 150 members. Five
of these largest lower houses are found in New England states that are
small in terms of geography or population, or both; the fact that the
constitutions in these states were all written between 1780 and 1820
suggests a historical reason for the large legislatures—particularly the
246-member Vermont House and the 400-member New Hampshire
House.[17]

State constitutions, while imposing serious limitations on legislative power, often grant the legislature powers that are not strictly
legislative. One route to constitutional amendment lies through the legislature (with approval at the polls); in the 37 states that lack the
constitutional initiative, this is the only route. Most states require legislative approval by a two-thirds or three-fifths vote or approval by two
successive legislatures. In most states legislative action is necessary to
start the procedure for calling a constitutional convention.

Legislative supervision of the administration varies considerably from state to state. The power of impeachment (the House presents the impeachment charge and the Senate tries the case) is a common but rarely used power. Most, but not all, governors must submit some of their appointments to the Senate for approval. In some states the legislature has authority that encroaches more seriously on the executive power, either through its ability to appoint certain executives or through the Senate's ability to veto the dismissal of certain officials or members of boards. Despite these surface manifestations of legislative strength, most legislatures are not effective in providing oversight of the administration, largely because of the constitutional restrictions limiting the length and frequency of sessions and because of legislative turnover and poor staffing.[18]

Innovations to Strengthen the Legislature.   As a result of constitutional limitations as well as tradition and practice, the state legislature remains today essentially a part-time body composed primarily of amateurs. This is the source of the sharpest contrast with Congress. Although this description fits every state legislature, there are some states, particularly the large industrial ones, in which the workload faced by the legislature has forced significant changes in its operations. These are the states in which annual sessions are most likely to be held, in which pay scales have been raised, and in which the greatest efforts have been made to provide more adequate staffs and office facilities for the legislature. In California, for example, each legislator has a two-room office and a secretary, as well as access to well-staffed service agencies. A dramatic example of an improvement in the physical environment is the new legislative building in North Carolina, which is strikingly modern in design and equipped with improved facilities, including a small office for each legislator.

With few exceptions, innovations have been made without changing the constitutional framework. The most important and most widespread steps have been designed to overcome the limitations of time through institutional devices. Interim committees have been used in most of the states, in some since the early part of the century, in order to permit a more detailed study of problems than is possible during the busy days of the regular session. As many as three hundred such committees have been in operation during some years. Some, though by no means all, of the committees are adequately staffed to permit research in some depth. Some states still rely primarily on interim committees: New York, California, and Michigan each average at least forty a year, with annual expenditures totaling over $2 million in New York and about $1 million in California.[19]

In most of the states (the number is now 39), the legislative council has superseded, although it has not entirely replaced, the interim committee as a device for carrying out studies and making legislative recommendations between legislative sessions. The legislative council movement started in Kansas in 1933 and gradually gained momentum; two-thirds of the councils have been established since the end of World War II. The legislative council is a committee of legislators, which averages about fifteen members, represents both houses and both parties, and usually consists of both legislative leaders and members appointed by the presiding officers of the two houses. The council is assisted by a permanent research staff; one of its advantages over the interim committee is that it can attract a better staff because of its continuity. The median annual budget is about $90,000. The council meets periodically to conduct studies, to authorize research projects, and to review and approve the findings of its research staff.

The councils vary widely in the scope of their legislative authority and in their practice with regard to making recommendations. Some councils simply transmit the research reports of their staffs to the legislatures. Others make specific legislative recommendations on the basis of staff reports. In a few cases the council's prestige is so great that its recommendations constitute the legislative agenda, at least with regard to major issues. In some states the legislative councils provide the legislature with an alternative to gubernatorial initiative, but in a few states the council works closely with the governor and serves, in effect, as an instrument of his leadership. Where there are sharp partisan divisions in the legislature, unanimous recommendations by the council are less likely. Whatever their influence may be as recommending bodies, the legislative councils (and in some states the interim committees) have served to bridge the gap between a part-time legislature and the continuing, complex legislative requirements of an urban society.[20]

Political Environment. The single factor that is most meaningful in explaining differences among state legislatures is the political environment. In a two-party state, the legislature is organized and its leaders and committees selected along party lines. To what extent the party serves as a cohesive force in explaining decision making, whether roles are perceived in partisan terms, whether party caucuses are functional and whether roll calls follow party lines—are questions explored in many of the subsequent chapters. All these considerations are potential characteristics of a two-party legislature. A legislature dominated by a single party is, in reality, a no-party legislature; we cannot expect to find partisan factors affecting any aspects of legislative behavior. The importance of party varies widely among two-party legislatures, but there are even greater variations between two-party and one-party legislatures. The role of the governor in the legislative process is important enough for it to be relevant also to include gubernatorial control in any catalog of party competition.

The student who is familiar with the literature on state politics must have noted that no two writers use the same criteria in defining categories of party competition in the states.[21] The reason is simply that different criteria are pertinent for different purposes. Since we are describing legislatures, we shall measure first, both the size of party delegations and the division of partisan control (in terms of party majorities) in the legislature and second, the partisan affiliation of the governor. Congressional and presidential elections are not relevant. No time period is perfect for our purposes. Party competition is increasing in some states, and this growth could be brought most sharply into focus by using a short time period; but the choice of a longer period can be justified because of the effect of custom on legislative practice. The period from 1947 through 1966 was chosen in order to balance these conflicting factors.

Tables 6.1a and 6.1b illustrate the wide range of partisan composition in state legislatures. In 5 Southern states (category A.1), Democratic control is absolute, Republican legislators are seldom if ever seen, and the result is a completely nonpartisan environment. In 6 other Southern states, Democratic control is just as complete for practical purposes, but there is a large enough group of Republicans to be identifiable as a minority party. In North Carolina, Tennessee, and Virginia these minority members come from pockets of traditional Republican strength in the mountains; in Florida, Georgia, and Texas they are a more recent phenomenon, representing the first products of Republican organizational efforts in metropolitan areas.

The next category of states (B) are those in which the legislative minority (though it has never attained a majority in recent years) is more significant as a minority party, and in which that party has captured the governorship at least once. All are states in which the minority party has consistently had at least recognizable legislative strength, and in most cases there has been an upsurge in that strength—however spasmodic—associated with the party's success in one or more gubernatorial elections.

The remaining states (categories C and D) are all competitive, in the sense that no party has consistently had a majority in both houses or control of the governorship, while minority legislative parties have consistently been strong enough to have at least a minimal impact on the legislative process. To set any higher standard of competition is to introduce distinctions among these "competitive" states. The states in categories C.1 and C.2 are those in which a single party either controlled both houses three-fourths of the time or controlled one branch nearly all the time and the other branch two-thirds of the time. The dominant party, except in New Mexico, Missouri, and Rhode Island, had been Republican. In some of these states the dominant party has usually held the governorship, in some it has been closely divided, and in three states (C.2) the party with a legislative minority has held the

Table 6.1a. STATE LEGISLATURES CLASSIFIED ACCORDING TO DEGREE OF ONE-PARTY CONTROL, 1947–1966*

A. 1. One-party States: Same party controlled the governorship and both houses throughout the period, and minority representation was negligible (all Democratic states).

Alabama	Mississippi
Arkansas	South Carolina
Louisiana	

2. One-party States: Same party controlled the governorship and both houses throughout the period, and minority representation was more than negligible (all Democratic states).

Florida	Tennessee
Georgia	Texas
North Carolina	Virginia

B. States with One Party Dominant: Same party controlled both houses throughout the period but did not always control governorship, and (except for Oklahoma) minority party occasionally had over one-fourth of the seats in at least one house.

DEMOCRATIC	REPUBLICAN
Arizona	Kansas
Kentucky	New Hampshire
Maryland	Vermont
Oklahoma	
West Virginia	

* Alaska and Hawaii are omitted from Tables 6.1a and 6.1b because of their brief terms as states, and Nebraska and Minnesota are omitted because they have nonpartisan legislatures. The time period is 1946–1965 for states with off-year elections: Kentucky, New Jersey, Virginia, Mississippi, and Louisiana.

governorship during a majority of the years in this period. Michigan is the most extreme example of this divided control.* The two

* Rhode Island has been put in category C.1 because the Lieutenant Governor assured Democratic control during all six years of even division in the Senate.

State	Senate			House			Governorship	
	D	R	Tie	D	R	Tie	D	R

C. 1. Limited Two-party States: Same party controlled both houses throughout most of the period and the governorship at least half the time.

State	Senate			House			Governorship	
South Dakota	2	18	—	0	20	—	2	18
North Dakota	0	20	—	2	18	—	6	14
New Mexico	20	0	—	18	2	—	12	8
New York	1	19	—	2	18	—	4	16
Maine	2	18	—	2	18	—	6	14
Iowa	2	18	—	2	18	—	8	12
Wisconsin	0	20	—	4	16	—	6	14
Wyoming	0	20	—	4	14	2	8	12
Missouri	18	2	—	16	4	—	20	0
Illinois	4	16	—	4	16	—	10	10
Rhode Island	8	6	6	20	0	—	14	6
Idaho	6	14	—	2	18	—	6	14

2. Limited Two-party States: Same party controlled both houses throughout most of the period but usually not the governorship.

State	Senate			House			Governorship	
Michigan	2	18	—	2	16	2	14	6
New Jersey	0	20	—	6	14	—	12	8
Ohio	4	14	2	4	16	—	12	8

3. Limited Two-party States: Two houses controlled by different parties during most of the period.

State	Senate			House			Governorship	
Nevada	0	18	2	20	0	—	12	8
Connecticut	14	6	—	2	18	—	14	6

D. Two-party States: Neither party had dominant legislative control, and in most cases party control of legislature approximated control of governorship.

State	Senate			House			Governorship	
Pennsylvania	0	18	2	8	12	—	8	12
Indiana	4	16	—	6	14	—	10	10
Washington	12	6	2	16	4	—	10	10
Massachusetts	8	10	2	16	4	—	10	10
Delaware	14	6	—	12	8	—	10	10
Colorado	6	14	—	10	10	—	12	8
Oregon	8	10	2	8	12	—	2	18
California	8	10	2	8	12	—	10	10
Utah	10	10	—	8	10	2	4	16
Montana	10	10	—	10	10	—	4	16

states in category C.3 differ in the sense that each party has a firm or nearly firm majority in one house while the governorship alternates between the parties.

The states in category D are those in which majority control of both houses of the legislature is shared most widely and there is some, usually considerable, rotation of the governorship. It is in these ten states that legislative competition is strongest, based on the criteria of size of party delegations and division of party control. This list contains some states that have long been competitive and others, like California and Oregon, where competition is quite recent.

The competitive nature of state legislatures is one of the variables determining the importance of partisanship in the legislative process. Some degree of competition is a prerequisite; we cannot expect to find any traces of partisanship in the legislatures in category A.1 and very few in those classified in A.2. (Partisanship is also absent, or disguised as factionalism, in the two nonpartisan states.) There are few traces of partisanship to be found in category B. The state legislatures where we find the most manifestations of partisanship (as described in subsequent chapters) include some but not all of those in category D and the various subcategories of C. The distinctions that we have made concerning levels of competition in these two categories do not provide clues to partisanship, which is found in some form at least as frequently in category C as it is in D.

Today there is a close balance between the parties in more states than at any other time in modern history. In the last decade the Democratic party has become potent in a number of Northern and Western states where it was once weak, and the Republican upsurge throughout the South and Border area has begun to manifest itself in some legislatures. This has not produced a reduction in divided government but contributed to its increase. It is common for a newly emerging party to capture the governorship for at least one or two terms before it is able to win a legislative majority in either house. In the period from 1931 through 1964 there were only 11 states that never had a division of party control among the governorship and the two legislative branches; these are the states in category A that were consistently Democratic. In 9 other states there was divided government for from two to eight years during the 34-year period, but all these were states in which a single party dominated the legislature all or nearly all of the time (most of them in category B). There were 19 states with divided government for from ten to sixteen years, and 7 states with divisions for half or more of the years (18 to 26 out of 34). Even during the more recent period, 1947–1964, the only states that were without divided government were those that had no rotation in the governorship or in legislative majorities.

During the two decades prior to 1950, a period for which V. O. Key studied party divisions, he found that in two-party states Democratic governors faced divided government half the time and Republicans less than one-fifth of the time. Since 1952, the proportion has remained the same for Democratic, but doubled for Republican governors.[22]

State legislatures differ from Congress because the constitutional curbs on the duration of sessions limit their effectiveness and the constitutional restrictions on the scope of their authority limit their power. On the surface, state legislatures appear to be almost perfect replicas of Congress in terms of organization, functions of leadership and committees, and procedures. The similarities of nomenclature are deceptive, however. The roles and functions of individual leaders and legislative institutions differ widely from state to state and, as the following chapters demonstrate, only occasionally approximate those in Congress. A search for the causes of these variations in most cases leads to the differences between one-party states, where party is a negligible factor, and two-party states, where it is a factor of varying importance.

NOTES

1. Max Farrand, *The Framing of the Constitution of the United States* (New Haven, 1913), p. 204.

2. George B. Galloway, *History of the House of Representatives* (New York, 1961), pp. 1–4; George H. Haynes, *The Senate of the United States* (Boston, 1938), vol. I, chap. 1.

3. James M. Burns, *The Deadlock of Democracy* (Englewood Cliffs, N.J., 1963), p. 17.

4. Neil MacNeil, *Forge of Democracy* (New York, 1963), pp. 23–38; Galloway, *op. cit.*, chap. 15.

5. Haynes, *loc. cit.*

6. William S. White, *Citadel* (New York, 1957), p. 68.

7. For a list of the sessions and their length, see the *Congressional Directory*.

8. Galloway, *op. cit.*, pp. 295–97; Bureau of the Census, U.S. Department of Commerce, *Historical Statistics of the United States, 1789–1945* (Washington, 1949), p. 293. There are some contradictions in these two sources concerning House membership.

9. For information on unicameralism see Belle Zeller (ed.), *American State Legislatures* (New York, 1954), chap. 4; A. C. Breckenridge, *One House for Two* (Washington, 1958).

10. Zeller, *op. cit.*, p. 16.

11. Duane Lockard, *The Politics of State and Local Government* (New York, 1963), p. 71.

12. Robert Dishman, *State Constitutions: The Shape of the Document* (New York, 1960), pp. 15–23.

13. Harvey Walker, *The Legislative Process* (New York, 1948), chap. 22.

14. *Book of the States, 1964–65* (Chicago, 1964), pp. 44–45.

15. For an example of the effect of a constitutional deadline on the legislative struggle, see Thomas Flinn, *Governor Freeman and the Minnesota Budget* (University, Ala., 1961).

16. *Book of the States, 1964–65,* pp. 38–39, 46–47.

17. *Ibid.,* p. 43.

18. Zeller, *op. cit.,* chap. 11.

19. *Ibid.,* chap. 8; *Book of the States, 1964–65,* pp. 70–71.

20. Zeller, *op. cit.;* *Book of the States, 1964–65,* pp. 67–73.

21. See Austin Ranney and Willmoore Kendall, "The American Party Systems," *American Political Science Review,* XLVIII (1954), 477–85; and Joseph A. Schlesinger, "A Two-dimensional Scheme for Classifying the States according to Degree of Inter-party Competition," *American Political Science Review,* XLIX, (1955), 1120–28.

22. The figures from 1931 through 1952 are taken from V. O. Key, Jr., *American State Politics* (New York, 1956), pp. 58–64.

[7]

Legislative Leadership

"EVERYONE knows something of leaders and leadership of various sorts, but no one knows very much. Leadership, especially in the political realm, unavoidably or by design often is suffused by an atmosphere of the mystic and the magical, and these mysteries have been little penetrated by systematic observation."[1] David Truman's comment is an appropriate introduction to the topic of legislative leadership; it should serve as a warning to avoid glib generalizations and the confusion of appearance with reality. We know that leaders are found in all legislative bodies, as in other organized groups. On paper there are striking similarities in the organizational structures of legislatures, but these formal similarities mask important variations. One source of this variety is the norms, developed over a period of time for the particular legislative body; these are related to legislators' expectations of the roles that leaders should play. Another source of variety is the skills and perceptions of the leaders themselves. Beyond that, actual patterns of leadership may be affected by the party balance in the legislature or the style of executive leadership in legislative matters.

THE NATURE OF LEADERSHIP

Leadership has been studied, for the most part, by sociologists and psychologists who have been primarily interested in groups that are smaller than the average legislative body. Efforts to discover those traits of character that are endemic to leaders have led to the conclusion, generally accepted by scholars, that these traits vary with the group that is being led. The traits necessary for a successful legislative leader are not exactly the same as those required by a football coach, a business executive, or even the leader of an urban political machine. Students of leadership have begun to focus their attention not so much on personality traits as on the relationships between leader and followers within the context of a given social situation. One writer defines leadership as "an interactional function of the personality and the social situation." A leader is "a member of a group on whom the group confers a certain status, and leadership describes the role by which the duties of this status are fulfilled."[2]

The requirements for successful leadership vary, even among groups as similar as American legislative bodies. One variable is the experience of the average legislator, another is the frequency and duration of the legislative sessions, and a third is the homogeneity of the legislature—in terms of party and type of constituency. Moreover, as Truman points out, the requirements for successful leadership "are likely to vary through time, depending upon the internal and external circumstances in which the group is operating."[3] The floor leader in Congress, for example, finds that both the necessity and the ability to initiate legislative programs are diminished when his party gains control of the White House. The power of the Speaker of the House was undermined early in the twentieth century because the incumbent proved unable to adapt to changes that had been wrought in the Republican party by the progressive movement.

Several characteristics common to most legislatures provide the prerequisites and limitations that distinguish this brand from other forms of leadership. Although some of the duties and powers of presiding officers are clearly prescribed in legislative rules, this is not true of floor leaders and other party officials in the legislature; their sources of authority are usually vague. Both types of leaders usually have an influence broader than that which is based on formal rules. As a consequence, legislative leadership is a variable, heavily dependent on the personal skills of leaders. There are wide variations in the strength of sanctions available to leaders, but leaders seldom have the power to influence significantly the members' chances for renomination and reelection. For this reason, legislative leaders must rely on persuasion, tact, and bargaining; their success often depends on their ability to sense the mood of the legislature. The legislative leader seldom gives orders to anyone.

Since legislative leadership is so dependent on individual skills, it is entirely possible that legislators who hold no formal position of leadership will exercise more influence than some of the formal leaders. In recent years Senators Richard Russell and Robert Kerr were sometimes described as more influential than some of the Democratic floor leaders who were their contemporaries. Robert A. Taft's influence among Republican senators was so great that the political office he held was of subsidiary importance; when he resigned as chairman of the policy committee to become floor leader, the locus of power simply shifted from one position to the other. Nevertheless, most legislative positions, whether party offices or committee chairmanships, carry with them both specific powers and opportunities. The ineffective legislator is not going to become influential by occupying a leadership post, but the effective legislator is likely to increase his power when he becomes a formal leader. Two examples from the Senate Foreign Relations Committee can be cited: Walter George was a respected and influential senator but never a spokesman on foreign policy until he became chairman of the committee, and Arthur Vandenberg lost some of his authority as a senatorial leader when he lost the committee chairmanship after the Democrats won a senatorial majority.

Truman suggests as a generally valid proposition that "the larger an organization, the more probable . . . is the convergence if not complete congruence of the 'formal' and 'informal' structures of influence and leadership." Truman believes that this results largely from the communications problem of a larger organization: the leadership is at the center of the communications network and has access to all components of the legislative system that are essential to leadership.[4] At the state level the convergence of formal and informal leadership is likely to result from another factor: the generally high turnover of legislators and the short and infrequent sessions common in most states reduce the likelihood that legislators will be able to gain and maintain broad influence outside the formal leadership posts.

FORMAL STRUCTURE OF LEADERSHIP

Presiding Officer of Senate. The presiding officer of the United States Senate is the Vice-President, and in 35 states the presiding officer of the Senate is the lieutenant governor (as is the presiding officer of the unicameral body in Nebraska). In the remaining 14 states the presiding officer is elected by members of the Senate.* Neither the Vice-President nor the lieutenant governor is regarded by the membership as a member of the legislative branch; he is an "outsider," a part of the executive, and consequently not to be trusted with as much power as is normally given to the presiding officer in those 14 states where he is elected. At the national level, the Vice-President's legislative powers, other than

* One of these 14 states is Tennessee where the presiding officer of the Senate holds the title of Lieutenant Governor but is a member of the Senate, elected by that body as its presiding officer.

breaking a tie on a roll call, are negligible. At the state level the lieutenant governor, who also can cast tie-breaking votes, often has to share power with an elected president pro tem or with a committee of Senate leaders. One obvious reason for the weakness of the position of either the Vice-President or the lieutenant governor is that he may be a member of the party that commands only a minority in the Senate. In states where divided government is most common, the lieutenant governor's influence is likely to be lowest.[5]

The Vice-President's most important task in the legislative process is to serve as a liaison man between the President and his party in the Senate. This was a role that could be performed well by Alben W. Barkley and Lyndon B. Johnson, both former floor leaders. During the first two administrations of Franklin Roosevelt, John N. Garner (the former Speaker of the House) kept the President informed about congressional opinion in both houses. On the other hand, during Roosevelt's third administration, Henry Wallace did not command the respect and did not have the rapport in the Senate that would have enabled him to serve this purpose. When the Vice-President serves in a liaison capacity, he is duplicating the job of the floor leader; the latter is responsible both to the senatorial party and to the President, while the Vice-President is responsible to neither. The lieutenant governor is in the same limbo of non-responsibility. Aside from his routine tasks as a presiding officer, the Vice-President or lieutenant governor has no *essential* part to play in the legislative process; if he succeeds in writing a bigger part for himself, it is only because his skill and advice made him valuable to the other actors in the legislative system. No Vice-President was better prepared than Lyndon B. Johnson to play a major legislative part, and there were a few signs at the start of his term that he intended to do so. The negative reactions of Democratic senators and the failure of President Kennedy to use the Vice-President in this fashion quickly relegated him to an intermittent backstage part.

When the presiding officer of the Senate is elected by that body, he is usually a figure of considerable power and influence in the legislature. Not only are his formal powers likely to be greater than a lieutenant governor's, but he is often—like the Speaker—a recognized leader of the legislative party. In states where the lieutenant governor presides over the Senate, the membership of the Senate selects a president pro tem. This is often, as in the United States Senate, largely an honorary title given to a senior member of the Senate, and it usually involves only the duty of presiding in the lieutenant governor's absence. Frequently the floor leader, rather than the lieutenant governor or the president pro tem, is recognized as chief of the legislative party. In a few states, however, the president pro tem is a powerful figure. South

Carolina and Kansas are examples of states where the president pro tem, with a long term of service, has made that position the most powerful one in the legislature.

Speaker of the House. The Speaker of the House in Washington and in the states is elected directly by the members of the House, and in every legislative system he is a figure of power. The Speaker of the House in most states is granted broad powers under the rules to appoint members to committees and to preside over the operation of the House; there are usually relatively few limitations on his freedom in the exercise of these powers. Comparable powers were gradually acquired by the Speaker of the United States House during the nineteenth century, but most of these were lost during the 1910–1911 revolt against Speaker Joe Cannon. In the United States House and in two-party states, the Speaker also serves as the leader of the majority party and is selected by the majority caucus. In one-party states he is likely to be one of the leaders in the dominant faction, usually a faction loyal to the governor. The Speaker combines many of the tasks performed by the presiding officer and the majority floor leader in the upper house. How party leadership is divided between the Speaker and the majority floor leader depends on custom and on the personal relationships between the two men.

The history of the United States House Speaker is a chronicle of individuals, strong and weak, in whose hands the Speaker's powers have waxed and waned. During the first two decades of the Republic, the Speaker was merely the presiding officer and, during Jefferson's Administration, one of the President's lieutenants. Henry Clay, who was elected Speaker as a freshman congressman in 1811 and served intermittently until 1825, was the first to make the Speaker the leader of the majority party or faction in the House. He came to power as a leader of the "war hawks" faction during Madison's Administration. He appointed his supporters to key committee posts, interpreted and applied the rules of the House, and insisted on the Speaker's right to participate fully in debate and voting. During the two decades before the Civil War, the Speaker's importance as a party leader declined as the slavery issue splintered the parties, making an effective majority impossible and leading to several deadlocks over the choice of a Speaker. Schuyler Colfax and James G. Blaine, who were Republican Speakers during and after the Civil War, were strong leaders in a period of congressional supremacy in Washington. Blaine acted more openly as a party leader, and used his authority over committee assignments more effectively as a means of control, than had his predecessors.[6]

The Speaker's power to interpret the rules and set the precedents of the House is a major source of his authority, one which was increasingly used by Speakers in the latter part of the nineteenth century. Speaker

John Carlisle asserted the Speaker's absolute discretion in recognizing members to offer motions or to participate in debate. Speaker Thomas Reed, who continued this practice, also prevented filibustering by refusing to accept motions that he considered dilatory and by counting as present members who refused to answer a quorum call. Reed also revitalized the Rules Committee, which he chaired and controlled, and through use of the "special rule" as the normal means of transacting legislative business, made that committee the most powerful in the House. These techniques of control were refined and strengthened by Joseph Cannon, who became Speaker in 1903 and ruled with an iron hand.

The revolt of 1910–1911 resulted from an alliance of Democrats and insurgent Western Republicans. It stripped the Speaker of his chairmanship and control of the Rules Committee, his power to name committee members and chairmen, and much of his discretion in recognizing members; it also established procedures for bypassing the Rules Committee and other committees. A century after Clay had demonstrated the potential power of the Speaker's office, that power once again depended largely on the skill of the incumbent rather than on the formal prerogatives of the office. "Henry Clay had mastered the House without the benefit of the rules available to Cannon, and Speakers who followed Cannon could learn from Clay's example."[7] For fourteen years after the revolt against Cannon, the speaker was primarily a presiding officer, and party leadership was in the hands of the floor leader. In 1925 Speaker Nicholas Longworth restored the Speaker's position as a political leader, and his successors—notably Sam Rayburn, during most of the 1940–1961 period—demonstrated the potency of this political influence. In Congress today the Speaker serves both as presiding officer and as leader of the majority party, unlike the Speaker of the British House of Commons, who presides with careful neutrality and does not even vote.

Floor Leaders and Whips. Until 1910, the majority floor leader in the United States House was appointed by the Speaker. Often the Chairman of the Ways and Means or Appropriations Committee was chosen, primarily because these committees handled so much of the important legislation. The floor leader was clearly a lieutenant of the Speaker. Since 1910 the floor leader in both parties has been elected by a secret ballot in the party caucus. During the interim of weak Speakers, the majority floor leader served as party chief, but since 1925 he has served in practice as deputy party leader, with responsibility for managing the legislative program from the floor. The majority floor leader in the United States Senate, on the other hand, has a responsibility for party leadership comparable to that of the Speaker; at the same time,

he is responsible for management of the legislative program. The minority floor leader in both houses is both the chief strategist and spokesman
for the party. There is a difference between the two senatorial parties
in leadership structure. The Democratic floor leader serves also as chairman of the policy committee and the caucus; the Republican party—
whether in the majority or the minority—divides these duties among
three men, and the floor leader has not always been the most influential
member of this triumvirate.

Both floor leaders in the Senate have a deputy leader, or party whip,
to assist in managing a bill on the floor and marshalling votes for it.
The much larger size of the House necessitates a more elaborate whip
organization. The first party whips in the House were appointed at the
turn of the century, but the use of assistant whips on a large scale was
a development of the early 1930s. Today the Republicans have a 17-
man organization, headed by a whip, a deputy, and three regional
whips; the Democratic whip organization has 20 members, headed by
the whip and his deputy. Both groups are organized along regional
lines, with each assistant whip responsible for one or more states. The
Republican Committee on Committees in the House chooses the whip,
who in turn chooses his assistants. The Democratic floor leader chooses
a whip, who picks his deputy, but the assistants are chosen in decentralized fashion by the deans or all members of the state delegations
for which the assistant is responsible.[8]

The whips in the House "are (1) responsible for the presence of
their fellow party members, but they must also (2) transmit certain
information to them, (3) ascertain how they will vote on selected important pieces of legislation, and (4) guide pressure to change the minds
of the recalcitrant and stiffen the wills of the wavering."[9] In a legislative body as large as the House, it is a major task to keep track
of the location of members and assure their presence on the floor
for important votes. This may involve persuading members not to leave
Washington or to return, arranging pairs when members must be away,
and telephoning members when the time for a vote approaches. One
congressman has said:

The key to effective whip action is timing. The Whip is on the Floor
surveying the scene and weighing alternatives. . . . He gauges the end of
general debate and estimates the time when a vote is likely. If he puts out a
call too soon, too urgently, many Members will assemble, take a quick
look, and then begin to fade until there is a critical deficiency when the
vote is taken. Yet, he can not defer too long, because a vote might come
unexpectedly.[10]

The tasks of transmitting information to members and of polling
members on their views are both important. A recent study concluded

that the polls conducted by the House Democratic whips in 1962 and 1963 were usually highly accurate (80 to 95 percent correct). One of the most serious mistakes the leadership can make is to seek a vote on an issue without accurately ascertaining whether or not it has the votes to win. Speaker McCormack and Minority Leader Halleck made greater use of the whip organizations than their predecessors did, and the Democratic whip organization, according to Ripley, "has become the focus of a corporate or collegial leadership in the House."[11] The Democratic whip organization, with its decentralized membership, is used more often as a two-way channel of communications, while the Republican whips more often attempt persuasion and pressure in dealing with members. There are enough examples of poor communications between the leadership and the rank-and-file in recent years to suggest that improvement in communication may be the most important task that the whip organizations can perform.

In a two-party state floor leaders have responsibilities like those of floor leaders in Congress, the extent of their influence depending on the structure and cohesion of legislative parties in the state. The place of the majority leader in the party hierarchy depends on the mode of his selection (by a caucus or by the Speaker, for example), and on the extent of partisan leadership exercised by the presiding officer. In a one-party state the floor leader is either a representative of the governor or a leader of the dominant faction in a legislative body; he acts much like a majority leader in a two-party state, but there is usually no counterpart to the minority leader. In a few one-party states, no one consistently serves as floor leader.

THE SELECTION OF LEGISLATIVE LEADERSHIP

In Congress and in two-party state legislatures, the Speaker is selected in the majority party caucus. The floor leaders are also normally chosen in party caucuses, although in some legislatures the Speaker selects the majority leader. The President rarely attempts to influence the choice of congressional leaders, although he may sway some votes when he does make such an attempt. There are a few states (mostly Southern) where the governor virtually appoints some legislative leaders, and others where his ability to influence the selection of leaders foreshadows the success he will have in working closely with the legislature to enact his program. More often the governor plays little or no part. (The factors determining the executive's influence over the selection of leaders are discussed more fully in Chapter 13.) With the exception of the chief executive, outsiders have little or no influence over the choice of leaders; legislators do not perceive this to be a legitimate concern of lobbyists. Polsby, in describing Carl Albert's victory over Richard Bolling in the 1962 contest for House Democratic leader, emphasizes that Albert commanded greater friendship and loyalty among Democratic representatives, while Bolling had much greater support from liberal interest groups outside the House, including the active assistance of the AFL–CIO and the NAACP. But few congressmen were swayed by this outside pressure, and some probably resented it; the fact that the vote was conducted by secret ballot in caucus enhanced the congressmen's ability to resist this pressure.[12]

One mode of leadership selection is inheritance. With one exception, every Speaker of the United States House selected in this century has been promoted from floor leader. Since 1947 the Senate Democrats have chosen three party whips to be floor leaders: Scott Lucas, Lyndon B. Johnson, and Mike Mansfield; in the fourth case the party whip, Francis Myers, had been defeated by the voters in November. Republican senators have not followed the principle of inheritance so closely, although in 1953, when he was forced to step down as floor leader because of illness, Senator Taft designated his own successor, William Knowland, who was confirmed as leader by the senators after Taft's death. In New Jersey, where leadership posts are rotated annually, the floor leader regularly succeeds the Speaker. In some other states the floor leader usually has the inside track when a contest arises for the speakership.

Another mode of selection involves a brief—though sometimes intense—contest for a leadership post between two (occasionally more) men with a claim to the position because of present legislative offices or their leadership of factions in the party. Although the floor leader has usually become Speaker of the United States House, some of them —including Sam Rayburn—have not won without a contest. Contests for the floor leadership in Congress are more common, particularly among Republicans. Although incumbent leaders are rarely challenged, in 1959 Republican representatives replaced their veteran floor leader, Joseph W. Martin, with his deputy, Charles Halleck; in 1965 Halleck, in turn, was replaced by Gerald Ford. These changes, accomplished both times by narrow majorities in the caucus, were motivated in each case not by liberal-conservative differences in the party but by a belief among younger representatives that the party needed more aggressive leadership in the wake of the 1958 and 1964 Democratic landslides. The close and rather bitter contest between Alben W. Barkley and Pat Harrison for the Senate Democratic leadership in 1937, in which Roosevelt took a hand, had overtones both of personal popularity and of loyalty to the Roosevelt Administration; Barkley won with Roosevelt's help.[13] In recent years the conservative wing of the Senate Republican party has held the floor leadership, but it has been challenged on several occasions by groups of Republicans supporting a more liberal candidate: Kenneth Wherry defeated William Knowland in 1949, and Everett Dirksen defeated John S. Cooper in 1959.

In some states the contest for the speakership has assumed the dimensions of a political campaign, with candidates openly soliciting votes over a prolonged period. In Florida the Speaker of the House is selected two years in advance, after a prolonged campaign in which the promises of choice committee assignments become the currency of bargaining. This pattern preserves control by a rural clique and minimizes the governor's influence on the choice.[14] In Texas the candidates for Speaker also start their campaigns early, seeking pledges of support not only from incumbents in the previous session but also from legislative candidates. One candidate for Speaker usually claims victory on the basis of these pledges after the primary election has been held. A winning candidate for Speaker in Texas is likely to build his coalition on the basis of ideological affinity, geographic proximity, personal friendships, and promises of committee assignments.[15]

The contest for the speakership is characterized by extensive campaigning not only in a few one-party states but also in some legislatures where the two-party system is so weak that the candidates often cross party lines in search for votes. In California the candidates for Speaker have been chosen from the majority party, but they have built winning coalitions by enlisting the support of members from the minority party, committee assignments being used to reward supporters. Although the minority party could enhance its power by voting as a bloc, its members are usually divided in their support for a candidate in the majority party. When a Speaker is selected with partial support from both parties he becomes more of a factional than a partisan leader, and both the organization and voting pattern in the legislature are likely to be factional rather than partisan.[16] A pattern of that sort can be observed in Arizona, although the minority Republican party is more likely to vote as a bloc in forming a coalition with a Democratic faction to elect a Democrat as Speaker.

Strict party voting in the choice of a Speaker is characteristic of a strong two-party legislature. Buchanan, whose study of the California legislature demonstrates how factional contests for the speakership undermine party cohesion, said: "The vote on organization is the indispensable glue for holding a legislative party together."[17] Even in a legislature with strong parties there are occasional examples of a break in party lines. In two recent sessions of the Illinois legislature, the minority party has been able either to elect one of its own members as Speaker by encouraging several majority members to abstain, or to swing its votes to a candidate for Speaker who had only minority support within the majority party.[18]

TENURE OF LEADERSHIP

One of the most important variations in state legislative practice has to do with tenure of leadership. Congressional leaders seldom retire and are rarely defeated by members of their own party; this pattern of longevity is duplicated in only about one-third of the state legislative bodies. It is more common for leadership posts at the state level to change hands every two or four years. A survey of the House Speaker and the president or president pro tem of the Senate (whichever is the top *elected* leader) from 1947 through 1964 showed that in only 31 of the 95 legislative bodies had there been at least one man with an extended tenure as leader (eight years in one-party bodies and six years in bodies that had some alternation in partisan control). Longer tenures were found in 17 one-party and 14 two-party bodies, shorter tenures in 42 one-party and 22 two-party bodies. Longer terms for the leadership tended to be more characteristic of states with strong parties and strong competition, either in the legislature or at the statewide level. But longer tenure was also found in states like California, with weak parties, and South Carolina, with one-party systems.[19]

A few examples will illustrate the differences. In South Carolina, the president pro tem of the Senate has held that post since 1942 (and has been described as the most powerful man in the government), and the Speaker of the House has served in that office almost continuously since 1937; the two men come from the same rural county. In Virginia the House Speaker has served since 1950, and in Mississippi the Speaker has served since 1944. After ten years, Speaker Bomar of Tennessee moved to the Senate in 1963 and was promptly elected president of that body. Among two-party states, the Rhode Island House Speaker has served since 1941, the Pennsylvania Senate president pro tem has held office since 1945, except for two years of Democratic control, and one New York House Speaker served from 1937 until 1959.

Long tenure does not guarantee effectiveness as a legislative leader, but it suggests that the leader has the full confidence of the dominant groups in the legislature. Moreover, during a prolonged term in office, the leader, like Sam Rayburn at the national level, can accumulate power through personal contacts, experience, and knowledge about legislative rules and techniques. Even where tenure is not so long, a legislative leader can emerge as a powerful figure, if legislative custom does not dictate rotation in office. Speaker Powell in Illinois, Speaker Unruh in California, and Senate President Powers in Massachusetts are examples of men who proved their strength and their independence of the governor during two or three terms of office.

At the other extreme, there are 23 legislative bodies in which there was a change in the leadership every two years (in New Jersey, every year) over the eighteen-year period starting in 1947; there were 41 bodies during that same period in which four-year terms either predominated or occasionally broke the two-year pattern. Shorter tenures do not guarantee weak leadership, but they are symptomatic of less independent authority on the part of the leaders. Two or four years is simply too short a time (particularly with biennial sessions) for a leader to develop personal bases of power, or to accumulate the knowledge and experience necessary for preeminence as a legislative leader.

If short tenure is generally a symptom of weakness, it does not mean that all leaders are equally handicapped by a short term. In some states where the job is rotated regularly, it seems to be little more than an honorary position, a reward for long service. On the other hand, some legislatures are like that in Virginia, where a small group of veteran senators have held the key positions in the Senate for many years while rotating the post of president pro tem among their number. A similar situation exists in Florida; although the post of presiding officer in both houses rotates every two years, it almost always stays under control of a small clique. Under these conditions, the leader may lack personal strength and prestige, but he can depend on the close support of the leadership group; this is a form of collective leadership.

Another pattern is evident in a few states, primarily in the South, where the leadership normally changes with every change in the governorship. This is a clue that the governor has a hand in the choice of the leadership. Where he does, the leader has less independent authority; his effectiveness in the legislative body depends in considerable part on the skills and political strength of the governor.

A survey of lower houses in 18 states for which data were available (in half of them, speakers had long tenure; in half, short tenure) sheds some light on the patterns of selecting the Speaker. The median age at which speakers were first selected was 47 in states where they had long tenure and 51 in states where they had short tenure; these are close to the median age for all legislators, as shown in the surveys cited in Chapter 5. In states where men served a short term as Speaker, they were usually elected to that office after six to twelve years of legislative service. Some speakers who served a long term had been chosen only after many years in the legislature, but in a few states men had been chosen early in their legislative careers and thereafter served long terms as Speaker. In general, seniority seems to mean less in the choice of state legislative than of congressional leaders. Most men who became Speaker had previously held one or more important leadership posts. In states with strong party competition, the Speaker is likely to have served as floor leader. Elsewhere, at least one key committee post is a steppingstone. In North Carolina, where a new Speaker is chosen every two years, he is likely to have chaired the Finance, Appropriations, or Judiciary committees. In New Jersey rotation has become an automatic annual affair, with men moving from the chairmanship of the Appropriations Committee to the post of floor leader to Speaker, after which they join the ranks of often influential ex-Speakers.

LEADERSHIP ROLES

If effective legislative leadership is dependent on personal qualities as well as formal powers and custom, it becomes particularly important to inquire into the role of the legislative leader. How does the leader perceive his job, his relationship to the legislative party, and his responsibilities to the President or governor? In tracing the history of the United States House Speaker, we have shown that the powerful Speakers were those who perceived their role as being that of a party leader as well as a presiding officer. The modern Speaker, in Congress and in the two-party states, perceives his role in terms of party leadership.

Serving Two Masters. There is a fundamental difference between the role of a Speaker or floor leader for the Administration party and that for the opposition party, a difference involving both the leader's policy-forming role and his loyalty. The opposition leader has greater freedom, which he does not necessarily use, to frame policy for his party. The leader of the Administration party faces the problem of role definition. Is he the leader of the legislative party who serves as an ambassador to the chief executive, or is he the chief executive's representative in the legislature? William S. White says that, except in times of crisis or during a period of unusually strong presidential influence (such as the early days of Franklin Roosevelt), the party leader "will not so much represent the President as the Senate itself."[20] David Truman, by contrast, argues that party leaders not only can but must serve two masters: "The fundamental complexity and subtlety of the role lie in the fact that the elective leaders are, and probably must be, both the President's leaders and the party's leaders." Truman admits that these requirements may not always be compatible, but says that "they are generally interdependent, in the sense that representing the President provides a focus and a part of the leverage for leadership of the Congressional party, and sympathetic reflection of the problems of legislative colleagues is an essential in advancing the President's program." He adds that the relative weight of the two requirements may vary from time to time, and that the requirement of loyalty to the congressional party lies nearer the surface, while loyalty to the Administration remains an implicit factor.[21]

When we examine the way in which individual congressional leaders appear to enact their roles we discover significant variations, but we find that leaders recognize that neither "master" can be completely ignored. Joseph Martin, who served as Speaker or floor leader during the first six Eisenhower years, makes clear in his autobiography his belief that the leader's job is to carry out the President's program unless he finds it absolutely impossible.[22] One observer of the Senate describes majority leader Scott Lucas as one who believed "that if a leader could not agree with his president 80 percent of the time, the leader should resign. In constant touch with the White House over a direct telephone, Lucas put Truman's program ahead of his own health and his political career."[23] As Speaker, Sam Rayburn bore the brunt of winning House acceptance for many programs of Democratic Administrations, and yet at times he negotiated stubbornly with these Administrations concerning the programs for which he was prepared to seek acceptance. Alben W. Barkley, who shared Rayburn's sense of responsibility to Democratic Presidents, demonstrated most dramatically the limits of this responsibility. He resigned as floor leader in protest against President Roosevelt's veto message of a tax bill and then accepted unanimous reelection by the party caucus. David Truman has pointed out that "Roosevelt's action undermined Barkley's value as the Administration's leader by treating him, implicitly, as exclusively that. Barkley's resignation and immediate reelection as majority leader restored the emphasis on his ties to his colleagues and reestablished the dual relationship, though not, apparently, in identical form."[24]

The problem of role conflict becomes more serious for a leader when there are major differences between his policy views and those of the President. In his brief months as Eisenhower's floor leader, Senator Robert Taft demonstrated, in roughly equal parts, a willingness to use his skill and his great influence in behalf of the President's program and a determination to influence the policy content of that program. Taft's biographer says that neither Roosevelt nor Truman "had so effective a Senate leader as Eisenhower had in Taft," but he adds that Taft negotiated legislative programs with the President substantially as a coequal.[25] Taft argued publicly and privately for cuts in Eisenhower's foreign aid program in the face of congressional hostility, but he spoke in the party caucus and voted on the floor against foreign aid cuts. He worked effectively in the Senate to secure approval of a nomination he personally opposed, the choice of Charles E. Bohlen as ambassador to Moscow, and then he passed the word to the White House: "No more Bohlens!"[26]

William Knowland, who succeeded Taft as floor leader, was frequently an effective proponent of Eisenhower's programs, but he had serious differences with the President on both the diplomatic and legislative aspects of foreign policy. Knowland's methods of resolving this role conflict can be illustrated in the case of the Bricker Amendment. This proposed constitutional amendment, which would have seriously hampered the President's conduct of foreign policy, generated support among many Republican senators—including Knowland—and strong opposition from Eisenhower. Once the President's opposition became clear, Knowland worked for months to bring about a compromise satisfactory both to the President and to a majority of Republican senators. He steered such a compromise to a favorable vote on the floor of the Senate, but then a further revision unacceptable to the President was adopted over his opposition, and Knowland had to make a decision on final passage of the often-revised amendment. He left the majority leader's desk to speak as an individual senator and announced that he would vote reluctantly for the bill. In a badly divided party, Knowland's sensitivity to senatorial opinion sometimes made him a valuable agent of compromise, but his influence in the Senate as a critic of the Administration declined, in part because the conflicts involved foreign policy, a field in which the President's preeminence is generally acknowledged by members of Congress.[27]

What role do legislative leaders play in the states? This varies with the governor's political effectiveness and particularly with his ability to dictate the choice of legislative leaders. Some legislative leaders, like those in Congress, serve two masters. But, in Northern states like New York, where the governor dominates a strong party, and in Southern states like Kentucky and Alabama, where the governor personally picks the leadership, the leaders are likely to see themselves as agents of the governor. Even in carrying out this role, they must report to the governor on the mood of the legislature and on the prospects for passing his bills, and in so doing they may act very much like agents of the legislative majority. In those states where the leaders are elected for relatively brief terms without gubernatorial interference, they are responsible primarily to the legislative majority that chose them. In other states where legislative leaders usually have longer tenure, they have an opportunity to develop their own legislative organization, which they not only serve but lead. The role of the majority leader may vary further, depending on whether he owes his being chosen to the governor, the legislative majority, or the Speaker. A leader chosen by the Speaker may operate primarily as his deputy. In a Southern state the floor leader is likely to be recognized as the governor's chief spokesman in the legislature.

The Opposition Leader. The leader of the opposition party escapes this kind of role conflict because he usually owes no responsibility to the chief executive. An exception may be made for the opposition leader in Congress, particularly one leading a majority party, whose role definition may include a sense of responsibility to provide support to the President on issues of foreign policy. Lyndon Johnson and Sam Rayburn clearly felt such a sense of responsibility on issues of foreign aid, reciprocal trade, and security treaties during the Eisenhower Administration. With this exception, the opposition leader is responsible solely to the legislative party which chose him.

The style of opposition leadership differs in a fashion that suggests distinct differences in the role perceptions of various leaders. These differences involve their responsibility for defining party policy, a duty of the Chief Executive in the Administration party. In the British parliamentary system, the leader of the opposition party in the House of Commons clearly has that responsibility because he is also the man who will become prime minister when and if the party wins an election. In this country, the identity of the opposition party's candidate for President is unknown in advance of the election year, but it is seldom the congressional leader.

Not since two former Speakers, James K. Polk and Henry Clay, contested the Presidency in 1844 has either party nominated a Speaker for President. Only once since the elections of 1884 and 1896 has either major party nominated a presidential candidate (James G. Blaine and William McKinley, in these two elections) who had served as an important party leader in Congress. The exception, Lyndon Johnson, was nominated for President only after his election as Vice-President and his succession to the Presidency following Kennedy's assassination. At the state level the chances of a legislative leader becoming governor are better, but still not great. In a study covering the years 1870 to 1950, Joseph A. Schlesinger found that over half of the governors had served in the legislature, one-fifth just before becoming governor, although the proportion in both cases had fallen in the later years. Only 7 percent of the governors had moved directly from a post of legislative leadership (Speaker of the House or president or president pro tem of the Senate) to the governorship. The legislature, and particularly legislative leadership, was most often the steppingstone to the governor's mansion in a few Northeastern and Southeastern states which had relatively low levels of party competition during the period studied.[28]

The contrasting perceptions with regard to the leader's role can be illustrated by the examples of Senators Robert A. Taft and Lyndon B. Johnson, two highly effective party leaders, both of whom also made serious bids for the presidential nomination. Taft, a man with sharply defined—though not doctrinaire—views on issues, sought to win the support of the Republican senatorial party for his views, not through bargaining but by intellectual force. Johnson was primarily concerned with discovering the policy position on which the largest number of Democratic senators could stand and with bargaining to obtain the largest possible number of votes for this position. William S. White has described the contrasting styles in these terms: "But where Johnson risked all for the sake of intraparty accommodation, Taft before him had been a great Senate leader precisely *because* his whole spirit was alien and hostile to party accommodation. Taft . . . had been a great leader *because* he was, in a way, always pointedly alone."[29]

The term "Mr. Republican" that was so often applied to Taft during the Truman Administration was appropriate because his viewpoints on domestic issues were broadly representative of those shared by most Republican senators, and because he articulated these viewpoints more clearly and forcefully than any of his colleagues. He used the Policy Committee (described in the next chapter) not so much as a sounding board but as an echo chamber for his ideas. His role was to define the party's record as an opposition party and in a few cases, such as the Taft-Hartley labor act, to enact major legislation in the face of the Administration's opposition. Taft was much less successful in defining party policy on international questions, both because of his own lack of interest and experience and because the Republican party was more seriously divided on this issue. In the later years of the Truman Administration, during the Korean conflict, the Republican party grew more unified in its criticism of the Administration's foreign policy, and as a consequence Taft's influence grew; then as always he won votes primarily from those who respected his views.[30]

Lyndon Johnson did not believe that he or the party could actually challenge the President's leadership or offer a comprehensive legislative program. (In 1956 he resisted demands that the party should frame its own program prior to the President's recommendations.) As a pragmatist, he was concerned with the possible, and this meant finding enough common ground among Democratic (and, if necessary, Republican) senators to pass legislation. Johnson held strong views on some issues, but in contrast to Taft, he seldom served as the initiator of or spokesman for a policy, with a few exceptions that occurred when he began to assume the role of presidential aspirant. The Bricker Amendment, which we used to illustrate Knowland's role, may be used again in the case of Johnson. Johnson opposed the most stringent versions of the Bricker Amendment, but he was not convinced that any such amendment would be dangerous. When he discovered that many Democrats supported some version of the amendment and others were under pressure from constituents to vote for some such measure, he worked out a compromise with Senator George and tried to get it enacted. Even more illuminating is Johnson's performance in the civil rights battles of 1957 and 1960. His own views were compatible with a "moderate" bill, and by 1960 he wanted to be identified with such a bill as a possible presidential candidate. His role during both legislative battles was that of a negotiator and mediator. He discovered what kind of bill could be passed without a filibuster, and then forced passage of the bill by warning Northern senators that any stronger bill would die in a filibuster and warning Southerners at the same time that he would help to break any filibuster against the compromise bill.

It is deceptive to draw too sharp a distinction between the role-concepts personified by Taft and Johnson. Taft, and others like him, have had to adjust their views to those of the partisan majority, and Johnson-style leaders have usually tried to raise the banner of compromise as close as possible to their own ideological position. This description of roles serves, however, to illustrate the difficulties faced by leaders whose viewpoints are out of tune with those of a majority in the legislative party. If they try to lead like Taft, by defining a clear policy, the chorus of agreement from party colleagues will be a feeble one; if they try to negotiate like Johnson, their policy preconceptions will warp their judgment in discovering the area of maximum agreement. Knowland tried to lead like Taft, but his views on foreign policy were doctrinaire; he lacked the flexibility to keep up with the changing views of Republican senators, more and more of whom were falling into step with President Eisenhower.

Opposition congressional leaders may differ in interpretations of the policy aspects of their role, but they have usually agreed in asserting that the responsibility for making party policy lies with the congressional party, through its legislative record, rather than with other elements of the national party. This was one of Taft's purposes in using the Policy Committee to make public policy statements. After the 1956 election, Chairman Paul Butler of the Democratic National Committee set up an Advisory Council to serve as a policy spokesman for the party outside of Congress. He invited the congressional leaders to join the group and was promptly rebuffed. Rayburn and Johnson recognized that, if they agreed to join the Advisory Council, its policy statements would limit their freedom of action in Congress. They denied that the congressional leadership had any responsibility to the national party, and their scarcely concealed hostility to the Advisory Council reflected a firm belief that policy leadership belonged in the hands of the congressional party.[31] Early in the Kennedy Administration this conflict was reenacted in the Republican party. When liberal Republicans in and out of Congress urged the creation of a new Republican organization patterned on the Democratic Advisory Council model but including congressmen, Republican congressional leaders made clear their hostility and their intention of running the congressional party without outside interference.

Leaders and Committees. There is one more factor that needs to be explained if we are to understand the role perceptions of congressional leaders in both the Administration and opposition parties; that is their relationship to the congressional committees. Party leaders recognize that rank-and-file congressmen respect the views of the standing committees and particularly the members of their own party on the committees. Moreover, the committee is able to make decisions on the specific provisions of a measure before the floor leader has any opportunity to seek changes in it. Party leaders may try to influence decision making within committees, but they proceed cautiously with any such approach, lest it arouse resentment and prove counter productive. The chairman of a committee, or the ranking minority member, often commands more respect in his party with regard to the issues handled by his committee than the party leader does. Matthews quotes one Senate floor leader as saying, "I always believed that it wasn't the leader's job to try to influence committee decisions. The leader's job is to take bills which have already been reported out of committee and placed on the Calendar and try to obtain as much party backing for them as he can."[32] Mike Mansfield, Senate Democratic floor leader, has repeatedly stated his view that policy cannot be made by the floor leader or a policy committee; it can be made only in the standing committees. Other floor leaders might not have stated the position in such absolute fashion. But the independent authority of the committees imposes serious limitations on the leader's freedom. His role is not strictly that of a follower of committee decisions, but neither is it that of a commander; his role is that of negotiating quietly with the committee members and seeking to refine committee decisions when they conflict with what he thinks a party majority will accept.

This restraint is in contrast with the authority assumed by party leaders in most states. Given broad authority in appointing committee members and wide discretion in assigning bills to committee, state legislative leaders are more likely to interfere directly in committee decision making when this appears necessary. They are more likely to have close working relationships with the chairmen of major committees; through them, the leaders can exert influence without openly interfering in the work of committees.

Rank-and-file Expectations. We have described leadership roles from the viewpoint of the leaders; it is also pertinent to examine the leadership role expectations of rank-and-file legislators. Our best information on this comes from the study of four state legislatures conducted by Wahlke and his associates.[33] Legislators expect the presiding officer to be fair and impartial in performing his functions, to maintain order, to follow the rules strictly, and to give individual members in both parties an opportunity to express their views. There is

wide agreement among legislators that the presiding officer's /
be that of an impartial referee. In two-party states, however,
stantial though smaller number of legislators also expect the Speake.
to play a partisan role—guiding the party program through the legislature and rallying party support for the program. Members of the majority
party are more likely than those in the minority to perceive the Speaker's
role in these terms. These expectations mean, of course, that the Speaker
is subject to role conflict. The authors of this study found that the conflict was seldom recognized by legislators, probably because some of
them saw only one aspect of the Speaker's role. They quote one legislator who was articulate about the Speaker's conflict:

> He must let every member have his views considered and yet retain
> enough control, influence and respect so that he can rally the support when
> he needs it. The speaker can't be a dictator or a neutral party; he must
> be a blend of the two, and this is very difficult to do successfully.
> He should be fair to both sides—except in a real pinch.[34]

The same role conflict is experienced in the Senate when the presiding officer is elected by a legislative majority. Where the lieutenant
governor presides, this conflict is largely removed; the lieutenant governor usually has the role of the impartial referee, and the president pro
tem or floor leader serves as a party leader.

The floor leaders escape this conflict; legislators recognize that their
role requires them to present and promote the legislative program of
the majority party or of the governor (in a one-party state), or in the
case of the minority leader to define and explain the minority party's
criticisms of bills. On the other hand, some legislators—especially from
states with weak party systems—stress the floor leader's responsibility
to encourage full debate and avoid unnecessary partisan conflict. Some
legislators emphasize the Administration floor leader's responsibility to
maintain liaison with the governor and other members of the Administration. The actual duties of floor leaders and the structure and cohesion
of legislative parties differ so widely from state to state that we need
more studies of legislators' role perceptions if we are to get a comprehensive picture of the leader's role.

The Powers of the Presiding Officer

The Speaker of the House and, where he is elected, the presiding
officer of the Senate in the states owe much of their authority to formal
powers granted in the legislative rules. The Speaker of the United States
House has formal powers that are significant, but—since the 1910–1911
revolt—less imposing than those of his counterparts in the states. The

Vice-President has little formal power as a presiding officer.

The Speaker of the House has authority to appoint members of the standing committees, and usually their chairmen, in the most states; Kentucky and Alaska are exceptions to this rule, while in two other states his choice must be confirmed by the House or a committee on committees. In 13 of the 14 states where the presiding officer of the Senate is elected by the members, he has the power to choose committees. In 13 of the states where the lieutenant governor presides, he has the power to choose committees; in 7, the president pro tem makes the selection; in the remainder, a committee or the full Senate chooses the committees.[35] The authority to choose committee members is one of the most powerful tools of leadership, and in most states it can be exercised without the deference to seniority that is necessary in Congress. There are likely to be other kinds of limitations on the leader's freedom to choose committees. In states with a frequent turnover and wide-open contests for the speakership, the Speaker often makes promises involving committee assignments during his campaign for office. In some states the governor takes a hand in assigning important committee chairmanships. The leader who has the formal power to choose committees often shares the responsibility of choice with other legislative leaders and in a two-party state usually delegates to the minority leadership the choice of minority members. The leader or leaders who, in practice, choose committees can use their authority to ensure that the important committees are tightly controlled by men who are loyal to the party or faction represented by the leadership. Occasionally the leadership's authority is challenged. In 1951 there was a prolonged but unsuccessful effort to deprive the California Speaker of his power to appoint committees and assign bills to them, an effort of rank-and-file members who believed that the Speaker had too much power and exercised it too arbitrarily.[36] Changes in the Senate rules regarding the lieutenant governor's authority are sometimes made when that office is won by a man who represents a party or faction different from that which controls the Senate. The Speaker of the United States House won the power to appoint committees during the First Congress. This power was often challenged, but it was repeatedly upheld by the House, and it was one of the most important methods by which strong Speakers achieved their control over the House, until the power was taken away from the Speaker by a change in the rules in 1911, which marked the culmination of the revolt against Speaker Cannon.[37]

A close corollary of the power to choose committee members is the authority to assign bills to committee, an authority exercised by the Speaker in 45 states, by the presiding officer of the Senate in 42 states, and by committees in the remaining cases. In many of these states, particularly in the case of the Speaker, the presiding officer has wide discretion in assigning bills. In the absence of jurisdictional rules, he can assign bills to those committees most securely controlled by the dominant group in the legislature. In many state legislatures a large majority of the bills—and nearly all important ones—are assigned to a handful of committees, usually bearing broadly descriptive titles, such as Judiciary, Executive and Legislative Affairs, or Finance and Taxation. The presiding officers in Congress have no such discretionary authority. The 1946 Legislative Reorganization Act specifies the jurisdiction of congressional committees in precise detail. In 1958 Speaker Rayburn did exercise his rarely used authority when he delayed for forty days assigning a labor bill to committee. Normally the assigning of bills to committees is handled routinely in Congress by the legislative clerks.

The Speaker of the House and occasionally the presiding officer in the Senate exercise significant discretionary authority in presiding over state legislative bodies. This is not so often a matter of rules as it is one of custom and precedent and the skills of a bold presiding officer. The presiding officer in a state legislature can act more boldly and arbitrarily than would be possible for the Speaker of the United States House because his actions are less publicized, he is less bound by tradition, most rank-and-file members are inadequately familiar with the rules and parliamentary practice, and in some cases his party or faction completely dominates the legislature. The presiding officer (particularly the Speaker) may be highly selective in recognizing members, or arbitrary in prolonging or cutting off debate. He may affect the decision on a bill through his judgment of voice votes, his failure to recognize demands for a roll call, or even his timing in closing the voting and recording votes when a mechanical voting device is used. We have noted that legislators expect their presiding officers to be fair, and it is usually true that a successful presiding officer must retain the respect of legislators in all parties and factions. It is also true that many actions of the presiding officer which appear abrupt and arbitrary to the newcomer in the gallery may be accepted by all legislators in the interests of expediting business. Nevertheless, when the leadership is short of votes and its legislative control is endangered, the presiding officer is sometimes able to assert that control through his skill and boldness in presiding.

The Speaker of the United States House cannot be so arbitrary, but he is far from being impotent as a presiding officer. For several decades prior to the 1910–1911 revolt, the Speaker had exercised absolute discretion in recognizing members who were seeking to make motions as well as those seeking to participate in debate. Since the revolt, the Speaker's discretion in matters of recognition has been limited. Rules and customs of the House require him to recognize certain members seeking to make motions, such as committee chairmen, and control over debate is largely handled by the member in charge of the legislation on the floor. Some discretion remains, but it is not an important source of power. Since 1890 the Speaker has had the power to refuse to entertain a motion that he considered dilatory; yet this potentially important power was never exercised by Speaker Rayburn during his long tenure.[38] The Speaker's discretionary authority is probably applied with greatest effect during votes. By failing to see enough members demanding a roll call, the Speaker may prevent a recorded vote and thereby facilitate a subsequent compromise in a conference committee. By delay in announcing the results of the roll call, the Speaker may give the floor leader an opportunity to persuade members to change their votes. A dramatic example of the Speaker's authority as presiding officer occurred in August, 1941, when a bill to extend the selective service law was in serious danger of defeat. Speaker Rayburn shared the Administration's belief that passage of the bill was vital to the nation's security. When the roll call had been completed with 203 "aye" votes and 202 "no" votes, Rayburn announced the result before any members could ask for a chance to change their votes. He agreed to a minority request for a recapitulation of the vote, then pounded the gavel and announced: "No correction in the vote, the vote stands, and the bill is passed and without objection a motion to reconsider is laid on the table." In eliminating the possibility of reconsideration, Rayburn acted arbitrarily and effectively to ensure passage of the bill.[39]

The Speaker of the United States House has one further important power. He has the authority to interpret the rules of the House, and in so doing to set precedents and revise the rules in important respects. In this task, he is aided by the House parliamentarian, who helps him to find those precedents that will justify the action he desires to take. Most of the important changes in House rules, including those enhancing the Speaker's power, have resulted from rulings by the Speaker. One writer has said: "The Speaker's power primarily has sprung from the political nature of his office: it has been he who has applied the rules and established the precedents that have controlled and guided the House of Representatives."[40] The rulings of the Speaker can always be overruled by a majority vote in the House, but such is the Speaker's traditional authority in this area that his rulings have rarely been questioned. Nicholas Longworth, who served in the late 1920s, was the last Speaker to have a decision overruled; this happened to him twice, but the effect of the second action was to reinstate his first decision.[41]

TECHNIQUES OF LEADERSHIP

At the national level the Speaker's influence is based less on these formal powers than on his skill as a political leader; the floor leaders, with even fewer formal powers, must rely on their own resources in developing political leadership. David Truman's comments on the congressional floor leader are perceptive:

A search for the substance and sources of power in the position, however, is frustrating, not because they do not exist but because they are tremendously varied and often inaccessible. One cannot draw up for this post a neat list of authorities and prerogatives that describes its power adequately if not exhaustively, as one can for a place in a tightly structured hierarchy. The sum total of influence in the role as played by any individual senator depends upon the skill with which he combines and employs the fragments of power that are available to him.[42]

What are these fragments of power? The floor leader of the majority party in the United States Senate or House is entitled to priority of recognition from the presiding officer, and he may occasionally gain significant tactical advantages from this right. In the Senate the majority leader shares with the majority policy committee the authority for scheduling legislation that is to be considered on the floor. The division of this responsibility between the leader and the committee varies from time to time, but some leaders have had little difficulty in winning committee approval for their proposals. In the House, this scheduling function is usually in the hands of the Rules Committee, and the floor leader's power is consequently reduced. In the states it is frequently the practice for the floor leader to determine priorities of bills to be taken up by the legislature, and this authority is facilitated by the custom of giving him priority of recognition on the floor.

An attribute, if not a power, of the floor leadership is that the occupant stands at the center of the legislative party's communications network. He is in a better position than an individual congressman to maintain contact with the White House, committee chairmen, and other congressmen. One observer has said that Lyndon Johnson's "greatest weapon was a communications system that bordered on the psychic."[43] Recent floor leaders, most notably Johnson, have made greater use of staff assistants to improve this communications network. Congressional leaders have often said that the leader must be able to "sense the mood" of the Senate or House, and this requires not merely intuition but also continuing contacts with the rank-and-file. Johnson, for example, was said to talk with every Democratic senator every day, a description that probably contains more truth than exaggeration. The floor leader should be able to judge better than anyone else the chances of a bill for passage; he should be more sensitive than anyone else to shifts in the wind of congressional opinion.[44]

"Most of the time the leader is cast in the role of someone trying to help you with your problems," according to one senator interviewed by Matthews.[45] The leader can help a congressman get more votes for a pet bill; as Huitt points out, this may involve providing "a respectable vote for a senator's bill or amendment that was bound to lose—a substantial boon to a man who wants his constituents to take him seriously."[46] The leader's success in providing votes is cumulative; once he has aided a congressman on a particular measure, he can call on that congressman for help on another. Although the leaders in Congress lack the control over committee assignments enjoyed by state legislative leaders, they usually have substantial influence on them. Illustrative of the tactics that a skillful leader can use to enhance his power is Lyndon Johnson's success in 1953 in persuading Democratic senators that seniority should play a smaller part in committee assignments and that each Democrat should have at least one major committee assignment. The leader's ability to do favors extends beyond the passage of bills and committee assignments. He can provide the congressman with an important speaker for a meeting in his district, better office accommodations on Capitol Hill, assignment as a special congressional delegate to an overseas conference, assistance in getting funds for a subcommittee, and a host of other favors that make congressmen indebted to the leader. We are not suggesting that the average senator's vote on an important bill can be bought by obtaining an audience with the President for the "Mother of the Year" who comes from his state. We are suggesting that the floor leader is in a position to help congressmen and that, through skillful use of these opportunities, he can create an atmosphere in which congressmen are favorably disposed to provide support for him, if that is at all possible.

There is another side to the coin. Favors that can be granted can also be withheld. In dealing with a recalcitrant congressman, the leader can persuade other congressmen to bury his favorite bill in committee or vote against it, or even to claim a committee assignment (on grounds of seniority) that the rebel had hoped to get for himself. Part of Lyndon Johnson's effectiveness as Democratic floor leader in the Senate was due to his willingness to take a "tough" line, to deny favors as well as to grant them. The resourceful leader, as Lyndon Johnson demonstrated, can endow the party leader's job with a power that some occupants of the post had never suspected was possible.

Every congressional leader has recognized, however, that his success depended more on persuasion and compromise than it did on favors and threats. House majority leader Carl Albert remarked: "If you can't win them by persuasion, you can't win them at all. If you whip them into line every time, by the time you reach the third vote you're through."[47] Albert studied party leadership under Speaker Rayburn, who said, "My experience with the Speakership has been that you cannot lead people by driving them. Persuasion and reason are the only ways. In that way the Speaker has power and influence in the House."[48] Lyndon Johnson, in echoing this theme, was underestimating his power but not straying far from an accurate description: "The only real power available to the leader is the power of persuasion. There is no patronage; no power to discipline; no authority to fire Senators like a President can fire his members of Cabinet."[49]

Lyndon Johnson's techniques present the best example of "persuasion" in action. He kept in constant touch with senators, finding out what they wanted, what compromises they might be willing to make, how strongly they felt about issues. He used his forceful personality to argue the cause of party unity and the necessity for compromise. He was conscious of the necessity for finding "face-saving" ways through which senators could change their position and facilitate compromise. If relations with a senator had temporarily cooled, he did not hesitate to use another senator or a staff aide as an intermediary. If he was unable to persuade a senator to vote favorably, it was sometimes possible to persuade him to pair with another senator who was going to be absent, to be absent himself, or at least to avoid public statements that would dramatize the party split.

Huitt has described Johnson's tactics as involving the "manipulation of the role perceptions of other senators." He tried to get senators to think as Democrats, not as liberals or conservatives. He tried to structure the votes in such a way that Democrats would find it possible to vote as a bloc. When liberal Democrats opposed one Eisenhower appointee because of his anti-labor record, Johnson persuaded Southern Democrats that the appointee's testimony before a Senate committee was so contradictory that he was flouting the dignity of the Senate. On other occasions, Johnson concentrated his efforts on a single senator, usually a Southern conservative, whose support he considered crucial because the senator would provide an "umbrella" that would make other senators feel that they could safely vote for the measure.[50]

Few leaders have had Johnson's skill in behind-the-scenes negotiations, and some have been too dogmatic to serve—like Johnson—as brokers of compromise. Differences in performance, as we suggested earlier, are also related to different conceptions of the leader's role. Johnson, though he did not share Taft's perception of the role as a policy-forming one, believed that the leader's role must be an active one; the leader must utilize a variety of powers and techniques in his effort to gain party consensus. Johnson shared with Rayburn and most recent congressional leaders a belief that leadership is largely personal; it is their scorn of most institutional devices that has stunted the growth of policy committees and party conferences as tools of political leadership.

NOTES

1. David B. Truman, *The Congressional Party* (New York: John Wiley and Sons, 1959), p. 94.
2. Cecil A. Gibb, "The Principles and Traits of Leadership," *Journal of Abnormal and Social Psychology*, XLII (1947), 267–84 at 284.
3. David B. Truman, *The Governmental Process* (New York, 1951), p. 190.
4. Truman, *The Congressional Party*, p. 97.
5. For an excellent description of the presiding officer's powers, see Eugene C. Lee, *The Presiding Officer and Rules Committee in Legislatures of the United States* (Berkeley, 1952).
6. Useful sources on the history of the speakership are: George B. Galloway, *History of the House of Representatives* (New York, 1961), chaps. 4, 5, and 7; Neil MacNeil, *Forge of Democracy* (New York, 1963), chaps. 3 and 4; George R. Brown, *The Leadership of Congress* (Indianapolis, 1922); Ralph B. Harlow, *The History of Legislative Methods in the Period before 1825* (New Haven, 1917), chaps. 8, 9, and 10.
7. MacNeil, *op. cit.*, p. 80.
8. Randall B. Ripley, "The Party Whip Organization in the United States House of Representatives," *American Political Science Review*, LVIII (1964), 561–76.
9. *Ibid.*, p. 562.
10. John W. Baker (ed.), *Member of the House*, (New York, 1962), p. 53.
11. Ripley, *op. cit.*, pp. 573, 574.
12. Nelson W. Polsby, "Two Strategies of Influence: Choosing a Majority Leader, 1962," in Robert L. Peabody and Nelson W. Polsby (eds.), *New Perspectives on the House of Representatives* (Chicago, 1963), pp. 237–70.
13. James M. Burns, *Roosevelt: The Lion and the Fox* (New York, 1956), pp. 309–10.
14. William C. Havard and Loren P. Beth, *The Politics of Mis-representation* (Baton Rouge, 1962), pp. 131–47.
15. Clifton H. McCleskey, *The Government and Politics of Texas* (Boston, 1963), pp. 123–25.
16. William Buchanan, *Legislative Partisanship: The Deviant Case of California* (Berkeley and Los Angeles, 1963), pp. 139–44.
17. *Ibid.*, p. 141.
18. For an account of one of these incidents, see Thomas B. Littlewood, *Bipartisan Coalition in Illinois* (New York, 1960).
19. The surveys of leadership turnover and the selection of Speakers are based on data in the Council of State Government's *Book of the States* and in legislative manuals and bluebooks for the appropriate years.
20. William S. White, *Citadel* (New York, 1957), p. 96.
21. Truman, *The Congressional Party*, pp. 298, 303.
22. Joe Martin, *My First Fifty Years in Politics* (New York, 1960), chaps. 1, 15, 16.

23. Ralph K. Huitt, "Democratic Party Leadership in the Senate," *American Political Science Review*, LV (1961), 333–44, at 336.

24. Truman, *The Congressional Party*, p. 306.

25. William S. White, *The Taft Story* (New York, 1954), p. 227.

26. *Ibid.*, pp. 230–41.

27. Malcolm E. Jewell, *Senatorial Politics and Foreign Policy* (Lexington, Ky., 1962), pp. 61–66.

28. Joseph A. Schlesinger, *How They Became Governor* (East Lansing, Mich., 1957), pp. 11–15, 51–58.

29. White, *Citadel*, p. 105.

30. Jewell, *op. cit.*, pp. 68–74.

31. Hugh A. Bone, *Party Committees and National Politics* (Seattle, 1958), pp. 219–33.

32. Donald R. Matthews, *U.S. Senators and Their World* (Chapel Hill, N.C., 1960), p. 126.

33. John C. Wahlke, Heinz Eulau, William Buchanan, and LeRoy C. Ferguson, *The Legislative System* (New York: John Wiley and Sons, 1962), chap. 8.

34. *Ibid.*, p. 183.

35. *Book of the States, 1964–65* (Chicago, 1964), p. 51.

36. Lee, *op. cit.*, pp. 42–47.

37. Brown, *op. cit.*, pp. 26–38, 143–71.

38. George B. Galloway, *The Legislative Process in Congress* (New York, 1955), pp. 348–49.

39. C. Dwight Durough, *Mr. Sam* (New York, 1962), p. 314.

40. MacNeil, *op. cit.*, p. 62.

41. *Ibid.*, p. 65.

42. Truman, *The Congressional Party*, p. 104.

43. Douglass Cater, "The Contentious Lords of the Senate," *Reporter*, Aug. 16, 1962, p. 27.

44. Matthews, *op. cit.*, pp. 126–29; Huitt, *op. cit.*, pp. 337–39.

45. Matthews, *op. cit.*, p. 127.

46. Huitt, *op. cit.*, p. 338.

47. MacNeil, *op. cit.*, p. 94.

48. *Time*, Oct. 13, 1961, p. 26.

49. *U.S. News and World Report*, June 27, 1960, p. 89.

50. Huitt, *op. cit.*, pp. 339–40.

[8]

Party and
Factional
Organization

ALL LEGISLATIVE bodies have leaders, though their roles and techniques of leadership differ from time to time and from place to
place. Congress and the state legislatures use standing committees with
substantive responsibilities (discussed in the next chapter), although they
vary in importance and in their methods of operation. The organizational
structure of majority and minority blocs differs substantially, however,
from one legislature to another and even in a single legislature over a
period of years. An organ such as a rules committee or a caucus may
be inconsequential in one legislature, of moderate importance in another, and the main arena for decision making in a third.

In a two-party state the organizational structure is partisan in nature,
and the cohesiveness of the party contributes to the effectiveness of
party organs. In one-party states the structure is factional in nature.
In either type of legislature the leaders usually have considerable discretion in determining what organs will be established and what tasks
they will perform. The leaders regard such committees as more or less
valuable tools for performing their own tasks more effectively, sharing
the workload, or improving communications with rank-and-file members
or with the leadership of the opposition. Often, particularly in smaller
legislative bodies, the leaders prefer to rely on informal methods and
make little use of such organizations. Occasionally a legislative majority
will establish a more formal structure in order to limit the authority

of one man and provide a degree of collective leadership. We noted in the previous chapter that such limitations are often placed on the power of a lieutenant governor who belongs to a party or faction different from a senatorial majority, and took note as well of the organizational changes that resulted from the revolt against a strong Speaker of the United States House early in this century.

FUNCTIONS

The presiding officer has leadership responsibilities for the entire legislature, but he and the floor leaders also act as party or factional leaders. Leadership committees likewise perform functions both for the legislature as a whole and for a party or faction, and it is useful to distinguish between these two kinds of functions. *Legislative management committees* are those that function to expedite the performance of legislative tasks. They may be used to recommend rules for the legislative body, to select the membership of committees, to assign bills to committees, or to determine priorities for scheduling legislation on the floor. All of these are responsibilities of leadership which may be performed by one man or by a committee, and all are essential functions for a legislative body. Where committees are used for these purposes, there is no consistent relationship between the titles used and the duties performed by them. In two-party legislatures the minority party is often, but not always, represented on these committees.

In a two-party legislature there are party organizations, which vary in form and importance; in other legislatures, factional organizations are sometimes found. The most common of these organizations is a party —or factional—*caucus*, which may meet only at the start of a session to choose party leaders, or may meet regularly during a session to discuss or take a stand on legislative issues. Some of the larger legislative parties also use a policy or steering committee to advise the leaders on policy and tactics. The essential function of party organizations is to provide a means of communication between the leaders and the led. The leaders may decide that such organizations are unnecessary or ineffective, for any of several reasons. The party or faction may be such a loose coalition that it lacks common purposes and agreed norms and rarely manifests cohesion in legislative voting. If so, regular meetings of caucuses or policy committees would be useless. Even in a more cohesive party or faction there may be little use for formal organizations. If the legislative party is small, the purposes of communication may be served by less formal devices. The styles and tactics of party leaders differ; some prefer to communicate with the rank-and-file through individual negotiations, an extensive whip organization, or other techniques.

In the few legislative parties where a serious effort is made to enforce party cohesion, a caucus is usually the vehicle for achieving that goal, and its decisions are frequently binding on the membership. In the larger number of legislative parties where caucus decisions are rarely considered binding, the caucus may strengthen party cohesion by serving as a source of voting cues for the member more effectively than an individual leader can. Legislators may give greater heed to party decisions arrived at after discussion in the caucus. The caucus occasionally serves a different purpose, one that causes some party leaders to avoid utilizing it: Rank-and-file legislators may perceive the caucus as the best vehicle for imposing restrictions on the leaders' freedom to determine policy stands and party tactics.

LEGISLATIVE MANAGEMENT COMMITTEES

Most legislative bodies have a rules committee, frequently chaired by the Speaker or presiding officer in the Senate and consisting of legislative leaders from both parties. It usually makes recommendations on changes in the rules, a power that occasionally assumes importance. It may have administrative functions: in California, the Rules Committee controls patronage, authorizes legislative expenditures, and screens resolutions creating interim committees.

Although the appointment of standing committees is normally in the hands of the presiding officer, in thirteen upper houses and two lower houses of state legislatures a committee has this function. In some other states an informal committee may advise the presiding officer. Such a committee is usually bipartisan; frequently it is called a Committee on Committees. In a few states, however, this function is performed by a committee with broader powers. In Congress, there are committees for both parties in both houses which make assignments to committees; their operations are described in Chapter 9. In five upper houses and three lower houses the referring of bills to committee is handled by a committee instead of by the presiding officer; this too is normally a bipartisan committee. One of the most powerful is the Reference Committee of the Ohio House, which is authorized to eliminate frivolous or duplicate bills.[1]

Once a bill has been reported by a standing committee, the responsibility for determining priorities for consideration on the floor is usually assumed by the leadership. In many states the majority leader makes this decision, and he is able to do so because the rules and precedents give him priority of recognition on the floor of the house. In other states this is the responsibility of the rules committee or of a separate calendar committee, for part or all of the session. Even though such a committee is usually bipartisan, it is normally under the firm control of legislators who are members of or loyal to the majority leadership. The committee's power derives primarily from the fact that in the course of setting priorities it may block action on a bill, at least long enough to ensure its defeat in the hectic closing days of a session.[2]

In Washington state the rules committees in both houses are the primary tools of legislative leadership. Though bipartisan in make-up, they are under majority control. They meet in secret, have jurisdiction over all legislation that comes from committees, and in the closing days of the session meet for many hours each day. New York is another state where the Rules Committee is similarly used in the interests of the majority party. The importance of such a committee increases in the closing days of a session when there is a log-jam of bills, and in several states the committee is not created, or is not authorized to set priorities, until the last few days or weeks of a session. Several of the states that use a rules or calendar committee are one-party states, such as Alabama, Tennessee, Virginia, South Carolina, and Kentucky, all states characterized by tight control exercised by the majority faction or the governor. In South Carolina a joint committee sets the date for adjournment and controls the bills to be acted upon, while the Rules Committee in each house determines priorities among these. The Kentucky rules committees are atypical in size, sometimes including as many as half of the members—still carefully chosen to ensure majority control. In that legislature these committees supersede the standing committees in the closing days of the session, and consequently can vote favorably on a bill that has been buried in one of the standing committees, a procedure that undermines the latter's authority.

At the state level the majority leadership normally has *de facto* control of priorities, either through the power of recognition or through its control of a rules committee, even though the rules committee is bipartisan. In Congress, there is a sharp difference in practice between the Senate and House. In the Senate, the scheduling power is in the hands of the majority floor leader and the Policy Committee. Although the internal operations of the Policy Committee are not publicized, it appears that the majority leader makes recommendations on scheduling and is rarely overruled by the Policy Committee. There are some differences, stemming from changes in leadership. Scott Lucas and Ernest McFarland were guided more by the Democratic Policy Committee than Lyndon Johnson was in later years. It is important to point out, however, that the Senate policy committees rarely block floor consideration of a bill that has been reported out by a standing committee, except in the closing days of a session, when some measures must be abandoned because of the shortage of time; at this point the scheduling function assumes its greatest importance.

United States House Rules Committee. The Rules Committee of the House is a unique kind of rules committee, in the sense that the majority leadership does not consistently have firm control over it. It is a bipartisan committee, with ten majority and five minority party members. Although the 2 to 1 ratio might appear to ensure majority control, since the later years of the New Deal the liberal Democrats have had, at best, only a tenuous hold over the committee, and often a coalition of conservative Democrats and Republicans has been able to block legislation. At times the chairman has been a conservative Democrat, like Howard Smith of Virginia, the chairman since 1955, who has not been consistently responsive to the wishes of the Democratic leadership in the House. The House Rules Committee has the authority to order a "special rule," which is the normal method for bringing measures to the House floor unless they are privileged measures (such as appropriation bills). The Rules Committee also can limit debate and amendments through its special rule. To a far greater extent than the Senate policy committees, the House Rules Committee has used this authority to prevent, delay, or force modifications in measures that have emerged from the standing committees.

The House Rules Committee developed its great power at a time when it was under the firm control of the majority leadership. Speaker Thomas Reed, who served intermittently during the 1890s, first recognized the value of the committee as an instrument of control by the leadership. The Speaker had been chairman since 1858 and the committee's powers had been expanded gradually by a series of rulings by the Speaker. Reed not only chaired the committee but controlled its five-man membership by appointing top lieutenants as majority-party members. He also gave the committee authority to determine the legislative program of the House, by developing the special rule as the regular method for handling most major legislation in the House. Under Speakers Charles Crisp and Joseph Cannon, the Rules Committee continued to grow in power and to become a "sleeping giant," in the words of Haines. In the 1910–1911 revolt against the Speaker, one of the first and most important steps taken was to remove the Speaker from the Rules Committee and deprive him of authority to appoint its members. *But the authority of the committee was not significantly reduced.* The committee was enlarged, and the approximate 2 to 1 party ratio soon became an established pattern. The Rules Committee was generally responsive to the majority party leadership in the years between the 1910–1911 revolt and 1937. But the growth of the seniority system gave the Rules Committee the same independence from majority leadership control that other congressional committees have enjoyed in the last half-century. Since 1937 the Rules Committee has often exercised that independence. It is true that the party leadership has considerable influ-

ence over the choice of members, but Democratic leaders have considered it necessary to retain geographic balance and consequently to
appoint Southerners who might at times rebel against the leadership.[3]

Liberal Democrats have followed two strategies alternately in trying to prevent a conservative coalition from using the Rules Committee
to block legislation. One line of attack is to change the membership of
the committee to make it more responsive to the Democratic majority;
the second is to make it easier to remove from the committee's jurisdiction bills that have become stalled. Speaker Rayburn was not enthusiastic
about either approach, but by 1961 the Republican membership on
the committee had grown more conservative, the deadlock had become
more serious, and President Kennedy had come into office with a
broad legislative program. Rayburn became convinced that change
was necessary, and he preferred to change the membership of the committee rather than to diminish its powers. Liberal Democrats who had
been pressing for reform were forced to follow his lead and adjust
their strategy to his.

Perhaps as a tactical maneuver, Rayburn initially suggested the
purge of one Democrat member: William Colmer of Mississippi, who
had actively supported an unpledged slate of electors in the 1960 presidential campaign. Moderate Southerners, who feared the establishment of
this precedent and believed that Rayburn had sufficient votes in the
Democratic caucus to accomplish it, sought a compromise. Rayburn then
shifted to what was perhaps his preferred tactic: enlargement of the
committee from 12 to 15, by adding two Democrats and one Republican,
and thus preserving the 2 to 1 ratio. This approach was more palatable
to some Southern Democrats, but it required approval by the whole
House, and the Republican leadership was determined to fight the
change. In one of the bitterest battles of recent years, foreshadowing
what lay ahead for the Kennedy legislative program, the House passed
the proposal by a mere 5 votes. Two years later, by a margin of 39
votes, the House made the fifteen-man figure a permanent part of the
rules.[4] Despite the change in membership, the liberal majority on the
committee was not completely dependable, in part because the Democratic leadership chose some new members for the committee who did
not have consistently liberal voting records.

Liberal Democrats have repeatedly proposed rules changes to make
it possible to bypass the Rules Committee, because the long-established
procedures are too awkward to be feasible. On several occasions they
have sought to restore the 21-day rule, which during the Eighty-first
Congress (1949–1950) made it possible for the chairman of a committee
that had reported a bill favorably to bring it to the House floor if the
Rules Committee had failed to approve a special rule for it after 21

days.[5] They also proposed a change in the discharge rule that would require the votes of fewer members to release a bill from the Rules Committee. When leaders of the Democratic Study Group (consisting of Northern, liberal Democrats) urged these reforms on Speaker Rayburn on several occasions, they found him consistently hostile. Rayburn distrusted institutional reforms. Although he could not exercise dependable control over the Rules Committee, he did exploit his friendship with individual members to win committee approval for most measures that he considered essential, and the committee often served his purposes by blocking or delaying bills or limiting amendments from the floor. Rayburn did not want to give authority to others—either committee chairmen or a designated number of House members—to bypass the Rules Committee, and perhaps to bypass him.

The 1964 election enhanced liberal Democratic strength in the House, and the Democratic Study Group was determined to effect a method for bypassing the Rules Committee. Its leaders reached agreement with Speaker McCormack on a plan that would weaken the Rules Committee and at the same time strengthen the Speaker. The rules change was approved by a 224–201 vote in the House; the votes of 16 Republicans were decisive because 78 Democrats opposed the change. The new rules permitted the Speaker to recognize a committee chairman (or a ranking member favorable to the bill) to call up a bill that had been held in the Rules Committee for 21 days, or to send a bill to a conference committee after it had passed the two houses in different versions. The new rules, if they remain in effect, will give the Speaker greater formal power than he has had at any time since 1911.

Members of the House Rules Committee exercise substantive control over legislation through their judgments about the merits of bills. A recent study of the committee members' perceptions showed that nearly all of them, liberals and conservatives alike, recognize this to be a major purpose of the committee, even though they sometimes vote for a rule for a bill that they oppose. Committee members also recognize the importance of regulating the time for debate and the kind of amendments to be permitted, as well as the closely related strategy of delaying a measure in order to permit "grass-roots" reaction to be felt in Congress. Through the use of these powers, the Rules Committee can dominate legislative strategy and often determine a bill's fate by prescribing not only its timing but also the form in which it will be voted on.[6]

Although some congressmen who are not on the committee, particularly liberal Democrats, would prefer a more neutral committee, there are no significant differences among Republicans, liberal Democrats, and conservative Democrats on the committee concerning the powers it does and should exercise. The differences have to do with another question: in whose interests should the committee exercise its powers? Most liberal Democrats on the committee see it as an instrument of majority leadership; as one member put it, "The whole function is as an arm of the leadership, an arm of the majority of the majority, which is the elected leadership of the House." Republican and conservative Democratic members are more likely to assert that the Rules Committee should represent a consensus of thinking in the House or a bipartisan majority. Members in both factions also recognize that at times the individual members will act in such a way as to protect their own constituency interests, even though one criterion for picking members of the Rules Committee is their relative freedom from constituency pressures.[7]

The Rules Committee of the United States House has impressive powers. Aside from private bills, noncontroversial legislation approved by unanimous consent, and such privileged measures as appropriation bills, legislation that is reported by a standing committee must receive a special rule from the Rules Committee to get consideration in the House, unless the Speaker exercises his authority to remove a bill after 21 days. The committee holds a hearing at which the leadership of the standing committee testifies; it may then grant a rule, refuse one, or perhaps delay while it negotiates informally with the standing committee on revisions in the bill. Occasionally the committee refuses even to grant a hearing, but few important bills have been blocked in this fashion. The number denied a special rule has usually been small, but some of these have been major bills. The largest number of refusals in recent years was 38 in the Eighty-first Congress (1949–1950)—the Congress in which the 21-day rule was in effect. The number in the remaining Congresses from the Eightieth through the Eighty-fifth ranged from 7 to 14. Measures pertaining to veterans affairs, public power, reclamation, and conservation (usually bills with a high price tag), as well as some civil rights bills, have been particularly vulnerable to rejection by the committee. Not every bill given a special rule by the Rules Committee has been called up by the House leadership; an average of five bills in each Congress have not been in recent years. The importance of the committee's authority cannot be measured entirely by the number of rules rejected. The committee, by delaying or threatening to block approval of a special rule, has forced revision and modification of bills by the standing committees.[8]

The Rules Committee may grant either an open or closed rule: The closed rule either imposes an absolute ban on amendments or permits only certain amendments or only amendments by members of the standing committee. Between 1939 and 1956 the committee granted closed rules only 7 percent of the time. Closed rules, which are usually granted at the request of the House leadership, are generally reserved for such matters as tax and tariff bills, both because of the complex nature of the measures and their vulnerability to logrolling on the floor. With an open rule, a bill is subject to amendment by any member, who has five minutes to speak for it. The committee sometimes grants a rule waiving points of order against the inclusion of legislative matters in an appropriations bill. Such a rule, which was granted 47 times between 1939 and 1956, is usually the only occasion for appropriations bills to be channeled through the Rules Committee. The committee, in approving a special rule, always specifies the amount of time permitted for debate. The majority of these rules permit four hours or less for debate; over half of them permit only a single hour. Even major issues seldom receive more than a day or two of debate. The House may always refuse to accept the rule, but such action prevents consideration of the bill on the floor. Between 1937 and 1956 only nineteen rules were defeated, none of them closed rules; nearly all the defeats resulted from House opposition to the bill proposed for consideration, and not to the terms of the rule. Until 1965 the Rules Committee had authority to determine House action when the Senate and House disagreed on the provisions of a bill, unless a motion was passed by unanimous consent either to concur in Senate amendments or to seek a conference; the committee occasionally used this authority to block a conference committee on a bill, as it did with the 1960 aid to education bill.[9]

PARTY ORGANIZATIONS

The most common form of party organization is the caucus. In Congress and in two-party state legislatures each party holds a caucus to choose its leaders and its candidate for presiding officer of the Senate or House. In some legislative parties this is the only use made of the caucus; in others, it meets more often and serves other purposes. Caucuses have been powerful organs of party discipline during some periods of congressional history, but congressional caucuses today seldom meet and have little influence and no authority over the rank-and-file members. A survey conducted more than a decade ago showed that in only about half of the two-party states did party caucuses meet frequently to deal with important issues, and in only a few was there a regular weekly or daily caucus meeting.[10] Since that time, increased two-party competition has prompted greater use of the caucus in some states.

Caucuses in the States. In those states where the caucus assumes some importance, it usually meets at least once a week early in the session and more often, perhaps daily, late in the session, as the legislative tempo increases. The caucus serves primarily as a communications device. It gives the leadership a chance to explain which bills are of concern to the party and to urge a particular course of action with regard to these bills. It gives the rank-and-file members a chance to express their views. If it becomes clear that the party is seriously divided, the leaders have an opportunity to revise or delay the bill and thereby to prevent the division from being transferred to the floor of the house. If the caucus demonstrates that there is substantial agreement concerning a measure, the members may be more likely to go along with it in a roll call vote, but in most states the decisions reached in a caucus are rarely binding on the membership.

In a few states, however, the party caucus has assumed greater importance and has in reality become the decision-making center in the legislative system. In Connecticut binding decisions are reached in the caucus on most bills; both parties, particularly in the Senate, follow the practice described by Lockard for the Senate Democratic party:

The caucus of senators, which takes place daily, is the scene of some protracted disputes and debates on bills, but when the senators leave their caucus to come to the floor it is rare indeed for the disputes of the inner chamber to be brought out in Senate debate and rarer still for members to desert in a roll call.

In the daily caucus—to which normally is devoted far more time than that spent on the floor of the Senate—the procedure is to review the day's calendar of bills and to come to agreement on the party stand on all bills. All senators attend their respective caucuses, as do the state chairmen of the parties. . . . Discussion among the senators as to the bill and the appropriate position for the party to take on it may occupy minutes or hours. . . . On some bills, however, no agreement can be reached and each senator goes his own way. On Administration bills more formidable pressures are involved.[11]

The New Jersey caucus illustrates how powerful such a body can be, particularly in a negative sense, in a state with a strong two-party system. "The majority party caucus makes all crucial legislative decisions, both procedural and substantive, as a body. It decides who the officers will be, which bills will be advanced on the calendar and which will die, and how these bills will be combined or amended."[12] One result of this concentration of power is to reduce the authority of the standing committees virtually to the vanishing point; another result is to diminish the authority of party leaders, who may influence the decisions of the caucus but have little discretion in implementing its decisions. The Senate Republican caucus had become the focus of controversy in New Jersey because the apportionment system had given the Republican party control over the Senate throughout the period of Democratic administrations until 1966. Because the Republican caucus could effectively prevent any bill from reaching the floor, six or seven senators were able to block action or even debate on the governor's program in the twenty-one-man Senate. Prior to 1952, the caucus rules required an affirmative vote of eleven Republican senators (a majority of the Senate) to act, and this placed the veto power in even fewer hands. Governor Meyner made the caucus system a particular target of criticism during his campaigns for office, but was unable to prevent its use by Republicans in the legislature.[13]

The strong two-party systems in these states, with each party resting on a base of rather homogeneous constituencies, make a powerful caucus possible but not inevitable. Caucuses are important centers of decision making in Massachusetts, Rhode Island, and Pennsylvania, but are used less often in some other states with strong party systems. The differences may be the result of custom or of the varied preferences of party leaders. Caucuses appear more frequently in smaller legislative parties, and consequently more frequently in upper houses, because they become unwieldy and inefficient as a communication device in a large party. In some states the governor may encourage use of the caucus as a leadership device. Philip La Follette, Progressive governor of Wisconsin in the 1930s, used the caucus regularly to explain and defend his program to Progressive legislators; one writer describes the caucus as "a key factor behind the relentless display of party unity on vote after vote after vote."[14]

A minority party that achieves majority or near-majority strength in the legislature may adopt the caucus as a way of maintaining communication in the newly expanded group and developing an agreed position on issues in order to maximize party effectiveness. In California the Democratic party in the lower house started holding caucuses in the late 1930s, as the party won new legislative strength and captured the governorship. The practice was revived in the 1950s, when the party won majority status in the legislature, but the caucuses have been informal and not binding. The growing use of the caucus by a developing minority party may force the majority party to take similar steps in an effort to strengthen its voting cohesion. Wisconsin, Iowa, and South Dakota are among the states in which an increase in two-party competition at the legislative level has been accompanied by greater use of the caucus. Strong party leadership is possible through other institutional devices, but the caucus is effective only where the ingredients of party unity are already present.

The Congressional Caucus. Caucuses have been used in Congress intermittently since its first session, when the followers of Alexander Hamilton held meetings to reach agreement on the issues confronting

Congress. When Jefferson became President in 1801, his supporters made regular use of the caucus, which became—in the words of one authority—"the most noteworthy institution in Congress." Federalist newspapers frequently referred in scathing terms to this institution that the Jeffersonians had borrowed from the Federalists: "The Democrats in Congress are adopting of late quite an economical plan of making laws. All business is to be settled in *caucuses* before it comes before the House; and the arguments or motives be given in *newspapers* afterwards. The federal members are to be treated as nullities." The caucus was used to determine policy as well as to select candidates for Speaker and members of committees; party caucuses during the first quarter of the nineteenth century were used to nominate presidential candidates. Under Jefferson, the caucus was a device for effecting presidential leadership, and he sometimes presided at the meetings. After Henry Clay became Speaker in 1811, the House caucus became a tool of congressional leaders, under whom it remained an effective organ of party unity for several years. The caucus withered away in the years before the Civil War, because sectional conflicts caused divisions within the parties and the frustration of party leadership.[15]

Over the last century the caucus waxed and waned in Congress. It was more often an important institution in the House than in the Senate. The caucus was impotent when a party was seriously divided, and it was seldom used as a policy-making group by a party in the minority. According to Hasbrouck, "There appears to be a tendency to greater use of the caucus when a party first comes into power, before leadership has become localized in certain members of the party, or in the President." This corresponds to the pattern sometimes found in the states. Hasbrouck adds that "when there is a concentration of power in the hands of the Speaker or of other leaders, the caucus is little used."[16] Woodrow Wilson, writing in the early 1880s, emphasized diffusion of power among committee chairmen, and added: "At least there is within Congress no *visible*, and therefore no *controllable* party organization. The only bond of cohesion is the caucus, which occasionally whips a party together for cooperative action against the time for casting its vote upon some critical question."[17] As successive speakers developed the authority of that office, they began to employ the party caucus once again as a more effective body. James G. Blaine was one of the first to recognize its utility. Under Thomas B. Reed in the last decade of the century, "the caucus system never worked perfectly, but it worked effectually. It sought to commit members of the party, in secret and binding conference, to a party program agreed upon in advance of the action in the House, and it gave to the organization a powerful weapon for the coercion of recalcitrants within the party."

Conformity to the decisions of the caucus became a prerequisite for getting and keeping choice committee seats. Under Joe Cannon, the last in a series of strong Speakers, caucuses were used to ensure unity on particularly close or critical issues, but frequent caucuses appeared unnecessary because the other methods of control were so dependable.[18]

The House Democratic party took part in the 1910–1911 revolt against Speaker Cannon and helped to strip away many of his powers. In 1911 the party gained a majority in the House, and in 1913—with an increased majority—it faced the necessity of filling the power vacuum and developing the unity necessary to enact President Wilson's program. The answer of the Democratic party leadership was to use the caucus in both houses, but particularly the lower house, as the catalyst of unity. During Wilson's tenure, and particularly during his first Administration, the Democratic caucus functioned more effectively than any congressional caucus since. In Galloway's words, "The party caucus functioned as the keystone in the arch of party government in the House of Representatives."[19]

During this period the House Democratic caucus made decisions on legislative issues which were binding on Democratic members if passed by two-thirds of those voting, provided this represented a majority of the party membership. Even during this period of strict party discipline, the caucus rules provided that "no member shall be bound upon questions concerning a construction of the Constitution of the United States or upon which he made contrary pledges to his constituents prior to his election or received contrary instructions by resolutions or platform from his nominating authority." If a member decided to use one of these excuses to escape being bound, he had to give specific and prompt notice to the party leadership. Although the exemptions seem to leave wide opportunities for avoiding party discipline, in practice the caucus served with unusual effectiveness to cement party unity on major issues. Greater use of the caucus meant less independence for committees. The caucus sometimes reached agreement on the details of a bill before it was introduced, and its approval in committee became a mere formality. At times it issued instruction to committees, or to their majority membership, limiting the committees' freedom of action on certain topics. Instructions were also issued on occasion to the Rules Committee. Party control of the committees was also indicated by the frequent use of caucuses by the majority members of committees to agree on a stand to take in committee.[20]

After the House Democrats lost their majority status, their caucus quickly declined in importance; the Republican caucus flourished only briefly during the Harding Administration. The Republicans developed the *conference* as an alternative; this was a meeting of all the members without the authority to make binding decisions. In recent years the House Democratic caucus has not met more than a few times during a session, usually when a particularly important bill has been pending. Although its decisions can be made binding by a two-thirds vote, this practice has not been followed for years, and even a show of hands is rarely taken on a legislative issue. During the critical struggle over enlarging the Rules Committee in 1961, Speaker Rayburn called a Democratic caucus and won its endorsement for the proposal; he did not seek a binding decision, however, even though he probably had the necessary two-thirds majority. House Republican conferences have been called more often, particularly in recent years, with the similar purpose of generating maximum Republican unity on an issue but without any binding decisions. Republican congressmen believe that, when a vote taken in the conference indicates substantial party unity, this has a significant psychological impact on many members, particularly those without strong views or commitments.[21]

In the Senate both parties have a conference, the decisions of which are not binding on the members. The Republican conference, like its counterpart in the House, has met more frequently in recent years than the Democratic conference, and it has been more formally organized. During the latter Eisenhower years, when the Policy Committee meetings were open to all Republicans, the two institutions in effect merged for a time. The Senate Democratic conference has seldom been used in recent years to discuss policy matters. During his last years as chairman, Lyndon Johnson yielded to demands for meetings on policy questions, but the few conferences that were held were not particularly productive and the practice was abandoned.

Caucuses or conferences have been little used in recent years because both parties have been so often divided on issues that it has proved impossible to employ them as devices for binding the membership and because, in the absence of this purpose, the leadership—particularly on the Democratic side—has not considered them to be useful. Most leaders share the views of House Speaker Rayburn and Senate floor leader Mansfield that caucuses are usually "a waste of time." It is difficult to get a large turnout of congressmen because of the burden of their other responsibilities. The caucus, particularly in the House, is too large and unwieldy for meaningful debate or for the development of compromises. Disagreements in caucus are often leaked to the press, with possibly embarrassing results. A more serious liability is that, in Rayburn's words, "You lose more votes than you gain." Huitt has explained the reason: "Party members frequently stand together for different reasons, but talking about these reasons may only open old wounds and drive them apart." The party leaders prefer to negotiate compromises more quietly. Senator Mike Monroney, one of the authors of the 1946 Legislative Reorganization Act, has pointed out that the Senate adopted policy committees in 1947 precisely because caucuses led to diffusion more often than to unity in party policy. There is one final, and important, reason for the leaders' suspicion of the caucus: they view it as a device for limiting their authority or at least their freedom of action in planning tactics and negotiating compromises that may produce maximum agreement in the party.[22]

Policy Committees. The use of policy or steering committees to plan tactics or to determine party policies has not been common in most state legislatures. The leaders frequently confer among themselves, of course, but seldom in any formal way or according to any schedule. The leaders of the Administration party in both houses are likely to meet jointly with the governor. In Illinois, during the 1953–1960 period, the Republican leaders from both houses held regular weekly meetings with the Republican governor, but there were no regularly scheduled bicameral meetings of Democratic leaders. The Republicans in Rhode Island have used a policy committee for periodic conferences among the leaders of both houses and certain members of the state central committee, a practice that works well only when similar interests and viewpoints predominate in both groups.[23] Although a number of state legislative parties include a policy or steering committee in their organizational structure, the practical use of such committees varies with the preferences of the legislative leadership. In strong two-party states, caucuses are more likely to assume importance than policy committees, except perhaps where the legislative party is too large for the effective functioning of a caucus. The tasks of tactical planning, discussion, and communication of policy decisions are performed either by the caucus or by informal leadership groups. Consequently, policy committees have rarely become established components of the legislative party structure.

Most congressional institutions have greater durability than their counterparts in the states, and the larger size of congressional parties (compared to those of most states) creates greater problems of communication for the leadership. For these or other reasons, policy or steering committees have assumed greater—although intermittent—importance in Congress. When the Republicans became the majority party in the United States House in 1919, they established a Steering Committee as a part of the structure of House leadership that replaced the strong Speaker who had dominated the party before 1911. In the 1920s the House Republican leadership made considerable use of the Steering Committee as a board of strategy; in order to diversify leadership, standing committee chairmen were excluded from the Steering Committee. During the same period a Senate Republican Steering Committee existed on paper, but it seems to have been used less by the leadership. Proposals for joint meetings of the two Republican steering committees were seldom implemented in practice.[24] During the 1940s Senator Robert Taft breathed considerable life into the Senate Republican Steering Committee, but the Senate Democratic Steering Committee in that period is best described by the frequently cited phrase: "It seldom meets and never steers." A House Democratic Steering Committee was established in 1933 and served some purposes, but during the 1940s it withered from lack of use by Speaker Rayburn.

The La Follette-Monroney committee, in its 1946 report on the organization of Congress, recommended the creation of policy committees with paid staffs in the Senate and House. The version of the 1946 Legislative Reorganization Act that passed the Senate included a provision for policy committees, but in the House these were omitted as a result of the opposition of Speaker Rayburn and other leaders in both parties. The Senate established policy committees with paid staffs for the upper branch in a 1946 appropriations act. Although the House Republicans transformed their steering committee into a policy committee in 1949, it did not emerge as a functioning group until Charles Halleck became Republican leader in 1959. After Rayburn's death, efforts were made to establish a Democratic policy committee in the House, but the only result was the reestablishment, on paper, of a steering committee.[25]

The pressure for policy committees has sometimes come from rank-and-file congressmen who were dissatisfied with the leadership, but the success of the committees has always depended on the willingness of the party leadership to use them. In the House, Rayburn and Martin preferred the customary, informal techniques of leadership and distrusted formal institutions that might tend to undermine their authority. Although Martin acceded to rank-and-file pressure for the establishment of a Republican policy committee in 1949, his chairmanship of the committee guaranteed that it soon deteriorated into an ineffective discussion group meeting occasionally.[26] In the Senate, although Alben Barkley held rather regular meetings of the Democratic Policy Committee, he used it cautiously and viewed it with some suspicion as a possible limitation on his freedom and authority as a floor leader. His successors as floor leader, Scott Lucas and Ernest McFarland, relied on it more as an asset in leadership. Robert Taft saw the Republican Policy Committee primarily as a device for committing the Senate Republican party to a program that was in accord with his own views on public policy; he recognized that the Republicans needed to confront the Truman Administration with an organized program. The importance that Taft assigned to the committee was indicated by the fact that from 1947 through 1952 he chose to serve as its chairman rather than as floor leader.[27]

Whatever their views about the functions of the policy committee, the party leaders have been careful to maintain control over its membership. Membership on the nine-man Senate Democratic Policy Committee does not rotate, and consequently it has gradually come to resemble a council of elders. In 1963 it included four of the eight Democrats with the longest senatorial seniority. Barkley originally bypassed the senior members of the Senate in order to pick men who were more pliable and responsive to his leadership, and Lucas and McFarland chose men who were close to them politically and personally. Johnson tended to choose men who represented sources of power and influence in the Senate.[28] The choices made by these various leaders led to overrepresentation of the South and West and a stronger voice for senators representing the moderate viewpoint typified by Johnson. In 1959 Johnson invited the members of the Calendar Committee, which consisted of three—and later four—junior senators, to participate in the Policy Committee meetings; this added both youth and some geographic balance to the committee. In 1960 Johnson defeated a move by Senator Gore in the caucus to enlarge the Policy Committee.

Membership on the Senate Republican Policy Committee rotates, except for leaders serving in an *ex officio* capacity. Taft kept the membership of the committee largely conservative, although in 1949 he yielded to liberal pressure for an expansion of the committee to permit better representation of other viewpoints. During the Eisenhower Administration, as the committee declined in importance as a policy-planning group, its membership varied in size. At one time it was enlarged to include all members facing reelection, and during the last five years of the Administration all Republican senators were invited to attend, a practice that practically eliminated the distinction between members and nonmembers.[29]

The House Republican Policy Committee is more broadly representative than either of the Senate bodies. In addition to the *ex officio* members, the committee includes members from each of nine geographic regions in proportion to the number of Republican representatives from each region and a member representing each of the recent groups of new members (Eighty-seventh Congress, Eighty-eighth Congress, etc.). The pressure of junior members has gradually had the effect of increasing the proportion of Republicans with low seniority on the Policy Committee.[30]

There are contrasts in the operating style of the three committees. The Senate Republican Policy Committee is the most institutionalized;

its staff is the largest and carries out an elaborate research and publicity program for the Policy Committee. The committee has been chaired, not by the floor leader, but by a senior member of the party; since Taft left the chairmanship, the chairman has been clearly subordinate to the floor leader in influence but has appeared to work closely with him. The Democratic Policy Committee in the Senate has consistently been chaired by the floor leader, and its membership, without rotation, has tended to be more representative of power centers in the party. It has always been a more informal body. As one writer describes it, "The Democratic Policy Committee will meet—perhaps—once a week, and when it does the thing seems simply to happen and members will stroll in, usually late, with the air of a man dropping into another's office to have a drink and, having nothing better to do at the moment, to pass the time of day."[31] Bone has concluded that the Democratic Policy Committee is "potentially a more important device than its Republican counterpart" because it is better adapted to the informal pattern of personal negotiation that characterizes senatorial leadership, while the Republican committee "seems a bit superimposed and synthetic."[32]

Theoretically, the Republican House Policy Committee is a more informal body: it is not formally established by law and has no appropriations for its staff. In recent years, however, it has resembled the Senate Republican Policy Committee. Although its staff is a small one borrowed from other committees, it has produced some research and publicity material. Although it is dependent on the floor leader for staff and resources, it has a separate chairman. The committee meets regularly, takes formal votes on some issues, and circulates notice of its decisions to all Republican representatives. In recent years, according to Charles O. Jones, its most careful student, it has become the most effective of the policy committees on the Hill.[33]

What is the purpose of policy committees—what tasks do they actually perform? The La Follette-Monroney committee that recommended their establishment said that their purpose should be "to formulate the over-all legislative policy of the two parties." Although the committee was sensitive to "the need for freedom of action on the part of the individual Member," it expressed the belief that "if party accountability for policies and pledges is to be achieved, stronger and more formal mechanisms are necessary."[34] This perception of the policy committees' purposes has been shared by few if any of the congressmen who have served on the committees. In the case of the Administration party, members of the policy committee have recognized the validity of Taft's assertion. "When our party controls the White House, most of the Republican policy is made there anyhow." Even in the opposition party, members of the policy committee have usually doubted that it was either possible or desirable to formulate "an over-all legislative policy" that would be acceptable to most members of the party. Senate floor leader Mansfield has consistently maintained that policy "is made in the legislative committees and is determined by a majority of the members of the committees. The policy committee, so-called, cannot go against the wishes of the legislative committees. All the policy committee can do is to expedite legislation. . . ."[35]

Robert Taft was probably the only leader of a policy committee who tried to make it a vehicle for formulating policy. During his six years as chairman (1947–1952), Taft dominated the Republican Policy Committee; in White's words, "It became, and pretty correctly so, the custom to consider Taft *as* the policy committee."[36] He dominated the committee because of his detailed knowledge of legislative measures and the force and persuasiveness with which he argued for adoption of his views. When there was near unanimity on the committee and its members sensed a high level of consensus in the senatorial party, the committee often took a formal stand on a measure or an amendment, and this stand was sometimes publicized.

Others who have served on one or another of the policy committees have had a more limited view of their purpose. Jones' description of the House Republican Policy Committee fits the other committees: Its primary role is one of communication—"that of enabling the Party better to discover bases for unifying House Republicans."[37] The House Republican Policy Committee occasionally discusses bills that are still in a standing committee and expresses its views to Republican members of that committee. More often it discusses bills that have emerged from committee and listens to an explanation from members of the committee; this is an important part of the communication process. Then it becomes the Policy Committee's task to determine, through discussion, whether there is sufficient consensus in the party to justify taking a position on the measure. In Jones's words, "The Policy Committee is a device for effecting unity, not division, and there is no point in putting individual members on the spot."[38] The committee tries to find the common ground that will make an agreed position possible. If the committee can agree on a position, it must decide on the best method for implementing it (proposing an amendment, moving to recommit, etc.). The members may agree on a procedural tactic, such as trying to cut the scope and cost of a proposed program, without agreeing on the major question involved. Once a formal position is agreed on, notice of it is sent to all House Republicans. Occasionally the decisions are announced publicly.

Lyndon Johnson had similar views about the function of the Senate Democratic Policy Committee, but he used it in a much less formal, more personal way. Bone's description of the committee under Johnson is an apt one: "In Democratic circles on the Hill the Democratic Policy Committee is often spoken of as the 'personal staff of Senator Johnson.' "[39] Johnson used the members of the committee to assist him in finding a basis for unity and compromise in the party and to rally support for a measure embodying that compromise. The committee, meeting less regularly, took formal stands on issues less often and did not follow any formal procedure for notifying rank-and-file members of its decisions. Public statements by the committee were rare. Johnson was particularly sensitive to the danger that formal stands by the committee, even if unpublicized, might drive away potential Republican votes from the measure being supported. Johnson adapted the committee to his own personal style of leadership, and in that sense made it an effective vehicle of communication and consensus; however, his techniques did not enhance the value of the committee as an institution.[40]

If the policy committee of the Administration party cannot be an effective policy body, it still can perform a useful service as a channel of communication. During the Eisenhower Administration, Republican leaders in the Senate used the Policy Committee as a liaison device. They developed the practice of reporting to the Policy Committee on their weekly meetings at the White House, and the committee served as a forum in which the reactions of senators could be expressed and their views reported at subsequent White House meetings. Occasionally cabinet members attended the meetings to give briefings and exchange views. For these reasons all Republican senators were eventually invited to attend the meetings. When the House Republican Policy Committee was revived during the last two years of the Eisenhower Administration, it served a similar function.[41] The Senate Democratic Policy Committee during Democratic Administrations has not assumed comparable liaison tasks, although its members have sometimes been briefed on White House meetings; its primary duties have been to plan tactics and schedule legislation.

It is difficult to prove what success the policy committees have had in unifying the parties, since the committees avoid taking a stand unless there is already substantial unity in the party. There is evidence that the members of policy committees are more likely than nonmembers to support the decisions of these groups; sometimes members will go along with decisions that we would not expect them to accept if they were not members. Jones found that House Republicans as a whole provided over 90 percent support for decisions of the House Republican Policy Committee in 1961 and 1962. The greatest unity came when its recommendation was for outright opposition to a measure supported by the Kennedy Administration. In the Senate, during the period of

Taft's chairmanship, there were sometimes instances of Republican senators giving unanimous or virtually unanimous support to a recommendation of the Policy Committee concerning a measure that would not normally generate such unity; in a few cases its recommendations appeared to be ignored.[42]

Party Organs as Instruments for Control of the Leadership. Party leaders in Congress have used policy committees and caucuses when and to the extent that these organs have served them. There have been efforts in recent years by some members of Congress to reshape them into instruments through which the party leaders can be made more responsible to, and more clearly controlled by, the rank-and-file congressmen. A few liberal Democratic senators have tried, and failed, to accomplish three things: to strengthen the caucus (or conference), to strengthen the policy committee, and to make various party organs more broadly representative—that is, more representative of liberal viewpoints. These efforts were most pronounced during the last two years of the Eisenhower Administration; they resulted from dissatisfaction both with the style of Johnson's leadership and with his failure to advance more boldly certain of the liberal programs sought by some members of the Senate Democratic party.

The boldest and broadest attack on Johnson's leadership was launched by Senator William Proxmire in 1959. He put into words the sense of frustration that underlay this criticism of Johnson's leadership when he complained that

The typical Democratic Senator has literally nothing to do with determining the legislative program and policies of this party in the Senate. . . . The cold fact is that Democratic policy in the Senate is made entirely on an ad lib, off-the-cuff basis. The initiative as well as the final decision is almost always resolved by the majority leader himself on the basis of his own judgment of what is desirable and what is possible. . . . And the critical point is that he does it without the overall conscious guidance of Senate Democrats either in caucus or in policy committee.[43]

To remedy this situation, Proxmire relied primarily on the party conference. He proposed that a conference should be held on all major issues and that, in most cases, the questions facing the conference should be put to a vote. It is significant that neither Proxmire, nor any other senator who proposed revival of the conference, suggested that its votes should be *binding* on members of the senatorial party. Proxmire did believe that decisions of the conference should be binding on the floor leader; should he be unwilling to implement these decisions, he should let the assistant floor leader take the reins while the measure was before the Senate. Proxmire's concept of the conference was clearly that of an organ for restricting the floor leader's freedom of action, but it was not widely shared among Democratic senators.[44] A year later a group of five liberal Democrats (Proxmire, Humphrey, Douglas, Clark, and McNamara) made a more modest proposal—that conferences be held more regularly. Johnson headed off formal action to this effect by agreeing to hold conferences whenever any senator requested it. Although several conferences were held in succeeding weeks, the failure of this device to become an established pattern reflects a growing recognition, even among the liberals, that the conference is awkward and inefficient as a communication device, as well as the reluctance of nearly all senators to follow Proxmire's plan of binding the floor leader through formal conference decisions.

A second proposal of the liberal Democrats was to strengthen the Policy Committee. Senator Proxmire criticized the committee because it did not draft an over-all legislative policy, but his primary attention was focused on the conference. A year later, in 1960, Senator Albert Gore offered a motion in the Democratic conference to make the Policy Committee's membership larger and more representative and to define its function clearly as that of making party policy. In explaining his proposal on the floor of the Senate, Gore made it clear that he wanted to restore to the committee the purpose envisioned for it by the La Follette-Monroney committee in 1946: "I want to have formulated a legislative policy of the Democratic party." Moreover, Gore criticized the view that the Policy Committee "is merely an arm of the Democratic leadership of the Senate"; in his view "the Democratic policy committee is, or should be, an agent of the conference of Democratic senators." Gore won only 12 votes for his motion in the Democratic conference; most Democratic senators were unwilling to challenge Lyndon Johnson's leadership and/or did not view the Policy Committee as a policy-making body.[45]

A part of Gore's defeated proposal was to enlarge the Policy Committee membership in order to make it more representative, and to provide for the election of new members by the conference rather than their appointment by the floor leader. This part of his proposal was renewed in 1961. At that time, as a compromise, the Democratic conference agreed that members of the Policy Committee, and of the Steering Committee as well, should be nominated by the floor leader and approved by the conference membership, and that both committees should be representative of variations in geography and viewpoint in the senatorial party. There was no increase in membership and no rotation. The victory of liberal Democratic senators appeared to be an empty one, however, as long as the powers of the committee were not increased, and Floor Leader Mansfield was clearly opposed to such a step.

In 1963, when Senator Joseph Clark launched his attack on what he called the "Senate establishment," he concentrated his efforts on changing the Steering Committee. Clark realistically decided that control of major standing committees was more important than control of the policy committees. He tried unsuccessfully to persuade the Senate to enlarge several of these committees. Within the Democratic caucus he tried in vain to enlarge the Steering Committee, which determines assignments on standing committees.[46]

The revolt against Johnson's leadership failed in part because he was an effective leader, and Democratic senators were reluctant to damage that effectiveness, even though some of them disagreed with his policies. Successful legislative leadership demands a high level of flexibility and finesse. If the policy committee, or the caucus, is used as a policy-making body rather than as an instrument of communication, it almost inevitably becomes a straitjacket for the floor leader. Johnson was a successful leader, and as Senator Monroney said, "In Oklahoma when we win six years in a row, we simply do not consider changing the split-T formation," and neither—he might have added—do we start voting on plays in the huddle.

The 1959 revolt in the House Republican party resulted from a widespread belief that floor leader Joe Martin's leadership had become ineffective. It also resulted from a desire among more junior Republicans to make their voices heard by the leadership. Some of those who supported Charles Halleck in his contest against Martin made the revival of the Policy Committee a condition for their support. Halleck responded to this pressure by reestablishing the committee under the leadership of John W. Byrnes and giving it his support. Continued dissatisfaction with the leadership led to a second revolt in 1963, during which the rebels chose Gerald R. Ford (who subsequently replaced Halleck in 1965) as chairman of the party conference, succeeding Charles A. Hoeven. At the same time the rebels were able to increase the representation of junior members on the Policy Committee. It is noteworthy that Republican rebels were not seeking to make either the Policy Committee or the conference into a policy-making group, the decisions of which would be binding on either the rank-and-file or the leadership. Their objectives were to strengthen these two groups as organs of communication through which the leadership could become more aware of and more sensitive to the viewpoints of the rank-and-file. There seems to have been some confusion about whether the Policy Committee or the conference was more effective for this purpose, but the Policy Committee has been used more regularly because its smaller size makes its use more feasible. Such institutional devices cannot guarantee that the leadership will be sensitive to rank-and-file opinion, however accurately communicated; thus, the dissatisfaction persisted in

Republican ranks and led initially to the replacement of one member of the leadership, the conference chairman, and later to Halleck's removal.

Interviews with a substantial number of congressmen several years ago revealed that junior members of the House were concerned about the weakness of communication in the House: "Those who are in control run the legislative program without much consultation. Certainly they haven't always been responsive." "One of the real problems here is that we don't know the party position except on something like the override of the veto." "A lack of communication is also apparent in connection with committee activities. There are so many non-major issues coming before us that it is impossible to keep up." Congressmen, particularly the younger members, not only wanted better opportunities to express their viewpoints to the leaders; they also wanted the leaders to keep them better informed both about party positions and about general legislative developments.[47]

It was the strength of these sentiments that led Republican representatives to choose new leadership that was pledged to revive both the Policy Committee and the conference in the House. Democratic representatives, however, although they were agreed on the need for better communication, were divided about the institutional remedies. Some favored the holding of frequent caucuses: "The leadership is opposed to the caucus idea, but a discussion group caucus rather than a policy making caucus would be very helpful to me and others." "True, there might be dog fights, and we might come out worse in some respects, but on the whole it would be worth it. It is very important to have an expression from all House members." Others accepted the view of the leadership that the caucus, at least for the Democrats, would be likely to intensify differences in the party; some felt that "if you have good leadership which gives you results, there is no need for a caucus." Democratic members at that time showed little interest in the development of a policy committee and little understanding of its functions.[48] The failure of the 1962 effort by some liberal Democrats to get such a committee established resulted not only from the opposition of party leadership but also from the failure of many junior members to recognize its potential value.

NOTES

1. *Book of the States, 1964–65* (Chicago, 1964), pp. 51–53.
2. Eugene C. Lee, *The Presiding Officer and Rules Committee in Legislatures of the United States* (Berkeley, 1952), pp. 19, 23, 26, 34–36.

3. George B. Galloway, *History of the House of Representatives* (New York, 1961), pp. 134–55; George R. Brown, *The Leadership of Congress* (Indianapolis, 1922), chaps. 6, 11, 12.

4. Milton C. Cummings, Jr., and Robert L. Peabody, "The Decision to Enlarge the Committee on Rules: An Analysis of the 1961 Vote," in Robert L. Peabody and Nelson W. Polsby (eds.), *New Perspectives on the House of Representatives* (Chicago, 1963), pp. 167–94; Neil MacNeil, *Forge of Democracy* (New York, 1963), chap. 15.

5. Galloway, *op. cit.*, pp. 150–55.

6. Robert L. Peabody, "The Enlarged Rules Committee," in Peabody and Polsby, *op. cit.*, pp. 133–45.

7. *Ibid.*, pp. 145–51, quote at p. 148.

8. James A. Robinson, "The Role of the Rules Committee in Arranging the Program of the U.S. House of Representatives," *Western Political Quarterly*, XII (1959), 653–69.

9. James A. Robinson, "The Role of the Rules Committee in Regulating Debate in the U.S. House of Representatives," *Midwest Journal of Political Science*, V (1961), 59–69.

10. Belle Zeller (ed.), *American State Legislatures* (New York, 1954), pp. 194–97.

11. Duane Lockard, *New England State Politics* (Princeton, N.J., 1959), pp. 281–82.

12. J. C. Wahlke et al., *The Legislative System* (New York, 1962), pp. 55–56.

13. Bennett M. Rich, *The Government and Administration of New Jersey* (New York, 1957), pp. 80–81.

14. David Carley, "Legal and Extra-legal Powers of Wisconsin Governors in Legislative Relations," *Wisconsin Law Review*, vol. 1962, p. 285.

15. Ralph V. Harlow, *The History of Legislative Methods in the Period before 1825* (New Haven, 1917), pp. 143–45, 183–91, 205–06; Galloway, *op. cit.*, pp. 128–31.

16. Paul D. Hasbrouck, *Party Government in the House of Representatives* (New York, 1927), p. 28.

17. Woodrow Wilson, *Congressional Government* (Cleveland, 1956), p. 80.

18. Brown, *op. cit.*, p. 92; Hasbrouck, *op. cit.*, p. 28.

19. Galloway, *op. cit.*, p. 137.

20. Wilder H. Haines, "The Congressional Caucus of Today," *American Political Science Review*, IX (1915), 696–706.

21. Cummings and Peabody, *op. cit.*, p. 175; Charles L. Clapp, *The Congressman* (Washington: The Brookings Institution, 1963), p. 298.

22. MacNeil, *op. cit.*, p. 109; Ralph K. Huitt, "Democratic Party Leadership in the Senate," *American Political Science Review*, LV (1961), 341; *Congressional Record*, Mar. 9, 1959, p. 3562.

23. Gilbert Y. Steiner and Samuel K. Gove, *Legislative Politics in Illinois* (Urbana, 1960), pp. 12–13; Duane Lockard, *op. cit.*, p. 218.

24. Paul D. Hasbrouck, *op. cit.*, pp. 92–96; Brown, *op. cit.*, pp. 212–19, 252–72.

25. Hugh A. Bone, "An Introduction to the Senate Policy Committees," *American Political Science Review*, L (1956), pp. 341–42; Charles O. Jones, *Party and Policy-making: The House Republican Policy Committee* (New Brunswick, N.J., 1964), chap. 2.

26. Jones, *loc. cit.*

27. Bone, *op. cit.*, pp. 342–45; Malcolm E. Jewell, *Senatorial Politics and Foreign Policy* (Lexington, Ky., 1962), chap. 5.

28. Huitt, *op. cit.*, pp. 341–42.

29. Jewell, *loc cit.*

30. Jones, *op. cit.*, chap. 3.

31. William S. White, *Citadel: The Story of the U.S. Senate* (New York, 1957), p. 210.

32. Bone, *op. cit.*, p. 357.

33. Jones, *op. cit.*, chap. 1.

34. U.S. Congress, Joint Committee on the Organization of Congress, *Organization of Congress*, Report No. 1011, 79th Cong., 2nd Sess., 1946, p. 12.

35. William S. White, *The Taft Story* (New York, 1954), p. 215; the Mansfield quotation is from the *Congressional Record*, Jan. 11, 1960, p. 236.

36. White, *The Taft Story*, p. 61.

37. Jones, *op. cit.*, p. 7.

38. *Ibid.*, p. 72.

39. Bone, *op. cit.*, p. 344.

40. *Ibid.*, pp. 352, 357; Jewell, *op. cit.*, pp. 101–04.

41. Jewell, *op. cit.*, pp. 91–96; Jones, *op. cit.*, chap. 4.

42. Jewell, *op. cit.*, pp. 86–90, 106–09; Jones, *op. cit.*, chap. 4.

43. *Congressional Record*, Feb. 23, 1959, p. 2814; Mar. 9, 1959, p. 3559.

44. *Congressional Record*, Feb. 23, 1959, pp. 2814–20; Mar. 9, 1959, p. 3566.

45. *Congressional Record*, Jan. 11, 1960, pp. 228, 235.

46. Joseph S. Clark, *The Senate Establishment* (New York, 1963). This volume contains the text of relevant discussions on the floor of the Senate from the *Congressional Record*.

47. Clapp, *op. cit.*, p. 292.

48. *Ibid.*, pp. 299–301.

[9]

The Committee Structure

COMMITTEES are an integral part of the legislature. They are used to facilitate the performance of significant legislative tasks, but the nature and scope of these tasks and the independent power exercised by committees vary greatly from one legislative body to another. The increasing complexity and variety of the issues that face legislatures place greater demands on the legislators' time and necessitate specialization and the division of labor. This is the purpose most universally served by committees. The committee system is the best method that legislators have been able to devise to provide careful and discriminating scrutiny of proposed legislation and legislative oversight of executive agencies. The committee system is the main line of defense relied on by congressmen and state legislators to halt the twentieth-century trends that threaten to turn legislative bodies into rubber stamps for the executive. The authors of the 1946 Legislative Reorganization Act, who were interested in enabling Congress to play a stronger role vis-a-vis the President, sought to achieve this aim primarily through making the committee system more effective: streamlining the structure, clarifying the jurisdiction of each committee, improving the staffs, and permitting congressmen to concentrate more of their time on fewer committees.

The committee has other functions. It is a vital link in the communications network essential to any legislative system, the main channel used by executive agencies for conveying information and proposals to the legislature. The committee plays a part in the establishment of norms and the allocation of roles to legislators (as described in Chapter 18). The committee, through its public hearings, provides a cathartic—

or safety-valve—mechanism for the expression of group and individual viewpoints. Committee members, and occasionally a whole committee, often serve as representatives or spokesmen for interests more effectively than would be possible without the committee system. To the extent that legislative bodies perform adjudicative functions (settling individual grievances or investigating crimes), this work is usually done in committee.

The two most important functions of legislative committees with respect to the larger political system are the making of decisions with regard to legislation and the authorization and oversight of administrative actions. It is in the exercise of these two functions that we find the greatest variety among legislative bodies. If legislators frequently follow the advice of committees, this means that the most important legislative decisions are usually made in committees—that legislative power is decentralized. If the committees are effective in administrative oversight, the executive may have to take its cues in policy making from these committees rather than from laws passed by the whole legislature. In both cases, the committees become the primary source of legislative leadership.

In the preceding chapters we have described another source of leadership: the political parties or factions that are found in most legislative bodies. There is an inherent contradiction between party and committee leadership. Party leadership is centralized; committee leadership is decentralized. Where committees are strong and independent, party leadership is weak. Where party leadership is strong, the committees are either weak or simply agents of the party leaders.

In the British House of Commons, where the political parties are strong and unified, the committees are relatively weak. The standing committees are large, they lack continuing jurisdiction over specific substantive areas, and they have a fluctuating membership. They are not sources of power but vehicles for detailed work. One authority has given this description:

Committees are utterly subordinate to the whole House in their status and role. They do not possess the power of life and death over bills such as is enjoyed by the committees of the U.S. Congress or even Continental legislatures. They are lowly handmaidens to help clean up amendments, and their work is sandwiched in between Second Reading of an *already formulated* bill and Report (to the House) and Third Reading, when their work will be reviewed.[1]

Party leaders have resisted efforts to increase the role of committees in the House of Commons because they realize that this would undermine party control and create barriers to the smooth and orderly approval of legislation proposed by the ruling party.

By contrast, the committees of Congress are strong, proud, and independent. Some of them date back to the early days of the Republic. The jurisdiction of each committee is carefully defined in the standing rules of the two houses, which were made more explicit by the 1946 Legislative Reorganization Act. Each committee jealously guards its jurisdictional prerogatives. The senior members of committees have often served twenty years or more, long enough to have become experts in the field, well able to handle the complexities of modern legislation and capable of holding their own in encounters with officials of the executive departments. Each committee determines its own rules and operating procedures, giving the chairman more or less power as it sees fit. The committees determine what bills will be reported out and which will be buried in obscurity, and congressional rules and traditions offer only the narrowest of opportunities for a congressional majority to extricate a bill that has been buried in committee. Favorable committee recommendations are not always followed on the floor of Congress, but the greater the strength of committee support for legislation, the greater its chances for passage.

The weakness of the party system in Congress results directly, although not entirely, from the independent strength of committees. Although the majority party has proportionate majorities in each committee, party lines are often crossed in the voting within committee, and party leaders have great difficulty persuading members to follow their wishes with regard to bills in committee when the views of these committee members are substantially different. The seniority system used in selecting committee chairmen frequently promotes to the chairmanship a man who is out of step with the opinion of his party with respect to the issues under his jurisdiction, yet the seniority tradition protects him from the loss of his post, however heretical his views.

The congressional committee system is duplicated at the state level in form, but not usually in substance. The committees in state legislatures bear subject-matter titles similar to those in Congress, but jurisdictional rules and traditions are weaker, and legislative leaders may assign most of the important bills—whatever their subject—to a few dependable committees. State legislative committees do not have the time and the staff for a careful, expert scrutiny of bills. Most legislatures lack a strong seniority system; consequently, the committees lack the hard core of veteran members, independent of party control, who can make a committee both expert and independently powerful.

The fact that state legislative committees are usually not independent centers of power does not mean that their role is insignificant. They may provide the means for the dominant faction or party to control the legislative process, through the party leaders who chair the important committees and the loyal party majorities on these committees. In other states the committee role may be a more perfunctory one, as the members concern themselves with technical details and perfecting amendments to a bill. In most states there is strong party or factional leadership in the legislature, and the committee system is designed not to conflict with that leadership.

There are several factors that provide clues to the function of committees. Each will bear some analysis. The first is simply the committee structure in legislative bodies. The second is the method of choosing committee members and chairmen. The third is the internal structure of committees, including the role of the chairman and the part played by subcommittees.

THE STRUCTURE OF COMMITTEES

Congress. The three major categories of congressional committees are: standing or permanent committees; special or select committees; joint committees representing both houses. Conference committees, used to adjust Senate-House differences over the terms of a bill which has passed both houses, are ad hoc groups selected from the standing committees which had original jurisdiction over the bill in both houses.

The standing committees are the most important, because of their permanence and because, as a rule, they are the only ones that can report bills. In its earliest sessions, Congress relied primarily on a large variety of select committees, but these gradually declined in importance during the nineteenth century. The first standing committees were established in 1789; by 1822 there were 15 standing committees in the Senate and 19 in the House. Many of these have persisted in name and function to the present. The number of committees grew until in 1946 the Senate had 33 and the House had 48.[2] This increase gave more congressmen a chance to chair committees, but it had several disadvantages. Congressmen, particularly members of the Senate, often found it impossible to attend meetings of all their committees (sometimes two or three at one time), to say nothing of devoting careful attention to the work of each. Some senators were on as many as ten committees. The large number of committees hampered the effort to provide better and larger staffs for all. The proliferation of committees had created jurisdictional disputes and inequitable workloads.

The 1946 Legislative Reorganization Act reduced the number of Senate committees from 33 to 15, and the House committees from 48 to 19. Since that time, each house has added just one committee, in 1958, to deal with problems of science, astronautics, and space (See Table

9.1). The reduction in committees was not easily accomplished, because it meant not only the abolition of 47 chairmanships but also thwarting the ambition of countless other members, who lost high seniority posts

Table 9.1. STANDING COMMITTEES IN CONGRESS*

Senate	House
Foreign Relations	Rules
Finance	Ways and Means
Commerce	Appropriations
Judiciary	
Appropriations	Foreign Affairs
Armed Services	Armed Services
Agriculture and Forestry	Interstate and Foreign Commerce
Interior and Insular Affairs	Judiciary
Banking and Currency	Agriculture
Labor and Public Welfare	Education and Labor
Public Works	Banking and Currency
	Public Works
	Post Office and Civil Service
	Science and Astronautics
Government Operations	Un-American Activities
Rules and Administration	District of Columbia
Post Office and Civil Service	Interior and Insular Affairs
District of Columbia	House Administration
Aeronautical and Space Sciences	Government Operations
	Merchant Marine and Fisheries
	Veterans' Affairs

* Senate committees are divided into major and minor committees, and those in the House are divided into three categories—exclusive, semiexclusive, and non-exclusive. Within each category committees are listed in order of the desirability of assignment to the committee, based on data concerning transfers among committees, with the more recent space committees listed last.

SOURCES: Adapted from George Goodwin, Jr., "The Seniority System in Congress," *American Political Science Review*, LIII (1959), 433; and Nicholas A. Masters, "Committee Assignments in the House of Representatives," *American Political Science Review*, LV (1961), 353.

on vanishing committees. The accomplishment of committee reform in the face of these obstacles testifies to the importance of the committee structure in the minds of congressmen. They believed that reform was necessary to revitalize the committee organization and they accomplished it.

Select, or special, committees of Congress are temporary, lasting only during the life of the Congress in which they were created. Their function is normally one of study and investigation, and, with occasional exceptions, they do not have the power to report bills to the Senate or House. As originally drafted, the Legislative Reorganization Act of 1946 banned the use of select committees; the Senate approved that version of the bill, but in the House this prohibition was removed.

The select committees in the House have four major purposes: to serve interest groups that feel they lack access to standing committees, to serve individual congressmen or make use of their particular talents, to evade standing committees when circumstances make it necessary, and to perform specific duties in areas of overlapping committee jurisdiction. In both houses a Select Committee on Small Business, which clearly serves a particular economic interest, has become a perennial committee, although theoretically it is still a select one. The space committees in both houses started out as select committees and later became standing committees, designed to deal with a new field that overlapped existing committees. The House Un-American Activities Committee was also initially a select committee. After the Marshall Plan was proposed in 1947, the Republican House leadership created a Select Committee on Foreign Aid, popularly known as the Herter committee, to study the question. The leadership bypassed the House Foreign Affairs Committee in an effort to get a more independent and critical evaluation of the aid program from a group that was broadly representative of opinion in the House.[3]

Since select committees cannot normally report legislation to Congress, what part can they play in the legislative system? Sometimes their recommendations lead to legislation. When this occurs, it is not because the select committees themselves are powerful. On occasion, however, the leaders of the committee do have the power and prestige necessary to win support in the standing committees and on the floor of both houses for legislation that has had its genesis in a select committee. In addition to its legislative role, the select committee may have an educational, promotional, or representative role, serving to lay the groundwork for long-run legislative objectives. The role of select committees in Congress might be compared with that of third parties in a two-party system. They serve individual or group interests that are not being served by the standing committee structure; sometimes, they promote causes effectively enough so that the standing committees must give attention to them. Despite their persistence on the congressional scene, however, they have neither displaced nor challenged the dominant position of standing committees in the structure of Congress.

Congress has not made extensive use of joint committees or joint action by the standing committees. It is often argued that joint hearings would save the time of Administration witnesses, but occasional experiments with such hearings have convinced members of both houses that this technique minimizes the chance that each congressman has for raising questions, because the joint committees are so large. Moreover, House members feel handicapped in joint hearings with senators, who have greater prestige. Though the professional staffs of the committees often cooperate and exchange information, the use of joint staffs is discouraged because one committee or the other might have its control over the staff diluted. Whatever the advantages of conducting committee activities jointly, these are obviously outweighed by the spirit of bicameralism, the jealously guarded prerogatives of the two Houses, and the significant differences in attitudes, operating procedures, and vested interests of Senate and House members.

The few existing joint committees of Congress resemble the select committees in their powers and purposes. They do not have the power to report bills to the Senate and House. They are used primarily to carry out studies and investigations or to supervise the work of administrative agencies. The Joint Economic Committee, for example, holds extensive hearings and makes recommendations to Congress on the President's annual economic report. The Joint Committee on Internal Revenue Taxation is composed of senior members from the taxing committees in the Senate and House, and provides a vehicle for them to coordinate activities and supervise a staff of taxation experts. Several other joint committees perform primarily housekeeping functions (Printing, Library, Disposition of Executive Papers, for example).

A unique example of a joint committee with power equal to or greater than that of most standing committees is the Joint Committee on Atomic Energy. This is the only joint committee that is authorized to report legislation. Its most important activities have been nonlegislative: supervising the atomic energy program and goading the administration into developing that program along the lines set by the committee. In this field the committee has been unusually vigorous and effective. Senator Henry M. Jackson has claimed that "in the case of certain vital policy decisions the urging from the Joint Committee has played so powerful a role that it can be said the Committee made the decisions, with the advice and consent of the executive branch."[4] The Joint Committee, established by the 1946 Atomic Energy Act, draws some of its power from specific provisions of that act (with 1954 amendments), which give it complete jurisdiction over atomic energy legislation, authority to make "continuing studies" of the atomic energy field and to make use of facilities of the executive department in its investigations, and the right to "be fully and currently informed" with regard to all activities of the Atomic Energy Commission and relevant activities of the Defense

Department. Moreover, the joint nature of its organization has given the committee stronger bargaining power with the Administration and greater influence in Congress.[5] The committee has sometimes been hampered by the rivalries between senators and representatives that have weakened other joint committees. In 1953 this led to a deadlock over the chairmanship, which was resolved after three months by agreement to rotate the chairmanship every two years between the Senate and House. Since the elimination of that divisive issue, the remaining undercurrent of friction has not been serious enough to damage the committee's effectiveness.[6] The authors of an excellent study on the committee conclude: "The Joint Committee on Atomic Energy is, in terms of its sustained influence in Congress, its impact and influence on the Executive, and its accomplishments, probably the most powerful Congressional committee in the history of the nation."[7]

State Legislatures. There has been a trend in the states toward the reduction in number and rationalization of committees, as shown in Table 9.2. From 1946 to 1963 the median number of Senate committees

Table 9.2. COMMITTEES IN STATE LEGISLATURES

| No. Standing Committees | No. States, Each Range | | | |
| | House | | Senate | |
	1946	1963	1946	1963
10 or under	0	5	0	5
11–20	2	15	8	21
21–30	9	16	15	18
31–40	15	4	13	4
41–50	12	8	9	2
51–60	7	1	2	0
61–70	2	0	1	0

SOURCE: *Book of the States, 1964–1965* (Chicago: Council of State Governments, 1964), p. 40.

dropped from 31 to 20, and in the House the reduction was from 39 to 22.[8] In sharp contrast to Congress, state legislatures operate in a procedural jungle when it comes to committee jurisdiction over bills. The legislative leaders frequently make it a practice to assign most of the important bills to a few committees, which often bear such vague titles as Executive and Legislative Affairs, Judiciary, or State Government. These are the committees dominated by members loyal to the legislative leadership. The result is that some committees are burdened with bills and others remain inoperative; some members are overworked and others have little to do when the committee sessions are held.

Connecticut, Massachusetts, and Maine have used joint committees for most legislative business for many years with considerable success. In the other states, however, joint committees are used only occasionally. The joint committee permits more careful consideration of bills without duplication of effort, offers better opportunities for hearings, and makes feasible more staff assistance. Joint committees might not appear feasible when different parties control the two houses, but in Connecticut, where this situation frequently prevails, the rules permit either the Senate or House members to report a bill separately to their chamber if joint approval in committee proves impossible. The success of the experiment in a few states has not contributed to its wider use in legislative bodies.

CHOICE OF COMMITTEE MEMBERS AND CHAIRMEN

The best clue to the part played by committees in a legislative system is the technique used to choose, and to retain or replace, committee members. When a legislative body is under tight control by party or factional leaders, these leaders will choose the members of key committees and even replace them with more loyal members if necessary. If power is decentralized, however, the committees may become the loci of power, and the members may have secured tenure on the committees.

In legislatures with two effective parties, the partisan make-up of committees approximates the proportions found in the house as a whole, and the chairman is normally a member of the majority party. In Congress this formula is adhered to closely, except for the Rules Committee, with a 2 to 1 majority; the Ways and Means and Appropriations committees had 3 to 2 majorities until the Democrats insisted on a larger proportion commensurate with their increased House majority in 1965. In state legislatures, even where both parties are strong, the formula is less exact. The majority party often has more than its share of committee seats, particularly on the more powerful committees. In Pennsylvania, for example, the majority party has maintained majorities of approximately 2 to 1 on committees, despite the fact that majorities in both houses have usually been very narrow in recent years.

In state legislatures that have weak party groups or are dominated by a single party, party membership may have little to do with committee assignments and the choice of chairmen. In California, where the tradition of legislative nonpartisanship (which lasted until the mid-thirties) extended to committee assignments, the majority party in recent years has had a majority on all committees but has not always held all chairmanships. In the California House this sometimes results from commitments made by a candidate for Speaker in his effort to win the votes of minority members.[9] In Kentucky, the Senate has sometimes established enough committees to give each member, including Republicans, a chairmanship, but in the House the Democratic majority has denied chairmanships and sometimes even seats on major committees to the growing Republican minority. The habit of giving occasional chairmanships to the minority Republican party in Arizona ended with the growth of the minority contingent in the House to greater numerical importance.[10] Among the other states where the minority party has sometimes held chairmanships are Washington, Oregon, Oklahoma, and Vermont.

We have already noted the inherent contradiction between party and committee leadership. Where the majority party leadership is strong, it must achieve its purposes in one of two ways: either by minimizing the importance of committees in the legislative process or by controlling membership on the committees. It may combine these techniques by bypassing some committees and assigning important bills to those committees that it controls.

State Legislative Committees. Seniority plays a relatively small part in the choice of committee members in most legislatures, primarily because a large proportion of legislators are freshmen and few of them have as much as ten years of seniority. In seeking choice committee assignments, freshmen may be handicapped, but they are not so completely excluded as their counterparts in Congress. Although the more senior legislators are likely to win chairmanships, in most states other factors assume greater importance than seniority in the choice of chairmen. Several years ago a survey showed that seniority was an important factor in the choice of chairmen in only fourteen senates and twelve houses.[11] There are only a few states in which committee chairmen have an assurance of continuity in their positions which approaches that enjoyed by chairmen in Congress.

The criteria used by the leadership in picking chairmen and the members of major committees include competence, experience in the subject matter, the maintenance of geographical balance, and an effort to respect the desires of members. In some states the legislative rules define the pertinent criteria. In California, seniority, preference, experience, and geographical balance are specified, and in Kentucky the rules require proportional geographic and partisan distribution of committee assignments (a requirement that is not always observed). In most state legislatures, however, the leadership is primarily interested in choosing chairmen and members of major committees who are loyal to the interests and sympathetic to the viewpoints of the majority and its leadership. If some or all committees are crucial in the legislative process, the leadership will pick members with great care. It should also be recognized that some committees, and in some states most committees, rarely handle important legislation or rarely make critical decisions on legislation. Appointments to such committees are likely to be made in a casual, haphazard manner. Once the major appointments have been determined, the leadership may be willing to follow the preferences of legislators almost entirely with regard to other committee assignments.

In states with strong legislative parties, the party leadership—occasionally with the help of the governor or party officials outside the legislature—chooses the committee chairmen and members. Seniority is usually of little importance. Members and even chairmen may be removed from important committees because their voting record is undependable or because they have proven to be inept. Pennsylvania is a good example of such a strong-party legislature. The party leaders are primarily concerned with picking chairmen, because in that legislature the chairman is the dominant force in the committee. The leaders seek men of demonstrated ability and loyalty, but in making appointments they must also maintain regional balance and recognize the claim of large-county delegations to some chairmanships. The more senior members head House committees and the major Senate committees, because they have had greater opportunity to demonstrate legislative skill and because seniority often provides a standard for balancing the claims of rival county delegations. But seniority does not determine the choice of specific chairmen; neither does it protect a chairman who has proven to be unsatisfactory to the leadership.[12]

In some legislatures, where parties are less important, the Speaker or Senate president makes committee assignments primarily on the basis of the legislator's loyalty to the majority coalition or faction headed by the presiding officer. Sometimes the dominant coalition represents identifiable regions of interests; in other cases it may be little more than a personal faction organized by the presiding officer. Particularly in the latter case, the presiding officer may have promised committee posts in order to win the votes necessary for his selection. This pattern of committee selection, though varying from state to state, is a common one in states lacking strong legislative parties. In recent years the Speaker of the Arizona House has been chosen by one Democratic faction, sometimes in coalition with the Republican delegation. Members of the majority coalition receive all or nearly all the assignments to major committees and the chairmanships. A turnover in the majority coalition has sometimes led to a complete replacement of committee chairmen.[13] A similar pattern of factional control is evident in the nonpartisan

Minnesota legislature, which is organized into Conservative and Liberal caucuses. In 1959 the majority Conservative caucus in the Senate held all seats on the Committee on Committees and the Committee on Rules, as well as a disproportionate majority and chairmanship of all other major committees.[14] In Florida an interlocking directorate of legislative leaders and committee chairmen has frequently dominated the legislature and provided firm leadership to the rural majority. In 1959, for example, 13 senators (out of 38) held 49 seats, including all chairmanships, on 6 important committees.[15] Texas provides a good example of a personal coalition constructed by the House Speaker, usually along liberal–conservative lines. Legislators who supported the Speaker in his campaign for that post receive the preferred committee assignments. Late in 1961 the Texas House amended its rules to provide that one-fourth of the committee assignments (but not chairmanships) were to be made on the basis of preference according to seniority. The change was repealed in the next session, before it took effect, when a new Speaker took office with strong majority support.[16]

Although the governor is likely to have an indirect influence on major committee assignments in strong-party legislatures, the best examples of gubernatorial determination occur in a few one-party states. In Alabama, Georgia, Tennessee, and Kentucky, at least, the governor is carefully consulted by the legislative leaders, who themselves have been chosen in line with the governor's wishes.

There are a few states in which senior legislators are able to gain and hold committee chairmanships on the basis of seniority. This is more often the case in a state senate. The rules of the New Mexico Senate state that seniority "shall prevail at all times in committee assignments, and the chairmen of committees shall be appointed by request of the senior members." In Virginia the chairmen of key committees in both houses have been men with ten or twenty years' seniority who have often held these chairmanships for many sessions and have not moved from one chairmanship to another. In the South Carolina Senate, similar power is exercised by a small group of senior senators, but there is some mobility from one chairmanship to another. In these two states the senior members ought to be able to use their chairmanships as independent bases of power, but in both states a small group of senior men exercise a form of collective leadership that precludes much conflict between chairmen and other legislative leaders.

Seniority and Congressional Committee Assignment. The seniority system is a frequent target of those who criticize Congress, and it is important to realize just how it operates. Seniority on a committee determines, virtually without exception, which member of the majority party will be chairman, but the influence of seniority on the initial choice of committee members is more complex. Since the committees vary in importance, most congressmen want a seat on one of the key committees; Senate and House Appropriations, House Rules, House Ways and Means, Senate Finance, and Senate Foreign Relations are among the most desirable. At the start of a congressional session, members in both houses make formal applications for seats on committees where vacancies exist. Each party determines how its seats on the committees will be filled.

The House, with its larger membership, has more formalized procedures. The Democratic members of the Ways and Means Committee constitute that party's Committee on Committees, and meet with the Speaker (if a Democrat) and floor leader. Each member screens requests for committee assignments from representatives in a designated number of states. These requests are channeled to the committee through the senior Democrat in each state delegation, and his influence may be important to the congressman seeking a choice assignment. The Ways and Means Committee is made up primarily of senior congressmen, and in the deliberations over committee assignments the more senior members carry particular weight. The Republican Committee on Committees serves no other function. It is composed of one member from each state with Republican congressmen, normally the senior member from that state; each member has as many votes as there are Republican representatives. The actual work of this group is delegated to a subcommittee, normally dominated by the states with the most Republican representatives, where the same voting pattern is followed. The consequence is to give the Republicans from such states as New York, New Jersey, Pennsylvania, Ohio, Illinois, Michigan, and California a dominant voice in choosing committee members. Though these are heavily metropolitan and industrial states, the senior Republican members from them are likely to represent the more rural, small-town areas of the states.[17]

Both party committees sometimes consult the senior members of their party on the committees where vacancies exist, and these members usually have what amounts to a veto power on new members. As one congressman described the process:

I don't see how the Committee on Committees could have the nerve to ram somebody down the throat of a committee chairman or ranking member who doesn't want that candidate. It would be natural to consult with your top man on the committee, and unless some unusual issue is at stake, his wishes would be adhered to.[18]

It is evident that the formal institutions in both parties for choosing committee members are seniority-conscious groups, and it is natural that these groups give considerable weight to seniority in making assignments. The party leaders might be expected to emphasize other factors, including the views of congressmen on policy questions. But the party leaders' part in the selection process is an informal one, dependent on their personal influence and political strength. According to one study of congressional opinion: "There is general accord that the leadership of both parties exerts much influence on committee assignments and that it should do so, but it seems clear that most House members feel that this power should be—and usually is—exercised with discretion and with a light rather than a heavy hand."[19] Party leaders concentrate their efforts on influencing choices for a few of the major committees, and in this respect they work closely with the senior members of the committee that makes the selections. Joe Martin has said: "In the four years that I served as Speaker no Republican went on an important committee without my approval."[20] Speaker Rayburn sought to make sure that the most promising congressmen who were beginning to make a good record were given assignments on major committees, where several years of seniority was necessary. He was particularly careful to guarantee that new members of the Ways and Means Committee were low-tariff men. The Democratic leadership has paid particular attention to this committee, both because of its jurisdiction over tariff and tax bills and because of its responsibilities for other committee assignments. New Democratic members of the Ways and Means Committee are nominated by the leadership and normally approved without question by the caucus, although in 1963 the caucus rejected one of the candidates proposed by Speaker McCormack.[21] Party leaders in the House have an influence over committee assignments that is often powerful, but it is exercised with a cautious restraint that is in striking contrast to the authority exercised by party leaders in many state legislatures.

In the Senate the procedures for choosing committee members are less formal, because of the smaller task involved, and the practices of the two parties are in greater contrast. Each party has a committee on committees, which is called the Steering Committee by the Democrats. The Democratic members are nominated by the floor leader and the Republican members by the conference chairman, both subject to approval by the conference. Republicans until recently relied heavily on the seniority rule to guide their decisions. The result was to deprive some of the most able younger senators of seats on the most important committees, relegating them to relative obscurity. Beginning in 1959, the more senior Republicans gradually yielded to the pressure of younger members and of the party leadership, and permitted junior senators to have at least one seat on a major committee. In cases of conflict over a particular vacancy on a key committee, however, the Republicans have in most cases continued to follow the seniority rule.

The seniority rule was just as important in the Democratic party until 1953 when the new floor leader, Lyndon Johnson, succeeded in gaining approval for a new policy, which gave less weight to seniority and guaranteed that each freshman senator would have at least one seat on a major committee. This made it possible to place such men as John F. Kennedy, Mike Mansfield, and Stuart Symington on major committees immediately. The result has been to give the most talented Democrats committee assignments that made them rather quickly into effective senators. Another effect of this new policy, and an important one, has been to give the floor leader greater influence over committee assignments. As floor leader, Lyndon Johnson had authority to fill vacancies on the steering committees; not until 1961 were these choices subject to approval by the party conference. Johnson's suggestions for committee assignments carried great weight in the Steering Committee, and he did not hesitate to use this influence to reward senators who were loyal to him. At the start of the 1959 session of the Senate, several Northern senators who had supported Johnson's stand against changing the rules to permit curbing filibusters by a majority vote received *two* choice committee assignments. Several of the Northern liberal senators who were less willing to work in harness with the Senate Democratic leadership found it difficult to get the committee assignments that they particularly wanted.

After Mansfield became floor leader, the Steering Committee appeared to act more independently, but Southern senators continued to have almost half the membership on the committee, and several Democratic liberal senators continued to feel discriminated against. Senator Joseph Clark of Pennsylvania took the lead in challenging what he considered conservative control of the Steering Committee. In 1961 he succeeded in getting more Northern representation on the Steering Committee, including his own membership, but he failed to get an enlargement of several committees so as to enhance liberal representation, and the Steering Committee continued to reflect conservative control. In 1963 Clark launched a public attack on what he termed the "Senate Establishment," a bipartisan coalition that guaranteed conservative control over several major committees. His speeches on the Senate floor did not prevent the Steering Committee from giving preferences to conservatives, however, and the Senate voted against Clark's motion to enlarge two committees that he considered to be dominated by conservatives, Finance and Appropriations.[22] In 1965 the Steering Committee was enlarged by the addition of two Midwestern liberals, and liberal Democrats fared better in committee assignments.

Seniority has not disappeared as a factor in committee assignments in either house. It is still difficult, particularly in the House, for freshmen to gain assignments on the most important committees. Yet seniority today is rarely the only factor taken into consideration. One congressman has aptly summarized its importance: "Seniority may control if all other things are equal. But other things usually are not equal. Sometimes you begin to think seniority is little more than a device to fall back on when it is convenient to do so."[23] What other criteria are used for selecting members on the key committees? Party leaders may be concerned with a record of party loyalty, particularly with regard to the issues under the jurisdiction of the committee concerned, but there are other factors that often overshadow policy positions and that are accepted as pertinent by other participants in the selection process. Geographic balance is considered important, and some of the larger state delegations have succeeded in establishing a claim to a seat on certain important committees. The Ohio Republicans, for example, insist that they must have one member on the House Public Works Committee. The members of the various committees on committees like to give the choice assignments to congressmen who have shown themselves to be "responsible." This is a term more often used than defined, but it suggests a congressman who is moderate and reasonable in his approach to issues, who contributes his share to the less-publicized committee chores, who works well with the leadership and other congressmen, who recognizes and accepts the congressional norms.[24] The description closely approaches William S. White's definition of members of the Senate "club."[25] In the House, there is suspicion of the member from a close district who is subservient to every whim of his district. The leaders who play a key part in selecting committee members are often men who have had little or no electoral opposition at home and who value their consequent freedom of action.

As a result of the process and criteria of selection, the members of the most important Senate and House committees tend to be experienced congressmen, moderate in their views, who have demonstrated a capacity for working within the system and cooperating with the leadership. In the House in particular (where there are greater contrasts between competitive and noncompetitive districts), they are likely to be men who are relatively immune from the tides of change in public opinion. A major political change that is manifested at the polls is not likely to have much direct or indirect effect on the most powerful congressional committees, except as it changes the party balance on committees. These aspects of the seniority system, however, do not bring about geographical distortion in the House, although they have produced some overrepresentation of Southerners on key committees in the Senate.

Although seniority is but one factor in determining committee assignments, it is, with rare exceptions, the only factor considered in determining retention on a committee. If a party's majority drops and it loses seats on a committee, it is the members with the least committee seniority who are dropped. Once a congressman has gained a place on a committee, the party leadership is unable to use the threat of removal to influence the congressman's vote. The power of the leadership to remove a committee member, which is so important in many states, has fallen into disuse since the days of the strong House Speakers, such as Joe Cannon. Congressmen are usually able to bolt their party in a presidential election (in the sense of actively supporting the other candidate) without risking their place on committees, so long as they do not leave the party.

In 1925 the Republican senatorial party took disciplinary action against Robert La Follette and three senators who had supported his campaign for President on the Progressive ticket. Two lost their chairmanships of committees, one was dropped from a committee, and all were dropped to the lowest rank on their committees. Since that time there have been repeated examples of congressmen supporting presidential candidates of the other party without suffering retribution with regard to their committee assignments. In 1953, when Senator Wayne Morse left the Republican party and became an independent, he was removed from two major committees and assigned to minor ones. Neither party was willing to let Morse, as an independent, sit on a major committee in place of a party member because the majority party balance was unusually narrow on the committees. Morse suffered because he had declared himself an *independent;* the bipartisan norms for committee assignments leave little room for independents.[26] In 1961 the Democrats, including Speaker Rayburn, came close to dropping from the Rules Committee a member who had bolted in the 1960 election. In 1965 liberal Democrats sought to discipline two House members who had bolted the Democratic ticket in 1964. The Democratic caucus voted by a substantial margin to drop them to the bottom of the party's seniority list, even below the incoming freshmen, in a move that may presage a gradual change in the House norms with regard to seniority.

Seniority and Chairmanships in Congress. Seniority on a committee is the sole criterion used in determining rank on the committee and in the selection of the chairman from the majority party. The chairman is the member of the majority party who has been on the committee the longest; if one senator is eligible to be chairman of two committees, he must take his choice of one, and the next ranking member chairs the other. The senator or representative of the majority party who stays on a committee long enough will eventually become chairman of it, and the time it takes depends on luck—the death, retirement, or electoral defeat of the man ahead of him. The members of the majority party with the greatest seniority in Congress are likely to have chairmanships.

In 1961 the eleven Democratic senators with the greatest seniority held 11 of the 16 chairmanships, and the eleven Democratic representatives with the greatest seniority (dating from 1913 to 1933) included the Speaker, majority leader, the chairmen of eight committees—including most of the important ones—and the second-ranking Democrat on the Rules Committee.

The accidental workings of the seniority rule and the desire of some congressmen to move to more important committees can result in relatively junior members rising quickly to the top of committees. An example is Pat McNamara, who entered the Senate in 1955 and was immediately assigned to the Labor and Public Welfare Committee and the Public Works Committee; by 1963 he had become second-ranking member of the first and chairman of the second, as a result of deaths, resignations, and transfers to other committees and to the White House. By contrast Paul Douglas, who entered the Senate in 1949 and had made one committee shift, was the third- and fifth-ranking member, respectively, of two committees in 1963. In the House, although half of the chairmen in 1961 had at least twenty years' seniority, there were several with only twelve to sixteen years. The most senior senators and representatives are likely to be found chairing the most powerful committees, because members are unlikely to gain access to such committees until they have had several years of congressional service. A classic example is Representative Sabath, representing a safe district in Chicago, who entered the House in 1907, joined the Rules Committee in 1922, became its chairman in 1939, and served as chairman or ranking Democrat for thirteen years.

A further effect of the seniority rule is that most subcommittee chairmen are senior members of the committees. On about two-thirds of the committees there are no exceptions to this rule, and on the rest there are only a few examples of congressmen being bypassed to give subcommittee chairmanships to junior members. Rarely does a committee chairman ignore seniority because of policy considerations in making subcommittee assignments. Moreover, the chairmen of subcommittees are likely to hold these positions with as much tenacity as committee chairmen do.

Effects of the Seniority Rule. What are the effects of seniority as it applies to committee chairmen? Most obviously, it places in the chairmanships men who are fully familiar with their committees' work, but who are also older, men on the average (in the first six postwar Congresses) 11 years older in the Senate and 6 years older in the House than their colleagues. Often a few of these will be men whose abilities are impaired by age. A more significant aspect of seniority is that it affects the geographical distribution of chairmanships, because only members from safe states or districts can acquire the seniority necessary to inherit a chairmanship.

As Table 9.3 shows, a large proportion of Democratic chairmen have come from the South, while the East and Midwest have had few chairmen, particularly in the Senate. Republican chairmen have been heavily concentrated in the Midwest and to a lesser extent in the East.[27]

Table 9.3. DISTRIBUTION OF CONGRESSIONAL SEATS AND
COMMITTEE CHAIRMEN BY GEOGRAPHICAL REGIONS, 1947–1958
(In percentages)

Region	Seats	Senate Chairmen		Seats	House Chairmen	
		Dem	Rep		Dem	Rep
East	25	12	37	30	17	31
Midwest	25	2	53	30	17	66
South	27	53	0	27	62	0
West	23	33	10	13	4	3
Total	100	100	100	100	100	100

SOURCE: Based on George Goodwin, Jr., "The Seniority System in Congress," *American Political Science Review*, LIII (1959), 421.

Table 9.4 shows that a disproportionate percentage of Democratic chairmen have come from one-party states and districts. Most of the one-party states that provide Democratic chairmen are in the South, but in the House a number of Democrats are reelected consistently enough from safe districts in metropolitan areas to acquire seniority and chairmanships. There were smaller proportions of Republican chairmen from safe districts (during the two brief periods of Republican control, 1947–1948 and 1953–1954), in part because there are fewer safe Republican states and districts and in part because of recent Democratic successes in formerly safe Republican seats.

The contrast between the distribution of seats and chairmanships evident in Table 9.4 is not due entirely to the operation of seniority. A more careful breakdown of the House districts (which are more consistent in voting patterns than states are) shows that a much larger proportion of Democratic representatives comes from safe seats. In absolute terms, the Democrats held 154 of the 221 districts classified as one-party, while the Republicans controlled 70 of the 119 with limited competition. The 95 seats that had full competition—that is, party turnover—were (by definition) controlled by neither party; on the average, in the five elections starting in 1952, the Republicans won 53. Republican chairmanships correspond almost precisely to Republican seats, in terms of the degree of competition in districts. On the Democratic side, the seniority rule is partially responsible for the high proportion of Democratic chairmen from one-party areas. It is Democrats, of course, who have chaired committees for most of the last 35 years.

One-party states and, to a greater degree, one-party districts are likely to be conservative, insulated from the liberal trends at the polls and immune to pressures from a President who owes his election (as do all Presidents since 1932) primarily to the voters in large metropolitan areas. (Democrats from safe metropolitan districts, on the other hand, are insulated from conservative trends.) James M. Burns has described very well the tactics and orientation of the congressman who achieves a chairmanship or a senior place on a major committee:

He placates the dominant social forces in the district; "protects" his district against hostile outside forces; does a great many individual favors; lobbies for benefits for the district; maintains a friends-and-neighbors political

Table 9.4. DISTRIBUTION OF CONGRESSIONAL SEATS AND COMMITTEE CHAIRMEN BY NATURE OF CONSTITUENCY, 1947–1962

(In percentages)

Competition in Constituency*	Senate			House		
	Seats	Chairmen		Seats	Chairmen	
		Dem	Rep		Dem	Rep
One-party	21	51	7	51	80	34
Some competition	25	3	40	27	18	37
Full competition	54	46	53	22	2	29
Total	100	100	100	100	100	100

* The categories of states in the Senate, following Goodwin, are the same described as "one-party," "modified one-party," and "two-party" by Ranney and Kendall, *Democracy and the American Party System* (New York: Harcourt, Brace, and World, 1956), pp. 161–64. The following procedures are used for classifying House districts: the five elections from 1952 through 1960 are the base; one-party districts are those consistently won by one party by at least 55%, those with some competition are those consistently won by a single party but sometimes with less than 55%, and those with full competition are those not consistently won by one party.

SOURCE: Figures for the Senate are an updated revision of a table in George Goodwin, Jr., "The Seniority System in Congress," *American Political Science Review*, LIII (1959), 425.

organization that scares would-be opponents out of the primary or trounces them if they come in; and comfortably overwhelms the opposition party's candidate—if there is one—on election day. His main commitment is to the *status quo*. He wishes nothing to disrupt his easy relationships with the public officials and private interests that rule the area. He views with alarm the great issues that sweep the nation and threaten to disrupt the familiar and comfortable politics of his district. . . .

And he remains invincibly local. By remaining in the orbit of his congressional area, he stays politically in the orbit of his party's local candidates and officeholders. Thus he operates in a world of political localism, for the electoral and other political forces in the area are largely activated by other local candidates.[28]

It is important to remember that the seniority rule not only creates chairmen but also maintains them. The national party leadership, unlike its counterpart in most state legislatures, has little more chance of removing a committee chairman than a President has of removing a Supreme Court Justice. Not since 1925 has a Senate chairman been deprived of his post.[29] It is quite possible for a committee chairman to be in disagreement with party leaders and a majority of the party on the major issues under the jurisdiction of his committee; it is also possible for him to use his position very effectively to undermine party policies. In recent years, Chairman Eastland of the Senate Judiciary Committee has stymied Democratic civil rights bills, Chairman Byrd of the Senate Finance Committee has delayed major tax legislation, and Chairman Smith of the House Rules Committee has delayed or blocked a multitude of legislative programs.

It is sometimes forgotten that the principle of seniority as applied to chairmen has become an inviolate one only during the last forty years. Half a century ago, when Woodrow Wilson became President, the Democratic majority made drastic changes in committee assignments, removing 28 senators either from chairmanships or from key committees and replacing them with senators—often quite junior—who were more loyal to the Wilson Administration. In recent years there has been no serious support in Congress for proposals to remove committee chairmen, most notably those of Senator Clark. In 1961 Clark found the Steering Committee hostile to his suggestion that it remove two chairmen who had failed to support Kennedy in the 1960 election: Harry Byrd and James Eastland.[30]

As often as the seniority base of chairmanships is attacked by outside critics or senators like Clark, it is defended by congressmen themselves. Most members, who have been slowly climbing the ladder, have a vested interest in the system. Senator Saltonstall has been quoted as saying, "The longer I stay in Washington, the more sympathetic I become with the system." Congressmen warn that, if seniority were abandoned, there would be a constant struggle for power, a perennial maneuvering to replace one chairman with another. Critics of the system argue with some reason that, although seniority is a factor in most institutions, it is not used in most as the sole criterion for advancement. In its struggle to preserve its power from encroachment by the Executive, Congress needs to be well led; the seniority system, however, often creates a vacuum in effective leadership. On other occasions, it makes Congress unresponsive to public demands and freezes into deadlock presidential-congressional relations.[31] The seniority principle, particularly as it affects chairmen, places severe limits on the effectiveness of party leadership in Congress. This is one side of the coin. The other side, equally important, is the fact that it—more than anything else—ensures that the congressional committees will be strong, independent centers of power.

INSIDE THE COMMITTEES

The Chairman. According to Matthews, "the chairman, with rare exceptions usually caused by gross senility or incompetence, is the most influential member of a Senate committee."[32] In William S. White's words, a Senate committee chairman, "unless he be a weak or irresolute man, is emperor."[33] The power of a congressional committee chairman rests on two legs: his formal power derived from the committee rules or practices, and his informal, self-created influence.

Congressional committee rules vary considerably in regard to the degree to which procedures are specified. The more explicit these details are, the less freedom a chairman has to run the committee in his own way. In a few cases, rank-and-file members have revolted against domination by the chairman and have succeeded in curbing his power by amending committee rules. It is more frequently true, however, that committee members acquiesce in the chairman's control and even permit him to ignore procedural requirements in the committee rules. There is a natural reluctance to challenge the exercise of power by a strong chairman. In this sense, the chairman's *de facto* power may depend not only on rules and precedents but on his political and personal strength.[34] According to one congressman:

There is great reluctance to challenge committee chairmen even though you don't agree with them. Everyone seems fearful; all members have pet projects and legislation they want passed. No one wants to tangle too much because they realize what the results would be.[35]

Although most congressional committees at present provide in their rules for a fixed meeting time, the chairman has the sole power to call meetings in some committees, and in all of them he can call—or refuse to call—additional meetings beyond those scheduled, and can determine the schedule for hearings. One of the most effective techniques, used occasionally by Chairman Howard Smith of the House Rules Committee, has been to delay meetings by simply leaving Washington for a few weeks to attend to work on his Virginia farm. The committee chairman normally controls the agenda of the committee, and he presides at its meetings. A determined chairman, with at least the tacit support of some members, can prevent another member from gaining a vote on a bill for many weeks by refusing to recognize him in meetings, bringing up other bills, ruling out of order the other member's motions, adjourning regular committee meetings early, and refusing to schedule additional meetings.[36] The chairman's powers are often well established by custom. In 1963, when Senator Harry Byrd's tactics delayed the Kennedy Administration's tax-cut bill, several senators in the Finance Committee moved to speed up the prolonged hearings scheduled by Chairman Byrd, but he easily defeated their proposal, pointing out that during his thirty years on the Committee all the senators who had served as chairman had been accorded the right to set the schedule of hearings. Except where committee rules leave him no discretion, a chairman can determine when a bill will be assigned and to what subcommittee for study, as well as which subcommittees have priority in reporting a bill to the full committee. The chairman appoints members of the staff and directs its activities. While theoretically serving the whole committee, the staff often gives its time and its loyalty primarily to the chairman. The chairman either manages the bill on the floor or determines who the manager will be. The floor manager in the House is responsible for allotting the limited amount of time available for debate. If the bill goes to a conference committee, the chairman frequently plays a dominant role there.

The rules and traditions of a committee are important determinants of a chairman's power, but a strong chairman can frequently either use or ignore the rules, according to his needs, while a weak chairman will not dare either to take full advantage of the rules or to bypass them. What makes a chairman strong? In the committees, knowledge is power, and the chairman often has more information and understanding about the measures coming before his committee than anyone else. He has been on the committee longer, perhaps twenty years or more. For example, Representative Carl Vinson was chairman or ranking Democrat on the Armed Services Committee from its establishment in 1947 until his retirement in 1964, and prior to that he had been a member of the Naval Affairs Committee since 1917 and had chaired it since 1931. The chairman, particularly in the House, devotes nearly all of his time to the work of his committee. Representative Wilbur Mills, who has served on the House Ways and Means Committee since 1943, probably knows more about tax laws than any man in Washington and delights in correcting the technical errors he discovers in the tax legislation written by Treasury Department experts.

The knowledge and experience of the chairman not only give him an advantage in dealing with other members of the committee; they force administrative officials to respect his views, and they command attention when a bill reaches the floor of the House or Senate. The committee chairman is a specialist, viewed by his colleagues as an authority (or *the* authority) on a given subject. He may have a little or no influence on legislation outside his committee's jurisdiction. In the Senate, where a lower order of specialization prevails, some senators also gain prestige and command respect as generalists or as party leaders. Senator Robert Taft, as chairman of the Labor Committee, and Senator Walter George, as chairman of the Foreign Relations Committee, commanded wide respect as political leaders and authorities on a wide range of issues. Most committee chairmen, however, have narrower bases of influence.

The seniority system promotes the senator with few skills and little influence as rapidly as any other, and some men who reach the chairmanship lack the ability that the post requires or have grown frail or senile while waiting for the chairmanship. When this happens, there is a power vacuum on the committee, and usually some other member or members step in to assume greater responsibility. Lacking the full prerogatives of the chairman, however, another member of the committee is seldom able to lead it with the firm hand of a strong chairman.

Subcommittees. We have described the powerful committees under strong chairmen as sources of a decentralized power structure in Congress. Many of the committees are further divided into subcommittees, where a major proportion of committee work is done. A congressional staff member has been quoted as saying, "Given an active subcommittee chairman working in a specialized field with a staff of his own, the parent committee can do no more than change the grammar of a subcommittee report."[37] Subcommittees may be symptomatic of the atomization of power within a committee and of loose control by the committee chairman, but they may be used as tools by the committee chairman in an integrated power structure.

There are several reason for the growing use of subcommittees, which in recent years have numbered around 250 in the two houses. The most obvious reason is the need for greater specialization than the committee structure permits, in order to cope with the variety and complexity of governmental problems and to permit individual congressmen to concentrate their time and attention on fewer subjects. In the case of the appropriations committees, the use of subcommittees is virtually essential if congressmen are to scrutinize the budget requests of all departments with care. Some of the factors which we have said caused the creation of select committees also lead to the establishment of subcommittees. They provide convenient channels of access for both pressure groups and governmental agencies. They make it possible to give attention to detailed, technical problems, such as improvements in judicial machinery, state taxation of interstate commerce, oceanography, and space sciences. Perhaps most important, they give experienced, able congressmen a chance to gain prestige and pursue their interests as subcommittee chairmen.

Despite the strong arguments for their use, subcommittees are not found uniformly in the committees. They are not used by the revenue-raising committees in either house, or by the House Rules and Un-American Activities committees (the latter is primarily an investigating body); they do not serve a major legislative purpose in either of the foreign affairs committees. In some cases, the extent of subcommittee use is explainable primarily in terms of the nature of the committee's work—whether it handles a few broad measures or a multitude of varied and technical ones. In other cases the use of subcommittees is a reflection of committee leadership, on the part of the chairman and other senior members on the committee.

The committee chairman, with support from his allies on the committee, may prefer to avoid subcommittees entirely. The Senate Finance and House Ways and Means committees have been run in such a centralized fashion by their chairmen, despite the fact that they deal with such diverse topics as taxes and reciprocal trade. Chairman Carl Vinson of the Armed Services Committee assigned bills to numbered subcommittees which had no specified jurisdiction—a technique of control that was followed by several other Southern conservative chairmen in the House. This prevents subcommittees from developing any independent proprietary interest in particular subjects within the committee's jurisdiction. A chairman may establish subcommittees to serve his own purposes. When Adam Clayton Powell became chairman of the House Education and Labor Committee, he found the existing subcommittees dominated by conservatives and promptly created additional subcommittees with parallel jurisdiction and liberal chairmen, to which he referred most of the important legislation.

The chairman has a variety of techniques that he can use to control subcommittees. The rules of about half the committees make him an *ex officio* member of all subcommittees, and though he seldom has the time to exercise the prerogative, he may be expected to take part in the deliberation and voting when a subcommittee is handling an important bill. Chairman Powell of the House Education and Labor Committee has developed a unique system for maintaining close supervision over subcommittees: an intercom system that allows him to sit in his office and listen to or participate in any subcommittee meeting. In some committees the chairman has considerable discretion in determining how quickly and to which subcommittee he will refer a bill. Although some subcommittees have a permanent staff of their own, the chairman usually has considerable freedom in assigning staff and providing funds for subcommittees; in the case of an investigating committee, the chairman can assign or withhold the power of subpoena.

In making appointments to a subcommittee and particularly in choosing its chairman, the committee chairman is frequently limited by the requirements of seniority. This is a matter of tradition, only rarely written into committee rules, and it is a tradition with which chairmen have sometimes been willing and able to break. They can sometimes choose which of the senior men will chair the most important subcommittees and may occasionally completely ignore a senior man. Conservative Democratic chairmen, of course, have little reason to violate the code of seniority, since the other senior members of the committee usually share their conservative views. Relatively few Northern, urban liberals hold high-ranking seniority on the major committees. In some committees other criteria than seniority are used. The House Agriculture Committee has a number of commodity subcommittees, and whenever possible the members are given their choice of seats on the subcommittees, a choice that corresponds with the most important commodities in their home districts.[38] The party ratios on subcommittees are less rigid than the ratio for the full committee, and the chairman has some discretion here, although he is likely to consult the ranking minority member in determining which minority members should serve on each subcommittee. Although most congressmen are able to cling to subcommittee positions as tenaciously as to committee seats, there are a few examples of chairmen who have taken members, and even subcommittee chairmen, off the subcommittee against their will.[39]

Most congressional committees fall into one of two patterns. In some cases the chairman plays a dominant role, and either minimizes the use of subcommittees or keeps a tight rein over them. In other cases the committee is run by a collective leadership which consists of the senior, and often conservative, members who chair the committee and the major subcommittees. Occasionally, however, this stable pattern is broken by revolt. In the early months of the Eighty-third Congress, for example, Republican Clare Hoffman ran the House Committee on Government Operations with an iron hand, primarily through the use of *ad hoc* subcommittees appointed by Hoffman with little consultation. The members revolted and voted to give virtual autonomy to five sub-committees, which would have broad powers to hire staffs and conduct investigations. Such insurrection in Congress is seldom tried, however, and even less often succeeds.

State Legislative Committees. The whole fabric of the committee system in the states makes it difficult for the committees to be tightly run citadels of power. The committees have little or no staff and budget, and they often function for only a few months during a legislative term. There are only a few states, such as North Carolina, in which subcommittees are extensively used; elsewhere there appears to be no need for such structural complexity. There is a large turnover of com-mittee membership in every session, which makes it difficult to develop widely accepted norms and traditions for committee operation or to accumulate a core of members who are experts on the subject matter with which the committee deals. Expert knowledge comes less from committee experience than from the custom of putting on committees legislators with specific occupational or professional experience. Lawyers are assigned to the judiciary committee, insurance men to the insurance committee, and farmers to the agriculture committee. Not only does this create obvious problems concerning conflicts of interests, but it may turn the committee into an arena for competing interest groups, each of which is directly represented on the committee.

The strength of congressional committee chairmen rests largely on the rigid seniority system. On state legislative committees the rate of turnover is usually high, not only for members but also for the chair-men. A 1950 study showed that there were only 15 states in which over one-third of the committee chairmen had served in the legislature for five or more terms; at the other extreme, there were 13 states in which over one-third of the chairmen had served only a single term.[40] The chairmen of major committees in the Missouri legislature usually do not hold seniority on the committee; they are often new members of the committee, and sometimes even freshmen legislators.[41] In the Texas House, over a period of six sessions, 70 percent of the members on the nine most important committees had had no previous experience on that committee. Half of the chairmen on these major House committees were new to the committee, and none had served on it for more than two previous sessions; chairmen of senatorial committees had more experience, but only half had more than a single session of committee experience.[42] Committee chairmen are unlikely to be powerful figures in a legislative system if some of them have had little legislative experi-ence and many of them have had little experience on their own com-mittee.

There are two patterns for choosing committee chairmen that tend to enhance their power. In a few states the chairmen of major committees hold their positions for long periods of time. In both Virginia and South Carolina the chairmen of most major committees are men with many years of legislative experience and usually long tenure on the committee. In some states with strong legislative leadership, the major committee chairmanships go to veteran legislators who are loyal to the leadership, but these men are likely to advance rather rapidly to more important committee and party assignments rather than to retain a specific chairmanship for many sessions. These chairmen are usually powerful, not because of their established reputation as subject-matter experts, but because they are skillful and trusted leaders of the majority party or faction. In Pennsylvania, for example, the chairmen dominate the committees to an unusual degree, but they do so as dependable agents of the majority party in the legislature.[43]

NOTES

1. Herman Finer, *Governments of Greater European Powers* (New York, 1956), p. 116.

2. For a chronology of standing committees, see George B. Galloway, *The Legislative Process in Congress* (New York, 1953), pp. 276–78.

3. V. Stanley Vardys, "Select Committees of the House of Representatives," *Midwest Journal of Political Science*, VI (1962), 247–65.

4. "Congress and the Atom," *Annals of the American Academy of Political and Social Science*, CCXC (November 1953), 77.

5. Harold P. Green and Alan Rosenthal, *Government of the Atom* (New York, 1963), pp. 25–30, 79–103.

6. *Ibid.*, pp. 54–56.

7. *Ibid.*, p. 266.

8. *Book of the States, 1964–65* (Chicago, 1964), p. 40.

9. William C. Johnson, "The Political Party System in the 1959–1960 California Legislature" (Unpublished M.A. thesis, University of California, 1960), pp. 40–43.

10. Dean E. Mann, "The Legislative Committee System in Arizona," *Western Political Quarterly*, XIV (1961), 925–41.

11. Belle Zeller (ed.), *American State Legislatures* (New York, 1954), p. 197.

12. Kenneth T. Palmer, "The Legislative Committee System in Pennsylvania" (Unpublished Ph.D. dissertation, Pennsylvania State University, 1964), pp. 19–35.

13. Mann, *loc. cit.*

14. G. Theodore Mitau, *Politics in Minnesota* (Minneapolis, 1960), pp. 59–62.

15. Loren P. Beth and William C. Havard, "Committee Stacking and Political Power in Florida," *Journal of Politics*, XXIII (1961), 57–83.

16. Clifton McCleskey, *The Government and Politics of Texas* (Boston, 1963), p. 125.

17. For a fuller description, see Nicholas A. Masters, "House Committee Assignments," *American Political Science Review*, LV (1961), 345–57.

18. Charles L. Clapp, *The Congressman: His Work As He Sees It* (Washington: The Brookings Institution, 1963), p. 194.

19. *Ibid.*, p. 192.

20. Joe Martin, *My First Fifty Years in Politics* (New York, 1960), p. 181.

21. Clapp, *op. cit.*, pp. 192–93.

22. Alan Rosenthal, *Toward Majority Rule in the United States Senate* (New York, 1962).

23. Clapp, *op. cit.*, p. 200.

24. Masters, *op. cit.*, pp. 351–55.

25. William S. White, *Citadel: The Story of the U.S. Senate* (New York, 1957), chap. 7.

26. Ralph K. Huitt, "The Morse Committee Assignment Controversy: A Study in Senate Norms," *American Political Science Review*, LI (1957), 313–29.

27. George Goodwin, Jr., "The Seniority System in Congress," *American Political Science Review*, LIII (1959), 420–27.

28. James M. Burns, *The Deadlock of Democracy* (Englewood Cliffs, N.J., 1963), 243–44.

29. Huitt, *op. cit.*, pp. 319–23.

30. Rosenthal, *loc. cit.*

31. See Goodwin, *op. cit.*, pp. 418–20, for a summary of the pros and cons.

32. Donald R. Matthews, *U.S. Senators and Their World* (Chapel Hill, N.C., 1960), p. 159.

33. White, *op. cit.*, p. 180.

34. For an excellent description of the chairman's sources of power, see Matthews, *op. cit.*, pp. 159–62.

35. Clapp, *op. cit.*, p. 223.

36. The chairman's ability to use his control over committee procedure as a powerful tool is well illustrated in Howard E. Shuman, "Senate Rules and the Civil Rights Bill: A Case Study," *American Political Science Review*, LI (1957), 961–62.

37. George Goodwin, Jr., "Subcommittees: The Miniature Legislatures of Congress," *American Political Science Review*, LVI (1962), 596. Goodwin provides a thorough analysis of varied uses of subcommittees in Congress which forms the basis of the description in this chapter.

38. Charles O. Jones, "The Role of the Congressional Subcommittee," *Midwest Journal of Political Science*, VI (1962), 327–44.

39. Clapp, *op. cit.*, pp. 225, 240–42.

40. Zeller, *op. cit.*, pp. 68–69.

41. Robert F. Karsch, *The Standing Committees of the Missouri General Assembly* (Columbia, Mo., 1959), pp. 17–18.

42. William E. Oden, "Tenure and Turnover in Recent Texas Legislatures," *Southwestern Social Science Quarterly*, XLV (1965), 371–74.

43. Palmer, *op. cit.*, pp. 60–63.

[10]

The Legislative
Bureaucracy

T HE SCOPE, magnitude, and complexity of modern governmental
activities have dictated increasing specialization and division of
labor in legislative systems. The most clearly manifest by-product of
legislative specialization has been the development since the late nineteenth century of staff operations to make available to congressmen and
state legislators personnel who are able to assist them in the performance
of their tasks. Legislative bureaucrats play functionally significant roles
in the legislative system. At the clerical level, the staff facilitates the
integrative function of the legislative system in so far as the members'
or committees' staffs are involved in office-management operations,
particularly those related to communication with interest-group representatives, constituents, or officials of the administration. Technical and
research staff operations may contribute to the management of conflicts,
to the extent that controversial issues can be converted into matters of
expert knowledge. The availability of staff to congressmen and state
legislators tends to increase the capacity of the legislature to be independent of the executive. One of the purposes of the provision in the
Legislative Reorganization Act of 1946 for increased member and committee staffs was to diminish the practice of borrowing staff from executive agencies, a policy that had tended to make congressional committees
dependent upon these agencies for facts and interpretation. Finally,
staffs provide a source of independence for legislative committees from
centralized political control by the party leadership. The relatively trivial
staff facilities for most state legislative committees is one of the factors
that help to account for the weakness of committees in state legislatures.
It should not be assumed that legislative bureaucrats are nothing

but "neutral servants," who unerringly supply the legislature with indisputably objective evidence. The staff members are inexorably involved in the political struggle within the legislative system, and their role behavior may have fundamental policy implications.[1] The legislator often prefers knowledge that supports his preconceptions, and the staff man himself is not devoid of political values that he may wish to see implemented by the legislature. Thus the staff may contribute to the development and crystallization of legislative conflict, and it may be directly involved in negotiations and bargaining among the conflicting interests that are focused upon particular issues.

TYPES OF LEGISLATIVE STAFFS

In general, there are two broad types of legislative staffs for American legislatures: the housekeeping staff, and the specialist, or professional, staff. The housekeeping staff performs clerical, secretarial, and service tasks of a relatively routine kind. The overwhelming preponderance of clerks and other staff assistance for Congress and the state legislatures has been occupied with records, schedules of witnesses for committees, clerical detail, general housekeeping duties of office supply and management, mail, services for constituents, and other routine work. The necessity for such routine assistance has been recognized by legislators in the United States, since the beginning of legislative operations, in the need to maintain records of proceedings. The growth in the numbers of housekeeping staff people is related to the increasing complexity of legislative work. Congressional committees first employed full-time clerks when the House Ways and Means Committee and the Senate Finance Committee first obtained regular appropriations for such assistance in 1856, though some clerical assistance for congressional committees was made available on a temporary basis as far back as the late eighteenth century.[2] Clerical services for state legislators probably is largely a late-nineteenth-century development, and even today anything like adequate clerical assistance for legislators is provided only in a minority of states.[3]

The specialist staff performs policy-related tasks, although their degree of involvement in policy may vary a great deal. The specialist staff may be characterized in terms of the following subtypes:

Research Staff. The research man gathers data and other information. His work may vary from routine collections of information (looking up references in the legislative library, or tabulating simple information) to major research investigations. Research-staff operations have been institutionalized at the congressional level in the Legislative Reference Service of the Library of Congress, an agency which was created in 1914. At the state level, institutionalized research operations may be associated with the legislative councils, which now exist in thirty-nine states, or with state legislative reference services. The first permanent legislative reference library was created in Wisconsin in 1901, and now every state except Nevada, North Carolina, and Utah has such an agency.[4]

Bill-drafting Staff. Bill drafters provide technical services to legislators in the preparation of legislation. The bill-drafting service for Congress is the Office of Legislative Counsel, established in 1918. The New York and Wisconsin state legislatures created bill-drafting assistance at the turn of the century, and this service is now available to legislators in every state except Idaho, Vermont, and Wyoming.

Investigating Staff. Experts in the arts and sciences of investigation are essential to the modern congressional investigating committee. The importance of a staff to a congressional committee is probably increased when

The chief function of that committee is the making of investigations by means of public hearings. Unless such hearings are planned with great care, the background of the subject under investigation thoroughly explored, and the potential contribution of each witness carefully estimated, an investigation is apt to prove aimless and fruitless.[5]

Lawyers and accountants are particularly needed by investigating committees. Although trained investigators on loan from the executive branch have been, and are still, used by congressional committees, and such committees frequently work in cooperation with executive investigating agencies (such as the Federal Bureau of Investigation), the tendency has been for committees to rely more and more on their own staffs.[6] Investigating staffs are much less available to state legislative committees, although there are some notable cases of their use at the state level.[7]

Subject-matter Experts. Traditionally, experts on taxation, social security, procurements, education, mental health, and other subject matter have been used by Congress and the state legislatures on a temporary loan basis from executive agencies, or have been in the employ of interest groups and associations with interests in particular subject-matter areas. Increasingly Congress, and especially congressional committees, have acquired their own expert staff; this has been particularly true since the passage of the Legislative Reorganization Act of 1946. Economists, accountants, lawyers with a specialist expertise, natural and physical scientists, and political scientists, to name a few, are now found in some numbers among the professional staffs of Congress. At the state level, permanent expert staffs are fairly uncommon, except in the areas of statutory revision and fiscal review and analysis. In 1961 only 27 states had professional staff assistance for one or more of the standing committees of their legislatures.[8]

Political Staff. Some staff operations are almost exclusively "political," and require personnel with political expertise. The legislative strategist, the "ghost" writer for political speeches and books, and the political campaigner are to be found particularly on the staffs of senators and representatives, and even sometimes on committee staffs.

STAFF ORGANIZATION

Considerations of staff organization must be divided into separate treatment of committee staffs and of those of individual legislators. Unfortunately, political scientists have devoted very little attention to systematic internal analysis of legislative staff organization. Congressional committee staffs have followed one of four fairly distinct patterns of staff management.[9] The most prevalent arrangement has been one in which there is no professional staff director; instead, a chief clerk is in charge of the clerical force. A second arrangement is one in which a professional staff director and a chief clerk have roughly equal status, each heading his respective components among the staff of the committee. In a third arrangement, a director of the professional staff, who is usually called "chief of staff," supervises the entire committee staff, and the chief clerk is his subordinate and assistant. Finally, in some committee staffs the positions of staff director and chief clerk are combined, although the duties performed by the chief clerk under other arrangements are usually, under these circumstances, delegated to an assistant clerk.

The routine clerical tasks are, in most congressional committee staffs, assigned among clerks in a fairly uniform way, with one clerk responsible for updating the committee calendar, one responsible for processing committee publications, another for maintaining committee files, another for handling mail, and so forth. Such tasks are often rotated among clerks so that each will ultimately become skilled in the handling of various types of clerical work.

The substantive expertise provided by the congressional committee staff may be organized in one of two alternative ways. On the one hand, each professional staff man may have "a clearly defined field of specialization covering certain classes of subjects considered by the committee," so that, "for example, during the 82d Congress, the four professional staff members of the House Committee on Interior and Insular Affairs specialized in the following fields respectively: irrigation and reclamation; territories and insular possessions; Indian affairs; and mines and mining." On the other hand, the professional staff may be "deemed equally qualified to handle any subject falling within the committee's jurisdiction," and duties may be assigned to aides "in a flexible fashion depending chiefly upon their relative availability."[10]

The two key aides of congressional committees, the chief clerks and the professional staff directors, have fairly clearly definable duties. The duties of the typical chief clerk have been described as follows:

> Whatever other duties he might perform on different committees during the period covered, the chief clerk's main responsibility was taking care of the administrative management aspects of the committee staff work. He was a sort of combined administrative officer and executive secretary. He saw that the committee, its subcommittees, and staff were supplied with the various institutional services essential to their operating properly; took care of the routine details of organizing hearings; gave out information about the committee's activities; and handled the bulk of the committee correspondence. In addition to supervising the clerical staff in discharging the above and related duties, he took the minutes, conducted roll calls, and tallied the votes taken at committee meetings.[11]

The professional staff director's duties can be summarized in the following categories:

> (1) He usually serves as the chairman's assistant and personal representative, assisting in planning and organizing the committee's work.
> (2) He acts as a liaison man between the rest of the staff and the members of the committee, serving as a channel through which assignments of work go from congressmen to staff.
> (3) He serves as an interpreter of congressional attitudes to the staff, anticipating congressional reactions to projected policy recommendations and advising other staff members accordingly.
> (4) He usually makes suggestions on the organization and content of committee reports and studies prepared by the staff, reviewing their work before its publication.[12]

There are many variations in the staff organization of the aides of individual members of Congress. The staffs of members of the House of Representatives are sufficiently small so that probably there generally obtains a relatively close working relationship between the member and each aide on a personal basis. Senate members' staffs vary more in size, and are more likely to be "bureaucratized." The types of Senate staff organization that have been observed are described as follows:

> It is possible to distinguish between two types of Senate offices, the bureaucratic and the individualistic. While very few offices are pure examples of either, most offices can be easily classified as tending toward one or the other. In the bureaucratic offices, the senator has delegated considerable

non-routine responsibilities to his staff, established a fairly clearcut division of labor and chain of command. The administrative assistant is really a "senator, junior grade," and under his direction other members of the staff specialize in such things as legislative research and speechwriting, answering the mail, press relations, or patronage matters. At the opposite end of the spectrum are the individualistic offices, "vest pocket" operations in which the senator has delegated only routine tasks and in which the staff has little influence and less authority. In these offices, a division of labor is relatively amorphous—"everyone does a little bit of everything in this office"—and the administrative assistant's job is reduced to that of a "paper shuffler."[13]

The role of the senators' staffs in policy making varies between individualistic and bureaucratic offices. In bureaucratic contexts, the staff serves as the important communications link between the senator and other members, lobbyists, newspapermen, executive officials, and constituents; in individualistic offices, the policy role of the staff is much reduced, and there is a tendency for the senator himself to handle all important matters.

No treatment of legislative staff organization would be adequate without some consideration to the staff of the legislative houses themselves. These aides constitute an important part of the housekeeping staff for legislatures, and usually include the clerk of the house, the sergeant-at-arms, the parliamentarian, and a variety of other officers. Unfortunately, we have no systematic data by means of which to generalize extensively about such aides, but it is clear that they may facilitate the performance of legislative tasks, ease the adjustment of legislators to the legislative system, and influence legislative policy making.

The integrative function of aides employed by the legislative bodies themselves can be illustrated by the following description of the activities of William M. "Fishbait" Miller, the majority Doorkeeper of the United States House of Representatives, and his associates:

"Fishbait" gets to know his future charges before they're elected. On even (election) years when Congress adjourns, "Fishbait," 50-year-old Chief Page Turner Robertson and Charles Hackney, Assistant Director of the House Telephone, scoot over to the National Democratic Congressional Campaign Committee. . . . By election night, "Fishbait" knows the Democratic candidates from A to Z.

A week or so after battle, victors trickle into the Doorkeeper's office, ripe for the "Fishbait Special." "Fishbait" welcomes them with courtly Mississippi charm in his green-carpeted, gilt-mirrored suite. Then, he personally conducts them on a leisurely tour. Here are the "fishbait special" ports-of-call:

First, the stationery room where the Congressman-elect pens a facsimile signature as pattern for his mailing frank. Second stop is *chez* Emmanuel

Ridgell, the House Office Building Superintendent. Mr. Ridgell explains the office situation, asks the newcomer to draw a metal disk from a box. The desk number determines priority on the office space list. Then, the Superintendent "shoos" them off to inspect a sample suite.

Afterward, the Doorman takes his new Congressman visiting. They drop into the Speaker's office to meet Mr. Sam's administrative assistant, John Holton, then call on assistants to the House Parliamentarian. Next, the freshman legislator is introduced to Joe Metzger, the Parliamentarian's secretary, an important "guy" to know, because he stopwatches the minutes allowed for House oratory. Last on the list is Lewis Deschler, the Parliamentarian who's been interpreting the rules for 30 years. Deschler sets the newcomer in the right groove by giving a 5- to 10-minute briefing on House procedure.

Next, the Congressman gets down to practical business. Ralph Roberts, the House Clerk, reminds him to file a campaign expenditures accounting and keep his certificate of election handy. Harry Livingston, Disbursing Office Chief, follows along, explaining that a Congressman may hire up to eight clerks, secretaries, stenographers. . . . And now comes the big moment when the happy Congressman is put on the payroll. He's in. It's Zeake W. Johnson, Jr., the House Sergeant at Arms, who turns the trick. . . .

But what of "Fishbait" himself? How come a doorkeeper is so important that he's constantly consulted by congressional VIPs and draws a cosy $18,150 annually? It's because his job is important. It was set up during the first session of our First Congress. . . . The job's purpose, according to the incumbent, is to take care of all the chores. The chores are something and under "Fishbait's" direction 250 to 300 employees handle them. They include House pages, working doormen and 40 custodians who keep the vast House spotless. "Fishbait" also supervises three barbershops; the document and folding rooms, and a snack bar in both Democratic and Republican cloakrooms. . . .[14]

At the state level, the staff assistance for the legislative houses is much less elaborate, and ordinarily the clerks of the House and Senate are the key figures. They are the chief administrative officers of the houses, and in many states serve over a long period of years. Perhaps largely because of their typically long tenure of service for essentially amateur legislative bodies, these clerks can come to have substantial influence on state legislation.[15]

CHARACTERISTICS OF CONGRESSIONAL STAFFS

While few comprehensive data are available for all the staff personnel employed by Congress, we do have some data for the description of characteristics of the "key" staff people, whose biographies appear in the *Congressional Staff Directory*. The information from these biographies is limited, and we do not know how adequate a sample of the total congressional staff these people are. Even so, an analysis of the 1,125 biographies in the 1963 *Directory* provides us with some interesting descriptive information.

Table 10.1 shows the assignments of congressional staffs. Of the 1,125 personnel considered for analysis, a higher percentage (54 percent) are assigned to the House of Representatives. The largest proportion of those in the "miscellaneous others" category are staffs of joint committees and the Library of Congress.

Table 10.1. ASSIGNMENTS OF CONGRESSIONAL STAFFS, 1963

Assignment	Number	Percent
House member	485	43
Committee	105	9
Staff	20	2
House of Representatives	610	54
Senate member	235	21
Committee	136	12
Staff	25	2
Senate	396	35
Miscellaneous others	119	10
Total	1,125	99*

* Total does not equal 100% because of rounding.

SOURCE: *Congressional Staff Directory*, 1963.

A preponderance of staff personnel employed by representatives and senators come from the members' own states, and the proportion of aides residing in the members' states is higher on the Senate side (70 percent) than on the House side (66 percent). In addition, administrative assistants who are the congressman's key aides are more likely to be residents of the member's state than others on his staff.

Congressional staff people are a highly educated category. The proportion of aides with college educations (97 percent) is higher than that for members of the House and Senate (see Chapter 5, Table 5.7). Table 10.2 shows the educational backgrounds of staff personnel, where such information is available. It is interesting to note the prominence of legal education here as elsewhere in the legislative system. Nearly two-fifths of the congressional staff have law degrees, and every staff position category, except those of "public relations" and "secretary," contains a considerable proportion of lawyers.[16] The high percentage of Ph.D.'s in the "other" category is to be accounted for by the fact that this category includes personnel employed by the Library of Congress, and the sizable percentage of lawyers in that category is explained by the fact that it includes the staff of the Office of Legislative Counsel.

Although a significant proportion of congressional aides have had legal training, a much smaller percentage enter staff service from private law practice, as Table 10.3 shows. Where a previous kind of experience was indicated in their biographies, most had had it in government work, either with administrative agencies (20 percent) or in other legislative staff work (26 percent). Legislative counsels, overwhelmingly lawyers, did tend to come from law practice, more than other staff positions did; clerks and staff directors tended to come to their positions from prior legislative staff work, more than did other types; public relations staff people tended to come from private business. Those in the "other" category, which includes mainly the staff of the Library of Congress, tended more than in other categories to come from administrative agencies, while field representatives and secretaries were more likely not to have indicated previous experience. Administrative and research assistants tended to be drawn heavily from administrative agencies, legislative staffs, and private business.

In summary, it can be said that the bulk (64 percent) of the 1,125 staff people who were examined work for individual members of the House and Senate. There is overwhelming male dominance in most staff positions, with the exception of secretaries. More than two-thirds of the individual members' staffs are recruited from the members' own states. Congressional aides are a highly educated group; 97 percent of the 1,125 individuals examined had college educations or beyond, and the largest number had law degrees. Finally, nearly half (48 percent) had previous experience in political life either with an administrative agency, a legislative staff, or a public elective office.

PARTISANSHIP IN CONGRESSIONAL COMMITTEE STAFFING[17]

The Legislative Reorganization Act of 1946 authorized each standing congressional committee to hire, by a majority vote of the committee, four professional staff members. The appropriations committees were allowed additional staff, and the act further authorized each committee to employ as many as six clerks. These staff members were to be chosen by the full committees on the basis of ability and without regard to partisan political affiliation. They were to serve the committee chairman, the ranking minority members, and the committee membership

Table 10.2. CONGRESSIONAL STAFFS, EDUCATIONAL BACKGROUND, 1963

(In percentages)

Educational Background	Staff Position								
	Admin. asst. (N=306)	Research asst. (N=58)	Counsel (N=96)	Clerk/ staff dir. (N=37)	Field rep. (N=13)	Public relations (N=19)	Secretary (N=72)	Other (N=132)	Total* (N=733)
Less than college	3	2	0	5	0	11	8	1	3
Bachelor's degree	47	45	1	43	31	68	56	22	37
Master's degree or postgraduate work	17	19	1	19	23	21	18	20	16
Law degree	30	26	97	30	46	0	17	37	38
Ph.D. degree	3	9	1	3	0	0	1	20	6
Total	100	101†	100	100	100	100	100	100	100

* The tabulation shows educational backgrounds only for those personnel for whom information was available (733 out of a total of 1,125).

† Equals more than 100% because of rounding.

SOURCE: *Congressional Staff Directory*, 1963.

Table 10.3. Congressional Staffs, Experience Prior to Present Position, 1963
(In percentages)

Previous Experience	Staff Position								
	Admin. asst. (N=514)	Research asst. (N=99)	Counsel (N=156)	Clerk/staff dir. (N=95)	Field rep. (N=37)	Public relations (N=39)	Secretary (N=284)	Other (N=254)	Total* (N=1,479)
None indicated	21	22	8	9	27	21	31	16	20
Administrative agency	15	25	22	23	19	10	18	33	20
Legislative staff	26	25	28	39	14	15	29	20	26
Political-elective	3	3	†	3	5	0	1	1	2
Private business	24	16	6	17	24	54	18	21	20
Law Practice	12	8	35	9	11	0	3	8	11
Total‡	101	99	99	100	100	100	100	99	99

* Total exceeds 1,125 because aides indicated more than one type of previous experience.
† Less than 1%.
‡ Some totals differ from 100% because of rounding.
SOURCE: *Congressional Staff Directory*, 1963.

as a kind of legislative "civil service." The original authorizations in the act now constitute an inadequate number of expert assistants for most of the committees of Congress, and many standing and special sub-committees now have their own staffs, including a full complement of professional staff assistants. Additionally, a number of committees (the House Committee on Education and Labor is a good example) have secured special permission from the parent chamber to hire professional staff assistants in excess of the stipulated number.

Although the act provides that staff members shall be available to the minority-party members of committees, and thus it might be said that the special needs of the minority are recognized, no provision is made for the designation of specific staff aides as minority assistants who serve exclusively the minority members. While this sometimes occurs in practice, the staffs of some congressional committees are often manifestly selected in such a way as to provide only a minimum of staff assistance to the minority members of committees.

Tables 10.4 and 10.5 indicate the majority- and minority-party identification of congressional committee staffs during the second session of the Eighty-seventh Congress. These tables suggest that there are two types of congressional committee staffs, with regard to their partisan composition. One is the highly professionalized, nonpartisan staff, illustrated by the House Foreign Affairs Committee, the Senate Foreign Relations Committee, and the Armed Services committees of both houses. These committees appear to recruit their staffs on a nonpartisan basis. Even where committees have both majority and minority staffs, the two may be integrated and may work together. Such was the case, for example, with the staff of the House Committee on Interior and Insular Affairs during the Eighty-second Congress, when the minority clerk performed the same duties as the other assistant clerks working for the committee. Again, the assistant chief clerk of the Senate Interstate and Foreign Commerce Committee during the Eighty-second Congress, a minority appointee, did not execute "any assignments of a partisan character for the minority members of the committee."[18] In neither case did these minority staff people assume the position of chief clerk when the party control of the Congress shifted with the Eighty-third Congress.

Another type of committee staff is the partisan staff, where party affiliation is a very important criterion in staff selection; here the minority staff services only minority members of the committees, while majority staff appointees serve only majority members of the committees. In the partisan staff, minority members are appointed by and work only for the ranking minority committee member. They may, as was the case in the Senate Labor and Public Welfare Committee staff in the Eighty-second Congress, be completely isolated physically from

Table 10.4. MAJORITY AND MINORITY COMMITTEE STAFF MEMBERS,
U.S. HOUSE OF REPRESENTATIVES, 1962*

Committee	Total Staff	Majority (Dem)	Minority (Rep)
Agriculture	11	10	1
Appropriations	61	48	13
Armed Services	15	†	†
Banking and Currency	14	12	2
District of Columbia	9	8	1
Education and Labor	47	45	2
Foreign Affairs	15	†	†
Government Operations	49	46	3
House Administration	6	4	2
Interior and Insular Affairs	9	7	2
Interstate and Foreign Commerce	25	†	†
Judiciary	43	42	1
Merchant Marine and Fisheries	9	8	1
Post Office and Civil Service	16	†	†
Public Works	45	40	5
Rules	3	2	1
Science and Astronautics	16	†	†
Un-American Activities	52	51	1
Veterans' Affairs	14	12	2
Ways and Means	21	17	4
Select: Small Business	20	18	2
Select: Export Control	4	†	†
Total	504	370	43

* Data for the table, effective April 11, 1962, were compiled by the office of Representative Fred Schwengel (R-Ia), and were checked by the Congressional Quarterly, Inc., prior to their use in the *Congressional Quarterly Weekly Report*, XX (May 4, 1962), 765.

† The committee staff is not organized in terms of majority and minority employees.

SOURCE: J. D. Cochrane, "Partisan Aspects of Congressional Committee Staffing," *Western Political Quarterly*, XVII (1964), 341.

the main committee offices and virtually unaware of the work of the majority staff. The House Education and Labor Committee provides another example of a staff in which majority and minority distinctions are sharp; the staff does not serve all the members of the committee, the minority has a very small amount of staff assistance, and intrastaff cooperation is minimized:

Table 10.5. MAJORITY AND MINORITY STAFF MEMBERS,
SENATE AND JOINT COMMITTEES, 1962*

Committee	Total Staff	Majority (Dem)	Minority (Rep)
SENATE			
Aeronautical and Space Sciences	12	11	1
Agriculture and Forestry	8	7	1
Appropriations	35	33	2
Armed Services	26	25	1
Banking and Currency	20	15	5
Commerce	30	26	4
District of Columbia	8	7	1
Finance	6	5	1
Governmental Operations	49	45	4
Foreign Relations	22	†	†
Interior and Insular Affairs	17	16	1
Judiciary	158	145	13
Labor and Public Welfare	32	24	8
Post Office and Civil Service	18	15	3
Public Works	17	14	3
Rules and Administration	14	11	3
Select: Small Business	18	17	1
Select: Aging	18	16	2
Total	508	432	54
JOINT COMMITTEES			
Atomic Energy	20	†	†
Defense Production	5	†	†
Disposition of Executive Papers	0	0	0
Economic	17	16	1
Internal Revenue Taxation	19	†	†
Library	0	0	0
Printing	9	8	1
Reduction of Nonessential Federal Expenditures	2	†	†
Total	72	24	2

* Data for the table, effective April 11, 1962, were compiled by the office of Senator Carl T. Curtis (R-Neb), and were checked by the Congressional Quarterly, Inc., prior to their use in the *Congressional Quarterly Weekly Report,* XX (March 16 and May 4, 1962), 449, 765.

† The committee staff is not organized in terms of majority and minority employees.

SOURCE: J. D. Cochrane, "Partisan Aspects of Congressional Committee Staffing," *Western Political Quarterly,* XVII (1964), 342.

When Representative John Lesinski (D.-Mich.), a liberal Northern Democrat, was chairman of the House Education and Labor Committee, John Graham, the minority clerk, and his assistant were completely isolated from the rest of the committee staff. The main committee offices were practically foreign territory to Mr. Graham. Whenever he entered them, the majority staff members would turn papers upside down so that he could not see what they were doing.[19]

This pattern of staff behavior changed markedly when Graham Barden (D-NC) became committee chairman; thereafter, unusual harmony developed between majority and minority staff members. But the more partisan structure of the staff of Education and Labor appears to have been reinstated under the chairmanship of Adam Clayton Powell (D-NY).

Between the extremes of highly partisan and very nonpartisan congressional committee staffs lie many variations. In some committee staffs, only the top staff people operate in partisan ways, while the bulk of the staff is nonpartisan in the sense of being accessible to all members regardless of their party affiliation. In some cases of that kind, the ranking minority assistant clerk may become chief clerk of the staff when the party composition of the house changes, and *vice versa*.

While partisan recruitment of committee staff personnel does not necessarily lead to partisan behavior on the part of the staff, the numbers of staff people designated as minority staff are remarkably small for committees that distinguish between majority and minority staff. Six House and three Senate committees are characterized by relatively nonpartisan recruitment of committee staff personnel, as are several of the joint congressional committees. The remaining committees are characterized by a substantial imbalance in the partisan recruitment of committee aides, which cannot be explained adequately in terms of party ratios on the committees themselves, or in terms of the workload which falls to the majority, and appears to be explainable largely in terms of purely partisan factors.*

CONGRESSIONAL STAFF ACTIVITY: THREE CASES

In order to illustrate the activities of congressional committee staffs, we have selected three brief case studies from the unfortunately meager

---

* Efforts were made in 1962–1963 to get increases in minority staffing. In February 1962, the Senate voted 30–55 on a partisan basis to reject a proposal submitted by Curtis (R-Neb) to establish a fixed ratio of minority staff personnel for Senate committees. In March and April resolutions were offered in the House by Schwengel (R-Ia) and Rhodes (R-Ariz) which would have permitted the minority members of a committee to hire approximately 40% of the staff. The Rhodes proposal was rejected, and the Schwengel resolution was ruled out of order. In October 1962, a

literature on this subject. The first deals with the organization and operations of the House Committee on Un-American Activities during the late 1950s. Congressional investigating committees sometimes undergo rapid changes in staff size and organization; large numbers of temporary investigative staff personnel may be used by such a committee to pursue specific topics. Temporary investigators are sometimes "borrowed" from executive agencies for such purposes. The House Un-American Activities Committee (HUAC) had an ignoble birth as a select committee in 1938, although it was made a standing committee in 1945. While investigations are frequently conducted by other committees and subcommittees of the Congress, HUAC is the only standing investigating committee. In regard to public prestige and popularity within the House, the committee has evoked a varied response.

The committee has relied largely upon its own staff; the size of the staff has been characterized by stable growth, and the staff is organized preeminently for the purpose of conducting investigations. Since investigating duties constitute an important activity of congressional staffs, HUAC provides an instructive and interesting illustration of staff organization.

Case 1: The HUAC Staff. The staff of the Un-American Activities Committee has been loosely organized into three divisions: investigations, research, and files. It is difficult to get a clear picture of the separate functions of these divisions or of the lines of communication which connect them to each other and to any central authority. The threefold division of responsibility has taken shape through the years, and specific duties have depended at any given moment upon the availability of personnel and upon the abilities and inclinations of the division heads.

The investigative unit has always been the most important part of the staff. The committee's staff heads—Adamson, Stripling, and Tavenner—have been closely identified with the work of this unit. Many of the committee's most famous investigations, such as those dealing with the motion picture industry and with Communist espionage, have been largely planned by this division. It has been responsible not only for the extensive field work which has had to be performed before public hearings could be held, but also for the actual conduct of these hearings. Members of the division . . . have often joined . . . in the questioning of witnesses, with particular reference to specific points which have been under examination by them.

Joint Ad Hoc Committee on Increased Minority Staffing was created, consisting of Senators Scott (Pa), Curtis (Neb), and Prouty (Vt) and Representatives Curtis (Mo), Lipscomb (Calif), and Schwengel (Ia). In January 1963, the House Republican Conference appointed a 12-man Committee on Increased Minority Staffing, with Representative Schwengel as its chairman. These committees have done some research and introduced new resolutions. Ranking Republicans on House and Senate committees have generally opposed these efforts on the grounds that they impair their working relationships with Democratic leaders.

The research unit has two primary responsibilities: feeding new materials into the committee's files by maintaining a careful watch of newspapers, periodicals, and other sources for information concerning the organizations and individuals considered to be inclined toward subversive activity, and preparing certain of the committee's written reports—in particular, those dealing with private organizations alleged to be Communist fronts, such as the Southern Conference for Human Welfare or the Congress of American Women.

The files unit, from the point of view of administrative organization, has had a purely ministerial function—that of maintaining the committee's extensive records in such physical condition that they are readily available to those who have authority to use them. The personnel of this unit has thus attracted little attention and has never been involved in controversy. But the files themselves have been the center of vigorous and persistent controversy. . . . The files are a voluminous mass of miscellaneous, undigested materials and information pertaining to thousands of organizations and perhaps one million individuals. Physically, the file material is of two types: a card index consisting of hundreds of thousands of entries, and a very much smaller number of folders containing exhibits and source materials. . . .[20]

A second activity of congressional committee staffs which can be illustrated here is that of supplying data, speeches, propaganda, and the like for sponsors of a bill. This kind of staff activity is exemplified in some detail in the following extract, dealing with the legislative campaign operations of the small staff of the House Banking and Currency Committee, which was involved in the passage of the Full Employment Act of 1946.

Case 2: The Full Employment Staff. No one who has dipped into the economic literature on employment policy can fail to recognize the technical complexities of the subject. One of the most significant contributions of the staff was the collection, analysis, and distribution of basic data about the background of full-employment thinking in this and other countries. In the preparation of this material, Gross [Bertram Gross, in 1945 the Staff Director of the War Contracts Subcommittee] used all possible public and private resources: universities, private research organizations, the Legislative Reference Service, and many of the departments and agencies of the Executive branch. . . .

One of the best examples of staff activity of this type was the preparation of a manual entitled "Basic Facts on Employment and Production." The Budget Bureau, with the assistance of the Census Bureau, the Bureau of Labor Statistics, the Bureau of Agricultural Economics, the Division of Research and Statistics of the Federal Reserve Board, the Treasury Department, and the National Bureau of Economic Research, organized the basic statistical data, and Sam Thompson, on loan to the Banking and Currency Committee from the Commerce Department, pulled the data together and with Bertram Gross prepared various notes commenting on special aspects of the material.

This thirty-five-page manual included "summary figures on population and the labor force; employment; production, income and expenditures; productivity; prices; consumer credit; and liquid assets available for the transition from war to peace . . . the history of Federal Government receipts, expenditures, surpluses, deficits, and the public debt, and a presentation of the relative position of the United States in the world economy."

To the sponsors of S. 380 and to others interested in full employment, the material gathered and prepared by the staff was of unquestionable value. Some of the ablest experts on employment policy in and out of the government made their advice available to Congress through the requests of the staff. And when employment schemes rolled in on the tide of mail from special interest groups or individuals, this material was screened and analyzed and briefed for the consideration of the busy sponsors.

A second important function performed by the staff was the preliminary drafting of speeches, articles, letters, press releases, memoranda, and reports for the various sponsors of the bill. . . . Between January, 1945, and February, 1946, Senator Murray alone issued over twenty-five long statements—written and oral—on full employment. These included statements on the floor of the Senate, testimony before the Banking and Currency Committee, and speeches before such diverse groups as the Chicago Reconversion Conference of the National Association of Manufacturers and the Hosiery Wholesalers National Association. . . .

One of the most interesting and perhaps significant activities of the staff was the development of a direct-mail technique which Gross had first explored in his work with the War Contracts Subcommittee. . . . When Gross began to work on the Full Employment Bill, he recalled the value of this consultation by correspondence. With Senator Murray's support, he chose 200 names . . . and in February, 1945, sent out copies of the Full Employment Bill along with a covering letter from Murray. The comments and criticisms of the businessmen were solicited, and a number of replies were received. . . . Later, in March and April, this consultation-by-mail technique was extended to include 1,500 public-opinion-formers all over the United States. . . . By these and other devices the staff rapidly increased the ferment of discussion on the full employment issue in and out of Washington, and was able to provide the sponsors of the bill with intellectual ammunition and support.

Much of the staff work on the Senate hearings was of course routine: answering requests from the scores of people who wanted to testify, sending out letters and telegrams to potential witnesses, preparing time schedules, and handling requests for information and printed and mimeographed material from individuals and organizations specially interested in the hearings. However, the staff worked closely with Senator Wagner in selecting witnesses and in preparing data and drafts for the testimony of Senators Murray, Thomas, O'Mahoney, and Patman. . . .

Strategically, . . . the proponents of the Full Employment Bill had three major jobs on their hands outside of Congress: (1) to arouse public interest, (2) to mobilize and unify the friends of the Full Employment Bill, and (3) to split the opposition.

. . . the staff used every possible device to get the full employment issue before the people. They worked closely with the press, especially with commentators and reporters whose liberal position could be trusted; they gave full cooperation to radio forums interested in securing speakers to debate the full employment issue; they made contact with the *March of Time* in the hope that a movie short would be made on the whole subject of postwar employment; they worked with state legislators and legislative representatives of liberal pressure groups in preparing "Little Murray Bills" which were to be introduced in the state legislatures along with a statement memorializing Congress to support the National Full Employment Bill. . . .

For a period of ten months (the staff) . . . had at their service virtually the entire resources of the Union for Democratic Action, a liberal organization which assumed the job of spearheading the liberal-labor fight for the Full Employment Bill. The Union for Democratic Action provided a full-time Washington representative in the person of Paul Sifton, formerly with the National Farmers Union, to work in the closest possible relation with the staff and the sponsors of S. 380 in building a strong liberal front for the passage of the bill. . . . By the time the Senate hearings were held, Gross and Sifton, with the active support of Senators Wagner and Murray, had organized an informal Continuations Group which met weekly to discuss liberal strategy for passage of the bill. . . .

Early in the fight, Gross wrote to various liberal businessmen in New York and New England who had supported Roosevelt in the 1944 election. He asked them for the names of other businessmen and industrialists who might be sympathetic to the Full Employment Bill. Through these and other contacts, relationships were established with two small business organizations [and] . . . their support and the qualified support of a small number of influential businessmen like Beardsley Ruml and Ralph E. Flanders made it possible for the sponsor of the bill to claim that ". . . small businessmen want full employment. . . . Enlightened big businessmen want full employment."

. . . During the months before the Senate hearings, the full employment staff maintained constant contact with representatives of the National Farmers Union and with strategically placed men in the Department of Agriculture in an attempt to educate the farmers to their "real" interest in full employment.

Realizing the growing power of the veteran in national affairs, the sponsors of the bill, largely through the staff, tried to gain the support of the leading veterans organizations. . . . Charles Bolte, Chairman of A.V.C., stated his organization's support in a letter to Senator Wagner on June 7, 1945, and Gross was quick to follow this up with an invitation to have Bolte testify before the Senate Committee.[21]

Finally, some congressional committees are involved, a few very deeply, in oversight of the administration. Staff practices in overseeing or checking on the administration of congressional enactments by executive agencies vary a great deal. Some committees are more active in this respect than others, and staff activities depend largely upon the expectations of members of the committees. The staff work of the Joint Committee on Atomic Energy, described briefly in Case 3, provides an example of a close and relatively harmonious relationship between a committee staff and an executive agency.

Case 3: The JCAE Staff. Few other legislative committees have made as great use of staff assistance in both technical and policy areas as has the Joint Committee on Atomic Energy. The JCAE has permitted, even encouraged, an unusual degree of creative initiative on the part of its staff. The staff has played such a crucial role, in fact, that one might properly inquire, not whether the Committee has maintained its expertness independently of information volunteered by the Executive, but rather whether it has not surrendered a portion of its prized independence to its own staff.

Besides the impressive abilities of staff professionals (which are indeed difficult to weigh against those of the staffs of other committees), there are four persuasive reasons for the effectiveness of the JCAE staff. First, the Committee's business has always covered a much narrower range than that of other committees; atomic energy has been a manageable field of endeavor for members and staff alike. Second, the relatively light legislative load, especially in the early years, and the fewer time-consuming, routine chores have allowed the JCAE professionals more time for studies in depth and self-education. . . . Third, there has been considerable continuity of personnel on the JCAE staff. . . . Finally, JCAE members have regarded the staff as unique and have taken unusual interest in its selection and activities. Unlike most committee staffs, there is no separate majority and minority staff. A single group of professionals services members of both parties and all of the subcommittees. . . .

Although the duties of JCAE staff professionals have covered a wide range—from preparing speeches for members to setting up hearings, arranging for witnesses, and preparing Committee documents for publication—undoubtedly the main job has been continuing liaison with, and scrutiny of, the AEC. . . . The staff men have accomplished this objective by going directly to the sources of information, the Commission's operating personnel. This direct contact has been maintained not only with personnel in AEC's Washington headquarters, but with field personnel as well. . . .

Seldom has the AEC attempted to escape the watchful eye of Committee staff members, who have generally been welcomed on their visits to AEC headquarters and field offices. That staff liaison has been so successful is due partly to the obligations imposed on the AEC by the statutory "fully-and-currently-informed" provision, partly to the cordial personal relationships between Committee and Commission staffs, and partly to the fact that the JCAE offers a promising avenue of appeal to bureaucrats and scientists who have had their proposals turned down by the Commission. . . .

In addition to the collection and processing of useful information, the staff has also played a more creative role. It has suggested problems for exploration, [and launched] the Committee on investigations that otherwise might not have taken place. In 1958 and 1959, for example, members of the

JCAE and the Committee staff became concerned about the safety and custody of nuclear weapons, particularly those assigned to NATO. In the summer of 1960, the staff embarked on a classified study, and in the winter staff members accompanied a special subcommittee on an inspection trip of nuclear-weapons installations in Europe. The outcome of JCAE investigation was a classified report to the president recommending electronic devices on nuclear weapons. "The idea of utilizing various electro-mechanical devices to improve U.S. custody and control of nuclear weapons," said Senator Anderson, "originated with the staff of the Joint Committee and, more specifically, our staff director."

Generally, staff members have worked up preliminary plans for hearings and then have discussed their ideas with the JCAE chairman. Their arguments have usually been so persuasive that hearings have been scheduled. The staff then determined the agenda of hearings, screened the information upon which members relied, participated in executive sessions, drafted Committee reports and recommendations, and assisted on the floor of the two chambers. By the subtle processes of inclusion and exclusion, it has been able at every stage of the decision-making process to structure alternatives and thereby influence the outcome.

Sometimes the Committee staff has felt it unnecessary to burden busy members with decisions that could be made at lower echelons. By working closely with AEC professionals, JCAE staff men have exerted influence even before problems have reached the attention of either commissioners or Committee members. Staff professionals have made special investigations of the AEC, during which they have been able to informally inject their views. Their influence thus extends well beyond the limits that their nominal positions would imply. They have conferred with AEC officials on policy questions in the effort to work out compromises and solutions on an informal basis. Thus, JCAE professionals have had the opportunity of participating in preliminary negotiations and have consequently influenced the nature of subsequent decisions.

Despite the powers delegated it, the JCAE staff has been limited in the arrangements it could negotiate independently of its patrons' desires or without their knowledge. Staff professionals have realized that the Committee, or at least the chairman and majority, must be sympathetic to the course they were taking. However aggressive and free-wheeling the JCAE staff in its dealings with the executive branch, it undoubtedly reflected the natural tendency of the Joint Committee itself. As long as the staff has worked in a direction approved by the chairman and Committee majority, it has been permitted wide scope for its energies. . . .[22]

STATE LEGISLATIVE STAFFING[23]

Generally speaking, the bulk of the staff services available to members of the American state legislatures is contained in the research arms of the legislative council organizations that are now operating in 39 states. The size of the staffs of these councils varies considerably from state to state, ranging from 2 or 3 to as many as 20. The staff director is the key figure in the research organization; typically, the directors of state legislative council staffs have served long tenure in their positions. Almost invariably, these men—such as Frederick Guild in Kansas, Emmett Asseff in Louisiana, Jack Rhodes in Oklahoma, and Earl Sachse in Wisconsin—have directed the research staffs in their states for a long time; some, like Dr. Guild, are identified with the beginning of the legislative council movement itself.

The policy position of the research staff, and its general effectiveness, are associated with the personality and capacities of the director. He may develop a viable and effective staff, intimately involved in the legislative policy-making processes, or he may, by ineptness or incapacity, wreck the research operation.

Nebraska is a case in point. One of the oldest councils, created in the heady atmosphere of a novel experiment in legislative organization, regarded as a vital element of the unicameral legislature, operating in the context of weak gubernatorial leadership, it was marked between 1937 and 1953 by a relatively undistinguished performance, largely as a result of the approach taken by its late director.[24]

In addition, the policy role of the staff is affected by the position of the council itself in the state's legislative system. In the *policy-planning* council situation, as typified by the Kansas Legislative Council, the council itself is an integral and immediate part of the legislative process; it regularly makes policy recommendations to the legislature, and tends to have a relatively high "batting average."[25] In such a context, the staff is an adjunct to an interim legislative committee that operates at the center of legislative activity, and "the significance of the council *does not* rest on the fact that it furnishes a valuable research product." Here, "the research function is an integral element, but its importance lies in the way in which it is deliberately and effectively subordinated."[26]

In the *research-type* council, illustrated by the Illinois Legislative Council, the research operation is purely informative and advisory. The council itself makes no recommendations to the legislature, and it operates on the periphery of the legislative process. Indeed, the council's principal role may be that of protecting and insulating the staff from policy influence and partisan politics. In this context, the research staff serves primarily to provide accurate information to individual legislators.

The workload of the Illinois council has grown slowly and steadily throughout the period of its existence; the director currently receives requests for a wide variety of services from individual legislators, "ranging from speech material to arguments in favor of or against a given measure, from help in handling a technically complicated inquiry from a constituent to somehow arranging for the reproduction of 150 copies of a letter." The council staff has come to be regarded by legislators as a major source of miscellaneous assistance as well as an almost unique clearing house of accurate information on practically any phase or problem of government in Illinois. . . .²⁷

In the case of the *governor's program* council, such as the Kentucky Legislative Research Commission, the research staff is in reality an arm of the executive branch, the Lieutenant Governor is the director of the Commission, and its policy role is dependent upon the legislative effectiveness of the incumbent governor. The governor has great influence upon the selection of council members, and its role is more that of promoting his program than program planning of its own.

NOTES

1. For example, Norman Meller, "The Policy Position of Legislative Service Agencies," *Western Political Quarterly*, V (1952), 109-23; Max M. Kampelman, "The Legislative Bureaucracy: Its Response to Political Change, 1953," *Journal of Politics*, XVI (1954), 539-50.

2. Kenneth Kofmehl, *Professional Staffs of Congress* (West Lafayette, Ind., 1962), p. 3; Lauros G. McConachie, *Congressional Committees* (New York, 1898), p. 65.

3. Belle Zeller (ed.), *American State Legislatures* (New York, 1954), pp. 156-59.

4. In this and succeeding paragraphs, references to staff development are drawn from George B. Galloway, *The Legislative Process in Congress* (New York, 1953), pp. 407-25; Zeller, *op. cit.*, pp. 124-62; and *The Book of the States, 1964-65* (Chicago, 1964), pp. 67-83.

5. Robert K. Carr, *The House Committee on Un-American Activities* (Ithaca, N.Y.: Cornell University Press, 1952), pp. 247-70, at pp. 247-48. Copyright 1952 by Cornell University. Used by permission of Cornell University Press.

6. M. Nelson McGeary, *The Development of Congressional Investigative Power* (New York, 1940), pp. 59-66.

7. For example, Vern Countryman, *Un-American Activities in the State of Washington* (Ithaca, N.Y., 1951), p. 22; Edward L. Barrett, *The Tenney Committee* (Ithaca, N.Y., 1951), pp. 18-19.

8. Council of State Governments, *Professional Assistance for Legislative Standing and Interim Committees and Legislative Leaders* (Chicago, 1961).

9. The following relies upon Kofmehl, *op. cit.*, pp. 39-51.

10. Quoted material from *ibid.*, p. 40.

11. *Ibid.*, p. 45.

12. *Ibid.*, pp. 46-49.

13. Donald R. Matthews, *U.S. Senators and Their World* (Chapel Hill, N.C.: University of North Carolina Press, 1960), pp. 83-84.

14. From an article by Mary Van Rensselaer reprinted in the *Congressional Record* (Appendix, daily edition), Feb. 2, 1959, pp. A731-2.

15. For example, Charles D. Hounshell, *The Legislative Process in Virginia* (Charlottesville, Va., 1951), pp. 8-9; see also Council of State Governments, *The Offices of Legislative Clerks and Secretaries in the States* (Chicago, 1957).

16. For an analysis and discussion of the prominence of lawyers on congres-

sional committee staffs, see Gladys M. Kammerer, *The Staffing of the Committees of Congress* (Lexington, Ky., 1949), and *Congressional Committee Staffing Since 1946* (Lexington, Ky., 1951), pp. 64–65.

17. This section relies heavily upon James D. Cochrane, "Partisan Aspects of Congressional Committee Staffing," *Western Political Quarterly*, XVII (1964), 338–48. See also Kofmehl, *op. cit.*, pp. 52–69.

18. Kofmehl, *op. cit.*, p. 58.

19. Powell had a wall built to reduce contact between Democratic and Republican staff members. For a brief discussion of "The Battle of Powell's Wall," see Claude Lewis, *Adam Clayton Powell* (Greenwich, Conn., 1963), pp. 97–98.

20. Excerpted from Carr, *op. cit.*, pp. 252–54.

21. Excerpted from Stephen K. Bailey, *Congress Makes a Law* (New York: Columbia University Press, 1950), pp. 67–78.

22. Excerpted from Harold P. Green and Alan Rosenthal, *Government of the Atom* (New York: Atherton Press, 1963), pp. 65–70.

23. This section is drawn primarily from William J. Siffin, *The Legislative Council in the American States* (Bloomington, Ind., 1959).

24. *Ibid.*, p. 195.

25. See William H. Cape and John P. Bay, *An Analysis of the Kansas Legislative Council and Its Research Department* (Lawrence, Kan., 1963).

26. Siffin, *op cit.*, pp. 92–93.

27. *Ibid.*, p. 146.

[11]

Legislative Procedures and Their Effects

FORMAL RULES and procedures are among the most important functional requisites of a legislative body. Together with the informal "rules of the game" discussed in Chapter 15, they constitute the primary means of normative regulation for legislators. It is difficult to imagine a legislature, or any other organization, existing and functioning for long without clearly defined rules. The importance of rules should be obvious to anyone who has attended a meeting in which the leading participants lacked knowledge of or agreement on procedural rules and has watched it degenerate into chaos. It may be helpful to distinguish between rules that help a group to maintain its existence and those that help it to achieve its goals. In addition, certain rules are part of the strategy of political conflict and may be viewed as serving the aims of particular groups, whether majorities or minorities. That is, some rules may be considered neutral, but others have a distinct effect on the legislative output. In a football game, for example, rules against unnecessary roughness might be considered neutral, but a rule change that facilitated field goals would help the team with a good kicker.

FUNCTIONS OF RULES

We can be more specific about the functions of rules in a legislative system. Fundamental for the existence of the legislature are rules that ensure stability, order, and predictability. Examples are rules that establish a regular order of business and assure orderly debate, as well as some of the organizational rules found in state constitutions. Several groups of rules can be related to the legislature's purpose as a lawmaking institution and not merely to the maintenance of its existence. Certain rules ensure the public and orderly consideration of bills—for example, the rules, often found in state constitutions, which require that bills be printed and read three times and that roll calls be recorded on the passage of all bills. Many rules serve to expedite legislative business—for example, the use of voice votes or standing votes, the handling of noncontroversial measures through unanimous-consent procedures, and the suspension of rules by an extraordinary majority. In legislatures where the committee system is important, rules and practices safeguard the prerogatives of the committee; these include rules on committee jurisdiction and rules and practices that discourage discharging bills from committee. The maintenance of strong committees is considered in many legislatures to be requisite for a high level of specialized competence, which in turn is essential for legislative independence from the executive.

A careful examination of those rules that are functional not for the legislature as a whole, but for some group within it, can tell us much about that particular legislature. Changes in rules are significant chapters in the history of a legislative body. Those rules that are not neutral may be classified according to the groups whose interests are served by the rule. Some rules serve the interests of a majority or its leadership. Rules that give the majority leadership control over the committee jurisdiction on bills, or over the timetable on the floor of the house, are designed for this purpose. Other examples are rules that permit a majority to cut off debate or to prevent the consideration of amendments. Other rules serve the interests of a minority; such rules may, of course, serve any minority that wants to delay or prevent action, but more particularly they benefit a minority party, faction, or regional grouping. Among examples of these are rules that permit unlimited debate or make it difficult to limit debate, as well as rules that require an extraordinary majority to transact certain kinds of business. Rules that affect timing are particularly important because the entire legislative process is a race against time, while rules that facilitate delaying tactics are among the most valuable weapons available to a minority. If a group with minority status in the legislature has effective control over a committee (as sometimes happens in Congress), rules designed to safeguard the committee's prerogatives and thus serve a legislative function may also serve the minority's interests.

Sources and History

The rules and precedents in Congress constitute a large, detailed, and complex body.[1] The Constitution provides broad authority for congressional rule-making: "Each House may determine the rules of its proceedings." The Senate and House have each adopted rules, which are printed in the Manuals of the two branches.* Both also make use of a manual prepared by Thomas Jefferson when he was serving as Vice-President. In addition, the rulings of the presiding officers of both houses have established precedents that affect the procedures to be followed. The rulings of the Speaker of the House, which have been more extensive and detailed, have been compiled in an eleven-volume publication[2] and summarized in a single volume of 498 pages.[3] Both houses have official parliamentarians, whose responsibility it is to supply the presiding officer and individual members with advice and information concerning interpretation of the rules and the pertinent precedents.

There is a significant difference between the two houses with regard to the status of rules. In the House, the rules are adopted at the beginning of each Congress, at which time the old rules may be re-adopted or modified; occasionally, changes have been made during the life of a Congress. The Senate, however, is a continuing body, in the sense that only about one-third of its members are elected or reelected prior to the opening of each Congress. Consequently, the Senate does not follow the practice of formally re-adopting the rules of the previous Congress. The rules may be modified, and efforts to change them are often made at the start of a new Congress, but the Senate is at all times bound by its previous rules. This is true even though all legislative business is considered *de novo* in the Senate, as well as in the House, at the start of a new Congress.

The continuity of Senate rules may seem to be a technicality, but it has played an important part in disputes over the filibuster. Opponents of the filibuster, who have tried to change the Senate rules in order to make it easier to stop debate, have been frustrated by the fact that the very proposals to change the rules have themselves been blocked by filibuster.† On several occasions, beginning in 1953, the proponents of rules changes have sought to persuade the Senate to accept the principle that rules were to be newly adopted at the start of each session; this would permit consideration of new rules under normal parliamentary

---

* The Legislative Reorganization Act of 1946 provided for changes in the rules of both houses, but included a provision that recognized the right of either house to make changes on its own authority in rules covered by the act.

† From 1949 until 1959, in fact, the Senate rules prohibited any motion to shut off debate—even by a two-thirds vote—on a motion to change the rules.

procedures of majority rule on all matters, including termination of debate.[4] Vice-President Nixon expressed his view as presiding officer that the Senate need not be bound by its previous rules. The Senate, however, expressed its approval of the principle of continuity in a series of votes, culminating in an amendment to the Senate rules, voted in 1959, which provided that "the rules of the Senate shall continue from one Congress to the next Congress," unless modified by the Senate. The dispute over continuity of the Senate shows how a rule that appears to be functional only for the legislative body may actually serve the interests of a single group.

A history of changes in the rules of the House is a significant chapter in the history of the House; in particular, it throws light on the conflict between majority and minority interests. Throughout the first hundred years of its existence, the House operated under rules that made it possible for a minority to delay and obstruct action on legislative matters. Little by little, changes in the rules enhanced the power of the majority and reduced that of the minority. These changes were often initiated by the Speaker; those Speakers who viewed their role as that of a party leader were the most aggressive in initiating changes that would serve the interests of the majority party. Often the changes initiated by the Speaker were consolidated through formal changes in the rules. In 1811, in an atmosphere of deadlock and division over foreign affairs, the House adopted the previous-question motion to permit cutting off debate. This proved inadequate to prevent filibusters, and during the 1840s the House adopted a one-hour limit for speeches and a five-minute rule for discussion of amendments. Basic revisions of the rules in 1860 and 1880 brought greater order and efficiency to the House, but did not substantially enhance majority power.[5]

It was Speaker Thomas Reed who initiated the devices that provided the majority with its modern control over the business of the House. By the simple device of counting as present members who were in the chamber but who refused to answer quorum calls, Reed eliminated the "disappearing quorum" as an effective tool of obstruction for the minority. He also declared his intention to reject any motions that were clearly dilatory in purpose. Reed's bold initiatives were promptly written into the House Rules in 1890. Reed also developed the "special rule" as the normal method of handling controversial legislation on the floor. Since special rules were the province of the Rules Committee, which was tightly controlled by the Speaker, this was an important technique of majority leadership. The famous revolution of 1910–1911 against Speaker Cannon, who had followed Reed and enlarged upon his techniques for control, stripped the Speaker of much of his power over the machinery of the House. The revolt, and the subsequent development of the seniority principle, made the committees independent of majority leadership. But the rules for procedure on the floor of the House that had been developed late in the nineteenth century remained in effect. House procedures today serve primarily majority interests, and leave little room for minority obstruction and little time for discussion and the proposal of amendments by individuals.

The rules of state legislatures, unlike those of Congress, are prescribed in some detail by constitutions. As we indicated in Chapter 6, these constitutional provisions sometimes impose serious limitations on the legislature's ability to adapt its procedures to its needs, but many of the constitutional requirements are ignored or evaded in practice. State legislative bodies develop formal rules, which are usually adopted with little change at the start of a session. Legislative procedure varies in particulars from state to state, but there are many similarities, often the result of the historical practice of copying the rules of a neighboring state or the rules of Congress. The variations reflect differences in environment and customs that have developed independently in the various states. What is lacking in most state legislatures is a body of precedents, either in written form or in the memories of veteran members, having to do with the detailed interpretation of the written rules. In the absence of detailed precedents, and with few members in most bodies who have a wealth of experience or parliamentary knowledge, the leadership usually can—if it chooses—run the legislature in an arbitrary fashion, with little regard to procedural niceties. Rules are a significant factor at the state legislative level, and a careful examination of them may provide useful clues to the power structure that has produced them. But in most state legislatures the rules are more flexible, less binding, and less comprehensive; consequently, written rules provide an imperfect guide to legislative practice.

PROCEDURES CONCERNING COMMITTEES

In the United States House of Representatives and in some state Houses, a member may introduce a bill simply by sending it to the Speaker's desk; in the United States Senate and most state Senates, the member must announce publicly that he is introducing a bill, and it must be read by title, a time-consuming chore in some legislatures. In order to expedite business and to prevent the crowding of the calendar late in the session, most states set a deadline on the introduction of bills for several days or weeks before the date provided by law for termination of the session.[6] The purpose of such deadlines is often evaded, however, either by the introduction of "skeleton bills," which may include only the title, or by the quite normal practice of consenting to late introduction by extraordinary majorities.

In Congress there are detailed rules concerning committee jurisdiction, which leave little if any discretion to the presiding officer in the matter of referring bills to committee and thus protect the committees' authority over particular categories of bills. In the states the presiding officer, or occasionally a committee, normally exercises broad discretion in referring bills and is consequently able to send important bills to dependable committees, either to ensure that they will be reported favorably or to guarantee that they will be buried (in what are often referred to as "graveyard" committees).

Procedure and practice with regard to the method of removing a bill from further consideration by a committee also tell us something about the importance of committees in the legislative system. Several states require committees to report out all bills—a requirement often evaded in practice. Although a discharge procedure is included in legislative rules, in most states it is rarely used. In the Arizona House, for example, a discharge petition has been used successfully only once since the attainment of statehood. This often results from a legislative norm with regard to the judgment and authority of committees, but in some states it means that the same majority party or group whose votes are necessary to a successful discharge motion has firm control over at least the most important committees.

Both branches of Congress have adopted procedures for drawing bills out of committees through discharge motions. These procedures have seldom been effective, except occasionally as threats, for two reasons: The procedures are difficult to effect and relatively easy to obstruct, and congressional norms discourage members from interfering with committee authority over bills. Taken together, the procedures and the norms have the effect of protecting the authority of committees, including the House Rules Committee, except in extraordinary circumstances. The discharge procedure is a safety valve, but a remarkably weak one. Since the action or inaction of committees often conflicts with the wishes of the majority leadership, it might be expected that the leaders would encourage use of the discharge procedure. In reality, congressional leaders have usually been reluctant to encourage the use of this device because it is one over which they have little control and, perhaps, because many of them are also seniority leaders on committees. The House discharge rule, in fact, was first adopted in 1910 as part of the revolt against the strong leadership of Speaker Cannon.

The discharge rule for the House provides that a petition to discharge a committee from further consideration of a bill must be signed by a majority of House members. Passage of a bill, of course, requires only a majority of those voting, and during several periods prior to 1935 the required number for discharge was less, either 145 or 150. The discharge motion may apply to any bill that has been in a committee for thirty days or in the Rules Committee for seven days. Once a majority have signed the petition, it is placed on the Discharge Calendar, where it must remain for seven days, whereupon any member who signed the petition may call it up for consideration by the House, but only on the second or fourth Monday of each month. If the House votes favorably, then the bill is considered immediately.[7] The procedure in the Senate appears on the surface to be simpler but is just as difficult to effect. Any senator may introduce a discharge petition, on which the Senate may vote the following day; if the vote is favorable, the Senate may start consideration of the bill the next day. This is a simple procedure for a bill that is relatively noncontroversial or has overwhelming support, but bills that are trapped in committee are likely to be highly controversial. A determined opposition group can prevent use of the discharge procedure because debate in the Senate is virtually unlimited and because the procedures for discharge and a vote on the bill require four separate motions, each of which is debatable. This procedure is not, for example, a practical way of getting a civil rights bill out of a hostile committee.[8]

Statistical summaries show that from 1923 through 1962, 344 discharge petitions were filed in the House, but only 18 bills that had been discharged from committees passed the House. Two of these became law: the Fair Labor Standards Act in 1938, and a pay raise for federal employees, passed over the President's veto in 1960. (The only bills successfully discharged from committees between 1953 and 1962 were federal pay-raise proposals.) Motions to discharge Senate committees from considering bills have been even less successful; only four such motions carried between 1909 and 1952.[9] The discharge procedure, particularly in the House, has a utility that is not measurable in the number of discharged bills, however. When the signatures on a discharge petition begin to approach a majority, a committee may decide to jump before it is pushed, and report the desired bill to the House. In 1960 and again in 1963, a campaign for signatures helped to persuade Chairman Smith of the Rules Committee to hold hearings on civil rights bills that had been stalled in his committee. Congressmen also sometimes sign a discharge petition to satisfy constituents or interest groups, with the assurance that not enough signatures will be collected to force action.

The Civil Rights Acts of 1957, 1960, and 1964 were passed despite the opposition of the Senate Judiciary Committee and without use of the cumbersome discharge procedure. In 1957, after passage of the bill in the House, proponents took advantage of a little-used rule that permitted a bill received from the House to be placed directly on the calendar, if anyone objected to its consideration in committee; the Senate overruled a point of order by Senator Russell of Georgia, who argued that other rules made referral of the bill to committee mandatory. The same procedure was used in 1964. In 1960, under similar circumstances, the leaders of the Senate succeeded in sending the civil rights bill that had been already passed by the House to the Judiciary Committee, with binding instructions to report it back within five days.

Other procedures exist for bypassing the House Rules Committee, but they are little used in practice. "Calendar Wednesday" is the name of a procedure adopted in 1909, under which committees may be called upon in turn alphabetically each Wednesday and given an opportunity to present bills that are not privileged and have not cleared the Rules Committee. This procedure is rarely used because it is awkward and out of line with normal procedures in the House. It has occasionally been used in an attempt to pass a controversial measure trapped in the Rules Committee. One weakness in this procedure, when it is applied to a measure as controversial as civil rights legislation, is that chairmen of committees having alphabetical priority can introduce bills approved by their committees as a delaying device if they are hostile to the controversial bill in question. In the years from 1947 through 1962, the committees were called on a total of only 16 Wednesdays (10 of them during the Eighty-first Congress), and only 25 bills were called up by committees (22 of them during the Eighty-first and Eighty-second Congresses).[10]

Another device for bypassing the Rules Committee is a motion for suspension of the rules, which is in order on the first and third Mondays. A bill taken up under such a motion cannot be amended and requires a two-thirds vote. Consequently, it is seldom a feasible device for passing highly controversial legislation, although it has been used with success for less controversial matters; the number of bills and resolutions passed under suspensions of rules ranged from 7 to 125, and averaged 46 a year between 1951 and 1962.[11] A more workable device is the 1965 rule, which authorizes the Speaker to call up a bill that has been in the Rules Committee for 21 days.

PROCEDURES TO EXPEDITE NONCONTROVERSIAL LEGISLATION

Legislatures handle a large quantity of noncontroversial bills and have devised procedures to pass them expeditiously once they have been screened by committees. In the United States House, this is accomplished by placing bills on special calendars. Bills that are on the House Calendar (public bills) or the Union Calendar (money bills) may be placed by a congressman on the Unanimous Consent Calendar. On the first and third Mondays, the bills on this calendar are reported by title and passed, one by one, without the formality of a vote, if there is no objection. A single objection is enough to prevent passage, and the bill will be reported out again on the next call of the calendar. If three congressmen then oppose passage, the bill is dropped from the calendar for the remainder of the session; if not, it is passed. Each party assigns to a small group of its members the task of reviewing bills on the Consent Calendar and raising objections when necessary. Between 200 and 300 bills a year are passed by this method. All private bills (such as private claims, land bills, and immigration matters) are placed on a Private Calendar, after review by subcommittees of the Judiciary Committee, and are considered in a similar manner. A private bill will be sent back to committee if there are two or more objections from the floor, but the committee may include such a bill in an omnibus bill, which is considered on the Private Calendar by majority vote. The House usually passes between 300 and 500 bills a year on the Private Calendar. Although the Legislative Reorganization Act of 1946 reduced the number of private bills by prohibiting legislation on certain subjects, private legislation still constitutes a drain on congressional time, made tolerable only because the careful review by subcommittees of the Judiciary Committee makes it possible for the Private Calendar to be handled in cursory fashion.[12]

The Senate achieves the same objective of expediting noncontroversial bills in simpler fashion. These bills are not placed on special calendars or considered on specific days; instead, approximately twice a month there is a call of the calendar that makes possible quick action on noncontroversial bills, both public and private. Both parties have committees to raise objections to bills so considered. This procedure is sometimes carried out under a unanimous consent agreement for passage of bills without objection; at other times, the procedure permits these bills to be passed by a majority vote, but this technique is not used for important, controversial matters. The Senate carries out much of its business under unanimous agreements, and as a consequence, it does not follow such rigid and complicated procedures as are common in the House.

In the states procedural rules vary but are seldom so detailed as those in the House. A mass of noncontroversial legislation is considered and passed expeditiously, but it is not usually passed by unanimous-consent procedures, although unanimous votes are common. Constitutional requirements in some states for roll calls on the final passage of all bills, although not always rigidly adhered to, are an impediment to rapid action. Some states have a special calendar for local bills, and whether or not this procedure is followed, local bills are often handled like private bills at the national level. In many state legislatures, approval is given without question or dissent to any purely local bill that has the support of any and all legislators from the county concerned; conversely, legislatures usually hesitate to act if this unanimity among the local legislators involved is lacking.[13]

CONTROL OVER AGENDA

As we have seen, in most legislative bodies procedural rules and practice make it difficult to place a bill on the agenda for consideration until it has been reported favorably by a committee. How is priority determined among the bills that have been so reported? Routine, non-controversial bills are usually handled quickly, in the order in which they were reported. In the United States House, more important legislation, unless it has a privileged status like appropriations and revenue measures, must receive a special order from the Rules Committee; in some state legislatures, the rules committee has similar authority, at least in the closing days of the session. (The operations of rules committees at both levels were described in Chapter 8.) It is the majority leadership that determines priorities among bills that have survived screening by committees and, where this requirement is applicable, by rules committees. In the United States Senate, the majority leader consults with his policy committee before setting priorities. In Congress, but not consistently in the states, the majority leadership is careful to give advance notice to the minority party about the schedule of major business. The authority of the majority leader to make the final determination of priorities, limited though it may be by prior committee decisions, rests less on formal rules than it does on customary procedure, and particularly on the common practice of giving priority of recognition to the floor leader. Thus, in a state legislature where the rules appear to give any legislator the right to move that a bill be called up for consideration, in practice the Speaker may recognize only the floor leader for that purpose, which gives him a power that may be far-reaching but entirely a matter of custom and precedent.

LIMITATION OF DEBATE

No procedural rules are more important to a legislative body than those that govern debate. Strict rules not only expedite business but serve the purposes of the majority; rules that are broadly permissive serve minority interests and sometimes, as in the United States Senate, make certain kinds of legislation almost impossible. A series of changes in the rules of the United States House during the nineteenth century transformed it from an ineffective body, in which the majority was frequently frustrated, to one in which business was conducted with great efficiency, if little deliberation. The most fundamental of these rules for stopping debate is the "previous question," which was adopted in 1811, a nondebatable motion to bring about a vote immediately on a pending motion or bill. Since that time the House has developed a series of procedures that drastically limit debate. Debate must be pertinent to the issue, no one may speak for more than an hour, and only five minutes are permitted for the proponents of an amendment and five minutes for its opponents. More significantly, most important legislation is considered under a special rule adopted by the Rules Committee, which limits the time for debate prior to amendment. More than three-fourths of the bills considered under this procedure are allotted either one or two hours for debate; only a small minority of highly important bills receive more than four hours. The time is evenly divided between proponents and opponents, and is allotted to individual congressmen by managers on each side.[14]

The practice in most state legislatures is to apply strict limits to debate. A study made more than a decade ago showed that, in nearly every lower house and in about three-fourths of the upper houses, the rules provided for the previous-question motion, in many cases by a simple majority vote. In some cases a brief amount of time was provided for debate after the previous question had been moved. About one-third of the state legislatures had special rules governing the closing of debate in one or both houses. In addition, most legislatures had limits on the length of time a member could speak, which varied from five minutes to one or two hours, as well as limits on the number of times a member might speak on a bill (usually once or twice).[15] Filibusters are rare in state legislatures, but they are not unknown in states where the rules for limiting debate are ineffective or can be evaded. The constitutional limitation on legislative sessions sometimes plays into the hands of those who are using debate in an effort to block legislation. In 1961 a bitter fight in the Alabama legislature over congressional redistricting was highlighted by a series of filibusters. A bill that would have divided the Birmingham district among surrounding districts was passed despite filibusters of 22 hours and 58 hours in the two branches, but an effort to override the governor's veto failed when the Senate session ended at midnight after 96 hours of unbroken debate.[16]

The United States Senate is the citadel of unlimited debate in this country. The rules of the Senate do not provide for a previous-question motion; debate can be limited only voluntarily or through approval of a cloture motion by a two-thirds majority. Debate is frequently controlled in the Senate by a unanimous-consent agreement. When the leadership has determined that there is consensus in the Senate on concluding debate, it will usually seek such agreement to vote at a given time and date; often the last few hours prior to a vote are divided equally between supporters and opponents. Early in the 1964 session, the Senate adopted a new rule that required all debate on amendments or on legislation to be germane for a three-hour period each day, immediately following the morning hour. The Senate overrode objections of veteran members, who argued that it would be unworkable, and also defeated a proposal by Senator Clark to adopt a requirement of germaneness less limited in duration.

The Senate adopted a cloture rule for the first time in 1917, after a filibuster had prevented passage of President Wilson's proposal for arming United States merchant ships, made prior to this country's entry into the war. The original rule provided that a two-thirds vote of those present and voting could end debate. After Southern senators discovered that the rule had a loophole preventing cloture on procedural motions, a compromise was adopted extending the cloture to apply to debate on any kind of motion, except a proposal to change the rules, but requiring a two-thirds vote of the total membership. In 1959 the present rule was adopted. It permits cloture to stop debate on any motion, and provides that, if sixteen senators sign a cloture petition, a vote will be taken after two days; a two-thirds vote of those present and voting is sufficient to effect cloture. Thereafter, each senator may talk for one hour prior to a vote, and dilatory motions or amendments are prohibited. Repeated efforts in recent years to make cloture easier by reducing the required vote to three-fifths or, after a certain number of days, to a majority have ended in failure.[17]

The word "filibuster" brings to mind Huey Long holding the floor for 15 hours and interspersing his remarks with recipes for pot liquor and turnip greens, or Wayne Morse talking for more than 22 hours against the tidelands oil bill, or Strom Thurmond setting a new record by talking 24 hours and 18 minutes against the 1957 civil rights bills. A one-man filibuster may be dramatic but it is not effective. The filibuster should be distinguished from extended debate that is designed to focus attention on an issue or to gain publicity for a particular viewpoint. The purpose of a filibuster is to talk a bill to death, to force the sponsors of legislation to abandon it. This purpose requires the concerted efforts of at least a few senators. If they are determined to, a group of eight to ten senators can prevent action indefinitely, even in the face of round-the-clock sessions, which have sometimes been held.

It is obvious that if the filibuster were used by every minority that strongly opposed a bill, it would be grossly dysfunctional for the senatorial system. The filibuster is tolerated in the Senate only because it is used sparingly; it is resorted to primarily when senators believe that fundamental rights of their constituents are being jeopardized. Liberals have conducted filibusters in recent years against the tidelands oil bill, the communications satellite measure, and a resolution to delay implementation of judicial decisions on reapportionment. But the technique has been used primarily by Southerners in opposition to civil rights measures or to proposed changes in the cloture rule. The filibuster today functions primarily in the interests of the Southern minority.

From the adoption of the cloture rule in 1917 until 1965, 32 votes were taken on motions to impose cloture, but only 7 of these efforts were successful. In 1962, when the Senate voted for the first time since 1927 to impose cloture, the issue was the communications satellite bill, and the 27 senators opposing cloture consisted largely of Southerners who had consistently opposed it and liberals—opposing the pending bill—who usually support cloture. Most recent attempts to impose cloture have related either to civil rights bills or to proposals to change the cloture rule. The first successful cloture motion concerning civil rights was the one that made possible passage of the 1964 Civil Rights Act; a second one was on the Voting Rights Act in 1965. In 1963, supporters of cloture came within ten votes of being able to halt debate on a motion to change the cloture rule.[18] The difficulty in mustering a two-thirds majority for cloture is a result not only of diehard Southern opposition but of the reluctance of some senators to limit the traditional right of unlimited debate and the consequent protection of minority interests in the Senate.

The Senate is likely to retain its status as a great deliberative body, in which speed and efficiency are often sacrificed in order to permit extended debate. But there are signs that the filibuster—the killing of a bill by talk—is losing its importance. The significance of the filibuster has to be measured not only by the number of occasions on which it is actually used, but also by the number of times bills are modified or abandoned because of the threat of a filibuster. For many years the filibuster was believed to make civil rights legislation impossible in the Senate. But major civil rights bills were passed in 1957, 1960, and 1964, and an anti-poll tax amendment was passed in 1962, although each of the civil rights bills that had passed the House was modified substantially before it passed the Senate as a direct result of the threat of filibuster. The persistent efforts to change the cloture rule and two recent successful applications of cloture have had some effect; the filibuster today is a less potent weapon than it was in the past.[19]

PROCEDURES REGARDING VOTING

Normally, before a vote is taken on passage of a bill, there is an opportunity for members to offer amendments. This is always the practice in the United States Senate, but in the House it is possible for the Rules Committee to limit amendments by adopting a closed rule. The closed rule may prohibit any amendments or it may limit amendments to those that cover certain topics or those offered by the standing committee that reported the bill. Closed rules, which are used on less than one-tenth of the measures considered, are applied most often to revenue measures and other highly complex legislation. Their purpose is to avoid amendments that serve purely local interests, which would result in "logrolling" tactics, or to avoid revisions that would have a chaotic effect on a particularly complicated measure. In some state legislatures the previous-question motion is often used not merely to halt debate but also to prevent the introduction and consideration of amendments. Where this is the practice, the motion is a powerful tool, in that it permits the majority party or faction to force the minority into a "take it or leave it" position, and to deny them even the chance of publicizing proposed revisions in the bill.[20]

When a vote is taken on amendments, those proposed by members of the committee normally have priority. In the Senate it is frequently the practice for a number of roll calls to be taken on proposed amendments prior to a vote on final passage of the bill. The House follows a different procedure for consideration of amendments; it is known as the Committee of the Whole. When the House is sitting as the Committee of the Whole, the Speaker selects someone else to preside, a quorum of only 100 members instead of a majority is required, and—most importantly—no roll call votes are taken on amendments. This has the effect of expediting voting, but it also means that, on many of the most important votes taken in the House, the individual votes are never recorded, and frequently the total number voting is low because of the low quorum requirement. When the bill is reported to the House by the Committee of the Whole, a single vote is taken to accept all amendments, although members may request a separate vote on individual amendments. It is also possible, though not usual, for a vote to be taken in the House on an amendment that has been defeated in the Committee of the Whole. The Committee of the Whole provides an expeditious means for considering amendments with a minimum of publicity about the position taken by individual members.[21]

One significant difference between Senate and House rules has to do with the nature of the amendments that are permitted. In the House and in the Committee of the Whole, an amendment must be germane to the bill and to the part of the bill being amended, and the presiding officer has the authority to exclude from consideration amendments that he regards as not germane; although his ruling is subject to appeal, the House rarely overrules the presiding officer. The importance of this rule was evident during the 1960 debate on the civil rights bill. Congressman Walter, presiding over the Committee of the Whole, ruled as not germane two amendments that had been eliminated from the bill by the Judiciary Committee: one pertained to the hiring policies of government contractors and one provided federal grants to aid state and local governments in achieving school desegregation. In the Senate, on the other hand, there is no requirement that amendments be germane. Amendments pertaining to civil rights have sometimes been offered in the Senate to bills dealing with entirely different subjects.[22] Another difference is a rule found exclusively in the Senate that a member who offers an amendment may withdraw it or modify it in any way, up to the moment when it is voted on. Thus, during the 1957 debate on civil rights, critics of the "jury trial" amendment said they were shooting at a "moving target," because its sponsors kept modifying the amendment until they were able to make it acceptable to a majority.[23]

The rules regarding voting on amendments, which are substantially the same in the two branches of Congress, are highly technical; on occasion, however, they may have a significant effect on the outcome of votes. After an amendment is offered, it is in order to offer a substitute for it, as well as an amendment both to the original amendment and to the substitute. So-called "third-degree amendments"—an amendment to the amendment to the amendment—are not permitted. When votes are taken, the voting follows a strict order: first, the amendment to the amendment, then the amendment to the substitute, the substitute, and finally the original amendment. A case study of the 1957 civil rights bill shows that this inflexible rule had the effect of making it difficult for liberal senators to carry out an effective voting strategy. (They were forced to vote on modifying Section III of the bill before a vote was taken on eliminating that section.) After amendments to a section of a bill have been considered, no separate vote is taken on that section of the bill.[24] William Riker has demonstrated that these voting rules sometimes have the effect of compelling the Senate or House to order its preferences in a nonrational way, principally because there is no vote on the section of a bill to which two or more amendments have been considered.[25] For example, suppose that one section of a bill authorizes the spending of $300 million for a certain purpose; an advocate of economy offers an amendment to cut the total to $200 million, and a member supporting a compromise position offers a substitute for the amendment to set the figure at $250 million. Let us further assume that, of 300 members voting, 120 prefer the highest figure, 120 prefer the lowest, and 60 prefer the compromise. It is evident that the compromise figure is preferred by 180 members to either the higher or lower figure. But it might well happen that the compromise figure of $250 million—being voted on first as a substitute—would lose; two-thirds of those (80 of 120) who desired a lower total might vote against it in the mistaken belief that their motion would win subsequently, and two-thirds of those (80 of 120) who desired the full $300 million might also vote against it in the accurate belief that compromise was unnecessary. The substitute would be defeated, 140–160, and then the more drastic cut would be defeated 120–180, but no vote would be taken on the $300 million figure, and unless still another amendment were offered, the total money voted would not accurately reflect the opinion of the House.

In addition to amendments, certain other motions may be made before a vote is taken on the bill itself. A motion to recommit a bill to committee is normally an indirect but effective way of killing it. Sometimes the motion will include instructions to the committee to make certain changes—often fundamental ones—in the bill, but such a motion is usually a method of demonstrating the nature of one's objection to a bill rather than a motion made with the expectation that the committee will act accordingly. A motion to table a bill is in effect a motion to kill the bill; since that motion is not debatable, it is a quick method of eliminating a bill without debate if there is majority sentiment against it. In the Senate it can also be used to table an amendment without debate; this is not feasible in the House, however, where the result of such a motion is to table the bill along with the amendment.

In most legislative bodies, voice votes are commonly used to determine the wishes of the majority unless a more exact count is dictated by the closeness of the vote, the desire of members, or constitutional requirements. A standing vote is sometimes used when the voice vote leaves doubt about the number on each side, and the United States House (because of its large size) frequently achieves greater precision with a teller vote, in which members file past one of the two congressmen appointed to count heads. A roll call may be demanded by one-fifth of those present in the Senate or the House (not when the latter is sitting as the Committee of the Whole). In the states, there are wide variations in the number of members needed to force a roll call, but a majority of the states require roll calls on final passage of all bills. In this latter category of states particularly, it is sometimes common practice to use some technique as a shortcut in calling the roll on noncontroversial measures (perhaps combining the roll calls on several bills, or recording as favorable all those who do not indicate otherwise). A mechanical voting device is used in thirty lower houses and six upper houses; this makes it possible to have roll calls without using shortcuts, whenever they are necessary or requested. A common practice in Congress is the use of *pairing*, a technique by which a member who has to be absent is paired with another member (either present or absent) who intends to vote on the opposite side of a question. Such pairs may apply to specific issues, or may be general pairs, agreed on by two members who usually oppose each other in their votes, to be effective whenever one or both are absent.[26]

When the roll is called in Congress or in a state legislature, it is possible for a member who was absent or who did not vote to have his vote recorded at the end of the roll call, but before the result is announced. It is also possible for a member to change his vote before the result is announced, and where a mechanical device is used he can change his vote at any time until the vote is recorded. These procedural rules are used by party leaders to assist in their efforts to corral votes. If a member is reluctant, for whatever reason, to support his party's position, he may withhold his vote to the end of the roll, in order to see whether the vote is close and what difference his vote will make. The leadership may occasionally persuade a member to change his vote if the change will be decisive for a partisan victory, and may even keep a few unrecorded votes or vote changes in reserve so as to counter similar strategy on the part of the opposition. The presiding officer may exercise some discretion in delaying the announcement of a vote to facilitate such changes.[27] The rules in Congress and in some states permit a motion to reconsider a vote by which a motion has been passed or defeated; often only one such motion to reconsider may be made, and it must be made within a day or two. To prevent reconsideration of a close vote, those who have won may move immediately to reconsider the vote and to table the motion to reconsider; this provides a quick way of eliminating the possibility of later reconsideration. In Kentucky this pair of motions is offered automatically (and called a "clincher motion") after passage of a bill and is passed without objection or vote.

NOTES

1. The best description and analysis of congressional rules are to be found in Floyd M. Riddick, *The United States Congress: Organization and Procedure* (Manassas, Va., 1949).

2. Asher C. Hinds and Clarence A. Cannon, *Precedents of the House of Representatives* (Washington, 1907), vols. 1–5; (Washington, 1935–1941), vols. 6–11.

3. *Cannon's Procedure in the House of Representatives,* House Doc. No. 741, 81st Cong., 2nd Sess. (1951).

4. George B. Galloway, *The Legislative Process in Congress* (New York, 1953), pp. 579–81. Galloway notes that the practice of continuity is not usual in state senates with overlapping terms of members.

5. Good sources on the history of House rules are Riddick, *loc. cit.;* George B. Galloway, *History of the House of Representatives* (New York, 1961), chap. 5; Neil MacNeil, *Forge of Democracy* (New York, 1963), chaps. 3 and 4.

6. Harvey Walker, *The Legislative Process* (New York, 1948), pp. 225–30.

7. Riddick, *op. cit.,* pp. 236–57; Galloway, *The Legislative Process in Congress,* pp. 539–40.

8. Howard E. Shuman, "Senate Rules and the Civil Rights Bill: A Case Study," *American Political Science Review,* LI (1957), 963–64.

9. James A. Robinson, *The House Rules Committee* (Indianapolis, 1963), p.

6; *Congressional Quarterly Weekly Report*, XXI (Dec. 6, 1963), 2130; Galloway, *The Legislative Process in Congress*, p. 548.

10. Robinson, *op. cit.*, pp. 8–9; Riddick, *op. cit.*, pp. 257–62.

11. Robinson, *op. cit.*, pp. 5–8.

12. *Ibid.*, p. 5; Riddick, *op. cit.*, pp. 228–35; Galloway, *The Legislative Process in Congress*, pp. 529–35.

13. See, for example, Ralph Eisenberg, "The Logroll, South Carolina Style," in Richard T. Frost (ed.), *Cases in State and Local Government* (Englewood Cliffs, N.J., 1961), pp. 155–63.

14. Galloway, *The Legislative Process in Congress*, p. 527; Riddick, *op. cit.*, pp. 308–10; Robinson, *op. cit.*, pp. 43–55.

15. Belle Zeller (ed.), *American State Legislatures* (New York, 1954), pp. 112–114.

16. *Congressional Quarterly Weekly Report*, XIX (Sept. 8, 1961), 1549, 1563.

17. Galloway, *The Legislative Process in Congress*, pp. 559–70; *Congressional Quarterly Weekly Report*, XX (Apr. 27, 1962), 660–62.

18. *Congressional Quarterly Weekly Report*, XX (Apr. 27, Aug. 17, 1962), 660, 1358–59; XXI (Feb. 8, 1963), 139; XXII (June 12, Sept. 11, 1964), 1169, 2123.

19. Shuman, *op. cit.*, pp. 955–75; Daniel M. Berman, *A Bill Becomes a Law* (New York, 1962).

20. Robinson, *op. cit.*, pp. 43–46.

21. Riddick, *op. cit.*, pp. 212–27, 362–64.

22. Berman, *op. cit.*, pp. 79–87.

23. Shuman, *op. cit.*, pp. 972–73.

24. Riddick, *op. cit.*, pp. 313–14, 364–65; Shuman, *op. cit.*, pp. 971–72.

25. William H. Riker, "The Paradox of Voting and Congressional Rules for Voting on Amendments," *American Political Science Review*, LII (1958), 349–66.

26. Riddick, *op. cit.*, pp. 298–300, 385–87.

27. MacNeil, *op. cit.*, chap. 13.

[Part IV]

PARTICIPANTS
IN THE
LEGISLATIVE
PROCESS

[Part IV]

I N THE TWO preceding parts of this book, we have examined the recruitment process for American legislators and its product, and we have described the structures of legislative institutions in the United States. But the borders of American legislative systems go far beyond the legislatures themselves. They encompass a wide variety of other individuals who play roles related to legislative action. Our analysis of legislative systems must take into account these other participants.

We have chosen to give attention in the following chapters to three sets of participants who are particularly relevant to American legislative activity. Lobbyists, the spokesmen for private-interest groups and associations, play representative roles in the legislative system. They speak for constituents who comprise the organized social, political, professional, ethnic, economic, and religious interests in American society.

Private-interest groups and associations have long been recognized as important elements in the American political process. The organizational and propaganda activities of the major American "pressure" groups have been described extensively. Usually these groups are analyzed in some sense in terms of their relationships with legislatures, but often their access to political power has been vaguely implied rather than examined specifically. We think that an analysis of interest-group politics vis-a-vis legislatures is most useful if the focus is upon the groups' representatives—the lobbyists. The AFL-CIO does not lobby in Congress; rather, individuals who represent the AFL-CIO, and whose roles can be identified, do. Congressmen do not react to or interact with the American Farm Bureau Federation (AFBF) as an organization, though they may have some diffuse image of that entity. Individuals who play roles as congressmen interact with other individuals who play roles as representatives of the AFBF. So our analytical focus is upon lobbyists, and this focus is consistent with the conceptual orientation outlined in Chapter 1.

The chief executive is not a member of the legislative body. The separation-of-powers ideology so long a part of American constitutional ideals (if not always of its practice) has probably dictated an undue stress in our political literature upon the separation between the legislative and executive branches of government. It would certainly be absurd today to talk about legislative action without reference to the role of the executive. In our common parlance, we have come to speak of one of the executive's roles as that of "chief legislator."

The President sets the agenda for Congress, provides almost all the important business, and customarily engages today in one legislative foray after another. His legislative role can easily be exaggerated, but it cannot be ignored. The state governor's legislative role varies considerably from state to state, but he is at least in every state a significant participant in legislative action.

In principle, it should be possible to identify those representatives of interest groups and agents of the executive branch who play roles in the legislative system. Constituent participants constitute a much more ambiguous category, and the boundary lines of the legislative system in regard to constituents are very complex and difficult to draw. Still, some constituents do play roles related to legislative action, and American legislators tend to respond to relevant constituents. They certainly are important participants in the legislative process. Since an American legislator's response to his constituents clearly constitutes an important factor in his own role definition, we think it is essential to stress the legislator's reaction to his constituency and to interchanges of communication between legislators and constituents.

These are not the only outside participants in legislative action. They are the ones we think are most important, and the ones we know most about. National, state, and local party leaders who are not themselves legislators may, in many cases, be participants in legislative action in the sense of playing roles in legislative systems. Judges of various kinds may play roles in legislative systems. We have made some references to non-legislative party leaders in Chapter 8, and to the involvement of courts in legislative apportionment in Chapter 3. In a later chapter (Chapter 19) we shall deal to some extent with administrative agents as they are involved in legislative-executive relations.

[12]

The Lobbyists

AMERICAN society is characterized by a multiplicity of private groups and associations that are more or less integrated into the political system. Because of the constitutional structure of the American governments, with their multifarious focal points of political decision making, and because of the fragmented and decentralized nature of the American political party system, private groups and associations tend to participate in the processes of public policy making through representatives of their own, distinct from those who are elected or appointed to public office.[1] These representatives are usually called *lobbyists*. The term lobbyist is a rather flexible one; it is sometimes used to refer to anyone who seeks to influence governmental decisions, including those of administrative agencies and courts. But its descriptive utility will best be maintained if we limit its inclusiveness to those representatives of private groups and associations who stimulate and transmit communication to a governmental decision maker in the hope of influencing his decision.[2] Here we are interested in representational communications directed toward American legislators.

The lobbyist plays a functional role in the American legislative system. He contributes to the maintenance of the legislative system by virtue of his key location in its communications structure. The lobbyist provides one of the important links between organized constituents and legislators, and communications flow in both directions (from organized group via lobbyist to legislator, and from legislator via lobbyist to organized group). This "two-step" flow of information is, in the American legislative system, probably prerequisite to its maintenance. In addition, the lobbyist's participation in the legislative system facilitates its contribution to the polity. The lobbyist's role is fundamental to both the crystallization and the resolution of political conflict and to the integration of the polity. He represents demands on the legislative system from organized citizens, he participates in the negotiation processes leading to their satisfaction, and his involvement in decisional processes facilitates support in the polity for public policy.

Lobbyists occupy a variety of positions vis-a-vis the groups or associations which they represent. Some are full-time employees of their organizations, directing or working in a Washington office, or serving as an executive director of an association. There are others, like many of those who are Washington representatives of corporations, who are in the position of endeavoring to justify political activities to companies whose interests are mainly directed elsewhere. And there are many lawyers and public relations professionals in both national and state capitals who have salaries or retainers from several organizations.

How Many Lobbyists?

One means of defining empirically the number of lobbyists at the national and state levels of government is to consider those who register under national and state lobby registration laws. While in all probability not all the individuals who should be regarded as lobbyists are required to register in those jurisdictions where such statutes exist, and while not all states have such enactments, we get a rough approximation of the extent of lobbying activity in this manner. The Federal Regulation of Lobbying Act of 1946, passed by Congress as part of the Legislative Reorganization Act, requires the registration of names and spending reports of anybody who "solicits, collects or receives money or any other thing of value to be used principally to aid in . . . the passage or defeat of any legislation by the Congress of the United States." Supreme Court interpretation of the statute has limited its application only to those who engage in direct communication with members of Congress; several large national associations do not file (e.g., the National Association of Manufacturers, the American Bankers' Association, the American Public Power Association, and Americans for Constitutional Action).[3] The number of lobbyists who are not registered because of the limited application of the act is not known. However, those who lobby probably tend to register with the Clerk of the House and the Secretary of the Senate. The rather ambiguous interpretation of the law makes it safer to register in order to avoid possible penalties.

State lobby regulation laws vary a great deal, although as of 1961, thirty-three states required the registration of lobbyists, and twenty-one required the filing of expense statements. In some states the law requires the lobbyists who are registered to wear identification badges; in some others, lobbyists are required to carry identification cards issued to them by the clerk upon registration.[4]

Under the federal law, 600 groups have filed as lobby organizations with the Clerk of the House since the law took effect in 1947. A total of 312 groups filed spending reports in 1961. As of 1965, 7,591 individuals and organizations had filed reports.[5] Although the total of registrations does not include an unknown number of those who do not register, it greatly exaggerates the number of active lobbyists before Congress at any one time—a number which probably does not exceed 700.

The number of lobbyists registered at the state level varies considerably from state to state. Table 12.1 indicates the number of lobbyists registered in a recent year for twenty-nine states. The number registered for these states ranges from 23 in South Carolina to 4,534 in Texas; the median number was 208. Obviously, the interstate variation can be accounted for, at least to a considerable extent, by differences in population size, urbanization, industrialization, political complexity, and by the nature of the legal registration requirements. To what extent each of these factors is at work we do not know.

Numerically, business groups and associations are more extensively represented in Washington than are other types of interest groups. Our data for the states are fragmentary, but we can show (as we do in Table 12.2) comparisons among groups and organizations registered in Washington and those in Nebraska, Oklahoma, Illinois, and Kentucky.[6] Insofar as national lobbyists are concerned, the percentage of business groups out of the total number of groups registered considerably underestimates the aggregate numerical presence of business lobbying. A study of a random sample of lobbyists registered with the Clerk of the United States House of Representatives during the first two quarters of 1956 showed that nearly 61 percent of those registered represented business groups, the largest component of which were spokesmen for small trade associations (about 40 percent of the total). Only 16 percent of the lobbyists represented labor organizations, only 5 percent farm organizations, and the remainder were scattered among a variety of organizational types.[7] We have some comparable analyses for lobbyists at the state level; studies of lobbyists for various years in Oklahoma, Illinois, and Kentucky indicate that the proportions of lobbyists in those states were distributed in about the same way as the groups they represented.[8] It is likely that at the state level, organizations will frequently tend to be represented by only one or two lobbyists.

Lobbying involves the expenditure of money for salaries, travel, research, public relations materials, entertainment, and the like. At the national level, reported expenditures annually total about $4 million—not a large amount, comparatively speaking. However, the reported figures probably represent only minimums because of the ambiguous nature of

Table 12.1. REGISTERED LOBBYISTS, SELECTED STATES

State	Year	Number
Alaska	1962	58
California	1961–62	534
Connecticut	1961	369
Colorado	1961	246
Florida	1961	576
Illinois	1959	541
Indiana	1961	300
Iowa	1961	193
Kansas	1961	412
Kentucky	1962	93
Maine	1961	131
Maryland	1961	247
Massachusetts	1960	301
Michigan	1962	221
Mississippi	1961	74
Montana	1961	208
New Hampshire	1962	88
New York	1962	129
North Carolina	1961	124
North Dakota	1961	280
Ohio	1961–62	348
Oklahoma	1961	62
South Carolina	1957	23
South Dakota	1961	91
Rhode Island	1962	100
Texas	1959	4,534
Vermont	1961	69
Virginia	1962	104
Wisconsin	1961–62	348

SOURCES: Edgar Lane, *Lobbying and the Law* (Berkeley and Los Angeles: University of California Press, 1964), p. 109; *The Book of the States, 1962–63* (Chicago: Council of State Governments, 1962), p. 86; G. Y. Steiner and S. K. Gove, *Legislative Politics in Illinois* (Urbana: University of Illinois Press, 1960), p. 47; S. C. Patterson, "The Role of the Lobbyist: The Case of Oklahoma," *Journal of Politics,* XXV (1963), 73.

the reporting requirements of the Lobbying Act. Lobbyist spending varies greatly from state to state, ranging from as high as $1,046,983 in California in 1963 to well below $100,000 in a given recent year in states like Alaska, Kentucky, Maryland, North Carolina, Virginia, and Ohio. There is also considerable interstate variation in the expenditures of business, labor, and farm groups, although the evidence available indicates that business groups, including trade associations, corporations, construction, communications firms, and loan, banking, and insurance companies, far outstrip other state lobby groups in lobbying expenditures.[9] Again, in all likelihood these figures reflect only bare minimums of expenditure. While we do not have accurate spending data for political interest groups,

Table 12.2. TYPES OF ORGANIZATIONS WITH REGISTERED LOBBYISTS
(In percentages)

Type of Organization	Washington, D.C. (1962)	Nebraska (1955)	Oklahoma (1961)	Illinois (1963)	Kentucky (1964)
Business	55	55	42	48	58
Labor	13	16	16	11	19
Farm	7	6	14	3	2
Professional	5	8	7	15	12
Governmental, citizens	17	10	14	16	9
Other	3	5	7	7	0
Total	100	100	100	100	100
Number	312	86	56	280	57

SOURCES: *Congressional Quarterly Almanac* (1962), p. 941; A. C. Breckenridge, *One House for Two: Nebraska's Unicameral Legislature* (Washington, D.C.: Public Affairs Press, 1957), pp. 92–93; the Oklahoma data appear in somewhat different form in S. C. Patterson, "The Role of the Lobbyist: The Case of Oklahoma," *Journal of Politics*, XXV (1963), 81. The Illinois and Kentucky data come from unpublished studies by S. C. Patterson and R. Hedlund (Illinois) and M. E. Jewell (Kentucky).

and the figures reported here are probably low estimates, lobbying expenses are much lower than the folklore of American politics would lead us to believe.

THE RECRUITMENT OF LOBBYISTS

A great deal more evidence than is now available is needed about the recruitment of lobbyists in terms of their social and political backgrounds. Reliable and systematic data are available only for samples of national lobbyists, and lobbyists in Oklahoma and Michigan.[10] These data give us a preliminary basis for comparison and analysis, but they mean that our generalizations must be taken as tentative.

In age, lobbyists in Washington, D.C., Oklahoma, and Michigan do not, as a group, differ much from legislators. Lobbyists are predominantly middle-aged men, with median ages in the fifties. About three-fourths of the sample of Washington lobbyists were between the ages of forty and sixty. Michigan and Oklahoma lobbyists were somewhat younger, although 69 percent of the former and 58 percent of the latter were over forty-five. Most lobbyists are also white, male, and Protestant.

If we take education, occupation, and income as indicators of socio-economic status, lobbyists would be classified as very high on the scale indeed. The median income of Washington lobbyists fell between $15,000 and $19,999; 64 percent of the lobbyists in Michigan and 47 percent of Oklahoma's lobbyists reported incomes of more than $10,000. On the whole, lobbyists are characterized by a high incidence of advanced formal education. Seventy-five percent of the lobbyists in the nation's capital had college degrees, and nearly half had graduate or professional training. In Michigan and Oklahoma, 48 percent of the lobbyists had college degrees, and more than one-fifth had graduate or professional degrees. Obviously, Washington lobbyists are better educated as a group than the lobbyists in the two state capitals.

Occupationally, national lobbyists tend to be recruited from government service more than from other occupations, and mostly from service in the executive branch. Former congressmen sometimes become lobbyists, but this is rather rare; less than 3 percent of the Washington lobbyist sample had ever served in Congress. In Michigan, 67 percent of the lobbyists in the sample had held public elective or appointive office, although a considerably greater proportion (24 percent) had served in the legislature than in Washington. Oklahoma lobbyists differed occupationally in this respect from both those in the national capitol and those in Lansing. Only 12 percent of Oklahoma lobbyists had held public office, and these had served in the legislature. Thus, legislative service is not a major source of lobbyist recruitment in Washington, D.C., and in Oklahoma, though it is somewhat more significant in Michigan.

Lobbying at the state level is largely a part-time activity. Most of the lobbyists in Michigan (50 percent) and Oklahoma (44 percent) served as officers or staff members of their associations. Otherwise, state lobbyists tend to be drawn from professional and business occupations; these occupational categories make a substantial contribution to Washington lobbying as well.[11]

What is the importance of legal training and practice for lobbyist recruitment? We noted in Chapter 5 the significance of the legal profession for the recruitment of legislators. For lobbyists the practice of law is not as important a prerequisite. While about 45 percent of the sample of Washington lobbyists had had legal training, only one-fourth carried on lobbying activities from a base in legal practice, and only about 10 percent came to lobbying directly from law practice. At the state level, lobbyist recruitment from legal training and practice may be much less important. Only 12 percent of the Michigan lobbyists and less than 10 percent of those in Oklahoma were lawyers. If there is a uniform difference between the occupational backgrounds of state and Washington lobbyists with respect to legal training, it may perhaps result from the more limited scope of lobbying at the state level. Interests may be more directly represented at the state level by the legislators themselves, many of whom are lawyers.

Only a very few registered lobbyists in Washington "can be said to have an over-all career pattern in lobbying. Even if careers in association work, which includes more than lobbying activities, are considered to be lobbying careers, less than one-fourth of the respondents have had over-all careers in lobbying. Those who have had predominantly lobbying careers received their training in a variety of professions."[12] There is no training program in educational institutions for lobbyists, and careers in lobbying are not those to which Americans usually aspire from an early age. Most men become involved in lobbying later in life, after a career in some other kind of activity has been well developed. In Michigan, the median years of lobbying experience for lobbyists was probably fairly high—9.5 years. Among Oklahoma lobbyists studied in 1961, 47 percent were registered for the first time, although 27 percent had been registered for four or more sessions.

Washington lobbyists are likely to be residents of the city, or of the suburban environs around it. In the states, lobbyists tend to be residents of the capitals, although a sizable proportion of state lobbyists are likely to come into the capital from some other city for the legislative session. Fifty-eight percent of the Michigan lobbyists and 65 percent of the Oklahoma lobbyists resided in the capital cities; the remainder were residents of other cities.

Lobbying is a fairly intense form of political activity, and it might be expected that lobbyists would be active in partisan politics. Most lobbyists are affiliated with one of the two major political parties, although the differences indicated in Table 12.3 are very interesting. Washington lobbyists were about evenly split in party preference; Oklahoma lobbyists were overwhelmingly Democratic at a time when their state legislature was also predominantly Democratic; Michigan and Illinois lobbyists were mostly Republicans in legislative settings that were fairly heavily Republican. There may be factors in lobbyist recruitment which result in the selection of lobbyists in such a way as to reflect the dominant political atmosphere of the system into which they are recruited.

At the same time, lobbyists are not, insofar as our evidence permits generalization, particularly active in politics. At the national level, nearly half the lobbyists had never been active in party politics, and only a fourth were active at the time they were interviewed. Few have been candidates for public office, and less than 10 percent held party office. Less than a third had ever made a contribution to party funds, although 42 percent had assisted in the raising of political funds. In Oklahoma only 7 percent of the lobbyists were political actives in the sense of hav-

Table 12.3. LOBBYIST POLITICAL PARTY AFFILIATION
(In percentages)

Party	U.S.	Oklahoma	Michigan	Illinois
Democratic	46	77	3	30
Republican	48	9	58	55
Independent	6	7	15	10
Not classifiable	—	7	24	5
Total	100	100	100	100

SOURCES: L. W. Milbrath, *The Washington Lobbyists* (Chicago: Rand McNally & Company, 1963), p. 77; S. C. Patterson, "The Role of the Lobbyist: The Case of Oklahoma," *Journal of Politics*, XXV (1963), 78; W. D. DeVries, "The Michigan Lobbyist: A Study in the Bases and Perceptions of Effectiveness" (Unpublished Ph.D. dissertation, Michigan State University, 1960), p. 67. The Illinois data are from an unpublished study by S. Patterson and R. Hedlund.

ing held party office, although political activity may be somewhat more important among Michigan lobbyists (where public office-holding is more prominent among lobbyists). It seems likely that strong party attachments, which might be indicated by the holding of a party office or a campaign for public office, "can be impediments to lobbyists who work with people in both parties."[13] DeVries asked his sample of Michigan lobbyists, "Do you find it necessary to work both sides of the aisle on most issues?" Eighty-five percent responded with a "yes" or "sometimes."[14] The lobbyist tends to limit his political activity to representations with the legislature; party activism and partisanship are probably dysfunctional for the effective performance of the lobbyist role.

Much has been said in the popular and even the scholarly literature of "pressure group" politics about the personality orientations and characteristics of lobbyists. Thurlow Weed, a prominent nineteenth-century politician whose reputation as a lobbyist was well deserved, is referred to by his biographer as a "wizard" and a "Lucifer," and it is clear that his political successes stemmed partly from his commanding personality.[15]

Lobbyists have been described as "snake-oil men," or "pernicious sugar men."[16] The personalities and motivations of lobbyists have been more often caricatured than adequately described and analyzed.

The evidence we have available to us about the personality characteristics of lobbyists is meager indeed. This evidence, from a study of a sample of Washington lobbyists, fails to support any hypothesis of the uniqueness of lobbyists in personality terms. The limited data suggest that "lobbyists do not seem to have personalities very different from the general population and certainly not much different from persons in other political skill groups."[17] Lobbyists are sometimes portrayed as conniving, devious, and unprincipled men, but there is no general evidence of this. On the contrary, the evidence does suggest that lobbyists do not, as a group, have unusual personality characteristics. Furthermore, they tend to think of lobbying as an honorable career in which they are likely to stay, and their motivations for entry into lobbying as a career do not appear to reflect particularly pernicious values.[18]

THE ROLE OF THE LOBBYIST

We have referred (in Chapter 1) to the importance of role allocation to the maintenance of legislative systems. The lobbyist is a distinctive actor in the legislative system, and he plays a representative role, just as the legislator does. While the role of the legislator tends to be diffuse and susceptible to conflicting expectations by relevant reference groups, the lobbyist role tends to be more specific. The "extensive internal conflict which the legislator experiences is virtually non-existent" for lobbyists.[19] The principal function of the lobbyist in the political system is to provide an essential connecting link between actors in official legislative roles and interest-group hierarchies in the society.

The role of the lobbyist, like other political roles, is likely to be played in somewhat different forms by different actors. That is to say, in playing the lobby role, individuals give that role various orientations. Five distinct lobbyist role orientations can be identified for analysis here: the Contact Man, the Campaign Organizer, the Informant, the Watchdog and the Strategist.

The Contact Man. The Contact Man plays a classic role as a lobbyist. He is the legislative representative who conceives his job to be that of making crucial contacts with the members of the legislative group. He devotes his time and energies to walking the legislative halls, visiting legislators, collaring them in the halls, establishing relationships with administrative assistants and others of the legislator's staff, cultivating key legislators on a friendship basis, and developing contacts on the staffs of critical legislative committees. The Contact Man is gregarious;

he likes to talk about the mundane routine of the legislative process; he concerns himself with the details. The Contact Man believes that the legislative goals of his organization can best be achieved through personal influence and personal contact with legislators. When faced with a legislative problem for his group, the lobbyist with a Contact Man orientation is likely to propose as the solution personally contacting as many members of the legislative body as possible and directly presenting the interest group's case.

All lobbyists may make contacts with legislators, but the Contact Man is a lobbyist for whom this is the primary, or most salient, orientation. There are important differences in the ubiquity with which this role is played—differences between national and state legislative systems, and differences among groups. At the national level, the complexity of legislative life has made contact work relatively impractical, and Washington lobbyists reported spending relatively little time in face-to-face contacting.[20] A lobbyist before Congress is probably likely to spend more time in face-to-face contact in the early stages of his career and then simply maintain his contacts by letter or telephone, although "fence-mending" personal calls are usually required in order to maintain continuous contact.[21]

Although Washington lobbyists reported spending relatively little of their time in direct contact work, more than 80 percent said they preferred direct methods, even though they were not able to employ them extensively.[22] Contact work is probably much more pervasive at the state level, where access to legislators is easier. Lobbyists in Oklahoma and Michigan emphasized this role; 54 percent of the Oklahoma lobbyists and 76 percent of the Michigan lobbyists could be classified as Contact Men.[23] The Washington lobbyist is much more likely to make his contacts through "intermediaries"—congressmen's friends, associates and constituents—than the state lobbyist. At the state level, the Contact Man is likely to be more effective, and to spend more time in lobbying activities, than lobbyists with primarily different orientations.

The Contact Man orientation is taken variously by lobbyists, depending upon the kind of organization they represent. This role orientation is predominant among lobbyists for labor organizations.[24] Among the lobbyists for business associations and companies, however, this orientation is much more uncommon.[25] It is clear that "representatives of organizations with high power at the polls spend more time with members of Congress than do representatives of organizations with little power." Thus groups vary in terms of the Contact Man orientation of their lobbyists.[26]

Contact operations are not, of course, indiscriminate. The Contact Man is likely to have his most persistent and regular contacts with friendly legislators—legislators who share at least a considerable proportion of the group's views. Again, legislative leaders are much more likely than rank-and-file members to be objects of contact work. Where party organization is strong within the legislature, contact activities tend to be concentrated upon the party leaders. In a highly partisan legislature like the Connecticut Senate, for example, contact limited mainly to party leaders has been maintained by some interest-group spokesmen, even when voting margins were slim for the group's proposals.[27] In Michigan, where party leadership has been relatively strong, only 39 percent of the lobbyists reported attempts to establish contacts with *all* legislators.[28] In Washington, maintaining contacts with 535 members of Congress is an unmanageable task for an individual lobbyist, except at the most rudimentary level of communication. The large national lobbying organizations divide the labor of lobbying so that each lobbyist has a limited number of members assigned to him for contact purposes.

The Campaign Organizer. The Campaign Organizer has a different conception of his role as a lobbyist from that of the Contact Man. Though he may make some contacts, this is not, for him, the important part of his job as a lobbyist. He conceives his job to be that of organizing mass grass-roots support for his organization's legislative program. He believes that his most important contacts are with leaders in the field and with rank-and-file members of his organization. He feels that the most effective lobbying for his group's program is achieved by demonstrating mass support for that program among the members of his organization "back home" who are the legislators' constituents. When a problem in legislative strategy is raised, the solution of the Campaign Organizer is to map out a nationwide or statewide campaign from the grass roots—television and radio programs, fact sheets on specific legislation for workers in the field, millions of leaflets for field distribution, delegations to the capitol, and letters to legislators. He sees the value of personal contact, but regards that as merely routine and by no means the most significant part of his own job. As one Washington lobbyist put it:

I'm convinced that the grass-roots support is the important thing rather than my contacts. I know this from my experience on the Hill where I have been on the receiving end. I can go up and explain the technical end of the thing, but it's the grass roots that lets the member of Congress know who is behind it. I would give 75 percent to the grass roots.[29]

The Campaign Organizer is more likely to be a Washington lobbyist than a lobbyist at the state level, although there are several case studies that describe the work of such lobbyists in their efforts to secure state legislation.[30]

The Informant.   The Informant is a lobbyist who conveys information to legislators, without necessarily advocating a particular position or program. He may lobby only by testimony, presenting information to a legislative committee as an "expert." He differs from the Contact Man in that his lobbying is often public and his contacts are frequently collective rather than individual. He may simply provide informational services for legislators. One Washington lobbyist, speaking of his congressman friends, said, "I will use my friends to get information for me; they are always calling me up about things I ought to know; but I will not ask favors of them. You can lose friends if you keep imposing on them."[31] The Informant is not a particularly numerous genre; in Oklahoma only 12 percent of the lobbyists could be classified as Informants, and in Michigan only 21 percent could be classified in roughly the same way.

The Watchdog.   This is the lobbyist who conceives of his job as that of scrutinizing closely the legislative calendars and watching legislative activity carefully, usually from a distance. His job is to be alert to developments in the legislative system that might affect his client group. Whenever legislation is proposed or introduced which affects his employer, his job is to signal his group so that it can attempt to bring pressure on legislators. His orientation is to alert the membership of his interest group to action when crucial legislative matters arise. He is a "listening post" for his organization, staked out in the capital to keep alert to developments that might affect his client. In performing this role he may seldom enter the legislative halls or talk to individual members; he may never leave his office downtown in the capital city. One Oklahoma lobbyist described his job in Watchdog terms:

> We attempt to keep our people informed about the merits of all legislation which has a direct effect on our business, as well as all legislation which has any effect on the state economy, and general interest. My member associations are kept informed on current legislative proposals via a legislative bulletin, and we make use of special bulletins and special committee actions when we wish to directly render an opinion concerning any act or prospective act.[32]

The Watchdog orientation was characteristic of about one-fourth of Oklahoma lobbyists in 1961, and it has been reported in other states among company lobbyists, oil lobbyists, and church lobbyists.

The Strategist.   A few lobbyists specialize in the formulation and development of legislative strategy; their orientation with regard to lobbying is a strategy-formulating one. The strategist plans legislative campaigns to be executed by other lobbyists. He may advise other lobbyists as to legislative strategy, and thus act as a "lobbyist's lobbyist." These lobbyists are rare, and we have little data about them. Only three of the hundred-odd lobbyists in Washington interviewed by Milbrath could be classified as Strategists, and his is virtually the only treatment of this type.

Such men must have an impressive array of talents: they must be exceptionally intelligent and perceptive; they must have an accurate and broad grasp of the political and governmental system; they must have intimate and detailed knowledge of the formal and informal rules of the policy-making process; and, perhaps most important, they must know the habits of thinking, quirks of mind, and patterns of action of the major players in the drama that they attempt to influence. With such requirements, it is not surprising that strategist-lobbyists are few.[33]

These lobbyist role orientations are not mutually exclusive: A Contact Man plans strategy, a Campaign Organizer makes contacts; both alert their groups to action and convey factual information. These are analytically distinct lobbyist orientations, in the sense that it is possible to type lobby roles in terms of the primacy and saliency of the lobbyist's orientation to his job.

THE TECHNIQUES OF LOBBYING

The literature of pressure-groups study is filled with descriptions of the tactics of organized groups.[34] We shall limit our focus in this chapter to the specific techniques used by lobbyists. Because reliable systematic data on lobbyists' techniques are available for only Washington, D.C. and Michigan lobbyists, we must be content with these, in the hope that our fund of knowledge will accumulate in the future.

Milbrath and DeVries asked lobbyists in Washington and Lansing to rate a variety of lobbying techniques on a scale ranging from 0 for not effective at all to 10 for very effective. In Table 12.4 we reproduce their data in part, indicating in the table only the mean, or average, scores for each technique.[35]

We have already indicated the extent to which Washington lobbyists engage in direct communication with congressmen. Though they spend relatively little of their time in direct communication, and there has been a shift from direct to indirect means of communication, Washington lobbyists continue to rate "personal presentation of viewpoints" highest as the most effective technique of lobbying. Michigan lobbyists rate this even higher than do those in the national capital. Direct contact is easier with state legislators than with congressmen because state legislators are more accessible.

In general, Michigan lobbyists rated techniques associated with communication to legislators through intermediaries considerably lower than did Washington lobbyists. For instance, letter and telegram campaigns were rated much lower by Michigan lobbyists than by Washington lobbyists. We shall deal in a later chapter with the importance of the mail to legislators. Suffice it to say here that organizations with

Table 12.4. LOBBYIST RATING OF TECHNIQUES

Technique	Mean Rating	
	Washington lobbyists	Michigan lobbyists
MEANS OF DIRECT COMMUNICATION		
Personal presentation of viewpoints	8.43	9.24
Presentation of research results	7.40	7.00
Testifying at hearings	6.55	6.64
COMMUNICATION THROUGH INTERMEDIARIES		
Contact by constituents	5.90	3.84
Contact by a close friend	3.76	2.73
Letter and telegram campaigns	4.55	1.73
Public relations campaigns	5.55	4.79
Publicizing voting records	2.05	0.84
METHODS OF KEEPING CHANNELS OPEN		
Entertaining	1.59	2.33
Giving a party	1.24	1.91
Bribery	0.10	0.00
Contributing money	1.88	0.87
Campaign work	2.28	1.21

SOURCE: L. W. Milbrath, *The Washington Lobbyists* (Chicago: Rand McNally & Company, 1963) pp. 213, 240, 257. As Milbrath points out, the mean is less than entirely satisfactory as a summary statistic for these ratings. They simplify our presentation however, and do no serious injustice to the data. The full frequency distributions are to be found at the pages cited above.

mass memberships (such as labor and farm organizations) rate letter campaigns higher than do other groups. At the state level, letter campaigns are much less commonly employed as a lobbying tactic than they are by national organizations. State legislators are in more immediate personal communication with their constituents. Furthermore, state legislators are less able to handle mail intake because of inadequate staff, and lobbying organizations may recognize this deficiency. A state legislator may be antagonized by a letter campaign because of the relatively greater burden it places upon him; he cannot hope to reply to large numbers of constituents who write. In addition, publicizing voting records, a technique used on the national scale most preeminently by the AFL-CIO, was not rated very highly by Washington lobbyists, and was on the average rated as very ineffective by Michigan lobbyists. Some state federations of labor imitate the national federation in the publicizing of voting records, but otherwise this is seldom done at the state level.

Entertaining and party-giving were rated higher by Michigan lobbyists than by Washington lobbyists. In all probability there is more lobbyist entertaining of legislators at the state level. State legislators are away from their home towns and from their homes and families when the legislature is in session. Few can afford to set up housekeeping in the capital city. The state legislator is more likely to need and seek entertainment of the sort the lobbyist may provide. At the same time, state legislators may be much more sensitive about the practice of lobbyist-provided entertainment than are congressmen. Among Wisconsin legislators, for example, it had always been regarded as proper for a member to accept meals and drinks from lobbyists, although some did not accept such favors on principle. Many Wisconsin legislators thought of this practice as a legitimate supplement to their low income, or as an acceptable practice among friends. This had been, until 1957, an accepted practice for many years. But some Wisconsin legislators got bad reputations by abusing this relationship with lobbyists. These "moochers" solicited favors from lobbyists; they might go to a restaurant with their friends, order a meal, and then afterward see a lobbyist sitting at another table and take their checks to him. They might insist that a lobbyist take them and their friends out for an evening "on the town." These moochers, few in number to be sure, took advantage of lobbyists and put them in an uncomfortable position. Some lobbyists refused to have anything to do with the moocher–legislators, but others felt that they had to cater to their demands for fear of losing crucial votes. In 1957 the Wisconsin legislature passed a law prohibiting lobbyists from buying meals and drinks for legislators. Few legislators privately believed in this enactment, but it passed the legislature because members were persuaded that it would improve their public-relations image.[36] We do not know to what extent lobbyists become ensnared in the entertainment dilemma, but it may be a deterrent to the use of entertaining as a lobbying technique in other states than Wisconsin. An Oklahoma lobbyist suggested a similar lobbying problem in that state: "Too many of our representatives are out for the dollar that is flowing around the capitol building. I was 'touched' a number of times in regard to our own bill." Certainly in a state where entertaining is restricted by law it is not likely to be rated as a very effective technique by lobbyists.

THE LEGISLATORS' RESPONSE TO LOBBYING

As a general proposition, American legislators tend to view lobbyists and lobbying as significant contributions to the effective operation of the legislative process. One congressman expressed the widely shared attitudes about lobbying among his colleagues:

A lot of people seem to think that lobbying is a bad thing. I think that is one misconception which still needs to be corrected as far as the general public is concerned. Lobbying is an essential part of representative government, and it needs to be encouraged and appreciated. [Lobbyists] are frequently a source of information. If they come to your offices and explain a program or factors contributing to the need for legislation, you get a better understanding of the problems and the answers to them. If you have your independence, and I think we all do, they can teach you what an issue is all about, and you can make your own decision. There can be bad lobbying technique, of course, but basically lobbying is a good thing.[37]

A state legislator explained:

Lobbyists are a vital part of the legislative process. Without them to explain, you couldn't get a clear picture of the situation. They can study and present the issues concisely—the average legislator has no time or inclination to do it, and wouldn't understand bills or issues without them. A professional lobbyist in ten minutes can explain what it would take a member two hours to wade through just reading bills. Both sides come around to you, so you can balance off all one-sided presentations (and they're all one-sided). A definite function is performed by lobbyists.[38]

In general, legislators react most favorably toward lobbyists in terms of the measure of public sentiment and the information, research, and support the lobbyist can provide, rather than in terms of pressures or assertions of demands.

American legislators are, on the whole, well aware of the presence of political interest groups, and are able to discriminate among them as to their relative influence. Our evidence at the state legislative level suggests that legislators' perceptions of relative group influence in the legislative process vary somewhat in different states. For example, in 1960 Indiana legislators were asked which were the "most powerful" lobbying organizations in the state. The results are summarized in Figure 12.1. The configuration of relative group influence perceived by state legislators in other states does not follow the Indiana pattern exactly, although labor, business, teachers', and governmental groups tend to have the highest perceived influence in the states for which data are available.[39] Business interests tend to be most salient for legislators at the state level, with educational interests second and labor interests

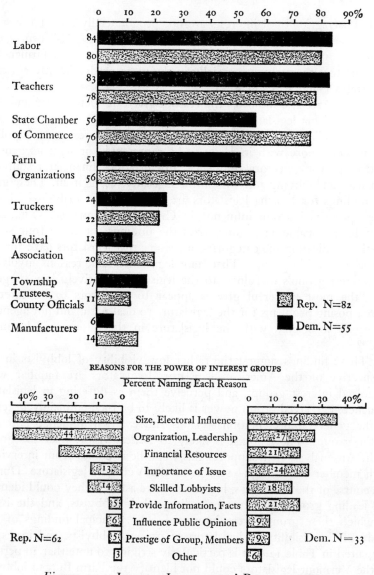

Figure 12.1. INDIANA LEGISLATORS' PERCEPTIONS OF
"MOST POWERFUL" GROUPS

SOURCE: K. Janda et al., *Legislative Politics in Indiana* (Bloomington, Ind.: Indiana University Press, 1961), p. 18.

third. That agricultural interests are not pronouncedly salient for state legislators in these states (Indiana, Ohio, New Jersey, California, and Tennessee) may be due to the more direct representation of farmers by the legislators themselves, especially in the more predominantly agricultural states (such as Tennessee).

Figure 12.1 also indicates the reasons given by Democratic and Republican Indiana legislators for their rankings of relative interest-group influence. Indiana legislators tend to associate the interest group's political influence more with its claim to be represented or with its general political power (electoral influence, organization, financial resources) than with its lobbying activities in the legislative arena itself. These general findings for Indiana legislators are supported by analyses of legislators' perceived group influence in California, Tennessee, Ohio, and New Jersey. Table 12.5 summarizes the findings for these four states together, indicating the categories of reasons that legislators gave for the power of specific groups. That state legislators rank reasons involving the interest group's usefulness to the legislature relatively low suggests that "the most powerful groups appear to legislators to be external forces, posing problems for the legislature to deal with, and not agencies intimately associated with the legislature in the business of lawmaking."[40]

These findings suggest the rather low visibility of lobbyists in the perspective of the American legislator. Legislators are familiar with organized interest groups, and perceive them as differing in legislative influence. Perceived group power is likely to be focused mainly in terms of the general representational claims and external influence potential of the groups. The lobbyist is likely to be less visible than the group itself. An analysis that supports this hypothesis comes from interviews with members of the 1951 session of the Vermont legislature. During the course of the interviews, legislators were asked if they could identify the leading groups in Vermont politics, their lobbyists, and the issues in which these groups were interested. The principal findings of this study of the visibility to legislators of groups, lobbyists, and issues are presented in Table 12.6. It is particularly striking to note that 30 percent of the Vermont legislators could not identify the Farm Bureau lobbyist, although he had been its president and lobbyist for a generation, and only about one-third of the legislators could identify the lobbyists for the Associated Industries of Vermont or the state AFL-CIO. Legislators most oriented to programs and policies as the focus of legislative activities were best able to identify lobbyists and organized groups' issues, while for the legislators least able to perceive the factional informal substructure of the 1951 session lobbyists and issues were least visible.[41]

The salience and visibility of lobbyists to legislators are likely to be

Table 12.5. REASONS FOR INTEREST-GROUP POWER GIVEN BY LEGISLATORS IN CALIFORNIA, TENNESSEE, OHIO, AND NEW JERSEY (In percentages)

Legislator's Reasons	Agricultural Groups	Business Groups	Labor Groups	Professional Groups	Governmental Groups
GROUP'S REPRESENTATIONAL CLAIMS (size, prestige, potential electoral influence)	43	19	34	44	39
GROUP'S INFORMATIONAL UTILITY (facts, knowledge, research)	6	5	3	4	8
GROUP'S LOBBYING ACTIVITY (entertainment, favors, skill, experience, money)	9	41	20	7	20
GROUP'S EXTRALEGISLATIVE POLITICAL ACTIVITY OR POWER (organization activity, publicity, campaign activity, letter-writing campaigns)	40	30	40	41	30
OTHER REASONS	2	5	3	4	3
Total	100	100	100	100	100
Number	87	464	188	367	88

SOURCE: J. C. Wahlke et al., *The Legislative System* (New York: John Wiley and Sons, 1962), pp. 334–35.

affected as well by the relationship between legislator and lobbyist. Lobbyists who are the close personal friends of legislators, or lobbyists for organized interests with which the legislator identifies, are not as likely to be identified as lobbyists as are group representatives who speak for interests inimical or hostile to those of the legislator. For instance, a Washington labor union lobbyist said:

> One time during the minimum wage battle, Senator —— began to weaken on the $1.00 minimum. Someone had touched his sympathy with a picture

Table 12.6. VERMONT LEGISLATORS ABLE TO IDENTIFY ORGANIZED
GROUPS, THEIR LOBBYISTS, AND ISSUES OF INTEREST TO THEM
(In percentages)

Question	Able to Recognize		
	Farm Bureau	AIV*	AFL–CIO
Group itself	100	63	78
Lobbyist	70	40	38
More than one issue	60	30	30

* Associated Industries of Vermont.

SOURCE: O. Garceau and C. Silverman, "A Pressure Group and the Pressured: A Case Report," *American Political Science Review*, XLVIII (1954), 685.

of what the bill would do to the sawmills of the South. He told me that he was contemplating making an exception in their case. I said, "—— (first name), if you even hint that you might back down from your previous position, this place will be swarming with lobbyists!" "Lobbyists," he said, looking around him, "I don't see any lobbyists around here." Then he realized that I was one and laughed. Hell, we don't think of ourselves as *lobbyists*![42]

While lobbying is a widely accepted practice in the American legislative system, and lobbyists are actors in it who are generally acceptable to American legislators, legislators vary in their orientations to lobbying activity by organized groups. Some legislators have relatively substantial knowledge about interest group activity and have a friendly attitude toward it. Legislators who fit this type have been called Facilitators. The "moochers" to whom we referred earlier in this chapter are facilitators of one kind (perhaps over-facilitators). A second type of legislator either has no strong affective orientation toward organized groups or has a very low level of knowledge about them; legislators of this type have been called Neutrals. Finally, legislators may be relatively knowledgeable about organized group activity and have a hostile attitude toward it. These legislators have been denominated Resisters in their lobbying orientation.

Interviews with legislators in California, Ohio, New Jersey, and Tennessee indicate that a substantial majority are of the Facilitator or Neutral type, although on the average about one-fourth can be classified as Resisters.[43] But Resisters were found to be relatively less well educated than other legislators, relatively less experienced in legislative work, and characterized by a lower sense of legislative efficacy. The Facilitators were found to be more sensitive to the complexity and multiplicity of interest-group politics, and seemed to play a more important part in the process of accommodation of conflicting interests. Furthermore, Facilitators appeared more often to be uncommitted to either pro-business or pro-labor interests, while Resisters were more often committed legislators. Among the ranks of Resisters are those who tend to be committed to one set of interests and hostile to others. Facilitators, on the other hand, more responsive to lobbying activities of a diverse kind, tend to be brokers of competing interests.

The American legislator is not to be viewed realistically as the pawn of contending forces. The legislator may influence the lobbyist as much as the other way round. He is no prostitute fallen prey to every seducer he encounters. Legislator-lobbyist relationships are reciprocal. But in this relationship, the legislator is more likely to have the upper hand. The legislator is often quite free to refuse to cooperate with lobbyists, without fear of electoral retaliation. Again, legislators may influence lobbyists by virtue of their friendly relations (the "friendship ploy"). Matthews points out that "friendship with a lobbyist can be as beneficial to a senator as to a lobbyist," because "it makes the lobbyist indebted to him, more sensitive to his political problems, less willing to apply 'pressure,' a more trustworthy ally."[44] Still further, legislators who deal with lobbyists as a part of the nature of legislative life build up "credit" with lobbyists just as much as the other way round, and legislators may influence lobbyists by calling in that credit. Finally, lobbyists are always susceptible to legislative attack; they are very vulnerable to legislative investigation and exposure, and "their public reputation is so low that public attack is bound to be damaging."[45] Lobbying is a part of the conflict-management process; it is an aspect of legislative bargaining, negotiation, and compromise. The legislator-lobbyist relationship is not a one-way street.

To the extent that we can talk meaningfully about lobbying in rather general terms, it is fair to say that lobbying in American legislative systems is not very effective in the sense of conventional popular conceptions of the shrewdness and manipulative ability of lobbyists. Lobbying activity is, in the main, directed at legislators who sympathize with the policy positions of the group or groups involved; lobbyists depend very substantially on their friends—those who sympathize with their cause. Much of lobbying involves the reinforcement and activation of sympathetic legislators, rather than the conversion of legislators from one policy position to another.

Assessments of lobbying effectiveness involve all of the unresolved problems of the measurement of influence. We must thus rely perforce upon crude and impressionistic evaluations of lobbying effectiveness. Impressions will vary where varying criteria of effectiveness are employed. The sensationalist muckraking exposé literature is not very helpful in our assessments of lobbying effectiveness. There is both historical and contemporary evidence for lobbying effectiveness, just as there is evidence of ineptitude in lobbying efforts. Some of the most effective lobbying in the recent history of the Congress has been done by the Railroad Brotherhoods and the oil and gas interests, and these lobbying efforts have been relatively narrow in scope.[46] On the other hand, there is reliable evidence that even large and important organized groups, such as business associations or labor unions, are on crucial issues often quite inept and ineffective in their lobbying efforts.[47] The key to successful lobbying in the postwar world has clearly been to communicate to policy-makers in the legislative body accurate parameters of popular sentiment.

NOTES

1. See Harmon Zeigler, *Interest Groups in American Society* (Englewood Cliffs, N.J., 1964); David B. Truman, *The Governmental Process* (New York, 1951); Donald C. Blaisdell, *American Democracy under Pressure* (New York, 1957).

2. Lester W. Milbrath, *The Washington Lobbyists* (Chicago, 1963), p. 8.

3. See *United States* v. *Harriss*, 347 U.S. 612 (1954).

4. Belle Zeller, "Regulation of Pressure Groups and Lobbyists," *Annals of the American Academy of Political and Social Science*, CCCXIX (1958), 94–103. See also Edgar Lane, *Lobbying and the Law* (Berkeley and Los Angeles, 1964).

5. *Congressional Quarterly Almanac*, XVIII (1962), 939, and *Congressional Quarterly Weekly Report*, XXIII (December 3, 1965), 1433–34.

6. See Charles D. Hounshell, *The Legislative Process in Virginia* (Charlottesville, Va., 1951), p. 45; also, William C. Havard and Loren P. Beth, *The Politics of Mis-representation* (Baton Rouge, La., 1962), pp. 220–25.

7. Milbrath, *op. cit.*, p. 31.

8. Samuel C. Patterson, "The Role of the Lobbyist: The Case of Oklahoma," *Journal of Politics*, XXV (1963), 81.

9. Lane, *op. cit.*, pp. 141–52.

10. This section relies primarily on Milbrath, *op. cit.*; Walter D. DeVries, "The Michigan Lobbyist: A Study in the Bases and Perceptions of Effectiveness (Unpublished Ph.D. dissertation, Michigan State University, 1960); and Patterson, *op. cit.*

11. An interesting description of some business lobbying activities is found in

Paul W. Cherington and Ralph L. Gillen, *The Business Representative in Washington* (Washington, D.C., 1962).

12. Milbrath, *op. cit.*, p. 72.

13. Milbrath, "The Political Party Activity of Washington Lobbyists," *Journal of Politics*, XX (1958), 346.

14. DeVries, *op. cit.*, p. 203.

15. Glyndon G. Van Deusen, *Thurlow Weed: Wizard of the Lobby* (Boston, 1947).

16. Kenneth G. Crawford, *The Pressure Boys* (New York, 1939).

17. Milbrath, *The Washington Lobbyists*, p. 107.

18. *Ibid.*, p. 136; DeVries, *op. cit.*, pp. 133–34.

19. Robert E. Lane, "Notes on the Theory of the Lobby," *Western Political Quarterly*, II (1949), 155; and E. Pendleton Herring, *Group Representation before Congress* (Baltimore, 1929), pp. 28–29.

20. Milbrath, *op. cit.*, pp. 116–19.

21. Donald R. Matthews, *U.S. Senators and Their World* (Chapel Hill, N.C.: 1960), pp. 180–81.

22. Milbrath, *op. cit.*, p. 212.

23. DeVries, *op. cit.*, pp. 97–99; Patterson, *op. cit.*, p. 85.

24. See Samuel C. Patterson, "The Role of the Labor Lobbyist" (Unpublished paper presented at the Annual Meeting of The American Political Science Association, Washington, D.C., 1962).

25. See Cherington and Gillen, *op. cit.*, pp. 45–70; and Raymond A. Bauer, Ithiel de Sola Pool, and Lewis A. Dexter, *American Business and Public Policy* (New York, 1963), pp. 350–57.

26. Milbrath, *The Washington Lobbyists*, p. 119.

27. Duane Lockard, *New England State Politics* (Princeton, 1959), p. 288.

28. DeVries, *op. cit.*, p. 199.

29. Milbrath, *The Washington Lobbyists*, pp. 238–39.

30. At the national level, see Edith T. Carper, *Lobbying and the Natural Gas Bill* (University, Ala., 1962); at the state level, see Rae F. Still, *The Gilmer-Aiken Bills: A Study in the Legislative Process* (Austin, Tex., 1950).

31. Milbrath, *The Washington Lobbyists*, p. 165.

32. See Gilbert Y. Steiner and Samuel K. Gove, *Legislative Politics in Illinois* (Urbana, 1960), p. 47; Cherington and Gillen, *op. cit.*, pp. 47–48; Robert Engler, *The Politics of Oil* (New York, 1961), p. 378; and Luke E. Ebersole, *Church Lobbying in the Nation's Capital* (New York, 1951), pp. 76–77.

33. Milbrath, *The Washington Lobbyists*, pp. 167–68.

34. See Truman, *op. cit.*, pp. 213–498.

35. Milbrath, *The Washington Lobbyists*, pp. 162–294; DeVries, *op. cit.*, p. 147; and Milbrath, "Lobbying as a Communication Process," *Public Opinion Quarterly*, XXIV (1960), 32–53.

36. Samuel C. Patterson, "The Role of the Deviant in the State Legislative System: The Wisconsin Assembly," *Western Political Quarterly*, XIV (1961), 463, 465–66.

37. Charles L. Clapp, *The Congressman: His Work As He Sees It* (Washington, D.C.: The Brookings Institution, 1963), pp. 162–63.

38. John C. Wahlke, Heinz Eulau, William Buchanan, and LeRoy C. Ferguson, *The Legislative System* (New York: John Wiley and Sons, 1962), p. 338.

39. *Ibid.*, pp. 314–16. A useful discussion of school lobbying is in Nicholas A. Masters, Robert H. Salisbury and Thomas H. Eliot, *State Politics and the Public Schools* (New York, 1964).

40. Wahlke et al., *op. cit.*, p. 335.

41. Oliver Garceau and Corinne Silverman, "A Pressure Group and the Pressured: A Case Report," *American Political Science Review*, XLVIII (1954), 685–686.

42. Matthews, *op. cit.*, p. 178.

43. John C. Wahlke, William Buchanan, Heinz Eulau and LeRoy C. Ferguson, "American State Legislators' Role Orientations Toward Pressure Groups," *Journal of Politics*, XXII (1960), 203–27.

44. Matthews, *op. cit.*, p. 189.

45. *Ibid.*, p. 190.

46. See Carper, *op. cit.*, pp. 36–38; and Engler, *op. cit.*, pp. 372–94.

47. The ineptitude of lobbying operations in congressional controversies over foreign trade legislation is particularly stressed in Bauer, Pool, and Dexter, *op. cit.*, pp. 323–99.

[13]

The Executive as a Legislative Leader

THE UNITED STATES CONSTITUTION is specific in its vesting of "all legislative powers herein granted" in the two houses of Congress. Similar provisions are found in state constitutions. Despite these clear constitutional assignments of legislative power, it has become customary to refer to the President or governor not merely as a partner in the legislative process but as the "chief legislator." Students will look in vain for amendments to the United States Constitution which expand the President's role in the legislative process. The only amendment affecting his power, the Twenty-second, restricts the President by limiting him to two terms. The grants of legislative authority to the President in the Constitution are few, though important: he shall make legislative recommendations to Congress, he may call special sessions, and he has the power to veto legislation (subject to overriding by a two-thirds vote in the Congress).

The case of the governor is different. It is possible to trace the trends in state constitutions that have enhanced his power in legislative affairs. Under early state constitutions the governor had a short term, exercised minimum powers, and was heavily dependent on the legislature. In the words of one writer, "The American governorship was conceived in mistrust, and born in a strait jacket, the creature of revolutionary assemblies."[1] During the Jacksonian period popular election of the governor became universal, the term of office was extended, and the veto became common. Later on in the nineteenth century, the proliferation of elected officials and boards and commissions reduced the governor's control over the executive branch and consequently his influence with the legislature. In the early years of the twentieth century, constitutional and statutory changes enhanced the governor's power, transforming him "from figurehead to leader" in the words of one writer. In many states his term was increased to four years and the item veto became more common. Programs to reorganize the state administrative structure and the development of the executive budget system, paralleling trends at the national level, strengthened not only the governor's administrative control but also his ability to influence legislative developments.[2]

EMERGENCE AS LEGISLATIVE LEADER

The emergence of the chief executive as chief legislator at both the national and state level has been due primarily to other factors. The growing demands on government and the growing complexity of these demands have increasingly forced the executive to take the initiative in the development of a legislative program. These trends did not evolve automatically; they were the product of strong executives with bold concepts of their responsibilities. The history of national government is the history of rivalry and shifts in the locus of power between President and Congress. Thomas Jefferson used many of the techniques of leadership that were duplicated or attempted a century or more later: he chose legislative leaders and made them responsible to him, used the party caucus effectively, drafted bills, and persuaded supporters to run for Congress. Under his successors the reins of leadership shifted to congressional leaders such as Henry Clay and John C. Calhoun. Although Andrew Jackson used the veto and patronage powers with unprecedented vigor, neither he nor other Presidents before the Civil War exercised such direct leadership of Congress as Jefferson had. Lincoln battled with Congress throughout the Civil War and accomplished some of his major objectives through bypassing it; the conflict was renewed during the next administration and came to a climax in the impeachment proceedings against Andrew Johnson. The remainder of the nineteenth century was characterized by congressional supremacy; the stronger Presidents resisted attempted congressional encroachments on presidential power, but they did not work effectively to enact legislative measures.[3]

It was three twentieth-century Presidents—the two Roosevelts and Wilson—who enabled the President to become the chief legislator. Each of these men came to Washington with experience in the states, where they had transformed the image of the governor into that of a leader with broad legislative as well as administrative responsibilities. Theodore Roosevelt started the practice of initiating a wide range of legislative proposals in messages to Congress, and Wilson dramatized his legislative recommendations by appearing personally before Congress to deliver them. Bills were drafted in the executive departments and forwarded without fanfare to Congress. Roosevelt and Wilson did not merely propose legislation; they recognized the need (in Rossiter's words) "to push politely but relentlessly" for enactment of their proposals, and they did so by writing letters to members of Congress, conferring with congressional leaders, and delegating members of the cabinet to lobby in caucuses and in the corridors of the Capitol.[4]

Theodore Roosevelt and Wilson, like several contemporary governors, recognized the President's tremendous potential as a leader of public opinion. Roosevelt described the White House as a "bully pulpit." He might be described as the first President with a sense of public relations, a flair for showmanship. Writing of his experience as governor of New York, he said:

In theory the Executive has nothing to do with legislation. In practice, as things now are, the Executive is or ought to be peculiarly representative of the people as a whole. As often as not the action of the Executive offers the only means by which the people can get the legislation they demand and ought to have.[5]

While he was still governor of New Jersey, Woodrow Wilson spoke in a remarkably similar vein:

The people are impatient of a President or a governor who will not formulate a policy and insist upon its adoption. They are impatient of a governor who will not exercise energetic leadership, who will not make his appeals directly to public opinion and insist that the dictates of public opinion be carried out in definite legal reforms of his own suggestion.[6]

Even earlier Wilson had written: "Opinion is the great, indeed the only coordinating force in our system," and the President draws his strength from "his close and special relation to opinion the nation over."[7] Although the Republican Presidents of the 1920s showed little understanding of public opinion, Franklin Roosevelt knew exactly what the earlier Roosevelt and Wilson were talking about. He had watched their performances closely, and he had followed their precepts as governor of New York. He came to the White House better prepared than any predecessor to lead public opinion, and he used the radio, the press conference, and speaking trips with unmatched skill.[8]

Wilson, described by one writer as "the first President to develop systematically the legislative powers of his office,"[9] was more conscious than his predecessors of his position as party leader. In one of his early appearances before Congress, Wilson said: "I have come to you, as head of the Government and the responsible leader of the party in power, to urge action. . . ."[10] Wilson believed in a disciplined congressional party, and was frequently able to use the Democratic caucus to achieve this end. It was this belief that led him to misjudge the popular temper and demand the election of a Democratic Congress in 1918. In the White House, Wilson personified the President he had described earlier in his writings: "He cannot escape being the leader of his party except by incapacity and lack of personal force, because he is at once the choice of the party and of the nation."[11] Wilson's Republican successors demonstrated such "incapacity and lack of personal force" for a dozen years, but Franklin Roosevelt reestablished the image of the President as a party leader. Party leadership in practice has never attained the ideal form envisioned by Wilson, but it has become an essential element of legislative leadership, as even a "nonpolitical" President like Eisenhower came to realize.

Richard E. Neustadt has pointed out that the exercise of legislative initiative used to be considered a way of distinguishing between "strong" and "weak" Presidents, a symptom of presidential intention to "dominate" Congress. "If these were once relevant criteria of domination, they are not so today. As things stand now they have become part of the regular routines of office, an accepted elaboration of the constitutional right to recommend. . . ."[12]

Since the turn of the century, congressional attitudes toward the role of the President have undergone a profound change. One senator described the senatorial mind at that time:

> The most eminent senators would have received as a personal affront a private message from the White House expressing a desire that they should adopt any course in the discharge of their legislative duties that they did not approve. If they visited the White House, it was to give, not to receive advice.[13]

Congressional perceptions of the President's role changed gradually. There were many congressmen who believed that Franklin Roosevelt's aggressive leadership must be the exception and not the norm and who therefore expected Senator Truman, when he became President, to restore to Congress its earlier monopoly of legislative matters.

Today congressmen may complain about specific cases of presidential action in the legislative sphere, but their broad perception of the President's role now coincides with reality. It was a senior Republican committee chairman who best exemplified this new attitude in 1953, when he told an Administration witness: "Don't expect us to start from scratch on what you people want. That's not the way we do things here —*you* draft the bills and *we* work them over."[14] Neustadt has listed some practical reasons why congressmen consider presidential initiatives a service rather than a threat:

> In practical effect they represent a means whereby Congress can gain from the outside what comes hard from within: a handy and official guide to the wants of its biggest customer; an advance formulation of main issues at each session; a work-load ready-to-hand for every legislative committee; an indication, more or less, of what may risk the veto; a borrowing of presidential prestige for major bills—and thus a boosting of publicity-potentials in both sponsorship and opposition.[15]

The men who set the precedents of strong gubernatorial leadership during the early years of the twentieth century were found primarily in the industrial states: Al Smith and Franklin Roosevelt in New York, Woodrow Wilson in New Jersey, Frank Lowden in Illinois, and Robert La Follette in Wisconsin. These were men who recognized that new demands were being placed on government in the larger states and that the governor must take the initiative to meet these reforms. Most of them initiated statutory or constitutional changes to strengthen the tools at the governor's command. It was Lowden (1917–1921) who reorganized the executive branch in Illinois to make the most of the agencies of government directly responsible to him, and it was Al Smith who established the executive budget system in New York in 1927. Both reforms were widely copied in other states, and both strengthened not only the governor's control over the executive branch but also his influence in legislative matters.

The most important changes wrought by these governors, however, were political rather than constitutional. They appeared in person before the legislature to present programs that became increasingly specific over the years. They used the veto, the special session, and messages to the legislature boldly and skillfully. Above all, they mobilized public support, with radio speeches, press conferences, and speaking tours across the state. They capitalized on the public demand for social reforms and on the tarnished image of the legislatures to force legislative approval of at least some of their major proposals. They transformed the governor into a legislative leader, a public figure highly visible to the voters. The precedents set by a few have been followed, with varying degrees of success, by scores of less famous governors in a majority of the states.

In some of the less urbanized states there have been fewer demands on government; in these states, particularly in the absence of strong, precedent-setting governors, it has not become customary for the governor to play a powerful and persistent part in the legislative process. In such states the legislators have a different perception of the governor's role; if a strong governor tries to reshape this role, he may encounter legislative resistance, and a successor with a narrower conception of his legislative role is unlikely to be bound by recent precedents. In more states the governor's role is comparable to the President's. State legislators have all the more reason to welcome gubernatorial intervention. They have fewer opportunities and resources than congressmen possess for studying the state's needs and developing legislative programs. In most states the gubernatorial message is the primary catalyst of legislative action.

Voters, as well as the legislators, expect the President and the governors to be legislative leaders. The chief executive is the most visible and articulate participant in the legislative process. He runs on a platform composed largely of legislative promises. To the extent that issues affect elections (and it is admittedly a limited extent), the voter judges a candidate largely on legislative issues, and the promises and performance of a presidential or gubernatorial candidate are better known and remembered than those of a legislative candidate. Duane Lockard has said: "People increasingly speak of a law being 'passed by the governor.' In sarcasm the storekeeper tosses coins into a can labeled 'Sales Tax' and says, 'A penny for the Governor.' "[16] The voter is often blissfully unaware of the problems an executive faces in getting his legislative program enacted. He does not understand the problems caused in some states by constitutional limitations, divided executive authority, or malapportionment. The public does not realize how seriously a President or governor is handicapped when the opposition party has a legislative majority; in fact, a large proportion of the public may not even be aware of that division in government when it occurs. The voter knows little about the chief executive's problems, but he has heard him make promises and legislative proposals, and is likely to hold him responsible for legislation that is passed or that fails. The chief executive has become the center of attention, the focus of conflict in nation and state.

In the opening chapter we described the legislative system as being composed of a complex of groups, with the legislature itself serving as the nucleus. The executive is one of these groups, comparable to lobbies or constituency groups, for example. These groups have in common the desire and some degree of ability to influence the legislative output. The trend of the twentieth century has been toward increasing this executive influence. At the same time the growing and conflicting demands for legislative action in Washington and in most state capitals have become focused on the chief executive. Presidents are widely criticized for their low batting average on Capitol Hill, and governors attribute their high political mortality rate in part to legislative deadlock. As we shall see in this chapter, the resources of constitutional power, opinion leadership, and party support on which the executive can draw are often insufficient for the demands placed on him.

There is another group in the legislative system that we will examine in order to shed more light on the executive: the administrative agencies. These are often a source of strength for the chief executive. But the bureaucracy has grown large and complex and its components often have enough legal independence to frustrate control from the White House or the executive mansion. They play an independent and sometimes contradictory part in the legislative process.

CONSTITUTIONAL SOURCES OF POWER

Legislative Recommendations. "He shall from time to time give to the Congress information of the state of the Union, and recommend to their consideration such measures as he shall judge necessary and expedient. . . ." Here, in Article Two, Section Three of the Constitution, is the constitutional base for the President's proposals to Congress. We have seen how strong Presidents, serving at times when public opinion and the needs of the nation demanded new policies of government, established precedents that have made executive initiation of legislation the accepted norm in our political system. In Franklin Roosevelt's time, this meant a wide variety of special messages, followed up by drafts of Administration bills. Presidents Truman and Eisenhower added a further refinement to this procedure: a detailed and comprehensive legislative package presented at the start of each session of Congress. As described by Neustadt, this development resulted in part from the 1946 Employment Act, with its requirement for an annual Economic Report to Congress, a report that has consistently included legislative recommendations. It developed also from the growing need for legislation to implement foreign policy and from President Truman's political tactics in dealing with a Republican Congress and in campaigning for reelection. In 1953 President Eisenhower had neither the time nor the inclination for such a comprehensive legislative program, and he sent a minimum number of recommendations to Congress during the session. At the start of the 1954 session and in subsequent years, however, the President presented a comprehensive program. Eisenhower had decided that he should present a legislative program, and his request to the departments for suggestions produced a flood of detailed measures. Neustadt's careful study makes it clear why the precedent established by

Truman was so powerful: it had taken root in the bureaucratic establishment, and from the Budget Bureau down to the internal components of departments, annual legislative proposals had become an established pattern, a norm.[17]

Legislative recommendations emerge from the departments not so much in response to bureaucratic ritual but as a result of departmental interests and policies that can be implemented only by legislation. These proposals are carefully drafted and, like the budget, sent to the President far in advance of presentation to Congress. Just as departmental budgets must be cut to avoid overcommitting the government's fiscal resources, legislative recommendations must be screened to avoid overcommitting the President's political resources. The White House staff and the Budget Bureau play a part in this screening effort, but the final decision, like that on the budget, must be made by the President. The President's State of the Union message, budget message, and Economic Report outline in considerable detail the legislative program that bears his endorsement. As the session progresses, the President will send more detailed messages on such topics as foreign aid, education, and housing, and loyal congressmen will be supplied with the drafts of bills. When the session is drawing to a close, the President may tell his legislative leaders which items he considers "must" legislation; with this step, the process of selection becomes more difficult and more crucial.

Presidential initiative, thus institutionalized, has become a permanent feature of the legislative process. We should be clear about its meaning. It does not mean that every legislative proposal originates in the mind of the President or within the confines of the White House. Most proposals come from the agencies of government and from interest groups, sometimes from agency–interest-group alliances. Congressmen play a role in the initiating process, as well. What the President does is to determine priorities and to focus attention and pressure on the high-priority measures. The departments provide him with the information and advice needed for making these choices, and then with some of the ammunition (drafts of bills and expert witnesses, for example) needed for securing congressional approval. Once the President has committed his prestige to certain proposals, he must make further choices, determining how to best use the resources of his office to advance his legislative program. In any session the President is able to win enactment of only part, and sometimes a small part, of his legislative program; few pieces of major legislation pass, however, that do not have his active support.

State constitutions provide governors with a comparable mandate to make legislative recommendations. The process by which a governor prepares a legislative program has been little studied,[18] but it appears to replicate the process at the national level on a smaller and less complex scale. State agencies have myriad suggestions for legislation. Some of them, on noncontroversial matters, do not need gubernatorial support. Some agencies in at least a few states have enough influence in the legislature to operate independently. But generally state agencies seek to gain a place for their major bills on the governor's list of recommendations, recognizing that this provides the best chance for passage.

The governor's legislative task is like the President's. The legislature deals with masses of trivial bills, more so than Congress, and the governor must determine priorities and provide direction. In states where the governor can depend on the loyal voting support of some legislators, this support applies primarily to legislation publicly advocated in gubernatorial messages. Even in states where party or factional alignments are weaker, there is often a strong disposition to support the governor's program whenever possible. Whatever the strength of its support, the governor's program becomes the focus of attention.

The Veto. The constitutional right to veto is a powerful negative weapon for both President and governor. The President has ten days in which to return a bill to Congress with his objections to it spelled out; a two-thirds vote in each house is necessary to override his veto. After Congress has adjourned, the President may exercise the "pocket veto" by simply failing to sign a bill within ten days. Comparable provisions for the veto are found in the constitution of every state except North Carolina. The only significant variation is in the size of the legislative majority needed to override, which ranges from a majority in a few states to three-fifths or two-thirds in most.

Beginning with Franklin Roosevelt, the veto became a significant presidential tool in dealing with major legislation. It is a powerful weapon because it is seldom reversed. A President can almost always rally more than one-third of Congress to his support. The President's prestige is involved in a veto, and members of his own party in particular want to avoid damaging that. The success record of vetoes is impressive. Up until 1961, only 73 had been overridden, out of 2,192. Andrew Johnson, who barely escaped impeachment, suffered 15 reversals out of only 28 attempted vetoes. In recent years, Franklin Roosevelt had 9 vetoes overridden (out of 631), Truman lost 12 (out of 250), and Eisenhower lost only 2 (out of 181). The record of gubernatorial vetoes is just as impressive. On the average only 1 or 2 percent of the vetoes are overridden in a year, and most of these are likely to be in a few states where governors are locked in partisan or factional struggles with a legislative majority. Even where such deadlocks prevail, the governor's veto is usually effective; in his twelve years of often bitter struggles with a Republican legislature, Governor Williams of Michigan (a Democrat) had only one veto overridden. In some states the veto has become almost invulnerable: only 3 vetoes were overridden in the last ninety years in Illinois, only one in fifty years in Pennsylvania, and none since 1838 in Missouri.[19] In states such as these, the final nature of a governor's veto is taken for granted, and there is seldom any effort made to override it. One factor that undoubtedly strengthens the governor's hand is that a high proportion of bills are passed in the closing days of a state legislative session, and consequently a high proportion of vetoes is of the "pocket" variety. In Alaska the new constitution provides for an additional legislative session to deal with bills vetoed after the close of the regular session.

The veto is essentially a negative weapon, but it may be used positively by the skillful executive. The threat to veto a bill can frequently lead legislators to improve the bill in order to make it acceptable. In four states—Alabama, Virginia, Massachusetts, and New Jersey—the governor has the power of executive amendment. In addition to the veto, the governor has the option of returning the bill to the legislature with amendments, and the legislature may adopt or reject these amendments. This device gives the governor more flexibility and formally makes the veto what it is informally: a positive tool.

In 41 states the governor has the item veto for appropriations bills. Since the governor can seldom risk vetoing a whole appropriations bill, this gives him a means of excluding unwanted additions to his budget. In some states the governor's budget is seldom tampered with and the item veto need not be used. Constitutional amendments to give the President the item veto on appropriations have often been proposed but never adopted. If we can assume that the item veto would be as effective as the regular veto, such an amendment would strengthen the President's authority over his departments by undermining their efforts to obtain increased sums from the appropriations committees; it would weaken the positive role of Congress in the appropriations process. "Much of the pressure now exerted on Congress would be transferred to the executive," as Herring has pointed out.[20] In lieu of the item veto, the President does have authority, occasionally exercised, to impound funds appropriated by Congress. This authority, first exercised by Roosevelt with regard to public works measures during World War II, was confirmed by an act of Congress passed in 1950.[21]

Special Sessions. The President has the power to call special sessions of Congress. This power has been used on occasion to meet particular emergencies; it has often been used as a political weapon to focus attention on presidential programs. Speaking to the Democratic national convention following his renomination in 1948, President Truman announced his intention to call a special session of the Republican-controlled Eightieth Congress. After Congress met and failed to act on most of his proposals, Truman had extra fuel for the fire of his election campaign against the Republican "do-nothing" Congress. In all states the governor has the power to call special sessions; in over two-thirds of the states this power is exclusively his, and in nearly half the states the governor alone can determine the subject matter. At the state level the special session assumes greater importance because regular sessions are fewer and usually shorter. The governor may call a special session to deal with a particular part of his program that was ignored in the regular session, or to enact a revised version of a bill he has vetoed. At the state level, the threat of a special session may be a powerful device for gaining action sought by the governor, just as the threat of the veto may block bills and amendments he opposes.

Term of Office. Most of the constitutional powers possessed by the governor do not vary significantly from state to state. All governors may propose legislation; all but one may exercise the veto, and the variations in requirements for overriding make little difference; all governors can call special sessions. There are significant constitutional differences in the governor's control over various components of the executive branch; these we shall examine later in the chapter. One remaining difference of great importance is in the governor's term. There are 15 states in which the governor has a four-year term of office, with no limit on reelection, and 7 other states where he can serve only two consecutive four-year terms. In the remaining 28 states, the limitations on his term constitute a serious obstacle to his effectiveness as chief legislator. In 15 states, mostly Southern, he has a four-year term but cannot be reelected. This reduces the governor's legislative effectiveness during the second half of his term and makes it difficult for him to build a political base in the legislature, particularly in one-party states. In 13 states the governor has a two-year term, but except for four-year limits in New Mexico and South Dakota, there is no limit on the number of successive terms possible. The two-year term gives the governor a minimum of time to build legislative support and to develop a legislative record before he must face the voters again. Most such governors are in highly competitive two-party states, where the two-year term increases the political mortality rate. The four-year governor normally faces the prospect of mid-term elections for half the Senate and all House members, elections that may deprive him of a working majority in the legislature. Only four states elect the governor and all legislators simultaneously for four years. Governors in two states, Kansas and New Mexico, sometimes face the unusual handicap of starting a two-year term with a Senate made up entirely of members who are serving for four years and were elected two years previously, senators who are obviously immune to the governor's mandate. The Twenty-second Amendment, by limiting the President to two terms, was widely believed to have weakened his effectiveness as a legislative leader during the closing years of his second term. President Eisenhower cast some doubt on this theory because he seemed to many observers to be a more aggressive legislative leader during his last two years in office. The questions remain to be answered by experience.

LEADERSHIP OF PUBLIC OPINION

Every recent President or governor who has been effective as a legislative leader has brought the force of public opinion to bear on the legislative body on behalf of his proposals. When the President wishes to, he can command newspaper headlines and television time as no member of Congress can, in order to capture the attention of the nation. A governor's impact on public opinion is far less but still exceeds that of legislators. In an age when the processes of government are complex and confusing to the average citizen, the chief executive of nation or state has visibility. The tools of public relations are available to any chief executive; it is his skill in using them that determines their effectiveness.

The press conference provides an example of how rapidly the innovations of strong Presidents—such as Franklin Roosevelt—become institutionalized, in an age when each President needs to utilize fully the resources of his office. The press conference has become a permanent institution, but the style has been affected by the personality of the President and by technological change. A small, almost intimate affair under Roosevelt, it gradually became larger and more formal; it was televised under Eisenhower and shown live under Kennedy. Lyndon Johnson, more accessible to the press than any President since Roosevelt, has varied the format, from occasional large-scale conferences on television to informal and even impromptu ones held, for example, on horseback at the Texas ranch or on the march around the White House grounds. At the state level the press conference remains a small, informal affair, comparable to the institution devised by Roosevelt in his days at Albany and carried by him to Washington. Often these are held once or twice a day.

The advent of television has given the chief executive an opportunity for direct, intimate contact with the American people. Franklin Roosevelt first recognized the value of radio as a means for communicating directly to the people. No President since Roosevelt has equaled his skill in personalized mass communications, but each has used radio and television in an effort to make his policies and legislative proposals understandable and acceptable to the public. Since Wilson's time and particularly since Roosevelt's time, Presidents have gone to the country on speaking tours designed to dramatize their legislative program through personal endorsement. Although the President can speak to people only by the thousands (by contrast with the millions reached by television), these trips are important because some of the talks are made to opinion leaders (newspaper publishers or business executives, for example) and others are delivered in sections of the country where the presence of the chief executive attracts attention and interest. Moreover, all these talks are reported in the press and reach millions of unseen readers.

The governor, although he attracts less attention, has the chance to be seen and heard in person by a larger proportion of his constituents. Some governors have weekly television reports or newspaper columns, and all of them have a multitude of invitations to dedicate highways, address graduating classes, and adorn state conventions. The governor can use these occasions to polish platitudes or to extol the virtues of the town where he speaks; he can also use them to generate public support for his legislative program.

The President and the governors of two-party states also influence public opinion by serving as party spokesmen. During the election campaign they define the issues and make the commitments that form the basis for their legislative programs. An incumbent chief executive, the party nominee, or one who seems likely to win nomination (depending on the timing and function of a convention) usually has a dominant voice in determining the content of the platform; the candidate who has not been able to dictate the platform can largely ignore it in his campaign. Voters who consider themselves Democrats may not agree with a Democratic governor's pronouncements but they are likely to identify these as party policy. Studies of voting behavior have shown a tendency for voters to approve many of the policy positions taken by the leader of the party with which they identify. The governor, as a party leader, speaks not only to loyal members of the legislative party but—with some effectiveness—to loyal and attentive voters as well, despite the vast public ignorance on most issues. The fact that the opposition party never has an undisputed leader, except during election campaigns, reduces the impact of the opposition leadership on public opinion.

These techniques for influencing opinion assume importance because legislators have some sensitivity to public opinion. If these techniques work perfectly, the chief executive will not only influence the thinking of the voters but will so impress them with the importance of an issue that they will deluge their legislators with demands to support the chief executive's program. To the extent that the legislator is sensitive to constituent opinion, he will then vote as the executive wishes. The many legislative successes of chief executives suggest that this model sometimes corresponds to reality, but the many examples of executive failure and legislative deadlock are proof that the model does not always work in this fashion. Why not? What weaknesses undermine the chief executive's control over the legislature through public opinion?

Although the President has a great advantage over any congressman in gaining access to the news media, he has to compete with every other source of news—from home-run hitters to movie starlets—in attracting public attention. The average citizen has only the most casual interest in the problems of politics and government, which he often finds complex, boring, and irrelevant to his personal life. The President cannot get and keep an audience simply by appearing before the television cameras. Neustadt has said of the President:

He has to ride events to gain attention. Most members of his public grow attentive only as they grow concerned with what may happen in their lives. . . . Without a real-life happening to hoist it into view, a piece of presidential news, much like the man's own voice, is likely to be lost amidst the noises and distractions of the day."[23]

In time of obvious crisis—the attack on Pearl Harbor or the discovery of missile bases in Cuba—the President commands attention. The President's legislative program seldom has enough intrinsic interest to attract such attention. Neustadt quotes Franklin Roosevelt's perceptive conclusion that

The public psychology and, for that matter, individual psychology, cannot, because of human weakness, be attuned for long periods of time to a constant repetition of the highest note in the scale. . . . Whereas in this country there is a free and sensational press, people tire of seeing the same name, day after day, in the important headlines of the papers, and the same voice, night after night, over the radio.[24]

An intensive campaign for a legislative measure, highlighted by a major television address, will have an impact—but not if it becomes a weekly feature. The President may decide that it is unrealistic to try to focus public attention on more than two or three measures during one session of Congress. In competing for public attention, the governor faces greater obstacles than the President. He is a less important figure and deals with problems that attract less attention. Except for desegregation crises in a few Southern states, it is difficult to think of recent state issues that would enable a governor to attract full public attention. The governor may devote a large proportion of his time to explaining his legislative program and still wonder whether anyone is listening.

The success of the President's program depends not only on public support for it but also on the President's prestige. Neustadt points out that congressmen—as well as the other actors on the Washington scene—are dependent in varying degrees on public support and are consequently interested in gauging the President's prestige. This prestige can be measured roughly by the public opinion polls, but it remains a vague thing, "a jumble of imprecise impressions held by relatively inattentive men." "Yet," Neustadt argues, "the prevalent impression of a President's public standing tends to set a tone and to define the limits of what Washingtonians do for him, or do to him"; among the most crucial of these Washingtonians are the congressmen.[25] The President's prestige may affect the success of his legislative program, but the effect is a subtle, unmeasurable one. One reason for this is that there seems to be little connection between the President's prestige and public understanding of and support for his legislative program. This was the finding of polls conducted during Kennedy's Administration, and it was also true during the New Deal: The public liked the President but was apathetic or hostile to important parts of his program.[26] If a chief executive's prestige is not necessarily an asset to his program and if his campaigns for public support often founder on apathy and ignorance about issues, perhaps he can seldom do more than generate public confidence—a willingness to give him and his program a chance. To focus this general support on specific measures, the executive must exercise political leadership in his direct dealings with legislators.

POLITICAL LEADERSHIP

The executive and the legislature are separate branches of government, independent in their electoral bases and distinct in the functions each performs. The division of power in our constitutional system breeds conflict, but the part played by the modern executive in the legislative process requires cooperation between the two branches. It is often said that party provides the cement of cooperation; this implies that the chief executive as a *partisan* leader can command the loyalty of his legislative party and can exercise certain kinds of partisan sanctions. But is this true? Neustadt asserts: "What the Constitution separates our political parties do not combine. The parties are themselves composed of separated organizations sharing public authority."[27] James M. Burns makes the same fundamental point in describing our "four-party system," two presidential and two congressional parties.[28] At the state level, if there is a significant level of two-party competition, we have greater reason to expect party cohesion.

In earlier chapters we have explored the leadership structure of legislative bodies and determined that in Congress and in some state legislatures this structure provides the basis for significant degrees of party cohesion. In Chapter 17, we shall summarize the research evidence that has shown party alignments appearing frequently in many legislative bodies—more frequently than any other form of alignment. Our purpose here is to determine what the chief executive contributes to party cohesion. David Truman concluded that in the Eighty-first Congress "the Democratic majority parties in the Congress worked as groups because of and in response to the initiatives of a Democratic Administration."[29] How often would this be true in Congress and in the states? What techniques can a chief executive use to engender party cohesion? What other kinds of techniques can he use, where partisan techniques are inadequate or impossible?

One of three possible political environments confronts the chief executive: He may command a party majority in the legislature. He may find the opposition in control of one or both branches of the legislature. He may, in some states, govern in a one-party environment, where the absence of a substantial opposition party eliminates the possibility of party leadership in the legislature. One of the four Congresses during President Truman's tenure and three of the four during the Eisenhower Administration were controlled by the opposite party. The five elections from 1952 through 1960 in the 32 two-party states led to opposition control of one or both houses 55 percent of the time for Democratic governors, and 39 percent of the time for Republican governors. No state with some alteration of party control has completely avoided divided government in recent years.

The greatest contrast in environments is that between a two-party and a one-party situation, because in the latter situation the executive must construct his own political organization and create his own personal loyalties in the legislature; he inherits no political support. In a two-party situation, the executive inherits a legislative party with some degree of organization, cohesion, and loyalty. If that legislative party lacks majority control, it still has some value, provided it is not too weak or divided, but it confronts the executive with certain problems. He must temper overtly partisan appeals, rely more heavily on public opinion, distribute patronage to both parties, and constantly base his tactics on the necessity of ultimate compromise with the opposition party. He must be effective both as a partisan and a bipartisan leader.

The Chief Executive and the Party Organization. Control over a strong party organization outside the legislature may be an asset to the chief executive who is seeking to enact a legislative program. At the state level, strong, well-organized parties are found more often in the industrial states of the East and Midwest, where party machines remain potent in large metropolitan centers. Party organization is weaker in the

West, where party loyalties and local machines are weaker. Though he wears the mantle of party leader, a governor does not automatically inherit *de facto* control of a strong party organization. Some governors have been powerful party leaders. Early in his term as governor, Thomas Dewey grasped firm control of the New York Republican party. Governor Mennen Williams, in alliance with labor leaders, captured and rebuilt the Michigan Democratic party. In such states as Indiana and Pennsylvania, the large amount of patronage under his control gives a governor great opportunities to dominate the party. The governor who wins nomination by defeating an entrenched organization may be handicapped in trying to control that organization during his term. A study of Massachusetts governors is probably typical of the situation in some other states where the organization lacks cohesion:

> Many of the twentieth-century Governors have risen swiftly in the party, created enmity, and sometimes taken short cuts in their pursuit of high office. At any rate, none of the recent Governors have relied on party organizations exclusively for their campaigns, and some scarcely used them. . . .
>
> Moreover, once a Governor was in office, efforts to build up the state party apparatus have generally been disappointing. . . . None could see any immediate use of the party machinery important enough to warrant a major effort to reorganize or streamline its operations while they were serving as Governor.[30]

Party leadership presents a different kind of challenge to the President because the federal nature of the national party structure makes impossible the tight control exercised by some governors over state parties. Modern Presidents have recognized the need to exert some type of influence over the national party. Theodore Roosevelt struggled for several years to wrest control of the party from Mark Hanna, one of the few national political leaders in our history. Roosevelt was working primarily to ensure his own renomination. Since that time most Presidents have been able to take renomination for granted, although Franklin Roosevelt maneuvered skillfully to eliminate opposition to his third-term nomination. Wilson gave up his efforts to reform the state parties because of the resistance of congressmen who had close ties to state organizations. Franklin Roosevelt played a larger part in state politics than any subsequent President. He used patronage to support one faction or another in state parties. He supported some Progressive Republican and Independent candidates, even against Democrats. He encouraged the formation of political alliances, such as the American Labor Party in New York, outside the Democratic party. These steps were taken primarily to strengthen his chances for reelection, to recruit support from those who were unwilling to work within the old-line Democratic parties. At times Roosevelt took steps in the direction of revitalizing the state Democratic parties, but he was unwilling to jeopardize the short-run prospects for reelection to obtain long-run goals. He left the parties largely as he had found them.[31] President Eisenhower, like Roosevelt, talked about party realignment, but he lacked the continuing interest necessary to reshape state parties.

The crux of the problem is congressional nominations. As Neustadt has said, "Until there is a marriage between presidential and congressional electorates, particularly at the stage of nomination, there will be no marriage between President and Congress."[32] Congressional influence in presidential nominating conventions has been shrinking since the "smoke-filled room" in 1920 that nominated Harding. There is no evidence that presidential influence over congressional nominations is growing. The importance of influencing legislative nominations can be illustrated in a few states where the governor has used this technique. Connecticut, New York, and New Jersey are examples of states where the party organization is relatively strong and the primary is a weak institution; the party leadership can usually persuade the local organization to deny renomination to a recalcitrant legislator, and while the sanction is seldom used, the threat of it is effective enough for it to be seldom needed. In Oregon and Colorado, states in which the primary is accompanied by local endorsement procedures, legislators are sometimes punished by the endorsing group for lack of party loyalty in the legislature. In states where the direct primary assumes greater importance, it is rare to find the governor openly involved in the legislative primary. In gubernatorial election years he has his hands full with his own race. Most governors probably believe that local reaction would range from hostile to apathetic and that they could not find enough local allies to make endorsements effective. The failure of a gubernatorial purge is a virtual guarantee that the legislator will be hostile at the next session of the legislature. In short, what the governor cannot do privately, he will not attempt to accomplish in open combat.

Recent Presidents have occasionally played a quiet part in congressional nominations—lending support to an incumbent, trying to prevent a damaging primary fight, persuading a strong candidate to run against an incumbent in the opposite party. The classic example of a public presidential effort to unseat his party's congressmen in a primary is Franklin Roosevelt's attempted "purge" in 1938; the failure of the "purge" largely explains why no President since Roosevelt has followed his example. Roosevelt endorsed several incumbent Democratic senators, but his real break with tradition came when he campaigned against several incumbent Democrats, including Senators Walter George of Georgia, "Cotton Ed" Smith of South Carolina, and Millard Tydings of Maryland. The incumbents endorsed by Roosevelt won, but so did those whom he opposed, and the venture entered the history books as a complete failure. The only incumbent who was purged, a conservative New York congressman who was chairing the House Rules Committee, lost not as a result of any public intervention by the President but as a consequence of quiet, effective political work on the scene by his lieutenants. A review of events in 1938 shows that Roosevelt undertook the purge without any clear idea about either objectives or tactics, and that the campaign was poorly managed from start to finish; Roosevelt was indecisive and his advisers were divided. William Riker, after describing the confusion and mistakes of the purge, concludes that failure was not due only to blundering. "Behind the blundering lies the fact of federalism. What this whole episode demonstrates more than anything else is the resistance of local politicians to national leadership."[33]

Perhaps the most effective use of presidential influence would be in elections rather than in nominations. In both presidential and mid-term election campaigns, recent Presidents have given increasingly direct support and endorsement to members of their congressional ticket. The President's time for personal campaigning is limited; there is no reason why he could not be more selective about his endorsements. There is some evidence that, during the Eisenhower Administration, some Republican candidates were embarrassed by their differences with the President, particularly on foreign policy, and some of the most isolationist grabbed quite frantically for the President's coattails. Although President Eisenhower bestowed his endorsements indiscriminately, he apparently considered the idea of selective endorsements; he told a press conference in 1958 that he would not support candidates who opposed him on several major issues: defense, foreign aid, trade, and economy in government.[34] As a technique for building congressional support for a program, such selective endorsements would be a very indirect form of pressure, but perhaps not a completely impotent one.

The Chief Executive and the Legislative Leadership. In dealing directly with Congress, the President must rely primarily on his party's leaders, as David Truman has explained:

Relations with the leaders of the Congressional party can be supplemented, as they often have been, but no substitutes have appeared on which he can rely with equal confidence. To the degree that the mechanism of the Congressional party is relied upon, however, it must be taken as it is, with the leaders it has produced. For a President to attempt to act directly as the leader of the Congressional party almost certainly would be to destroy, for the time being, this valuable, if variable, governing instrument.[35]

Matthews lists several practical reasons for the President's dependence on these leaders: he lacks the time and detailed knowledge for personal leadership; he is interested in the total legislative program, and therefore can deal more effectively with the party leaders, who are generalists, than with committee chairmen and other specialists; he can minimize his personal involvement in possible legislative defeat and reserve his direct intervention for major crises. Moreover, "if the Senate party leaders lose their prestige and effectiveness—and this they will certainly do, if they are perceived merely as presidential messenger boys—the president and his program are in serious trouble."[36] Finally, party leaders, who stand at the center of the congressional communications network, are better informed and better able to judge the political climate and the prospects for legislation than anyone else on Capitol Hill. Franklin Roosevelt devoted more time and attention to legislative matters than subsequent Presidents, but Burns has pointed out that he preferred to work through established congressional leaders and was criticized by rank-and-file congressmen—some of them more liberal than the leadership—who found access to the White House difficult.[37]

The regular channel for communications with the congressional party leadership is the weekly meeting, which has become another presidential institution since Franklin Roosevelt started the practice. The Vice-President, Senate floor leader, House Speaker (if a member of the President's party), House floor leader, and frequently party whips attend, along with committee chairmen or other important congressmen who may be invited on an ad hoc basis. Regular meetings minimize the chances for misunderstanding and may help to create a sense of rapport between the President and his party leaders. Whether this happens depends on the skill and candor of the participants and the degree of mutual trust that has developed among them. Senator Taft and later Senator Knowland used the White House meetings to lecture President Eisenhower on Republican policy; House floor leader Martin has characterized those meetings as "practically always . . . empty affairs," and others have described them as more formal and less effective than in the past.[38]

The governor's relationship to his legislature leaders is similar but not identical. He runs the risk of damaging their effectiveness if he bypasses them or ignores them too often, and he is dependent on their knowledge and advice concerning the legislative system. He can devote more time than the President to legislative matters, however, particularly during the rather brief periods when the major legislative decisions are being made. In addition to meetings as often as every day with his leaders, the governor may hold more conferences with individual legislators than the President would normally attempt. Although he may be bypassing the leadership, often the governor is simply using his prestige and persuasive powers to implement strategy that has been agreed upon with the leadership. The relationship between governor and legislative leaders is a variable one, dependent on the influence that the governor has over their selection.

If the President or governor must usually live with and work through his legislative leaders, it becomes important to determine how these leaders are chosen. The chief executive has much less chance to oust an incumbent than he does to influence the filling of a vacancy in the leadership. In Congress and in some state legislatures, there are few vacancies because leaders hold their posts with tenacity; in other states, a custom of rotation or short tenure offers the governor more opportunities to influence the choice of leaders. The chief executive may find that an established legislative leader holds the personal loyalty of his colleagues and is unwilling to adapt his views to those of the executive. In Massachusetts, for example, the former Senate President, John Powers, held such a position of strength and effectively led the Democratic opposition to the tax program of Governor Furcolo, also a Democrat. In Rhode Island, the Speaker and floor leader of the House (with a total of 80 years of legislative experience behind them) were so solidly entrenched for years that no governor would seriously consider challenging them. In California the speakership is frequently rotated, but the governor plays little part in the choice of a new Speaker, which is based on bargaining with individual legislators over a prolonged period.

It is rare to find a chief executive trying to oust a legislative leader, and even more rare to find him succeeding. Neither of the Roosevelts in the White House made such an effort, and Wilson only toyed with the possibility of reshaping legislative leadership. Taft initially gave support to the insurgents who were trying to reduce Speaker Cannon's powers, but he soon succumbed to pressure and supported the House and Senate leadership.[39] While Senator Knowland's differences with the Eisenhower Administration on foreign policy were a source of serious concern to the President, Knowland spoke for at least a substantial minority of senators, and the President could not make any move to displace him as floor leader without risking a bitter split in the party and, quite probably, a humiliating defeat. Eisenhower played a role in the removal of House floor leader Joe Martin in 1959, but it was in response to initiatives from Republican representatives who were seeking more aggressive leadership. Twice before, in 1955 and 1957, Eisenhower had halted a campaign in the congressional party to choose Charles Halleck as leader. In 1959 he took a hands-off attitude (although some White House staff members apparently worked for Halleck) and Halleck defeated Martin by four votes in the caucus.[40] Although party leaders at the state level seldom have the prestige and tenure of congressional leaders, it is unusual to find a governor removing an established leader. In 1921 Governor Sproul of Pennsylvania lost control of the leadership posts at the start of the session; when his program became bottled up in committee late in the session, a majority of legislators loyal to him elected a new Speaker in a rump session and passed his program. This example was as rare as it was dramatic.

When leadership posts are vacated, because of retirements or the custom of rotation, the governor has his best opportunity; his success or failure in influencing the choice may be an important test of his probable effectiveness as a legislative leader. In some states, however, the governor rarely makes any effort to influence the choice. A recent student of Wisconsin government has contrasted the experience of two governors there: Walter Kohler took no active part in the choice of leaders, and during his three terms had to work with House speakers who were reluctant to support his program; Philip La Follette "did everything possible to install his choices for legislative office," and "the governor's program was safe because the whole legislative machinery was under executive control."[41] A recent Republican governor of Illinois facing a Democratic majority was even able to determine which of two Democrats would become Speaker by swinging Republican votes to the candidate who would work more closely with the governor; his Democratic successor was able to secure reelection of the same Democratic speaker, despite a narrow Republican majority, by swaying a few Republican legislators.[42]

Presidents have seldom tried to exercise the same influence even in the choice of a new leader after the death or retirement of the incumbent. Thomas Jefferson played a larger part in the choice of leaders, and in their removal, than most modern Presidents. Franklin Roosevelt took no open part in the choice of party leaders, and if he played a more subtle role, it seems to have been largely lost to history. He may have provided quiet support for Rayburn's election as majority leader in 1937. That same year, when a bitter fight developed for the Senate leadership post, Roosevelt sent Alben Barkley a public letter that was interpreted as an endorsement, and more importantly, he worked behind the scenes to swing senators to Barkley's support. Barkley won by a single vote.[43] Neither Truman nor Eisenhower seems to have tried to influence the choice of new leaders. After Senator Taft's death, Eisenhower told his cabinet members to remain neutral and asked them to avoid even expressing personal views about a successor; he believed that a policy of non-intervention was essential to maintaining smooth relations with Congress.[44]

The situation faced by President Kennedy after Speaker Rayburn's death in 1961 illustrates and summarizes the dilemma of the President. Leadership positions, particularly in the House, are often inherited.

Although John McCormack, for a variety of reasons, was not Kennedy's choice for Speaker, the sentiment among House Democrats so strongly supported rewarding the veteran floor leader that it would have been foolhardy for Kennedy to oppose him. The contest for majority leader (and heir-apparent to the speakership) was between two men, Carl Albert and Richard Bolling, each of whom was friendly to the Administration. Polsby has neatly summarized the President's thinking:

To intervene in behalf of one friend would have meant sacrificing another. For the White House to intervene and lose would have been disastrous for its prestige and legislative program. To intervene and win would have been more satisfactory, but still would have involved (aside from the making of enemies) great exertion, the distribution of indulgences and "cashing in" on favors owed, all of which could otherwise be employed to improve the chances for passage of controversial reciprocal trade, medical aid, tax reform, and education bills.[45]

The governor in a one-party state is normally represented in the legislature by floor leaders. In the absence of an effective legislative party, these leaders are chosen by the governor and solely responsible to him. In addition, the governor of a one-party state often has much to say about the selection of the House Speaker and Senate president or president pro tem. Alabama, Georgia, Oklahoma, and Kentucky are examples of states where the legislature normally ratifies a Democratic governor's selection of these leaders; its failure to do so is a sign of rebellion and a portent of trouble for the governor's program. In Texas the governor has less influence, because the candidates for Speaker carry out an extensive campaign among House members and legislative candidates before the session starts. Past examples of open gubernatorial intervention in the speakership race aroused such legislative hostility that recent Texas governors have intervened quietly or not at all.[46] In Florida and South Carolina, the elective legislative officials are chosen by the clique that controls the legislature, and the governor is no more than a spectator viewing the contest.

Contact with Rank-and-file Legislators. Every recent President has used his persuasive powers directly on rank-and-file congressmen. Usually this has been done on the advice or with the approval of the congressional leadership, although occasionally press reports suggest that the President is bypassing the leadership. Sometimes the contacts have been in the nature of White House briefings on the virtues of an important legislative measure, and on other occasions the President has made his appeal on the basis of personal or party loyalty. Woodrow Wilson conferred frequently with congressmen both at the Capitol and at the White House. Calvin Coolidge's frequent breakfasts for congressmen had little impact because they were social events totally devoid of substantive discussion. Schlesinger reports that Franklin Roosevelt "spent long hours, in his office and over the telephone, persuading, reassuring, mollifying, and disciplining individual senators and congressmen." Roosevelt estimated that he averaged three to four hours a day on congressional relations during a session.[47] Since World War II, the other demands of the Presidency have reduced the time available for presidential liaison. Eisenhower started his Administration with Coolidge-like social luncheons for congressmen, and in later years made only occasional use of direct appeals to congressmen for support of legislation. Kennedy was more active, but had neither the time nor the inclination to duplicate Roosevelt's personal role in legislative liaison. Lyndon Johnson, who relied so heavily on personal persuasion while he was floor leader, has used persuasion techniques, notably telephone calls and invitations to the White House, on a scale reminiscent of Roosevelt.

The average congressman is surprised to pick up his telephone and hear the President's voice; he can probably remember the few times in his career when the President has asked him personally for support on legislation. If a call comes from the White House, the congressman is much more likely to find that a member of the President's staff is calling. The staff makes it possible for the President to conserve both his time and his prestige for crucial occasions. Wilson used liaison men on a quiet, informal basis, and Franklin Roosevelt used them more frequently and more openly, but still in an informal, unstructured fashion. The practice grew during Truman's Administration, and during the Eisenhower Administration the White House staff became more institutionalized, with responsibility for legislative liaison delegated to specific members of the staff. The organizational pattern has been followed by Eisenhower's successors. Is the staff used to bypass congressional leadership? This was apparently one of Wilson's purposes in choosing his own liaison men, and it must have occasionally motivated his successors. Members of the White House staff have several advantages over congressional leaders: they are chosen by the President and are loyal only to him. They can be used for communications purposes, sometimes with greater effectiveness than congressional leaders; they can provide an independent judgment about congressional opinion.

White House liaison men have become accepted by the congressional leadership and rank-and-file because they perform a variety of useful tasks and maintain a communications network between Congress and the White House more effectively than the busy President could do by himself. Despite occasional friction, liaison men and congressional leaders seem to have worked together relatively smoothly. Though complaints were heard about the lack of political finesse of Eisenhower's aides and the tough, tactless approach of some of Kennedy's "brash young men," the practice of using liaison men has grown despite these faults of some practitioners. It should be recognized that, however great their skill, these staff members have no political power except the President's; it is his prestige that sets the upper limit of their effectiveness. Although congressional liaison has been institutionalized, variations in practice continue from one Administration to another. Under the Eisenhower Administration, liaison was a low-pressure operation, considerable attention being devoted to providing services for congressmen and their constituents. Accounts of the Kennedy Administration suggest that his congressional liaison chief, Larry O'Brien, was given greater authority than the Eisenhower aides had, and that he ran a tough, demanding operation which, while it did not neglect service performance and patronage, focused mainly on the legislative program.[48]

Patronage. One of the tools of presidential leadership that is, of necessity, usually handled at the staff level is *patronage*. This term can be usefully defined to include not only jobs but all of the assistance the executive can provide for members of the legislative body. Job patronage is of limited value to the President for several reasons: A small proportion of federal jobs are outside of civil service and the most important of these must be filled largely on the basis of the availability of skilled personnel. On many local positions, such as postmasterships, the President must be guided by congressmen and local politicians; in filling these local slots, particularly, the President is likely to alienate as many politicians as he pleases. Most jobs must be filled at the start of the Administration, which leaves few for day-to-day bargaining. Job patronage can be a liability if mishandled, or an asset if handled skillfully, but it has declined in importance as compared with other forms of patronage. The President can add local projects to his legislative program—the dams, parks, hospitals, river improvements, and reclamation projects that mean much more to a district than jobs that would benefit a handful. Military installations may be even more important to the district's economy. The Kennedy Administration perfected another patronage device—permitting a congressman to make the announcement about any development of particular interest to his district, thus creating the impression that the congressman was instrumental in obtaining it, even if it was a defense contract awarded without regard to patronage considerations. The President can lend his presence, or that of other top officials, for election campaigns or a variety of speaking engagements, or he can meet or otherwise honor the congressman's constituents.

The President's patronage resources are varied but not unlimited, and he encounters a multitude of patronage demands in his efforts to advance a comprehensive legislative program. He may also encounter resentment, as Kennedy learned, if his tactics in dispensing patronage appear petty, threatening, or vengeful to congressmen. The President and his staff must be misers, spending patronage carefully to gain the maximum benefits. They must bargain with congressmen who are usually skilled bargainers, and they must compete with congressmen who have patronage to dispense, such as the key figures on appropriations committees. They must not alienate loyal congressmen by dispensing all the patronage to the waverers. They must handle patronage as a centralized operation, in order to avoid contradictory commitments; in the Kennedy Administration, this was done under the White House assistant for congressional liaison. Finally, and most important, because the supply of patronage always falls short of demand, the President and his staff must make hard decisions about priorities: which bills are most important, and which congressmen are keys to passage of these bills.[49]

The governor, with fewer demands on his time, devotes more personal attention to legislators than the President finds possible. Most governors also depend on staff assistance for this purpose, and in a few of the larger states there is a specific staff member assigned to legislative matters. Occasionally employees of state agencies may be borrowed for legislative liaison. Members of his staff represent the governor at committee meetings and caucuses, keep track of important bills in the legislative mill, service the requests of legislators, and generally duplicate the work of the White House staff. The governor sometimes appears personally at committee and caucus meetings. Most governors devote considerable time in the closing days of the session to face-to-face negotiations with individual legislators, where their skill and experience may be decisive in winning votes. On rare occasions governors may be found on the floor of the legislature, lobbying for their bills or watching a roll call vote, practices in which Huey Long engaged with a frequency and bravado that no one since his time has matched.

In dealing with legislators, the average governor relies on patronage to a greater extent than the President. In fact, the "average" governor is a myth; variations in patronage are among the major reasons why governors vary in legislative influence. In more than half the states there is a general civil service system, and in some states such a comprehensive one that only a few hundred jobs are available as patronage. In some states elected officials can make a large proportion of the patronage appointments independent of the governor; in some states the governor has extensive powers to fill local vacancies. Most of the major industrial states have general civil service systems, although some (notably Pennsylvania and Indiana) have several thousand patronage jobs available for the governor. The patronage opportunities seem to be greatest in the South, although these states vary widely in the scope of the governor's control over major departments. Some governors have access to jobs with interest groups or with contractors who seek favor with the state.

At the state level, as well as in Washington, the chief executive usually has many favors that he can dispense for the legislator's district: roads, parks, and institutions and services of all sorts. The governor may be inhibited by federal requirements, expert advice, or campaign promises in using these favors to bargain for legislative votes, but in most states they remain significant weapons in the governor's arsenal. With few exceptions it is true that constituents will be more impressed with a new or improved state project than they will by the legislator's voting record. Highways are particularly valuable as patronage, but they are beyond the scope of gubernatorial control in some states. Another form of patronage is the awarding of state contracts for everything from textbooks to liquor supplies; despite regulations concerning competitive bidding, it is sometimes possible to channel these contracts to the friends or supporters of a wavering legislator. Some of the patronage at the state level goes directly to legislators and their families. In those states that still permit dual office-holding, loyal legislators may expect to receive a remunerative position, at least between sessions. Legislators associated with legal, insurance, and other firms sometimes do business with the state, as one-fourth of the Maryland legislators did during the 1957 session.[50]

The state legislator is a part-time representative with a full-time, long-term interest in some other profession or occupation, in contrast to the congressman, who is primarily interested in his political career. This makes the state legislator more receptive than the congressman to patronage offers that personally benefit him. There are other reasons why patronage is more valuable to the governor than to the President: the former usually has proportionately more jobs and a greater number of specific projects that can be supplied for each district with a minimum of delay and red tape. The governor has less prestige, less influence over public opinion, and in some states less party organizational support, but he does have more patronage resources than the President.

The Political Environment. The President and the governor of a two-party state have certain advantages over the governor in a one-party state. They have an organized legislative bloc that is accustomed to viewing the executive's legislative program sympathetically. This legislative party is sometimes quite cohesive, and often demonstrates a sense of loyalty to the chief executive. Members of the legislative party have a stake in the success of the chief executive's program; some of them believe that their reelection is dependent on his victory at the polls. These assets, though significant, are often less potent in practice than in theory. In certain two-party states, there is little party cohesion in the legislature; in Congress, the cohesion varies widely from issue to issue. In some states party organization is weak or beyond the governor's control; the President is clearly the leader of the party, but it is a federal party and thus a fragmented one. Executive influence over legislative nominations is the toughest test of party leadership; it is a test passed by only a few governors; since Roosevelt took the test without adequate preparation and failed it, his successors have avoided it.

The governor of a one-party state lacks the dependable support of a legislative party; he must build a personal following from scratch in each new legislature. In the Southern states the one-term limitation on the governor makes difficult the formation of a cohesive legislative faction loyal to the governor. There are no legislators who link their political fortune with his. Nothing the governor does is likely to help or hurt the legislator at the polls, and both of them realize it. But the one-party governor has many of the assets of other chief executives. He has as great an opportunity to lead public opinion and to focus attention on his legislative program. He comes into office with some platform or program, which is perceived by the legislators and voters as a mandate deserving some respect. In many Southern states, as a matter of custom, he has an influence over the selection of legislative leaders that is as great as or greater than that of other chief executives. Patronage is not dependent on party government but on constitutional statutory provisions; it is a major resource of some two-party and some one-party executives.

The one-party governor has one frequently neglected but fundamental advantage over the two-party executive. In the two-party legislature there is always an opposition party, sometimes in the majority. This party has organization, continuity, and sometimes cohesion. Its members are invulnerable to most or all of the chief executive's blandishments. The opposition party tries to maintain unity in order to build a legislative record, and sometimes tries to discredit the executive by blocking parts of his program. As Senator Robert Taft often said, the business of the opposition is to oppose. In the one-party legislature, there is normally no group with the organizational structure or motivation to play the part of the opposition consistently. Opposition blocs that have been formed on one issue fade away on the next. There is no group whose regular business is to oppose. The seeming ease with which some Southern governors have been able to enact legislative programs is due in large measure to the absence of an opposition party and the resulting power vacuum. The exceptions prove the rule. Occasionally in Florida, Alabama, Louisiana, and Kentucky we find examples of strong opposition factions with at least enough continuity to last through a session of the legislature; as a consequence, legislative programs are sometimes deadlocked.[51]

Another factor that affects the chief executive's political leadership involves the constituencies to which he and a legislative majority are responsible. The arithmetic of the electoral college makes the President particularly sensitive to the needs of the large industrial states, which contain the major metropolitan centers; except for California and Texas, these are located in the East and Midwest. The distribution of electoral votes, because it is based on Senate as well as House seats, slightly favors the small states. But all the states follow the practice of awarding all their electoral votes to the presidential candidate who wins a plurality, and this practice forces the President to give highest priority to the needs of constituents in these large states when he prepares his legislative program. This industrial, metropolitan vote is not similarly overrepresented in Congress. There has been a moderate rural bias to House districting, a bias which is declining (see Chapter 3). In the Senate, the larger states as such are obviously underrepresented by the equal representation of each state. This factor is beginning to be offset by the growth in the number of senators who represent predominantly urban states. The difference in constituencies is an important—though declining—reason for the conflicts between President and Congress, a reason why party loyalties cannot completely bridge this gap.

In many states, malapportionment has made legislative majorities responsive to the interests of rural and small-town voters, while the governor has been more responsive to metropolitan interests. In the past, malapportionment has been the fundamental cause of deadlock between governor and legislature in Florida; to a considerably lesser extent it has caused conflict in some of the other one-party states, most of them less urban. In two-party states, malapportionment has its greatest impact where one legislative party is primarily metropolitan and the other primarily nonmetropolitan in its constituent base. The stage is set for conflict and deadlock, between a governor responsive to metropolitan interests and a party with a nonmetropolitan base, which owes its legislative majority to malapportionment. The more homogeneous each of the parties is—particularly in its legislative delegation—the more stubborn the deadlock. The experience of Michigan under Democratic Governor Mennen Williams is a classic example. On the other hand, if a single interest or a single type of constituency is dominant in a state, there may be a minimum of conflict between governor and legislature. In some of the rural states this helps to explain the low-pressure politics and the smoothness of gubernatorial-legislative relations that often prevail.

DIVERSITY AND COORDINATION IN THE
EXECUTIVE BRANCH

The chief executive is the most powerful, but far from the only member of the executive branch with an influence on the legislative process. The other agencies in the executive branch may be an asset or a liability to the "chief legislator." At the state level the governor's leadership of the executive branch is dependent on widely varying degrees of political and constitutional authority. The President has constitutional authority that would be envied by many governors, but this does not guarantee his control over the vast bureaucracy. Richard Neustadt has defined both the President's dilemma and his opportunity: "Presidential *power* is the power to persuade." Neustadt has aptly described the triangular relationship that is involved:

A great share of a President's potential trading-stock with Congress is actually in the hands of the executive departments: jobs, expertise, publicity, administrative actions of all sorts. No less a share of his potential leverage with the departments is actually in the hands of his congressional supporters: protection or defense, consideration or support, in every sort of legislative situation.[53]

Often it is the individual departments, and not the White House or governor's office, that can best help legislators to satisfy the requests of constituents. Recent Presidents have had to urge department heads to take into account congressional desires in recommending appointments, and sometimes the department heads have been unsympathetic. Some state governors have little direct control over the patronage in state agencies. In recent years some of the federal agencies have developed large staffs to deal with the requests of constituents that are forwarded by congressmen; the White House staff becomes involved in only a few of the most important requests. The agencies have standing rules which require that congressional correspondence be answered quickly. The requests come from constituents with widely varying problems: veterans whose checks have mysteriously stopped, students looking for a summer job in Washington, businessmen seeking exemption from a bureaucratic regulation, parents trying to bring servicemen home from abroad earlier than scheduled. In addition, the legislative liaison offices in each department handle congressional requests for information and help that are related more closely to legislative matters. Congressmen seek information for a speech, assistance in drafting a bill, approval of a proposed amendment.

The attention devoted by the departments to all kinds of congressional requests suggests a belief by the departments that such attention will help to secure congressional support for their legislative programs and budget requests. On a smaller scale, state agencies follow the same pattern of behavior for the same reason. It is worth emphasizing that, once the departments have built up a fund of credit and good will in the legislative body, they may draw on this fund in support of their legislative objectives, *whether these coincide with or contradict the chief executive's legislative program.*

In addition, the agencies bear most of the burden of defending and promoting a legislative program. Theirs is the responsibility for drafting a bill and carrying on the negotiations with interest groups on the terms of the bills. Spokesmen for the agencies testify before committees in support of legislation and before appropriations subcommittees in defense of their budgets and the record of the agency. The skill with which this testimony is presented is one of the important factors in the success of the program. Furthermore, top officials in the agencies lobby on behalf of their programs as persuasively and ubiquitously as possible. In sheer manpower, agency heads outnumber the chief executive, and agency assistants and liaison men outnumber those assigned to the chief executive. The President may pick a high administrative official largely because of his skill and popularity in dealing with Congress; examples of this are Cordell Hull in Roosevelt's Administration, George Marshall in Truman's Administration, and Douglas Dillon in Kennedy's Adminitration. A cabinet member who has lost support in Congress can become a serious liability, as Truman discovered with respect to Dean Acheson and Henry Wallace.

Although we often talk about the chief executive initiating legislative programs, the actual initiative usually comes from the agencies, which have far more detailed knowledge about the fields in which legislation may be needed. The typical pattern is for the agency to prepare a bill and send it to the chief executive, together with whatever budget request may be required, in the hope that the bill will become part of his legislative program. The President's role in the legislative process has become so pervasive that his failure to support a bill not only seriously handicaps it but often places the agency in the position of appearing to disregard the President's wishes if it persists in seeking congressional support. At the state level, where a much wider variety of minor bills are prepared by the agencies, the governor's unwillingness to endorse a measure often leaves the agency free to seek legislative support without any inhibitions.

The legislative activities of government agencies, though not a new phenomenon, have recently grown in importance and become more centralized in each agency. The major agencies of national government have a "chief lobbyist," who usually bears the formal title of "assistant to the secretary for legislative liaison." He is responsible for directing the handling of congressional requests for service and information. He acts as the political adviser to the department head and keeps him informed about congressional attitudes. He engages in lobbying, trying to coordinate his tactics with that of liaison men in the White House and to gain maximum White House support for his department's legislative program. Not the least of his jobs is to coordinate legislative liaison within the department. The bureaus within departments often advance their own parochial purposes by developing rapport with congressmen and congressional committees. The task of the agency liaison man is to reverse this trend toward decentralization without alienating members of Congress or destroying the advantages of the rapport developed by subordinate members of the bureaucracy. Agency liaison men are usually men with political and congressional experience, and some of them have largely succeeded in channeling liaison activity through their offices. Yet these officials, like their counterparts in the White House, lack personal authority and can be no more effective than their political chief.[54]

There are many specific reasons why agencies sometimes fail to work in harmony with the chief executive in support of his legislative program. The fundamental reason is that government comprises a vast array of interests. Each agency serves a different purpose, and many of them serve or represent interests outside of government. In pursuit of this purpose and in service to these interests, each develops certain policies and viewpoints. One reason why these policies come into conflict is that they cost money and consequently represent competing claims on the budget. In addition, they represent the conflicting interests and constituencies, domestic and foreign, that this government serves. There will inevitably be differences of opinion between diplomats and military men on a nuclear test ban treaty, between officials with domestic and foreign responsibilities over "dumping" American products abroad, between the Interior Department and the Health, Education, and Welfare Department over the relative priorities of reclamation projects and aid to education. These conflicts are not merely the result of bureaucratic rivalry and "empire-building," although these factors may contribute to dissension; they are inevitable in modern representative government.

When an agency undermines the chief executive's legislative program, it is usually the result of a tripartite alliance involving an agency (or one of its components), a group of legislators, and an interest group. When an agency's requests for funds are sharply cut in the executive budget, officials in the agency may leak this information to sympathetic congressmen and interest groups served by the agency; in hearings on the budget, committee members may encourage agency representatives to explain their need for additional funds, and the interest groups may carry out a campaign—in and out of Congress—for restoration of the funds. When the Hoover Commission recommended that the medical services of the Veterans Administration be transferred to a united medical agency and the President supported this suggestion, opposition came from the Veterans Administration, the veterans groups, and congressmen who had worked closely with veterans groups. There have been several occasions since World War II when military leaders in the Pentagon, seeking to enhance the military role of bombers, aircraft carriers, or infantry, challenged the President's budgetary decisions and received support from sympathetic congressmen. The ability of agencies to defy the President is dependent on their congressional allies and is enhanced by the independent power exercised by congressional committees, in which these allies are often ensconced.

Probably no agency has achieved greater independence from the President than the Army Corps of Engineers, which has responsibility for carrying out river and harbor development and flood-control projects. The Corps considers itself responsible to Congress, and its actions reflect this belief. It carries out studies authorized by Congress and by congressional committees, and in making recommendations it is sensitive to congressional wishes and local interests. Since the New Deal, the Corps has repeatedly come into conflict with the Interior Department and with other agencies that are interested in multi-purpose projects and the development of public power. With effective allies in Congress, the Corps has won many of its battles even though it lacked the support of the President. Presidential efforts to subordinate the Corps through governmental reorganization have several times been thwarted by Congress.[55]

The head of an agency in Washington must serve three masters, in addition to the President. He must espouse as effectively as possible the viewpoints developed by his subordinates, the viewpoints that have become departmental policy; he must serve interest groups, which are a source of his department's power; and he must serve Congress, particularly the congressional committees that review his budgetary requests and his legislative program. It is not surprising that agency heads sometimes resolve these conflicts by giving less than full support to the President's program.

The President has to be cautious about disciplining the agency or antagonizing its interest-group and congressional allies. He may need these allies to help enact a bill on which he and the agency are in accord; the agency's allies are often his. He may remove the head of the agency as a last resort, but this may be a costly move if it antagonizes these powerful allies. David Truman cites the example of Jesse Jones, who as Secretary of Commerce "operated with almost complete independence of Roosevelt, thanks to his following among important business elements and among the members of the Texas delegation in Congress and their allies."[56] When Roosevelt finally replaced Jones with Henry Wallace, a storm arose on Capitol Hill. The President's removal power, if cautiously used, has some importance. This is illustrated by the difficulties some Presidents have had with agencies whose heads are not subject to removal except for cause. An example would be Eisenhower's controversies, in the Dixon-Yates dispute and on other occasions, with the Tennessee Valley Authority, which had powerful friends in Congress.

At the state level we find examples of both greater and lesser control by the chief executive. The weakness of the legislative committee system, and the absence of vast bureaucratic power centers comparable to the Pentagon or the Agriculture Department, weaken the alliances of resistance to the governor's legislative program. On the other hand, in some states the governor's direct authority, and his power of removal, extend to so few of the state agencies that his ability to generate administrative support for his legislative program is seriously handicapped. The administrative reorganization movement of the last few decades has undoubtedly strengthened the governor's position both as an executive and as a legislative leader, but it has left some areas of state government virtually untouched. The proliferation of elected officials extends to most states: over half the states have six to nine elected officials in addition to the governor, and only eight states have three or less. The governor, particularly if he represents the traditional minority party, may find most of these offices controlled by the other party. In some states, particularly Southern states where the governor is limited to a single four-year term, other officials are free of this restriction and are frequently reelected for several terms. In some states the governor's authority over many appointed officials is limited by overlapping terms of board members and restrictions on removal without cause, a procedure that is cumbersome and difficult.

Florida provides us with an example of the correlation between administrative and legislative weakness in the governor's office. There are six other elected officials, who are rarely denied reelection and are consequently able to develop powerful bases of support among legislators and among their particular clienteles: farm groups supporting the commissioner of agriculture, county education boards and teachers organizations supporting the superintendent of education, and courthouse officials supporting the attorney general. Moreover, these elected officials constitute an administrative cabinet, on which the governor has only a single vote and which has many legal responsibilities, including authority over the budget.[57]

The chief executive has devised institutional techniques for controlling the executive branch, principally the executive budget. The federal budget act, passed in 1921, authorized the President for the first time to present a single budget to Congress and provided him with a Budget Bureau to assist in the task. In keeping with this, the Senate and House centralized their appropriations functions in single committees. Within a few years, during the economy-minded Coolidge Administration, the Budget Bureau was given authority to make recommendations to the President on the budgetary implications of all departmental proposals concerning legislation. The Budget Bureau has developed elaborate procedures for reviewing departmental budgets and has repeatedly cut these budgets, although the final determination has remained the President's.

The executive budget, inaugurated by Al Smith and made effective by Franklin Roosevelt in New York late in the 1920s, has become standard practice in most states. There are six states in which the budget is prepared by a board, on which the governor has a single vote; in Arkansas there is only a legislative budget, and in Texas the governor's budget has to compete with a legislative budget. In the vast majority of states the governor's authority over the budget, coupled with the item veto, provides his most effective control over administrative agencies, including those for which he lacks complete appointment and removal power. Agencies are seldom able to gain legislative restoration of funds that have been eliminated in the presidential or gubernatorial budgets.

The President's control over legislative recommendations of the departments has become institutionalized through the Budget Bureau. This development, described in detail by Neustadt, was started in 1934 by President Roosevelt, who recognized the importance of blocking agency support of bills that conflicted with his policies and also of making explicit which measures had his endorsement. In Roosevelt's words, "If I make every bill that the Government is interested in *must* legislation, it is going to complicate things . . . very much." This central clearance was designed to coordinate policy, and not merely, like earlier procedures, to control the costs of proposed legislation. Since Roosevelt's time, the clearance procedures have varied with personalities and circumstances, but they have gradually become part of the institutionalized Presidency. Clearance is carried out by personnel in the Budget Bureau, working closely with the White House staff. Neustadt, in explaining the development and survival of central clearance, emphasizes its value to the agencies: "Most measures of most agencies face an uncertain future in the legislative process. Whatever clearance brings by way of support, even acquiescence, from President and Budget Bureau, from other agencies, and, implicitly, their clientele, may help to reduce hazards, strengthen prospects in Congress." Central clearance provides a service to Congress, a dependable source of information about the Administration's stand on issues. Some congressional committees as a matter of routine request the Budget Bureau's evaluation of all bills that they consider. Neustadt concludes that central clearance serves both agencies and congressmen without restricting their freedom to maneuver, while it makes both groups conscious of Presidential authority. "The vitality of central clearance lies in the fact that it can satisfy, at once, both these conditions. The President, as he may choose, gains ample opportunities to make known his desires. But Congress and the agencies are not compelled to notice. And he, meanwhile, retains the right to alter course, or change his mind."[58]

The chief executive has constitutional and institutional resources for executive leadership that are valuable at the national level and variable in the states. His executive and legislative leadership are interdependent, and both are dependent on his public prestige and his skill in interpersonal relationships with administrators and legislators. The tasks of a chief executive who would lead, as Neustadt has vividly shown in his *Presidential Power*, require the imaginative conservation and utilization of all the resources of the office in order to maximize a power which is, essentially, the power to persuade.

NOTES

1. William H. Young, "The Development of the Governorship," *State Government*, XXXI (1958), 178.
2. Leslie Lipson, *The American Governor from Figurehead to Leader* (Chicago, 1939).
3. Wilfred E. Binkley, *President and Congress* (New York, 1962); George B. Galloway, *History of the House of Representatives* (New York, 1961), chap. 15. There is an excellent description of Thomas Jefferson's techniques of legislative leadership in Ralph V. Harlow, *The History of Legislative Methods in the Period before 1825* (New Haven, 1917), chap. 10.
4. Clinton Rossiter, *The American Presidency* (New York, 1960), chaps. 3 and 4; Binkley, *op. cit.*, chap. 10, 11.
5. Quoted in Edward S. Corwin, *The President: Office and Powers* (New York, 1957), p. 265.
6. Quoted in Arthur W. Macmahon, "Woodrow Wilson: Political Leader and Administrator," in Earl Latham (ed.), *The Philosophy and Policies of Woodrow Wilson* (Chicago, 1958), p. 100.
7. Quoted in Richard P. Longaker, "Woodrow Wilson and the Presidency," in Latham, *op. cit.*, p. 69.
8. James M. Burns, *Roosevelt: The Lion and the Fox* (New York, 1956), pp. 118–22; Binkley, *op. cit.*, pp. 291–92.
9. Lawrence H. Chamberlain, *The President, Congress, and Legislation* (New York, 1946), p. 17.
10. Quoted in Macmahon, *op. cit.*, p. 108.

11. Woodrow Wilson, *Constitutional Government in the United States* (New York, 1908), p. 67.

12. Richard E. Neustadt, "Presidency and Legislation: Planning the President's Program," *American Political Science Review*, XLIX (1955), 1014.

13. Rossiter, *op. cit.*, p. 111.

14. Quoted by Neustadt, *op. cit.*, p. 1015.

15. *Ibid.*, p. 1014.

16. Duane Lockard, *The Politics of State and Local Government* (New York, 1963), pp. 367–68.

17. Neustadt, *op. cit.*, pp. 980–1021.

18. See, however, Roy D. Morey, *Politics and Legislation: The Office of Governor in Arizona* (Tucson, Ariz., 1965).

19. Frank W. Prescott, "The Executive Veto in American States," *Western Political Quarterly*, III (1950), 97–111.

20. Pendleton Herring, *Presidential Leadership* (New York, 1940), p. 77.

21. J. D. Williams, *The Impounding of Funds by the Bureau of the Budget* (Inter-University Case Program, No. 28, University, Ala., 1955).

22. Angus Campbell, Philip E. Converse, Warren E. Miller, and Donald E. Stokes, *The American Voter* (New York, 1960), chap. 6.

23. Richard E. Neustadt, *Presidential Power* (New York, 1960), pp. 105, 102.

24. *Ibid.*, p. 103.

25. *Ibid.*, pp. 86, 87.

26. Burns, *op. cit.*, pp. 338–39.

27. Neustadt, *Presidential Power*, p. 33.

28. James M. Burns, *The Deadlock of Democracy* (Englewood Cliffs, N.J., 1963), especially chap. 10.

29. David B. Truman, *The Congressional Party* (New York: John Wiley and Sons, 1959), p. 290.

30. Robert C. Wood and Bradbury Seasholes, "The Image of the Governor as a Public and Party Leader: The Disintegration of an Image—Reflections of Five Governors," in Robert R. Robbins (ed.), *State Government and Public Responsibility, 1961: The Role of the Governor in Massachusetts* (Medford, Mass., 1961), pp. 92–93.

31. Burns, *The Deadlock of Democracy*, pp. 104–06, 130–36, 156–76.

32. Neustadt, *Presidential Power*, p. 191.

33. William Riker, *Democracy in the United States* (New York, 1953), pp. 285–93.

34. Malcolm E. Jewell, *Senatorial Politics and Foreign Policy* (Lexington, Ky., 1962), pp. 189–97.

35. Truman, *op. cit.*, p. 298.

36. Donald R. Matthews, *U.S. Senators and Their World* (Chapel Hill, N.C., 1960), pp. 142–43.

37. Burns, *Roosevelt: The Lion and the Fox*, pp. 347–50.

38. Joe Martin, *My First Fifty Years in Politics* (New York, 1960), p. 13; Robert Bendiner, "Pennsylvania Avenue Gets Longer and Longer," *Reporter* (Feb. 20, 1958), pp. 25–27.

39. Macmahon, *op. cit.*, p. 109; Burns, *The Deadlock of Democracy*, pp. 104, 109.

40. Martin, *op. cit.*, chaps. 1 and 2; *Time*, June 8, 1959, pp. 15–18.

41. David Carley, "Legal and Extra-legal Powers of Wisconsin Governors in Legislative Relations," *Wisconsin Law Review*, vol. 1962, pp. 333–34.

42. Thomas B. Littlewood, *Bipartisan Coalition in Illinois* (New York, 1960).

43. Burns, *Roosevelt: The Lion and the Fox*, p. 309.

44. Robert J. Donovan, *Eisenhower: The Inside Story* (New York, 1956), p. 112.

45. Nelson W. Polsby, "Two Strategies of Influence: Choosing a Majority Leader, 1962," in Robert L. Peabody and Nelson W. Polsby (eds.), *New Perspec-*

tives on the House of Representatives (Chicago, 1963), p. 259.

46. Fred Gantt, Jr., *The Chief Executive in Texas* (Austin, Tex., 1964).

47. Arthur M. Schlesinger, Jr., *The Age of Roosevelt*, vol. 2, *The Coming of the New Deal* (Boston, 1959), p. 554.

48. *Time*, Sept. 1, 1961, pp. 10–15.

49. Stanley Kelley, Jr., "Presidential Legislative Leadership: The Use of Patronage" (Paper presented at the annual meeting of the American Political Science Association, 1962).

50. See Coleman B. Ransone, Jr., *The Office of Governor in the South* (University, Ala., 1951), pp. 88–96; Robert Highsaw, "Southern Governor—Challenge to the Strong Executive Theme," *Public Administration Review*, XIX (1959), 7–11.

51. For a description of the Florida situation, see William C. Havard and Loren P. Beth, *The Politics of Mis-representation* (Baton Rouge, La., 1962), chaps. 5 and 7.

52. Neustadt, *Presidential Power*, p. 10.

53. "The Presidency at Mid-century," *Law and Contemporary Problems*, XXI (1956), 627.

54. These comments are based largely on the unpublished research of Abraham Holtzman.

55. David B. Truman, *The Governmental Process* (New York, 1951), pp. 410–15. Arthur A. Maas, "Congress and Water Resources," *American Political Science Review*, XLIV (1950), 576–92.

56. Truman, *The Governmental Process*, p. 407.

57. Havard and Beth, *op. cit.*, chap. 7.

58. Richard E. Neustadt, "Presidency and Legislation: The Growth of Central Clearance," *American Political Science Review*, XLVIII (1954), 641–72, especially 650, 670–71.

[14]

The Legislator and His Constituents

I N THE TWO previous chapters we described the importance of lobbyists and executive agents as participants in the legislative process. In
this chapter we shall deal with the constituent as a participant, indicating
some of the problems of legislator response to constituent participation,
and suggesting some of the occupational role strains created for the
legislator by his constituents. Here our treatment must, of necessity,
be in rather general terms; we deal specifically with constituency effects
on the voting behavior of legislators in Chapter 17.

It has become a part of the common lore of the "legislative way
of life" that a legislator, to survive politically, must maintain constant,
persistent, favorable, and even perhaps obsequious relations with his
constituents. In reality, the conventional wisdom is, as usual, both right
and wrong. Legislators in the United States are deeply concerned,
sometimes even obsessed, with their image among their constituents; but
constituents do not, on the whole, reciprocate with commensurate
concern about their legislators. A theory of representation adequate to
describe and explain legislator-constituent relationships in the real world
cannot rely upon the existence of highly attentive constituents who,
as a body, watch closely the work of their legislators.

CONSTITUENTS AND THE SALIENCY OF LEGISLATORS

Sample surveys and public opinion polls have since the 1930s supplied substantial data about constituents—voters—in the United States. Our purpose here is not to develop these data; they are treated at length in numerous studies of the electorate.[1] It is more pertinent in this context to summarize our knowledge about the cognitive orientations of constituents toward their legislators. The simple fact is that constituents have remarkably little knowledge about their legislators. National surveys conducted by the American Institute of Public Opinion have consistently shown the low level of saliency of legislators for American adults. In 1945 a representative adult sample of the population was asked, "Do you happen to know the names of the two United States Senators from this state?" Only 35 percent of the sample correctly named both of their senators, and 22 percent could name only one. In 1954 a similar query was put to an adult sample, and only 31 percent were able to identify both of their senators.[2] Congressmen are somewhat less visible. In 1947 the AIPO asked its sample, "Can you remember off-hand the name of the United States Congressman from your district?" Only 38 percent were able to do so correctly. By 1965, 43 percent could name their congressman.

If we lower the cognitive hurdle somewhat, we can indicate to what extent constituents know how many senators and representatives they have. For instance, in 1945, 55 percent of the adults interviewed were able to state the correct number of United States Senators from each state, although in 1954 only 49 percent were able to do so. In 1954 only 11 percent of the AIPO sample were able to answer correctly to "How many states will elect members of the House of Representatives this fall? how many will not?"

Following the congressional elections in 1958, the Survey Research Center interviewed a sample of constituents living in a sample of 116 congressional districts. It was found, among other things, that only 47 percent correctly attributed control of the Eighty-fifth Congress to the Democrats. Beyond that, "of the people who lived in districts where the House seat was contested in 1958, 59 percent—well over half—said that they had neither read nor heard anything about either candidate for Congress, and less than 1 in 5 felt that they knew something about both candidates."[3] Eliminating nonvoters from this analysis does not improve the saliency of congressmen very much; 46 percent of those who went to the polls in 1958 admitted that they had done so without having read or heard anything about either candidate. The incumbent congressman is more visible than his opponent. In districts where there was a contest in 1958, 39 percent of the constituents sampled knew something about the congressman, while only 20 percent reported knowing anything about his opponent.

If the saliency of American congressmen and senators is relatively low, constituents are more aware of congressional *activity*, at least of the more dramatic sort. There are occasions when popular awareness of congressional activity reaches rather impressive levels. Consider, for example, the findings from surveys of samples of the adult population taken between 1947 and 1954, as shown in Table 14.1. Sizable proportions of the adult population have at least heard of congressional activity of the kinds reported here, and these are obviously the kinds of newsworthy activities that are likely to have been brought to public attention via the mass media. But public awareness of dramatic congressional activities which involve questions of public policy cannot be taken to mean that constituents evaluate their legislators primarily in policy terms. The 1958 Survey Research Center interviews with constituents in 116 congressional districts led to the following conclusions about the image of the congressman which constituents reflect:

> Our constituent interviews indicate that the popular image of the Congressman is almost barren of policy content. A long series of open-ended questions asked of those who said they had any information about the Representative produced mainly a collection of diffuse evaluative judgments: he is a good man, he is experienced, he knows the problems, he has done a good job, and the like. Beyond this, the Congressman's image consisted of a mixed bag of impressions, some of them wildly improbable, about ethnicity, the attractiveness of family, specific services to the district and other facts in the candidate's background. By the most reasonable count, references to current legislative issues comprised not more than a thirtieth part of what the constituents had to say about their Congressman.[4]

Constituents are not, generally speaking, particularly aware of the issue positions of their legislators, and they tend to evaluate legislators more in terms of non-issue factors, which are only remotely related to policy orientation.

The saliency of legislators for constituents is a variable of very great interest, but we know woefully little about the correlates or determinants of saliency. It is, however, very clear that there is a generally low level of saliency among constituents regarding Congress. We do not have parallel data of even this general sort for state legislators.[5] However, if anything, it seems very likely that state legislators are less visible to their constituents than are congressmen, though we have to rely on the impressions of state legislators themselves. Here are some comments from interviews with state legislators, which indicate their impressions of their saliency with their own constituents:

There isn't much interest in my county. The local newspaper gives me the only indication as to how my constituents feel. I think I'd say they were disinterested. If they are not affected by the legislation, they don't care. Sometimes someone will tell them to come up here and tell me how to vote on a

Table 14.1. EXPOSURE TO CONGRESSIONAL ACTIVITY

Question	Year	Percent Who Responded "Yes"
Have you followed the arguments in Congress for and against cutting down on the money for the Army and Navy?	1947	43
Have you heard or read about the House Un-American Activities Committee?	1949	64
Have you heard or read of the Kefauver probe of gambling?	1951	72
Have you heard or read about the U.S. Senate Committee's investigation of Howard Hughes (the airplane manufacturer)?	1947	76
Have you heard or read about the congressional committee's investigation of Hollywood?	1947	77
Have you heard or read about the congressional spy hearings?	1948	79
Have you heard or read anything about the congressional investigation of the quarrel between Senator McCarthy and Army Secretary Stevens?	1954	87

SOURCE: Hazel Gaudet Erskine, "The Polls: Exposure to Domestic Information," *Public Opinion Quarterly*, XXVII (1963), 491–92.

certain bill, but they don't know what the bill is about. They are pitifully ignorant of how you spend state money. People often fight for legislation, like education, that would hurt the county taxwise. Thirty PTA women once came to see me about education. I explained to them my position, but they don't know and don't care.

I don't think my constituents have the slightest idea of what the legislature is for. They're very poorly informed, speaking in general terms, of course. There are always the people who are close to you and they come to ask questions, so they know a little more, but there is just too much apathy on the part of the rank and file. Constituents have the impression that we're in session all the time and are surprised to learn that we have only one session every two years. This is because they see Congress news all year. I am thought of like a representative in Washington. People ask me to support federal bills, and ten to one, ask me, "How are things in Washington?"[6]

Well over half the legislators in California, Ohio, New Jersey, and Tennessee who were asked about their constituents characterized them as uninformed about the legislature or the work of the legislator.

The American legislator is not generally very visible to his constituents, even to those who go to the polls to vote for him, and the American constituent is poorly informed of the identity of his legislator, the work of his legislature, or the policy position of his representative. But these things are not true of all constituents. There are attentive publics in every legislator's constituency, and he responds to them. The legislator may endeavor to widen the attentiveness of his constituent-public, or he may attempt to restrict it, but he does respond to it. He communicates with some of his constituents, and they with him. These attentive constituents have a variable impact upon the legislator's policy position, as we shall see in a later chapter, but he does organize his work around them.

LEGISLATOR-CONSTITUENT COMMUNICATION

Most state legislators are in almost constant touch with at least some of their constituents. They live with their constituents, earn their living among them, and in many cases were born and raised within easy distance of most of them. The legislative session is relatively brief, and even during the session they are home for part of the week. Their communication with their constituents is largely that of personal contact on a fairly continuous basis. There are, of course, some exceptions to these generalizations. A few rural state legislators represent geographically enormous districts with constituents so scattered that contact is difficult to maintain. The urban legislator elected at-large in a metropolitan county, may, like the Los Angeles state senator, have millions of constituents—more than most congressmen. The state legislator elected from a district within a metropolitan center may have difficulty maintaining contact with his constituents when, for example, not even the press, which covers the entire metropolitan area, is very accessible to him. While we know very little in detail about the communications practices of state legislators, we can assume that they tend to be informal. When we deal with the routinized and formalized mechanisms of legislator-constituent communication, we discover its full complexity through examining these mechanisms in use by a remote and professionalized legislative body like the Congress.

Congressmen, like state legislators, apparently rely most heavily upon personal contact as a source of information from their constituents, with the mail, newspapers, party organization, and opinion polls taking on importance in that order (among the factors considered in Table 14.2). As often happens, what is most important is least understood.

Table 14.2. EXTENT OF RELIANCE UPON VARIOUS COMMUNICATION CHANNELS BY CONGRESSMEN FROM 116 DISTRICTS, 1958

(In percentages)

Extent of Reliance	Source of Information				
	Personal contact	Mail	News- papers	Party organiza- tion	Opinion polls
A great deal	62	25	5	8	6
Quite a bit	19	30	27	10	7
Some	8	23	24	15	11
Not much	8	19	29	28	15
None	2	3	15	39	61

SOURCE: Warren E. Miller, "Policy Preferences of Congressional Candidates and Constituents" (Paper presented at the 1961 Annual Meeting of the American Political Science Association).

We know almost nothing about the nature of personal contacts between legislators and constituents in any systematic way. Personal contacts are intensified during the legislators' campaign for election, and constituents come to Washington (or to the state capitals) in considerable numbers to see their representative. Congressmen and senators from districts near Washington are particularly likely to have a high degree of interpersonal contacts with constituents. A congressman from southern Maryland or northern Virginia may see constituents daily, and in fairly large numbers. They come to his office in downtown Washington, or they call him on the telephone. Similarly, some congressmen are frequently in their district offices (the best illustration of this being the New York City members of the so-called "Tuesday–Thursday Club"), where they hold forth for constituents. On the other hand, Southern congressmen and those from the West have constituent visitors rather infrequently, and may make quite an occasion of such a visit.

The Mail. Although personal contact with constituents is apparently the channel of legislator-constituent communication most relied upon, the most regular and pervasive is the mail. The revolution in mass political letter-writing which occurred in the 1930s had a tremendous effect upon congressional mail. According to reports in *The New York Times*, incoming congressional mail reached 50,000 pieces daily in early 1934, and by February of the following year 40,000 pieces had gone to the Senate alone. The *Times* reported estimates by congressmen that their mail in 1946 had risen 100 percent over the last prewar session, and in 1954 the Senate Postmaster estimated incoming mail at 25 percent higher than it had been the preceding year.[7] It has been estimated that the House Post Office handled nearly 23 million pieces of incoming mail in 1962.[8] Senator Hubert Humphrey's experience illustrates the increasing mail load: "In my first year in the Senate— 1949—an average of 150 letters were received each day. Today (April 1963), the daily average is between 800 and 1,000 letters."[9]

At the same time, the percentage of a congressman's or senator's constituents who write is small, though growing. The Gallup Poll in 1946 reported that 15 percent of a sample of the adult population of the United States said that they had at some time written or wired their congressmen or senators. In response to a 1954 Roper Poll, 20 percent of the respondents indicated that they had written or talked to their congressman or senator, or other public official.[10] The constituents from whom a member of Congress receives mail are not likely to constitute a representative sample of opinions in his constituency. Letter-writers differ significantly from the general population in occupational status, education, and level of political activity. Metropolitan legislators receive disproportionately more mail than their brethren from rural districts, because people who live in urban areas are more inclined to be letter-writers.[11] On some issues, so few constituents may write that legislators get virtually no guidance from the mail about constituency opinions.

As a result, congressional mail is not likely to be a good estimate of public opinion in a legislator's constituency. For instance, business leaders are more likely than others to write their congressmen. In a study of foreign-trade legislation, a sample of business leaders selected from the heads of firms with more than 100 employees was questioned about writing congressmen. The investigation revealed that

Three-fourths of our sample said that at some time they had communicated with Congress on some issue other than foreign-trade policy. By size of firm the percentages were 88 (large), 79 (medium), and 71 (small). By a large margin, the heads of business organizations are more inclined than the average citizen to act on the assumption that one writes his representative or senator on matters of public policy in which he is concerned.[12]

There are some pieces of evidence on specific issues of the inaccuracy of the mail as an estimate of public opinion.[13] A legislator who relies heavily on the mail as a communications channel to his constituents, and who is not aware of the potential distortions it can represent, may be bewildered by adverse reactions.

Massive letter-writing campaigns, often inspired by pressure groups, have varying effects under different conditions. If mail is demonstrably inspired, it may be heavily discounted by the legislator. If a legislator is unaccustomed to getting large amounts of mail from his constituents, a massive influx of mail may influence his behavior considerably. Thus, Southern congressmen, who get less mail than their colleagues from Northern states, were heavily influenced by the large amount of constituent mail on foreign-trade legislation in 1955, much of it inspired by the American Cotton Manufacturers Institute.[14] Furthermore, the extent of constituent interest in and support for a legislative proposal may be highly overestimated by legislators if the influx of mail is great. For instance, sensitivity among United States Senators to the Bricker Amendment issue appears largely to have been the result of the large amount of mail they received, especially during 1954, even though polls indicated very little general public interest in this issue.[15]

Congressional mail is very diverse in tone, subject matter, quality, and content. A sizable proportion of the mail is "junk"—press releases, printed materials, magazines, and other printed propaganda material. In addition, members receive a considerable amount of "fan" mail—requests for autographs or photographs—and this kind of mail is increasing in volume. Again, a relatively small but regular volume of "crank" or "crayon" mail is received by congressmen. A letter addressed in crayon is quickly spotted, and (unless it is from a child) is likely to have been written by a constituent who is living in an institution where sharp pencils are not permitted. The "crank" mail is often annoying to congressmen and their staffs, although some of it is unwittingly witty. A constituent once wrote to Senator Bartlett (D-Alaska) as follows:

> I voted for you 3 times and I think you are wonderful. Please send me $900 at once so I can buy an ice box and repaint my car. P.S. The 3 times I voted for you were in the election of 1946.[16]

Another wrote Congressman Arends (R-Ill):

> I understand that you have free mailing privileges. I am sending you all my Christmas cards. Would you be good enough to drop them in the mail for me?

A young man once wrote to Senator Chaves (D-NM):

> Although I'm not through school yet, I'm interested in a Political Career.

By a slight oversight and through no fault of my own, my Father and Mother were never married. Some people tell me Congress is just the place for me. What do you think?

While the amount of junk, fan, and crank mail varies in volume from time to time and from member to member, it has been estimated that, on the average, about a fourth of the congressional mail is of these kinds.[17]

Another large category of congressional mail is "inspired" or "stimulated" by private interests, public officials, lobby organizations, and the like. On the average, a substantial proportion of the congressional mail is inspired, perhaps as much as a fourth of it. However, on some occasions and with regard to specific issues, the proportion of inspired mail is much higher. During congressional consideration of reciprocal-trade legislation in 1954, it has been estimated that 40 percent of the protectionist mail was stimulated by the Westinghouse, Dow, Monsanto, and Pittsburgh Plate Glass companies and that three-fourths of the anti-protectionist mail was inspired by the League of Women Voters.[18] Inspired mail is usually easy to identify because of the similarity of the messages. But what is stimulated mail is not always easy to define; the voluminous mail in 1959 during congressional consideration of labor reform legislation (the Landrum-Griffin Act) was overwhelmingly inspired—by the labor unions, the trade associations, corporations, the President, "Bobby" Kennedy, and Jack Paar, as well as by congressmen themselves.

Between one-third and half of the congressional mail relates stories of distress, asks for redress of grievances, or requests help. This "case" and "issue" mail is various, including requests for information or for statements of the congressman's viewpoint, as well as for help with administrative agencies or for the introduction of private legislation. The case mail involves regular intervention by members of Congress in the administrative process, and requires members to develop established relationships with administrative agencies. A considerable amount of executive branch time is consumed in the processing of case mail to congressmen, and some members believe that it is in this process that Congress most effectively engages in surveillance or "oversight" of the administration.[19]

In addition to the evidence in Table 14.2, there is overwhelming testimony in the comments of senators and representatives as to the importance of the mail, and most of them insist that every letter from a constituent must be answered.[20] A good illustration of the importance of the mail for members of Congress is provided by congressional action on foreign-trade legislation in the mid-1950s:

Despite the fact that, on issue after issue, the mail has been shown to be not representative—in 1954–1955 it was about ten-to-one protectionist—and despite the fact that there is no reason to suspect that letter-writing on any given issue has any relationship to voting or political influence, the mail is nevertheless seen as the voice of the district or state. As is to be expected, many congressmen and senators run counter to the mail in obedience to dictates of conscience, party, or committee; but, when they do so, many of them appear to think that they are defying something very significant.[21]

Beyond this, it was found that

The mail is the congressman's main source of information on foreign-trade policy. Whenever we asked a congressman if he had heard anything about foreign-trade policy, he almost inevitably answered in terms of mail. We cannot say whether this is true of other issues, but it is our distinct impression that congressmen are far more conscious of what the mail says about foreign-trade legislation than they are about any other exposition of foreign-trade matters.[22]

So significant is the mail to members of Congress that they tend to inspire a considerable amount of mail themselves.

Once a congressman becomes accustomed to a heavy mail, he tends to worry if it drops off. So important does he regard mail to his success that he actively seeks it. The special mailings to particular groups, for example, constitute an important means by which legislators try to stimulate correspondence with residents of their districts.[23]

In their campaigns, members of Congress often urge voters to write them. Congressmen frequently initiate correspondence with constituents by mailing letters of condolence or congratulation to persons whose names are culled from the columns of local newspapers. Over 90 percent of the members of Congress send newsletters to the residents of their districts or states (the franking privilege permits them to do this at public expense), and the newsletters often contain explicit invitations to reply. The legislator's mailing list may be his most prized, and closely guarded, possession.[24]

Why is the mail given a position of such importance? We find the best answer to this question in an article by Lewis Dexter, who explained it this way:

In the first place, members of their staffs spend an enormous amount of time on mail. And having invested that time on it, they like to feel that it means something.

Second, a great deal of the time Congressmen operate in a pretty complete vacuum so far as the voters of their district go. Most people seem to know what they are supposed to do (if even in some cases merely so that they can protest or revolt). The mail gives a sense that one is doing something that excites large numbers of people.

Third, . . . many Congressmen are irritated and annoyed because they come to Washington expecting to do and be something important; and because of the complexity of government and the seniority system they find they are hampered and shut off from effective action at every turn. Granted this rather general exasperation, handling mail is almost the only thing on which a Congressman finds himself quite free; he can write any sort of letters he likes without let or hindrance from anybody. Thus letter writing becomes a disproportionately significant aspect of his job, for it represents the freedom and importance that he thought he would find when he got to Washington (but rarely does).

Fourth, most Congressmen genuinely treasure the right of petition and the opportunity of the individual citizen to complain about mistreatment. This right has great importance on many issues where bureaucrats mistreat individuals or overlook individual rights.

Fifth, whether realistically or not, some Congressmen actually believe and many others like to feel that on any issue of national significance, rational communication between them and any constituent is possible. For this reason they spend a quite irrational amount of time on correspondence that is essentially academic in the sense that it is fairly clear that no political or legislative purpose is really served by the time they give it.[25]

Congressional Polls. The use of polling methods to get estimates of the views of constituents has been increasing since World War II. While only about one-fourth of the congressmen interviewed in 1958 indicated that they relied upon opinion polls (see Table 14.2), some members of Congress apparently give much more than the average weight to polls. A 1954 survey of members of the House of Representatives indicated that 15 percent of the members were using polls, had used them in the past, or intended to use them; by 1961 this proportion had increased to 30 percent.[26] The relatively greater attention given to polls by some members is indicated in the comments of one congressman:

> Since people more often write letters when they are against something, mail can be a useful reflection of the intensity and degree of organization of the opposition to a particular issue. *But I would put greater—though also limited—trust in polls and surveys.* Most useful, I think, are the views of my friends and associates in the district. And I place great stock in the impressions I have received myself from many years in public life.[27] (italics added)

A study of the delegation of representatives from one state, Washington, indicates that congressmen from that state attach a great deal more than the average importance to their polls.[28]

Congressional polling of constituents ordinarily involves staff personnel in the congressman's office in preparing and mailing a questionnaire to each constituent on the mailing list, which usually includes a disproportionate number of the congressman's avid supporters. Some congressmen have sought to develop more or less refined sampling methods for their polls; in other cases members have persuaded district newspapers to run their questionnaires, urging readers to return them to the congressman. In any event, the sampling problems involved in the polling done by most congressmen are enormous, and the representative adequacy of most congressional polls is, at best, unknown. Still, some members claim to rely heavily upon them, referring to the poll results as indicating "definite trends in the thinking of the people of the district."[29] When questionnaires are used, usually thousands are mailed to district residents, and thousands are returned. Processing these returns makes for very substantial staff effort, but the large numbers may serve to convince congressmen who use polls that the results are "representative" of constituent opinions. To illustrate some of the factors in congressional polling, we have assembled some information about the polls of thirteen members of Congress who questioned their constituents in 1961–1962, and we show this information in Table 14.3. These are members who published their poll results in the *Congressional Record*. The relatively low return rate for these polls is probably typical of congressional polls in general.

Another source of difficulty in congressional polling stems from the questions asked. Since the polling device may be used for public relations or campaign purposes or to reinforce the congressman's own preconceptions, as well as to get information, biased or distorted questions are often asked. In addition, questions are often included in congressional polls which call for a quite unreasonable amount of information on the part of the ordinary citizen. Illustrations of these two difficulties in survey questions can be found in a 1962 poll by a New York congressman. He asked one biased question: "Do you believe that United States and free world policies have been that of vacillation, conciliation, appeasement, and retreat?" Seventy-nine percent of his constituents who replied said, "Yes." He asked another question calling for a very great deal of technical information: "Admiral Rickover states our Navy is technologically obsolete. Do you favor equipping naval vessels with ICBM's for ICBM mobility and dispersal advantages?" About 90 percent who replied said "Yes."[30]

The mails and polling do not, of course, exhaust the channels of communication between legislator and constituent. A legislator is very often a public-relations man, and he may pay a great deal of attention to the press in his district, county or state. Both national and state legislators have the newspapers, especially the weekly press, at their disposal as a potential mode of communication to constituents, and legislators often utilize the press as a means of gauging public sentiment.

Furthermore, radio and television broadcasting of "reports to the people" has become common legislative practice. In spite of his low visibility to his constituents in general, the American legislator is substantially concerned with his communications to and from them.

In the face of their relatively low saliency among constituents, the concern of American legislators with constituency communications and

Table 14.3. POLLING CONSTITUENTS BY SELECTED CONGRESSMEN, 1961–1962

Congressman	State, District	Political Party	No. Questionnaires Mailed	Percent Returned
H. T. Schneebeli	Pa. (17th)	R	185,000	11
J. T. Broyhill	Va. (10th)	R	70,000	23
C. R. Jonas	N.C. (8th)	R	45,000	12
J. J. Rhodes	Ariz. (1st)	R	25,000	23
T. M. Pelly	Wash. (1st)	R	40,000	23
S. L. Devine	Ohio (12th)	R	20,000	32
E. C. Gathings	Ark. (1st)	D	8,000	17
E. Y. Berry	S.D. (2nd)	R	—	11
T. C. Tollefson	Wash. (6th)	R	65,000	21
A. Pirnie	N.Y. (34th)	R	60,000	18
W. E. Minshall	Ohio (23rd)	R	135,000	19
J. S. Clark	Pa.	D	10,000	16
J. G. Beall	Md.	R	8,000	28

SOURCE: *Congressional Record* (Daily Edition, Appendix), 1962, pp. A1985, A2180, A2205, A2482, A2785, A2906, A3102, A3162, A3316, A3376, A3597, A3892, A7109.

their representative image is, in a sense, contradictory. This apparent contradiction can be explained, in part, by the tendency of legislators to overestimate their public visibility. The constituents with whom the legislator has contacts personally, through the mail, or via the communications media are not likely to be representative of the adult population of his district as a whole, or even the voting population. The legislator is likely to perceive his constituents, not as atomized, but as organized into groups or blocs. His contacts are with organized group leaders or with constituents who are more politically active and informed than the average citizen.

But the legislator's concern with constituency opinion, even though he may realize that he is not very visible to many of his constituents, has a sound basis in the electoral facts of life. In the first place, the degree of party regularity in the voting behavior of his constituents is substantial. The legislator "starts with a stratum of hardened party voters, and if the stratum is broad enough he can have a measurable influence on his chance of survival simply by attracting a small additional element of the electorate—or by not losing a larger one."[31] The legislator's communications with constituents and his legislative record may have a substantial bearing on his success at the polls, even though most of his constituents are not aware of his record and only marginally aware of his existence. In the second place, the nomination process itself involves a meaningful, though less tangible, kind of electoral sanction, where "the customary norms of the constituency which must be met if a person is to be 'available' as a candidate limit the field to those candidates with broad views consonant with those of the district."[32] Finally, the image of the legislator is not created for all constituents by way of direct communication; rather, the legislator's image is filtered through agents intermediary between legislator and constituent—the news media, interest groups, ethnic groups, and party organizations. While the legislator's own response, in terms of his perception of constituency expectations, may not be directly reflected to his constituents, it may affect the cues given to them by these intermediaries.

There are also intangible cultural factors in the consonance of outlook between legislators and constituents, to the extent that such agreement exists. The legislator tends to respond to his constituency in the way he organizes his work and represents himself to "his people," even though they may know little about him or his record and he may have little evidence of their opinions through external communication. The legislator may have very reliable intuitions about his constituents because he shares their cultural values, and he may respond in their terms "without any conscious interchange of ideas or beliefs."[33]

The legislative office in America is a response-oriented institution. Its principal response is to the constituency. We shall refer to the sum total of behavior patterns associated with the legislative office—the responses of representative and staff—as the "institutionalized legislator." We turn now to a brief consideration of the organization of the legislative office.

THE INSTITUTIONALIZED LEGISLATOR

Legislative service is not a leisurely way of life. In general, legislators are harried men; they ordinarily have more work to do than the time available makes it possible for them to do thoroughly. The legislative workload has increased substantially since the 1930s, although "errand-running" or service activities occupy a large share of the time of the legislator's office.[34] These increases in the burden of legislative work have given rise to the institutionalized legislator. The institutionalization of the legislative office can be seen as varying from the lonely state legislator who, virtually without staff assistance of any kind, performs by himself as best he can both service and legislative work, to the United States senator with a highly organized office and staff of twenty or thirty assistants and secretaries. The complex institution that is known to the outside world as "Senator Javits" is, merely to cite one illustration, a highly organized administrative apparatus.

The legislative office, especially at the national level, has become fairly highly bureaucratized. The state legislative office is more individualistic and less highly organized, although this varies from state to state. Bureaucratic tendencies not unlike those observable for congressmen have developed noticeably in the more industrial urban states. And in most states some legislative offices are relatively highly organized —those of presiding officers and committee chairmen.

The office of a member of Congress is largely occupied with constituent-service activities. "Most congressional offices," writes a student of the House of Representatives, "are more concerned with activities not strictly legislative in character than they are with legislative ones." While "representatives generally assign as much of the extra legislative work as possible to their staff," still "constituent-oriented activities usually occupy the major portion of their own time."[35] While most of the work of a congressman's office is performed in the District of Columbia, ordinarily with inadequate physical facilities, most members also maintain some kind of office in their districts as well. In 1963, of the 435 members of the House nearly 300 were renting office space in their districts, paid for from a rental allowance that each member receives.[36] This office space houses the legislator and his staff, which varied in 1963 from three to ten assistants, although the House as a whole employs about 4,500 people. Even so, the facilities available to a congressman are seldom adequate to meet the demands placed upon the office. According to one congressman,

It is true that we just don't have much time to legislate around here . . . all this nonlegislative work which our office gets means that I don't get any help from anybody there on research or speeches or things like that. My staff is busy taking care of constituent matters, case work, and such things. My press man helps some on political speeches but not very much. It would be helpful to have someone who could assist me in carrying out my legislative role.[37]

Senate offices are larger than those in the House office buildings, and some are "the fastest-growing 'bureaucracies' in Washington." A fairly typical Senate office has been described in the following way:

One walks in the door and there is a receptionist, eager to have you sign the guest book, to give you a gallery visitor's card and a tourist's map of Washington, to talk about "home." In the same narrow room, decorated with pictures of the state's industries and tourist attractions, are three or four other girls . . . typing and answering the constantly ringing telephone. Next door, in another room or two there are more typists, the senator's administrative assistant, a legislative assistant or two, and perhaps an executive secretary. Beyond this, a tranquil oasis amid the noise and clutter of the "outer" and "working" rooms, is the senator's private office.[38]

House and Senate offices seem fairly similar in appearance, but in actuality there are considerable variations among them. Members of Congress are free, within the limitations of space and their office-expense and clerk-hire allowances, to organize their offices as they wish. No two offices are quite the same, and staff members with the same titles may have different duties and responsibilities. On the House side,

There is no clear pattern in office organization, particularly where the duties of the top assistant are concerned. Some first assistants perform little more than routine responsibilities; others are in every sense advisers and assistants. As one congressman said, "I think every office is run differently and shaped after the personality of the congressman."[39]

Matthews argues that "the way a senator staffs and organizes his office," can tell us "a great deal about him as a man, what his problems and preoccupations are, and how he defines his role."[40]

The most time-consuming activity of the legislative office is the processing of the mail. Most members of Congress answer all mail from their districts or states, and some answer all letters whether they are from constituents or not. The regular constituent issue mail is divided into those that can be answered by use of one of the standard form letter replies and those that the congressman or senator ought to see. The case mail is usually handled by an assistant who specializes in its processing; in Senate offices where more than one case-mail "expert" is employed there may be "area specialists"—one for veterans' cases, one for social security, another for immigration cases. Most of the routine mail can be answered with form letters, a process that is described accurately in the following commentary about it on the Senate side, where in one office "about five hundred letters daily are opened, classified, and tabulated by some half-dozen staff members."

They decide which letters can be answered with form replies, which need the attention of one of the Senator's assistants, and which few the

Senator must see himself. (He once said that if he had to see more than 4 percent of his mail, his staff wasn't doing its job.) His form replies have, in general, been drafted by an assistant, but approved by the Senator. They have been transcribed onto player-piano-like rolls which operate electric typewriters, so that a typist need type only the address and the salutation and turn the machine loose to finish the letter. This is done in one of the rooms which house a pool of automatic typewriters in the basement of the Old Senate Office Building. When the letter and envelope have been completed, an automatic pen traces the Senator's signature, in ink, from a matrix cut from an authentic signature. So the constituent back home gets what appears to be a letter dictated and addressed to him personally, and signed by the Senator. In fact, the Senator never saw either the constituent's incoming letter or his reply. He will, however, see a monthly tabulation of letters received.[41]

Members of the House of Representatives are more likely than senators to read their mail—because it is a more manageable job—and some regard reading their own mail to be an important aspect of maintaining constituency contact. But in many House offices it is impossible for members to read more than a few selected letters, and the use of the automatic typewriter and signature machine is increasing—a sign of the bureaucratic times.

But the fact that the processing of congressional mail is more bureaucratic than it used to be does not mean that congressmen are any less concerned about it. Being unable to read it all worries some congressmen; they begin to feel they are losing touch. One congressman's comments reflected this source of anxiety with regard to his case mail:

Unless you retain a fairly direct interest in the so-called routine case work you may find the staff takes it too much in stride, without realizing that for the individual involved it is a matter of great importance. I sometimes find an irritated letter from a constituent saying, "Why haven't you been able to help me?" or "Why haven't I gotten an answer?" Had I known about those cases perhaps I would have been able to accelerate them more than the staff did. So, I always find myself looking over their shoulder saying, "What is this case?" and asking them to put anything unusual on my desk.[42]

If a member of Congress mails questionnaires to his constituents and takes seriously the tabulation of the results, this can be a major effort for his office. Congressman Jerry Voorhis (D-Calif) provides us with an illustration of the office problems created by the use of polls:

Once I prepared a questionnaire for our district, asking the people's opinions on a number of important questions which Congress was about to have to decide. I sent it to more than 30,000 people, the extent of my mailing list at that time. A little over ten percent of them responded by filling out the questionnaire and sending it back to me. For more than a week we worked at night, tabulating and compiling the results of the people's votes, and even then had to hire extra help.[43]

It would be a mistake if the impression were left that legislative life is a kind of Hobbesian nightmare. Legislators often complain about the meager political awareness of their constituents, and congressmen, in particular, about the tremendous burden of nonlegislative work upon which they must concentrate most of their time. But, generally speaking, the service activities are accepted by congressmen as part of their job, and for those employed in a legislative office life is never dull or unduly exasperating. The excitement of legislative politics comes from being in the swim, even if the main arena is some distance off.

NOTES

1. Two samples are Angus Campbell, Philip E. Converse, Warren E. Miller, and Donald E. Stokes, *The American Voter* (New York, 1960); and William N. McPhee and William A. Glaser, *Public Opinion and Congressional Elections* (New York, 1962).

2. The figures in this and the following paragraph can be found, developed in greater detail, in Hazel Gaudet Erskine, "The Polls: Textbook Knowledge," *Public Opinion Quarterly*, XXVII (1963), 137–38; and *Gallup Political Index*, V (October, 1965), 18.

3. Donald E. Stokes and Warren E. Miller, "Party Government and the Saliency of Congress," *Public Opinion Quarterly*, XXVI (1962), 540.

4. *Ibid.*, pp. 542–43.

5. For a fragment of data, see Lewis A. Dexter, "More on Voters' Information About Candidates," *PROD*, I (March 1958), 36–38.

6. John C. Wahlke, Heinz Eulau, William Buchanan, and LeRoy C. Ferguson, *The Legislative System* (New York: John Wiley and Sons, 1962), pp. 296, 301–02.

7. Leila A. Sussmann, *Dear FDR: A Study of Political Letter-writing* (Totowa, N.J., 1963), p. 12.

8. Charles L. Clapp, *The Congressman: His Work As He Sees It* (Washington, D.C.: The Brookings Institution, 1963), p. 69.

9. Hubert H. Humphrey, "Modernizing Congress," *AFL-CIO American Federationist* (April 1963), p. 2.

10. Sussmann, *op. cit.*, p. 134.

11. An analysis of some of the general characteristics of letter-writers and non-letter-writers is in *ibid.*, pp. 135–38.

12. Raymond A. Bauer, Ithiel de Sola Pool, and Lewis A. Dexter, *American Business and Public Policy* (New York, 1963), p. 201.

13. See, for example, Sussmann, *op. cit.*, pp. 76–77; Rowena Wyant, "Voting Via the Senate Mailbag," *Public Opinion Quarterly*, V (1941), 359–83; L. E. Gleeck, "96 Congressmen Make Up Their Minds," *Public Opinion Quarterly*, IV (1940), 3–24; and Robert A. Dahl, *Congress and Foreign Policy* (New York, 1950), pp. 34–35.

14. Bauer, Pool, and Dexter, *op. cit.*, pp. 359–61.

15. Malcolm E. Jewell, *Senatorial Politics and Foreign Policy* (Lexington, Ky., 1962), pp. 182–83.

16. The letters are reproduced in Juliet Lowell, *Dear Mr. Congressman* (New York, 1948), pp. 12, 23, and 38.

17. See Ellen Davis, "Don't Write Your Congressman, Unless . . . ," *Harper's* (June 1961), p. 13.

18. Bauer, Pool, and Dexter, *op. cit.*, p. 439.

19. Donald R. Matthews, *U.S. Senators and Their World* (Chapel Hill, N.C., 1960), p. 225; Clapp, *op. cit.*, pp. 75–84.

20. Matthews, *op. cit.*, pp. 219–20; Clapp, *op. cit.*, pp. 73–74; Jerry Voorhis, *Confessions of a Congressman* (Garden City, N.Y., 1947), pp. 40–54; Al Toffler, "How Congressmen Make Up Their Minds," *Redbook* (February 1962), p. 129.

21. Bauer, Pool, and Dexter, *op. cit.*, p. 438.

22. *Ibid.*, p. 436.

23. Clapp, *op. cit.*, p. 74. See also John W. Baker (ed.), *Member of the House: Letters of a Congressman by Clem Miller* (New York, 1962).

24. Clapp, *op. cit.*, p. 89.

25. Lewis A. Dexter, "What Do Congressmen Hear: The Mail," *Public Opinion Quarterly*, XX (1956), 18.

26. Carl Hawver, "The Congressman and His Public Opinion Poll," *Public Opinion Quarterly*, XVIII (1954), 125, and *The Congressman's Conception of His Role* (Washington, D.C., 1963), p. 102.

27. Davis, *op. cit.*, p. 20.

28. John H. Kessel, "The Washington Congressional Delegation," *Midwest Journal of Political Science*, VIII (1964), 1–21.

29. Comment made by Representative Tom V. Moorehead, Ohio Republican; see *Congressional Record* (Daily Edition, Appendix), 1962, p. A4033. For an analysis of one congressman's polling, see Frank V. Cantwell, "The Congressional Poll—Six Years' Experience," *Public Opinion Quarterly*, XVIII (1954), 130–35.

30. See *Congressional Record* (Daily Edition, Appendix), 1962, p. A2789. See also Richard A. Brody and Edward R. Tufte, "Constituent-Congressional Communications on Fallout Shelters: The Congressional Polls," *Journal of Communication*, XIV (1964), 34–49. For an extended analysis of congressional polling methods, including sampling and questionnaire construction, see Leonard A. Marascuilo and Harriett Amster, "Survey of 1961–1962 Congressional Polls," *Public Opinion Quarterly*, XXVIII (1964), 497–506; and Hawver, *The Congressman's Conception of His Role*, pp. 195–211.

31. Warren E. Miller and Donald E. Stokes, "Constituency Influence in Congress," *American Political Science Review*, LVII (1963), 55.

32. V. O. Key, Jr., *Public Opinion and American Democracy* (New York, 1961), p. 497.

33. Harold F. Gosnell, *Democracy: The Threshold of Freedom* (New York, 1948), pp. 137–38.

34. Several descriptions of "a day in the life of a legislator" are available in the literature. For example, see Stephen K. Bailey and Howard D. Samuel, *Congress at Work* (New York, 1952), pp. 96–135; Baker, *op. cit.*, pp. 66–68; Matthews, *op. cit.*, pp. 80–81; Voorhis, *op. cit.*, pp. 291–301.

35. Clapp, *op. cit.*, pp. 51–52.

36. *Ibid.*, pp. 55–60.

37. *Ibid.*, p. 61.

38. Matthews, *op. cit.*, p. 83.

39. Clapp, *op. cit.*, p. 63.

40. Matthews, *op. cit.*, pp. 83–84.

41. Davis, *op. cit.*, p. 14.

42. Quoted in Clapp, *op. cit.*, p. 74.

43. Voorhis, *op. cit.*, p. 300.

[Part V]
THE LEGISLATURE AS A SOCIAL SYSTEM

I T HAS now become rather commonplace to observe that a legislative body, like other human groups, is a social system in the sense that it is characterized by widely shared standards of proper conduct, or norms; that each position in the legislative structure has associated with it expectations about the behavior of men who occupy these positions; and that these expectations about positions, or roles, are interlocking in an interactional system. In the subsequent chapters, we deal with the observed norms of Congress and state legislatures and with the network of those roles that seem to be most notable in American legislatures. In principle, these analyses could be enlarged to include all the elements of the legislative system, but the accumulated research is limited primarily to the legislatures themselves.

If we are to begin more adequately to understand and explain the legislative policy-making process, we must learn about the context, or setting, in which policy is or is not made. We need to understand the unwritten rules of the legislative game in order to make sense out of the things that legislators do and say (or fail to do and say), to assess the situational limitations or possibilities for public policy, and to be aware of the strategic implications of the norms of the legislature in the use of written rules or formal organization. Our ability to explain legislative behavior depends, among other things, upon our understanding of how legislators perceive their jobs and how those with whom they interact expect them to behave.

[15]

Legislative Norms

Every human group or institution develops within a context of normative standards of proper conduct, which the participants uphold. The *norms*—those widely held expectations of what members must do, should do, or ought to do in particular circumstances, and the violation of which leads to some kind of sanction or punishment—are acutely significant in political subsystems as highly stylistic and institutionalized as legislative systems are.[1] Legislative norms are, in some particulars, so highly authoritative, persistent, stable, formalized, and legitimate that they are elaborately codified and come to constitute the written rules of legislative bodies. Otherwise, standards of proper conduct in legislative settings may be informal and unwritten, although they need not be thereby less authoritative or sanctioned. Thus, we may speak of the norms of legislative systems in terms of their relative formality or, in a sense, of their visibility. Figure 15.1 provides an illustration of the manner in which legislative norms may be classified in terms of their visibility; it indicates an intermediate category which has analytical virtue when this crude typology is applied to certain American legislatures, such as the United States Senate. Highly formalized legislative norms—the written rules of procedure, standing orders, precedents, and rulings of the chair—are so commonplace and so highly visible to the most casual observer of legislative life that they are seldom treated as norms. Though discussion of the written rules clearly belongs in any general analysis of legislative norms, they are so independently significant for any understanding of legislative decision making that we have treated them separately in an earlier chapter (Chapter 11). Our concern in this chapter will, therefore, be restricted to the so-called "unwritten rules of the game," the informal norms which, along with the written rules, are associated with the control, consensus-building, socialization, and cognitive functions that maintain the legislative system.

We are in a position to describe and illustrate the most notable norms that have been observed to operate in congressional and state legislative systems, and we can illustrate the application of sanctions under some circumstances. Contemporary legislative research does not permit us to deal systematically with the development of legislative norms, nor

DEGREE OF FORMALITY OR VISIBILITY	DESCRIPTION	UNITED STATES SENATE
High	Highly formalized, written rules	Rules and standing orders of the senate, committee rules, precedents, rulings of the chair
Intermediate	Well-established, traditional unwritten rules	Senatorial courtesy, the seniority rule
Low	Informal, unwritten rules	Apprenticeship, specialization, courtesy, reciprocity, institutional patriotism, etc.

Figure 15.1. TYPOLOGY OF LEGISLATIVE NORMS

can we synthesize data (because we know of none) which take us very far in the explanation of policy effects.

THE PROFESSIONAL AND AMATEUR LEGISLATURE

Not only can we expect legislative norms to vary in terms of their formality or visibility, but also we can expect them to vary in terms of the degree of institutionalization of the legislature. The norms of a legislative system (or of any other social system, presumably) are likely to be more highly structured, more highly traditionalized and legitimized, more authoritative, more strongly institutionalized, more widely and intensely accepted, and probably more rigidly and overtly enforced, the more permanent and professionalized is the legislative institution. At least in a limited way, it adds to our perspective of legislative norms to contrast the professional and amateur legislature in terms of descriptive normative differentiation. Figure 15.2 indicates the kind of comparison being suggested. Where the legislature itself is highly professionalized, its normative underpinnings are likely to be more highly structured, consistent and sanctioned than would be expected to be true of a more amateur legislature. This distinction between professional and amateur legislatures corresponds roughly to the differences between Congress

	PROFESSIONAL	AMATEUR
Characteristics	High status, meets regularly, lengthy sessions, well-established, legitimate, has relatively high public respect and esteem, long history, relatively well-integrated, highly formalized, stable, complexly organized	Low status, meets periodically or irregularly, brief sessions, less well-established, relatively low public esteem, brief or cloudy history, fewer traditions, relatively disintegrated, informal, instable, simply organized
Norms	Coherent and congruent, highly structured, pervasive, highly institutionalized, widely and intensely accepted, well-established, regular, automatic sanctions	Contradictory, incoherent, unstructured, erratic, only moderately institutionalized, unevenly recognized and accepted, erratic application of sanctions

Figure 15.2. NORMATIVE DIFFERENCES IN PROFESSIONAL
AND AMATEUR LEGISLATURES

and most, but not all, of the state legislatures, and we would expect to find congressional norms more highly developed than those prevalent in the legislatures of the states. As Milbrath has written in a different context, "The policy-making process in the state capitals is more informal; there is less structure, less rigid adherence to rules, and less permanent record-keeping. There also seems to be less personal commitment by the actors to the success of the system and to the building of long-range personal reputations."[2]

UNWRITTEN RULES: CONGRESS

Traditional Norms. Two congressional norms that are highly visible are those of *senatorial courtesy* and *seniority.* The former applies to the Senate in its constitutional role of giving its "advice and consent" to presidential nominations for federal appointments, and has been practiced since the Washington Administration. "The custom of senatorial courtesy is the sanction by which a majority of the Senate may require the President to nominate the candidate proposed by the senator or senators from the state in which the office is located, provided they belong to the same party as that of the President."[3] If the President nominates a person to serve as a federal judge, for example, in Illinois, and an Illinois senator of the President's political party declares that person to be "personally obnoxious" to him, the Senate will not ordinarily confirm the appointment. The objecting senator may be expected by his colleagues to present reasons for his objections, but this has not always been required. In fact, the person nominated by the President may not be disliked by the objecting senator; he may simply prefer, or have recommended, someone else. Thus, in 1951 the Senate rejected two nominations for judgeships in Illinois because Senator Douglas "stated that the manner of their selection was personally obnoxious to him."[4] Douglas had recommended other men for these posts, which recommendations President Truman had not followed, and Douglas thought that his candidates were more worthy. But the norm of senatorial courtesy is not absolute; it is interlaced with other senatorial norms, and it has not always been successfully invoked. Harris suggests the interdependence of senatorial courtesy with other Senate norms when he outlines the standards of the Senate for invoking it:

> In passing upon a personal objection of senators to a nomination, the Senate takes into account the standing of the senator, as well as the grounds of his objection, and whether the office is one located within the state of the senator or is a national office. When the Senate has declined to honor an objection it is usually due to the fact that the objecting senator is not in good standing with his colleagues. . . . A senator who has not shown the usual courtesies to his colleagues may be denied the courtesy of the Senate.[5]

Senatorial courtesy is seldom invoked, but this is because senators are almost invariably consulted in the nominating process, and virtually make federal appointments of some judges and administrators in some of the lower levels of administration in the federal field service. Thus, senatorial courtesy, while it is an unwritten rule, has drastically modified those provisions of Article II of the Constitution which provide for the appointing powers of the President.

The seniority rule applies most directly to the selection of congressional committee chairmen, a process which we have described in detail in Chapter 9. However, its application is much wider than simply to the selection of committee chairmen, and it pervades the whole life of the Congress. Members of the House and Senate are ranked according to the length of their uninterrupted service in the house. For senators, the ranking commences on the opening day of the Congress to which they are first elected. Senators elected or appointed to fill an unexpired term begin to accrue seniority on the day their state governor certifies their appointment, or, if they are elected, when the senator takes the oath of office, provided the Senate is in session. House procedure is much the same, except that, for some purposes, House members receive more credit for nonconsecutive service (i.e., representatives with three non-consecutive terms are ranked above those with two consecutive terms).[6] Seniority in the respective houses of Congress confers status upon a member which affects much of his legislative life, and especially the perquisites available to him. Office space is assigned on a seniority basis, seating at official dinners is based upon seniority, and committee assign-ments are usually, if not always, made on the basis of seniority.[7] "In no other place," writes Galloway, "does seniority or length of service carry so much weight as it does in the Congress of the United States."[8]

Informal Rules. Closely related to the seniority norm is that of *apprenticeship.* New members of the House and Senate are expected to exercise restraint in their participation in debate, to show respect for their elders, and to perform some of the more unexciting chores of the house like that of presiding over floor debate in the Senate. Roland Young has pointed out:

New members continually identify themselves in a remarkably short time with what might be called the congressional point of view, but the period of full maturation, when the politician becomes also a seasoned legis-lator trusted fully by his colleagues, may require several years. Until relatively recently, the Senate expected a new member to remain sedately quiet for most of his first term in office, but with the greater number of Senators who serve for a single term, this practice is no longer followed. In both Houses, new members are tested and trained before they are given major responsibilities and before their words carry weight.[9]

At one time new members of both houses were expected not to par-ticipate in legislative debate at all—to be "seen but not heard." The increasing numbers of new members and the complexity and volume of legislative work have reduced this stricture considerably, but freshmen legislators are still warned not to speak too frequently and on too many subjects. "Don't try to go too fast," Speaker Rayburn told new members. "Learn your job. Don't ever talk until you know what you're talking about. . . . If you want to get along, go along."[10]

Freshmen who ignore this advice—and some do—irritate their peers and are often the subject of sanctions. "He talks too much" is a description often heard in connection with a few members. At times these men cannot understand why they are passed over for assignments for which they are intellectually prepared. The blunt truth is that colleagues do not wish to see them get ahead or to work with them, despite their qualifications.[11]

While the rigidity of congressional expectations regarding the apprenticeship of new members has undoubtedly been relaxed in the postwar period, it is still very real to freshman congressmen. Although the sanctions for deviation are unevenly applied, and in any event are not likely to be severe, the pressures toward conformity with the apprenticeship norm are very pronounced. For an illustration of this point from the House of Representatives, consider the comments of Jerry Voorhis, who served in the House for ten years:

> For what seemed to me a very, very long time (actually it was only a few weeks) I managed to observe the "freshman rules." Day after day I listened, without participating, to debates on subjects in which I had a most active interest. At the close of the sessions I would return to my office with every organ of my body feeling as though it had been tied in knots. It was as if the thoughts I had felt impelled to express had somehow congealed within me and reposed like heavy stones all through my physical being.
> Such experiences were not confined to those first few weeks. From time to time through my congressional career I heeded the counsel of friends who told me I was inclined to speak too often and on too many subjects. At times I persuaded myself that I was not adequately prepared to enter actively into a certain debate or to make a statement on the floor on some subject even though I had a deep conviction that it was somehow my duty to do so. But always I suffered profound regret and the almost physical pain which I have just described. I learned that for me, at least, the role of the comparatively silent men who move about the chamber with calm assurance, speak but seldom and are heard, therefore, with presumably greater effect was an impossible one. For better or for worse I had to do the job in the only way I could do it and live at peace with myself. When there was something I believed ought to be said in the House I had to say it.[12]

Voorhis understood the norms of the legislative group; he conformed to them only with great discomfort, psychological strain, and perhaps physical agony, and he deliberately decided that he would have to risk sanctions by deviating from the norm. Severe sanctions did not follow, although he was often reminded of the displeasure of his colleagues.

An illustration from the Senate is the case of William Proxmire (D-Wis). Proxmire's accommodation to the apprenticeship norm is described by Huitt as follows:

> Throughout the spring of 1958, for roughly half his first session in the Senate, Proxmire strove earnestly to be a model freshman senator. He worked hard on his committees and took care of his constituents. He ac-

cepted cheerfully a mammoth portion of the burden of freshmen of the majority party, presiding over the Senate. He did much more than his share; an unofficial tabulation midway in the session showed that he had sat in the chair longer than anyone else and about sixteen times as long as Vice President Nixon. . . .

But Proxmire had not satisfactorily answered the question that mattered most to him: How much could he talk on the floor? Ordinary prudence, as well as Senate practice, counsel a neophyte to bide his time before exercising very freely his undoubted right to speak at any time. But to a man like Proxmire the life of the Senate is the debate on the floor. Not to be there and participate is to deny himself equal membership in the Senate. Proxmire said of a freshman colleague who seldom spoke: "He might as well not be a senator!"

Nevertheless he forbore, trying to find socially acceptable ways to take some part. The "morning hour," that period at the beginning of each day when senators introduce bills and insert material in the *Congressional Record,* seemed safe enough so he quickly became a regular contributor to the *Record.* He entered colloquies on the floor only when specifically invited to do so by senior members. He cautiously scheduled his first major speech for the day before the Easter recess when most members would be gone, having been assured that this was an appropriate time for a freshman to talk. . . .

But almost as if he could not help himself, Proxmire became steadily more active in debate until he was one of the busiest men on the floor. Then came the first warnings that he was "talking too much." The warnings were characteristic of the operations of the Senate. None of them was direct. They came in friendly tips: someone heard an unnamed person say it; the report was passed on to a Proxmire staff man for what it was worth. Or a very senior senator in the chair would pointedly overlook Proxmire standing at his desk, to recognize other members ahead of him out of turn.

Proxmire retired, brooding, to his office. He was puzzled and frustrated. He believed that he *had* exercised great restraint. He had kept his speeches short, except when asked by a party floor man to help kill time.[13]

Proxmire's immediate reaction to the cues that he was thought to be violating the apprenticeship norm was to withdraw entirely from debate; however, his retirement was brief. He decided not to worry about his Senate influence, and to talk whenever he chose to do so. He then pursued a variety of issues in Senate debate, including mutual security, social security improvement, the Lake Michigan water diversion bill, and the Democratic Senate leadership itself. While his behavior was widely disapproved, his deviation was tolerated by a Senate that was predisposed to apply severe sanctions only in the most outrageous cases.

Two of the norms of the Congress have to do with the nature of the taskload of the legislative bodies. One prescribes concentration by the member upon *legislative work,* the other prescribes *specialization.* Matthews points out that "the Senate folkways . . . prescribe that a senator place first priority upon being a *legislator*."[14] A member of the House is often "told that the committee system is the core of the legislative process and that the best way to attract the favorable attention of his colleagues is to participate wholeheartedly in his committee work," where "he should develop a specialty and concentrate on it, playing down other interests he may have that fall within the jurisdiction of other committees."[15] A member of Congress is expected to devote his major efforts to legislative tasks, and to give secondary priority to personal advancement or publicity. This emphasis upon the workload of the legislature produces the commonplace disparity between "inside" and "outside" prestige—some of the most respected and effective legislators, with high inside prestige, are little known outside the institution. As Harry S Truman once observed, "the real business of the Senate was carried on by unassuming and conscientious men, not by those who managed to get the most publicity."[16]

In addition to the expectation that members of Congress devote their main efforts to legislative work, members are expected to develop a specialty. Specialization of tasks is probably essential in a modern legislative body, which has a limited amount of time and a complexity of tasks to perform. A member is expected to specialize in the relatively few matters that are of special importance to his state or district, or that are immediately connected with his own committee work, so that he can speak as an expert on those subjects. Specialization may be a more powerful norm in the United States House than in the Senate. It does seem clear that House members, to be maximally effective, are required, more than senators, to develop expertise in a single subject-matter specialty. Such expertise enhances the influence and effectiveness of the member; when he speaks in debate, he is listened to because he is regarded as an authority. And while the specialization norm may have become more important in the last forty years, it has been important for a much longer time. It is said, for instance, that Representative Nelson Dingley (R-Me) advised Champ Clark (D-Mo) to specialize if he wished to "make a great name for himself in Congress." Himself a specialist on tariff legislation, Dingley advised:

I have been in Congress for many years and I have watched and studied men as they have come and gone. . . . If a man be a specialist on a subject, if he knows more than the ordinary congressman knows or can hope to learn by mere dabbling, then he can compel Congress to listen to him, and he rises to be a power. That is the secret of success here.[17]

Two additional congressional norms are associated with the manner in which legislative business is conducted; these are the norms of *interpersonal courtesy* and *reciprocity*. Interpersonal courtesy among legislators helps to resolve conflict in an atmosphere relatively free from invective and personal attacks upon members. Representatives and senators are forbidden by the formal rules from questioning the motives of another member, criticizing another state, or making reference to members of the other chamber. Members address their remarks in debate to the chair—to "Mr. Speaker" or to "Mr. President"—rather than to another legislator. Impersonality in reference to other members is adhered to, so that members do not refer to one another by name; rather, a representative refers to the "gentleman from New York," or a senator to the "senior senator from Rhode Island." A congressman may engage in mudslinging in his campaign, but not on the floor of the house. As one House member put it, "we acknowledge that a person does a little bit of demagoguery with his people, but snow is for the folks."[18] Interpersonal courtesy makes it possible for competitors to cooperate.

Reciprocity is so fundamental a part of the American legislative process that we can scarcely do it justice in a few sentences. It is pervasive in the congressional system, and may take the forms of personal exchange of assistance or favors, compromise and negotiation over the provisions of legislation, or "logrolling" (trading of votes). Members are expected to play the game of exchange and mutual aid, especially where the immediate concerns of their own constituents are not directly involved. Much reciprocal behavior is both private and subtle, but it cannot be doubted that it is there. In referring to his colleagues, for example, a House member observed:

When one of them votes with you on something in which you're interested, it is pretty tough to turn him down when he comes to you later and wants some assistance on a matter of importance to him. There is a great deal of logrolling in Congress, and it's not going to be changed. It is particularly apparent on a close vote. Now I vote against any farm bill despite the fact that members who would like my support on those bills often support me on other things. People know my stand on the farm situation, and they just don't bother trying to get me to go along. This doesn't affect our relationship on other things, however, I think most of us recognize a cardinal rule in the House and that is that you don't ask a member to support you if such support is going to be going against his district or against a particular project in which he happens to be interested. We all respect one another's views on those matters.[19]

Legislative reciprocity emerges most visibly when the Congress considers public works appropriations bills, and other "pork barrel" legislation. Perhaps the operation (as well as the frustrations) of reciprocity in the life of the Senate is best illustrated by the candid reflections of Senator Paul Douglas (D-Ill) when the public works bill was considered in 1956. Douglas said:

This bill is built up out of a whole system of mutual accommodations in which the favors are widely distributed, with the implicit promise that no one will kick over the applecart; that if Senators do not object to the bill as a whole, they will "get theirs." It is a process, if I may use an inelegant expression, of mutual backscratching and mutual logrolling.

Any member who tries to buck the system is only confronted with an impossible amount of work in trying to ascertain the relative merits of a given project; and any member who does ascertain them and who feels convinced that he is correct is unable to get an individual project turned down because the Senators from the State in which the project is located, and thus is benefiting, naturally will oppose any objection to the project; and the other members of the Senate will feel that they must support the Senators in question, because if they do not do so, similar appropriations for their own states at some time likely will be called into question.[20]

It is probably important to stress that not all legislation that is enacted by the House and Senate is the result of such implicit bargaining, or such pervasive reciprocity. Furthermore, it is an understatement to say that our knowledge of the place and impact of reciprocity on decisional processes in Congress is incomplete. At the same time, it is clear that congressmen widely share expectations that representatives ought to behave in these terms.

A further consideration of congressional norms leads us to expectations about *institutional patriotism.* Members of Congress are expected to have an emotional attachment to the institution, and in particular to the house of which they are members. House members tend to regard themselves as the "real" representatives of the people and more responsive to their needs than senators; they tend to hold to the Protestant ethic of work, and believe that they are harder-working than members of the Senate; they tend to regard senators as too publicity-seeking and the Senate as too "clubbish."[21]

If the members of the House of Representatives are prone to express their chauvinism in terms of relatively invidious comparisons with senators, members of the Senate are likely to express their institutional patriotism in much more sweeping ways. Senators are inclined to refer to the Senate as "the greatest deliberative body in the world," and they are certainly expected to believe it. And, if William S. White's observations are roughly accurate, those senators who are most influential in the Senate are most likely to have internalized the norm. Speaking of the "Inner Club," White says:

Those who belong to it express, consciously or unconsciously, the deepest instincts and prejudices of "the Senate type." The Senate type is, speaking broadly, a man for whom the Institution is a career in itself, a life in itself and an end in itself. This Senate type is not always free of Presidential ambition, a striking case in point having been the late Senator Taft. But the important fact is that when the Senate type thinks of the Presidency he thinks of it as only *another* and not really a *higher* ambition, as did Taft and as did Senator Russell of Georgia when, in 1952, he sought the Democratic Presidential nomination.

The Senate type makes the Institution his home in an almost literal sense, and certainly in a deeply emotional sense. His head swims with its history, its lore and the accounts of past personnel and deeds and purposes. To him, precedent has an almost mystical meaning and where the common run of members will reflect twice at least before creating a precedent, the Senate type will reflect so long and so often that nine times out of ten he will have nothing to do with such a project at all.[22]

A senator is expected to champion the Senate, to respect it, and to honor it. When he defiles the Senate—in its terms, when he abuses the "honor of the place," as defined in a rather neo-Victorian style—he exposes himself to perhaps the severest sanctions the legislative body can apply. The most celebrated illustration of the application of sanctions by the Senate for the violation of its norms is that of the late Senator Joseph McCarthy (D-Wis), who as Chairman of the Permanent Subcommittee on Investigations of the Committee on Government Operations engaged in a Communist witch-hunt during 1953-1954, which focused mainly upon the Department of State and the United States Army. In December 1954, the Senate voted to censure McCarthy for his conduct. But the Senate did not censure his browbeating witnesses before his Subcommittee, indiscriminately accusing people of being Communists and traitors, or even abusing the investigatory powers of Congress. McCarthy was censured, and his power deflated, because he attacked the integrity of the Senate itself. The language of the censure resolution, in a certain sense, permits the Senate to explain itself.

SECTION I: Resolved, that the Senator from Wisconsin, Mr. McCarthy, failed to cooperate with the Subcommittee on Privileges and Elections of the Senate Committee on Rules and Administration in clearing up matters referred to that subcommittee which concerned his conduct as a Senator, and *affected the honor of the Senate* and instead, repeatedly abused the members who were trying to carry out assigned duties, thereby obstructing the constitutional processes of the Senate, and that the conduct of the Senator from Wisconsin, Mr. McCarthy, is *contrary to Senatorial traditions* and is hereby condemned.

SECTION II: The Senator from Wisconsin (Mr. McCarthy) in writing to the chairman of the Select Committee to study censure charges (Mr. Watkins) after the Select Committee had issued its report and before the report was presented to the Senate charging three members of the Select Committee with "deliberate deception" and "fraud" for failure to disqualify themselves; in stating to the press on November 4, 1954 that the special Senate session that was to begin November 8, 1954 was a "lynch party";

in repeatedly describing this special Senate session as a "lynch bee" in a nationwide television–radio show on November 7, 1954; in stating to the public press on November 13, 1954 that the chairman of the Select Committee (Mr. Watkins) was guilty of "the most unusual, the most cowardly thing I've heard of" and stating further: "I expected he would be afraid to answer the questions but didn't think he'd be stupid enough to make a public statement"; and in characterizing the said committee as the "unwitting hand-maiden," "involuntary agent," and "attorneys in fact" of the Communist Party and in charging that the said committee in writing its report "imitated Communist methods—that it distorted, misrepresented, and omitted, in its effort to manufacture a plausible rationalization" in support of its recommendations to the Senate, which characterizations and charges were contained in a statement released to the press and inserted in the *Congressional Record* of November 10, 1954, *acted contrary to Senatorial ethics and tended to bring the Senate into dishonor and disrepute,* to obstruct the constitutional processes of the Senate, and to impair its dignity; and such conduct is hereby condemned.[23] [Italics added]

But the censure of McCarthy for a failure of loyalty to the Senate meant much more than the terse language of the resolution suggests. Politically, he was effectually stripped of power in the Senate; he was ignored; he was given the "silent treatment," almost the severest sanction a group can apply to one of its members.[24]

A final congressional norm which deserves some mention in this analysis has to do with the loyalty of members of Congress to their political party. The party norm is not clear-cut and unambiguous in the American Congress. The congressman is subjected to a variety of pressures in his decisional behavior, some of which may be conflicting; political party pressures (either strategic or psychological) are difficult to sort out from the maze of pressures he feels. Further, when the outcomes of congressional votes are certain, party pressures may not be pressed strongly. Thus, while there are among congressmen widely shared expectations that members ought to support their party, the machinery for the implementation of such expectations is not particularly well-developed and severe sanctions are seldom applied for violating expectations of party loyalty. Even when members of the United States Senate have failed to support, and have actively opposed, their party's presidential candidate in a national election, seldom have such sanctions as deprivation of committee assignment been imposed.[25] But we know a great deal more about the party voting of legislators than we do about how partisan norms are invoked; we fully synthesize party voting data for legislators in Chapter 17.

Conformity to Norms. It is clear that normative rules of conduct exist in American legislative systems. The norms we have described here deal explicitly with the legislative institution itself, but presumably more thorough research would reveal norms that regulate conduct more

widely in American legislative systems, including the behavior of newspapermen, lobbyists, bureaucrats, and so forth. Of course the norms
existing within the legislative body are not universally accepted by all
legislators, nor are they consistently adhered to, but our knowledge of
the correlates of normative conformity is very limited. Matthews, in
his study of the "folkways" of the United States Senate, explored the
effects of four factors that influence conformity to Senate norms: previous training and experience, political ambitions, constituency problems,
and political ideology. His data support the hypothesis that the recruitment function affects normative conformity so that those senators
"elected relatively early in life with considerable political experience
seem to conform most readily and often," while "amateur politicians,
men who have entered politics relatively late in life after distinguished
business and professional careers, have the hardest time of all."[26] State
legislators and judges who moved to the Senate seemed to conform most,
while former state governors and former federal executives in the Senate
were less likely to accept the norms of the Senate. (The measures of
conformity used by Matthews were frequency of floor speaking and
an index of specialization based upon the number of bills a senator introduced which were referred to the two committees receiving the
greatest number of his bills.) Furthermore, Matthews' data suggest that
senators with political ambitions beyond the Senate (such as the Presidency) are less likely to conform to the institutional norms, and
that senators elected from competitive two-party, or complex urban-
industrial, constituencies are more likely to deviate from the norms.
Finally, Senate liberals are more likely to be nonconformists than are
conservatives. These findings comport with the status of the norms
themselves—they tend to support, reinforce and buttress the status quo
in the legislative body. Since rural, conservative, and safe-district senators
are overrepresented in the Senate, and have set many of its norms,
liberal senators who face electoral insecurity are most likely to seek to
upset the status quo. But, at least with respect to the success senators
have in getting their bills passed, Matthews' data show that conformity
to Senate norms is related to "legislative effectiveness."[27]

Conformity to congressional norms is seldom obtained by overt
threats of sanction, or by the formal application of sanctions to deviant
legislators. While the sanctions that support congressional norms are not
fully understood or documented by adequate research, the pressures to
normative conformity are impressive. We have available to us a few
illustrations of the formal application of sanctions (such as the McCarthy
censure), and we are aware of the existence of a variety of informal
sanctions. Congressmen may get interpersonal cues from other members,
which indicate disapproval of violations of the rules of the game. *Selective
inattention*, manifested by personal avoidance, exaggerated inattention

in debate, or ignoring suggestions and requests, constitutes an observable sanction for normative violations. *Process sanctions* are known to have been applied to legislators, as in instances where bills are mysteriously "misplaced," neglected, or ignored. Though a member who persistently violates the norms is very likely to be tolerated, his behavior is not likely to be regarded as legitimate.

STATE LEGISLATIVE NORMS

The norms we have discussed with respect to Congress—senatorial courtesy, seniority, apprenticeship, legislative work, specialization, interpersonal courtesy, reciprocity, institutional patriotism, and party loyalty —are certainly applicable to any discussion of the unwritten rules of the state legislative game. An inventory of the normative expectations of legislators in five states (California, New Jersey, Ohio, Tennessee, and Wisconsin) indicates that in these states there exists a wide range of expected behavior. The interview responses of these states' legislators were coded into a total of 42 categories, based upon asking legislators to name the " 'rules of the game'—that a member must observe to hold the respect and cooperation of his fellow members."[28] These categories were:

1. Performance of obligations
2. Respect for other members' legislative rights
3. Impersonality
4. Self-restraint in debate
5. Courtesy
6. Openness of aims
7. Modesty
8. Integrity
9. Independence of judgment
10. Personal virtue
11. Decisiveness
12. Unselfish service
13. Advance notice of changed stand
14. Openness in opposition
15. Sociability
16. Conciliation
17. Agency for party or administration
18. Restraint in opposition
19. Application
20. Respect for other members' political rights
21. Objectivity
22. Agency for legislative party
23. Gracefulness in defeat
24. Ability and intelligence
25. Non-venality
26. Restraint in bill-introduction
27. Maintenance of confidences
28. Avoidance of trickery
29. Apprenticeship
30. Caution in commitments
31. Commitment to job
32. Institutional patriotism
33. Respect for opposition groups
34. Negotiation
35. Limits to negotiation
36. Seniority
37. Acceptance of committee system
38. Self-restraint in goals
39. Senatorial courtesy
40. Compliance with group
41. Limits to partisanship
42. Abstinence from dilatory actions

The parallels between congressional and state legislative norms suggest the wide generality of the legislative way of life in the United States. Yet the more transient, more temporary, less stable, less professionalized character of state legislatures provides, in general terms, a more flexible group life than is true of the national Congress.

Because Congress is more highly institutionalized than state legislatures (or certainly most of them), its norms tend to be more *institution-oriented*. While institution-oriented norms (seniority, legislative work, apprenticeship, institutional patriotism, specialization, etc.) are not alien to the state legislative system, they are apparently far less salient for state legislators (in the sense of being important rules of the game). The norms of the American state legislatures appear to be more *individual-oriented*. The standards of proper individual conduct that are widely accepted in our society—those of simple honesty, trustworthiness, respect for others, sociability, openness, and sportsmanship—are given preeminence as state legislative norms, and are probably given greater emphasis and held with greater intensity in the state legislative setting than among the general population. Wahlke, Eulau, Buchanan, and Ferguson found that the rules of the game most frequently mentioned by state legislators were those involving performance of personal obligations and commitments, respect for other members' legislative rights, and impersonality, including observance of the "golden rule."[29]

The most frequently mentioned normative expectation among state legislators in four states (California, New Jersey, Ohio, and Wisconsin), and the third most frequently mentioned expectation in another (Tennessee), was *performance of obligations*. State legislators overwhelmingly expect their colleagues to keep their word and abide by their commitments. This expectation of reliability is illustrated in the comments of a Wisconsin legislator: "Keeping your word is an unwritten law among assemblymen. You vote the way you say you will or you explain why you changed your mind. You just don't double-cross people."

Almost as important among legislators in these states are standards of fairness and helpfulness in playing the legislative game—reciprocity. State legislators expect that members of the legislature will support the local bills of others, respect a member's amendments to his own bill, and refrain from unnecessarily objecting to another member's local bill before legislative committees. Again, the norm of *interpersonal courtesy* has special importance in state legislative systems. As one state legislator said,

> You have to have respect for other people's opinions and refrain from personal abuse. I mean you have to exhibit a spirit of cooperation regardless of party or urban–rural residence. You might even vote with the other

group when you think they are right. Also, give constructive criticism—don't tear a bill down just because it was introduced by a certain party or individual. Don't make fun of ridiculous measures either, or ridicule witnesses when they come before committee. You have to hear everybody and not abuse or hurt anybody's feelings.[30]

In keeping with our postulation of the difference in the salience of norms between the professional and amateur legislature, it may be noted that the norm of specialization, or something close to it, is scarcely mentioned by state legislators. While such a process occurs in state legislatures, it does not have a powerful normative status.

Interstate Variations. We have contrasted state legislatures and the Congress, but this comparison should not obscure the important differences in norm structure from one state legislature to another. Each state legislature operates within its own political system and is embedded in its own political culture. Thus, in the relatively competitive two-party states of Wisconsin, Ohio, and New Jersey, party norms are much more frequently salient for legislators than in factional, nonpartisan or one-party states (such as California or Tennessee). In Wisconsin, where a fairly lively two-party politics has prevailed since the early 1950s, members are expected to support their party on procedural motions and party platform legislation, as a minimum. As one Wisconsin legislator put it: "It's absolutely necessary for a member to vote with his party on party platform bills. It's your bible, and if you don't want to belong to that religion, you should get another bible."[31] Wahlke and his associates found that behavior supportive of party or administration was given greater emphasis by legislators in New Jersey and Ohio, both with competitive two-party politics.[32]

In terms of the data available, California presents some interesting contrasts with other states. In a state that was for many years characterized by partisan immobility because of nonpartisanship, direct legislation, and cross-filing, the California legislature (particularly the Assembly) has been one in which individual members, rather than party organizations or other agencies, have played key roles.[33] "California legislators," note the authors of the celebrated four-state study, "put a premium upon abiding by commitments made, upon notifying other members in advance when finding it necessary to change their positions on an issue, upon refraining from embarrassing fellow members politically with their constituents, and upon accepting the decisions and operations of the committee system," and they were found to be less likely to insist that members refrain from extralegislative publicity, playing to the galleries, or other "prima donna" behavior.[34] The emphasis upon interpersonal individual behavior among California legislators seemed to reflect the individualistic political culture of that state.

Both in Tennessee and Wisconsin, greater emphasis than in the other states for which we have comparative material was placed upon individual self-restraint. Fifty-nine percent of the 119 Tennessee legislators interviewed by Wahlke made mention of the norm against talking too much in floor debate, a proportion far greater than in other states. In Wisconsin, a great deal of emphasis was given to proscriptions against excessive talking in debate. One Wisconsin legislator said, "A legislator shouldn't talk too much and should confine himself to the issue. Any legislator who can't speak his piece in five minutes is no good."[35] Another distinguished between talking by leaders, or by legislators whose knowledge was respected for what it could contribute, as opposed to rank-and-file oratory:

Talking on the floor by floor leaders and their assistants is quite proper. That's their job. But from there on there are a lot of people who have a habit of getting up and talking, and it doesn't make much sense. They don't contribute knowledge or information, they just invite publicity. The old-timers get disgusted with this more than anybody else. They know it doesn't change any votes, and they've heard all the arguments before.

Another important source of interstate variability in normative emphasis may be those expectations that have to do with the behavior of lobbyists. We noted in an earlier chapter that American legislators tend to view lobbyists as playing functional roles in the legislative system, although there are variations from state to state in the proportions of legislators who have a "positive image" of lobbying. But we know very little about legislative expectations regarding lobbying. Presumably, lobbying norms do exist in all American legislative systems. One kind of lobbying norm was uncovered in a study of the Wisconsin legislature, and it had to do with legislators' expectations about the behavior of other legislators in their relationships with lobbyists.

[The] norms of the Assembly prescribed that it was permissible for a member to accept meals and drinks from lobbyists. There were a number of members who did not do so because of personal convictions, but most members agreed that such behavior was all right for others if they wished to do so. However, "chiseling" or "mooching" from lobbyists violated the norms of the Assembly. It was all right if a lobbyist invited a member to lunch, but a member who mooched from a lobbyist was an "outlaw."[36]

Another legislative norm, observable in at least one state, prescribes the way in which lobbyists should behave with respect to legislators. The norm requires the privacy of legislator-lobbyist relationships and proscribes making lobbying activities public. In Iowa, early in 1964, a lobbyist for the Asphalt Paving Association of Iowa made public letters to a state senator in which he impugned his personal integrity, accused him of favoritism toward the cement industry, and revealed his private conversations with the senator. He was severely chastised both by legislators and other lobbyists for violating the rules of the game. As one lobbyist said:

No experienced lobbying group would state its complaint in a public letter. If the lobbyist felt a senator was being unfair to his industry, he would have gone quietly to a friendly senator or to the majority leader to correct it.

A business lobbyist pointed out that the lobbyist had also violated the norm of impersonality: "The asphalt people broke another rule. The Senate itself has a written rule that senators do not question each other's personal motives in debate on the Senate floor."[37]

Sanctions. State legislators are quite conscious of a variety of sanctions which may be imposed upon a member who violates the rules of the game. While punishment is seldom so severe as to involve virtual expulsion (as was essentially the result of the McCarthy censure by the United States Senate), the sanctions are, while subtle, severe enough to be salient to legislators. Republican members of the 1957 Wisconsin legislature who deviated from the party norm were quite aware of attempts by the party to purge them at the polls, and they could cite specific cases where violators were relieved of their committee chairmanships. Legislators interviewed by Wahlke and his associates had no difficulty in delineating the ways in which the norms were enforced; most of them made reference to obstruction of their bills, ostracism, and mistrust as the probable consequences of nonconformity.[38] But beyond specific sanctions recognized by legislators, the rules of the game are significant because they are both widely accepted and regarded as functional for the legislative system. The norms of American legislatures are not catechisms which legislators can recite by rote, slogans suitable for framing to be hung on the legislator's office wall, or "pious platitudes about good behavior." Enforcement of the rules of the game may be variable, but it is real. At the same time, sanctions seldom need to be applied, and the really remarkable conformity to legislative norms would "seem to be obtained not primarily through members' fear of such punishment but through their general acceptance of the functional utility of the rules for enabling the group to do what a legislature is expected to do."[39]

Conclusion. The unwritten rules of the game in a legislative system must be understood in order to comprehend fully the written rules that may be invoked or who may invoke them and under what circumstances. This point is particularly well illustrated from the few studies extant of state legislative norms. It is clear, for instance, that in the states studied the rules permit objection to unanimous-consent requests, but the unwritten rules almost invariably prohibit such objection. Rules regulating debate may be vitiated by informal norms; the rules of procedure in the Wisconsin Assembly contain a straightforward provision for moving the previous question to end debate, but a norm intensely held among members prohibits invoking the rule under any circumstances.

The functional contributions of legislative norms are significant, even though they are unmeasured (and perhaps unmeasurable). The norms contribute to the socialization function, providing new members with cues by which they can shape their behavior along appropriate lines. They support the control and consensus-building functions of the legislative system by advancing the group solidarity and cohesion without which the system could not function, promoting the predictability of the behavior of legislators within the system, limiting the chanprinting conflict, and expediting legislative business. They provide an important element in the culture of the system, and thus contribute to cognitive sharing—making it possible for members to operate on similar premises, to share meanings, to see things in about the same ways.

In this chapter we have dealt with the expectations of proper conduct by legislators in general. There are other norms in a human system which are concerned with specific locations that people occupy in the system. Those legislative norms that are focused on, relate to, and describe specific positions in the legislative structure constitute *roles;* we turn to these special kinds of norms in the next chapter.

NOTES

1. George C. Homans, *The Human Group* (London, 1951), pp. 124–25.

2. Lester W. Milbrath, *The Washington Lobbyists* (Chicago, 1963), p. 302.

3. Joseph P. Harris, "The Courtesy of the Senate," *Political Science Quarterly*, LXVII (1952), 39.

4. George B. Galloway, *The Legislative Process in Congress* (New York, 1953), p. 577.

5. Harris, *op cit.*, p. 51.

6. George Goodwin, Jr., "The Seniority System in Congress," *American Political Science Review*, LIII (1959), 413.

7. Galloway, *op. cit.*, pp. 367–68.

8. *Ibid.*, p. 367.

9. Roland Young, *The American Congress* (New York, 1958), pp. 62–63.

10. Neil MacNeil, *Forge of Democracy: The House of Representatives* (New York, 1963), p. 129.

11. Charles L. Clapp, *The Congressman: His Work As He Sees It* (Washington, D.C.: The Brookings Institution, 1963), p. 11.

12. Jerry Voorhis, *Confessions of a Congressman* (Garden City, N.Y., 1947), pp. 28–29.

13. Ralph K. Huitt, "The Outsider in the Senate: An Alternative Role," *American Political Science Review*, LV (1961), 568–69.

14. Donald R. Matthews, "The Folkways of the United States Senate: Conformity to Group Norms and Legislative Effectiveness," *American Political Science Review*, LIII (1959), 1067.

15. Clapp, *op. cit.*, p. 12.

16. Quoted in Matthews, *loc. cit.*

17. Quoted in MacNeil, *op. cit.*, p. 130.

18. Clapp, *op. cit.*, p. 13.

19. *Ibid.*, pp. 180–81. For a discussion of reciprocity in the congressional committee context, see Richard F. Fenno, Jr., "The House Appropriations Committee as a Political System: The Problem of Integration," *American Political Science Review*, LVI (1962), 316–19.

20. *Congressional Record*, June 13, 1956, p. 9153; quoted in Matthews, *op. cit.*, p. 1072.

21. Clapp, *op. cit.*, p. 35.

22. William S. White, *Citadel: The Story of the U.S. Senate* (New York, 1956), pp. 84–85. See also White, *The Taft Story* (New York, 1954), pp. 195–205.

23. Quoted in Richard H. Rovere, *Senator Joe McCarthy* (Cleveland, 1960), pp. 229–30.

24. For impressions of the effects of the censure upon Senator McCarthy's prestige, status, and physical and mental health, see Rovere, *op. cit.*, pp. 239–48; and White, *Citadel*, p. 133.

25. Ralph K. Huitt, "The Morse Committee Assignment Controversy: A Study in Senate Norms," *American Political Science Review*, LI (1957), 313–29.

26. Matthews, *op. cit.*, p. 1088.

27. *Ibid.*, pp. 1085–86.

28. John C. Wahlke, Heinz Eulau, William Buchanan, and LeRoy C. Ferguson, *The Legislative System* (New York: John Wiley and Sons, 1962), pp. 143, 146–47.

29. *Ibid.*, p. 144.

30. *Ibid.*, pp. 144–45.

31. Samuel C. Patterson, "The Role of the Deviant in the State Legislative System: The Wisconsin Assembly," *Western Political Quarterly*, XIV (1961), 462.

32. Wahlke et al., *op. cit.*, p. 150.

33. *Ibid.*, pp. 43, 59–60; and William Buchanan, *Legislative Partisanship: The Deviant Case of California* (Berkeley and Los Angeles, 1963).

34. Wahlke et al., *op. cit.*, p. 150.

35. This and the following quotation appear in Patterson, *op. cit.*, p. 463.

36. *Ibid.*

37. *Des Moines Sunday Register*, Mar. 29, 1964, p. 1–L.

38. Wahlke et al., *op. cit.*, p. 154.

39. *Ibid.*, p. 168.

[16]

Legislative Roles and Informal Organization

THROUGHOUT this book, our conceptualization of the activity, action, and behavior that goes on within the fluid boundaries of American legislative systems has been somewhat eclectic because we recognize that a variety of scientifically and politically relevant factors contribute to the understanding of legislative situations. We have given attention (and will do so further, in later chapters) to the legislature as a law- or policy-making institution, but we have also sought to show that conceiving the legislative system solely in instrumental terms (as a sort of policy-making factory) is inadequate and incomplete. We have eschewed the policy-making approach because, among other things, (1) a considerable amount of politically relevant representational behavior occurs in legislative systems which is not immediately or directly related to specific policy outcomes, and (2) even where policy outcomes are considered, more fundamental than the policy processes themselves are those behavioral conditions that affect the policy configuration of a legislative system.

One set of "behavioral conditions" which we regard as most important involves the legislative norms, and the ways in which those norms are focused around specific locations in the structure of the legislative system, so as to constitute expectations about the behavior of individuals there. We have defined "role" in Chapter 1 as consisting of a pattern of reciprocal expectations of proper conduct among those who occupy positions in the structure of the legislative system. An exhaustive description of the role structure of a legislative system would involve a complete map of the interactions among participants and a definitive analysis of the sum total of behavioral expectations that participants share about each system position. Legislative behavior research has by no means provided adequate empirical data for such a complete description. It is, however, now possible to enter into the role structure of American legislative systems to some extent—at least to the extent of examining *some* of the variations in the legislative role.

The norms of the larger society, as well as those operating in the legislature itself, define the generalized role of the American legislator. However, the American legislative system is an open society in the sense that, within the framework of a rudimentary consensus, considerable flexibility is possible in the legislator's definition of his job. We will, in this chapter, be concerned with the role *orientations* of congressmen and state legislators—that is, with the patterns of variability that have been observed in the role conceptions of American legislators. While we have used role as an interpretive concept in earlier chapters, we here synthesize research that bears directly upon legislative role systems.

All of this sounds very promising, but in fact our claims are modest. As the reader will discover, our analysis rests more on the importance of the subject than on any plethora of empirical material. The data available to us are uneven, and our commentary about state legislative roles can be much more systematic than it can about congressional roles. In the latter case, we must be more general and illustrative.

A LEGISLATIVE ROLE MODEL

Role theory of legislative behavior has been adequately developed, so that our analysis can proceed tentatively around a model of legislative role orientations of the sort depicted in Figure 16.1. Here we take the perspective of the legislator, and attempt to show the major components of role orientation for him. We have placed the legislator in the context of a legislative input-output scheme in which the inputs into the system are the demands made, the expectations held, and the support and resources provided by constituency, interest group, party, and the bureaucratic components of the system. The outputs are shown as decisions (action on bills and resolutions), policies (to include formulations of goals and means not necessarily enacted into law), and services; to make the model more complete, we indicate the feedback from outputs to inputs.

Our model suggests eight categories of orientation for the legislative role. While it draws very heavily upon the study of the role structure of four state legislatures, it is a useful, if not entirely satisfactory, con-

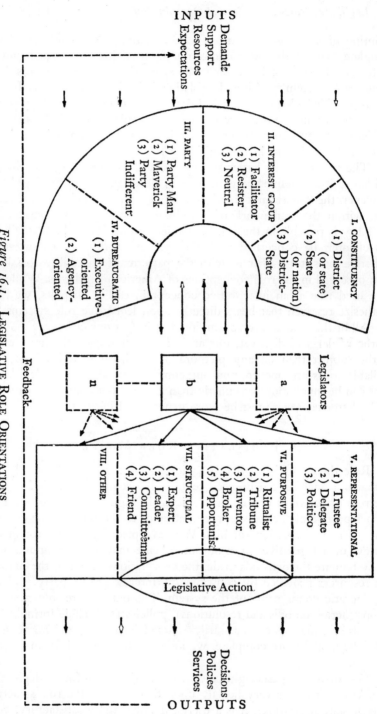

Figure 16.1. LEGISLATIVE ROLE ORIENTATIONS

ceptualization for the analysis of both congressional and state legislative roles.[1] The specific role orientations depicted in Figure 16.1 can be described briefly as follows:

I. CONSTITUENCY ROLE ORIENTATIONS: orientations in which the geographical entity of the constituency is the focus of representation.
   A. *District-oriented (or state-oriented)*. The legislator conceives his job explicitly as that of sponsoring and supporting legislation for the benefit of the constituency from which he is elected.
   B. *State-oriented (or nation-oriented)*. The legislator overcomes the parochial interests of county, district, or state, and conceives his job in terms of the general policy; the state legislator concerns himself more with broad state policy as opposed to the narrower interests of his county or district; the congressman concerns himself more with national programs and policies than with his district or state.
   C. *State-district-oriented (or district-nation, state-nation-oriented)*. The legislator gives analytically undifferentiated weight to the interests of his own constituency and of the larger political system.

II. INTEREST-GROUP ROLE ORIENTATIONS: orientations of the legislator toward political interest groups.
   A. *Facilitators*. Legislators who are knowledgeable about group activity and have a friendly attitude toward pressure groups.
   B. *Resisters*. Legislators who are knowledgeable about group activity and have a hostile attitude toward it.
   C. *Neutrals*. Legislators who have little knowledge of pressure group activity, or no strong attitudes toward it, either favorably or unfavorably.

III. PARTY ROLE ORIENTATIONS: the legislator's conception of his job as a member of the political party to which he belongs.
   A. *Party Man*. The legislator who conceives of his job as supporting the program of his party or its leaders, regardless of his own judgments or the consequences of party loyalty.
   B. *Maverick*. The legislator who sees his job as taking a course independent of partisan programs or leadership, and who votes with the other party with some regularity.
   C. *Party Indifferent*. The legislator who eschews partisan considerations, who conceives his job after his election to be that of representing all citizens regardless of party; for him party has little salience.

IV. BUREAUCRATIC ROLE ORIENTATIONS: orientations of the legislator toward the executive (governor, President), or toward the administrative apparatus.
   A. *Executive-oriented*. The legislator who sees his job as that of spokesman for the executive officer in the legislative body, who considers his job to be that of introducing the governor's or President's program, defending the executive's bills, and seeking their passage, and who may defend the executive generally; or the legislator who sees his job as opposing the executive.

B. *Agency-oriented.* The legislator who sees his job as that of spokesman for, or opponent of, some governmental administrative agency.
V. Representational Role Orientations: the orientation the legislator
takes with regard to the way in which decisions are to be made, regardless of whether his focus of representation is district, political party,
interest group, administrative agency, or a combination of these.
A. *Trustee.* The representative who sees himself as a free agent, required to make decisions according to principles, conviction, and
conscience.
B. *Delegate.* The legislator who thinks that his decisions ought not
be premised upon his own independent judgment, but that he ought
to consult his constituents, accept their instructions, or even follow
their mandate when it may differ from his own convictions.
C. *Politico.* The legislator who expresses both Trustee and Delegate role
orientations.
VI. Purposive Role Orientations: the legislator's orientation to the purposes and processes of the legislative institution.
A. *Ritualist.* The legislator whose concept of his role involves the technical routines of legislative work—committee work, rules and procedures, progress of bills, and so forth.
B. *Tribune.* The legislator who conceives his job as that of discovering
popular feelings and desires, defending popular interests, or advocating popular demands.
C. *Inventor.* The legislator who sees his major tasks as those related
to the creation, formulation, and initiation of public policy.
D. *Broker.* The legislator who conceives his job in terms of compromising, arbitrating, coordinating, and integrating conflicting demands
and interests within the legislative body.
E. *Opportunist.* The legislator who accepts only the bare minimum of
expectations about the legislative role, and uses his legislative office
to play essentially non-legislative roles.
VII. Structural Role Orientations: the orientation of the legislator toward other critical legislative roles (experts, leaders), or to critical
structural features of the legislative institution (committees, informal
groups or cliques).
A. *Expert.* The legislator who regards himself, and is regarded by
others, as having special subject-matter expertise.
B. *Leader.* The legislator who performs integrative and directional
functions, gives cues to others for their behavior; this includes occupants of official leadership positions (speaker, floor leaders, whips,
committee chairmen), and informal leaders.
C. *Committeeman.* The legislator whose conception of his job is as
a member of a legislative committee or subcommittee.
D. *Friend.* The legislator whose role conception includes interpersonal
relations vis-a-vis his legislative friends and companions.

The legislature is a role *system* in the sense that roles are interrelated in a network. In principle, the legislative system as a whole can be viewed as a role system in which the roles of legislators, lobbyists, constituents, administrative officials, party leaders, the executive, and perhaps other relevant actors are interrelated. Our model focuses only upon the legislator's role and deals with it in terms of his role orientations. This restriction in practice is called for by the limited empirical evidence now available. But within these limitations, it is possible to view the legislative role system through the interpenetration of role orientations. A legislator's "role-set" may consist in a variety of combinations of orientations; thus, a representative may be a District-oriented-Facilitator-Delegate-Broker-Tribune, and perhaps also an anti-Agency-oriented-Expert-Maverick. In actual, ongoing legislative institutions, a variety of combinations of role orientations are possible in principle and observable empirically.

Constituency Role Orientations. It certainly seems safe to say that a substantial proportion of American legislators, both national and state, are oriented to the geographical territory within which they are elected and feel responsible for the interests of their districts. We lack systematic and inclusive evidence on this point with respect to congressmen, although a number of distinguished commentators have alleged that congressmen are more committed to their district (or their state, in the case of United States Senators) than to the more ambiguous entities of the state or nation as a whole. In the congressman's scheme of values, says Galloway, "the interests of the district come first, of his state second, and of the nation third."[2] Of course, a representative may identify his district's interests and the state or national interests as synonomous, but the extent to which congressmen select one area focus over another is impressive. One congressman expressed the district-oriented focus in an almost classic way:

> My first duty is to get reelected. I'm here to represent my district. . . . This is part of my actual belief as to the function of a congressman. . . . What is good for the majority of districts is good for the country. What snarls up the system is these so-called statesmen—congressmen who vote for what they think is the country's interest . . . let the Senators do that. . . . They're paid to be statesmen; we [members of the House] aren't.[3]

The incompleteness of the communications between congressman and constituent (which we noted in Chapter 14) does not obviate the predominant district-orientation that appears to characterize members of the Congress. Given the nature of the legislative recruitment function both for national and state legislatures in the United States, the localistic orientation of American legislators is not surprising.

Investigations of the constituency role orientations of American state legislators indicate the generality of District-oriented foci in American legislative systems. As one Wisconsin legislator put it:

An assemblyman's job is representing his county or district. He should serve the interests which are most important in that county. His task is to determine what the major interests in the county are, and then see how proposed legislation would affect those interests.[4]

Interviews with all or nearly all of the members of six state legislatures, in which members were asked to develop their own role conceptions, provide the basis for making some interstate comparisons in constituency role orientations. These orientations, for the four states investigated by Wahlke, Eulau, Buchanan, and Ferguson, are shown in Table 16.1. The

Table 16.1. CONSTITUENCY ORIENTATIONS OF LEGISLATORS, 1957
(In percentages)

Constituency Orientations	Calif. (N=113)	N.J. (N=79)	Ohio (N=162)	Tenn. (N=120)	Total (N=474)
District	35	27	28	21	27
District and State	14	28	25	8	19
State	20	14	16	9	15
No mention	31	31	31	62	39
Total	100	100	100	100	100

SOURCE: H. Eulau, J. C. Wahlke, W. Buchanan, and L. C. Ferguson, "The Role of the Representative: Some Empirical Observations on the Theory of Edmund Burke," *American Political Science Review*, LIII (1959), 753.

table indicates a higher proportion of District-oriented legislators in every state except New Jersey, where a very slightly higher proportion were District-and-State oriented. Also the table illustrates the empirical reality of the constituency orientation of legislative roles. At the same time, these data create some difficulties which make them less than definitive. In three of the states studied by Wahlke and his associates, nearly one-third of the legislators interviewed could not be classified for this kind of analysis, and in Tennessee nearly two-thirds could not be classified. In all probability the data in Table 16.1 underestimate the extensiveness of District-oriented representatives in American state legislatures. At any rate, studies of the legislators in Wisconsin and Pennsylvania, where the problem of missing data was not so serious as for the states reported in Table 16.1, suggest a considerably higher proportion of District-oriented legislators. Sorauf found that, of Pennsylvania legislators in 1958, 35 percent of the Democrats and 56 percent of the Republicans could be characterized as District-oriented.[5] Again, data gathered by Patterson for the 1957 session of the Wisconsin Assembly, when coded according to the categories utilized by Wahlke and his associates, reveal a much higher proportion of District-oriented representatives than is reported for any of the states shown in Table 16.1. Interview data were available for 90 percent of the members of the Assembly; of the total (N=89), 70 percent were District-oriented.[6]

Of course, interstate variations in constituency role orientations are to be expected and can, to some extent, be understood in terms of interstate differences in political culture. In Pennsylvania a substantial amount of localism in state politics based on a tradition of party fragmentation may help to explain its legislators' District orientation. In Wisconsin political independence is a well-established norm, and there is some evidence to suggest its special legislative impact.[7]

There are legislators in every state, and in Congress as well, whose area focus is broader. Table 16.1 shows that 9 to 20 percent of the legislators in California, New Jersey, Ohio, and Tennessee were State-oriented, and the data for the 1957 Wisconsin Assembly show that 17 percent were State-oriented. This orientation is illustrated very well by the comments of one state legislator:

> Well, I consider the state legislature to be like a board of directors of a great state on the same plane as in a large corporation. I feel the legislator has two basic responsibilities—to represent their own section, but beyond that to exercise judgment in representing all the people of the state. You should look at a problem in terms of what is best for the state today and in the future. . . . I would go with the general good of the state over the county. . . .[8]

The District-state oriented legislators, who constitute about a quarter of the legislators in New Jersey and Ohio, 14 percent in California, and 10 percent or less in Wisconsin and Tennessee, appear to give important weight in their role conceptions both to state and district, although "these hyphenated legislators may more resemble district-oriented than state-oriented respondents in attitudes and behavior."[9]

We would expect the area focus of the legislative role to have a relationship to the political milieu in which the legislator is elected— representatives from politically competitive districts should be more District-oriented than those from "safe" districts, while legislators elected from one-party districts should be more State-oriented. This set of expected relationships between political environment and role conception is borne out by the data for California, New Jersey, Ohio, and Wisconsin; in none of these states is the relationship simply an artifact of rural-urban differences in the political competitiveness of legislative districts.[10]

The constituency role orientations of legislators are closely tied to certain of the service outputs of the legislative system, and in particular to "errand-boy" and educational activities. We noted in Chapter 14 some of the errand-boy activities of congressmen in handling case mail, and while such activities do prevail in state legislatures, they are perhaps less important there than in Washington. Similarly, educational activities are more notable at the congressional level. Speeches, newspaper columns, newsletters, and other communications devices are common for the performance of these educational activities. The newsletter is perhaps the most notable. About 90 percent of the members of Congress use newsletters to constituents, and these newsletters increasingly have an educational purpose.[11] As we would expect, District-oriented legislators (among state legislators, at any rate) are more likely to engage in these service activities than are State-oriented legislators.[12]

Interest-group Role Orientations. In Chapter 12 we discussed the role orientations of lobbyists, and suggested the legislators' role responses to interest groups. The only data that fulfill the Facilitator-Neutral-Resister conceptualizations are those from interviews with legislators in California, New Jersey, Ohio, and Tennessee.[13] These data indicate that in the relatively pluralistic states of California, New Jersey, and Ohio, where pressure politics is fairly highly developed, about two-fifths of the legislators take the Facilitator orientation, about one-fifth the Resister orientation, and the remainder are Neutrals. More than three-fourths of the Tennessee legislators were either Neutrals or Resisters, which suggests both that absence of partisanship does not necessarily increase the importance or salience of interest-group politics for legislators and that underdeveloped pluralistic group life, along with negative legislator attitudes toward interest-group activity, may provide a political culture that lessens the importance of pressure-group politics for legislators.[14]

Party Role Orientations. In the following chapter we will deal in some detail with the party voting behavior of American legislators. But the party attachments of legislators can be viewed in terms of their normative expectations about conformity to party. Orientations toward political parties are ambiguous in American politics, and it is not always clear whether legislators, in verbalizing their expectations about partisan behavior, are referring to the legislative or the extralegislative parties. The legislative party in Congress "appears to extend little beyond the survival of the group as a scheduling device and as a means of allocating instrumental rewards such as committee assignments."[15] But, as Truman has suggested,

Even these seem in many instances to be contingent upon the satisfaction of norms deriving from elsewhere in the political system, upon the reconciliation of the legislator's multiple group memberships. Yet the norms do seem at times to include more than procedural functions. When the competing demands of loyalties outside the legislative party are not dominant, the norms of the legislative party apparently can reach into areas of significant substantive policy.[16]

Without minimizing the importance of party orientations in the Congress, we must point out that the scope of party orientations may vary considerably among members, even when they are party-oriented. The fragmentation and localism of American party organization make the congressional district a rather autonomous unit in the party structure. Legislators who have the same party label may respond to their party in different ways, because the scope of their focus is their district party rather than the national party. And, when the congressman owes his election to a well-organized, well-disciplined district party organization, he may even be relatively free from national-party and other pressures.

Indeed, there is considerable reason to believe that a strong local party organization either insulates him or screens out the conflicting pressures so that he finds it easier to clarify and vote his personal convictions. Professional party men tend to be reluctant to tell each other how to do their jobs. Contrariwise, when the district party organization is inchoate, factional, and the incumbent is highly dependent upon his own personal organization, he is much more exposed to conflicting group demands and to claims placed upon him by personal-financial and friendly sources of support.[17]

Where legislators who are party-oriented conceptualize their roles in terms of the legislative party, they may conceive of the legislative party in different ways. Differences in the meaning of party orientation can be observed not only in different legislatures, but also within the same legislative body. Party-oriented legislators who were members of the 1952 session of the Massachusetts legislature fell into three categories in terms of the meanings they gave to party: those who saw party as a vehicle for the advancement of class or ideological forces, those who defined party issues by the activity of the party leaders, and those who were principally oriented to the party program.[18] Differences between Republicans and Democrats in their party orientations were not significant among Massachusetts legislators, although Leiserson found that Republican congressmen were somewhat more party-oriented than Democrats (on the strength of interviews with a small sample of members of the United States House of Representatives).[19]

The Party Man is the legislator who votes with his party and supports his party's program. As a Party Man in the 1957 Wisconsin Assembly put it: "It's absolutely necessary for a member to vote with his party on party platform bills. It's your bible, and if you don't want to belong to that religion, you should get another bible."[20] The Party Man gives great weight to party in orienting his behavior; he supports the party leadership; he may support the legislative party even when the party position is at variance with his own preferences. But his party expectations do not necessarily require blind loyalty to party. Studies of state legislators' party orientations indicate that Party Men may deviate from the decisions of party caucuses if they do so within the party framework and explain their problems to party colleagues (usually at the caucus). The most generally acceptable reason for departing from party loyalty among Party Men arises when the legislator believes that the interests of his district require him to act contrary to a party position. But in partisan state legislatures few representatives are likely to perceive significant differences between party role expectations and the interests of their district. For instance, among party-oriented Republicans in the Wisconsin Assembly, more than three-fourths said that conflicts between the interests of their party and the interests of their districts were "infrequent."[21]

Among state legislators, the extent of party role orientations varies greatly. Obviously, such orientations are not meaningful in nonpartisan or one-party legislatures. In states such as Wisconsin, New Jersey, Ohio, and Massachusetts party role orientations have great importance, and expectancies related to party are frequent. We would expect party role behavior to be more intensely and widely expected as partisan competition increases in the legislature. In some states, like California, where the legislature is changing from nonpartisan to partisan, party-oriented role-playing appears to be increasingly expected. But the data are not conclusive; Sorauf found a relatively low incidence of party-oriented expectations in the highly partisan Pennsylvania legislature.[22]

Party role orientations are clearly affected by the majority-minority status of the legislative party. A legislative party with a large majority may tolerate more deviation from party positions than one that is functioning under circumstances where the margins are close between parties. Again, the minority party member may exhibit very limited party role orientations, as is illustrated by the following comments by two Democratic members of the Wisconsin Assembly:

The Democrats are in the minority, so the only thing we can do is hold them on the line—we have to hold them to the manual.

A minority member should try to get his party's program through. But when you're in the minority, you have a hell of a time getting anything through, except pointing up what's wrong with the majority party.[23]

The legislator who eschews partisan expectations about his behavior, who serves in a legislature where partisan expectations are not relevant, or who endeavors to "rise above party," we shall call an Indifferent. Presumably legislators in nonpartisan and one-party state legislatures

could be said to be Indifferent with respect to their party role orientations. But even in partisan legislatures, some members may be Indifferents
—like the Wisconsin legislator who said: "I never listen to anything that
goes on in caucus. Everybody in caucus speaks for his own selfish interest in their district." Sometimes the hopelessness of minority status
appears to be the basis for the Indifferent orientation. In the 1957
Wisconsin Assembly some Democrats defined their roles in such a way
as to minimize their partisan obligations and maximize cooperation with
the Republican majority.

> A minority member can't get anything passed if you become a red-
> hot party man. They don't hold it against our floor leader or assistant floor
> leader; that's their job. But if any other member gets violently partisan he's
> in trouble. They won't let him pass any legislation. It's better to have a re-
> cord of accomplishment.

Another Wisconsin legislator illustrates the Indifferent who rises above
party:

> I was elected to the Assembly on a party vehicle, but after the election
> an assemblyman represents all the people of his district and should conduct
> his job on a nonpartisan basis. There have to be two parties, but I supported
> beneficial Republican legislation. If you can't get your bill passed you support
> a similar Republican bill. There should be closer harmony between the
> parties on bills that benefit the people.[24]

The Indifferent role orientation hangs between the Party Man and the
Maverick. He may or may not vote consistently with his party on party
issues, but he does not attach great importance to partisan expectations.
   The Maverick regularly and persistently deviates from the position
of his party; he takes an independent course; he has a reputation for
deviancy and independence from party, and other members expect him
to behave that way. Senators Wayne Morse (D-Ore) and William
Proxmire (D-Wis) are good illustrations of Mavericks in the United
States Senate, where Mavericks have been not at all unusual. Maverick
role expectations have not been widely characteristic in American state
legislatures. Of the members of the four state legislatures studied by
Wahlke and his associates, half or more did not make reference to
Maverick orientations. The percentages of these legislators referring
to Mavericks in their legislatures were:

Tennessee	6
New Jersey	30
California	39
Ohio	50

But in a state like Wisconsin, where political independence in the legislature is supported by norms in the wider political community, Maverick orientations are much more notable and more widely expected. Almost all the Republicans in the 1957 session of the Wisconsin Assembly recognized and identified a Maverick role.

Intralegislative variations in party role orientations are related both to the majority-minority status of the legislative party and to the degree of electoral competition in legislative districts. The strength and flexibility of the party role tends to be greater where the legislative party is the majority, and lesser for minority party members. Mavericks tend to be elected from districts that are atypical of their party, or where electoral margins are close. But interstate variations in party role orientations are more complex, involving important differences between states in their political environments or cultures. A partisan political culture might be defined as one in which party conflicts are perceived as highly relevant and important, where emotional involvement in and attachment to party is significant, and where political actors evaluate positively party influence in policy-making. Since these kinds of attitudes and beliefs about partisanship vary from state to state, the political cultures in which legislatures act are clearly varied. Attitudes toward, and presumably enactment of, party roles will tend to vary in terms of the partisan political culture; one correlation analysis among the factors suggested here has provided support for the proposition that "the more a legislature's political culture is party-oriented, the more likely will legislators look on the role of the party man as a positive asset of his total legislative position."[25]

Bureaucratic Role Orientations. Legislators may be executive-oriented or agency-oriented (or both) with reference to the executive branch of government. In state legislatures, the "Governor's man" is a common role orientation, though it may take various forms and have varied results. In some states, especially those of the South and Southwest, the state governors have often been in a position to designate their legislative leaders, who occupy the official leadership positions in the legislature.[26] But these relationships are not always stable. In California, for instance, the floor leader had been considered the governor's spokesman in the Progressive days, but this practice was abandoned in the 1920s. Thereafter, in the individualistic and relatively nonpartisan California House, the chairman of the Ways and Means Committee came to be recognized as the spokesman for the governor, while the majority floor leader came to represent the institutionalization of opposition to the governor.[27] The highly atomized legislative politics of Florida has tended to make gubernatorially oriented legislative roles untenable, and the governor is often required to bargain individually with legislators.[28] Of course, executive-oriented roles are more general in American legislatures, and go beyond those who are gubernatorial spokesmen to include any legislator who defines his job in terms of executive leadership. Legislators who take their cues from the governor and whose role expectations are executive-oriented are fairly common in partisan legislatures, where the governor shares the same party identification as the legislative majority, as well as in nonpartisan or one-party legislatures, where the governor is the dominant legislative leader.[29]

In Congress, and in a few state legislatures, executive-oriented roles are patterned institutionally so that it is possible to describe the legislative role structure crudely in terms of "administration supporters" and the "loyal opposition." But executive-legislator interaction in the national Congress is much more complex and ambiguous than it is in most states. In Congress, official and informal leadership roles are very unlikely to be played by different individuals, and the President is usually required to rely upon his party's congressional leaders, even though their loyalties and orientations tend to be directed toward the legislative institution. While "the fundamental complexity and subtlety of the role lie in the fact that the elective leaders are, and probably must be, both the President's leaders and the party's leaders," congressional leaders are usually disposed to "play down their spokesmanship for the President."[30]

In addition to executive orientation, American legislators may be agency-oriented. Their formal legislative positions, the nature of their constituencies, or their substantive legislative interests may lead them to orient their jobs toward a specific administrative agency or set of agencies. Legislative committee structure and norms of specialization frequently facilitate agency orientation, especially among congressmen. Some members of Congress, typically those who have served for many years, know certain administrative agencies or departments intimately, and frequently have had more experience with them than the agency heads themselves. These members may come to take very personal interests in agency operations, and have great influence upon agency policy.[31]

The relationships between legislators and bureaucrats, while they are persistent (especially in the case of congressmen) and often mutually agreeable, tend to be characterized by suspicion, jealousy, and hostility. "The role of the legislator versus the bureaucrat is an old one," Huitt has observed, "rooted in an institutional jealousy never hard to arouse."[32] And the tensions in legislator–agency relationships may be quite impersonal, as was reflected, for example, in the exchange between Senator Robert A. Taft and Chester Bowles (who was Director of Economic Stabilization) during hearings before the Senate Committee on Banking and Currency on the question of price controls after World War II. Taft told Bowles:

I don't distinguish you from the administration. The administration has one policy; you are the Director of Economic Stabilization. What your particular views are makes no difference to me. You are carrying on the policies of the administration. When I say "You" I should be more explicit. I mean the administration. I am not attacking you personally on it, or anything of the sort. I am criticizing your analysis of the situation which is only affected by administration policy; not what you personally think. That makes no difference to me.[33]

The resentments and hostilities of legislators toward administrators is often reflected in the context of committee or subcommittee hearings. While "there is seldom the element of direct challenge to the personal status of the legislator, . . . the authoritative and self-assured way in which the administrator disposes of his own knowledge and the legislator's questions can . . . become a source of uneasiness," because "the administrator deals self-confidently with a matter which the legislator does not always grasp with the same measure of self-confidence."[34]

Tensions between legislators and administrators are very well illustrated by Freeman's analysis of the relationships between bureaucrats in the Bureau of Indian Affairs and congressional committees, especially the House and Senate Committees on Indian Affairs. He concluded that:

The committee member's role, in which he is expected to choose wisely among policy alternatives as well as to represent his local constituency, tends to create blocks against his receptivity to the views of bureau leaders, despite their often alleged superior technical knowledge. The committee member frequently feels a strong urge to protect his status as the lawmaker in the face of bureaucratic challenge. Consequently, the committee member often prefers information and suggestions about policy from sources other than bureau leaders and their allies. Furthermore, he may frequently play something less than a neutral role in the deliberations within the sub-system by giving encouragement to non-bureau spokesmen. Certainly, even if the committee member does not feel especially sensitive about his status relative to that of bureaucrats, on occasions in which the committee member's interests lie counter to the bureau leader's, he may find it convenient to pretend that the bureaucrat is attempting to preempt the legislative function and to lay claim to a superiority of knowledge that is based on theory rather than on practicality.[35]

Members of Congress have, and must virtually cultivate, regular and personal relationships with bureaucrats. Their need for information is enormous, and administrative agencies often provide the only expertise available. The frequent recourse to personal intervention with administrative agencies on behalf of constituents "has greater consequences than the maintenance of a sensitive attachment of the legislator to his audible constituency. . . . It fosters in him a particular attitude of personal ex-

pectancy toward the bureaucracy and towards the individual administrator."[36] Robinson has estimated that 75 percent of the members of the
House and Senate discuss some topic with the Department of State each
week, and most of these communications concern the representative's
constituents. In interviewing a sample of congressmen, Robinson investigated the association between approval of State Department foreign
policy and various aspects of the communications linkage between congressmen and the Department. He found that "statistically significant relations do not exist between Congressmen's satisfaction with the way the
Department of State handles requests from constituents and satisfaction
with foreign policy," but

Significant relations are observed between satisfaction with other aspects of
the communications network linking Congress and the Department and
foreign policy. These include the Department's record for answering requests
for policy information, volunteering information to Congress, and perception
of the weight of Congressional opinion in the Department's formulation of
policy.[37]

Representational Role Orientations. Legislators' role orientations
may differ in terms of their style of representation. The Trustee sees
himself as a free agent, premising his decision-making behavior upon
what he considers morally right and just, and following the dictates of
his judgment and conscience. John F. Kennedy, when he was still a
United States Senator from Massachusetts, once articulated a Trustee
conceptualization of the legislative role. He said:

The voters selected us . . . because they had confidence in our judgment
and our ability to exercise that judgment from a position where we could
determine what were their own best interests, as a part of the nation's
interests. This may mean that we must on occasion lead, inform, correct and
sometimes even ignore constituent opinion, if we are to exercise fully that
judgment for which we were elected.[38]

In the same vein, a state legislator clearly set forth the Trustee orientation when he explained his conception of the legislator's job:

I have never subscribed to the theory that I'm here to reflect the views of
my constituents. I'm here to vote as I see it. You can't vote by what you
think the constituents' thinking is. You don't know what that thinking is. . . .[39]

But surely a substantial proportion of American legislators are inclined to a non-Burkean formulation of the legislative role. The Delegate
thinks of his job in terms of reflecting constituent opinion. Among a large
number of illustrations of this role orientation, here are two expressions
of it from Wisconsin legislators:

I regard myself as the servant of the people, not their master. Whether

I believe in something or not, I go along with the people in my district when I'm voting on legislation. Daylight saving is a good example. I was personally opposed to it, but the people in my district wanted it, so I voted for it.

Another said:

My duty is to go to Madison and vote the way the people in my district want me to, whether I personally agree with it or not. I'm not going to Madison to do what I want, but what the people want.[40]

The Politico is an intermediate type, the legislator who is sometimes a Trustee, sometimes a Delegate, or who reconciles both orientations. One state legislator who appeared to combine both Trustee and Delegate orientations said:

There is a line of demarcation between what they want at home and what you think is good for them. I haven't been too disturbed by that yet but it could become a major problem. I don't think I could ever settle just where the line is. It is too flexible. Each piece of legislation must be considered individually to determine it. . . .[41]

It is possible to compare the representational role orientations of legislators in six states; such a comparison is made in Table 16.2. These

Table 16.2. DISTRIBUTION OF REPRESENTATIONAL ROLE
ORIENTATIONS, 1957
(In percentages)

Representational Role Orientation	Calif. (N=49)	N.J. (N=54)	Ohio (N=114)	Tenn. (N=78)	Wis. (N=89)	Pa. (N=106)
Trustee	55	61	56	81	21	33
Politico	25	22	29	13	4	27
Delegate	20	17	15	6	66	39
Not classifiable	—	—	—	—	9	1
Total	100	100	100	100	100	100

SOURCES: J. C. Wahlke et al., *The Legislative System* (New York: John Wiley and Sons, 1962), p. 281; F. J. Sorauf, *Party and Representation* (New York: Atherton Press, 1963), p. 124; Patterson's unpublished study of the 1957 Wisconsin Assembly.

data present numerous anomalies. Wahlke and his associates argue, apparently *post facto*, that legislators ought to be found to be predominantly Trustees because the business of government has become so complicated and technical that people are neither capable of nor interested in giving their representative instructions. But it might be argued that legislators are increasingly able to get their constituents' opinions, given rapid transportation and communication, polls, and the like. Certainly governmental life is simpler in Tennessee than in California, New Jersey, or Ohio, and yet 81 percent of the Tennessee legislators were found to be Trustees.

Wahlke and his associates found a relatively low proportion of Delegates in California, New Jersey, Ohio, and Tennessee. Yet in the Wisconsin Assembly, two-thirds of the legislators were Delegates, and a preponderance of Pennsylvania representatives were Delegates. The complications of modern government are not likely to have been less serious in Wisconsin and Pennsylvania than in the states Wahlke and his associates studied. We can at present offer no rationale to reconcile these anomalies in the data except to say that the findings for Wisconsin and Pennsylvania cast grave doubt upon the conclusion that "the trustee role is the easiest and the delegate role the most difficult to take."[42] But Table 16.2 does demonstrate the empirical possibility of categorizing legislators analytically in terms of the stylistic dimension of representation.

Purposive Role Orientations. One cannot observe the floor action of an American legislature without being impressed with the importance of the *process*—the rules of procedure, the steps in the passage of legislation, the importance of committee work and the ritual of floor debate and action. In some legislatures, particularly the amateur state legislative bodies, there are members who are very minimally adapted to the legislative role. They may be process-oriented only to the extent of sitting in the audience, hardly participating at all—they are simply Spectators. Others' purposive orientations may be more to their private occupational and career ambitions than to legislative processes. These members may use legislative office primarily to advertise their private occupations. They are Advertisers, lacking both the commitment to legislative work and the patience to master legislative skills. Still other members may be minimally adapted to the legislative role in terms of their general reluctance to enact it fully. The Reluctant finds the legislature populated by strangers with different backgrounds and values than his own, he finds the pace of legislative processes suspiciously swift, and he may be baffled, confused and discomfited by the complicated processes of lawmaking.[43] Legislators whose adaptation to the legislative process is more fully developed are likely to have a fairly wide range of role orientations.

In state legislatures a high proportion of representatives undoubtedly orient their jobs with regard to decision making in terms of the legislative rituals—and they can be called Ritualists. Perhaps the leading illustration of a Ritualist in the United States House of Representatives is H. R. Gross (R-Ia), whose only important claim to fame in the House has been his mastery and skillful use of the rules of procedure—especially his objections to unanimous-consent requests—so as to obstruct legislation and frustrate the leadership. Clearly, the legislative body would be immobilized if a large proportion of the membership were not oriented toward the mechanics of the legislative process.

Other orientations toward legislative purposes are important, too. Some legislators approach their tasks as advocates and defenders of popular wishes, needs, and desires—and these representatives can be called Tribunes. Others are innovators and creators of policy directions or programs—the Inventers. Still others mediate and negotiate conflicting interests—the Brokers. Many legislators play a combination of these roles.

The only careful study of these analytical role types, that of California, New Jersey, Ohio and Tennessee, indicates that the Ritualist orientation is most common in all states. The Broker orientation is taken by more than one-fourth of the legislators in New Jersey, Ohio, and California, but it is less important in Tennessee, where presumably interest-group conflict is not so complex. Tribune and Inventor orientations were found to be most important in New Jersey, where at the time party control of the legislature and the governorship was divided, and where, therefore, greater expressions of legislative initiative were to be expected.[44]

Structural Role Orientations. We discuss the roles of committee members and legislative leaders elsewhere, the former in Chapter 18 and the latter in Chapter 7. Readers interested in these roles should turn to the relevant sections of those chapters.

The role of the Expert is a particularly important and functional role-orientation, given the increasing specialization of American legislatures and the significance of specialization in the normative systems of these bodies. While the committee structures of legislatures provide the basis for the organization of legislative specialization, some legislators have reputations for, and respond to expectations about, specialization in particular policy arenas. With regard to Congress, expert role-playing is familiar. Well-known Senate experts like Fulbright (D-Ark) on foreign affairs, Morse (D-Ore) on labor law, Javits (R-NY) on legal matters, and Monroney (D-Okla) on legislative reorganization, and less familiar House specialists like Vinson (D-Ga) on defense, Fogarty (D-RI) on medical research, Kilday (D-Tex) on military regulations, Mills (D-Ark) on taxation, and Judd (R-Minn) on Asian policy, testify to the Expert role in the Congress.

Attributions of and expectations about expertise in state legislatures are no less important, although the state legislative Expert is perhaps less visible to the ordinary citizen. Considerable consensus among legislators who have been interviewed systematically suggests the functional importance of the Expert in the state legislature.[45] The subject-matter fields of legal problems, taxation, education, agriculture, conservation, labor, and local government tend to be those with which state legislative Experts deal most.

The Expert role carries with it considerable responsibility—"There is the feeling that the legislator-expert should play a dual role, responsible in some degree to his colleagues."[46] As one of the Experts in the 1957 Wisconsin Assembly put it: "I am very careful when I take a stand on bills to make sure that my vote is absolutely right and based on my very best judgment, because people respect my experience and I know they follow my vote. It is a very great responsibility."[47]

State legislative Experts tend to base their expertise upon their extralegislative occupational experience more than upon other factors, whereas congressmen may be more likely to develop expertise other than that which might be expected on the basis of their occupational experience. Finally, while partisan considerations are involved in expectations about Experts, these representatives tend to have reputations for special knowledge which cross party lines.

Role Interrelationships and Conflict. The role-orientations of American legislators are interrelated, and we would expect to find some kinds of orientations going naturally together. Thus, representational and constituency role orientations are, in a sense, complementary. We would expect the District-oriented legislator to take the Delegate orientation more than State-oriented or State–district-oriented representatives would, and we would expect the State-oriented legislator to take the Trustee orientation more than others. The data for state legislators confirm these expected combinations of role orientations. Wahlke and his associates found this to be the case in California, New Jersey, Ohio, and Tennessee, and the data in Table 16.3 support these findings for Wisconsin.[48] A complete map of the role structure of the legislative body would include analysis of the interpenetrations of each type of role orientation with all of the others, and an attempt at such an analysis with partial data has been made for the four legislatures studied by Wahlke and his associates. Their analysis suggests that "through the use of nonconventional analytical categories, in our case derived from a role analysis of legislators, we can describe the structure of a legislative chamber, not as it is embodied in rules and bylaws, . . . but as it represents a system of action."[49]

At the same time, the legislative role is particularly susceptible to conflicting expectations. Many a legislator has been torn between the demands of his constituents, political interest groups, and party leaders. Role conflict resolution is a social-psychological process about which we know rather little, but it is possible in legislative settings to observe behavior from which we can infer the existence of such a process.[50] Perhaps the problems of Silvio O. Conte (R-Mass) will serve as an adequate illustration of the occupational role strains that can be experienced by a congressman:

When I returned to my district office there were long and loud complaints that I was spending too much time there and should be in Washington. Then when I didn't make it for several weeks, others said, "Who does that guy think he is? We only see him during elections."

Table 16.3. CONSTITUENCY AND REPRESENTATIONAL ROLE ORIENTATIONS, WISCONSIN ASSEMBLY, 1957

(In percentages)

Representational Role Orientation	District-oriented (N = 62)	State-district-oriented (N = 9)	State-oriented (N = 15)
Trustee	13	34	53
Delegate	74	56	47
Politico	5	10	0
Not classified	8	0	0
Total	100	100	100

SOURCES: J. C. Wahlke et al., *The Legislative System* (New York: John Wiley and Sons, 1962), p. 281; F. J. Sorauf, *Party and Representation* (New York: Atherton Press, 1963), p. 124; Patterson's unpublished study of the 1957 Wisconsin Assembly.

When I came home shortly after being sworn in, driving my old car, they were upset because it looked like something farmers use to haul trash. But, by gosh, when I bought a new one, they were sure the lobbyists had gotten to me already.

The first time I came home wearing an old suit people said, "Look at him! Just an old bum." Yet when I bought a new suit, I heard, "He's gone high-hat with that Ivy League suit of his."

One Sunday I missed church because I was tied up talking with constituents and some people said that being down in Washington had made an atheist of me. Several weeks later, when I was again back home and did get to church, they said, "Why that pious fraud! He's just trying to dig up votes!"[51]

We do not wish to minimize the importance of role conflict in legislatures, or to make light of the difficulties, tensions, and agonies which individual legislators may experience in resolving conflicting expectations about how they should perform their jobs. On the other hand, some legislative role conflicts are probably fairly easily resolved, in at least two respects. First, the legislative process involves a multiplicity of decisional points, and the legislator can be guided by different orientations at different times. Jones's analysis of members of the House Agriculture Committee suggests how congressmen may resolve conflicting demands by taking different role orientations serially:

> The representative on the House Agriculture Committee can view his composite role retrospectively as one in which he has taken several separate actions to make up a total pattern in regard to the omnibus farm legislation. He also can recognize that on different occasions he felt differing demands upon him in his several capacities, as a member of a party, a representative of a constituency, a member of a committee, of a Congress, of interest groups, etc. He was able to reconcile, compromise or avoid some of the inherent conflicts in these demands, at least in part, because of the multiple action points.[52]

Second, a very common kind of potential legislative role conflict, that between constituency expectations and demands as opposed to others, is probably quite easily resolved by American legislators by simply deferring to constituency demands. While American legislators probably do not often perceive constituency versus state or national differences, or constituency-party differences, as very salient ones, even when they do they are likely to opt for the constituency expectations.[53]

INFORMAL LEGISLATIVE ORGANIZATION

The most visible features of the internal organization of legislative bodies are the structures of leadership, committee, and party. Not so visible, but perhaps equally important to the maintenance of the legislature, are the informal, unofficial organizations, committees, or cliques with which legislators associate, and within which friendship roles are enacted. We shall briefly discuss several types of informal legislative groups: friendship cliques, social groups, policy groups, and state delegations.

Although we have much to learn about the influence of legislative friendships upon policy making, we do have some clues to their importance. At least some members of Congress are convinced that the bipartisan exercises in the congressional gymnasium have policy implications. One congressman said:

> The gymnasium group is about the most influential one in the House. That isn't a joke either. Actually a lot of work is done in the gym. You can accomplish a lot on an informal, casual basis. You can discuss informally things you don't want to call a man about. One important value of the gym

is that it crosses party lines. You have an opportunity to get to know better the guys in the other party.[54]

Some legislatures have fairly highly developed friendship clique structures. Perhaps the best illustration of such a structure is the 1957 session of the Wisconsin Assembly, where friendship cliques were so well developed that some cliques had names familiar to the representatives. The major cliques in this legislature are depicted sociometrically in Figure 16.2, which shows these friendship groups by party affiliation. Some of these cliques had distinguishable "styles of legislative life," and there was a very marked tendency for clique members to vote together on the floor. Comparative analysis of friendship choices in four other state legislatures (California, New Jersey, Ohio, and Tennessee) has indicated "that the political roles of a legislator . . . are more compelling than his social role as a friend . . ." but "the latter does have an effect in the one chamber where we were able to test it," although "on the whole it was not large."[55]

Legislative social groups are fairly common in American legislatures, though they have been commented upon most in regard to Congress. The classes of entering freshman congressmen (87th Club, 88th Club) and their outgrowths with broader memberships, like the Chowder & Marching, SOS, and Acorn Republican groups, illustrate the rather active social life of national representatives. The House and Senate prayer breakfast groups, which include members of both parties, meet weekly for breakfast and prayer, and the "bonds between members of this group are unusually strong and . . . often expressed in acts of legislative cooperation."[56] The policy-making impact of such social activities may not be great, but under certain circumstances they may have important policy implications.

There are a number of congressional policy groups of an informal character; the best known congressional unofficial group, however, is the Democratic Study Group.[57] It was formally organized by liberal Democratic representatives late in the 1959 session of Congress, the outgrowth of an informal grouping developed in the two preceding years. Like their Republican counterparts at this time, many of the younger Democratic representatives were dissatisfied with the performance of the party leadership and were frustrated by their inability to make their own voices heard by the leadership. The Democrats in this group were distinctly liberal in orientation and represented primarily urban areas in the North and West; to a greater extent than was true of the Republican dissidents, viewpoints on policy issues provided the best clue both to the unity of this group and their differences with other members of the House Democratic party. Their dissatisfaction with the party leadership resulted from the belief that it was too cautious and too willing to compromise with more conservative elements in the party. The Democrats, unlike the Republican dissidents, decided to work through a distinct organization.

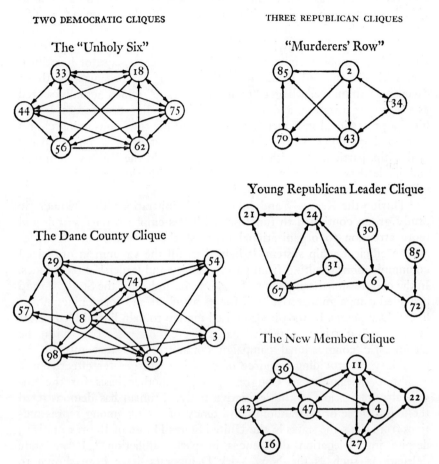

Figure 16.2. THE FRIENDSHIP CLIQUE STRUCTURE OF
THE WISCONSIN ASSEMBLY, 1957

SOURCE: S. C. Patterson, "Patterns of Interpersonal Relations in a State Legislative Group: The Wisconsin Assembly," *Public Opinion Quarterly*, XXIII (1959), 101–109.

Liberal Democratic representatives organized not only to make their voice more powerful but in order to serve their own needs. They needed information about the substance of issues, agreement within the group on tactics, and voting cues on the many detailed provisions of legislation that come to a vote. Kofmehl, who has conducted the most comprehensive study of the group, defines it as "an institutional response to these needs for improved communications." Obviously the organization had no sanctions that it could impose on disloyal members; one source of its effectiveness was that its membership was voluntary and that individual congressmen could avoid interaction with the group on specific issues when they found it necessary. The members perceived the group as a service agency, providing information, facilitating prompt communications among members, and giving members a sense of identification with like-minded Democrats. The group was organized with an executive committee, a larger "policy committee" which actually served as a whip organization, and a variety of fact-finding task forces. It also hired a professional staff member to perform the time-consuming chores that no single congressman could handle. It put pressure on the party leadership, particularly with regard to reforms in the Rules Committee, and its leaders frequently worked closely with the party leadership, when there was agreement on policy and tactics.[58]

During the Kennedy and Johnson Administrations, the Democratic Study group continued to function, with less emphasis on research and more attention to organizational matters—the coordination of tactics and an efficient whip system. It helped to fill the vacuum in organized communications resulting from party disunity and leadership techniques. In the congressional campaigns of 1960, 1962, and 1964, the Study Group provided campaign material both for its members and for nonincumbent liberal Democrats. In 1964 it also raised money to help liberal Democrats in marginal districts—a tactic that reflected dissatisfaction with the Democratic congressional campaign committee and that offered the possibility of providing a source of cohesion and greater effectiveness.

State delegations in Congress provide another basis for the unofficial organization of the legislative body. Truman has demonstrated the high degree of nonrandom consistency of voting among representatives from the same states in the United States House of Representatives, despite intradelegation differences in party affiliation.[59] Large state delegations, such as the New York Democrats, have been shown to provide information, advice, and voting cues to members.[60] Some small state delegations have been shown to be highly unified, especially where members of both parties in the delegation can unite in a bipartisan effort to defend state interests.[61] In some states the delegation from a major metropolitan center may form a group of comparable cohesion and importance within the legislative party.

These informal or unofficial groups, friendship cliques, social groups, policy groups, and state delegations complement the role structure of the legislature. As significant structural features of legislative institutions, these groups perform important functions for the maintenance of the legislature. The friendship and social groups tend to contribute most to the socialization function, but they may also provide companionship and status reassurance. All these kinds of unofficial groups facilitate communication, which is especially important in larger legislative bodies. They provide channels of access to committee or party leaders for rank-and-file representatives, and make more efficient the communication of influence and intelligence to leaders. Again, informal legislative groups constitute cue-giving or decision-facilitating mechanisms in the legislative body, including the providing of cues to members about voting. Finally, these groups contribute to legislative solidarity—facilitating the strategy of bloc voting, and also permitting representatives (from the same state, for instance) to present a united front to the electorate.

NOTES

1. The scheme that follows adheres closely to that of John C. Wahlke, Heinz Eulau, William Buchanan, and LeRoy C. Ferguson, *The Legislative System* (New York: John Wiley and Sons, 1962), pp. 170–413. See also David Easton, "An Approach to the Analysis of Political Systems," *World Politics*, IX (1956–57), 383–400; and Gabriel A. Almond, "Comparative Political Systems," *Journal of Politics*, XVIII (1956), 391–409.

2. George B. Galloway, *The Legislative Process in Congress* (New York, 1953), p. 374.

3. Lewis A. Dexter, "The Representative and His District," *Human Organization*, XVI (1957), 3. See also Raymond A. Bauer, Ithiel de Sola Pool, and Lewis A. Dexter, *American Business and Public Policy: The Politics of Foreign Trade* (New York, 1963), pp. 403–32, 445.

4. The quotation is from Patterson's unpublished study of the 1957 session of the Wisconsin Assembly. For additional illustrations, see Wahlke et al., *op. cit.*, pp. 289–90.

5. Frank J. Sorauf, *Party and Representation: Legislative Politics in Pennsylvania* (New York, 1963), p. 124.

6. From Patterson's unpublished study of the 1957 Wisconsin Assembly.

7. See, for example, Wilder W. Crane, Jr., "Do Representatives Represent?" *Journal of Politics*, XXII (1960), 295–99.

8. Wahlke, et al., *op. cit.*, p. 290.

9. *Ibid.*, p. 291.

10. The data for California, New Jersey, and Ohio appear in Wahlke et al., *op. cit.*, pp. 292–93.

11. Charles L. Clapp, *The Congressman: His Work As He Sees It* (Washington, D.C., 1963), pp. 89, 100; for a good illustration of a series of congressional newsletters with a primarily educational purpose see John W. Baker (ed.), *Member of the House: Letters of a Congressman by Clem Miller* (New York, 1962), pp. 1–140.

12. Wahlke et al., *op. cit.*, pp. 304–08.

13. *Ibid.*, pp. 323–42; John C. Wahlke, William Buchanan, Heinz Eulau, and LeRoy C. Ferguson, "American State Legislators' Role Orientations Toward Pressure Groups," *Journal of Politics*, XXII (1960), 203–27; and Samuel C. Patterson, "The Role of the Deviant in the State Legislative System: The Wisconsin Assembly," *Western Political Quarterly*, XIV (1961), 465–66.

14. For a study that deals with Facilitator, Resister, and Neutral orientations in the Wisconsin Assembly with regard to branch banking legislation, see Wilder Crane, Jr., "A Test of Effectiveness of Interest-group Pressures on Legislators," *Southwestern Social Science Quarterly*, XLI (1960), 335–40.

15. David B. Truman, "The State Delegations and the Structure of Party Voting in the United States House of Representatives," *American Political Science Review*, L (1956), 1045.

16. *Ibid.* See also David B. Truman, *The Congressional Party: A Case Study* (New York, 1959).

17. Avery Leiserson, "National Party Organization and Congressional Districts," *Western Political Quarterly*, XVI (1963), 643.

18. Corinne Silverman, "The Legislators' View of the Legislative Process," *Public Opinion Quarterly*, XVIII (1954), 184–88.

19. Leiserson, *op. cit.*, p. 647.

20. Patterson, "The Role of the Deviant in the State Legislative System," p. 462.

21. *Ibid.*, p. 468. See also Sorauf, *op. cit.*, p. 125.

22. Sorauf, *op. cit.*, p. 124.

23. From Patterson's unpublished study of the 1957 Wisconsin Assembly.

24. *Ibid.*

25. Wahlke et al., *op. cit.*, p. 371.

26. For a good example, see Hallie Farmer, *The Legislative Process in Alabama* (University, Ala., 1949), p. 168.

27. William Buchanan, *Legislative Partisanship: The Deviant Case of California* (Berkeley and Los Angeles, 1963), p. 91.

28. William C. Havard and Loren P. Beth, *The Politics of Mis-representation: Rural-Urban Conflict in the Florida Legislature* (Baton Rouge, La., 1962), pp. 196, 202.

29. For example, see Oliver Garceau and Corinne Silverman, "A Pressure Group and the Pressured: A Case Report," *American Political Science Review*, XLVIII (1954), 672–81; and George A. Bell and Evelyn L. Wentworth, *The Legislative Process in Maryland* (College Park, Md., 1958), p. 26.

30. Truman, *The Congressional Party*, pp. 298–300.

31. For a good illustration, see Rowland Evans, Jr., "The Sixth Sense of Carl Vinson," *The Reporter* (Apr. 12, 1962), pp. 25–30.

32. Ralph K. Huitt, "The Congressional Committee: A Case Study," *American Political Science Review*, XLVIII (1954), 349.

33. *Ibid.*, pp. 345–46.

34. Edward A. Shils, "The Legislator and His Environment," *University of Chicago Law Review*, XVIII (1951), 577. Surely a leading example would be that of Congressman Otto Passman (D-La). See Rowland Evans, Jr., "Louisiana's Passman: The Scourge of Foreign Aid," *Harper's Magazine* (January 1962), pp. 78–83.

35. J. Leiper Freeman, *The Political Process: Executive Bureau–Legislative Committee Relations* (Garden City, N.Y., 1955), p. 67.

36. Shils, *op. cit.*, p. 573.

37. James A. Robinson, *Congress and Foreign Policy-making* (Homewood, Ill., 1962) pp. 189–90.

38. Irwin J. Schulman, "The Case Against the 'Fireside Chat,'" *New York Times Magazine* (June 14, 1964), p. 70.

39. Wahlke et al., *op. cit.*, p. 275.

40. Patterson's unpublished study.

41. Wahlke et al., *op. cit.*, p. 279.

42. *Ibid.*, p. 286.

43. James D. Barber provides a lucid development of these orientations in his analysis of freshman Connecticut legislators. See his *The Lawmakers: Recruitment and Adaptation to Legislative Life* (New Haven, Conn., 1965).

44. Walhke et al., *op. cit.*, pp. 245–66. A somewhat similar formulation can be found in Garceau and Silverman, *op. cit.*, pp. 682–89, where some purposive

orientations are characterized as "policy-oriented," "program-oriented," "faction-oriented," and "non-generalizers."

45. Wahlke et al., *op. cit.*, pp. 193–215. See also Wayne L. Francis, "Influence and Interaction in a State Legislative Body," *American Political Science Review,* LVI (1962), 953–60.

46. *Ibid.*, p. 209.

47. Patterson's unpublished study.

48. Wahlke et al., *op. cit.*, p. 396.

49. *Ibid.*, p. 423.

50. See William C. Mitchell, "Occupational Role Strains: The American Elective Public Official," *Administrative Science Quarterly,* III (1958), 210–28.

51. *Washington Post and Times Herald* (Apr. 5, 1959), pp. E1–2.

52. Charles O. Jones, "Representation in Congress: The Case of the House Agriculture Committee," *American Political Science Review,* LV (1961), 367. For a comment along similar lines with reference to the Pennsylvania legislators, see Sorauf, *op. cit.*, p. 126.

53. This statement is illustrated for congressmen on the foreign trade issue in Bauer, Pool, and Dexter, *op. cit.*, pp. 444–50.

54. Clapp, *op. cit.*, p. 40. See also Samuel C. Patterson, "Patterns of Inter-personal Relations in a State Legislative Group: The Wisconsin Assembly," *Public Opinion Quarterly,* XXIII (1959), 101–09.

55. Wahlke et al., *op. cit.*, p. 235.

56. Clapp, *loc. cit.*

57. For example, see Neal A. Maxwell, "The Conference of Western Senators," *Western Political Quarterly,* X (1957), 902–10.

58. Kenneth Kofmehl, "The Institutionalization of a Voting Bloc," *Western Political Quarterly,* XVII (1964), 256–72.

59. David B. Truman, "The State Delegations and the Structure of Party Voting in the United States House of Representatives," pp. 1023–45.

60. Alan Fiellin, "The Functions of Informal Groups in Legislative Institutions," *Journal of Politics,* XXIV (1962), 72–91.

61. John H. Kessel, "The Washington Congressional Delegation," *Midwest Journal of Political Science,* VIII (1964), 1–21.

[Part VI]

THE LEGISLATURE
IN ACTION

M OST OF this volume has been devoted to legislative inputs: the selection of legislators; the factors affecting their roles; the legislative structure, norms and power distribution; the impact of outsiders on the legislative process. Now we focus primarily on the outputs in the legislative process.

Roll call analysis provides our best technique for evaluating the decisions recorded on the floor of the legislature. Most important and controversial issues that reach the floor are tested in roll calls, and these provide data that are precise and susceptible to measurement and analysis through relatively sophisticated techniques. These techniques give us evidence of role behavior that sheds light on legislative roles. When votes are taken, the groups that serve as potential sources of voting cues range widely through the legislative system, as we have seen. Under what circumstances does each group become salient for the legislator? When is he subject to conflicting pressures, and how are these resolved? Some of the answers are to be found in an examination of roll calls.

Many legislative decisions are reached in committees, where the process of decision making is often hidden from public view. But we know something about the sources and effects of committee norms, the factors that make certain committees cohesive and influential, the purposes served by hearings, and the mysteries of the conference committee. Committees not only make preliminary decisions on bills, but also provide the best mechanism for oversight of the executive through control of appropriations, investigations, and other forms of continuing control. Whether committees are effective mechanisms depends in part on the degree of subject-matter specialization and the adequacy of time and staff. It is in these respects that congressional committees are more successful than those in most states.

[17]

Legislative
Voting Behavior

"THE YEAS and nays have been ordered. The clerk will call the roll." The clerk begins to read the names of congressmen. Bells ring in the chamber and in congressional offices. Members come hurrying into the chamber. Party leaders anxiously check off names as the roll call proceeds. Visitors in the gallery sense an air of excitement and suspense as the roll call nears the end with the outcome still in doubt. This scene is repeated in state legislatures, where it is often possible for spectators to watch the drama being enacted electronically, as the lights on the scoreboard switch back and forth from red to green. Are the drama and excitement real, or are we simply watching the formal ratification of agreements negotiated behind the scenes, in committees or in meetings of the leadership? Does a study of roll call voting tell us anything that is not already obvious from our study of other aspects of the legislative process?

We have said that resolving conflicts is one of the important legislative functions, and we have emphasized the decisional aspect of this function. The decisions embodied in bills are the most important legislative output. The roll call is a significant, but not always decisive, step in the decision-making process. At one of the earlier stages in the legislative process, negative decisions may have precluded a roll call vote, or a positive decision—such as committee approval of a noncontroversial measure—may have assured consensus and unanimity in the vote. At an earlier stage the bill may have become a party issue, and the size and cohesion of the party majority may assure passage on the floor. Unanimous and one-sided votes are common, especially in those states that have a roll call on every bill. But in any legislative body there will be some issues that remain in doubt until the vote has been taken on the floor. Whether the vote is close or one-sided, whether or not preliminary decisions have foreshadowed the outcome, the vote on the floor is an essential part of reaching decisions on bills.

Beyond this, the roll call is of interest to us because of what it reveals about the legislator. If he is forced to choose among the competing demands of his constituents, his party leadership, and his committee colleagues, he may resolve the conflict by playing different roles in public and private. His public role, at least, stands revealed by the nature of his vote, and it is largely on the basis of this vote that he will be judged by most of those who are making demands on him. Whether his vote represents an agonizing choice or follows inevitably from past actions, it is an important act from the viewpoint of the legislator.

In the last fifteen years students of the legislative process have focused much of their attention on roll call voting and have applied new and sophisticated statistical techniques to its measurement. The principal reason for this has been well stated by David Truman:

> Roll call votes . . . have the great advantage of being "hard" data. Like statistics on elections, they represent discrete acts the fact of whose occurrence is not subject to dispute. They do not depend for their validity as data upon verbal reports of action or upon the impressions of fallible observers. . . . In the Congress, moreover, the "yeas and nays" closely approximate a record of the principal actions of the two houses.[1]

In Congress the accuracy of this "hard data" is almost perfect. In some states, short cuts in the roll call procedure sometimes leave doubt about precise accuracy in the case of noncontroversial issues, but the records are likely to be accurate for closely contested bills. Our concern in this chapter is with the meaning of roll calls, the light that they shed on the political forces operating in the legislature, and not the more technical and methodological problems involved in roll call analysis (some of these are discussed in Chapter 21).

In Congress a roll call vote is taken only when the motion being voted on concerns a controversial or highly important matter; consequently, as Truman has said, the roll calls represent a record of the principal congressional actions. In the states, however, the constitution often requires a roll call on final passage of every bill; the usual consequence is that a large proportion—sometimes as many as 90 percent —of the roll calls are unanimous or nearly unanimous. Analysis of roll calls that approach or achieve unanimity is of little value because the record does not reveal any differences among the legislators. They may be voting together for different reasons—and these differences may be significant—but this possibility is not demonstrated by the roll call statistics. Unanimity on a roll call usually means that legislators are taking their voting cues from the same sources or from sources who are in agreement. Before a bill reaches the floor it has been screened, carefully or perfunctorily, by a committee and by the majority—and perhaps minority—leadership. When the majority floor leader calls up a measure and no objection is raised by the minority leader or anyone else, the legislator recognizes that the bill is acceptable to the committee and to his leadership, two of the main sources of his voting cues. If he has no reason to believe that the measure will arouse criticism in his district and has no personal objection to it, the legislator can be expected to vote favorably.

Most bills on which voting is unanimous can be described as non-controversial. If the issue arouses controversy, some one or more of the groups that are sources of voting cues is likely to raise an objection with enough force to guarantee dissenting votes. A few of the bills that pass with little dissent are matters of great controversy, perhaps even of serious conflict among interests or between parties. In these cases the controversial points are negotiated and settled in committee or at some other point prior to action on the floor. These decisions are fully as important as those that are recorded in roll calls, but we have no way of measuring them in the sense in which roll call votes can be measured. When we exclude unanimous votes from analysis, we are excluding many trivial issues and a few important ones, just as we are excluding negative decisions that prevent an issue from coming to a vote. We are including those votes that provide some clue to the conflicting forces and pressures at work in the legislative system.

Roll call statistics can tell us *how* legislators vote. They can show how often Republicans vote together, or Southerners, or Catholic members, or representatives of urban constituencies. The roll calls cannot tell us *why* legislators vote that way. Does Congressman Brown support the federal aid-to-education bill because he is a Democrat, because he represents a low-income urban constituency, because he is a former high school teacher, or because a close friend is sponsoring the measure? We cannot *prove* causal relationships from roll call statistics. Roll call statistics do provide evidence—hard, measurable evidence—that may be added to our other sources of knowledge about the legislative system, so as to provide the basis for judgments about the importance of party, constituency, and other sources of voting cues.

PARTY AS A REFERENCE GROUP

Studies of roll call voting in Congress and in some of the two-party state legislatures have shown that on nonunanimous roll calls, the voting follows party lines more often than it is related to sectional, urban-rural, or other factors that have been tested. Occasionally the voting pattern on a particular roll call can be better explained by some factor other than party, but voting follows party lines (more or less perfectly) on the largest proportion of roll calls. This statistical fact suggests the strong possibility that the party is an important source of voting cues, a reference group (which we defined earlier as a group to whose norms the actor refers for his behavior). But there are other possible explanations for the prominence of party alignments in voting. If a high proportion of the Democrats who support federal aid to education represent Northern urban constituencies, are most of these congressmen using the constituency as their only reference group? Behind the mask of a "party vote" is there some other factor—constituency, region, personal conviction—that actually explains the vote?

To bolster the statistical evidence for describing the party as an important reference group, we must recall other evidence about the party. We know that Congress and many state legislatures are organized along party lines, that caucuses are active in some states, that friendship groups tend to be intraparty more than interparty, and that partisan leaders in both the executive and legislative branches apply rewards and sanctions primarily to members of their own party. We frequently hear legislators saying that they prefer to "go along" with the party whenever possible. As Matthews has said, in describing the United States Senate, "Party 'discipline' may be weak, but party 'identification' is strong."[2] We know that on many issues the pressure for conformity to a party position is immediate and direct, whereas constituency pressures are often distant, vague, ill-informed, and contradictory. There is ample evidence to bear out the assumption that, where statistics demonstrate that party alignments are frequent, party is an important reference group. In fact, the symptoms of party identification and activity are most apparent in those states with a high level of party alignment on roll calls; where both kinds of evidence are strong, we have reason to describe the party as a source of voting cues, a reference group.

This does not necessarily mean that the legislator is always conscious of the party as a reference group. But often he will be. He will know how the caucus has voted or he will go to the floor leader and ask about the party's position. On other occasions the party is a less conscious source of voting cues. Wilder Crane, in an analysis of the Wisconsin legislature, found that, when there was a clear party opposition in the roll call, legislators often did not explain their votes in terms of the party as a reference group. A member's views on issues (like those of a voter) are shaped over a period of time by party identification. The interests of party and constituency often overlap, and the legislator is more likely to explain his vote in constituency terms although the party may have been a more immediate and specific reference group. A vote may be motivated (as Crane found it often was) by respect for another legislator who is sponsoring the bill, and this friendship is often affected by party ties.[3] George Young, in a study of the Missouri House, estimated that on about half of the roll calls with high party voting, legislators were simply voting to support a party colleague's motion; only about one-fifth of party roll calls involved bills discussed in caucus and about the same number involved other questions on which the party had taken a public stand.[4] In a two-party legislature it is party leaders who determine the timing and often the form (with or without amendments, for example) of voting, and in this indirect sense party is also a reference group.

It makes a difference what perception the legislator has with regard to party. Wahlke and his co-authors found that legislators in New Jersey and Ohio, where the level of party voting is high and party structure is visible, ranked party as a more important factor than did their counterparts in California and Tennessee, where the overt evidence shows party to be weak. Specifically, legislators in the first two states ranked party conflict as much more important than did those in the latter two, when compared to other types of conflict (such as urban-rural or among interest groups). Legislators in the first two states responded more favorably to questions concerning the parties as cue-giving groups. (Example: "If a bill is important for his party's record, a member should vote with his party even if it costs him some support in his district.") Legislators in the first two states also evaluated party influence as being higher. There were differences between the responses of Democrats and Republicans in some states, differences that corresponded to contrasts which were evident in their organizational and voting cohesion. Where party voting is evident in the roll calls and where there is organizational evidence of party activity, legislators are likely to regard party as an influential factor in legislative conflict, and we can expect to find the party appearing frequently as a reference group when the roll is called.[5]

Measuring Variations among Legislative Systems. Roll call studies have demonstrated that in some legislative bodies voting according to party is frequent on controversial questions, in others it is rare, and in still others party appears to be completely absent as a factor in voting. Before we consider the reasons why party becomes a reference group for certain legislators on some roll calls in a particular legislature, we should describe and seek to explain the variations that occur from one legislature to another. Comparative data are limited not only by a paucity of studies but also by variations in the measuring tools that are used by students of particular states. Because of variations from state to state in the frequency of roll calls, it is necessary for comparative purposes to eliminate unanimous roll calls and, where possible, roll calls with a small number of dissenters (usually under 10 percent).

One rough but easily comparable measure of party voting is the percentage of roll calls on which a majority of Democrats vote against a majority of Republicans. One measure of party unity is the index of cohesion. If all members of a party vote the same way, the index is 100; if three-quarters vote one way, the index is 50; if they are evenly divided, the index is 0. The index of cohesion may be found by subtracting the percentage in the minority from that of the majority in a party. Then the average index of cohesion may be calculated, or the percentage of roll calls on which the index of cohesion was above a certain level may be recorded. A good measure of partisan alignment is the "party vote," on which the two parties took opposite sides and each had a high index of cohesion, perhaps 60 or 80.

Table 17.1 uses several of these measurements to show the extent of party voting in a number of the states in which roll call studies have been made. Despite slight variations in the standards used for the various studies, it is evident that party is a far more important reference group in southern New England and New York than it is in California and that a number of state legislatures may be located between these two extremes. It is also clear that in some states, such as California, party alignments have changed in importance over a period of years.

A number of studies of congressional party alignments make it evident that Congress ranks somewhere between the two extremes, with less party voting than is found in a few states but more than is found in most. In recent years, the proportion of roll calls on which a majority of the two parties take opposite stands has varied considerably, but has averaged a little under half. Key found that, in selected sessions from 1933 through 1945, the Democratic index of cohesion averaged 46 in the Senate and 59 in the House; the index was 70 or better on 22 percent of the Senate roll calls and 44 percent of those in the House. Republican cohesion was greater: the index averaged 52 in the Senate and 66 in the House; it was 70 or better on 32 percent of Senate roll calls and 54 percent of those in the House. Turner used the measurement of a party vote (the two parties opposed, each with a cohesion index of at least 80) for selected House sessions from 1921 through 1948, and found that it varied by from 7 to 31 percent per session and averaged 17 percent.[6] *Congressional Quarterly* figures for recent years show that, on issues on which the President has taken a stand, he can count on the support of about three-fourths of the members of his own party and almost half of the opposition congressmen (see Table 17.2).

Reasons for Variations in Party Voting. What are the characteris-

Table 17.1. PARTY VOTING IN SELECTED STATE LEGISLATURES, NONUNANIMOUS ROLL CALLS*

State	Roll Calls, Majority of Both Parties Opposed						Average index of cohesion (median of sessions)				Year
	Total % such roll calls		%, each party has 80 index of cohesion		%, each party has 60 index of cohesion		Senate		House		
	Senate	House	Senate	House	Senate	House	D	R	D	R	
R.I.	96	96	—	—	92	88	95	95	99	98	1931, 1937, 1951
Conn.	90	83	—	—	71	77	88	86	87	80	1931–1951
Mass.	82	87	32	34	36	56	84	63	82	66	1931, 1937, 1951†
N.Y.	62	61	52	56	—	—	—	—	—	—	1947, 1949†
Pa.	64	81	22	30	25	30	—	—	—	—	1945†
Pa.	34	43	—	—	—	—	—	—	—	—	1951
Pa.	—	29	—	—	—	14	—	—	—	—	1959
Pa.	56	—	—	—	24	43	—	—	—	—	1962†
Mich.	52	61	15	—	26	—	—	—	—	—	1935, 1949, 1955, 1957†
Ohio	53	40	15	7	—	13	67	73	57	55	1949†
Ill.	—	54	—	17	—	26	—	—	—	—	1949–1957
Ill.	—	—	—	—	32	—	—	—	—	—	1937, 1951
Maine	—	—	—	—	—	—	—	—	—	—	1931, 1937, 1951†
N.H.	72	68	—	—	30	18	95	32	71	48	1945†
Wash.	71	51	9	9	—	—	83	62	58	52	1953, 1955, 1957†
Kan.	—	73	—	—	—	—	—	—	49	29	
Ky.	54	41	27	7	—	—	—	—	—	—	1944, 1946†

Roll Calls, Majority of Both Parties Opposed

State	Total % such roll calls		%, each party has 80 index of cohesion		%, each party has 60 index of cohesion		Average index of cohesion (median of sessions)				Year
	Senate	House	Senate	House	Senate	House	Senate D	Senate R	House D	House R	
Colo.	36	38	6	7	—	—	—	—	—	—	1941, 1947†
Mo.	23	36	I	9	—	—	—	—	—	—	1945–1946†
Mo.	—	—	—	—	—	21	—	—	—	—	1955, 1957†
Calif.	20	32	—	I	—	—	—	—	—	—	1947–1949†
Calif.	—	34	—	—	—	—	—	—	—	—	1957†
Calif.	3I	49	I	3	—	—	—	—	—	—	1959†

* All figures in this table are percentages of the total roll calls in a session with certain categories excluded from the total. In all states unanimous roll calls are excluded. For those legislative sessions marked with a dagger, roll calls with 10% or less of the members (or in some cases, of both parties) voting in the minority are also excluded. The average index of cohesion in the five New England states includes only those roll calls on which the parties were in opposition; for Ohio and Kansas it includes all roll calls listed in the other columns for those states. Kansas roll calls exclude those with less than 20% in opposition.

SOURCES: These figures are based on the following sources cited in the footnotes to this Chapter: Lockard (ftnt. 7), Jewell (ftnt. 18), Sorauf (ftnt. 9), Flinn (ftnt. 18), Grumm (ftnt. 19), Young (ftnt. 4), Buchanan (ftnt. 20); and on W. J. Keefe, "Parties, Partisanship and Public Policy in the Pennsylvania Legislature," American Political Science Review, XLVIII (1954), 450–64; D. R. Derge, "Urban-Rural Relationships in the Illinois General Assembly, 1949–1957" (Paper presented at the 1958 meeting of the Midwest Conference of Political Scientists); R. S. Friedman and S. L. Stokes, "The Role of Constitution-Maker as Representative" (Unpublished paper).

tics of legislative and political systems where the party is an important reference group for legislators? An absolute prerequisite is the existence of two parties in the legislature. Where a single party consistently has a monopoly or an overwhelming majority of legislative seats, the party is not a reference group for legislative voting. In a state where a minority party consistently holds a bloc of roughly 10 or 15 percent of the legislative seats, the minority party has little incentive to achieve voting cohesion, and as a consequence the members of the majority party see no need to maintain voting cohesion. Excluding the legislatures dominated by a single party, however, we find no close correlation between the intensity of two-party competition for legislative seats and the degree of party cohesion. New York has a high level of party cohesion despite firm, usually consistent Republican majorities; some of the Western states have much less party cohesion despite turnover in party majorities. As long as the minority party is strong enough in the legislature to win an occasional vote by maintaining unity and securing defections from the majority, both parties have some incentive to maintain unity, and closer competition or more frequent turnover does not necessarily produce more party cohesion.

On the basis of the small number of studies summarized in Table 17.1, and more impressionistic analyses available concerning some other states, it is possible to describe the geographic variations in party voting. Voting along party lines occurs most frequently in some of the most industrialized and urbanized two-party states in the Northeast and Midwest. A moderate level of party voting occurs in other states in this region which have substantial urban populations and in some of the Border areas and states farther West. Among the two-party states, party alignments appear to be weakest in some of the less urbanized states, particularly in the Border and Western areas.

If there is a rough approximation between party voting in the legislature and the urban and industrial characteristics of states, what more specific causative factors can be found? In states with high party voting, each of the parties is likely to be relatively homogeneous in its composition. The Democratic party draws its electoral strength from the metropolitan centers, and particularly from labor groups, Catholic voters, racial and ethnic minorities, and persons with below-average incomes. The Republican vote is in the higher income sections of the metropolis, the towns and smaller cities, and some of the farm areas. This is the familiar political pattern in the industrial North that grew out of the New Deal realignment. The operation of the single-member district system (and multi-member districts, in the absence of proportional representation) creates an even sharper polarization of party strength. Republican voters in the metropolitan areas (particularly in multi-member districts) and rural Democratic voters are unrepresented in the legislature. In most of the heavily urban states shown in Table 17.1, upwards of three-fourths of the Democratic legislators and only about one-third of the Republicans come from a few metropolitan areas. The result of this polarization is that each legislative party is quite homogeneous in the constituencies represented by its members. There is a maximum of opportunity for agreement on issues within each party and a minimum of likelihood that legislators will be torn between loyalty to the legislative party and loyalty to the constituency. In most of the states where party voting is more frequent than in Congress, the constituencies of the two parties are much more homogeneous than is the case with the congressional parties. In less urbanized states, the urban-rural polarization is either missing or less sharply defined, and the Democratic party—whether or not it is strong in the large cities— often draws much of its legislative membership from farming areas or areas of traditional party strength.

Some of the states with a high level of party voting appear to be characterized by issue-oriented party systems. Lockard attributes party cohesion in the Connecticut legislative party to the ideological similarities within each party: the Democrats are generally liberal, and the Republicans are generally conservative.[7] In looking for other examples of issue-oriented parties, we think of New York, with its Democratic heritage of Smith, Roosevelt, and Lehman; Michigan, with its parties sharply oriented toward labor and business, respectively; Rhode Island, where the Democratic party is heavily committed to the labor and welfare policies of union interests. In these and other states, the two parties are likely to draw their votes from the same interests that the national parties do in the North. The two parties in such a state appear to stand for different things, at least in the minds of some voters; they are not merely benefiting from traditional voting habits.

We must be extremely cautious, however, in attributing party cohesion to the issue-orientation of parties. Voting behavior research has shown that few voters have clear perceptions of the issues for which the two national parties stand; even fewer have any clear ideological attachment to a party. They are more likely to perceive a party in terms of the groups or classes that are allied with it or benefit from its programs.[8] Perceptions of issues at the state level are probably even weaker. In states where the most perceptive observer finds it hard to define the issues that separate the parties, it is clear that this factor is an obstacle to party cohesion. Where there appear to be differences in the issue-orientation of parties, this fact is primarily important as a symptom of the differences in constituency interests represented by the two parties. Sorauf's analysis of the Pennsylvania parties is pertinent and broadly applicable:

So, the parties achieve an indirect responsibility to an inarticulate ideology —the common interests and goals of the similar constituencies from which they draw their most loyal partisans. It is in the support of this inarticulate ideology and the gubernatorial program, rather than in that of a spelled-out party program, that this party discipline is used. The legislative party merely mobilizes the cohesive party vote from among its basically non-ideological ranks.[9]

Some of the states with a high level of party voting are among those with the strongest state and local party organizations in the country. In his study of New England political systems, Lockard gives weight to this factor: "If the organization is well-led, clearly identifiable, and powerful enough to give a boost to the career of the ordinary member of the party in the legislature, then the likelihood is that it can have a considerable influence on the way members vote. Disciplinary action against the recalcitrant may be rare, but the fact that rewards and punishments are possible is a spur to regularity." Lockard lists, as one of the characteristics of cohesive, strong party organizations, "great party influence in the making of legislative party decisions."[10] Strong local party organizations may result in a highly cohesive party delegation from a particular county in the legislature, but the local party is likely to take an interest in only a small proportion of legislative issues. If a strong state party organization is to have any direct effect on the cohesion of the legislative party, it must be able to dispense rewards and sanctions; for the state organization to affect a legislator's chances for renomination, it must apply pressure to those local organizations that control or effectively influence nominations. Lockard found this to be true in Connecticut: "The close contact maintained between the state leadership and local organizations permits the virtual elimination of some recalcitrants from political activity."[11]

A more typical situation, even in states with strong party organizations, is probably that described by Sorauf: "A great gulf yawns in Pennsylvania—and in most other states—between the local, constituency parties and the legislative party. Communication between them is erratic and desultory at best, and, although the legislative party may have to support a state-wide platform or a governor's program, the local parties may freely keep eyes and heart close to local bread-and-butter issues."[12] This would also be an apt description of the relationship between congressional and state parties. If local parties have little interest in state issues, only the most extreme pressure from a state party organization is likely to compel them to discipline a maverick legislator. The state party that is out of power does not have the means to exert such pressure. Whether the administration party seeks to do so is largely dependent on the governor, and we have seen in Chapter 13 that the governor seldom finds the party organization to be a valuable tool of legislative leadership. The President's partisan weapons are also relatively weak. Strong party organization and cohesive legislative parties may coincide because of a common cause, such as homogeneous parties growing out of urban-rural polarization, but there are relatively few states (such as Connecticut and New York) where party organization directly enhances legislative cohesion.

In Chapter 8 we described the party organs that assume varying degrees of importance in state legislatures: caucuses, policy committees, and individual leaders who fill a party role. In several of the states with the highest party cohesion in voting, the caucus meets regularly and frequently makes binding decisions; in others, the party leaders are recognized as powerful figures. In states such as Kansas and California, a gradual increase in party cohesion has coincided with the increased frequency of caucuses. The fact that the caucus functions regularly, or that skillful leaders have an acknowledged party role, may mean that a legislative party achieves greater cohesion than it would if party organs were absent or ineffective. These organizational devices make it possible to communicate the norms of partisan behavior and, more specifically, information about the leadership position on bills. They make the party more visible to the legislator as a reference group. The absence or ineffectiveness of such party organs can be expected to make the legislative party less cohesive than it might potentially be. The existence of effective party organs is not, however, an adequate explanation of cohesive party voting; we are forced to explain why party organs are more effective in some two-party legislatures than in others.

Among the two-party states, legislative systems vary widely as to the importance of party voting. The most common attribute of legislatures with strong party alignments in voting is the presence of parties that are highly homogeneous as a result of the urban-rural or socioeconomic polarization of constituencies. In many of these states the parties may be described very loosely as issue-oriented, and the state party organizations are often strong; it is usually difficult, however, to demonstrate a direct impact of either factor on legislative party cohesion. In the legislatures where such aspects of the party system are conducive to party voting, party regularity becomes one of the legislative norms. The new legislator quickly learns that, when the party takes a position on certain issues, a degree of conformity is required. We showed in the previous chapter that different legislators interpret their roles—including the party role—differently. Where party regularity is a widely accepted norm, the party role is accepted by more legislators and party homogeneity reduces the role conflict between party and constituency. In these states, party regularity can be understood best not as a discipline, but as a custom or habit. The legislator becomes accustomed to the party as a reference group. He "goes along" with the party and "follows the leadership" unless "pressure from constituents is heavy" or he has "strong personal convictions."[13] The function of the caucus or other leadership devices in this environment is largely one of efficient communication: to make it clear to the legislator when the party has taken what stand on an issue, and to reinforce—rather than to enforce—the norm of conformity to the party's position.

MAJORITIES AND MINORITIES

In a legislative body where party voting has some importance, does the majority party manifest greater voting unity than the minority party and does the administration party have more unity than the opposition party? There are four possible categories of legislative parties to consider: majority-administration, minority-administration, majority-opposition (what David Truman calls the "truncated majority"), and minority-opposition. We must keep in mind the possibility that one party may have consistently greater unity than the other, whatever its majority-minority status or its relationship to the administration.

Truman suggests that presidential preferences provide the congressional leadership with leverage that is useful and perhaps essential to their efforts to achieve party cohesion. The opposition party, on the other hand, "seems to have encountered special obstructions to coherent and programmed voting behavior." The difficulties faced by the opposition party leadership are intensified by the fact that the President's appeal is not merely partisan, so that his legislative proposals do have an influence on at least some opposition congressmen; this is particularly true in foreign affairs. The opposition leadership lacks "not only most of the means of developing an alternative program but also the leverage of an alternative 'outside' source of legitimacy."[14] Truman studied a Congress in which the Democratic party was both the majority and the administration party. His analysis of the President as a source of program and of leverage for the leadership suggests that in a period of divided government, it would be the administration party rather than the majority party in Congress that would be more cohesive.

Truman's appraisal of the Eighty-first Congress is based on a thorough and sophisticated analysis of voting blocs within each Senate and House party. He concludes that the two parties differed in the fluidity of their voting structure. In both branches "the minority party recurrently appeared to be more fluid, almost regardless of its relative cohesion. . . . The minority's voting structure, more than the majority's, tended to shift, not quite from issue to issue, but from one cluster of votes to another." The elected minority leaders were collectively less united and there was less agreement between minority floor leaders and seniority leaders than was true in the case of the majority party. In the Senate the majority party was more cohesive (as measured by the cohesion index), but in the House the majority was—by a smaller margin—less cohesive than the minority party.[15]

In an effort to measure the stability of party voting patterns in the Eightieth, Eighty-third, and Eighty-fourth Congresses by means of a scaling technique, Anderson found clear-cut evidence of a difference between the parties only on roll calls concerning liberal-conservative issues. With regard to these, the majority party in Congress had more stability than the minority party, not only when the majority was the administration party but also (contrary to Truman's hypothesis) when it was in opposition.[16]

Although it may be more meaningful, as Truman suggests, to measure stability and fluidity rather than cohesion, the only comparable data over an extended time period are the figures on party unity compiled by the *Congressional Quarterly*, some of which are summarized in Table 17.2. While the standards of measurement have varied over time, it is possible to contrast the cohesion of the two parties in any given session and throughout the time periods when the same standards were used.[17] Variations in party cohesion from year to year may be caused by changes in the distribution of roll calls among issues or changes in membership. But if one party (Democratic or Republican, administration or opposition) consistently achieves greater cohesion, that fact should be meaningful.

A study of the *Congressional Quarterly* figures from 1949 through 1964 covering roll calls with the parties opposed (as well as those with parties in agreement) shows that the differences between the two parties were seldom great and averaged only 2 or 3 percentage points—hardly a major difference, given the roughness of the measuring device. In the Senate the administration party had slightly higher cohesion in most sessions than did the opposition party, but in the House there was no consistent difference in cohesion between administration and opposition parties. In both houses the sharpest contrast between the two parties occurred in the Eighty-third Congress (1953–1954), the only Congress in which the Republican party was both the majority and the administration party. The fact that Republican cohesion was substantially greater than Democratic cohesion in that Congress but not in the remaining Eisenhower Congresses suggests that a majority in Congress is at least as important as control of the White House in producing

Table 17.2. SUMMARY OF CONGRESSIONAL ROLL CALLS, 1949–1964

(In percentages)

Classification of Roll Calls		1949–52		1953–54		1955–60		1961–64	
		Senate	House	Senate	House	Senate	House	Senate	House
% roll calls, two parties in opposition	Range	58–64	51–66	47–52	38–52	30–53	40–59	36–62	46–55
	Median	64	54½	—	—	40½	48½	44	49½
Average vote for party with two parties in opposition*	Range D	78–82	76–80	74–76	74–81	60–72	65–79	61–69	69–73
	R	75–80	80–83	82–90	84–84	64–75	65–77	64–68	70–74
	Median D	82	80	—	—	69	70	65½	71
	R	76½	81	—	—	70½	69½	66	72½
Av. vote in support of President as % of times voting†	Av., administration party	—	—	81	80	79	68	75	83
	Av., opposition party	—	—	49	48	52	54	49	42

* From 1949 through 1954 this is the average percentage of times a member voted or announced a stand in agreement with his party out of the total number of votes and announced stands. From 1955 through 1964 this is the average percentage of times a congressman voted in agreement with his party out of the total number of roll calls in this category; consequently, the percentages are lower.

† The Congressional Quarterly figures show the average percentage of votes in support of, and in opposition to, the President's position. These figures were used to calculate support for the President as a percentage of total votes cast.

SOURCE: *Congressional Quarterly Almanac,* vols. V–XIX (Washington: Congressional Quarterly Service, 1949–1963); *Congressional Quarterly Weekly Report,* XXII (Oct. 30, 1964), 2588–97.

greater party unity. The Republicans' party-unity score averaged slightly higher than that of the Democrats throughout the 1949–1964 period.

Another way of evaluating the President's effect on party voting is to look at the *Congressional Quarterly* figures of support for the President on those issues on which he took a stand. The average senator of the administration party supported the President on three-fourths to four-fifths of the votes that he cast; in the House the figure was occasionally lower. Opposition congressmen in both houses supported the President a little less than half the time, although the proportion was slightly over half for Democrats during the 1955–1958 period. It is evident that the administration party was much more united in support of the President's program than the opposition party was in voting against it.

There was no consistent pattern in the state legislatures of greater cohesion for either the administration party or the majority party. There is some evidence that, when a majority of both parties are aligned on the same side of an issue, there is more likely to be some dissent in the minority party. For most states we do not have data available over a long enough time span to determine with any certainty which differences are due to majority-minority status and which to differences in the nature of the Democratic and Republican parties. In Ohio, a state with a moderate degree of party cohesion, data from a number of sessions suggest that, when the Republican party was in the majority, it had greater cohesion, but when the Democrats had a majority, there was little difference in cohesion between the two parties. There is evidence from both Ohio and Pennsylvania that a party which holds a narrow legislative majority has a particularly strong incentive for maintaining cohesion.[18] A minority party may achieve a high level of cohesion when it captures the governorship, as the Democratic party did in the Illinois legislature at the start of Adlai Stevenson's term as governor in 1949. In Kentucky, where the minority Republican party is seldom cohesive, the winning of the governorship and the growth in the size of the legislative party brought about a higher level of cohesion during the legislative sessions of 1944 and 1946.

Kansas provides an illustration of the changes in level of party cohesion that occur when a minority party increases its strength. As the Democratic party in the House grew from an ineffective minority of 20 out of 125 in 1953 to a strong minority of 56 in 1959, and when it became the administration party in 1957 and 1959, the level of two-party conflict (as measured by an index of unlikeness) grew steadily, and the average index of cohesion for the Democratic party also grew. There was a significant difference between Democratic voting patterns in the Kansas House and Senate in 1959. In the Senate the small Democratic delegation voted as a group only in opposition to Republican proposals, but in the House the Democrats were strong enough to force votes on their own measures and to provide greater support to the governor. The most regular, or typical, Democrats in the House—unlike those in the Senate—did not appear to be merely a negative image of the most typical Republicans.[19]

PARTISAN ISSUES

Studies of roll call voting in a variety of legislatures have produced remarkable consensus on the issues that are most likely to result in party alignments. Even in states with high party cohesion, a substantial number of bills produce roll calls—sometimes sharply divided roll calls —on which party appears to have had no effect. Whether party cohesion is high or low in a state, it is more likely to appear if the measure fits into one of three categories: (1) issues involving the prestige and fundamental programs of the administration, (2) social and economic proposals for welfare programs or the regulation of business or labor— issues associated with the "liberal-conservative" dichotomy, (3) issues involving the special interests of the parties or legislative organization and procedure.[20]

Administration Issues. In state legislatures the administration party is more likely to unite on measures that involve the governor's prestige; for political reasons the opposition party is also more likely to unite on such issues. In most states the governor commits his prestige to the support of (or in opposition to) only a small number of bills and remains neutral on most others, even on some advocated by his administrative agencies. In states with high party cohesion, the governor's stand on an issue becomes the signal for party conflict and the absence of such a stand makes party conflict unlikely. Some of the states where party voting in the legislature is rare are ones in which the governor seldom takes a clear, forceful stand on issues.

In the absence of precise state-by-state information on the governor's stand on various issues, we must try to identify the kinds of issues that are most likely to involve the prestige of the governor. These include virtually all taxation and appropriations bills, confirmation of the governor's appointments, and most measures that directly affect the administration of state government. A variety of studies ranging from New England through New York, Pennsylvania, Ohio, and Illinois to California indicate that money bills are consistently among those on which party cohesion is strongest. Cohesion is at least as high on the smaller number of controversial appointments and on proposals by the opposition party to curb the governor's control over state administration. It is also probable that many of the social and economic measures discussed below which produce the highest cohesion are ones that form a part of the governor's program or have been written into the platforms of one or both parties.

The President differs from governors in that he takes a public stand on a much larger proportion of the measures that occasion roll calls in Congress. Since the *Congressional Quarterly* began compiling indexes of support for the President in 1953, it has identified a presidential position on about half the roll calls in Congress. Its calculations for all issues do not indicate any consistently higher cohesion for issues on which the President is publicly committed. Perhaps the best way to study the impact of the President's prestige on congressional voting is to examine roll calls on foreign policy. Although the President can count on bipartisan support for most measures that involve foreign commitments, this support has usually been stronger from the administration party. The *Congressional Quarterly* figures show that President Kennedy received much stronger support on foreign policy from Democrats in both houses. President Eisenhower received (from 1955 through 1960) somewhat greater support from Republicans in the Senate, but in the House Democratic support was greater in some sessions.[21] Republicans strongly supported Eisenhower's collective-security proposals, the issue that most directly affected the President's prestige. He won increasing numbers of Republican votes, many of them reluctant, for continuation of large-scale foreign aid. Although he had to depend more on Democratic than on Republican votes for his reciprocal trade proposals, it was this issue—on which Eisenhower was taking the traditional Democratic position—that prompted the largest increase in Republican support: from less than one-fourth to over one-half of the senators. The Truman Administration had a remarkably high level of Democratic congressional support for its foreign policy measures, while the level of Republican support gradually declined during the latter years of the Administration.[22]

The President's preeminence in foreign policy matters is so widely accepted by both Congress and the public that congressmen of both parties hesitate to vote against his foreign programs. But members of the Administration party evidently believe that the President's prestige is most directly involved on foreign policy issues. Moreover, they are more likely than the opposition to have confidence in the President's implementation of these programs and consequently more likely to provide voting support.

Social and Economic Issues. A second broad category of issues on which party cohesion is high includes health, education, and welfare services, all kinds of labor legislation (from minimum wages to restrictions on unions), and measures to regulate business. A large proportion of the domestic issues that arise in Congress are in these categories. There is evidence from many of the industrial states of the Northeast and Midwest, together with California, which indicates that these issues constitute a large bloc (perhaps one-fourth) of those on which party voting occurs. Some of these are issues that might be expected to arise more often in industrial and highly urban states, but even when they come to a vote in more rural, low-cohesion states, clear-cut party alignments are seldom found. There are several possible reasons why legislators in states with high party cohesion might be expected to follow party lines on such issues. Most of these are issues of broad public concern, which are likely to be included in the platform of a party or the program of a governor. In a state where the parties each represent districts that are relatively homogeneous in economic terms (this is characteristic of states with high party cohesion), it is on issues of this kind that the two parties are likely to represent clearly conflicting interests. More broadly, we might say that in the heavily urban and industrial states the two parties have come to resemble the national parties in terms of image and programs; consequently, we would expect party cohesion to be particularly strong on these economic and social issues.

Party Issues.   William J. Keefe concluded from a study of Illinois and Pennsylvania: "A large number of party conflicts develop on issues the primary concern of which is the party organization, not the public. The party, in this sense, is a pressure group." Such issues frequently occasion party votes in most New England states. Even in California, where party organizations have been weak, measures that have to do with elections and party organization have produced the highest level of party cohesion. In Congress, on the other hand, the proportion of such issues is quite small. There is often some overlap between these issues and those involving the prestige of the governor; an example would be a bill affecting the civil service. Some of the measures in which the parties have a strong interest also have important public consequences, but frequently the issues in dispute are of concern only to the politicians. Party-interest issues are not so easily recognizable as, for example, economic and social issues are. The party may have an interest in the patronage implications of a bill to transfer functions from one unit of local government to another, or to increase the number of judges in a district court. Keefe has determined that party interests are most often revealed in bills designed to protect or enhance the status of one party, to jeopardize that of the other, to embarrass state or local administrations controlled by the opposite party, to secure favorable election laws, to offset electoral defeats in city governments, and to increase access to all forms of patronage.[23] These issues are of such little public importance and such slight interest to the voter that the legislator can be expected to regard the party as the only important reference group; moreover, a high level of party cohesion on roll calls of little interest to the public is not a meaningful measure of party responsibility. If this is the only category of measures on which a substantial proportion of high-cohesion roll calls occur, as appears to be true in some states, the importance of party voting must be discounted.

A closely related area that often produces perfect party cohesion is roll calls on legislative organization—the election of the Speaker, and any questions that may arise concerning party prerogatives in the legislature. In his study of California, where party unity has not been automatic on such roll calls, Buchanan emphasizes that disunity on organizational votes can produce cracks in the party structure that may have lasting effects throughout a session. He concludes that "The vote on organization is the indispensable glue for holding a legislative party together."[24]

INTRAPARTY BLOCS

Regionalism in Congress. There is a wealth of information from congressional voting studies which demonstrates that, although party alignments are more consistently important than regional alignments, regional blocs within the parties can be identified on certain issues. Within the Democratic party two blocs stand out: one consists largely of Southern congressmen, and the other consists primarily of non-Southerners (this we can loosely call a Northern bloc). David Truman, whose study of the Eighty-first Congress is the most thorough analysis of intraparty blocs available, determined that the Democratic party in both houses was divided into two clearly definable blocs along North-South lines, while the Republican blocs were more fluid. Truman's description of the Southern bloc in the 1949–1950 House could be applied quite accurately to both branches of Congress in recent years:

Despite a fluidity in the Southern wing that was much more striking than that among the Northerners, however, the evidence is clear that there was a solid and sharply identifiable die-hard element among the Southern Democrats, whose opposition extended well beyond the issues of intense regional loyalty to almost the whole range of questions growing out of the strains and stresses to which the American society is subjected in the midtwentieth century.[25]

On only a handful of roll calls, usually those concerning racial questions, does a majority of Southern Democrats vote in opposition to a majority of Northern Democrats and Republicans. More common, and more significant, is the "conservative coalition" of Southern Democrats and Republicans opposed to Northern Democrats, which in recent years has occurred on about one-fifth of the congressional roll calls. The strongest manifestations of the conservative coalition have been on labor legislation, a variety of welfare questions (housing, health, education), taxation, and civil rights.[26]

The blocs within the Republican party are less clear-cut and stable and do not have a readily definable regional base; they vary from one domestic issue to another, but assume a more consistent pattern on issues of foreign policy. Ever since the 1920s the Northeast has been the dependable source of internationalist voting in the Republican party, and the Midwest and West Coast sections have ranked next. The Plains States (since the 1920s) and the Mountain States (since World War II) have been the centers of isolationist voting. Although congressmen from all sections of the party increased their support of foreign programs during the Eisenhower Administration, the regional contrasts remained strong.[27]

The cautious student of congressional voting hesitates to attach great importance to such an imperfect pattern of regional blocs, except in the case of issues like civil rights on which the motivations for regional differences are clear. David Truman has described geographic cleavage in a legislative party as "a symptom whose origins are multiple and complex and are not readily susceptible to isolation and rating except in general terms." He warns that regional variations may be "less geographic than demographic, reflecting rural-urban differences rather than, for example, market or commodity specializations."[28] The regional variations in voting are not merely a reflection of urban-rural differences. Several studies indicate a persistence of regional differences when urban-rural factors are held constant, particularly in the House, where the size and variation of districts makes such manipulation possible. There is no doubt, for example, that Northern urban Democrats have a more liberal voting record than Southern urban Democrats, and the same distinction applies to Northern and Southern rural Democrats.

Urban-Rural Differences. Within the congressional parties, are there differences in the voting behavior of urban and rural congressmen (or more exactly, those representing metropolitan and nonmetropolitan constituencies)? If these distinctions exist, they must be looked for in the House, where the districts are more homogeneous than entire states. Turner, in his study of the 1921–1944 period, found urban-rural differences to be less important than sectional differences and, in the case of Democrats, less important than the proportions of foreign-born in a district.[29] MacRae's scale analysis of the Eighty-first Congress indicated that there were some urban-rural differences on welfare issues but that, in the case of Democrats, these were less clear-cut than sectional differences.[30] In recent years Southern Democratic congressmen representing metropolitan areas have voted with the "conservative coalition" only slightly less frequently than nonmetropolitan Southern congressmen have. Recent voting records suggest that some of the most conservative as well as some of the most liberal Republicans represent metropolitan districts. A study of foreign policy and defense roll calls in the House from 1945 to 1962 showed that the urban-rural factor is second only to party as a factor explaining the vote. A partial correlation measurement (which makes it possible to weigh each variable separately while controlling others) showed that urbanization was a significant variable on half of the roll calls (as compared to 84 percent for party and one-fourth for section). On about 8 percent of the roll calls, it was the only significant variable.[31]

Studies of state legislatures in which party is an important reference group have consistently shown that urban-rural voting occurs less often on roll calls than does party voting. In some states one legislative party represents almost exclusively metropolitan districts while the other is overwhelmingly nonmetropolitan. In these cases it is impossible to distinguish the effect of the two factors on voting, although it is clear that the resulting homogeneity of the parties contributes to their cohesiveness. David Derge, in studies of two states—Illinois and Missouri—with parties that are less homogeneous, found that metropolitan legislators from the two parties seldom voted together with a high degree of unity, and there were few roll calls on which metropolitan legislators were aligned against nonmetropolitan legislators. On measures primarily affecting metropolitan areas, Derge found that there were frequently interparty splits among metropolitan legislators and that other legislators tended either to support their party colleagues or to vote against measures that lacked bipartisan metropolitan support. The splits among metropolitan legislators may be caused by struggles for partisan advantage, or by the fact that the legislators represent voters with conflicting viewpoints on such issues as annexation, taxation, and welfare services. This is particularly likely if Democrats represent the central cities and Republicans represent the suburbs. Similar conclusions have resulted from studies in Ohio, where neither party was divided often along urban-rural lines, and Kansas, where partisan differences (as measured by an index of likeness) were at least twice as great as urban-rural differences in the 1955 and 1957 sessions.[32]

The Legislator and His District

Urban-rural variations, like regionalism, provide a guide to intraparty differences that is convenient for descriptive purposes, but too crude for any detailed, precise analysis. For this purpose we must shift our focus to the individual legislator and examine the factors that influence his voting decisions. In the previous chapter we discussed the variety of roles played by legislators, many of them pertinent to voting decisions. Legislators may rely primarily on their own judgment, playing the role of Trustee, or they may accept the role of Delegate and look to the constituency (or some part of it) as a reference group—a source of voting cues. (The delegate is almost always district-oriented rather than state-oriented.) We have emphasized the importance of the party as a reference group, and we may designate those who rely most on the party as Party-loyalists. A legislator may look to an interest group as a source of voting cues (usually it is one within his constituency). Likewise the President or governor, a legislative committee, a state or local delegation, or some other grouping may be a significant reference group for the legislator on some issues.

The average legislator does not self-consciously choose one or another role, but every legislator is aware of his need to make choices and to maintain some kind of balance among the pressures exerted on him. Not all legislators make the same choice, and for this reason it is possible to describe them as playing different roles. We must realize, however, that in assigning a role to a legislator, we are applying a stereotype to him and that his role is likely to vary more or less from issue to issue. Sorauf's description would fit many legislators:

The average legislator appears, then, to make no firm commitment to constituency, party, or self. Their demands on him and their sanctions over him shift from issue to issue. Both the shifting political demands and the finely balanced equities of choice force him to choose only tentatively and cautiously, one issue at a time.[33]

We are interested primarily in role conflicts: Under what circumstances do they arise and how are they reconciled? Often the legislator does not recognize any conflict in roles, usually because some of his potential reference groups remain silent. We have emphasized that the legislative party does not take any stand on many of the issues that come to a vote, even in states where party discipline is strong. On many issues the legislator looks in vain to his constituency for voting cues: "I don't know how my constituents see things. I don't have a crystal ball that tells me how my constituents feel." "You can't vote by what you think the constituents' thinking is. You don't know what that thinking is."[34] Conflict between a legislator's views and those of his constituents is reduced by the fact that he is a product of the district, often a lifelong resident; as one Pennsylvania legislator said, "A man usually agrees with his district, since he's one of them and typical of them."[35] In a relatively homogeneous party, conflict between party and constituency is minimized by the fact that the party is most likely to take a stand in favor of those measures that are supported by strong interests in most of the constituencies.

District Characteristics. It is not possible to measure the impact of all the reference groups that may be involved in role conflicts. Enough research has been done to permit some observations about the resolution of conflicts between party and constituency; a few of these studies also provide hints about the effect on voting behavior of personal viewpoints and particular statuses and group loyalties within the legislature. Duncan MacRae has advanced the thesis that "representatives who come from districts that are most typical of their parties tend to show highest 'party loyalty' on roll calls; those who come from districts atypical of their party tend to cross party lines more often."[36] The term "typical" is used here to refer to districts that rank highest in some characteristic which distinguishes districts of one party from those of the other party. This is logically consistent with our finding that the most homogeneous parties are likely to have the highest cohesion. In a relatively homogeneous party the legislator from a typical district is less likely to be cross-pressured on those issues on which his party has taken a stand.

In a general way, this thesis fits our common knowledge about Congress. It is the Southern, and often rural Southern, congressmen who vote most often against the measures supported by the Northern, urban, Democratic majority; several of the most prominent Republican mavericks represent urban constituencies. Does this "common-sense" thesis stand up against more rigorous analysis? The few studies available indicate that the Democratic congressmen who vote most consistently with the party have been those from Northern metropolitan districts, with a high proportion of foreign-born or (in more recent years) non-white population. Rural Republicans are likely to have a more loyal voting record than those who represent the kind of metropolitan district that usually votes Democratic.[37] But these studies have remained somewhat inconclusive because they have not undertaken a comprehensive exploration of all the factors that might be pertinent. Moreover, the importance of constituency characteristics varies with the issue. MacRae found that during the Eighty-first Congress constituency factors were of little importance on questions of foreign aid, of moderate importance on welfare issues, and of greatest importance on agricultural issues. Other studies have emphasized the strength of constituency influences on roll calls concerning agriculture as well as reciprocal trade bills.[38] Presumably the congressman perceives constituent interest to be stronger and more unified on some topics than on others.

In most states the variations from district to district are much less extreme than in Congress, but the relationship between party loyalty and constituency characteristics appears to be an important one. An increasing number of state studies, involving more sophisticated techniques of analysis, provide evidence for this conclusion. Studies in Massachusetts and Pennsylvania have demonstrated that in one or both parties legislators from the most typical districts (measured in terms of urban-rural characteristics and income levels) vote more consistently with the parties. In Pennsylvania this proved to be the case in the House but not in the Senate, which has longer terms and larger districts.[39] In the Ohio House, the most loyal Democrats and the least loyal Republicans represented districts that were more urban and had a large proportion of their working force engaged in manufacturing and mining.[40]

Competitive Nature of District.   Does a legislator who holds office precariously by a narrow electoral margin resolve conflicts between party and constituency any differently from the legislator whose tenure appears to be secure? One frequently suggested hypothesis is that the legislator who is electorally insecure must be particularly sensitive to constituent opinion and must resolve any conflicts that exist in favor of his constituents' preferences. In a state like Michigan, where most Democrats represent safe metropolitan seats and most Republicans represent safe nonmetropolitan seats, electoral security may promote disciplined party voting, but its effect is difficult to measure. It is often true that state legislators of both parties from typical districts have safe election margins and those from untypical districts do not. Several of the studies which indicate that larger electoral margins promote party loyalty have not isolated this factor from the characteristics that make a district typical. Studies of the Pennsylvania House, for example, suggest that legislators who deviate from party loyalty are most likely to come from atypical, closely competitive districts, but these studies do not distinguish among atypical districts, with various levels of competition.[41] The size of the electoral margin is of less importance in a typical district, where the likelihood of conflict is reduced, but in the untypical district we might expect the freshman legislator who barely won his seat to be more sensitive to constituent pressures than the veteran of several terms whose personal popularity has won him increasingly comfortable margins at the polls. We can word our original question differently: Does the legislator who resolves party-constituency conflicts in favor of the constituency do so as a result of his political anxiety and insecurity?

The evidence at the state level is contradictory. Studies in Massachusetts and Wisconsin show that the mavericks in at least one party were usually legislators who had been elected by small margins.[42] But in Ohio the traces of correlation between electoral margins and party loyalty were small and inconsistent, and they appeared only in the most typical districts, where such a relationship is least explainable. In Kansas, the Democratic legislators whose voting records were closest to that of the party leaders were primarily freshmen who had been elected by small margins.[43] If electoral insecurity is a reason why some legislators from untypical districts vote against their party, that has not yet been demonstrated by roll call studies at the state level.

At the congressional level a variety of studies using different techniques and different time periods have also produced conflicting conclusions. One study of the Eighty-first Congress (1949–1950) concluded that Republicans, but not Democrats, "showed some indication of heightened responsiveness to constituency characteristics when they had narrow electoral margins."[44] No such relationship was found for either party in a study of Northern districts during the Eighty-seventh Congress (1961).⁴⁵ In the South, most Democrats have had low records of party loyalty despite a level of electoral security that until recently has been high. But a study of Southern congressmen in the first session of the Eighty-eighth Congress (1963) concluded that these congressmen were more likely to support the Democratic Administration's program if their districts had provided electoral support to Democratic presidential candidates and that the effect of this factor was independent of constituency characteristics.⁴⁶ In Congress, as in state legislatures, we need more extensive and more sophisticated research in order to isolate the effects of electoral margins on roll call voting.

The SRC Study of Constituent-Congressional Relationships. Without discounting electoral insecurity as a variable affecting the votes of some legislators, we must look for evidence of some other variable that might increase the constituency's importance as a reference group. We have already said that there is no party-constituency conflict on some issues because the legislator is unable to discover what views, if any, his constituents have. In Chapter 14 we described some of the obstacles that are faced by legislators in gauging district opinion. It is reasonable to suppose that some legislators will be better able than others to perceive constituent opinion, for any of several reasons: longer tenure, greater efforts at perception, or greater consensus in the district. If this variable is an important one, the veteran legislator from a safe district (with a clearly discernible majority) might be expected to rely more on constituent opinion. This hypothesis implies that the legislator turns to the constituency as a reference group, not reluctantly, out of fear of reprisal, but willingly, when the demands of that group are clear enough to perceive.

Support for this hypothesis comes from the most intensive analysis of the relationship between the legislator and his district that has been carried out at the congressional level; this was conducted by the Survey Research Center of the University of Michigan. Interviews with incumbent congressmen and a small sample of voters in 116 congressional districts immediately after the 1958 election, together with analysis of roll call records in the Eighty-fifth Congress, made it possible to measure relationships among four factors: district attitudes, the congressman's attitudes, the congressman's perception of district attitudes, and his voting record. A scale analysis was used to determine both attitudes and roll call positions regarding three issue areas: civil rights, social welfare, and foreign policy. These issues comprise only a fraction of the measures dealt with by Congress in a session, but they are obviously among the most important issues, those that frequently recur.⁴⁷

Table 17.3 includes some of the most important relationships that

have been found to exist. It can be better understood by referring to
the diagram used by the Survey Research Center to illustrate its analysis
(see Figure 17.1). Columns 1 through 4 correspond to the numbered
relationships in Figure 17.1. Column 5 is a multiple correlation, expressing the combined relationship of the representative's attitude and his
perception with his roll call behavior. Column 6 shows the relationship
between the constituency's attitude and the representative's roll call
behavior.

The first conclusion to be drawn from these compilations is that

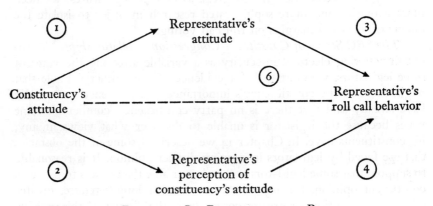

Figure 17.1. DIAGRAM OF REPRESENTATION RELATIONSHIPS

the congruence between constituent attitudes and the roll call record
varies greatly from issue to issue. In the case of civil rights, the relationship is a close one: the congressman's voting record is more closely related to his highly accurate perception of district attitudes than to his
own attitude, but this correspondence is closer than it is on other issues.
These two factors—his attitude and his perception—are highly predic-
tive of the congressman's roll call behavior. There is a much less impressive relationship between constituent attitude and roll calls in the case
of social welfare issues; roll calls are tied more closely to the congressman's attitude than to his perception of district attitudes. This is an issue
that is more likely to divide constituents along party lines, and consequently it is one on which the congressman's attitude and perception
are closer to the viewpoints of those who supported him in the election
than of those who did not. In the area of foreign policy, there is no
significant relationship between district attitude and roll call vote. The
correlation between the congressman's vote and the views of his constituents is in fact slightly negative; his own views have little connection
with those of his constituents, and his perception is not very good. A
substantial number of congressmen—particularly those from competitive

districts—have acknowledged their reliance on the Administration as a reference group for voting on foreign policy. Among those who emphasized this, there was a low multiple correlation (0.21) of roll call behavior with candidate attitudes and perceptions; for congressmen who were not so disposed to follow the Administration, the comparable figure was 0.63. With the exception of the representatives who follow the Administration's lead on foreign policy, the combined impact on the congressman's roll call record of his own views and his perception of district attitudes is remarkably high for all issues.

Further analysis of the two issues—welfare and civil rights—that are most affected by constituent attitudes demonstrates the importance of distinguishing between safe and competitive districts and between majority and minority constituents (that is, those who supported the congressman and those who opposed him in 1958). The designation of districts as safe or competitive is based on the congressman's evaluation. The difference between these two types of districts is great, and it does not follow the pattern we might expect (see Table 17.3). In safe districts, the roll call behavior of congressmen is related more closely to his perception of district attitudes than it is to his own attitude on issues; in competitive districts, greater importance attaches to the congressman's own views. Although perceived constituency views have greater effect on the civil rights issues, the same differences between safe and competitive districts are found for both issues. The congressman from a safe district, whom we might presume to have the greatest flexibility, sticks closest to the views of his district. The congressman from a marginal district, whom we might expect to be sensitive to constituent views, relies more on his own viewpoint and, in the case of welfare legislation, casts votes almost entirely without regard to the perceived views of his constituents. The most logical explanation for this paradox is that the congressmen from safe districts are better able to become familiar with district attitudes. They have somewhat longer tenure and their perception of majority opinion in safe districts is much more accurate than is true of congressmen in competitive districts. During the survey, congressmen from competitive districts more often expressed doubts about their own assessment of constituent attitudes. This line of reasoning suggests that the congressman from a competitive district is not necessarily less sensitive to his constituents' views but is rather less able to measure them with any sense of accuracy; consequently, he is forced to follow his own viewpoint.

Table 17.3 shows that voting records correspond more closely to the attitudes of majority constituents than to those of minority constituents (except in the case of the civil rights issue in competitive districts). In safe districts, where the views of minority constituents can

Table 17.3. Representation Relationships of Congressmen

	Coefficients of Correlation*					
Issues Competition in District and Constituency Groups†	(1) District attitude & candidate attitude	(2) District attitude & candidate perception of district	(3) Candidate attitude & roll call behavior	(4) Candidate perception & roll call behavior	(5) Roll call behavior correlated with candidate attitude & perception of district	(6) District attitude & roll call behavior
Foreign policy	.06	.19	.42	.49	.56	−.09
Social welfare ENTIRE DISTRICT	.21	.17	.61	.54	.70	.28
Civil rights	.39	.63	.77	.82	.88	.57
SAFE DISTRICT						
Social welfare Majority	.39	.38	.30	.56	.73	.60
Minority	.26	−.13	.30	.56	.73	.04
COMPETITIVE DISTRICT						
Social welfare Majority	.27	.03	.75	.05	.77	.08
Minority	−.38	.11	.75	.05	.77	−.34

Coefficients of Correlation*

Issues	Competition in District and Constituency Groups†	(1) District attitude & candidate attitude	(2) District attitude & candidate perception of district	(3) Candidate attitude & roll call behavior	(4) Candidate perception & roll call behavior	(5) Roll call behavior correlated with candidate attitude & perception of district	(6) District attitude & roll call behavior
Civil rights	**SAFE DISTRICT**						
	Majority	.54	.78	.23	.70	.89	.64
	Minority	.31	.24	.23	.70	.89	.23
	COMPETITIVE DISTRICT						
	Majority	−.16	.23	.50	.34	.65	−.08
	Minority	−.14	.44	.50	.34	.65	.01

*Figures in columns 1, 2, and 6 are simple product-moment correlation coefficients. Those in columns 3 and 4 are normalized regression coefficients showing the relationship of candidate attitude or perception to roll call behavior, with the other predictor controlled. Figures in column 5 are the product-moment coefficients of multiple correlation, expressing the combined relation of candidate attitude and perception with roll call behavior.

†Districts are divided into safe and competitive districts according to the designation of the congressman. The majority and minority constituents whose attitudes are measured separately are those who voted for and those who voted against the 85th Congress incumbent (or his successor) in the 1958 election.

SOURCE: Based on data from publications by the staff of the Survey Research Center of the University of Michigan, cited in footnote 47.

be safely ignored, the correlations between the views of majority constituents on the one hand and candidate attitude, candidate perception,
and roll call behavior on the other hand are much higher than other
correlations among these same factors. In competitive districts, where
it is more difficult to distinguish what majority opinion is, the differences
are less clear.

We can shed a little more light on the congressman's perception of
constituent attitudes by contrasting those who make greater and those
who make lesser efforts to gain information about these attitudes, through
personal contact, mail, polls, etc., as revealed by the congressional interviews. Using the social welfare issues as an example, the authors of this
study found that those congressmen who made greater efforts to determine constituent opinion voted more in accord with perceived constituent attitudes and less in accord with their own views; both their
perception and their own attitude were closer to constituent attitudes.
However, the congressmen who were less zealous in measuring constituent opinion had a voting record and personal viewpoints that were
more in accord with majority constituent opinion in their districts than
was true of their colleagues.

This study by the Survey Research Center, without focusing directly on party-constituency conflict, provides clues to variables in the
constituency as a reference group which are pertinent to this conflict.
The constituency provides strong voting cues on some issues, few if
any cues on others. The legislator is better able to perceive constituent
opinion if he is familiar with the district and if a majority viewpoint is
visible, both being more frequent conditions in safe districts. He need
not satisfy all constituents but can take his cues from the majority, if he
can identify that majority with some degree of certainty. The legislator
has some area of choice, but he cannot always choose his role freely.
The legislator from the marginal district who relies heavily on his own
viewpoints may have been forced into the Trustee role because the
Delegate's role requires a level of information about constituent opinion
that he too often lacks. On a few issues (such as civil rights) even the
most secure legislator must, or thinks he must, play the role of Delegate.

INFORMAL REFERENCE GROUPS IN THE LEGISLATURE

In the previous chapter we described some of the informal groups
with which a legislator has contact. Because it is through such friendship
groups that legislative norms and opinions on issues are often transmitted
to the legislator, it is reasonable to suppose that these groups are sometimes a source of voting cues, particularly if other sources (party, constituency) are weak on a particular issue. In the 1957 session of the
Wisconsin Assembly, intraparty cliques tended to have distinct voting

patterns on some issues.[48] Until more research on such friendship groups has been undertaken, we can only hazard the prophecy that more adequate understanding of these groups would reveal a substantial effect on voting. Another study of Wisconsin illustrates a slightly different aspect of legislative friendship: legislators have often said that their votes on issues were influenced by their attitude toward the sponsor of the bill; when the legislator is free from party or constituent pressure, such a casual and seemingly irrelevant factor may become important.[49]

The strongest evidence of voting cohesion in informal groups pertains to the state Democratic and Republican delegations in the national House. This is partly a consequence of the greater homogeneity of districts: Democratic districts in Massachusetts have much in common with each other but little in common with Democratic districts in Tennessee. Beyond that, the state party delegation represents a natural friendship group, with common interests and background. The new member of Congress turns naturally to party colleagues from his own state for advice, information, and quite possibly voting cues. Truman's analysis of the larger House delegations in the Eighty-first Congress provides convincing evidence that, particularly when party cohesion is weak, the state party delegation is an important source of voting cues. The proportion of congressmen who voted more often with one or more state colleagues than with others in their party was much larger than would be the product of chance. In a few state party delegations, cohesion was based more narrowly in a single metropolitan district—such as Chicago, where the local Democratic organization has unusual influence over congressional voting—but this local cohesion was less important than statewide party cohesion.[50] A few scattered examples—New Hampshire, Wisconsin, and California—suggest that there may be particularly strong cohesion in city delegations within some of the parties in state legislatures.

VOTING IN ONE-PARTY LEGISLATURES: AN UNFILLED VACUUM

In those state legislatures that are completely dominated by a single party, the party is not a source of voting cues. The constituency remains a reference group of intermittent importance, lobbyists remain eager to provide advice, and informal legislative groups probably take on greater importance. But there is commonly no substitute for party. Only rarely does any factional grouping demonstrate voting cohesion on a significant number of roll calls, and even more rarely does such a faction retain its identity and cohesion beyond a single session of the legislature.

In many one-party states, the governor is the most visible source of voting cues; those measures that have his endorsement have the best chance of passage, and those that he opposes face serious obstacles to their obtaining a legislative majority. The governor often has no dependable, cohesive faction to support his program, nor does he face a cohesive opposition. In his effort to win votes for his program, he is entirely dependent on his skill in using the resources of his office: patronage, public relations, and the rest. In some one-party states, these resources are sufficient to assure the governor of legislative support for the major bills in his program. Georgia, for example, is a state in which the governor has traditionally been strong. In the legislative sessions from 1955 through 1961, the Georgia legislators passed 57 of 62 bills that typified major parts of the governor's program. Of these 57 bills, in the Senate 43 passed unanimously, and only 2 had negative votes from over 10 percent of the members; in the House 24 passed unanimously, 26 were opposed by less than 10 percent, and 7 were opposed by over 10 percent.[51]

In a few states, a bifactional system has evolved in the legislature as a result of the personality and program of a governor. During Jim Folsom's tenure in Alabama, factions supporting and opposing his administration could be identified, and they voted with at least moderate cohesion on some roll calls.[52] The bifactionalism evident in Kentucky Democratic primaries seldom extends to legislative issues, but in 1958— during the second session of A. B. Chandler's administration—there was a sharp factional split on a number of important roll calls, some of which the governor won only by enlisting Republican support. In neither of these states have legislative factions been consistent and consistently strong from one administration to the next. The bifactionalism in Louisiana, which had its origins in Huey Long's reign and its roots in deep socioeconomic conflicts, has persisted in the legislature for several decades. Although it varies in intensity and in the nature of alignments from one administration to the next, legislative factionalism has a continuity and a significance in Louisiana which exceed those in other Southern states.[53]

Fragments of research provide some clues in a few other states about factional alignments that are not directly related to the governor. The Minnesota legislature, which is formally nonpartisan, is organized into Liberal and Conservative caucuses; the Liberal caucus has close ties with the Democratic-Farmer-Labor party, while the Conservative caucus has somewhat weaker Republican ties. These groups vote with high cohesion on organizing the legislature, and there is some evidence of cohesion on a number of other roll calls.[54] An analysis of factions in the California Assembly during the 1947–1955 period, when party lines were weak, reveals the existence of two factions that took opposite sides on several roll calls that involved contests for the speakership and other organizational issues. The importance of these factions as reference groups can be traced in a small number of the most important policy questions that came to a vote during this period. The factions were each bipartisan and biregional; each included a nucleus of members with highly consistent voting records on the fourteen roll calls under consideration. The California factions were unusual in that they appear to have assumed greater importance than the parties as reference groups.⁵⁵

Regional or urban-rural alignments seldom appear with any regularity in roll call votes of one-party states. One exception appears to be the Florida Senate, where Parsons found "a quite stable, cohesive bifactionalism."⁵⁶ In most one-party states, the metropolitan legislators are badly outnumbered and consequently have little incentive for cohesion. There are some issues on which urban-rural splits frequently develop: the allocation of state funds, apportionment, "moral" issues such as liquor laws and betting, and—in the South—certain racial questions. Important though these issues may be, they do not arise often enough or produce clear-cut alignments consistently enough to make urban and rural blocs visible in roll call analysis.

The most thorough study of urban-rural voting in a one-party state is Murray Havens's analysis of the 1955 and 1956 sessions of the Alabama House. He concluded that differences in the voting of urban and rural legislators were statistically significant on slightly more than one-fourth of the seriously contested roll calls. Many of these dealt with reapportionment; often urban-rural conflict was absent on issues—such as municipal or farm legislation—where it might have been most expected. The outnumbered urban legislators sometimes formed a coalition with Northern rural legislators. In short, there were no consistently cohesive urban-rural blocs, but rather a network of coalitions shifting from one issue to the next.⁵⁷

The 1959 session of the Oklahoma House provides a final example, and probably one that could be duplicated in many states, of voting in a one-party state. The voting pattern of individual legislators was consistent enough to permit the creation of 7 scales (each of which met standard tests of scalability) pertaining to the governor's program, labor and welfare, schools, campaigns and elections, public morals, appropriations, and taxation. But rank-order correlation analysis showed that these scales represented independent and largely unrelated dimensions of voting behavior; only the governor's program scale was associated to any extent with the others. Support for the governor's program came primarily from leaders, freshmen, and legislators from competitive districts. (The Republicans held 9 of 119 seats.) Members from competitive districts were more likely to support stricter regulation of campaigns. On most scales, metropolitan legislators could be distinguished from all others, but on tax legislation metropolitan and rural legislators formed an alliance against urban and semirural legislators. The school scale was related to the income level of districts. Voting on appropriations and labor and welfare legislation was related to membership on the committees that were handling these questions. The analysis of Oklahoma stands as a warning against efforts to find simple explanations of voting behavior—particularly in one-party states. It suggests that "in the absence of party as a reference group, the legislator is likely, consciously or unconsciously, to respond to different pressures in different voting areas."[58]

PARTY COHESION AND PARTY RESPONSIBILITY

Patterns of roll call voting are fundamentally different in legislatures where party is a reference group from what they are in those where it is not. Where party is a reference group, it is usually pertinent not to the mass of trivial and local legislation considered in many states but to the issues of greatest concern to the administration, the party interests, or the public. Party alignment is strongest in the two-party industrial states, where both parties have a high degree of constituent homogeneity and in Congress, where the parties are heterogeneous enough to permit only a moderate level of party cohesion. In such legislatures, party loyalty is a norm rooted in custom; it is often supported internally by such institutional devices as the caucus and enhanced externally by strong executive leadership. No system of factions, whatever their constituent base, has equaled the stability and continuity of the voting alignments that are frequently characteristic of party voting.

Party cohesion in the legislature is not the same thing as party responsibility. The concept of responsibility requires not only cohesive parties but also regular two-party competition for legislative seats and public awareness of the legislative record. The extent and limitations of two-party competition were discussed in Chapter 4. There is not consistent competition for all Southern congressional seats or for all legislative seats, even in strong two-party states, but the likelihood of party competition in two-party areas is greater than the likelihood of primary competition in one-party areas.

V. O. Key contrasted the function of parties and factions in a system of representation in these words:

Under a system of fluid factions . . . the voters' task is not simplified by the existence of continuing competing parties with fairly well-recognized, general-policy orientations. . . . Factions that form and reform cannot become so identified in the minds of the electorate, and the conditions of public choice become far different from those under two-party conditions.[59]

Buchanan noted that, when legislative partisanship was weak in California, factions lacked the electoral base "that would enable them to clarify issues, formulate programs, present the voters with meaningful choices, or assume responsibility for their actions." As Buchanan points out, the individual citizen must expend large amounts of time and effort if he wishes to follow legislative developments in detail.[60] We know that the average citizen is almost totally ignorant of legislative voting records or even of the substantive character of legislative issues. The disillusioning finding of the Michigan Survey Research Center bears repetition: Only 3 percent of its respondents in 1958 could identify a single policy stand taken by their congressman on any given major issue. This does not mean that responsible government is impossible, but rather that it is a meaningless concept to most voters unless they can use the party as a crutch.

It is well to recall, as Sorauf reminds us in his study of Pennsylvania, that the party seldom presents a comprehensive legislative program to the voters, that local parties and legislative candidates pay little attention to issues, and that most voters have only a vague awareness of whatever policies are advocated. Party discipline, where it exists, is rooted in the social and economic homogeneity of interests and political values in the constituencies of each party. Such disciplined parties are responsible in the sense that the voter can confidently expect the party to represent these interests. In particular he can expect the administration party to support major programs of the governor who has espoused these interests in his campaign. This "inarticulate ideology" based on constituent interests may be—as Sorauf describes it—only "a reasonable substitute for party responsibility," but it makes legislative politics more meaningful for the voter than is possible in a one-party state.[61]

NOTES

1. David B. Truman, *The Congressional Party* (New York, 1959), p. 12.
2. Donald R. Matthews, *U.S. Senators and Their World* (Chapel Hill, N.C., 1960), p. 123.
3. Wilder Crane, Jr., "A Caveat on Roll-call Studies of Party Voting," *Midwest Journal of Political Science*, IV (1960), 237–49; see also his "The Legislative Struggle in Wisconsin: Decision-Making in the 1957 Wisconsin Assembly" (Unpublished Ph.D. dissertation, University of Wisconsin, 1959). The "unconscious" party votes are discussed in Fred I. Greenstein and Elton F. Jackson, "A Second Look at the Validity of Roll Call Analysis," *Midwest Journal of Political Science*, VII (1963), 156–66.
4. George D. Young, "The Role of Political Parties in the Missouri House of Representatives" (Unpublished Ph.D. dissertation, University of Missouri, 1958), pp. 151, 203.
5. John C. Wahlke, Heinz Eulau, William Buchanan, and Leroy C. Ferguson,

The Legislative System (New York: John Wiley and Sons, 1962), pp. 350–71, 423–27.

6. Julius Turner, *Party and Constituency: Pressures on Congress* (Baltimore, 1952), pp. 24, 31; V. O. Key, Jr., *Southern Politics in State and Nation* (New York, 1950), p. 370; Roland Young, *Congressional Politics in the Second World War* (New York, 1956), p. 269.

7. Duane Lockard, *New England State Politics* (Princeton, N.J., 1959), pp. 291–92.

8. See, for example, Angus Campbell, Philip E. Converse, Warren E. Miller, and Donald E. Stokes, *The American Voter* (New York, 1960), chap. 10.

9. Frank J. Sorauf, *Party and Representation* (New York: Atherton Press, 1963), p. 151.

10. Lockard, *op. cit.*, pp. 156–57, 325.

11. *Ibid.*, p. 298.

12. Sorauf, *op. cit.*, p. 146. The situation in Ohio is similar to that in Pennsylvania; see Thomas A. Flinn, "Party Responsibility in the States: Some Causal Factors," *American Political Science Review*, LVIII (1964), 61.

13. Wahlke et al., *op. cit.*, pp. 362–63.

14. Truman, *op. cit.*, pp. 289–90, 292, 309–10.

15. *Ibid.*, pp. 178, 281.

16. Lee F. Anderson, "Variability in the Undimensionality of Legislative Voting," *Journal of Politics*, XXVI (1964), 568–85.

17. All figures have been calculated from volumes of the *Congressional Quarterly Almanac*. Note that the percentage of support for the party's position on issues with the party taking opposite stands dropped from 1955 on, partly because the basis of calculation was changed in such a way that the failure to vote lowered the congressman's party unity average. The CQ figures for presidential support throughout the period have been recalculated to prevent nonvoting from lowering the level of support.

18. Flinn, *op. cit.*, pp. 60–71; Flinn, "An Outline of Ohio Politics," *Western Political Quarterly*, XIII (1960), 719; Malcolm E. Jewell, "Party Voting in American State Legislatures," *American Political Science Review*, XLIX (1955), 779–80; Sorauf, *op. cit.*, p. 137.

19. John G. Grumm, "Party Responsibility in the Kansas Legislature" (Unpublished paper presented at the Wichita Conference on Politics, April 1959); and "A Factor Analysis of Legislative Behavior," *Midwest Journal of Political Science*, VII (1963), 336–56.

20. See, for example, Jewell, *op. cit.*, pp. 788–90; Lockard, *op. cit.*, pp. 71–72, 117, 154, 214, 280; William Buchanan, *Legislative Partisanship* (Berkeley, 1963), pp. 111–115.

21. *Congressional Quarterly Almanac* (1953–1964).

22. Malcolm E. Jewell, *Senatorial Politics and Foreign Policy* (Lexington, Ky., 1962), chaps. 2 and 3.

23. William J. Keefe, "Comparative Study of the Role of Political Parties in State Legislatures," *Western Political Quarterly*, IX (1956), 726–42. Keefe's findings are presented in greater detail in "The Party as an Interest Group in the State Legislative Process" (Unpublished paper presented at the annual meeting of the American Political Science Association, September 1957).

24. Buchanan, *op. cit.*, p. 141.

25. Truman, *op. cit.*, chaps. 3 and 5, p. 167.

26. *Congressional Quarterly Almanac* (1958–1964).

27. Jewell, *Senatorial Politics and Foreign Policy*, chap. 2; George L. Grassmuck, *Sectional Biases in Congress on Foreign Policy* (Baltimore, 1951), chap. 7; H. Bradford Westerfield, *Foreign Policy and Party Politics* (New Haven, Conn., 1955), chaps. 2 and 3.

28. Truman, *op. cit.*, p. 78.

29. Turner, *op. cit.*, chaps. 4–7.

30. Duncan MacRae, Jr., *Dimensions of Congressional Voting* (Berkeley, 1958), chap. 3.

31. Murray C. Havens, "Metropolitan Areas and Congress: Foreign Policy and National Security," *Journal of Politics*, XXVI (1964), 758–74.

32. David R. Derge, "Metropolitan and Outstate Alignments in Illinois and Missouri Legislative Delegations," *American Political Science Review*, LII (1958) 1051–65; Flinn, "The Outline of Ohio Politics," pp. 717–18; Grumm, "Party Responsibility in the Kansas Legislature."

33. Sorauf, *op. cit.*, p. 126.

34. Wahlke et al., *op. cit.*, p. 296.

35. Sorauf, *op. cit.*, p. 124.

36. Duncan MacRae, Jr., "The Relation between Roll Call Votes and Constituencies in the Massachusetts House of Representatives," *American Political Science Review*, XLVI (1952), 1046–55, 1055.

37. Turner, *op. cit.*, chap. 8; Lewis A. Froman, Jr., *Congressmen and Their Constituencies* (Chicago, 1963), chaps. 7 and 9.

38. MacRae, *Dimensions of Congressional Voting*, chap. 3; J. Roland Pennock, "Party and Constituency in Postwar Agricultural Price-support Legislation," *Journal of Politics*, XVIII (1956), 167–210; Jewell, *Senatorial Politics and Foreign Policy*, chaps. 2 and 3.

39. MacRae, "The Relation between Roll Call Votes and Constituencies in the Massachusetts House of Representatives"; Sorauf, *op. cit.*, p. 142; Thomas R. Dye, "A Comparison of Constituency Influences in the Upper and Lower Chambers of a State Legislature," *Western Political Quarterly*, XIV (1961), 473–80, 480.

40. Flinn, "Party Responsibility in the States," pp. 61–66; Grumm, "A Factor Analysis of Legislative Behavior."

41. Sorauf, *op. cit.*, p. 141; Dye, *op. cit.*, p. 477.

42. MacRae, "The Relation between Roll Call Votes and Constituencies in the Massachusetts House of Representatives"; Pertti Personen, "Close and Safe State Elections in Massachusetts," *Midwest Journal of Political Science*, VII (1963), 54–70; Samuel C. Patterson, "The Role of the Deviant in the State Legislative System: The Wisconsin Assembly," *Western Political Quarterly*, XIV (1961), 467–68.

43. Flinn, "Party Responsibility in the States," pp. 66–69; Grumm, "The Systematic Analysis of Blocs in the Study of Legislative Behavior, *Western Political Quarterly*, XVIII (1965), 350–62.

44. MacRae, *Dimensions of Congressional Voting*, p. 286.

45. Froman, *op. cit.*, chap. 9, p. 121.

46. Thomas A. Flinn and Harold L. Wolman, "Southern Democratic Congressmen: The Reflection of Constituency in Roll Call Voting" (Unpublished paper, 1964).

47. A preliminary description and analysis of these data can be found in Warren E. Miller and Donald E. Stokes, "Constituency Influence in Congress," *American Political Science Review*, LVII (1963), 45–56; Warren E. Miller, "Majority Rule and the Representative System" (Unpublished paper presented at the annual meeting of the American Political Science Association, September 1962); Miller, "Policy Preference of Congressional Candidates and Constituents" (Unpublished paper presented at the annual meeting of the American Political Science Association, September 1961). A fuller analysis of the data will appear in a forthcoming volume, *Representation in the American Congress*.

48. Samuel C. Patterson, "Patterns of Interpersonal Relations in a State Legislative Group: The Wisconsin Assembly," *Public Opinion Quarterly*, XXIII (1959), 101–09.

49. Crane, "The Legislative Struggle in Wisconsin."

50. Truman, *op. cit.*, chap. 7.

51. Hugh M. Thomason, "The Legislative Process in Georgia" (Unpublished Ph.D. dissertation, Emory University, 1961), pp. 207–09.

52. Murray C. Havens, *City Versus Farm?* (University, Ala., 1957), p. 54.

This analysis covers only the 1955 and 1956 sessions.

53. Allan P. Sindler, *Huey Long's Louisiana* (Baltimore, 1956).

54. G. Theodore Mitau, *Politics in Minnesota* (Minneapolis, 1960), chap. 3; Thomas A. Flinn, "The Policy Process: The Minnesota Governor and Legislature in 1955" (Unpublished Ph.D. dissertation, University of Minnesota, 1957).

55. Buchanan, *op. cit.*, chap. 5.

56. Malcolm B. Parsons, "Quasi-partisan Conflict in a One-party Legislative System: The Florida Senate, 1947–1961," *American Political Science Review*, LVI (1962), 605–14.

57. Havens, *City Versus Farm?*

58. Samuel C. Patterson, "Dimensions of Voting Behavior in a One-party State Legislature," *Public Opinion Quarterly*, XXVI (1962), 185–200, 200.

59. Key, *op. cit.*, p. 303.

60. Buchanan, *op. cit.*, p. 83.

61. Sorauf, *op. cit.*, pp. 150–151

[18]

Legislative
Committees
at Work

Vᴵˢᴵᵀᴼᴿˢ to the Senate or House who do not see their congressman on the floor are usually told that he is in a committee meeting, "where the real work goes on." The press of varied and complex legislative business forces both Congress and state legislatures to delegate a large share of the decision making to committees. In Chapter 9 we described the function of committees in the legislative system, their organizational structure, and the techniques used for choosing members. In this chapter we shall examine their operation and their methods of reaching decisions on legislation. With rare exceptions it is the practice to refer all bills and resolutions to a committee after introduction in the first house and, after passage there, to repeat the process in the second house.

In some committees a bill will be assigned first to one of several subcommittees. Where subcommittees are used, the hearings are conducted and the significant decisions made at that level; approval by the full committee is usually a matter of routine. We shall examine four stages of committee (or subcommittee) action. In the hearing, the committee members play a variety of roles other than that of a neutral judge. In the executive session, decisions are made about how to amend the bill and whether to report it; we are concerned with the factors that tend to produce (or reduce) consensus regarding these decisions. When the bill is considered on the floor, a number of variables determine how much weight the committee's recommendations will have. After a bill has passed both houses in different versions, a conference committee, chosen from members of the original Senate and House committees, often has wide latitude in determining the final contents of the bill.

THE HEARINGS

The Purpose of Congressional Hearings. A hearing is usually necessary before a congressional committee will vote on a bill. Approval of a bill without a hearing is rare; on the other hand, there is no guarantee that a bill will receive a hearing. This initial decision on the bill is primarily in the hands of the committee or subcommittee chairman, although he may be persuaded by pressure from other members. It is at this stage that many bills are given a quiet burial because of their trivial or unrealistic nature, because the chairman judges that they will not engender enough support for serious consideration in Congress, because of the overwhelmingly negative pressure of interest groups, or because the committee or its chairman is hostile to those bills. The decision to hold hearings on a bill indicates that it is going to receive serious consideration because the committee members are interested in it or because they believe the interest of outside groups is sufficient to warrant a hearing.

Hearings serve several purposes, recognition of which facilitates an understanding of the various roles that committee members play. The hearings provide an opportunity for interested groups and individuals to present their viewpoints and their versions of the facts to a committee. This is by no means the only route of access that interest groups have to Congress, but it is the open, formal, direct route. Hearings provide the committee with one of its best means of obtaining information. One of the committee's functions is fact finding. This does not mean that committee members are necessarily impartial, but usually they are interested in gaining information, even if it is only to reinforce their preconceptions. Sometimes the need for information is great enough to justify a broad investigation of the whole problem, perhaps lasting for months, while on other occasions the study is limited to the specific provisions and immediate implications of a bill. In either case, the fact-finding role is pervasive for committees.

Because committee members are not merely neutral judges, they sometimes use the hearings for another purpose: to develop support for, or opposition to, a bill. The chairman may accomplish this purpose by the timing of the hearings, the selection and priority of witnesses, and the use made of staff resources during the hearings. Other members may use friendly or hostile questions to witnesses in order to achieve the same end. The purpose of these maneuvers may be the narrow one of persuading undecided committee members, or it may be the broader one of generating public interest and support that will impress Congress as a whole. When the committee chairman solicits testimony from a long series of distinguished witnesses or schedules a prolonged and highly publicized investigation, his purpose is usually to attract attention to a problem and to inform the public and Congress about the viewpoint he supports. Also, as Congressman Clem Miller once explained, "Many times, the hearings seem to be *pro forma*, just going through the motions, with the key decisions already made. They resemble a large verbal orchestration, as a 'record' is carefully shaped under the vigilant gavel of the chairman."[1]

The Setting. The stage for committee hearings is usually set by the chairman, whose decisions may affect the outcome by affording a significant advantage to one side or the other. The chairman who is trying to enhance the chances of a bill may decide that hearings should start quickly or else should be postponed until group support can be organized. He may hold prolonged hearings in order to develop public and congressional interest and support, or he may decide that brief, little publicized hearings will be more effective because they arouse less opposition.[2]

One provision of the 1946 Legislative Reorganization Act was designed to limit the chairman's freedom to hold hearings behind closed doors. The law requires public hearings, except where a majority of the committee votes for closed hearings. Nevertheless, a substantial number of committee hearings are closed. Calculations by the *Congressional Quarterly* show that in recent years about 35 percent of committee hearings have been closed. More than half the hearings have been closed in the case of the committees of both houses that deal with foreign affairs and taxation. All House Appropriations Committee hearings and subcommittee hearings are closed.[3] In national defense or foreign policy matters, the reason may be security. In the case of the House Appropriations subcommittees, closed hearings are designed to discourage pressure from interest groups. Closed hearings may facilitate the gathering of information quietly and free from pressure, but they are often used by committee members to serve their own purposes of promoting or burying proposed legislation.

The chairman schedules the witnesses. Although the committee can sometimes hear all who want to testify, this is likely to be impossible in the case of major pieces of controversial legislation. Then the chairman may make choices, which are not always impartial. The chairman's power, however, is not merely negative; he may recruit witnesses who support his point of view on legislation. On sharply divisive issues, a committee sometimes divides the time of the hearings equally between supporters and opponents, giving two members of the committee supervision over the witnesses on each side. When the hearings take on an investigatory nature and the committee surveys a broad area of concern, the staff plays a more important role, subject to the chairman's direction, in recruiting witnesses, questioning them, producing evidence, and even carrying out extensive investigations of its own as a prelude to the hearings.

One aspect of the hearings over which the chairman has no control is the presence of committee members. Congressional hearings are normally held in the morning, when the Senate and House are not in session. But there are many other demands on a congressman's time. Other committees or subcommittees of which he is a member may be meeting simultaneously. Occasionally he finds it necessary to testify before another committee. There are unavoidable meetings with constituents, conferences with other congressmen on legislative strategy, and appointments with government officials in order to serve the needs of constituents. The result is that there is rarely full attendance at a hearing; often only a small fraction of the committee members are present, and witnesses become accustomed to seeing congressmen wandering in and out of the hearings. One of the chores of an effective lobbyist is to make sure that some committee members who are sympathetic to his cause will be present to support his testimony with friendly questions.

Normally a witness is given a chance to make a prepared statement first, although there is no guarantee that he will not be interrupted by questions. When a large number of committee members are present, protocol requires that members be permitted to ask questions in order of seniority. This may leave the junior member with little to say. In smaller hearings, the questioning is likely to be more informal. On occasion staff members may ask most of the questions or may supply the committee members with questions to use during the hearing.

The Roles of Committee Members. We can identify a variety of roles assumed by committee members, which reflect a variety of views about what is expected of them by constituents, pressure groups, and fellow congressmen, among others. As Huitt has said, "The congressional role probably is most usefully conceived not as a single role but as a multiplicity of roles, defined for the congressman by the varying expectations of the groups which he represents or with which he identifies."[4] The most obvious clues to these roles can be found in the committee hearings, particularly at the congressional level, where hearings are frequent and well publicized. An identification of these roles demonstrates why committee members seldom act as impartial judges at hearings; outside groups usually have a claim on their loyalties. A word of caution is necessary here, however. Because hearings are usually public, the roles of committee members during a hearing are likely to be affected more by the expectations of outside groups than is necessarily true within the committee itself. As we shall see, some of the roles that are emphasized in hearings may be modified or subordinated within the committee in response to the expectations of other committee members.

Sometimes the committee member interprets his role in national terms. One example of this is the Administration Loyalist. He cooperates closely with administration witnesses, feeding them questions that advance their argument, but he sharply challenges witnesses who are critical of the administration. One of the handicaps faced by any administration is that it cannot automatically depend on having a loyal supporter in every committee hearing, although there will frequently be some member or members playing this role. On issues of foreign policy, a member of the opposition party may even assume this role, as Senator Vandenberg did in guiding the hearings on the Marshall Plan in 1947. Cohen describes the role played by senators of both parties during hearings of the Senate Foreign Relations Committee on the Japanese peace treaty in 1952:

> There appeared to be an implicit set of ground rules agreed to by almost everybody according to which no questions likely to prove embarrassing would be asked. Most of the questions, in fact, seemed to be set up in such a way as to give Mr. Dulles [who had negotiated the treaty and was the key witness] excellent opportunities to make his major points, and he always cheerfully obliged. . . .
> Sometimes the questions which the Senators asked of Administration witnesses inadvertently led into areas of controversy, exposing for a moment the still-raw nerve ends of a policy dispute. Generally, when this happened, the line of questioning was brought to a quick close, before the real substance of the disagreement was drawn into public view.[5]

A natural counterpart to the Administration Loyalist is the Opposition Spokesman, which is likewise a role not played consistently by most congressmen. Senator Robert A. Taft is perhaps the best recent example of a congressman who assumed this role in most committee hearings. In a study of hearings on price control in 1946, Huitt found that most congressmen were concerned with the effects of price control on particular interests and constituents, but for Senator Taft "the price control contest was simply one round in a continuing battle with the Administration."[6]

Congressmen very often assume more parochial committee roles.

Most of the major pressure groups have at least one Advocate on the committees that concern it most. He serves as a source of information, a prompter during the hearings, and a spokesman in the closed sessions. The congressman's loyalty may be based on personal conviction or association, agreement on specific policy objectives, political alliance, or campaign contributions. A congressman working in alliance with a lobbyist who is giving testimony may work out in advance a series of questions that will help the lobbyist, or warn him about the kinds of questions he may expect from hostile members of the committee. Just as some congressmen serve as Advocates for an interest group, others serve as Critics. In 1955, when the spokesman for the Vigilant Women for the Bricker Amendment testified before a Judiciary subcommittee, Senator Bricker, naturally enough, congratulated the women on their fine work, but Senator Kefauver suggested that the organization should have registered with Congress as a group engaged in lobbying. Gross cites the example of Senator Forest Donnell, who regularly interrogated witnesses in support of national health insurance to determine the strength of the organizations they represented and whether the organization had actually endorsed the position taken by the witness.[7] This is a favorite tactic of committee members who are skeptical of or hostile to certain pressure groups.

A closely related role of a committee member is that of Representative of a local constituent interest, organized or unorganized. In his study of price-control hearings, Huitt uses the example of Senator McFarland of Arizona, who showed great interest in subsidies for lead, zinc, and copper industries important to his state, and guided the testimony of witnesses for those industries, but showed little interest in other aspects of the hearing. A congressman may, in fact, seldom appear at hearings until the subject matter touches on constituent interests. Huitt points out that, when these regional or local interests are involved, the congressmen are likely to be better informed than when they are dealing with broader issues.[8] Sometimes the makeup of a committee guarantees that most attention will be focused on local interests. Jones has described the makeup of commodity subcommittees of the House Agricultural Committee, which are composed to a large extent of members from a constituency where that particular commodity (corn, cotton, or peanuts, for example) is important.[9]

Sometimes the congressman is representing not a general constituency interest, but a particular constituent—perhaps a businessman; this might be called the Errand Boy role. During the price-control hearings cited by Huitt, Senator Capehart wanted information for several constituents about pricing policies on trousers, Senator Hickenlooper wanted to secure records about quotas and prices for meat, and Senator Tobey wanted to know why one of his constituents was not permitted by the government to fabricate lumber that he had logged himself.[10] This is an important role, one assumed on some occasions by nearly all congressmen who are seeking public redress for bureaucratic mistreatment of their constituents. Behind the scenes, the congressman may use his committee position to get a favor for an important business constituent, or for the broader purpose of getting projects and benefits for his district.

In addition to the broader national roles and the interest and constituency roles already described, some congressmen play roles that derive peculiarly from their position on a committee. Every congressman with a few years of committee experience becomes an expert on some topic. Though this is a role played by many, we can identify as the Expert the member who subordinates other roles to this one, who takes great pride in displaying to administration witnesses his superior knowledge and proficiency in the techniques of government.

One role is particularly associated with investigating committees, but it is popular enough to emerge at almost any point in a hearing. That is the role of Prosecutor. The congressman may be interrogating an evasive bureaucrat, an erring labor leader, an unrepentant Communist, or simply a presidential appointee who is lacking in humility. The role of Prosecutor comes easily to the many congressmen who are former lawyers. It is a natural role for committee members, who are traditionally suspicious of administrative officials and are sometimes frustrated by the difficulty of penetrating to the depths of the complex process by which policies are made and administered in Washington.

Hearings in State Committees. In some state legislatures committee hearings are a rarity; at the other extreme, in a few states they are required on all bills. The variation in practice is wide, but generally speaking, committee hearings play a smaller role in the legislative process of most states than they do in Congress. There are several reasons for this. The shortage of time is an important obstacle, particularly in legislatures where most of the important controversial legislation is referred to a few committees, or in states where the session is limited to two or three months. The large number of committee assignments for each member sometimes reduces attendance at those hearings that are held. The lack of a professional staff makes it difficult or impossible for most legislators to be prepared to question witnesses who appear at the hearings.

Often the absence of hearings can be explained simply by the absence of witnesses. In contrast to most congressional legislation, a large proportion of the bills considered by state legislatures deal with issues of trivial, technical, or local importance, issues unlikely to stir much public interest. It is not surprising that no one requests a chance to be heard before a committee on many such bills. In a number of states it is the practice to hold a hearing whenever there is a demand for it; in most cases there is no demand. In some states, however, an observer cannot escape the suspicion that committees discourage persons and groups from appearing at hearings by failing to publicize the time and place of such hearings, or by avoiding the holding of hearings so regularly that interested citizens are led to believe that they do not have any chance to testify. Sometimes hearings are scheduled with little notice, so as to accommodate the spokesmen for only one point of view. Hearings on the budget, at which administration officials in particular are invited to testify, are more common and more extensive than hearings on other issues, but in some states even budget hearings are rare.

Variations in the frequency and importance of committee hearings result in part from differences in the independent authority exercised by committees. The states where hearings not only are frequent but also have a significant impact on the decision-making process are primarily those in which legislative parties are weak. Examples of this include New Hampshire, Tennessee, California, and Oregon; another example is Nebraska, where procedural rules assure that adequate publicity and time will be provided for committee hearings. There are a number of other states where hearings are held regularly on important bills or upon request, but these hearings are usually *pro forma* affairs, serving only the purpose of permitting interest groups to be heard and to put their views on record. New York, where joint hearings are held with adequate notice on major bills, and Connecticut, which also makes frequent use of joint hearings, are states in which the crucial decisions are nevertheless more often made by the party leadership or in caucus than in committee. In Illinois, hearings are always held if the sponsor of the bill requests it; if he does not, the bill dies a quiet death. Illinois committee hearings are usually brief, informal affairs at which testimony is heard quickly, a minimum of questions are asked, and a quick vote is taken. Illinois committees usually give routine approval to bills and leave the question of their passage to the party leadership.

In some states where partisan or factional leadership is particularly strong, committees seldom hold hearings, except perhaps on appropriations bills. In both New Jersey and Pennsylvania, the committee chairmen serve as agents of the party leadership and the caucus. In Pennsylvania, the chairman may consult extensively with the interest groups affected by a bill, but he seldom holds a formal hearing. In Kentucky, hearings are infrequent and are not always held, even when requested by major interest groups on important bills. Infrequent and poorly publicized hearings are also the rule in a few states that lack strong party or factional leadership, such as North Carolina.[11]

In state legislatures, the roles of committee members may not be so clearly defined or apparent, so long as the spotlight of publicity seldom shines on the committee. In those states where committees are primarily tools of the legislative leaders, we may assume that the role of members is primarily that of Loyalists. They do not act independently, but follow the leadership. The role of a pressure-group Advocate is a familiar one in many legislative committees, and it is enhanced by the frequent practice of weighting a committee heavily with members who have a personal interest in the subjects under the committee's jurisdiction. The role of Expert is often combined with that of Advocate. It may be difficult to find unbiased experts for state legislative committees, since most members have a primary profession that overshadows their legislative career. On an insurance committee, for example, there will be a number of legislators who are considered experts because that is their profession, but who cannot separate their expert knowledge from their advocacy of the viewpoints held by the insurance profession. Under these conditions, lobbyists are likely to have unusually easy access to the committee, and in some committees lobbying by outsiders is unnecessary because of the work already being done by insiders. This becomes a more serious problem when the committee deals with regulatory legislation. Several years ago, the Alabama Senate committee on banking had a majority of bankers as members and, in another example, the alcoholic beverage committee of the Maryland House was made up largely of members with a financial interest in some aspect of the liquor business.

Behind the Scenes

Executive Sessions. If the "real work" of Congress is conducted in committees, the "real work" of the committees can be said to occur in the executive sessions. Important though the hearings may be in developing congressional and public support for a bill, it is in the executive session of the committee or subcommittee that the vital decisions must be made. There are serious gaps in our knowledge about Congress and about the legislative history of bills, because these committee decisions are made in secret. This secrecy facilitates the informal give-and-take necessary to produce legislation and permits congressmen to abandon or revise their stands on issues without embarrassment. From time to time word leaks out to the press about developments in committee, and occasionally a chairman will give out information directly about decisions reached. But the process of decision making remains relatively obscure.

The cloak of secrecy that frustrates historians and political scientists does not necessarily keep interest groups and administration officials in ignorance about committee decisions. Committee members friendly to an interest group or loyal to the administration have no qualms about transmitting information about what is going on in the committee, even occasionally during the meetings. Sometimes an outsider, particularly one who represents a government agency, is permitted to attend these executive sessions. No form of access could be of greater importance to a group or agency. Gross quotes an official as describing the Navy Department's tactics with regard to a bill: "We'll develop our position when we go down to the Hill and meet in executive session to help the committee mark up the bill."[12]

Nowhere is the power of the committee or subcommittee chairman more important than in the executive sessions. It is usually up to him to decide which representatives of interest groups or agencies, if any, may attend the executive sessions. He can influence the bill by the timing of meetings and by his conduct of them. Most executive meetings of committees, however, are not run in formal, parliamentary fashion. The "marking up" of a bill normally is done through a process of informal consensus. The bill is read, section by section, with the committee discussing any suggested changes and usually reaching agreement without a formal vote, except on major amendments. As the details in the bill are ironed out, only a few of the best informed members of the committee are likely to be active. At this stage, the advice of the committee staff is usually important. The committee may spend weeks in the marking up stage if it is dealing with a thorough revision of the tax code or some equally technical subject. In other cases, the whole process may take only a few hours. Sometimes the committee is dealing with a single bill, but more often it has a variety of bills and revised drafts, and its first decision must be to determine which one offers the best starting point.

The decisions that are made in executive sessions of the committee are of vital importance for two reasons: They usually determine the detailed contents of the bill passed by that house, and they may determine whether or not the bill passes. Decisions on the detailed provisions of a bill made in a subcommittee are seldom reversed in the full committee. On the floor of the House no more than a few amendments are likely to be offered and even fewer passed; some bills reach the floor under rules prohibiting any amendments. The Senate is likely to make more revisions in the bills that come from its committees, but even these revisions usually leave most provisions of a bill unchanged.

If the committee members accurately reflect or anticipate congressional attitudes on an issue, their revisions may clear the way for passage of a bill that would have been doomed in its original version.

By limiting the scope, paring the cost, or adding provisions sought by particular interests, the committee may effectively pacify potential opponents. Senator Arthur Vandenberg, who chaired the Foreign Relations Committee during 1947 and 1948, was a master at foreseeing and eliminating obstacles. When he discovered that opponents of Greek-Turkish aid were arguing that the Truman Administration's program bypassed the United Nations, Vandenberg amended the bill in committee to provide that the program would be canceled if the United Nations declared it to be undesirable or unnecessary. He sponsored a number of minor amendments to the bill for the Marshall Plan, and once, when committee members argued that a clause referring to the "impact on our domestic economy" was too vague, he said, "I can tell nineteen different Senators on the floor of the Senate who are worried about something—your problem is taken care of by that clause in the bill."[13] If the committee members are out of step with a congressional majority, their revisions may inadvertently doom a bill. In 1953 Senator John Bricker introduced a constitutional amendment affecting the conduct of foreign policy. It had 64 cosponsors, enough to guarantee passage by the necessary two-thirds vote if none were lost. The Judiciary Committee, where isolationist sentiment was disproportionately strong, added provisions which made the amendment much more restrictive. The result was to scare off several cosponsors and to stir up strong enough opposition both in the Administration and in the Senate to defeat the proposal by a single vote, even though the Judiciary Committee's additions had been eliminated before the final vote.

If the committee decides against reporting the bill, its decision is almost always final. Although the rules of both houses make it possible for a bill to be extricated from committee and brought to the floor by a majority of the congressmen, the procedure is seldom used, both because it is cumbersome in practice (see Chapter 11) and because congressional norms dictate respect for the authority of committees. The committee's decision to report the bill may be made unanimously or by a divided vote. The committee usually makes a written report explaining its recommendation, and the nature of any division within the committee becomes apparent only if the minority chooses to file a dissenting report. On rare occasions the committee may report a bill without any recommendation concerning its passage, but congressional committees (unlike those in some states) do not report a bill with negative recommendations.

Congressional Committee Unity and Diversity. In Chapter 1 we discussed the concept of legislative bodies as systems and as subsystems within larger political systems. A congressional committee is, of course, an important subsystem in Congress. The norms of the committee are shaped in part by the larger unit, Congress, and its purposes are closely related to those of Congress, in the sense that most committee decisions have effect only when ratified by Congress. Congressional committees have a group life of their own, with traditions, objectives, and norms growing out of a long history and a high degree of independence.

Like any political group, the congressional committee has certain common objectives and elements of diversity. The primary objective of the committee may be defined as maximizing its power and influence in order to get its decisions accepted by Congress. Richard Fenno, who has made a pioneering analysis of the committee as a system, defines the task of maximizing internal unity and minimizing diversity as *integration*. Integration becomes possible when the broad common objectives are translated into a degree of consensus on the substantive policy goals of the committee and effective committee norms with regard to its operating methods.[14]

Any congressional committee has many sources of diversity. One potential source is subcommittees, which operate as subsystems within the committee, with their own traditions, objectives, and norms that may be in conflict with those of the committee. Every committee is divided into Democratic and Republican members—another potential source of great diversity. Not only are the purposes of the two party groups likely to differ, but the members of each have strong ties with members of Congress outside the committee who may not share the committee's norms. There are other sources of diversity present from time to time in most committees. Some members have deep loyalties to a region, a state, a constituency. Some share the views of pressure groups with regard to the issues facing the committee. Members have conflicting philosophies of government, related but not limited to the conflicts between Democratic and Republican programs. Another conflict smoldering below the surface in some committees is that between veteran members of both parties and the relative newcomers.

These sources of diversity account for the variety of roles (already described) which become apparent in committee hearings. In fact, committee members have two kinds of loyalties, which are reflected in two kinds of roles. There is a loyalty to the committee, which requires that the congressman's role be based on the norms set by the committee. There is also a loyalty to outsiders—the various constituencies of party, state, and interest group, which require a congressional role as an advocate for such a group. Actually this role conflict experienced by the committee member is no different from that experienced by all members of the congressional system. Committee hearings are usually open; consequently, the congressman generally finds it necessary to conform to the expectations of his outside constituencies with regard to his role. He may appear as uncompromising as they are, loyal to their viewpoints and acting as a spokesman for their demands. In the sanctuary of the executive session, however, the committee member can subordinate, though not necessarily abandon, this role and emphasize a different role, which is based on the committee norms and the expectations of his fellow members. We may say that integration in a committee depends on its success in substituting one role for another.

The formula for successful committee integration is easily expressed: that which unites the committee must be more important than that which divides it. To begin with, there must be consensus in the committee concerning its major purposes. Fenno, who has cited the House Appropriations Committee as a model of integration, has described the agreed purpose of that committee as being *"to guard the Federal Treasury,"* a purpose which the committee members agree implies "the task of *cutting whatever budget estimates are submitted."* This is not merely a cliché but an apt description of the major purpose underlying the committee's activities and accepted by all or nearly all its members. The words of committee members underline the strength of this norm: "It's a tradition in the Appropriations Committee to cut." "You're grounded in it. . . . It's ingrained in you from the time you get on the Committee." Fenno suggests that consensus on purpose in this particular committee is facilitated by the fact that the members are dealing with money decisions, which can always be compromised at some dollars-and-cents level, rather than with policy decisions, which are not only more difficult to compromise but also force members into specific and inescapable public commitments. The character of the committee may facilitate the growth and survival of committee norms. The Appropriations Committee is one of the most attractive in the House. Members who join it have already had some House experience; they are chosen in part because they have already made an impression as responsible legislators who conform to the norms of the legislative process. Once on it, they stay; the committee has unusual stability of membership.[15]

The Senate Foreign Relations Committee might be cited as another that has attained a high degree of integration, at least in the post-World War II period. Although this committee deals with important and often highly controversial issues of foreign policy, it has achieved a large measure of internal agreement on its broader purposes. One of these is to provide support for internationalist policies—that is, those policies that constitute our commitment to leadership of the Western world. Another purpose on which there appears to be consensus is that of supporting the Administration, whether it is Democratic or Republican. While this cannot be absolute and inflexible, the Foreign Relations Committee appears to start its deliberations with the assumption that the President bears primary responsibility for the conduct of foreign relations and that Congress must be prepared to give legislative support to his policies. The Foreign Relations Committee also benefits from its institutional characteristics; it is a high-priority committee with stable membership.[16]

In contrast to these two committees is the House Education and Labor Committee. Fenno has described the reasons for its lack of integration: It deals with highly controversial issues, on which party and interest-group differences are sharply defined. In addition to strong outside pressures on members, the committee lacks the prestige, the stability of membership, and the traditions that could establish committee norms and reduce conflict among groups within the committee.[17]

There are several ways in which committees can overcome the potentially centrifugal force of subcommittees. One is to avoid establishing them, another is to use *ad hoc* committees instead, and a third is to assign only minor chores to subcommittees, as is often done in the Senate Foreign Relations Committee. The House Appropriations Committee may be used again to illustrate the means by which harmony among subcommittees may be maintained without reducing their power. Fenno has described the norms that serve this purpose: The members usually specialize in only one of the few subcommittees on which they serve, they normally accept the recommendations of each subcommittee without dissent, and members of a subcommittee generally support its recommendations before the full committee. If these principles of specialization, reciprocity, and subcommittee unity can be maintained, a high level of committee integration is possible within the framework of powerful subcommittees.[18]

The perceptive reader may raise a question at this point about such integration as that achieved by the Appropriations Committee. Has the committee gained its life by losing it? Has it achieved the illusion of power and harmony by subcontracting decisions to subcommittees? To a considerable extent, the answer is "Yes." This may appear to be a paradox, but in the eyes of committee members it is not a contradiction. They would argue that the common goal of cutting the budget can be accomplished skillfully and carefully only if each subcommittee is given wide latitude and if its recommendations are accepted by the committee. Subcommittee specialization is viewed as an essential means to the committee's goals.

This point becomes clearer if we recall that most of the major congressional committees are dominated by a bipartisan coalition of senior members. The ranking members of subcommittees are the same men as those who dominate the committee. These men, usually from safe constituencies, are insensitive to electoral trends and tides of public opinion. They are predominantly conservative, bound together by com-

mon goals and attitudes. While the level of integration and the extent
of decentralization on the Appropriations Committee are both above
average, it is possible for other committees to be integrated, despite the
existence of strong subcommittees, if a majority of members, particularly
the senior ones, share a common outlook on political issues and agree on
committee norms. One of the important norms is an adaptation of a
familiar congressional norm: younger members are expected to let the
more senior members—of both parties—play a predominant role in
decision making. New members are expected to ask few questions in the
hearings, to follow the lead of the veterans in executive sessions, and to
adapt quickly and quietly to the committee's norms. The newcomer who
offers an amendment to a subcommittee recommendation and fails to
gain any votes in the executive session of the full committee soon learns
to accept committee norms.

Potentially, political parties are just as disruptive a force as subcommittees, perhaps more so. Party loyalty is a strong force in Congress.
As a subsystem of Congress, the committee cannot escape politics. Each
committee member has ties to party colleagues outside the committee.
The party makeup of each committee is based on that in the parent
body. But if committee integration is to be meaningful, partisan influences must be minimized. The committee member never completely
abandons his role as a party member, but this role is most evident in
public—on the floor or in hearings—where his ties to other party members are most binding. Seldom do Democrats and Republicans operate
as cohesive blocs within a committee. Party-line voting in committee is
unusual, but when a committee is divided on an issue, party differences
often form the basis for this division.

There is no exact way of measuring the extent of party voting in
committees, because the voting is conducted in secret and the results
only occasionally leak out to the press. The committee vote on reporting
a bill is usually indicated by majority and minority reports, but these
provide no clues about voting on amendments. Donald Matthews has
measured committee unity in the Senate by analyzing roll call votes
concerning bills that came from each committee. His study assumes
what is probably true most of the time—that committee members are
consistent in their voting in committee and on the floor. He found that
the Foreign Relations Committee was most united, that the high-prestige
committees that deal with appropriations, taxation, and armed services
were nearly as united, and that committees that deal with particular interests, such as agriculture and labor, were the least united.[19]

A few examples will illustrate the variations in partisan influence
in committees and the techniques that have been used to minimize this
influence. During an eleven-year period concluding in 1957, the House

Appropriations Committee filed 141 reports on measures, and minority reports were filed with only 9 of these—a remarkable record of unity. In all other cases dissenters—if any—reserved their right to disagree on the floor, but avoided public disagreement with the majority. This committee operates with a nonpartisan staff unaffected by changes in party control. The chairman and ranking minority member of the committee and its subcommittees traditionally work closely together. The chairman and ranking minority member of the committee are both *ex officio* members of all subcommittees. Subcommittee chairmen consult the ranking minority member on agenda, preparation of the committee reports, and other relevant matters. This close working relationship was personified by Democrat Clarence Cannon and Republican John Taber, who for two decades worked closely together while exchanging roles as chairman and ranking minority member. They served as a model for other congressmen, particularly subcommittee chairmen, to follow.[20]

The Senate Foreign Relations Committee is another example of a committee that has reduced partisanship to a minimum. During the Eightieth Congress, the Republican-controlled Committee gave unanimous support to the Truman Administration's policies on "47 critical occasions," according to Arthur Vandenberg. In the postwar period there was unanimous support for such major programs as Greek-Turkish aid, the European Recovery Program, the North Atlantic Treaty, and the Point Four Program. There was minimum dissent to the initiation of foreign military aid in 1949 and the resolution to defend Formosa in 1955. When conflict occurred in the committee, it was usually over details rather than on the main principles involved, and it sometimes followed party lines. For example, there were divisions in the committee primarily along party lines on foreign aid to China in 1949, the holding of secret hearings on General MacArthur's dismissal in 1951, amendments to the Formosa resolution in 1955, and the resolution for aid to the Middle East in 1957.[21]

Unity on the committee was in part the result of the attitude that members brought to the committee and the familiarity with foreign affairs which they gained while serving. It was also partly the result of efforts by various chairmen. Senator Arthur Vandenberg, for example, placed a high priority on unanimous reports, devised compromises to make them possible, steered the committee away from conflicts on such partisan issues as aid to China, and tried to minimize changes in the partisan makeup of the committee, despite changes in Congress. The bipartisanship exhibited on major foreign policy issues since World War II has been facilitated by, and in turn has furthered, bipartisan cooperation on this committee and its counterpart in the House. One important aspect of this smooth working relationship was the close personal cooperation between top Administration officials and opposition leaders in the Senate, such as Arthur Vandenberg and Walter George.

There are several reasons why party lines might remain sharp and clear in a committee, why party roles might not be subordinated to committee roles. Some committees, such as the labor committees, deal with issues on which party stands are sharply defined and on which there are few neutrals; these stands often involve the role of government in economic affairs, the welfare state, and the vital interests of major pressure groups that are aligned with parties. On these issues most congressmen are deeply committed to their constituencies.

The House Agriculture Committee is an example of a committee in which party lines are strong, largely because the committee deals with price support programs for specific commodities, and "the Republicans and Democrats have constituency interests in different commodities," as a study by Jones has shown. He points out that "the sectional character of American party strength results in Republican and Democratic commodities. Cotton, rice, and tobacco are Democratic commodities; wheat, corn, and small grains are Republican commodities." This not only makes it difficult to achieve bipartisan agreement; it also makes it difficult to achieve committee integration. There are subcommittees for each of the major commodities, and the partisan-tinged competition among the various commodity programs makes it difficult to achieve either subcommittee unity or committee acceptance of proposals made by a majority of a subcommittee. One aspect of the problem is that a subcommittee dealing with a commodity of the greatest interest to Republicans, such as wheat, has a majority of Democrats (when the Democrats control Congress). The difficulty that Congress has had in passing agricultural legislation is due in no small part to the identity between party and commodity that makes it difficult for the Agriculture Committee to unite behind agricultural bills.[22]

The commodity interests of the Agriculture Committee are just one example of constituency influences that force the committee member to play a partisan role. The member of the Agriculture Committee who represents a district with major cotton interests must be a spokesman for cotton, and there are so many "cotton Democrats" on the committee that all Democratic members must support them. The member of the Labor and Education Committee who represents a district where labor unions are strong must be sensitive to the views of organized labor, and most *Northern* Democrats, at least, find themselves more or less in this position. On the other hand, members of the Appropriations Committee, whatever the dominant groups in their constituencies, are not committed to any particular level of government spending for any specific program.

A symptom of a high level of partisanship on a committee is any cohesive party group operating within the committee. Representative Clem Miller described a subcommittee in which majority members caucused between the hearings and the start of the subcommittee executive session in an effort to work out agreements on the details of a bill so as to maintain maximum unity in the full subcommittee.[23] It is obvious that such a caucus is likely to produce rigid party voting in committee and to destroy committee integration. Experienced congressional observers agree that such caucuses in committee are rare, which helps to explain why the party role is subordinated to other roles in committee.

Diversity in State Committees. Everything that we have said about state legislative committees in this chapter and in Chapter 9 should have made it clear why such committees are usually poorly integrated, why they seldom have definable norms affecting the members. The committees have not developed a set of norms and customs or agreed on objectives over a period of years, nor do they have a stable membership to perpetuate patterns of action over a prolonged period. Members come and go rapidly on most state committees, and few serve for more than four or six years. In the short run, the committees do not have time enough for studies of legislation that might bring about committee consensus strong enough to override partisan, interest-group, or local loyalties of the members.

Some state legislative committees serve as the agents of the majority leadership—partisan or factional—in the legislature. Under these conditions the committee will probably be sharply divided along partisan or factional lines. In a typical legislative committee in Pennsylvania, the bulk of the work is done by the chairman and a small core of majority-party members. Once these few have reached a decision, a committee meeting will be called to ratify it, and the minority party members are usually powerless to prevent majority approval of the decision.[24] In some one-party states, the most important committees will be responsive in a similar fashion to the wishes of the governor and the legislative leadership. Where partisan or factional influence is less, the committee members are more likely to be swayed by the demands of their local constituency interests or pressure groups. In any case, if the committee is poorly integrated and lacks well-recognized norms, the role of committee members will be determined by the expectations of those outside the committee. In the privacy of the committee deliberations, and not merely in the hearings, the committee member is likely to be a Party Loyalist or an Advocate of parochial interests. The nature of the committee system at the state level virtually guarantees a lower level of integration and less salient group norms than have been achieved by most congressional committees.

COMMITTEE INFLUENCE ON THE FLOOR

The purpose of efforts to achieve unity in a committee is to maximize its influence on the floor, to gain passage of bills in the form recommended by the committee. There is evidence that some committees are more successful than others on the floor of Congress. Why? Does unity in committee enhance the prospects for passage of bills on the floor of the Senate or House? The best statistical evidence of this has been collected by Matthews in his study of the Senate. Because there is little evidence on voting in committee, he based his analysis on a comparison between the roll call votes of committee members and those of all other members during the Eighty-fourth Congress. He found that all motions on the floor concerning a bill were passed when they were supported by 80 percent or more of the members of the committee that had reported out the bill. If from 60 to 79 percent of the members supported it, there was a 90 percent chance of its passing. Below that level of committee support, the proportion of motions that passed quickly dropped. If 20 to 40 percent supported it, there was a less than 20 percent chance of passage; if support went below 20 percent, no bills were passed.[25]

Matthews also found that the committees with the greatest prestige seemed to have greater success in achieving agreement between the majority of the senators and a committee majority in roll calls. While the highest prestige committees had the greatest internal unity and also the greatest agreement with a majority of the Senate, the "interest" committees (such as Agriculture, Labor and Public Welfare, and Banking and Currency) had the least unity of all classes of committees, but were second to the prestige committees in the degree of agreement between their views and those of the Senate.[26] Fenno, in his study of the high-prestige and well-integrated House Appropriations Committee, found that 87 percent of the committee's recommendations about the size of appropriations were accepted by the House, and in one-third of the cases these recommendations were exactly what Congress enacted into law.[27]

It is difficult to measure the impact of committee voting on the floor, not only because it is difficult to gauge accurately the voting of committee members, but also because it is not always possible to determine when committee members are leading congressional opinion and when they are reflecting it. (Passage of a bill unanimously after unanimous committee approval might seem to be a perfect example of strong committee influence, but it might simply mean that the bill involved a noncontroversial issue.) Most of the major international programs of the Truman Administration had united support of the

Senate Foreign Relations Committee, and most passed with limited opposition in the Senate, generally less opposition than contemporary observers had expected. The Point Four program of technical aid was the only major program that a majority of Republican voters opposed, despite unanimous committee approval; in this case committee unanimity had less effect, but it was probably the reason why enough Republicans voted favorably in the Senate to assure passage by a single vote. During the Eisenhower Administration the committee's unanimous approval of Charles Bohlen's nomination as Ambassador to Moscow and its nearly unanimous approval of the Formosa resolution were major factors in undermining opposition, which in each case was potentially strong. The Foreign Relations Committee has an unusually high "batting average" in the Senate. Robinson calculated that from 1949 through 1958 the Senate passed 91 percent of the bills and resolutions reported to it by that committee.[28]

Committee integration requires the subordination of partisanship, but voting on the floor of Congress is substantially affected by party. Democrats in Congress often look upon the Democratic members of a committee as the party's leaders with regard to the issues handled by that committee; the same is true for Republicans. This helps to explain the impact of unanimous or nearly unanimous committee reports. If most Democrats and most Republicans on a committee have approved a bill, it is likely to pass that house of Congress with strong bipartisan support. This is one reason why majority party leaders are often reluctant to seek amendments on the floor if there has been a large measure of agreement in committee on the version of the bill reported. In case of a conflict between the Democratic leader and most Democrats on the committee, the rank-and-file Democrats sometimes feel greater loyalty to the committee. If a bill is reported from committee with majority and minority reports closely following party lines, the stage is set for a struggle between the parties on the floor of Congress. The degree of committee unity significantly affects floor action, not merely because congressmen defer to committee members as specialists, but also because they regard them as their party's specialists. In this sense, committee members have an additional role to play, that of Party Specialist. Committee members are probably more likely to affect their party's stand on an issue on the floor than they are to be affected by that stand in their committee deliberations.

The impact of a committee on floor decisions can be regarded in two ways: the impact on Democratic and on Republican congressmen. The recommendations of Democratic committee members, for example, might have greater impact than the recommendations (whether the same or different) of Republicans on the committee, either because of greater unity among the committee Democrats or because Democratic congressmen have greater respect for the views of the committee members of their own party, and are more likely to take their voting cues from them. During the Truman Administration and the early Eisenhower years, the Senate Foreign Relations Committee's recommendations carried great weight, not only because of unity on the committee but also because the leadership of both parties deferred to outstanding committee leaders such as Arthur Vandenberg, Tom Connally, Walter George, and other widely respected senators. Cohen noted some contrasts between the two parties, however, during the 1952 debate on the Japanese Peace Treaty: Democratic senators generally let Democrats on the committee speak for them in debate, but Republicans were less likely to defer to Republican committee members.[29] In the later Eisenhower years, although the level of unity on the Foreign Relations Committee remained high, neither party contingent in the committee had leadership that was so widely respected in the Senate. Democratic unity on the floor declined, while Republican unity on foreign policy issues grew—apparently in response to the continuing demands of a Republican Administration.

A party contingent on a committee may be particularly powerful if it includes several congressmen who either hold formal party posts or exercise broad influence in the party. For example, the growing support accorded by Republican senators for the Eisenhower Administration's requests for foreign aid funds probably resulted in part from the presence on the Appropriations Committee of an unusually high proportion of ranking Republicans. The party contingent on a committee may also be more influential if it includes several senior members of other prestigious committees. The greater specialization necessary in the House virtually precludes the possibility of party leaders playing such a direct role on standing committees or of overlapping membership of senior men on major committees.

Because state legislative committees lack the prestige, resources, and experience of congressional committees, we would not expect their recommendations to carry comparable weight on the floor of the legislature. Whether this is true, however, depends on the influence of alternate sources of leadership. In most state legislatures committee decisions on killing legislation are final. Rarely are successful efforts made on the floor to discharge a bill from committee. In some states the rules require committees to report out all bills (a rule sometimes evaded in practice), and in a few other states (such as New Hampshire and Illinois) the committees customarily report out most bills. If there is neither strong partisan nor factional leadership, the legislators may be dependent on the leadership of committees. This may be less a result of the committees' institutional strength than of the respect that cerain committee chairmen and members command as experts on substantive fields.

In states where there is strong partisan or factional leadership, the committees have less independent influence on legislative decisions concerning major legislation. They may serve as agents of the majority leadership, reporting, revising, or burying bills in accord with the wishes of that leadership. In Arizona, where the committees are carefully controlled by the dominant faction, they "play a critical role in the legislative process," and very few bills are reported out by committees which fail to pass on the floor.[30] In other states, such as Illinois, Pennsylvania, and New Jersey, the committees may almost completely surrender their responsibilities to the caucus or party leadership. In Illinois, the committee is "of scant importance" as an "independent determinant of the fate of legislative proposals." In Pennsylvania, the committees "are creatures of a disciplined and cohesive majority political party," and their reports carry weight only because they are in accord with the views of the majority caucus. Committee chairmen in Pennsylvania sometimes release tentative reports on bills in order to determine consensus in the caucus. In New Jersey, the caucus determines which bills should be reported from committee. Where partisan or factional leadership is so strong, the committees may retain some authority and influence over the fate of minor bills that do not interest the majority leadership. The Pennsylvania committees make independent decisions "only on items which do not deeply involve the interests of major groups in or outside of the Assembly."[31]

CONFERENCE COMMITTEES

When a bill passes the Senate and House in different versions and neither house is willing to accept the other's bill, a conference committee is used to adjust the differences. This device, patterned after the conference committee used in the British Parliament as early as the sixteenth century, was first adopted by Congress during the early days of its first session in 1789. The rules and precedents surrounding the conference committee evolved gradually, but by 1852 the major governing principles had become well established.[32] The conference committee plays a powerful role in the legislative process because its reports are not subject to amendment and are usually accepted by both houses. In order to avoid deadlock in a bicameral system, there must be some locus for final decisions, some group charged with reconciling differences. In Congress this is the part played by the conference committee, an *ad hoc* body consisting of senior members from the Senate and House committees that originally reported the bill. While minor differences between the Senate and House versions of bills are sometimes reconciled without resort to the committee, the more important and complex the bill, the greater is the need for a conference committee. In the Eighty-second Congress, 90 of the 217 public laws that were enacted went through a conference committee.

Tactical Considerations. A conference committee becomes necessary whenever the house that first passed a bill refuses to accept the amendments adopted by the second house. If the differences are trivial, the first house will probably accept the amendments in order to expedite matters. On major bills, it is often taken for granted that a conference will be necessary. There are occasions, however, when congressional leaders will try to avoid a conference despite major differences between Senate and House bills. In the closing days of the session, sponsors of a measure may fear that the delay caused by conference action would be fatal or that opponents of the bill would be strong enough in the conference committee or on the floor to defeat it if given another chance. Democratic leaders blocked a conference committee on the 1957 civil rights bill, for example, because they were afraid that if the concessions made to Southerners in the Senate were eliminated in conference, the bill would be destroyed by filibuster in the Senate. Republican leaders —including President Eisenhower—wanted a stronger bill and wanted specifically the elimination of the "jury trial" amendment for contempt cases. A compromise involving minimum changes in the Senate bill was finally engineered by leaders of both parties without resort to a conference committee.

Since conference committees are usually required for major legislation, many tactical decisions on the floor of the Senate and House are made in anticipation of developments in the conference committee. For example, the floor leader for a bill often faces a dilemma when an influential member of the Senate or House offers an amendment which the leader considers damaging but not destructive. If he opposes the amendment, he runs the risk of precipitating a floor fight and perhaps losing votes for the bill itself. He may decide to accept the amendment without a vote, and work for its elimination in the conference committee. One of the factors that determines the outcome of conference committee deliberations is the presence or absence of recorded votes in either house on specific amendments. Consequently, the sponsor of an amendment, if he is reasonably sure of strong support, may ask for a roll call vote to record the strength of that support. The same logic may require that a roll call vote be avoided. The House Appropriations Committee has often made deep cuts in the appropriations for foreign aid. Unless they were quite sure that they had the votes to raise the figure, Democratic leaders have often avoided a roll call on that issue, anticipating that the Senate would increase the appropriation and that a better result could be obtained in the conference committee in the absence of recorded votes in the House. Another consequence of the reliance on conference committees is that, in the appropriations process, one committee will make deeper cuts and the other larger restorations of funds because both realize that the final figure will be a compromise. The same tactic of starting the bargaining process prior to the conference committee is also applied to other legislation. The sponsors of a bill or the leadership in one house will seek the adoption of amendments likely to be unacceptable in the other house in order to use these as pawns in the bargaining process. Even the threat of a filibuster by senators against an amendment adopted by the House may be used as a bargaining weapon by Senate conferees.

Choice of Participants. Members of conference committees are formally chosen by the presiding officers in both houses, but they always follow the advice of the chairmen of the committees that handled the bill. In recommending those to serve on conference committees, the chairmen usually choose only the senior members of both parties, frequently including themselves on committees for major bills. If a bill was handled first in a subcommittee, its senior members will also usually be included. Although the chairman seldom ignores seniority in his choices, he has some discretion, particularly in determining how many members to put on the conference committee. Conference committees on appropriations are chosen from the senior members of the subcommittees, although in the House the committee chairman and ranking minority member are also regularly included. There seems to be a greater tendency in the Senate than in the House to use the senior members, and occasionally all members, of subcommittees on conference committees. The result is that relatively junior members of the Senate serve occasionally on conferences, while House conferees are nearly always men with substantial seniority.

Theoretically the members of a conference committee should represent the viewpoints of each house as accurately as possible. The reliance on seniority in the choice of members makes it possible, however, that a majority of the senators or representatives on the committee will be men who voted against the bill or—more likely—who voted against the majority in their house on one of the amendments that is in dispute between the two houses. Under these conditions, there is a danger that the conferees of one house will surrender without a fight to the demands of the other house. This was what occurred in March 1959, when a conference committee met to consider an unemployment compensation bill. A major point in dispute was an amendment liberalizing the bill adopted only in the Senate, an amendment opposed by four of the five Senate conferees, and dropped from the bill by the conference committee after a twenty-one-minute session. This incident led Senator Joseph Clark to propose an amendment to the Senate rules to provide that a majority of Senate conferees "must have indicated by their votes their sympathy with the bill as passed and their concurrence in the prevailing opinion of the Senate on the matters of disagreement with the House." Despite Senator Clark's persistence, his amendment to the rules has remained buried in the Senate Rules and Administration Committee. A study by the *Congressional Quarterly* to determine the frequency of the practice that Senator Clark sought to correct disclosed only four such instances among conference committees during the 1958 session of Congress, and not all of these produced the one-sided effect feared by Clark.[33]

Behind Clark's criticism of the procedures for choosing committees is his concern, and that of other liberals, that the seniority system gives conservatives from safe districts disproportionately greater representation on conference committees, in addition to the predominance they enjoy in committee chairmanships and on the high-prestige committees. There is no doubt that conference committees are dominated by men with great seniority. Among these, the two chairmen or ranking members who represent each house are likely to be the most influential, perhaps more powerful in conference than they are in their own, larger committees. The senior senator normally serves as chairman of the conference committee, although one of the demands made in 1962 by Chairman Clarence Cannon of the House Appropriations Committee during a prolonged dispute with his counterpart in the Senate was that the chairmanship rotate. Skillful, determined leaders can guide a conference committee, often with great effectiveness. In his study of the 1946 Full Employment Act, Stephen Bailey describes the critical role of an effective chairman:

Major credit for keeping the discussions moving must go to Senator Alben Barkley. Whenever the discussions became tense and acrimonious, Barkley, as chairman, relieved the tension with a joke or a gentle whim. He performed what John Chamberlain has called the function of the "master broker"—the classic job of statesman-politician: the discovery of areas of agreement.[34]

The conference committee does not operate in total isolation, however. Occasionally the floor leaders of one or both parties will intervene, usually in an effort to end a deadlock, though the committee leaders are jealous of their prerogatives and do not often welcome such intervention. In 1948 the conference committee was deadlocked over the foreign aid appropriations bill. Members from the House Appropriations Committee who were seeking a sharp cut believed that the senators would give in to make possible adjournment of Congress before the imminent national party conventions. Republican leader Robert Taft warned that he would force Congress to reconvene after the conventions if necessary, and his announcement ended the stalemate on the Senate's terms.

Members of the committee staffs are frequently participants in conference committee deliberations, and experts from the government departments and agencies are often invited to attend. Whether the latter are invited into all the conference sessions, or wait outside the doors to be consulted on specific points, depends on the attitude of the chairman. Controversy occasionally arises over permitting outside experts to attend. In one famous case, after a conference committee had become deadlocked over the 1935 Public Utilities Holding Company Act, the House conferees went so far as to obtain a vote from the House endorsing their demand that one of the senatorial advisers be barred from the conference. The victim, Benjamin Cohen, had played a key part in the main issue in dispute.[35] The advice of government officials may carry more weight during conference sessions than at earlier stages in the legislative process. If there is a difference of half a billion dollars, for example, between the foreign aid funds approved by the two houses, the government agency that handles foreign aid can expect that its advice will often be followed concerning the priorities for restoring funds that have been cut. If an amendment that has been introduced and passed on the floor in one house will have damaging consequences, perhaps not foreseen by its sponsor, government officials can probably get it quietly removed in the conference committee.

Occasionally the President intervenes in conference committee deliberations, on the advice of White House staff members, departmental officials, or legislative leaders. Intervention may take the form of letters (publicized or private), telephone calls, or perhaps meetings with the conference committee or its leaders at the White House. In recent years, publicized letters to conference committees handling foreign aid bills have become almost a routine tool of presidential influence. Gilbert Steiner, in his comprehensive survey of conference committees during the 1930s and 1940s, reports several examples of compromises effected by President Roosevelt. In 1933, the Senate and House versions of a banking act embodied fundamental conflicts in philosophy and interests, but Roosevelt devised an ingenious and complex compromise enthusiastically accepted by the conferees and by both houses. Sometimes presidential intervention has backfired. In 1934, when Roosevelt publicly intervened in a conference committee dispute over administration of the

Securities Exchange Act, he embarrassed his own supporters on the conference committee (who had been appointed in place of more senior members), and the deadlock was not broken until the White House announced that Roosevelt had no intention of interfering in the conference decision. The veto power provides the President with a potent weapon on occasions, particularly if he is willing to risk defeat of any legislation on the issue in dispute. In 1932, after a conference committee had reached agreement on the terms of the Emergency Relief and Construction Act, President Hoover called the conferees to the White House and informed them that he would veto the bill they had agreed to. The bill was revised to meet his objections.[36]

Stephen Bailey's study of the 1946 Full Employment Act illustrates several aspects of presidential influence on conference committees. The initiative for presidential intervention came from a well-organized lobby of liberal and labor groups which was disappointed by the watered-down version of the bill passed in the House and urged President Truman to threaten a veto of a weak bill. As a result, Truman wrote to the Senate and House chairmen warning that "no bill which provides substantially less than the Senate version can efficiently accomplish the purposes intended." He repeated his request in a radio speech and in a message to Congress. The effectiveness of this White House pressure was weakened, however, by the fact that the Administration did not submit a specific compromise proposal to the conference committee. Such a proposal was drawn up by Secretary of the Treasury Fred Vinson, but the President never authorized its use because of opposition by another high official and presidential confidant, John Snyder. A combination of political pressure from the White House and expert advice from agency officials is more effective than either technique used alone in influencing a conference committee.[37]

Exercise of Power. Though outside influences are often important, the reins of power are held by the conference committee members. If politics is the art of the possible and the essence of the legislative process is compromise, then the conference committee is the epitome of legislative politics. Nowhere in the legislative process are congressional skills —skills born of experience, knowledge, and patient attention to the specialized demands of committee work—put to a greater test. Formal votes in conference are relatively rare; each provision must be acceptable to a majority of conferees from each house. The conference usually proceeds informally, relying on consensus whenever possible. The conference may be a matter of minutes or of weeks. Some controversies are minor and easily settled; often a simple trade will give each side the provisions it values most. Appropriations bills are particularly negotiable because the level of funds is easily adjustable and because, as a last resort, the conferees can usually compromise at the halfway point. In some cases, however, one house has completely rewritten the bill passed by the other, or there are a few points of profound difference between the bills—perhaps on emotionally charged or politically explosive issues.

Conferees may debate the substance of the points in controversy, but one of their major tactics is to persuade their colleagues that one house feels more strongly about an issue than the other house and should be permitted to have its way. This is often the reason why the floor managers of bills will either seek or avoid a recorded vote. Sometimes, when a conference is pending, one house or the other will vote to "instruct" its conferees to insist on a particular provision in dispute, though the conferees are not bound by the "instruction." Sometimes, as a bargaining tactic after conference sessions have started, the conferees for one house will take the issue back to the floor to get a vote supporting and insisting on a specific provision (particularly if there has been no previous separate vote on that provision). Occasionally, the conferees from one house will ask those from the other house to obtain such a vote in order to give the former an excuse for receding from their stand on the issue. Since the conferees must justify to their own house the reasons for concessions (sometimes in broad terms, sometimes in detail), such a face-saving device is occasionally necessary.

The Senate and House meet on equal terms in the conference, though on rare occasions the threat of a Senate filibuster may strengthen the hand of Senate conferees. Steiner determined from a detailed study of 56 conference committees from 1928 through 1948 that House influence was greater in 32 cases, that Senate influence was greater in 15, and that there was substantially equal influence in 9. House influence was greater in all conferences on taxation and appropriations bills, which are always initiated by the House, and in most conferences on agricultural bills, concerning which representatives may have more specific constituency interests.[38]

Much that we have said earlier about the roles of congressmen in committee is applicable here. In the privacy of the conference committee, the congressman's role as an agent of his district, a pressure group, or his party is usually overshadowed by his committee role. As a conferee he formally assumes another role—that of representing the majority viewpoint in his house. We have seen that this role may conflict with any or all of the other roles, including that of the committee member. There is no certainty that this special role of the conferee will supplant others, but there are circumstances under which it does; the most rigid deadlocks often result from loyalties to the majority of each house, loyalties that frustrate efforts at compromise.

Theoretically, conference committees may not consider any provisions of a bill except those in disagreement between the two houses; they may not add provisions on their own initiative or exclude or modify provisions agreed on by the two houses. For many years the rules and precedents of both houses have imposed such restrictions. However, when one house has rewritten a bill passed by the other house in substantially different form, the conference committee has wide discretion in further rewriting the bill. This often occurs in the passage of major pieces of legislation. Conference committee reports which appear to violate these rules are subject to a point of order in either house. Such points of order are occasionally made but very seldom sustained; in voting on them, the congressmen seem to pay little attention to the proper interpretation of legislative rules and vote, according to their viewpoints, on the substantive issue involved. Senator Alben Barkley, for example, in arguing against a point of order challenging the conference report on the 1940 Transportation Act, stressed the preeminent importance of the bill to the national transportation system, and in defending the conference report on the Selective Service Act that same year, he expressed the view that "the American people are not very much concerned about the technical interpretation of the language of the conference report."[39] In 1951, when Republican leaders challenged a conference report that gave the President greater flexibility to transfer money between economic and military foreign aid funds than either house had provided, the issue was decided by a roll call vote that rather accurately reflected the attitude of senators toward foreign aid.

Although conference committees have often been criticized for exceeding their authority, Steiner concluded from his comprehensive study that in only 3 out of 56 cases had the conferees made changes beyond the scope of Senate-House differences; in each case they were on sound legal ground, because one house had substituted a new bill for that written in the other house. Steiner concludes that, although occasionally acting recklessly or in contradiction to the congressional majority, the conference committee has not been "a consistently irresponsible 'third house' of Congress"; rather it "appears to be a better reflection of the notions of House and Senate than may have been believed."[40]

Limited Use in the States. When there are differences in state legislatures between the versions of bills passed in the two houses, some machinery is necessary for resolving the differences. Often, when minor bills or trivial amendments are involved, the amendments of the second house will be accepted by the first, perhaps because this is the only way to ensure passage in the hurried closing days of a session. When differences remain, the task of resolving them may be delegated to a conference committee, or it may be handled, perhaps more informally, by the leadership of the two houses. It is evident that conference committees are used much more frequently in some state legislatures than in others, but the reasons for these variations are obscure because little research has been done on the conference committee.

Appropriations measures are sent to conference committees more often than other categories of bills. In some states, appropriations bills are regularly sent to conference, and in others this is the only type of bill that is likely to require a conference. In states where the committees play a decisive part in the decision-making process, conference committees are likely to be used—at least on the most important and controversial legislation in a session. In states where there is strong party leadership, the conference committee may simply ratify the decisions made by these leaders; on other occasions, the party leaders or the governor may be unwilling to delegate (even formally) the settlement of controversies to a conference committee. New York and Alabama are examples of states with strong legislative leadership where little or no use is made of the conference committee.

NOTES

1. John W. Baker (ed.), *Member of the House: Letters of a Congressman by Clem Miller* (New York, 1962), p. 8.

2. For an excellent, detailed description of hearings, see Bertram M. Gross, *The Legislative Struggle* (New York, 1953), chap. 15.

3. *Congressional Quarterly Weekly Report*, XIX (Dec. 22, 1961), 1961–63.

4. Ralph K. Huitt, "The Congressional Committee: A Case Study," *American Political Science Review*, XLVIII (1954), 345. Huitt's article provides the best analysis of committee roles as revealed in hearings. The roles we have delineated are derived in part from his descriptions.

5. Bernard C. Cohen, *The Political Process and Foreign Policy: The Making of the Japanese Peace Settlement* (Princeton, N.J., 1957), pp. 155–56.

6. Huitt, *op. cit.*, pp. 345–46.

7. Gross, *op. cit.*, p. 305.

8. Huitt, *op. cit.*, p. 347.

9. Charles O. Jones, "The Role of the Congressional Subcommittee," *Midwest Journal of Political Science*, VI (1962), 327–44.

10. Huitt, *op. cit.*, p. 348.

11. Henry W. Lewis, *Legislative Committees in North Carolina* (Chapel Hill, N.C., 1952), pp. 35–38; Gilbert Y. Steiner and Samuel K. Gove, *Legislative Politics in Illinois* (Urbana, Ill., 1960), pp. 71–83; Kenneth T. Palmer, "The Legislative Committee System in Pennsylvania" (Unpublished Ph.D. dissertation, Pennsylvania State University, 1964), pp. 105–08.

12. Gross, *op. cit.*, p. 309.

13. Arthur H. Vandenberg, Jr. (ed.), *The Private Papers of Senator Vandenberg* (Boston, 1952) pp. 388–89.

14. Richard F. Fenno, Jr., "The House Appropriations Committee as a Political System: The Problem of Integration," *American Political Science Review*, LVI (1962), 310–24.

15. *Ibid.*, pp. 311–15.

16. Malcolm E. Jewell, *Senatorial Politics and Foreign Policy* (Lexington, Ky., 1962) pp. 134–39.

17. Fenno, *op. cit.*, p. 324.

18. *Ibid.*, pp. 315–17.

19. Donald R. Matthews, *U.S. Senators and Their World* (Chapel Hill, N.C., 1960) pp. 168–69.

20. Fenno, *op. cit.*, pp. 317–18.

21. Jewell, *op. cit.*, pp. 118–26, 134–37.

22. Jones, *op. cit.*, pp. 329, 332, 340–44.

23. Baker, *op. cit.*, p. 14.

24. Palmer, *op. cit.*, pp. 60–64.

25. Matthews, *op. cit.*, p. 170.

26. *Ibid.*, pp. 169–71.

27. Fenno, *op. cit.*, p. 323.

28. James A. Robinson, *Congress and Foreign Policy-making* (Homewood, Ill., 1962) p. 95.

29. Cohen, *op. cit.*, p. 204.

30. Dean E. Mann, "The Legislative Committee System in Arizona," *Western Political Quarterly*, XIV (1961), 925–41 at 938.

31. Steiner and Gove, *op. cit.*, p. 82; Palmer, *op. cit.*, pp. 199–201.

32. Ada C. McCown, *The Congressional Conference Committee* (New York, 1927) pp. 254–57. This is the best source of information on the early history of conference committees.

33. *Congressional Quarterly Weekly Report*, XVII (May 1, 1959), 597–98. The problem that concerned Clark was not a new one. In 1933 several important amendments adopted in the Senate were abandoned or watered down in conference, and Senator La Follette, the author of one of these, charged that the Senate conferees had violated "all the unwritten rules of the Senate, in that they have frankly and obviously abandoned the position of the Senate because, forsooth, a majority of the Senate conferees were not in sympathy with the attitude of the Members of this body." Gilbert Y. Steiner, *The Congressional Conference Committee* (Urbana, Illinois Studies in the Social Sciences, vol. XXXII, 1951) p. 93.

34. Stephen K. Bailey, *Congress Makes a Law* (New York, 1950) p. 227.

35. Steiner, *op. cit.*, pp. 98–99.

36. *Ibid.*, pp. 37–38, 94–96, 130–33. Steiner's study is the best recent survey of the conference committee; it includes a wealth of detail in 56 brief case studies.

37. Bailey, *op. cit.*, pp. 221–22.

38. Steiner, *op. cit.*, pp. 170–72.

39. *Ibid.*, p. 106.

40. *Ibid.*, pp. 174, 176.

[19]

The Legislature
and the Executive:
Oversight,
Supervision, Control

I N CHAPTER 13 we viewed the executive as an actor in the legislative
system. We now view the legislature as an institution engaged in the
policy activity of overseeing, supervising or controlling executive
agencies. The terms oversight, supervision, and control, while they are
not unambiguous, tend to denote analytically distinct degrees of legislative influence upon agencies of administration. When an individual
legislator observes closely and becomes familiar with the organization
and policy implementation of an administrative agency, or when a
legislative committee by contact, observation, or investigation places
itself in the posture of a "watchdog" over agency activities, we speak
of these legislative-executive relationships in terms of *oversight*. When
the influence of individual legislators or legislative committees constitutes
substantial involvement in the formulation or implementation of administration policy, producing changes in policy emphasis or priority, we
speak of these relationships as legislative *supervision*. When the legislature directs administrative organization and policy, or requires legislative
clearance for administrative decisions, it is meaningful to talk of the legislative-executive relation as one of *control*. In effect, these terms crudely
demarcate cut-off points on a continuum of variable legislative-execu-

tive relations, from little legislative influence upon administrative policy to substantial legislative control over executive agencies. The real virtue of the distinction between oversight, supervision, and control is the fairly important one of maintaining alertness to rather wide variations in the relationships between legislatures and executive agencies. Thus, legislative committees could be classified as primarily engaged in oversight, supervision, or control. In the national Congress, for instance, the House Armed Services Committee could, as we shall see, be typed as an oversight committee, the appropriations committees as mainly supervisory, and the Joint Committee on Atomic Energy as a control committee. We shall, in the proper place, illustrate these variations in legislative influence upon administration.

Legislative influence upon administrative agencies fulfills at least three purposes from the point of view of the legislative branch. The varied relationships between legislative institutions and executive agencies provide mechanisms by means of which the legislature can test and attempt to secure the compliance of administrative agencies with legislative policy and can hold agencies accountable to legislative intentions. Again, legislative investigation, review, and even involvement in administrative policy making provide the legislature with mechanisms for the evaluation and assessment of legislative policy, exposing gaps between expected and actual performance, and providing legislative policy makers with cues to needed changes in law or informal legislative-executive agreements. Finally, legislative oversight, supervision, and control provide relationships between legislators and administrators such that there can be reciprocal and sustaining support for public policy. Administrative agencies need legislative support, both to maintain their existence and to legitimize their programs; legislative support tends to facilitate support for administrative policies in the larger political community.[1]

PROBLEMS OF LEGISLATIVE–EXECUTIVE RELATIONS

The web of government is far too complex to enable us to treat legislative-executive relations in the United States in detail. Legislative surveillance of administrative agencies is highly decentralized and, at all levels of American government, administration has become enormously large and farflung. In our treatment here, it is necessary to select major problems to deal with, to focus upon the most useful among a wide variety of examples of legislative-executive relations. It is possible to consider the relationships between legislative bodies and administrative agencies in terms of the problems that these relationships raise for legislatures.

Atomization. Legislative innovation and response to executive agencies are highly atomized. Not only are a very large number of legislative committees and subcommittees typically involved, but individual legislators who regularly have interpersonal contacts with individual bureaucrats are persistently involved in the administrative process. While analyses of legislative-executive relations ordinarily focus attention upon legislative committee activities, the contacts between legislators and administrators, usually stimulated by constituency demands, may constitute the most pervasive and fundamental form of legislative oversight. These interpersonal relations have mutual cognitive and affective value; they permit legislators and bureaucrats to become knowledgeable about each other's workways, and they tend to facilitate mutual understanding. In addition, the reciprocity made possible by many opportunities for mutual aid at this level of interpersonal relations between legislators and administrators probably makes a significant contribution to the functional integration of the legislative and executive branches of government in the face of constitutional, or formal, separation of powers.

Since American legislators are predominantly constituency-oriented, legislator-bureaucrat contact tends to be motivated by demands from the legislators' constituents. As one Democratic congressman said of his relations with the National Labor Relations Board: "We never think twice about calling the Board and asking for a little special handling of some cases; not just to speed things up but to look a little differently at the case."[2] But beyond the legislator making demands upon the administrator in behalf of his constituents, legislator influence upon agency policy may very frequently be informal, interpersonal, and individual. For instance, in describing relations between congressional Appropriations Committee members and the War Department in the early 1940s, Huzar points out that "many controls which might have been included in statutes are contained, instead, in understandings between members of the Appropriations Committees and officials of the War Department." These "administrators have a well-recognized responsibility to take legislators into their confidence about their operating plans," and "they have a recognized obligation to adhere to the plans Congress approves not only by formal legislation but also by gentlemen's agreements."[3]

Congressional and state legislative institutions are thus highly atomized with respect to their relations with executive agencies. The legislatures are characterized by multiple focal points of influence and intervention in administrative activity. Every legislator, and a host of committees and subcommittees, are involved, and legislative influence is thereby dispersed and decentralized. This dispersal and decentralization create serious problems for coordinated and integrated surveillance of the executive branch.

Strategic Conditions. As a result of his observation of relationships between congressional committee members and independent regulatory agencies, Scher has identified several strategic conditions for legislative oversight, supervision, and control. He suggests that a congressman, faced with the problem of deciding whether to devote his time and energy to reviewing agency procedure and policies or engaging in new legislative activity, can be expected to ask himself "What's in it for me?" The decision to get involved may be governed by the following strategic considerations:[4]

(1) Congressmen tend to see opportunities for greater rewards in the things they value from involvement in legislative and constituent-service activity than from participation in oversight activity.

(2) Committee members tend to view the agencies as impenetrable mazes and to believe that any serious effort at penetrating them poses hazards for the inexpert Congressman which outweigh any conceivable gain to him.

(3) Congressmen who have established mutually rewarding relationships with agency people tend to be reluctant to initiate or become actively engaged in a close review of that agency's affairs.

(4) Congressmen tend to view their personal contacts with the agencies as more efficient than committee investigations for serving constituent and group needs.

(5) Committee members will tend to avoid agency review if they expect it will provoke costly reprisals from powerful economic interests regulated by the agencies.

(6) Congressmen who perceive that gains to themselves can be had by loyalty to the President can be expected to avoid close examination of the performance of agency officials appointed by the Executive.

(7) As committee routines become fixed, for all of the foregoing reasons, in ways that make no regular provision for agency oversight, in the absence of powerful external stimuli they tend to resist change.

Scher found congressional oversight of federal regulatory agencies to be intermittent, characterized by long periods of inactivity punctuated by bursts of oversight. He concluded that "committee leaders can be expected to involve committee resources in studies of agency performance if and when the likely gain in things valued by Congressmen is gauged as greater than any prospective loss in those things."[5] These strategic conditions are then pertinent:[6]

(1) When the leadership of the majority party in Congress believes it can cause sufficient embarrassment, with accompanying profit for itself, to a past or current opposition President who is held responsible for the performance of his agency appointees, committee oversight tends to be used for this purpose.

(2) When the committee leadership or powerful committee members believe that constituent or group interests important to them cannot be satisfied

by the routine personal intercessions between Congressman and agency, committee review tends to be used as a substitute.

(3) When Congressmen perceive a threat, particularly from the President, to their traditional prerogatives of primacy in relation to the regulatory agencies, committee interest in the agencies is a likely response.

(4) When, periodically, interest builds in Congress for revising regulatory policy, committee attention to the regulatory agency tends to occur as a by-product.

(5) When the committee leadership becomes convinced that interests to which it is opposed can be substantially advanced by the exposure of dramatic evidence of agency failure, it can be expected to move first to neutralize or minimize these gains by initiating its own inquiry.

In general, American legislatures are today better equipped to evaluate, to assess, and even sometimes to develop and integrate ideas, than they are to innovate or stimulate the invention of ideas. Strategically, legislatures are better able to "check and balance when there are, within the politically alert public, sets of ideas and interests which check and balance each other, thus creating a situation within which [they are] able to *sift, winnow,* and *judge.*"[7]

Generalist-Specialist Tension. We have referred elsewhere (in Chapter 16) to some of the occupational role strains experienced by the American legislator in his relationships with bureaucrats. It is appropriate to advert here to potential problems of legislative-executive relations which arise in the contact between citizen legislators and administrative experts. At least three aspects of this problem can be pursued. On the one hand, legislators may regard the work of administrative agencies as simply too complex and technical for effective legislative supervision. As one United States House committee member said of the work of overseeing the federal regulatory agencies: "The [regulatory] agencies' work is pretty technical. Most of us just don't know enough about it to even begin to ask intelligent questions."[8] Again, legislators may themselves define technical and nontechnical questions in such a way as to confine their involvement in administration to manageable and desirable proportions, from their own point of view. Dexter, in describing the oversight activities of the House Committee on Armed Services, points out that "Congressmen tend to regard as 'technical' such questions for 'professional' military men as the nature of war plans," but "they regard as 'non-technical' and fit subjects for their consideration such matters as the way in which oil is stored at overseas installations or how service credit shall be allocated for ROTC or military academy training."[9] Congressmen "will evaluate or try to evaluate the efficiency of given types of rifles or waste in the procurement of military overcoats," but "they have recently shown little interest in stimulating the invention and development of newer types of weapons or innovations in 'grand strategy.' "[10] That is left up to the experts.

Finally, of course, legislators may resent the greater knowledge of administrators, or may be suspicious of their credentials as experts. Legislators may understand different versions of the facts, and tend to substitute what they consider to be their own expertise for that of administrators. Thus Freeman, in explaining some of the factors in the receptivity of members of the congressional committees on Indian Affairs to the policy viewpoints of the Bureau of Indian Affairs, points out that committee members came to view the administrators as attempting to secure and expand their own administrative structure and, in their arguments before the committees, to rationalize their own interests and challenge the members of the committees for the loyalty of their Indian constituents.

By this light, personnel of the Bureau became "theorists" who knew too little at first hand about either Indians or the law. Reflected in the frames of reference of some committee members were those ancient criteria of practical knowledge and ability, whereby bureaucratic attorneys are deemed impractical if they have "never tried a case," and public servants are written off if they have "neither carried a precinct nor met a payroll." A great deal of time was spent in trying to show that the Commissioner could not know as much about the needs of Indians in the various states as did the legislators from those states.[11]

Legislative Role Perceptions.   The legislator's response to executive agencies will depend upon how he perceives his job as a representative. He may be agency-oriented in a positive direction and take the posture of defending the agency from attacks upon it, or he may play a hostile role. Whether the legislator plays the role of Agency-defender or Agency-detractor is likely to depend upon a variety of factors in the situation, including the partisan affiliation of the President who appointed the agency officials, the comity of interpersonal relations between the legislator and the agency chiefs,[12] his satisfaction with the information furnished about administration policy,[13] and the legislator's perception of constituency expectations and demands.

The latter is likely to be especially compelling in the American legislator's view of his role as an Agency Overseer. Legislators are likely to become heavily involved in administrative processes on behalf of explicit demands made upon them by their constituents. For example, witness the views of United States Senator Everett Dirksen (R-Ill) about communication with agency officials on behalf of his constituents:

Ever since 1933, when I came here as a freshman Congressman, I have been calling every agency in Government in the interest of my constituents.

I expect I am going to continue to do it whether this becomes law or not, and I am afraid this bill [to bar *ex parte* communications by "any person" in adjudicatory proceedings] is not going to become law with my sanction, because I don't go that far.

I make the case just as clear as crystal, so the whole world may know. But now let's get the specific examples. There is an airline, let us say X, based in Chicago. I know the president and all the personnel and a good many of the pilots. There is another airline based in Missouri, my neighboring State. I don't know very much about it. But there is a petition or an application pending before CAB [Civil Aeronautics Board], and they both want to be certified for a stop in Iowa, so I call up this Chairman of the CAB and I say: "Look, Mr. ——, X Airlines has an application pending. I know these people, they are good, reliable operators; they are good, solid citizens. I just want to know what the status of the matter is."[14]

Furthermore, legislators are likely to view their role in overseeing executive agencies in terms of the perceived effects of agency behavior upon the legislator's own constituents or clientele. In analyzing congressional committee oversight by focusing upon the relations between the House Education and Labor Committee and the National Labor Relations Board, Scher explained that

The Southern Democrat's concern for his small employer constituents typically was compatible also with his own antagonism toward the organizing activity of unions. The Northern Democrat reacted vigorously in behalf of "his people" when his own sympathies placed him in the camp of organized labor confronting what he saw as a hostile coalition of employers and an unfriendly regulatory agency.

In cases where a committee member's own constituents were adversely affected by agency action, the member's reaction was more or less vigorous depending on the extent, if any, of his personal association with the group values of employers or unions. The member's intercession with the agency for its treatment of an employer constituent took on the character of a routine inquiry when the member's own ideological predispositions were with the rights of labor. On the other hand this same member's reaction to adverse agency treatment of a union in his district bore all the earmarks of a free-swinging, no-holds-barred encounter between committee member and offending agency. Where a member's own constituents were not affected by agency decisions brought to the committee for review, the member's response to agency conduct was governed by the extent of his identification with the values of the affected groups, labor or employer. The intensity of a committee member's reaction reached its peak, then, when the case before the committee found an injured constituent's interests coinciding with the Congressman's own group values.[15]

The legislative oversight role will also bear a relationship to the perceptions the legislator has toward the Administration and the obligations and responsibilities of his committee. Some legislative committees are hardly involved in oversight activities at all, because the committee chairmen or powerful committee members conceive their role in such a way as to eschew oversight activities on the part of their committee. Such has been the case with the United States Senate Committee on Banking and Currency, whose chairman, Senator A. Willis Robertson (D-Va), "used his powers primarily as a restraining influence on his committee. . . . His conception of the proper function of a committee places little emphasis on oversight. . . . He feels that the committee should not, in the words of a colleague, 'be poking around the agencies and stirring things up.' "[16]

Some legislative committees engage in what might be called selective oversight. Their members conceive their role to be that of observing and reviewing selected or limited aspects of agency operation. The United States House Committee on Armed Services is perhaps the best available illustration. Not only does this committee tend to defer to the appropriate appropriations subcommittee in the matter of review of important substantive policy issues regarding the military establishment, but within its own purview the committee tends to select a substantively narrow range of oversight interests.[17] The committee members have little inclination to raise or consider broad issues of military policy involving weapons, personnel, appropriations, military objectives, organization, or administration. The main concern of the House Armed Services Committee is the location of military, air, and naval installations and the purchase, sale, or transfer of properties by the Department of Defense. As one of the members of the Committee staff said: "Our committee is a real estate committee. Don't forget that. If you study our committee, you are studying real estate transactions."[18]

The appropriations committees of the Congress, especially the House Committee, exemplify a more pervasive role conception on the part of committee members vis-a-vis the administrative agencies. In their posture of guardians of the federal treasury, members of the House Committee tend to engage in the most detailed and sweeping oversight of the general government, largely with the object of reducing budgetary requests.[19]

No greater control over executive policy making and implementation exists than that of the Joint Committee on Atomic Energy. Members of this congressional committee conceive their job as that of recommending programs and policies both to the Atomic Energy Commission and to Congress. The Joint Committee is so heavily involved in atomic energy policy formulation and execution that it is difficult to tell where the legislative process leaves off and the administrative process begins. "The Joint Committee on Atomic Energy is, in terms of its sustained influence in Congress, its impact and influence on the Executive, and its accomplishments, probably the most powerful Congressional committee in the history of the nation."[20]

Legislative Organization. Two aspects of legislative organization can be developed here with respect to legislative oversight, supervision, and control of the administration. One has to do with the *jurisdiction* of legislative committees to engage in surveillance over executive agencies. At the congressional level, the Legislative Reorganization Act of 1946 endowed all congressional standing committees with wide jurisdiction to engage in oversight activities. Section 136 of the act provides that "each standing committee of the Senate and the House of Representatives shall exercise continuous watchfulness of the execution by the administrative agencies concerned of any laws, the subject matter of which is within the jurisdiction of such committee. . . ." Furthermore, the act especially gave the committees on government operations authority to investigate and oversee federal agencies. State legislative committees seldom have such pervasive jurisdiction. Again, the specific jurisdiction of each congressional standing committee varies considerably. Where more than one committee has jurisdiction over legislation affecting the same executive agency, the agency may be able to develop multiple sources of support in Congress and thus benefit from the dispersion of congressional resources for oversight. Thus, the military and defense establishment may utilize its support from the House Armed Services Committee so as to bolster its efforts before the Defense Appropriations Subcommittee for increased appropriations. Both cooperation and conflict between legislative committees may benefit the administrative agency whose budget or program is under review.[21] The congressional Joint Committee on Atomic Energy is perhaps a unique legislative committee in the pervasiveness of its jurisdiction and in the importance of its statutory basis as an institutional factor in its unusual accretion of power. The Atomic Energy Act of 1954 empowered the Joint Committee to take jurisdiction over "all bills, resolutions or other matters in the Senate or the House of Representatives relating primarily to the Commission or to the development, use, or control of atomic energy."[22] This broad committee jurisdiction both enhances the committee's position with regard to other congressional committees that might claim jurisdiction over particular programs and also makes it clear to the Atomic Energy Commission that it must deal with the committee. The AEC has not been able to develop competing bases of support in other congressional committees. When the Joint Committee's authority to use executive facilities, authorize appropriations, veto proposed AEC actions, and require information from the executive branch is added to its sweeping jurisdiction, it becomes easy to understand the substantial control that the Joint Committee exercises over the commission.[23]

The second relevant problem of legislative organization involves the structural-constitutional factor of *bicameralism*, a factor to be reckoned with in the case of the national Congress and of every state legislature except that of Nebraska (where, as a matter of fact, we know little of the variable effects of unicameralism). One aspect of the problem that bicameral legislative organization raises has to do with the nature and extent of cooperation and conflict between house and senate committees engaged in oversight activities. The generally low level of coordination between house and senate committees is likely to impinge upon the effectiveness of the legislature in the performance of its oversight tasks.

In the supervision of administration through the budgetary process, the respective committees of the United States House and Senate take quite different positions, and their members play different roles. The House committee members, as we have already suggested, tend to play the role of guardian of the exchequer, cutting the budgets of administrative agencies whenever possible. The Senate Appropriations Committee, on the other hand, takes the position of an appellate court with respect to executive agencies, and its members tend to play the role of hearing appeals from House Committee budget cuts. The difference in the perspectives of the two congressional committees is illustrated very well by the remarks of Senator Dirksen (R-Ill). Referring to a House Committee decision to cut the number of employees for a particular agency from ten to six, Dirksen said: "It was great, good fun when I was on the House Appropriations Committee to cut four [positions]. Too often you discover that the six positions depend in large measure on the four. You just wasted the money for the six. I would rather give you nothing or whatever it takes to do a good job."[24]

A second problem that bicameralism raises for legislative oversight, although closely related to the first, involves the position taken by the respective legislative houses on administrative agency programs. The case of the reduction of the RS-70 bomber program that occurred in 1962 is an example of this kind of problem. In preparing the federal military budget for the 1963 fiscal year, Secretary of Defense Mc-Namara, with the support of the President, proposed drastic cuts in funds for the development of a supersonic reconnaissance strike bomber (the RS-70) and the elimination altogether of plans for the mass production of these bombers. While only a relatively small amount of money was involved, this proposal stimulated substantial opposition on the part of powerful individuals in Congress and in the Defense Department. The principal congressional opponent of the cutback plan was Representative Carl Vinson (D-Ga), venerable chairman of the House Committee on

Armed Services. In the Department of Defense, Air Force Chief of Staff General Curtis LeMay vocally supported the buildup of manned bombers and opposed the RS-70 reduction. However, Secretary McNamara won the support of Congressman George Mahon (D-Tex), chairman of the Defense Appropriations Subcommittee, and under his guidance the House of Representatives supported the Defense Department in its final appropriations bill. The Senate did not support the RS-70 reduction and appropriated the $491 million that Representative Vinson and General LeMay wanted for the bomber program. The conference committee finally agreed upon the spending of $362 million, but Secretary McNamara privately negotiated a tacit agreement with the House conferees that he would not spend all that the conference committee had authorized. The Defense Secretary stood on his constitutional prerogative of refusing to spend money on a program with which he disagreed, even though Congress had appropriated the necessary funds. Thus, "Congress may authorize expenditure, but it can do little to bring it about unless it is able to persuade the President and the administrative agencies concerned that its policy position is appropriate. A united Congress has a good chance for success in this endeavor, but a divided legislature has little hope."[25]

An extremely important factor in congressional policy initiation, especially in attempting to counter the policy position of an executive agency supported by the President, is that of the fragmentation of the policy processes of Congress in relation to the Administration. When the two houses of a legislature are divided and the chief executive supports the bureaucracy, imposing legislative policy on an executive agency is very difficult, and legislative oversight is thereby substantially vitiated.

Staff Involvement. A further problem of legislative-executive relations is the extent to which the legislative committee or individual staffs are involved.[26] At the state levels, if any kind of effective legislative oversight exists at all, some legislative staff person is likely to be the one who does it. About half the states have year-round staffs for the specific purpose of budgetary and fiscal review, and this tends to be the major, if not the only, continuing legislative oversight of the state executive agencies.[27] At the congressional level, however, the staffs of some committees have a very prominent place in the oversight process.

The staff of the congressional Joint Committee on Atomic Energy, one of the most effective operations, maintains very close contact with the operating personnel of the Atomic Energy Commission, including its field personnel.[28] The committee staff has been described as being more knowledgeable about the commission's field activities than the AEC's own Washington staff. One of the major purposes of the JCAE staff has been to keep committee members informed, although it has also played the more creative role of suggesting problem areas for exploration and initiating committee investigations. Perhaps the importance of this particular committee staff is suggested most pointedly by the fact that the executive director of the staff, James T. Ramey, was appointed a member of the commission in 1962.

The well-integrated and nonpartisan staffs of the congressional appropriations committees have a more significant part in oversight activities than do most committee staffs. Reciprocal confidence between the Appropriations Committee staff and the budget officers of executive agencies is made necessary by their mutual dependence, and "many agencies choose to keep subcommittee staff informed months and sometimes years ahead on new developments."[29] When hearings are in progress, contact between committee staff and agency budget officers may be as frequent as several times a day; clearly the staff plays an important part in the budgetary oversight process.

At the same time, legislative staff aides are by no means a match for the enormous pool of experts upon whom an executive officer can call for intelligence and information. The personnel of executive agencies are not only more numerous, but have a greater opportunity to specialize; they are free of the necessity of periodic exposure to the electorate, and have a tremendous advantage over the congressional committee staff in knowledge of and experience with the operating end of agency activity. Even an enlarged legislative committee staff would be required to get much of its information about agency activities from the agency personnel themselves.

Anticipated Reactions. A number of students of legislative-executive relations have noted the phenomenon of anticipated reactions (sometimes called feedback, or "strategic sensitivity") in the relationships between legislative committees and executive agencies.[30] It involves the bureaucrats' abilities "to anticipate or to recognize the expectations of committee members, to gauge the timeliness of a request, and to be cognizant of the claims, demands, and expectations which others direct at committee members immediately, but which are ultimately directed at the bureau itself."[31] The bureau officer who learns to take a role in his relationships with legislators which is formulated in terms of legislators' expectations about the proper behavior of representatives of administrative agencies maximizes his chances of successful legislative-executive relations. Administrators get many cues about the behavior expected of them by legislators through legislative committee hearings, personal contacts between legislators and agency leaders, or contacts with a committee staff. American legislators tend to expect bureaucrats to be hard-working, economy-minded, honest and straightforward, trustworthy, well-informed, friendly, and respectful of the legislative body. The complexity of modern government requires considerable mutual confidence between legislators and administrators, and such confidence "is achieved by gearing one's behavior to fit in with the expectations of committee people."[32]

A good illustration of administrators anticipating the reactions of legislators about their behavior is provided by the budget process. Members of the congressional appropriations committees tend to take the role of guardians of the treasury; their principal objective has been to reduce governmental expenditures, or at least to keep them to a mimimum. The budget officer from an executive agency, therefore, "needs to show that he is also a guardian of the treasury: sound, responsible, not a wastrel; he needs to be able to defend his presentations with convincing evidence and to at least appear to be concerned with protecting the taxpayer."[33]

Like the lady who gets a "bargain" and tells her husband how much she has saved, so the administrator is expected to speak of economies. Not only is there no fat in his budget, there is almost no lean. Witness Dewey Short, a former Congressman, speaking on behalf of the Army: "We think we are almost down to the bone. It is a modest request . . . a meager request. . . ." Agency people soon catch on to the economy motif: "I have already been under attack . . . for being too tight with this money. . . ."[34]

Perhaps one of the most outstanding federal administrators of this century was William A. Jump, who served in the Department of Agriculture for many years. His successful relations with the Congress apparently resulted very largely from the fact that he was able to take the role expected of him by congressmen. When "a question would arise as to whether or not an expenditure of funds for a given purpose was authorized by the appropriation . . . Mr. Jump never took a purely legalistic approach . . . but often consulted with the chairmen of the committees to find out their position."[35]

LEGISLATIVE CONTROL OF EXECUTIVE ORGANIZATION

American legislatures can, and many do, exercise considerable control over administrative organization and reorganization, personnel recruitment and policy, and administrative procedures and rules.[36] Executive agencies and their programs must have authorization in the laws enacted by legislatures. The detail of statutory authorization varies a great deal, although there is a tendency for legislatures increasingly to prescribe administrative organization, procedures, and programs in greater detail.[37] By appropriations and civil service legislation, controls are imposed by legislatures upon the recruitment, loyalty, promotion, salaries, duties, and numbers of administrative personnel. And, in the last three decades, with the increasing necessity for legislative delegation of wide discretionary authority to administrative agencies, legislatures have attempted to devise adequate mechanisms for controlling the use of administrative discretion.

A potentially important method of control is legislative approval of executive appointments. The United States Senate gives its advice and consent to thousands of appointments, most of them routine. The senators' interest in the average appointment is limited to preserving their control over patronage through the technique of "senatorial courtesy" described in Chapter 15. Occasionally, with respect to more important appointments, senators question the competence of a nominee or possible conflicts of interest arising from his appointment; rarely do these doubts lead to rejection of a nominee. In only a small proportion of controversies over appointments are there any policy implications. Sometimes senators regard a nominee as a symbol of a disputed policy; the criticism directed by a few Republican senators at Charles Bohlen, President Eisenhower's nominee as Ambassador to Moscow, grew out of Bohlen's presence at the disputed Yalta Conference and more broadly out of his identification with the foreign policies of the Truman Administration. On rare occasions the policy implications are more than symbolic. In 1949, when the Senate rejected President Truman's renomination of Leland Olds to the Federal Power Commission, the debate was concerned with his personal characteristics, but the struggle actually involved the scope of the commission's regulatory authority, and the major opposition came from oil and gas interests.[38] The Senate has traditionally been reluctant to reject cabinet appointees; only eight such cases are on record, just two of them since 1868. Despite this tradition, in 1959 the Senate narrowly rejected President Eisenhower's nomination of Lewis Strauss, a former commissioner of the Atomic Energy Commission, as Secretary of Commerce. At issue in this heated controversy were Strauss's views on public power, his record with the AEC, and his attitude toward legislative-executive relations, but questions of personality and his personal relations with senators were inextricably involved in his defeat.

The chief executive's power to dismiss his appointees is obviously a vital part of his executive authority, but the extent of senatorial control over dismissals was long an unsettled constitutional question. The impeachment proceedings against President Andrew Johnson resulted from his refusal to abide by a law that required senatorial approval of dismissals. In the 1926 Myers case, the Supreme Court held that the President has exclusive authority to dismiss administrative officials, a decision modified in 1935 to provide that Congress might limit presidential authority to remove members of independent regulatory commissions.[39] In a number of states there are constitutional or statutory limitations on the governor's power to remove, except for cause, numerous officials and members of commissions, who are appointed for fixed terms despite their importance as policy makers. Though control of the legislature by the opposition party sometimes leads to rejection of gubernatorial appointments, it is these restrictions on the removal power that constitute the most serious restrictions on governors.

Perhaps the most direct and visible legislative control over administrative organization and procedure has been that of the so-called "legislative veto." In the early New Deal days, when economic crisis made necessary the delegation of what was then thought to be sweeping discretionary power to administrative agencies, Congress sought to retain some check upon the procedures, rulings, and organization of the new federal agencies. In the field of executive reorganization, for instance, in the 1932 reorganization law Congress required that a President's reorganization plans be submitted to Congress sixty days before going into effect, subject to disapproval by a resolution of either house. This precedent has been followed in subsequent legislation dealing with executive reorganization. Under such legislation, Congress twice rejected presidential reorganization plans submitted by President Truman to create a Department of Health, Education and Welfare (finally accepted shortly after President Eisenhower took office) and rejected a reorganization plan of President Kennedy's, which would have created a Department of Urban Affairs.

Legislative clearance of administrative decisions dates at least back to the practice, developed in the 1920s, of review and approval by the congressional Joint Committee on Internal Revenue Taxation of certain tax refunds made by the Internal Revenue Service.

This committee oversight arrangement grew out of a "prior reporting" requirement regarding particular tax refunds of the Bureau of Internal Revenue contained in the Urgent Deficiency Act of 1927. The statutory stipulation directed the Bureau to report all tax refunds involving more than $75,000 to the Joint Committee on Internal Revenue Taxation sixty days before they were actually paid. Although the statutory language did not explicitly grant a veto power to the joint committee, an arrangement soon developed whereby only the committee-approved decisions would be carried out.[40]

Such clearance continues to exist, accomplished for the most part by the staff (and particularly by the chief of staff, Colin Stam) of the Joint Tax Committee.[41]

Formal statutory requirements for legislative committee clearance of administrative procedures, rules, or decisions began with the passage by Congress of a naval public works statute in 1944, which authorized the Secretary of the Navy to acquire land for the establishment of naval shore facilities, but only after the review and approval of the naval affairs committees.[42] A more recent illustration is provided by a rider attached to the defense appropriations bill passed by Congress in 1955. It provided that:

> No part of the funds appropriated in this Act may be used for the disposal or transfer by contract or otherwise of work that has been for a period of three years or more performed by civilian personnel of the Department of Defense unless justified to the Appropriations Committees of the Senate and House of Representatives, at least ninety days in advance of such disposal or transfer, that its discontinuance is economically sound and the work is capable of performance by a contractor without danger to the national security; provided, that no such disposal or transfer shall be made if disapproved by either committee within the ninety-day period by written notice to the Secretary of Defense.[43]

Although the rider was later removed, and Congress does not now have the statutory authority to intervene and prevent the Defense Department from closing commercial or industrial installations, Congress has used the veto technique on a variety of other matters, especially on government purchases, land acquisition, sale of surplus property, conservation and reclamation projects, deportations, and exchange of military information and atomic energy materials.[44] The most all-encompassing legislative veto powers are those in the hands of members of the Joint Committee on Atomic Energy.[45]

Somewhat similar developments have been occurring in some of the states. Administrative procedures acts in five states (Connecticut, Kansas, Michigan, Nebraska, and Virginia) contain legislative review provisions. In these states, administrative regulations must be submitted to legislative review, and rules disapproved by the legislature are void. Wisconsin experimented for a time with legislative invalidations of administrative rules.[46] But the Michigan statute has been in effect longest (since 1947). It states: "The legislature reserves the right to approve, alter, suspend or abrogate any rule promulgated pursuant to the provisions of this act." It requires that all rules promulgated by executive agencies be submitted to each member of the legislature prior to the regular session; those disapproved by concurrent resolution are void. Between sessions, the clearance process is performed by a joint committee on administrative rules, which has the power to suspend rules until the next legislative session. In practice, this joint committee performs a continuous clearance of administrative rules. One significant result of the Michigan law has been to reduce the issuance of formal rules by Michigan administrative agencies.[47]

Legislative clearance is a method of control over administration with considerable appeal to legislators who wish to secure or maintain current supervision of the uses of delegated authority. The usual mechanisms of legislative oversight—reporting, budget review, investigation—tend to be *ex post facto* in nature, and they are therefore somewhat limited in usefulness. Furthermore, legislative clearance may be appealing to administrative officers who desire the favorable reaction of the legislature to their use of delegated authority. "Committee clearance helps to decrease the guesswork in such calculations and predictions," and thus "promotes security and stability." Requiring that each use of administrative discretion be accompanied by legislative committee acceptance "assures the agencies of approval and support by the most influential units of the legislative branch."[48] At the same time, legislative committee clearance does tend to reduce the supervisory capacity of the chief executive and to some extent of the legislative body as a whole.

OVERSIGHT BY INVESTIGATION

One of the most important, and sometimes the most spectacular, devices for legislative oversight of administration is the committee investigation. Legislative committee investigations have come into public prominence since World War II, largely because of the improprieties in state legislative and congressional committee investigations of internal Communist, or allegedly subversive, activities.[49] While the loyalty of officials in the executive agencies of government was at least the original focus of most of these inquiries, committees investigating un-American activities have seldom limited themselves to the narrow confines of legislative-executive relations; these investigations have almost invariably broadened their scope. Perhaps the most bizarre legislative investigation in American history was the so-called Army-McCarthy Hearings in the spring of 1954, which involved the erratic Senator Joseph McCarthy of Wisconsin.[50] Peculiar as the McCarthy investigations were, and significant as they were for understanding the temper of American society in the 1950s, they teach us little about legislative-executive relations beyond indicating legislative excesses, the failure of legislatures to impose restraints upon investigating committees under some circumstances, and the extent to which investigations of certain kinds can distort and inflate individual legislators' reputations.

State legislative investigating committees have been subjected to very little study, although they appear to operate only sporadically and irregularly. But congressional investigations have increased significantly in number since standing congressional committees obtained wider investigative authority and greater resources with the enactment of the 1946 Reorganization Act. Since 1950, Congress has conducted each year some 200 investigations, covering a very wide range of subjects. Most of these investigations have a distinctive and legitimate legislative purpose and bear some relation to the specific legislative enactments that are, in part at least, their result. Some congressional committee investigations, rather than having a directly law-making purpose, provide a means by which the committees can supervise executive agencies through examining their implementation of delegated power in particular circumstances. Also, investigations may have a primarily informational purpose, simply helping legislators to keep up with events.

Legislative investigations of executive agencies may be generated by many, and even mixed, motives. Partisan advantage is often involved: "When the Republicans captured control of Congress in 1946, it was virtually a political obligation to set about discrediting the Democratic administration through investigations—with an eye to the 1948 election."[51] Investigations may be instigated by legislators because of the anticipated personal profit in the form of national publicity and popularity. Suspicion or evidence of malfeasance, wrongdoing, illegal activity, or improper conduct on the part of administration officials may trigger congressional investigations—such as the celebrated investigation of the Teapot Dome scandals during the Harding Administration by the Senate Committee on Public Lands and Surveys.[52] Again, investigations may be forthcoming because legislative leaders have come to feel that administrative agencies are not doing the job that the legislature intended. For example, in 1957, when Speaker Sam Rayburn urged the creation of the Special Subcommittee on Legislative Oversight of the House Committee on Interstate and Foreign Commerce to investigate the work of the independent regulatory commissions, Bernard Schwartz, the controversial chief counsel of the subcommittee, felt that Rayburn had been motivated by a genuine conviction that the regulatory agencies he had helped create were being "run by men who have been out of sympathy with their objectives."[53]

But if legislative investigations are often designed to curb executive agencies by means of probing and public disclosure, it is clear that there are great institutional and interpersonal restraints upon penetrating investigations of the behavior and conduct of administrative officials.[54] In addition, as often as not, legislative committee investigations seem to be designed to help the chief executive or an executive agency, and congressional-administrative cooperation in the development (or squelching) of investigations is not uncommon. In some cases, legislative inquiries have been designed primarily to reinforce the recommendations of the President for major legislation. Thus, "exposures in 1933 and 1934 by the Senate committee investigating stock exchange practices and banking, for example, contributed markedly to the enactment of such Administration-supported legislation as the Banking Acts of 1933 and 1935, the Securities Act of 1933, and the Securities and Exchange Act of 1934."[55] Cooperation between a congressional committee and an administration agency may occur when the agency wishes to get information that only an investigating committee can acquire by using its subpoena power. Thus, it is said that "the Senate Committee on Interstate Commerce conducted an inquiry into the financing of railroads partly for the purpose of acquiring information which the Interstate Commerce Commission felt it did not have the power to obtain. . . ."[56] Finally, congressional leaders may initiate an investigation by a committee or subcommittee led by congressmen friendly to the Administration in order to circumvent an investigation by hostile members, a factor which appears to have been important in the authorization of the so-called Truman Committee, created in 1941 to investigate defense mobilization.[57]

One of the important sources of conflict between legislative investigating committees and executive agencies comes in connection with the right of committee access to the papers and files of executive agencies, and the correlative right of executive agencies, under presidential authority, to withhold information that the President regards as contrary to the public interest. Congressional dependence upon information from executive agencies is acute, and congressional reaction is often heated when information is denied. Such conflict has arisen in recent years, for example, in connection with loyalty-security investigations, in the so-called Dixon-Yates affair, in the abortive 1957 regulatory commission investigation, and in 1958–1959, when the International Cooperation Administration refused to furnish the Senate Foreign Relations Committee with a file of evaluation reports on the operation of the foreign aid program.[58]

AUTHORIZATION AND APPROPRIATIONS

The most substantial and detailed legislative supervision of executive agencies is in the area of fiscal control, the central processes of which are the authorization for the expenditure of funds, the appropriation of funds, and the audit or review of their actual expenditure. At the congressional level, the primary units for fiscal supervision are the appropriations committees, although the Joint Economic Committee, the Committees on Government Operations, and the General Accounting

Office also have important parts to play in the fiscal review process.[59] While we cannot examine congressional fiscal surveillance in detail, we can observe some of its main characteristics.

Authorization-Appropriations Tension. A fundamental characteristic of the congressional budget process is the distinction between *authorization* and *appropriation*. Authorization is accomplished by the substantive legislative committees (on agriculture, interstate commerce, foreign affairs and so forth), and involves setting a ceiling of expenditure for substantive governmental programs. Substantive committee authorizations for programs "may be open-ended, requiring no further action by the legislative committee; they may be multi-year or lump sum, expiring when either the time or expenditure limitation is exceeded; or they may be annual—i.e., requiring action by the legislative committee concerned *each* fiscal year."[60] Programs must be authorized before funds can be appropriated for their implementation. The appropriations committees allocate funds to be expended for programs already authorized. But the control of the appropriations committees over the purse strings gives them a crucial opportunity to make policy. This control, when they wish to exercise it, frequently leads to tension between the appropriations committees and the substantive committees. Such tension is clearly indicated by the following comments of a member of the House:

> Theoretically the weapons system is authorized by the Committee on Armed Services, but that is only in theory. On the missile programs that have been permitted to go ahead, decision is made by the Appropriations Committee through the language of reports and through riders. The committee which heard all the testimony and is presumed to have special competence is not the one which makes the decisions. If we are going to take the trouble to develop men with specialized knowledge in a given field, then we should give them the right to sit in and second guess on Appropriations. There is no point in having hearings before Armed Services and then have the final decision made by Appropriations.[61]

Appropriations-authorization tension is mitigated to some extent in the Senate, where members of the Appropriations Committee serve on a larger number of other committees and where the Senate committee is not so much inclined as is the House committee toward budget reduction.

Decentralization of Decision Making. The atomization of legislative control of administrative agencies is nowhere more clearly illustrated than in the appropriations process. That appropriations decisions are highly decentralized is primarily a function of the congressional norms of specialization and reciprocity. The crucial unit of appropriations decision making is the subcommittee. The subcommittees of the House and Senate committees on appropriations are highly independent and autonomous and subject to very little direction or coordination from the parent committees. As Macmahon observed a good many years ago:

It is not the Congress, not the House or Senate, not even the appropriations committee as a whole that should be thought of as abstractions, set against administration. The reality is a handful of men from particular states or districts, working with a particular committee clerk on a multitude of details.[62]

Budgetary Restraint and Complexity. Budgeting for a modern government is extremely complex, and the armada of officials in executive agencies who prepare and justify the President's budget far outnumbers the congressional subcommittees and their small staffs. Ranking subcommittee members have had long experience in supervising budget items within their jurisdiction, but they must, of necessity, concentrate their attention on a few details. Perhaps there is often a tendency to dwell excessively on trivial detail, as, for instance, when Representative Mahon's House Defense Appropriations Subcommittee, during consideration of the defense budget for fiscal 1950, devoted as much time in hearings to the price of oats the Army intended to buy for horses as it did on the impact of the defense budget on the North Atlantic Treaty, and far more time on appropriations for the National Board for the Promotion of Rifle Practice.[63]

The question of how much money should be spent for a government program is often without a determinate answer. The amounts of money that executive agencies request, and the amounts Congress appropriates, are not, however, unrestrained. As Schilling points out with regard to the defense budget:

Neither the Executive nor Congress approaches the defense budget as an ad hoc problem, intent on a free-ranging examination of all possible alternatives before making a choice. On the contrary, members of the Executive and Congress start their thinking about the budget with a common and very narrow range of figures in mind. The area of their choice is closely limited by the prevailing climate of opinion regarding desirable and possible defense budgets. All figures outside these limits, in either direction, are rejected out of hand as manifestly undesirable, infeasible, or just plain inconceivable.[64]

The executive agencies develop their figures and justifications with an eye to what Congress will approve, and the subcommittees operate in a climate of expectation about what the agencies want and will spend.

Reduction of Budget Estimates. It is part of the prevailing normative structure of the congressional appropriations committees to economize. The resulting behavior can be fairly easily observed by looking at Richard Fenno's tabulations of the appropriations histories of 36 bureaus for 1947 to 1962, as shown in Table 19.1. It is apparent that the Budget Bureau estimates were reduced by Congress about three-fourths of the time. However, one ought not to infer from these comparisons that the appropriations subcommittees never increase expenditures; programs that have strong congressional support are sometimes appropriated greater amounts than the executive agencies request. The National Institutes of Health, for example, got an appropriation in 1961

Table 19.1. CONGRESSIONAL CUTS IN BUDGET BUREAU ESTIMATES
(In percentages; N=444 cases)

	Budget Estimate		
Difference	Compared to House committee recommendation	Compared to House bill	Compared to final appropriation
No difference	18	18	15
Estimates greater than recommended	74	74	67
Estimates less than recommended	8	8	18
Other	*	*	—
Total	100	100	100

* less than 1%

SOURCE: Richard Fenno, *The Power of the Purse: Appropriations Politics in Congress* (Boston: Little, Brown and Co., 1966), chaps. 8, 9, 12.

of $160 million in excess of the amount the agency had requested.[65] Furthermore, reduction in an appropriation for an agency may be followed by a deficiency or supplementary appropriation, which awards the agency as much as, or more than, it originally requested. The Appropriations Committee may endeavor "to keep the total appropriation figure down for a while to demonstrate that it was economizing," and then make restitution of the funds later.[66]

Adoption of Committee Recommendations. It is uncommon for the recommendations of appropriations subcommittees to be rejected or fundamentally altered by the full committees. In addition, as is indicated in Table 19.2, the recommendations of the appropriations committees are overwhelmingly adopted without change on the floor of the House and the Senate.[67] Members of the subcommittees are regarded as men with special expertise, whose judgment really ought not to be

Table 19.2.   ADOPTION OF COMMITTEE RECOMMENDATIONS*
(In percentages)

	Recommendation	
	Senate committee compared with Senate bill	House committee compared with final House bill
No difference	88	90
Committee recommendation greater than bill	3	5
Committee recommendation less than bill	9	5
Other	—	†
Total	100	100

* The data for this table are based upon the same 444 cases shown in Table 19.1.

† Less than 1%.

SOURCE: Richard Fenno, *The Power of the Purse: Appropriations Politics in Congress* (Boston: Little, Brown and Co., 1966), chaps. 9 and 11.

questioned on the floor. Such an attitude is suggested by the remarks on the House floor by Representative Carl Vinson (D-Ga), chairman of the Armed Services Committee, in urging the adoption of the defense appropriation bill in the form reported by the Appropriations Committee:

They [the subcommittee] deserve the support of every member of this House because they are in a far better position to know the needs and necessities of national defense than you and I, who have not given . . . [the bill] the complete and detailed study it should have.[68]

That the appropriations committees make public policy along with allocating funds can hardly be questioned. The committee hearings provide a public opportunity for members of the committees to give cues to executive officials and to extract promises from them about policy, and committee reports may contain specific expressions of the agreements and understandings between subcommittees and officials about the manner of spending funds.[69] Carroll's observations of the relations between officials of the Department of State and the appropriations subcommittees led him to conclude that:

> Prudent administrators carefully read the hearings and reports of the committee because they know they will be questioned on their compliance with the advice the next time they appear before the subcommittee. These subcommitteemen, so free with advice, control the lifeblood of any policy—money—and the administrators are acutely aware of this simple fact. It is often wiser to please the money committee than to placate the legislative committee which authorized the policy, if the two do not agree.[70]

In addition, policy decisions and directives may actually be written into appropriations acts. It is not uncommon for appropriations bills to contain detailed restrictions on the salaries and employment of personnel, earmarking funds for specified purposes, spending without prior committee approval or other congressional action, and administrative expenditures.[71] Finally, the committees engage in year-round surveillance of executive agencies through studies and investigations of the expenditure of appropriated funds conducted by committeemen and members of the committee staffs.

In addition to its controls over executive agencies through budget authorization, allocation, and review, Congress created its own staff agency to audit federal expenditures when it enacted the Budget and Accounting Act of 1921. The General Accounting Office, headed by the comptroller general, was authorized to investigate the receipt and disbursement of public funds and to report to Congress. In addition to audit reports, the comptroller general may recommend ways of achieving greater economy and efficiency in governmental expenditures and report on fiscal control practices in executive agencies or on violations of law in expending funds. The staff of the GAO may be used to help congressional committees conduct investigations or prepare analyses of budgetary implementation and execution.[72]

State Legislative Fiscal Control. As we suggested earlier in this chapter, legislative review of the state budget is the major instrument for oversight of the executive branch at the state level. The governor is the budget-making authority in most American states; only in Arkansas does the budget-making authority reside exclusively with a legislative agency. In a number of states, however, legislative committees or staff personnel participate to some degree in the process of budget formulation. In New York, for example, the chairmen of the House and Senate appropriations committees and their staffs participate in executive budget hearings and are usually consulted by the governor before he submits his budget, which then is customarily considered briefly without legislative hearings and passed without change. The Texas budget process is unique because both an executive and a legislative budget are submitted to the legislature. The legislative budget is prepared by a Budget Board composed of the presiding officers and four members of each legislative house and its permanent staff. The staff prepares budget estimates, conducts investigations, holds hearings on budget requests, and prepares a draft budget for the board. The board reports to the legislature independently of the executive, and during sessions the staff of the board becomes the staffs of the House appropriations and Senate finance committees.[73]

About three-fourths of the state legislatures have available to them some kind of fiscal oversight machinery, although in only twelve states are budget review and analysis, continuous study of revenue and expenditures, and legislative post-auditing all performed. In some states one or more of these activities are engaged in by the legislative interim committees; in some, permanent fiscal review committees and staffs are provided.[74] But in most state legislatures budgetary control is minimal. Commonly, the governor and executive agencies prepare the budget. Legislative committees and staffs, because of their small numbers and limited time, can engage in only the most cursory review of the executive budget, which is enacted without opportunity for much review and often without significant change; there is also little oversight following statutory enactment. Illinois is a fairly typical state. There, hearings before the appropriations committees, while they provide some opportunity for legislators and citizens to become better informed about executive agency policy, are largely perfunctory. The legislature gets the governor's budget in April and must adopt it before the biennium and the legislative session end in June; thus only a very short time is available for budgetary consideration. Seldom are objections raised to executive agency budgetary items; legislative consideration constitutes little danger to the integrity of the governor's estimates.[75]

A significant factor in state legislative supervision, oversight, and control of the budgetary process is the fairly widespread use of segregated or earmarked funds. This results when state revenue legislation specifically pledges the expenditure of revenues for a designated purpose, e.g., when gasoline taxes or motor vehicle license fees are specifically earmarked for the highway fund to be spent for highway construction and maintenance, rather than going into the general funds of the state for regular government operating expenses. Where they are used often, such earmarked funds tie revenues to specified programs, and leave little flexibility or initiative to either executive or legislative branches for fiscal planning and management. Where, as in some states, half or more of the state money is earmarked, the sphere and scope of legislative control is obviously very limited.[76]

The emphasis of this chapter has been upon some of the salient characteristics of the legislative process of sifting, winnowing, and judging the organization, programs, policies, practices, and spending of executive agencies. We have dealt primarily with the activities of Congress for two reasons: in most state legislatures, oversight—except perhaps for the budget—has been minimal; further, descriptive literature on legislative-executive relations is much more adequate at the national than at the state level. The paucity of systematic research is, however, much more impressive than the plethora of descriptive, and frequently repetitive, commentaries. Here is an area of legislative research that is badly in need of expansion.

NOTES

1. Roland Young, *The American Congress* (New York, 1958), pp. 165–67.
2. Seymour Scher, "Congressional Committee Members as Independent Agency Overseers: A Case Study," *American Political Science Review*, LIV (1960), 919.
3. Elias Huzar, *The Purse and the Sword* (Ithaca, N.Y., 1950), p. 354; and William W. Boyer, *Bureaucracy on Trial* (Indianapolis, 1964), pp. 44–46.
4. Seymour Scher, "Conditions for Legislative Control," *Journal of Politics*, XXV (1963), 526–40.
5. *Ibid.*, p. 541.
6. *Ibid.*, pp. 541–50.
7. Lewis A. Dexter, "Congressmen and the Making of Military Policy," in Robert L. Peabody and Nelson W. Polsby (ed.), *New Perspectives on the House of Representatives* (Chicago, 1963), p. 312.
8. Scher, "Conditions for Legislative Control," p. 533.
9. Dexter, *op. cit.*, p. 321.
10. *Ibid.*
11. J. Leiper Freeman, *The Political Process: Executive Bureau–Legislative Committee Relations* (Garden City, N.Y., 1955), p. 59.
12. A good example is the well-known antagonism that existed between U.S. Senator Clinton Anderson (D-NM) and Admiral Lewis Strauss when Strauss was Chairman of the Atomic Energy Commission. Senator Anderson served on the Joint Committee on Atomic Energy. "Much of the Joint Committee's history between 1954 and June, 1958, was colored by the personal enmity between Anderson and Strauss." See Harold P. Green and Alan Rosenthal, *Government of the Atom* (New York, 1963), pp. 59–60.
13. For example, James A. Robinson, "Process Satisfaction and Policy Approval in State Department-Congressional Relations," *American Journal of Sociology*, LXVII (1961), 278–83.
14. U.S. Senate, *Administrative Procedure Legislation, Hearings before the Subcommittee on Administrative Practice and Procedure of the Committee on the Judiciary*, 86th Cong., 1st Sess., pp. 92ff; quoted in Scher, "Conditions for Legislative Control," p. 536.
15. Scher, "Congressional Committee Members as Agency Overseers," p. 919; and Aaron Wildavsky, *The Politics of the Budgetary Process* (Boston, 1964), pp. 47–51.
16. John F. Bibby, "Legislative Oversight of Administration: A Case Study of a Congressional Committee" (Unpublished Ph.D. dissertation, University of Wisconsin, 1963), p. 146.

17. Bernard K. Gordon, "The Military Budget: Congressional Phase," *Journal of Politics*, XXIII (1961), 689–710; and Dexter, *op. cit.*, pp. 305–24.

18. Dexter, *op. cit.*, p. 312.

19. Wildavsky, *op. cit.*, pp. 47–62; and Richard F. Fenno, Jr., "The House Appropriations Committee as a Political System: The Problem of Integration," *American Political Science Review*, LVI (1962), 310–24.

20. Green and Rosenthal, *op. cit.*, p. 266.

21. Jurisdictional conflicts between committees may, of course, make for disadvantages from the point of view of the executive agency. For an interesting discussion of this possibility in connection with legislative authorization of military weapons systems, see Raymond H. Dawson, "Congressional Innovation and Intervention in Defense Policy: Legislative Authorization of Weapons Systems," *American Political Science Review*, LVI (1962), 42–57.

22. Quoted in Green and Rosenthal, *op. cit.*, p. 79.

23. *Ibid.*, pp. 79–103.

24. Wildavsky, *op. cit.*, p. 52; and Huzar, *op. cit.*, p. 39.

25. See Peter Woll, *American Bureaucracy* (New York, 1963), p. 128.

26. Various kinds of staff oversight activities are briefly described in Kenneth Kofmehl, *Professional Staffs of Congress* (Lafayette, Ind., 1962), pp. 127–31.

27. See Kenneth D. Patterson, "Legislative Budget Review: An Economist's Viewpoint," *Public Administration Review*, XXIV (1964), 7–13.

28. This paragraph is based upon Green and Rosenthal, *op. cit.*, pp. 67–70, 107.

29. Wildavsky, *op. cit.*, pp. 55–56, 83–84.

30. See Boyer, *op. cit.*, p. 42; Freeman, *op. cit.*, pp. 34–35; Wildavsky, *op. cit.*, pp. 41–42 and 74–83; and William E. Rhode, *Committee Clearance of Administrative Decisions* (East Lansing, Mich., 1959), pp. 67–68.

31. Freeman, *op. cit.*, p. 34.

32. Wildavsky, *op. cit.*, p. 74.

33. *Ibid.*, p. 75.

34. *Ibid.*

35. O. B. Conway, Jr., *Legislative-Executive Relationships in the Government of the United States* (Washington, D.C., 1953), p. 5.

36. Judicial organization and rule-making are, of course, subject to legislative oversight, supervision, and control as well, though these are much more sporadic than oversight of the executive. The oversight process does not differ greatly, although oversight of the judiciary may generate more ideological conflict. On the attempt of one state legislature to reorganize the state judiciary, see Gilbert Y. Steiner and Samuel K. Gove, *Legislative Politics in Illinois* (Urbana, 1960), pp. 164–98. See also C. Herman Pritchett, *Congress Versus the Supreme Court* (Minneapolis, 1961); and Walter F. Murphy, *Congress and the Court* (Chicago, 1962).

37. This general subject is treated by Joseph P. Harris, *Congressional Control of Administration* (Washington, D.C., 1964), pp. 15–45, 163–248. Few studies have been made of the activities of state legislatures in state administrative reorganization, but see Steiner and Gove, *op. cit.*, pp. 134–63, for a treatment of the efforts of the Illinois legislature to reorganize that state's financial administration; and Thomas H. Eliot, *Reorganizing the Massachusetts Department of Conservation* (University, Ala., 1953).

38. James N. Rosenau, *The Nomination of "Chip" Bohlen* (New York, 1962); Joseph P. Harris, "The Senatorial Rejection of Leland Olds: A Case Study," *American Political Science Review*, XLV (1951), 674–92.

39. *Myers* v. *United States*, 272 U.S. 52 (1926); *Humphrey's Executor* v. *United States*, 295 U.S. 602 (1935).

40. Rhode, *op. cit.*, p. 34.

41. Kofmehl, *op. cit.*, pp. 129–30.

42. Rhode, *op. cit.*, pp. 9–10.

43. Edith T. Carper, *The Defense Appropriations Rider* (University, Ala., 1960), p. 14.

44. Harris, *op. cit.*, pp. 204–48; and Rhode, *op. cit.*, pp. 8–49.

45. Green and Rosenthal, *op. cit.*, pp. 87–89.

46. Boyer, *op. cit.*, pp. 146–50.

47. Ferrel Heady, *Administrative Procedure Legislation in the States* (Ann Arbor, Mich., 1952), pp. 49–62; see also Glendon A. Schubert, Jr., Helenan Sonnenburg, and George Kantrowitz, *The Michigan Athletic Awards Rule* (University, Ala., 1955).

48. Rhode, *op. cit.*, p. 68.

49. For congressional investigations, see Alan Barth, *Government by Investigation* (New York, 1955); Robert K. Carr, *The House Committee on Un-American Activities* (Ithaca, N.Y., 1952); and Telford Taylor, *Grand Inquest* (New York, 1955). For state legislative investigations, see Edward L. Barrett, *The Tenney Committee: Legislative Investigation of Subversive Activities in California* (Ithaca, N.Y., 1951); and Vern Countryman, *Un-American Activities in the State of Washington: The Work of the Canwell Committee* (Ithaca, N.Y., 1951).

50. See Emile de Antonio and Daniel Talbot, *Point of Order! A Documentary of the Army-McCarthy Hearings* (New York, 1964); and Richard H. Rovere, *Senator Joe McCarthy* (New York, 1959).

51. Harris, *op. cit.*, p. 263.

52. *Ibid.*, pp. 258–59.

53. Bernard Schwartz, *The Professor and the Commissions* (New York, 1959), p. 7.

54. These restraints may have serious consequences for staff recruitment and performance. See *ibid.*, pp. 7–21 and 52–112.

55. M. Nelson McGeary, "Congressional Investigations: Historical Development," *University of Chicago Law Review*, XVIII (1951), 431.

56. *Ibid.*

57. Donald H. Riddle, *The Truman Committee* (New Brunswick, N.J., 1964), p. 14.

58. See Francis E. Rourke, "Administrative Secrecy: A Congressional Dilemma," *American Political Science Review*, LIV (1960), 684–94; Schwartz, *op. cit.*, pp. 66–68; and *Congressional Record* (Daily Edition), Sept. 12, 1959, pp. 17749–80.

59. An excellent brief review of the budgetary process will be found in John S. Saloma III, *The Responsible Use of Power: A Critical Analysis of the Congressional Budget Process* (Washington, D.C., 1964), pp. 1–21. Also see Robert A. Wallace, *Congressional Control of Federal Spending* (Detroit, 1960).

60. Saloma, *op. cit.*, p. 15.

61. Charles L. Clapp, *The Congressman: His Work As He Sees It* (Washington, D.C.: The Brookings Institution, 1963), p. 220.

62. Arthur W. Macmahon, "Congressional Oversight of Administration: The Power of the Purse," *Political Science Quarterly*, LVIII (1943), 181.

63. Warner R. Schilling, "The Politics of National Defense: Fiscal 1950," in Warner R. Schilling, Paul Y. Hammond, and Glenn H. Snyder, *Strategy, Politics, and Defense Budgets* (New York, 1962), p. 92.

64. *Ibid.*, p. 96.

65. Harris, *op. cit.*, pp. 81–83.

66. Holbert N. Carroll, *The House of Representatives and Foreign Affairs* (Pittsburgh, 1958), p. 155.

67. See also *ibid.*, p. 154.

68. *Congressional Record* (Apr. 7, 1952), p. 3641, quoted in Harris, *op. cit.*, p. 69.

69. Huzar, *op. cit.*, pp. 354–59; Carroll, *op. cit.*, pp. 161–66.

70. Carroll, *op. cit.*, p. 162.

71. *Ibid.*, pp. 166–69; Harris, *op. cit.*, pp. 93–97.

72. Harris, *op. cit.*, pp. 128–52.

73. See Kenneth Patterson, *op. cit.*; Belle Zeller (ed.), *American State Legislatures* (New York, 1954), pp. 172–88; Council of State Governments, *Fiscal Serv-*

ices for State Legislatures (Chicago, 1961); and Vernon A. McGee, "A Legislative Approach to State Budgeting," *State Government*, XXVI (1953), 200–04.

74. A detailed summary and tabulation of fiscal services available in the states is provided in the Council of State Government publication entitled *Fiscal Services for State Legislatures* (Chicago, 1961).

75. Steiner and Gove, *op. cit.*, pp. 78–81.

76. Zeller, *op. cit.*, pp. 177–79.

[Part VII]
CONCLUSION

AMERICAN legislatures are suitable subjects both for speculation and investigation. As social scientists, we speculate and investigate in order to describe, build theories, and test ideas. But American legislatures have been made the subject, over a long period of years, of more general speculation about how they might be better organized, what better purposes they might serve, and what more democratic rules they might adopt. Proposals for legislative reforms have usually had their roots in the advocacy of specific kinds of public policy. And policy change through legislative reform may sometimes be cloaked in rationalizations about legislative efficiency, more harmonious legislative–executive relationships, more tidy and rational legislative processes, or in more general postulates about the representative efficacy of responsible party government. Frustrations about public policy may be taken out in attacks upon the legislative bodies themselves.

A modern industrial society which is undergoing the world revolution of our time would surely suffer if its legislative institutions were not able to change in order to meet the new challenges and requirements of peace and order, or even if there were not sturdy debate—and new ideas—about how to make legislative bodies more effective in terms of contemporary necessities and demands. Our era virtually demands of us that we be inventive and imaginative.

Speculation without investigation is often the product of excessive impatience. Patience has its limits, however; there is a great compelling urgency in our century to act for human survival. At the same time, investigation of legislative systems is really just getting started; it does not, like rocket flights to the moon, capture popular imagination or government financial support. Speculations about how legislatures might more effectively meet the challenges of our time are often not founded on the results of investigation. There are great and yawning gaps in our simple, descriptive knowledge about legislative institutions, and we are only beginning to have some systematic, empirical understanding of behavior in those institutions and of the patterns of behavior around them. Except for the most mechanical trivialities, significant legislative reform involves changes in attitudes and behavior. And we can scarcely hope to alter attitudes and behavior, if we have hardly begun to understand or explain them.

Thus, it seems appropriate first to close the argument of this book with a chapter that summarizes briefly a variety of reform proposals of contemporary interest which have been directed toward legislatures, and then to consider some lines of research along which we can advance our knowledge of legislative behavior.

[20]

Problems of Legislative Systems

THE ENDURING motif in both popular and academic discourse about American legislatures has been that of reform. No institutions have been more maligned in popular commentary, except perhaps those of organized crime and prostitution. Legislatures have been criticized because they have done too much or too little, because they have interfered with the executive or become "rubber stamps," because they have deliberated too speedily or acted too slowly, because they represented the people too precisely and sensitively or not accurately enough, because they acted in too partisan a fashion or lacked party responsibility, because their leaders were autocratic or ineffectual. The mechanics of the legislative process, as well as the moral turpitude and wisdom of legislators themselves, have been subjected to a stream of criticism in the American literature.

Reform movements directed toward changing the face of American legislatures have their substantial genesis in the progressive politics of the late nineteenth century. In the years around the turn of the century, state legislative reform focused upon the creation of library, reference, and research services. In the interwar years, a variety of procedural reforms were attempted by state legislatures, with varying success. Split legislative sessions, often with one session devoted exclusively to budget and fiscal matters, were experimented with, and advocates of legislative reform pressed for annual legislative sessions. A number of states began to install electrical voting machines to make roll call voting more efficient. Greater control by the state legislature over state fiscal policy was sought by reformers in the form of legislative budget review and audits, proposals for legislative budgets, and the creation of fiscal review offices. A movement for uniform state legislation in a variety of policy areas was afoot, and uniform codes were advocated, as well as a Model State Constitution, with detailed recommendations for uniform state legislative organization. The unicameral movement stimulated wide discussion and controversy, and attracted national attention under the leadership of Senator George W. Norris of Nebraska; it had its only success when Nebraska adopted the unicameral form in 1934.[1] A more successful effort, beginning in the 1930s, was the legislative council movement.[2] These efforts were the result of organized reform activity, sparked in the early years by the American Legislators' Association, and later by its offspring, the Council of State Governments.

Congressional reforms in the early twentieth century were highlighted by the direct election of United States Senators, accomplished by a constitutional amendment which went into effect in 1913, and by the substantial modification of the written rules of the House of Representatives that was the product of the revolt against Speaker Cannon in 1910–1911.[3] The development of increased presidential initiative during the New Deal, and the events of World War II, gave added impetus to congressional reform movements. In 1941 the American Political Science Association created a Committee on Congress, and placed it under the chairmanship of George B. Galloway. Its report stimulated widespread interest in congressional reorganization.[4] In 1945, Congress created a Joint Committee on the Organization of Congress (widely known as the La Follette-Monroney committee), and this committee selected Dr. Galloway as its staff director. As a result in large part of the work of the Joint Committee, implemented by the American Political Science Association's Committee on Congress and a citizens' committee called the National Committee for the Strengthening of Congress, Congress enacted the Legislative Reorganization Act of 1946. The continuing interest of the organized political science profession in legislative reform is indicated by its creation of a Committee on Political Parties in 1946, which made detailed recommendations on congressional party organization in its 1950 report, and also by its Committee on American Legislatures, chaired by Dr. Belle Zeller, which made sweeping proposals for state legislative reform in its 1954 report.[5]

LEGISLATIVE ANALYSIS AND REFORM

Nothing perhaps is more forcefully suggested by our analysis of Congress and the state legislatures than that American legislatures are highly institutionalized groups and that changes in their fundamental structure and behavior patterns have been infrequent over their fairly long histories. The legislative analyst *qua* analyst views change in legislative systems as a subject of study; he knows that institutional and behavioral changes have occurred, can occur, and will occur in the future. Our attempt to hew to a functional perspective on American legislative systems makes us highly skeptical about the prospects for success of the numerous and sometimes gratuitous proposals to reform American legislatures. We are not opposed to reform nor, as legislative analysts, are we in a position to promote or advocate particular reforms. Our position simply is that reform proposals have to be viewed in the light of the functional maintenance and product of legislative systems, and are most likely to be meaningful and workable when they are based upon knowledge of legislative behavior, rather than simply upon popular stereotypes of some "ideal" legislature. As Huitt has said about Congress,

There is nothing about the procedures or structure of Congress that should be defended for its own sake. Congress, like other institutions, goes about its business in certain ways because at some time or other in its history these ways have proved to be convenient to most, or enough, of the members. These ways are continued so long as they are more convenient to maintain than to change, or so long as they work to the advantage of interests strong enough to preserve them.[6]

Not only is it important that reformers be knowledgeable about the institutions and behavior they seek to alter, in order to maximize their chances for success, but they must also be aware that changes in legislative structure or procedure may have unanticipated consequences, which may or may not be desirable from their point of view. Changes in form may not produce the desired results. "It is unlikely," Huitt suggests, "that the political scientists and members of Congress who rationalized the standing committee structure in the 1946 Act, reducing the number and spelling out the jurisdiction of the respective committees, ever intended that a Senate majority leader would find himself with no place to send a civil rights bill but to a committee whose chairman was implacably opposed to it."[7] Serendipity is a risk of (and perhaps the spice of) life and ought not to deter those who wish to remold legislative structure and procedure, but it is well to be aware of it.

Most of the proposals of contemporary interest for reforming American legislatures can be grouped into four categories: (1) suggested improvements in the efficiency and conduct of individual members, (2) changes in the written rules to promote procedural efficiency, (3) proposals having to do with the operations and effectiveness of legislative political parties, (4) schemes for reorganizing the committee systems. We shall examine these four summary categories in the sections which follow. The list omits geographical reforms—apportionment and districting—which are considered in detail in Chapter 3. We also omit possible reforms in the regulation of lobbying activities, because in this area the principal reform proposal has simply been that all state legislatures adopt the reporting-and-disclosure legislation which Congress and a number of states have already enacted or that present legislation be more rigorously enforced.[8]

LEGISLATIVE REPRESENTATION

Three kinds of proposals have been advanced that have to do with the individual legislator and how he behaves as a representative. One goes to the heart of legislator-constituent relations by condemning the "localism" of American legislators, and urging that this be abolished.[9] Presumably this means that legislators, instead of being errand boys for their constituents, should learn to play more statesmanlike roles. Party government on the British model is the principal vehicle by means of which this role change is to be achieved, but also involved are suggestions that legislators be admonished to behave in terms of national, as opposed to parochial, interests, or that better men be elected to the legislatures.

Another kind of proposal has to do with the personal and public ethics and moral conduct of legislators. It has been argued that a few legislators who abuse their privileges have, by their unethical and immoral conduct, brought into disrepute the entire legislative process. It has been suggested that Congress and the state legislatures regulate themselves by adopting codes of ethical conduct for legislators and by requiring members to disclose their financial holdings so as to make it possible to control potential conflicts of interest between legislators' official duties and their private gain.[10]

Finally, a large number and variety of proposals have been made which aim to improve the efficiency and productivity of individual legislators. Usually these proposals deal with legislative mechanics and management—providing larger, more diversified, and better managed staff facilities; increasing legislators' salaries; lengthening terms of office; providing modern physical facilities in which legislators can work; or automating some routine tasks performed in legislative offices. A number of legislators, especially members of the United States Senate, have recently complained of the burdens of legislative work, and recommended improvements.[11] Those who urge the reduction of "localism" frequently suggest that, if legislators learned to play nation-oriented or state-oriented, instead of local-oriented, roles, the problem of overwhelming constituency or errand-boy burdens would be automatically alleviated. More feasible and perhaps more practical in this connection has been the suggestion, made recently by members of Congress, that a new "office of complainer" be created to dispense equity and cut red tape for constituents who have legitimate grievances.[12]

LEGISLATIVE ROADBLOCKS

A large assortment of reform proposals have been offered which are designed to improve the procedural efficiency of American legislatures. Annual sessions of state legislatures, unicameralism at the state level, use of electrical or electronic voting machines, better record-keeping and administrative procedures are typical of proposals in this direction. It has been suggested that some rather modest alterations in the rules of procedure of the Congress would promote efficiency. Thus Senator Humphrey proposed:

... more efficient scheduling of the work days of Congress. Certain days could be scheduled specifically for floor debate and action by the full House or Senate. Other days could be restricted exclusively for hearings and action by the Congressional committees.

... modification of the "Morning Hour" in the Senate, in which members read miscellaneous speeches of marginal or undated importance and insert various articles into the Congressional Record.

... a requirement in the Senate that members restrict their remarks to the issue formally listed as the business of the Senate.... This "Rule of Germaneness" now applies only to debate in the House of Representatives.*

... a summer recess of Congress of at least three weeks....

... modification and adoption of the British "Question Period," in which Administration leaders would report on and answer questions of general importance before the full Senate and House. This would save time, help to keep members of Congress better informed on Administration programs and policy, and sustain the necessary frequent contact between the Executive and Legislative branches of government.†[13]

Proposals to change the rules of legislative bodies, while they may be clothed in arguments about the contributions of rules change to legislative efficiency and economy, are often motivated by specific policy preferences. Unlimited Senate debate, a target of most congressional reformers, has most often been attacked by those who were seeking

---

* In 1964 the Senate adopted a rule requiring that all debate be germane for a three-hour period each day.

† Stephen Horn has examined this proposal, as well as the more general notion that cabinet members ought to be seated in Congress, in *The Cabinet and Congress* (New York, 1960). Three-fourths of a sample of congressmen questioned in 1957 were opposed to the idea of creating a "question period." Horn favored it.

passage of civil rights legislation. Probably no American legislative procedure has been more vehemently attacked than the Senate rules that permit filibustering.[14]

In recent years, the fiscal machinery of American legislatures has been an important focal point of proposed reforms. It is often argued that the central part that legislatures can play in modern government is that of fiscal control. Proposals to modernize taxation and budgetary processes have included legislative budgeting, special budgetary legislative sessions, more use of joint fiscal committees, omnibus appropriations legislation, biennial appropriations, and the item veto for the executive.[15]

ATTACKS ON THE POWER STRUCTURE

Any change in the status quo of a legislative system, and thus any change in legislative organization or rules, may affect, or be seen as affecting, the power structure of the system. Reforms that constitute direct attacks on the legislative power structure, or that substantially affect persons in key locations in the system who play roles involving high degrees of influence in decision making, are likely to be most heatedly debated and most difficult to secure. Such reforms are seldom proffered solely for the sake of efficiency or neatness. Rather, they are usually advanced in order to give the advantage to those who support particular kinds of public policy, and to take advantages away from others (those who occupy the power structure). It is not unusual for such reforms to be motivated by a desire to make the legislative body more amenable to the program and policies of the executive branch.*

Contemporary legislative reform proposals which most immediately involve attacks on the legislative power structure are those that have to do with committees and party organization. The principal thrust of the Legislative Reorganization Act of 1946 was against the congressional committee system; at the state level, there is also frequent insistence upon a reduction in the number of legislative committees. Wider use of joint committees as a means of coordinating and integrating the two houses of a bicameral legislature is proposed regularly. In recent years, advocates have urged the creation of at least three new joint congressional committees: on fiscal policy, on national security, and on congressional organization and operations.[16] Again, those who wish to secure legislative committee reforms have often focused their attention upon

---

* Perhaps it can be said, in an oversimplified way, that some "liberals" tend to define an effective legislature as one that adopts whatever the executive proposes, and that some "conservatives" define it as one that rejects most of the administration program.

investigating committees, urging their abolition or the adoption of adequate rules of conduct.[17]

Perhaps the most penetrating attacks upon the congressional power structure have come from those who have sought to reform the seniority custom for the selection of committee chairmen and from those who have attempted to reduce the control of the House Committee on Rules over the legislative agenda in that body. Senator Richard L. Neuberger (D-Ore) once characterized the seniority norm as "rigid, inflexible and unyielding—particularly in the vital realm of committee chairmanships."

An isolationist may head the Armed Services Committee at the height of American involvement in a world-wide conflict, and in that post he stays if seniority put him there. If seniority installs a foe of conservation as chairman of the committee charged with protecting America's dwindling supply of natural resources, draft horses and wainrope cannot drag him out of this seat. And if the allies or beneficiaries of special interests become the heads of key committees responsible for regulating those same special interests—well, that is seniority.[18]

Since seniority is not just simply a mechanism for the selection of congressional committee chairmen, but is rather a pervasive basis for the acquisition of status in the congressional setting, it is often attacked as one of the major obstacles to "responsible" party leadership. It is sometimes said that the operation of seniority in the selection of committee chairmen could be materially vitiated by requiring that chairmen be elected by a secret ballot of committee members.[19]

The House Rules Committee is attacked as the major congressional bulwark against the program of the Administration. It has even been characterized—in a somewhat self-consciously exaggerated way—as a "third house."[20] "Today the House Rules Committee is perhaps the single most powerful committee of the Congress," says Senator Clark. "It exercises enormous power to flout democracy . . . [and] a high price is often exacted for what, in a democratic legislature, should be done as a matter of course, not as a matter of bargaining with a ruling clique."[21]

Proposals to reform the House Rules Committee have involved a wide range of changes. If the seniority rule were not used to determine the chairmanship, Judge Howard W. Smith, a conservative Democrat from Virginia, might not hold the post. In 1961, when two Catholic members joined with the conservative coalition to block clearance of the Administration's federal aid-to-education bill by a vote of 9 to 6, the effort to liberalize the committee by enlarging it proved only partially successful.[22] In the past, reformers have sought in vain to change the rules so that chairmen of other committees could extract bills from the Rules Committee after a certain period (as was true in the Eighty-first Congress) or so that the discharge procedure could be used more easily. In 1965 the House voted to give the Speaker authority to bring bills to the floor after 21 days in the Rules Committee, and the committee lost its authority to send bills to a conference committee. Both reforms, if they remain in effect, should substantially diminish the committee's power.

A much more fundamental attack upon legislative power structures than reforms of committee systems is represented by the so-called "responsible party government" school of thought. Consider the sweeping assertion that "the fundamental basis of all legislative improvement in the United States, both national and state, is no doubt a root-and-branch reform of our system of party politics with a view to creating more responsible party government."[23] These advocates urge the creation of competitive two-party politics in all, or most, congressional districts, the development of clearer legislative programs by the national party organization, more frequent and effective use of party caucuses and policy committees, the creation of joint House-Senate leadership conferences, binding caucus decisions, legislative scheduling in the United States House by a party leadership committee rather than the Rules Committee, and national party financing of congressional campaigns.[24]

Party government advocates are urging a fundamental alteration in the American political system. As Burns has said, in discussing the need for new party leadership in Congress as a way of eliminating the role of seniority in status conferral, "What the defenders of the seniority rule are really saying is that given our present congressional party system, a seniority rule is inevitable. And in this they are correct. By the same token, an end of the rule *depends on the end of the system*."[25]

It seems unlikely that fundamental changes in the political systems of the United States will occur, barring a catastrophe which would set in motion social forces of an unexpected sort. Evolutionary modifications and improvements in American legislatures are occurring, and should continue to occur. In historical perspective, it is probably correct to say that American legislatures have not fundamentally changed, at least in many ways, for about two hundred years. Unless American society undergoes a radical transformation, American legislatures are likely to continue very much as they have. Many of the more or less superficial reforms of the nineteenth and twentieth centuries have provided demonstrations of Alphonse Kerr's classic adage, "Plus ça change, plus c'est la même chose."

The proposing and debating of legislative reforms is probably, in itself, functional for the maintenance and operation of the legislative system. The legislature, T. V. Smith used to argue, performs an important "aesthetic function." Smith contended that the high morale of legislative groups makes it "possible for representatives amiably to 'stand the gaff,'" and "this we-group bulwark gives opportunity for a great many good citizens to do a great deal of criticizing harmlessly."

Legislators become scapegoats, as it were, to bear away without much social damage vague aggressions which, did they not achieve catharsis through expression, might well totalize into attacks upon public order. . . .

It is safe to say that no other institution today has half the effectiveness of the legislature in soaking up and sterilizing the wastage produced in society when the will to perfection meets the will to power in the lives of good men and women.[26]

Before legislative analysis can effectively deal with problems of reform, indicate their probability of success, and predict their consequences, we shall probably need to learn a great deal more about legislative systems. Most of the systematic research on American legislatures dates from the post-World War II period. This book is testimony to the considerable knowledge that exists about American legislative systems, but it is also a study in the limitations of our knowledge. In the next chapter, we shall describe some research perspectives for legislative analysis in the future.

NOTES

1. There is a substantial literature, mostly hortatory, on the unicameral movement. See John P. Senning, *The One-house Legislature* (New York, 1937).

2. A twenty-year period is summarized in Harold W. Davey, "The Legislative Council Movement in the United States, 1933–1953," *American Political Science Review*, XLVII (1953), 785–97.

3. George B. Galloway, *History of the House of Representatives* (New York, 1961), pp. 97–118.

4. See *The Reorganization of Congress: A Report of the Committee on Congress of the American Political Science Association* (Washington, D.C., 1945). Galloway also wrote two major books stressing congressional reform. See his *Congress at the Crossroads* (New York, 1946, and *The Legislative Process in Congress* (New York, 1953), especially pp. 591–670.

5. See Belle Zeller (ed.), *American State Legislatures: A Report of the Committee on American Legislatures of the American Political Science Association* (New York, 1954); and *Toward a More Responsible Two-party System: A Report of the Committee on Political Parties of the American Political Science Association* (New York, 1950).

6. Ralph K. Huitt, "Congressional Reorganization: The Next Chapter" (Paper presented at the annual meeting of the American Political Science Association, 1964), p. 4.

7. *Ibid.*, p. 5.

8. Zeller, *op. cit.*, pp. 214–39.

9. For instance, see Daniel M. Berman, *In Congress Assembled* (New York, 1964), pp. 402–03.

10. See Galloway, *The Legislative Process in Congress*, pp. 380–91; and Joseph S. Clark, *Congress: The Sapless Branch* (New York, 1964), pp. 206–08.

11. See Clark, *op. cit.*, pp. 55–79; A. S. Mike Monroney, "Wanted: New Machinery for Congress" (Address delivered at the University of Iowa, Iowa City, December 1963). Senator Hubert Humphrey often wrote in this vein: see "Modernizing Congress," *AFL–CIO American Federationist* (April, 1963), pp. 1–4; "To Move Congress Out of Its Ruts," *New York Times Magazine* (Apr. 7, 1963), pp. 39, 129–32; and "The Legislature," in *The Mazes of Modern Government* (Santa Barbara, Calif., 1964), pp. 14–20. See also Bertram M. Gross, *The Legislative Struggle* (New York, 1953), pp. 412–46; and Zeller, *op. cit.*, pp. 89–104, 141–62.

12. Senators Humphrey and Monroney and Congressman Henry Reuss (D-Wis) have publicly proposed such a new institution.

13. Humphrey, "To Move Congress Out of Its Ruts," p. 130. See also Clark, *op. cit.*, pp. 189–206, where he advances a longer and more sweeping list of congressional reforms, as does former Senator Kenneth B. Keating (R-NY) in *Government of the People* (Cleveland, 1964). Senator Clark had edited a useful collection of reports and articles under the title *Congressional Reform: Problems and Prospects* (New York, 1965). A view of congressional reform more akin to our own is reflected in the papers presented to The American Assembly late in 1964, and published under the editorship of David B. Truman, *The Congress and America's Future* (Englewood Cliffs, N.J., 1965).

14. The literature on the so-called cloture rule in the U.S. Senate, which makes filibustering possible, is voluminous. A basic volume is Franklin L. Burdette, *Filibustering in the Senate* (Princeton, N.J., 1940). The subject is treated in almost every book on Congress and in many popular commentaries. For current arguments, see Clark, *op. cit.*, pp. 189–201, and Richard B. Russell, "Russell Defends the Filibuster," *New York Times Magazine* (Mar. 15, 1964), pp. 20, 113–14.

15. See Galloway, *The Legislative Process in Congress*, pp. 655–64; and Clark, *op. cit.*, pp. 204–05.

16. See John S. Saloma III, *The Responsible Use of Power: A Critical Analysis of the Congressional Budget Process* (Washington, D.C., 1964); Humphrey, "The Legislature," pp. 17–18; and Galloway, *The Legislative Process in Congress*, pp. 660–61.

17. The literature on investigating committee reform, and especially on the question of abolition of the House Committee on Un-American Activities, is substantial. A good brief analysis is in Galloway, *The Legislative Process in Congress*, pp. 627–44.

18. Richard L. Neuberger, "A Senator's Case against Seniority," *New York Times Magazine* (Apr. 7, 1957), p. 15.

19. See, for instance, *ibid.*, p. 44; Clark, *op. cit.*, p. 185.

20. Robert Bendiner, *Obstacle Course on Capitol Hill* (New York, 1964), p. 140; Tom Wicker, "Again That Roadblock in Congress," *New York Times Magazine* (Aug. 7, 1960), pp. 14, 64–69.

21. Clark, *op. cit.*, p. 135.

22. See H. Douglas Price, "Schools, Scholarships, and Congressmen: The Kennedy Aid-to-Education Program," in Alan F. Westin (ed.), *The Centers of Power* (New York, 1964), pp. 53–105.

23. Zeller, *op. cit.*, p. 213.

24. The basic arguments and proposals of the party government school are old ones, dating at least from the writing of A. Lawrence Lowell and Woodrow Wilson. The contemporary versions of this point of view are in H. H. Wilson, *Congress: Corruption and Compromise* (New York, 1951), pp. 234–44; James M. Burns, *Congress on Trial* (New York, 1949), and *The Deadlock of Democracy* (Englewood Cliffs, N.J., 1963), especially pp. 323–40; Bendiner, *op. cit.*, pp. 207–219; Clark, *op. cit.*, pp. 166–76, and (with others) *The Senate Establishment* (New

York, 1963). The basic document still is "Toward a More Responsible Two-party System," *American Political Science Review* (supplement), XLIV (1950), especially pp. 56–65.

25. Burns, *The Deadlock of Democracy*, p. 329. Italics added.

26. T. V. Smith, "Two Functions of the American State Legislator," *Annals of the American Academy of Political and Social Science*, CXCV (January 1938), 187.

[21]

Legislative
Behavior Research

LEGISLATIVE behavior research may be taken to refer to "analyses whose data directly concern those human beings known as representatives, the persons who constitute the various representative bodies historically known to man."[1] Although legislative behavior research is sometimes thought of as a recent, and even an upstart, orientation to the study of legislative politics, political scientists and historians have actually been interested in the behavior of representatives in some systematic way since before the turn of the century.[2] While much of the classical writing on the legislative process in the United States has been descriptive, therapeutic, and hortatory, there is not much to be gained from condemning the intellectual tradition of institutional legislative analysis, nor is there any need here to embellish or defend behavioral analysis of legislative systems. We take it as a truism that legislative bodies must be understood as institutions and that fundamental to any explanation of legislative phenomena is the analysis of the behavior of participants in the legislative system. Behavioral analysis of legislative systems is marked by a primary emphasis on the part of the investigator upon the characteristics, motivations, perceptions, and behavior of individuals. But its purview need not be limited only to legislators; it may include analysis of a variety of actors in legislative systems.

Behavioral analysis of participants in legislative systems has yielded three fairly discrete types of research: that which focuses upon recruitment, that which emphasizes individual motivations and behavior, and that which studies legislative decision making.

Recruitment

In Chapter 5 we reviewed a mass of material related to the kinds of individuals who are recruited to serve in American legislatures; elsewhere, we discussed the recruitment of other actors in legislative systems (staff in Chapter 10 and lobbyists in Chapter 12). Studies of the recruitment of legislators range widely and exhibit great variety, but they tend to be highly descriptive and to focus upon social and political background characteristics. Seldom have such studies probed the explanations for the differential recruitment of legislators with particular characteristics. Much is made, for example, of the prominence of lawyers in American legislatures, but there are few empirical efforts to explain why lawyers are present more prominently in some American legislatures than in others. (Efforts to explain cross-national variations in the recruitment of lawyers as legislators are also uncommon.)[3] Studies of the recruitment of nonlegislator participants in legislative systems are rare.[4]

Another neglected aspect of recruitment analyses has to do with the functional and decisional consequences of differential recruitment in legislative systems. Do social and political background characteristics make any difference in terms of legislative representation or policy outcomes? Some attention has been given to the latter (policy outcomes), especially with respect to lawyers.[5] The functional consequences for the representation of variations in recruitment—whether a lawyer is a more "effective" legislator, or better epitomizes the "representative" for constituents—are only beginning to be investigated.

Individual Motivations and Behavior

Another body of legislative behavior research is mainly concerned with the individual motivations and behavior of actors in the legislative system. Assessment of personality factors in the behavior of individuals in this setting is limited to a study of a small sample of state legislators and the analysis of a few variables for a sample of Washington lobbyists.[6] These studies suggest the need for much more, and more adequate, analysis of individual psychological factors. A larger category of research includes studies which deal in some way with the interpersonal communications and interactions among participants in legislative systems. Some have dealt with relationships between legislators and their constituents, principally with a view of assessing the legislators' response to constituency communication.[7] Others describe the normative settings in which individual legislative behavior proceeds.[8] Some deal with the interpersonal relations and contacts among legislators.[9] A growing body of research uses the concept of role as a key analytical device.[10] An extremely important development has been the effort in recent research to correlate the mutual or reciprocal perceptions of legislators and constituents.[11]

Research in this category has scarcely exploited to the full the opportunities and the methodological capacities of modern social research. The implicit or explicit models for these investigations have varied widely from those that postulate decisional rationality to fairly sophisticated perceptual, personality, or sociometric models. Furthermore, most of the research on the individual motivations and behavior of legislators is rather fragmentary, and few efforts have been made to replicate or develop these studies. Finally, most of these investigations deal with legislators, and we know much less about other participants in legislative systems.

LEGISLATIVE DECISION MAKING

By far the most numerous studies of legislative behavior involve aggregate analyses of legislative decision making. These studies have two principal purposes: to reveal the decisional substructure of the legislative institution and to describe the impact of certain social and political forces upon collective legislative action or both. Those that operate on the decisional or attitudinal structure of the legislature seek to reveal voting blocs or attitudinally homogeneous subgroups. Those that seek to explain some part of the collective behavior of legislators in terms of "outside" pressures have involved, typically, analysis of the effects of political party affiliation, constituency characteristics, sectional cleavages, or pressure group activity.[12]

Usually such investigations use roll call data for analysis. Roll call voting is so common in American legislatures that a very substantial amount of data are generated. These data are rather easy to gather, and can be manipulated statistically in fairly sophisticated ways. Certainly the quantitative analysis of roll call data is much more highly developed than are methods of analysis in other areas of legislative research.

One other type of decision-making analysis is the case study. The case study differs from roll call analysis in important ways. In the case study, usually only one legislative policy output is analyzed, although a series of decisions leading up to it may be included. And the analysis can seldom be quantitative, since a range of decisions is not usually involved. A fairly large number of case-policy analyses are available, usually highly descriptive and limited in their generalizability to discrete circumstances.[13] Case studies of the passage of individual bills may very well involve the description and analysis of behavior, but extant studies seldom use the same standards for the selection of evidence. It is sometimes said that case studies do not "add up" to anything theoretically, and their contribution is doubtful for scientific purposes. Even if case studies could be made comparable and were numerous enough to provide for generalization about uniform or persistent patterns of behavior, other methods can probably provide roughly the same knowledge in more systematic form. But case studies are useful for some purposes, and those who are just beginning to do legislative behavior research may find that case studies provide a useful research experience.

Sources of Data and Methods of Research

The sources of data for legislative behavior research are of three major kinds: documents, direct observation, and interviews. Documents have provided the traditional material for legislative analysis, and still constitute an important source of data. The documents of American legislatures are extensive in scope and provide a great deal of detail, although in some states there is less documentation than is found in Congress.[14] That behavioral study can proceed exclusively through the use of legislative documents has been demonstrated in a study of congressional committee members' roles.[15] Social background and recruitment studies tend to rely primarily upon documentary and bibliographic sources.[16] Roll call data for virtually all American legislative bodies are readily available in the official legislative records and journals.[17] Census materials that provide data for legislative districts are generally available; they have also been prepared in convenient form for congressional districts.[18]

Direct observation methods are not so common in legislative behavior research, and data from direct observations of legislative systems (or segments of them) are uncommon.[19] It is often thought that legislatures are too large for practicable direct observation in any systematic way, although this may be mainly because of limitations in our methodological creativity. Much understanding of an impressionistic sort can be obtained about legislative bodies by observing them at work, but it also seems clear that systematic direct observation could provide important data, especially for small and more easily observed legislative groups, such as municipal councils and legislative committees.[20]

Systematic Interviews. Interviewing legislators is not a particularly new method of gathering information, but it has been a major method of gathering systematic data about legislative behavior only since the 1950s. Legislative research which utilizes systematic interviewing has taken a variety of forms. We can think of the interviewing of legislators as being accomplished in two major ways: *focused* interviewing and *standardized* interviewing. Focused interviewing involves employing a list of topics to be covered or a list of general questions to be asked in the interview situation; the same topics or questions may not be used, however, with all respondents. Standardized interviewing involves the administration of a standard schedule of questions to all respondents; it includes the mailed questionnaire technique.

Focused interviewing is surely the most common kind of legislator interviewing, although its methods and techniques have varied greatly. Clapp tape-recorded the conversations of 36 congressmen meeting in the Brookings Institution Round Table Conference on Congress, whose discussions were based upon a previously distributed agenda.[21] Jones interviewed 30 members of the House Agriculture Committee of the Eighty-fifth Congress.[22] Matthews' study of United States senators was based in important respects upon focused interviews with 25 senators, 62 staff members, 14 lobbyists and 8 journalists.[23]

Standardized interviewing of legislators is less common, especially as applied to congressmen. A number of recent studies report standard interviews with state legislators, among them those by Wahlke, Eulau, Buchanan and Ferguson, Patterson, Sorauf, and Francis.[24] The fact that congressmen will submit to standardized interviewing has been demonstrated by Robinson; it is reinforced by successful interviews with a sample of congressmen by the trained professional interviewers of the Michigan Survey Research Center.[25] There is ample evidence that survey interviewing of legislators is quite possible and that it yields uniquely significant data.

Roll Call Analysis. Roll call analyses have served a variety of research purposes, of the sort that we have described at some length in Chapter 17. Here we can comment briefly on the principal techniques of roll call analysis: index construction, cluster bloc analysis, cumulative scale analysis, and factor analysis.

The use of *indices* constructed from roll call votes dates from the seminal work of Lowell around the turn of the century.[26] This work was further developed by Rice and Beyle, but few advances were made thereafter until after World War II.[27] The most common indices in the literature of political science have been those of party voting, cohesion, and likeness. Since 1947, the *Congressional Quarterly* has provided periodic computations of indices from congressional roll calls, such as administration support scores, conservative coalition support scores, party unity scores, and party voting indices.[28] Indices of party voting have simply been the percentages of roll calls taken by a legislative body in which some given proportion of the members of one party have voted together against that same proportion of the members of the other party. Lowell, Turner and Jewell defined a party vote as a roll call on which 90 percent of the members of one party vote Yea and 90 percent of the other party vote Nay.[29] But other criteria have been employed: Keefe used 80 percent agreement, whereas the *Congressional Quarterly* requires only a majority.[30] If the analyst is interested simply in the extent to which members of legislative parties vote on opposite sides, the percentage of party voting has value, and can be used for comparative purposes. Whether the cut-off point for roll calls is to be a majority of party members, 80 percent, 90 percent, or some other figure is largely arbitrary, though of course the percentage of party votes in American legislatures will tend to decrease as the cut-off point is raised. Comparative analysis would be facilitated if some agreement were reached so that everyone used the same definition.

The index of cohesion is a measure of intraparty agreement. Developed originally by Rice, it has been used recently by Turner, Jewell, and Truman. It is computed by taking the number of votes cast by the members of the party in a majority on a roll call and dividing it by the total number of party members who voted, then subtracting 50 from this percentage and multiplying by 2. The index ranges from 0 to 100.

$$IC = 2 \; [100(M/T) - 50]$$

where IC = Index of cohesion

M = Votes cast by majority

T = Total party vote

If 75 members of a legislative party of 100 vote Yea on a roll call, $IC = 50$. A series of roll calls can be selected for analysis, yielding average indices of cohesion for interparty or interlegislative comparisons.

The index of likeness measures the difference between two groups in the degree of support (or opposition) given a motion. It is computed by subtracting the percentage of Yea (or Nay) votes cast by one group from the percentage of Yea (or Nay) votes cast by another, and then subtracting the result from 100.

$$IL = 100 - (R - D)$$

where IL = Index of likeness

R = % of yea or nay votes of group R

D = % of yea or nay votes of group D

Like the cohesion index, the index of likeness may vary from 0 to 100; an index of 0 would reflect complete dissimilarity of voting behavior, and an index of 100 would reflect complete similarity. Turner, Crane, and Flinn have published research reports utilizing the index of likeness,[31] where the arithmetic mean of the indices derived from separate roll calls was used as the index of likeness for a selected series of votes.

These indices are very useful if the purpose of analysis is to describe and compare classes or groups of legislators in terms of their gross characteristics. For example, suppose we were interested in selecting a set of roll calls that were characterized by high cohesion within parties and a set characterized by low intraparty cohesion in order to examine the voting of the congressmen from our state under these two differing circumstances. The index of cohesion would provide the basis for selecting these roll calls for analysis.[32] Or suppose we wanted to analyze sessions of Congress that were highly partisan, in order to compare them with those in which partisanship was minimal. Indices (or percentages) of party voting using the 90 percent criterion have been computed for a number of nineteenth- and twentieth-century sessions of Congress. These indices (see Figure 21.1) show the generally low level of party voting in Congress, and provide us with a quantitative basis for comparing sessions of Congress over time. Party voting scores are measures of members of Congress in the aggregate. We are usually more interested in index scores for individuals, and we could construct individual party loyalty scores by using the percentage of times a member voted with his party on party votes. Indices of cohesion and likeness are aggregate measures for groups or classes of legislators; they have the disadvantage of presenting difficulties in generalizing about the behavior of individuals when such scores are correlated with other variables or characteristics.[33]

Index scores from roll call votes which provide individual scores (such common indices as party loyalty, administrative support, liberalism-conservatism, and support for a larger federal role) may very well violate some very elementary assumptions about the cardinality of the data. Suppose legislators A and B have party loyalty scores of 50, based upon 10 party votes in the legislature, which would indicate that each voted with his party on 5 of the 10 issues. Their index scores are the same, but the scores do not tell us on which five of the ten issues these members supported their party. Legislator A may have cast a pro-party vote on roll calls 1, 3, 5, 7, and 9, while legislator B may have cast his pro-party votes on issues 2, 4, 6, 8, and 10. To infer a similarity in the voting behavior of these two legislators by assigning to both of them a party loyalty score of 50 is to do substantial violence to logic! Though these individual scores may not have clear meaning, indices of this type will continue to be used in legislative behavior research, and may provide crude orderings of legislators which are empirically useful. The fact that different response patterns may lead to identical index scores may not be a serious drawback. Whether it is or is not is ultimately a matter of conceptual clarity and empirical investigation.

Cluster bloc analysis was first suggested by Rice for use with legislative roll call data, and later more fully developed by Beyle.[34] The probability assumptions incorporated into Beyle's model have been shown to be erroneous, and his preoccupation with tabulating votes either on the prevailing or the losing side seems puzzling; nevertheless, his basic method of constructing cluster blocs is still very useful.[35] The utility of cluster bloc analysis has been demonstrated in the monumental

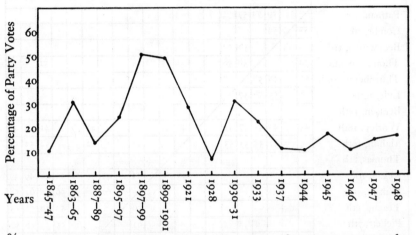

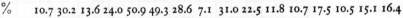

Years														
1845–47	1863–65	1887–89	1895–97	1897–99	1899–1901	1921	1928	1930–31	1933	1937	1944	1945	1946	1947	1948

% 10.7 30.2 13.6 24.0 50.9 49.3 28.6 7.1 31.0 22.5 11.8 10.7 17.5 10.5 15.1 16.4

Figure 21.1. PARTY VOTING IN CONGRESS, 1845–1948

SOURCES: J. Turner, *Party and Constituency: Pressures on Congress* (1951), p. 28. The figures for 1895–97 were provided in a letter to Patterson from Duncan MacRae, Jr., April 16, 1964.

work of David Truman.[36] This kind of analysis involves counting the number of agreements on roll calls between pairs of legislators, and entering these frequencies into a matrix (illustrated by Figure 21.2). It is necessary to manipulate the matrix by reordering members so that the ones with the highest paired agreements will be listed along the main diagonal of the matrix. The example provided by Figure 21.2 shows two clusters in one matrix, one in the upper left corner and the other in the lower right corner. The frequencies in the cells of the matrix are numbers of paired agreements on 74 House roll call votes for members of the Texas Democratic delegation in the Eighty-first Congress. The cluster bloc method involves summarizing the voting agreements of individuals over issues. It can reveal the interagreement structure of the legislative body at the roll call stage.

Cluster bloc analysis poses some methodological problems. Since it summarizes individuals without regard to issues, the cluster bloc itself tells us nothing about the kinds of issues over which the legislators are agreed. It shares with index construction the problem of handling missing data (mainly absences); absences will lower a legislator's total number of agreements. More importantly, the Beyle-Truman technique

Member and District	\	1	2	3	9	10	14	15	18	19	8	16	5	6	7	11	12	13	20	17	21
								District Numbers													
Patman, 1st	\			59	54	57															
Combs, 2d		52	\	54																	
Beckworth, 3rd		59	54	\		58	54														
Thompson, 9th		54			\	58	58					55							52		
Thornberry, 10th		57		58	58	\	57														
Lyle, 14th		53		55	58	57	\			54											
Bentsen, 15th			51					\													
Worley, 18th		43		44	45	47	45		\	46	43					48		41		43	41
Mahon, 19th				52	55	51	53			\		52				52	52	52		52	51
Thomas, 8th											\										
Regan, 16th										46		\	53	49		52	50	48	49	49	
Wilson, 5th												53	\	61		59	56	58	61	58	
Teague, 6th													50	\		52	53	48	51	55	
Pickett, 7th													61		\	60	55	53	58	57	
Poage, 11th				46	50	52	48		48	52		47	47	46		\	51	46	49		47
Lucas, 12th												59		60			\	57	58	56	58
Gossett, 13th												56	53	55		57		\	54	56	58
Kilday, 20th												58		53		58	54		\	56	
Burleson, 17th												61		58		56	56	56		\	56
Fisher, 21st												58	55	57		58	58	52	56		\

Figure 21.2. CLUSTER BLOC SHOWING AGREEMENTS WITHIN THE TEXAS DELEGATION ON 74 ROLL CALLS, U.S. HOUSE OF REPRESENTATIVES, 81st CONGRESS

SOURCE: D. B. Truman, "The State Delegations and the Structure of Party Voting in the United States House of Representatives," *American Political Science Review*, L (1956), 1041.

does not provide a completely satisfactory guide for assigning legislators to clusters or for deciding what the cluster limits are.[37] Preparation of cluster blocs by hand for a legislative body of any size is laborious and involves a great deal of clerical work, although such analysis even for large legislatures would not present difficulty if computer facilities were utilized.

Scale analysis of legislative roll call votes stems from the cumulative scale model invented by Louis Guttman, and has been used for roll call analysis by MacRae, Belknap, Price, Aydelotte, Lingoes, and Patterson.[38] While the technology of scale analysis is rather complex, the basic logic is elementary. Perhaps Price's "building" example illustrates its logic as well as any. Suppose a man from Mars wanted to compare the heights of buildings in New York City, but had available to him no quantitative measurement concepts (metrics such as inches or feet). He could pick a series of buildings, rank-order them in terms of their heights, and use the rankings to classify all buildings in the city. Figure 21.3 provides a simple illustration. Buildings as high as the Empire State Building are also as high as the Chrysler Building and the

	As High As			Not As High As		
Class	Empire State Building	Chrysler Building	Guggenheim Museum	Empire State Building	Chrylser Building	Guggenheim Museum
Type I	X	X	X			
Type II		X	X	X		
Type III			X	X	X	
Type IV				X	X	X

Figure 21.3. PRICE'S BUILDING EXAMPLE OF CUMULATIVE SCALING

SOURCE: H. D. Price, "Are Southern Democrats Different? An Application of Scale Analysis to Senate Voting Patterns," in N. W. Polsby, R. A. Dentler, and P. A. Smith, (eds.), *Politics and Social Life* (Boston: Houghton Mifflin Company, 1963), p. 743.

Guggenheim Museum (type I); buildings not as high as the Empire State, but as high as Chrysler, are also as high as the Museum (type II), and so on. All the buildings in the city can be classified as falling into one of these categories in terms of their relative height, since the result is ordinal measurement of building height.

Exactly the same logic may be used to rank-order legislative issues, using roll call votes and groups of legislators who exhibit similar responses to these issues. With roll call data, the result of scaling will not be a perfect scale pattern of the sort idealized in Figure 21.3. Deviations will occur because of idiosyncracies in the voting responses of legislators, because our scales may not be perfectly unidimensional, or because of "measurement" errors. A "real-world" legislative scale is illustrated by Figure 21.4, which shows scale patterns for a sample of members of the Wisconsin Assembly in 1957 on ten "liberal-conserva-

Legislator	Scale Score	Conservative 1	2	3	4	5	6	7	8	9	10	Liberal 1	2	3	4	5	6	7	8	9	10
Baumgart	10	X	X	X	X	X	X	X	X	X	X										
Genzmer	10	X	X	0	X	X	0	X	0	X	X										
Grady	10	X	X	X	X	X	X	X	X	X	X										
Harper	10	X	X	X		X	X	X	X	X	X									(X)	
Hutnik	10	X	X	X	X	0	X	X	X	X	X										
Lewison	10	X	X	X	X	X	X	X	X	X	X										
Marotz	10	X	X	X	X	X	X	X	X	X	X										
Peters	10	X	X	0	X	X	0	X	X	X	X										
Rice	10	X	X	0	X		X	X	X	X	X									(X)	
Stauffer	10	X	X	X	X	X	X	X	X	0	X										
Abraham	9		X	X	X	X	X	X	X	X	X	X									
Anderson, J.	9		X	X	X	X	X	X	X	X	X	X									
Blanchard	9		X	X	X	X	X	X	X	X	X	X									
Huibregtse	9		X	X	X	X	X	X	X	0	X	X									
Metzner	9		X	X		X	X	X	X	X	X	X								(X)	
Pommerening	9		X	X	X	X	X	X	X	0	X	X									
Rewald	9		X	X	X	X	X	X	X	X	X	X									
Seymour	9		X	X	X	X	X	X	X	X	X	X									
Cane	8			X	X	0	X	X	X	X	X	X	0								
Heider	8			X	X	X	X	X	X	X	X	X	X								
Leonard	8			X	0	X	X	X	X	X	X	X	X								
McEssy	8			X	X		X	X	X	X	X	X	X							(X)	
Morton	7				X	0	0	X	X	0	X	X	X	X							
Sullivan	7	(X)			X	X	X	X	0	0	X	X	0								
Clemens	6					X	0	X	X	X	X	X	X	X	X						
Crawford	6					X	X	0	X	X		X	X	X	0						
Guell	6	(X)				X	X	X	X	X	X	X	X	X							
Haase	6					X	0	X	X	X	X	X	X	X	X						
Hagen	5						X	X	X	X	X	X	X	X	X	X					
Jahnke	5					(X)	X	X	X	X	X	X	0	0		X					
Schmidt, W.	5		(X)				X	0	X	X	X	0		X	X	0					
Peterson, J.	4			(X)				X	X	X	X	0	X		X	X	X				
Schmeischel	4		(X)	(X)				X	X	X	X	X		X		X	X				
Crowns	4					(X)			X	X	X	X	X	X	X	X		X			

Legislator	Scale Score	Conservative										Liberal									
		1	2	3	4	5	6	7	8	9	10	1	2	3	4	5	6	7	8	9	10
Lynch	3								X	X	X	0	X	X	0	0	0	X			
Timmerman	3								X	X	X	X	0	X	X	X	X	X	0		
Kostuck	2									X	X	X	X	X	X	X	X	X	X		
Coggs	1										X	X	X	X	X	X	X	X	X	X	0
Flannigan	1										X	X	X	0	X	X	X	X	X	X	
Hardie	1										X	X	X	X	X	X	X	X	X	X	X
Huber	1										X	X	X	X	X	X	X	X	X	X	X
Lauby	1										X	X	X	X	X	X	X	X	X	X	X
Luebke	1										X	X	X	X	X	X	X	X	X	X	X
Mogilka	1										X	X	X	X	X	X	X	X	X	X	X
Murphy	1										(X)	X	X	X	X	X	X	X	X	X	
Perala	1										X	X	X	X	X	X	X	X	X	X	X
Riehle	1										X	X	X	0	X	X	X	X	X	X	
Sokolowski	1										X	X	X	X	X	X	X	X	X	X	X
Warren	1										X	X	X	0	X	X	X	X	X	X	
Anderson, N.	0											X	X	X	X	X	X	X	X	X	X
Crane	0										(X)	X	X	X	X	X	X		X	X	X
Duffey	0											X	X	0	0	X	0	X	X	0	0
Molinaro	0											X	X	X	X	X	X	X	X	X	X
Naleid	0											X	X	X	X	X	X	X	X	X	0
Risser	0											X	X	X	X	X	X	X	X	X	X

* Circled items are errors.

NOTE: Coefficient of reproducibility $= 1 - \dfrac{\text{Sum of errors}}{\text{Total responses}} = .97$

Coefficient of scalability $= 1 - \dfrac{\text{Sum of errors}}{\text{Maximum errors}} = .94$

SOURCE: Patterson's study; the complete scale was used in S. C. Patterson, "Legislative Leadership and Political Ideology," *Public Opinion Quarterly*, XXVII (1963), 406-07.

tive" issues. It will be noted that both assemblymen and issues are ranked and that a remarkably consistent and systematic pattern of voting behavior is manifested.

Scale and cluster bloc analysis obviously have much in common, since legislators who have the same scale scores constitute a perfect cluster bloc for the issues under analysis, and two-dimensional cluster blocs can be constructed by cross-tabulating two or more scales.[39] However, these two types of analysis may or may not produce the same results, depending, among other things, upon the nature of the content of legislation under analysis.[40] Similarly, scale analysis and analysis based upon indices indicate quite different orderings of legislative choices, insofar as comparisons have been made.[41]

Numerous methodological problems are involved in using scale analysis with legislative roll call votes; perhaps the most notable of them are those of selecting roll calls to be scaled, treating the problem of missing data (absences, nonvoting), and testing the adequacy of the scale. The problem of selecting the universe of roll calls to be scaled has been handled in a variety of ways. In early scale analyses, the investigator chose roll calls for scaling by virtue of the content of the issues. He might select all civil rights roll calls, or all roll calls involving labor-management relations—issues or motions that he thought ought *prima facie* to belong to the same universe of content. This procedure works well enough, though it may leave the investigator in doubt about whether all scalable roll calls in the total population of roll calls have been discovered, and it is not entirely objective.

More objective methods of selecting universes of roll calls for analysis are now available, and ought to be used in future work. These methods involve successive comparisons between pairs of roll call votes as a means of selecting a homogeneous and scalable subset of votes. This can be done by using the conjunction count technique, in which each pair of roll calls is cross-tabulated by using fourfold tables, and arbitrary minimums are set for the so-called "zero cell" of these tables.[42] MacRae's "exponential model" simplifies this process somewhat.[43] Also, the paired comparisons can be evaluated using correlation techniques; this method has been adapted for computer processing, using programs that produce Kendall's Q correlation matrices.[44] Roll calls which share high intercorrelations (Q's) are selected for scaling. Finally, inter-item coefficients of reproducibility can be used to select scalable subsets of roll calls.[45]

Missing data lead to a number of difficulties in scale analysis, the main problem being that of assigning a scale score to a legislator when there is an absence in his voting pattern that occurs at a cut-off point in the scale. Scale analysis makes it possible to deal with absences in much more satisfactory ways than do index construction or cluster bloc analysis, but it does not resolve all the difficulties. Roll calls with the same (or roughly the same) marginals can be used together to construct one artificial or contrived item, and this procedure can help to reduce the effects of missing data. Scoring conventions have been developed to assign a scale score to a member where there is missing data for him at a cut-off point (by listing all possible scale assignments, averaging them, and rounding toward the median of the scale).[46]

Finally, scale analysis involves the problem of the adequacy of scales. The principal problems in this connection are those of dealing with "errors," responses that do not fit perfect scale patterns, and those that deal with the item marginals. Whether or not a scale contains too many errors has largely been resolved by using Guttman's coefficient of reproducibility, which "is secured by counting up the number of responses which would have been predicted wrongly for each person on the basis of his scale score, dividing these errors by the total number of responses and subtracting the resulting fraction from 1."[47] Menzel's coefficient of scalability provides a means of assessing the adequacy of the item marginals in a scale.[48] Obviously, if all of the issues selected for scaling passed the legislature 90–10, and a yea vote was counted positively for the scale in each case, the coefficient of reproducibility would be highly inflated by virtue of that fact; Menzel's coefficient tests the scale for adequate dispersion in item marginals. In addition, though they have been little used in scaling legislative roll call votes, significant tests have been developed for cumulative scales.[49]

Factor analysis is becoming more widely used in studies of legislative roll call votes. Multiple factor models are very complex, and although they can be used fairly easily, now that "canned" computer programs are widely available, they should not be used by those who do not understand the requirements of the statistical models. The student who enters the world of factor analysis will find that it is filled with disputants (mainly psychologists) over methods and applications. We cannot possibly discuss here the disputes that emerge in the factor analysis literature, much less resolve them.[50]

Factor analysis is a statistical technique that reduces the number of variables in a correlation table to a smaller number of artificial variables (or vectors), which may be said to constitute underlying or latent factors. Any correlation matrix can be factored, and thus the factor analysis can be interpreted only in terms of the logic or political relevance of the correlations. If the correlations do not make sense, the factor analysis will not make them more meaningful. Again, any table that represents correlations among variables may be factored in an infinite number of ways; the factor "solution" is indeterminate—it is not unique. The political scientist must select from an infinite number of possible alternative solutions; although analytical solutions are likely to be widely used, with the present availability of computer facilities, there has been insufficient experience with factor analysis of legislative data to warrant uncritical acceptance of any particular solution. Finally, the analyst must interpret the factors produced by the analysis. The factor loadings can (when the factor matrix is post-multiplied by its transpose) reproduce the original correlation matrix, but the political scientist has the problem of trying to determine what the factors are. This problem is a serious one, and probably involves as much art as science.

Two types of factor analysis have been applied to legislative roll call data: R technique and Q technique. The factor analysis in both cases may be exactly the same; the two techniques really only describe the nature of the correlations to be factored. R technique involves correlations of a series of roll call votes over a population of legislators; the correlations are between roll calls for all legislators.[51] This technique resembles scale analysis—and to some extent, analyses based upon indices —in that factor loadings from it are related to, or define, dimensions of issues or attitudes. The original factor models developed by Thurstone were designed to deal with correlations between items (or tests) for a population of individuals, and this technique presents fewer logical difficulties, in terms of the statistical models.

Q technique, or obverse factor analysis, involves correlation of a series of legislators over a population of roll call votes; the correlations are between legislators.[52] This kind of factor analysis resembles cluster bloc analysis in that the factor loadings will have legislators loaded on them; legislators with high loadings on a factor will constitute a cluster. By contrast, in R technique the factor loadings are for issues or motions. The major difficulties with Q technique arise in connection with the between-person correlations. The statistical problems here are fairly complex, and it is not our purpose to deal with them. Suffice it to say that a fundamental difficulty is that Q correlations require ipsative data —"The scores should be distributed about the mean of an individual for each individual, not about the mean of the population for each test."[53] In addition, the means for all individuals must be the same. Roll call data do not meet these requirements, and inter-individual correlations will be biased unless the data are transformed.[54]

Q and R techniques are useful for different purposes. The two techniques produce the same results only under very limited conditions. Comparisons between the two techniques for legislative data are very few indeed, although it seems fairly clear that Q technique, like cluster bloc analysis, tends to obscure the attitudinal dimension of the data.[55]

Factor analysis and scale analysis may be used together. The loadings from an R-type factor analysis may be converted into scales "arraying the representatives according to cumulative scores for each factor."[56] Or the scale analysis may precede the factor analysis. Factor analysis may be used as a way of "scaling scales" by intercorrelating Guttman scales and then factor-analyzing those correlations.[57] This latter procedure is very alluring, and probably the more promising of the two, although it involves overlooking the fact of the nonlinearity and nonmetric character of the scale scores.

NEED FOR COMPARATIVE RESEARCH

Legislative behavior research can best be pursued within the realm of what in political science is rather loosely referred to as the "comparative method." The most serious general weakness of the body of knowledge about legislative life is the lack of comparative perspective. As Eulau has pointed out, "discourse on 'comparative method' in political science was, quite properly, appropriated by the students of 'comparative government' who, in doing so, inadvertently expropriated the rest of the discipline."[58] But such an accident of history need not now serve to deter comparative analysis of American legislative institutions or to inhibit cross-national comparisons of legislative functions and behavior on the part of students of American legislatures.

Comparative research is imperative, if we are to build high-order empirical generalizations about legislative behavior. Generalizations developed in one legislative setting should be examined in another, both in order to identify uniformities and regularities in legislative behavior and to specify the unique or limiting characteristics of particular legislative systems. As Suchman has said,

Ultimately, a comparative methodology professes to provide a logic of analysis whereby the general nature of a phenomenon may be specified and the conditions that give rise to its specific manifestations explained. It attempts to do this by showing that the "causes" for a phenomenon discerned in one cultural context are equally "causal" when they occur in another cultural context. If they are not the same, or similar, then the cultural context is analyzed for the limiting conditions of the phenomenon in question.[59]

In terms of comparative legislative analysis, achievement of such a goal may be in the distant future. But some contemporary legislative research has approached this goal, and it should certainly be our "guiding star."

We can discern at least five distinct types of legislative comparison: (1) intra-institutional or subsystem comparison, (2) interstate or intercommunity comparison, (3) interlevel (national-state-local) comparison, (4) cross-national comparison, (5) historical comparisons. The first category, intra-institutional comparison, involves comparison of subsystems within a given legislative system. This is perhaps best illustrated in contemporary research by the work done by Fenno on congressional committees.[60] Interstate comparative analysis has as its leading example the work of the State Legislative Research Project.[61] Intercommunity legislative analysis is much needed and very uncommon in the literature.[62] Descriptive interlevel comparisons which include national and state legislatures are true of few general works on the legislative process in the United States (including this book), but interlevel hypothesis-testing is rare.[63]

Similarly, cross-national legislative analysis has tended, where it has been done at all, to be descriptive—involving data that describe institutional characteristics, practices, and procedures.[64] Cross-national behavioral data for individual legislators are essential for further development of comparative legislative research, and there are signs of effort in this direction.[65] Comparative analysis of legislative systems or subsystems within a single national culture reduces the difficulty of controlling cultural variation. Cross-national comparison raises the serious problem of conceptual equivalence. Legislative analysts have scarcely touched the problem of whether similar legislative structures or practices have the same meaning or function in different cultures, or indeed of whether the concept "legislature" itself is conceptually equivalent across cultures.

Finally, the historical comparison of legislative behavior is almost nonexistent.[66] Political scientists have ignored the legislative institutions of the past, and political historians have virtually done so. Legislative behavior research is seriously in need of developmental analysis showing similarities and differences in legislative institutions and behavior across time.

Until legislative behavior research develops a fully comparative methodology, a great deal of substantive knowledge needs to be filled in. We have much to learn about specific national, state, and local legislatures. We need to know more precisely how the political party system affects the legislature: its organizational structure, voting patterns, legislative turnover, and relations with the executive. The data necessary for comparative analysis can be found in states with one- and two-party systems, as well as in those in which a two-party system is emerging. The states in transition provide particularly valuable laboratories. Does party consciousness in the legislative party appear first in the emerging minority party? How quickly do the roles of the leadership change in a period of partisan change?

One advantage of tracing change in a single state is that the interstate variables (such as socioeconomic and historical factors) can be controlled. For this reason executive-legislative relations can be studied profitably within one state over a period of several administrations as well as on an interstate basis. Each governor has a personal impact on the office, and in some states changes in the term of office or legal or political aspects of the governorship make for a particularly timely study.

In states where the governor's legislative role has been minimal, how does he change the expectations of legislators and the public concerning this role? What happens when a weak governor comes into office in a state where the governor has traditionally been strong? In addition to probing these broader questions, we must collect specific, comprehensive evidence about the variety of techniques used by governors. How much patronage does a governor have, and how does he use it? How does he handle individual legislators and leaders? How does he perceive public opinion as a force to be mobilized in support of a legislative program?

Comparatively little is known about the legislator's campaign for office. How is he recruited? How much help, if any, does he get in his campaign? What is the voter's perception of and knowledge about legislative candidates? State legislative races have been almost completely ignored by the practitioners of survey research. How do the legislator's experience in a campaign and his perception of the electorate affect his roles as a legislator? Role analysis has been devoted almost entirely to questioning legislators. There are vast opportunities for correlating the roles articulated by legislators with such factors as the nature of their constituency, their electoral background, and the likelihood of competition in subsequent elections.

We have a dearth of factual information about the operation of committees and caucuses and the techniques of leadership practiced at the state level. Once this information has been collected and analyzed, it could be compared with legislators' perceptions concerning both leaders and the institutions of leadership. Do legislators perceive accurately interstate differences in the power of a Speaker or in the functions of committees in the legislative system? How does a legislative leader's role vary with differences in the mode of his selection? The scarcity of information on the organization and operation of legislative bodies is not limited to the states. One startling example of our information gaps is the lack of any adequate study of the Speaker of the United States House of Representatives, perhaps the second most important political figure in the country.

Methods of legislative research are developed to the point where we need to begin to apply them more, simply to provide a greater abundance of descriptive data. Some rather sophisticated techniques of legislative roll call analysis have already been described. What is probably needed more than further technical development is wider application of the methods that we now have available. The use of the same technique, the same measuring stick, for a variety of states and for legislative sessions under a variety of partisan conditions would strengthen our comparative analysis of legislative systems.[67]

RESEARCH AND THEORY

The technological progress in legislative behavior research and an insistence upon comparative legislative analysis must be anchored in, and contribute to, *theory*. A few political scientists have been concerned about the gap between research and theory in legislative behavior inquiry. As Wahlke and Eulau noted several years ago:

> Research on legislative behavior has been more sensitive to problems of technique than to problems of conceptual clarification. Yet, the most sophisticated technical developments, to be fruitful from the point of view of advancing knowledge about legislatures and legislative behavior, are meaningless unless research findings are presented in a theoretically, or at least conceptually, viable framework which will give more than *ad hoc* significance to the great variety of factors that constitute the legislative process.[68]

It may even be that the development of sophisticated methodological devices tends to inhibit, rather than facilitate, conceptual and theoretical advances. We now have the capacity to process tremendous quantities of data, and it may be tempting to do so without adequate theoretical clarification. If we have no adequate theoretical criteria for the selection of variables for analysis, there may be a tendency to treat all variables as if they were equally important. This would certainly be very unfortunate.

Structural-functional, systematic conceptual framework of the kind proposed by Wahlke and his associates, which we have utilized loosely in this book, are improvements over having no conceptual scheme at all. Yet we have a long way to go in theorizing about representation, the functions of legislatures and legislative systems, and decision making in legislative settings. Legislative behavior research must be accompanied by a constant concern for conceptual and theoretical development beyond mere operationalism.

NOTES

1. John C. Wahlke, "Behavioral Analyses of Representative Bodies," in Austin Ranney (ed.), *Essays on the Behavioral Study of Politics* (Urbana, Ill., 1962), p. 173.

2. Norman Meller, "Legislative Behavior Research," *Western Political Quarterly*, XIII (1960), 131–53.

3. See David Gold, "Lawyers in Politics: An Empirical Exploration of Biographical Data on State Legislators," *Pacific Sociological Review*, IV (1961), 84–86; Albert Somit and Joseph Tanenhaus, "The Veteran in the Electoral Process: The House of Representatives," *Journal of Politics*, XIX (1957), 184–201; and Heinz Eulau et al., "Career Perspectives of American State Legislators," in Dwaine Marvick (ed.), *Political Decision-makers* (New York, 1961), pp. 218–63.

4. The best example is Lester W. Milbrath, *The Washington Lobbyists* (Chicago, 1963).

5. See Donald R. Matthews, *The Social Background of Political Decision-makers* (New York, 1954), especially pp. 38–41. See also David R. Derge, "The Lawyer as Decision-maker in the American State Legislature," *Journal of Politics*, XXI (1959), 408–33; "The Lawyer in the Indiana General Assembly," *Midwest Journal of Political Science*, VI (1962), 19–53; Duncan MacRae, Jr., and Edith K. MacRae, "Legislators' Social Status and Their Votes," *American Journal of Sociology*, VI (1961), 599–603; and Samuel C. Patterson, "Intergenerational Occupational Mobility and Legislative Voting Behavior," *Social Forces*, XLIII (1964), 90–92.

6. John B. McConaughy, "Certain Personality Factors of State Legislators in South Carolina," *American Political Science Review*, XLIV (1950), 897–903; Lester W. Milbrath, "Latent Origins of Liberalism-Conservatism and Party Identification: A Research Note," *Journal of Politics*, XXIV (1962), 679–88; and Lester W. Milbrath and Walter W. Klein, "Personality Correlates of Political Participation," *Acta Sociologica*, VI (1962), 53–66.

7. A good recent example is Richard A. Brody and Edward R. Tufte, "Constituent-Congressional Communication on Fallout Shelters: The Congressional Polls," *Journal of Communication*, XIV (1964), 34–49.

8. See Donald R. Matthews, "The Folkways of the United States Senate: Conformity to Group Norms and Legislative Effectiveness," *American Political Science Review*, LIII (1959), 1064–89; compare Allan Kornberg, "The Rules of the Game in the Canadian House of Commons," *Journal of Politics*, XXVI (1964), 358–80. See also John C. Wahlke et al., *The Legislative System* (New York, 1962), 141–69.

9. Samuel C. Patterson, "Patterns of Interpersonal Relations in a State Legislative Group: The Wisconsin Assembly," *Public Opinion Quarterly*, XXIII (1959), 101–09; and Garland C. Routt, "Interpersonal Relationships and the Legislative Process," *Annals of the American Academy of Political and Social Science*, CXCV (1938), 129–36.

10. Heinz Eulau et al., "The Role of the Representative: Some Empirical Observations on the Theory of Edmund Burke," *American Political Science Review*, LIII (1959), 742–56; and Ralph M. Stogdill, Omar S. Goode, and David R. Day, "The Leader Behavior of United States Senators," *Journal of Psychology*, LVI (1963), 3–8.

11. Warren E. Miller and Donald E. Stokes, "Constituency Influence in Congress," *American Political Science Review*, LVII (1963), 45–56.

12. For example, see David B. Truman, *The Congressional Party* (New York, 1959); Julius Turner, *Party and Constituency: Pressures on Congress* (Baltimore, 1951); and Duncan MacRae, Jr., *Dimensions of Congressional Voting* (Berkeley, 1958).

13. Perhaps the outstanding case study in print is Stephen K. Bailey, *Congress Makes a Law* (New York, 1950).

14. See Laurence F. Schmeckebier and Roy B. Eastin, *Government Publications and Their Use* (Washington, D.C., 1961), especially pp. 119–77. *Ex post facto* editing of some legislative documents restricts their utility for some purposes. See, for instance, Howard N. Mantel, "The Congressional Record: Fact or Fiction of the Legislative Process," *Western Political Quarterly*, XII (1959), 981–95.

15. Ralph K. Huitt, "The Congressional Committee: A Case Study," *American Political Science Review*, XLVIII (1954), 340–65.

16. Donald R. Matthews, *U.S. Senators and Their World* (Chapel Hill, N.C., 1960), pp. 267–68.

17. Congressional roll calls are neatly summarized and subjected to preliminary analysis in the *Congressional Quarterly Weekly Report* and the *Congressional Quarterly Almanac*.

18. U.S. Bureau of the Census, *Congressional District Data Book* (Districts

of the 88th Congress)—A Statistical Abstract Supplement (Washington, D.C., 1963).

19. Routt, *op. cit.*, provides a rather unique illustration of direct-observation data.

20. A variety of techniques of small group research are available for potential use. See Sidney Verba, *Small Groups and Political Behavior* (Princeton, 1961); and Robert F. Bales, *Interaction Process Analysis* (Cambridge, Mass., 1950).

21. See Charles L. Clapp, *The Congressman: His Work As He Sees It* (Washington, D.C., 1963), pp. 1–7.

22. Charles O. Jones, "Representation in Congress: The Case of the House Agriculture Committee," *American Political Science Review*, LV (1961), 358–67; and "Notes on Interviewing Members of the House of Representatives," *Public Opinion Quarterly*, XXIII (1959), 404–06.

23. Donald R. Matthews, "Interviewing Procedures," *U.S. Senators and Their World*, pp. 269–72.

24. Wahlke et al., *op. cit.*, pp. 435–63; Patterson, "Patterns of Interpersonal Relations," *loc. cit.*; Frank J. Sorauf, *Party and Representation: Legislative Politics in Pennsylvania* (New York, 1963), pp. 155–62; and Wayne L. Francis, "Influence and Interaction in a State Legislative Body," *American Political Science Review*, LVI (1962), 953–60.

25. James A. Robinson, "Survey Interviewing among Members of Congress," *Public Opinion Quarterly*, XIV (1960), 127–38; Miller and Stokes, *loc. cit.* Systematic interviews with lobbyists have also been successful. See Milbrath, *The Washington Lobbyist*, pp. 359–66.

26. A. Lawrence Lowell, "The Influence of Party upon Legislation," *Annual Report of the American Historical Association*, I (1901), 321–543.

27. Stuart A. Rice, *Quantitative Methods in Politics* (New York, 1928), pp. 207–27; Herman C. Beyle, *Identification and Analysis of Attribute Cluster-Blocs* (Chicago, 1931).

28. The CQ indices have been rather seldom used, even though they are readily available for further analysis. But see Lewis A. Froman, "Inter-party Constituency Differences and Congressional Voting Behavior," *American Political Science Review*, LVII (1963), 57–61. Truman and Matthews have used similar indices. See Truman, *op. cit.*, pp. 326–29; Matthews, *U.S. Senators and Their World*, pp. 276–81.

29. Turner, *op. cit.*, pp. 23–24.

30. William J. Keefe, "Comparative Study of the Role of Political Parties in State Legislatures," *Western Political Quarterly*, IX (1956), 726–42; Malcolm E. Jewell, "Party Voting in American State Legislatures," *American Political Science Review*, XLIX (1955), 773–91.

31. Thomas A. Flinn, "Party Responsibility in the States: Some Causal Factors," *American Political Science Review*, LVIII (1964), 62; Wilder Crane, Jr., "A Caveat on Roll-call Studies of Party Voting," *Midwest Journal of Political Science*, IV (1960), 237–49; and Fred I. Greenstein and Elton F. Jackson, "A Second Look at the Validity of Roll-call Analysis," *Midwest Journal of Political Science*, VII (1963), 156–66.

32. This, in effect, was what was done by David Truman. See his "The State Delegations and the Structure of Party Voting in the United States House of Representatives," *American Political Science Review*, L (1956), 1023–56.

33. Essentially the problem is that of ecological correlations. See W. S. Robinson, "Ecological Correlations and the Behavior of Individuals," *American Sociological Review*, XV (1950), 351–57; and Austin Ranney, "The Utility and Limitations of Aggregate Data in the Study of Electoral Behavior," in Ranney, *op. cit.*, pp. 91–102. See also John G. Grumm, "The Means of Measuring Conflict and Cohesion in the Legislature," *Southwestern Social Science Quarterly*, XLIV (1964), 377–88.

34. See especially Beyle, *op. cit.*, pp. 26–83.

35. See Samuel P. Hayes, Jr., "Probability and Beyle's 'Index of Cohesion,'" *Journal of Social Psychology*, IX (1938), 161–67.

36. Truman, *The Congressional Party*, pp. 45–48, 320–30.

37. An effort has been made to resolve this problem by using correlation techniques. See John G. Grumm, "The Systematic Analysis of Blocs in the Study of Legislative Behavior," *Western Political Quarterly*, XVIII (1965), 350–62.

38. MacRae, *op cit.*, especially pp. 289–323; George M. Belknap, "A Method for Analyzing Legislative Behavior," *Midwest Journal of Political Science*, II (1958), 377–402; H. Douglas Price, "Are Southern Democrats Different? An Application of Scale Analysis to Senate Voting Patterns," in Nelson W. Polsby, Robert A. Dentler, and Paul A. Smith (eds.), *Politics and Social Life* (Boston, 1963), pp. 740–56; William O. Aydelotte, "Voting Patterns in the British House of Commons in the 1840s," *Comparative Studies in Society and History*, V (1963), 134–63; James C. Lingoes, "A Multiple Scalogram Analysis of Selected Issues of the 83rd U.S. Senate," *American Psychologist* (Abstract), XVII (1962), 327; Samuel C. Patterson, "Dimensions of Voting Behavior in a One-party State Legislature," *Public Opinion Quarterly*, XXVI (1962), 185–200.

39. See Price, *op. cit.*, pp. 749–50.

40. See MacRae, *op. cit.*, p. 303.

41. See *ibid.*, pp. 303–08, where party-unity indices and 6 cumulative scales for the 81st House of Representatives have been compared.

42. William O. Aydelotte, *op. cit.*, pp. 139–40; Matilda W. Riley, John W. Riley, Jr., and Jackson Toby, *Sociological Studies in Scale Analysis* (New Brunswick, N.J., 1954), chap. 15.

43. Duncan MacRae, Jr., "An Exponential Model for Assessing Fourfold Tables," *Sociometry*, XIX (1956), 84–94.

44. This technique is illustrated in Duncan MacRae, Jr., "Intraparty Divisions and Cabinet Coalitions in the Fourth French Republic," *Comparative Studies in Society and History*, V (1963), 164–211. Duncan MacRae, Mildred Wilkerson, and Theodore M. Feely, Jr., have developed a computer program for the IBM 1401 which produces, among other things, a matrix showing the Q correlation between all roll calls in a data deck. This program has been modified and rewritten for the IBM 7044 by James Whitely at the University of Iowa Computer Center.

45. James C. Lingoes, "Multiple Scalogram Analysis: A Set-theoretic Model for Analyzing Dichotomous Items," *Educational and Psychological Measurement*, XXIII (1963), 501–24.

46. MacRae, *Dimensions of Congressional Voting*, p. 321.

47. Samuel A. Stouffer et al., *Measurement and Prediction: Studies in Social Psychology in World War II*, vol. IV (Princeton, N.J., 1950), p. 77.

48. Herbert Menzel, "A New Coefficient for Scalogram Analysis," *Public Opinion Quarterly*, XVII (1953), 268–80.

49. See Philip C. Sagi, "A Statistical Test for the Significance of a Coefficient of Reproducibility," and Leo A. Goodman, "Simple Statistical Methods for Scalogram Analysis," both in *Psychometrika*, XXIV (1959), 19–43. See also Lingoes, "Multiple Scalogram Analysis: A Set-theoretic Model for Analyzing Dichotomous Items," pp. 509–10.

50. The basic statistical models for factor analysis are presented in L. L. Thurstone, *Multiple-factor Analysis* (Chicago, 1947). See also Harry H. Harmon, *Modern Factor Analysis* (Chicago, 1960); and Benjamin Fruchter, *Introduction to Factor Analysis* (Princeton, N.J., 1954). That this is a rapidly developing research tool is indicated by Chester W. Harris, "Some Recent Developments in Factor Analysis," *Educational and Psychological Measurement*, XXIV (1964), 193–206.

51. The best illustration of R technique with legislative roll call data is Chester W. Harris, "A Factor Analysis of Selected Senate Roll Calls, 80th Congress," *Educational and Psychological Measurement*, VII (1948), 583–91. See also Carl D. McMurray, "A Factor Method for Roll Call Studies," *American Behavioral Scientist*, VI (1963), 26–27.

52. The best example of Q technique is John G. Grumm, "A Factor Analysis of Legislative Behavior," *Midwest Journal of Political Science*, VII (1963), 336–56. See also Lingoes, "Multiple Scalogram Analysis: A Set-theoretic Model for Analyzing Dichotomous Items," pp. 517–18.

53. J. P. Guilford, *Psychometric Methods* (New York, 1954), p. 530.

54. See J. P. Guilford, "Preparation of Item Scores for the Correlations between Persons in a Q Factor Analysis," *Educational and Psychological Measurement*, XXIII (1963), 13–22.

55. See Lingoes, "Multiple Scalogram Analysis: A Set-theoretic Model for Analyzing Dichotomous Items," p. 518.

56. McMurray, "A Factor Method for Roll Call Vote Studies," p. 27.

57. See Lingoes, "A Multiple Scalogram Analysis of Selected Issues of the 83rd U.S. Senate," p. 327.

58. Heinz Eulau, "Comparative Political Analysis: A Methodological Note," *Midwest Journal of Political Science*, VI (1962), 397.

59. Edward A. Suchman, "The Comparative Method in Social Research," *Rural Sociology*, XXIX (1964), 126. See also Roy C. Macridis, *The Study of Comparative Government* (Garden City, N.Y., 1955).

60. Richard F. Fenno, Jr., "The House Appropriations Committee as a Political System: The Problem of Integration," *American Political Science Review*, LVI (1962), 310–24; and Frank J. Munger and Richard F. Fenno, Jr., *National Politics and Federal Aid to Education* (Syracuse, N.Y., 1962), pp. 106–36.

61. John C. Wahlke, Heinz Eulau, William Buchanan, and LeRoy C. Ferguson, "The Annals of Research: A Case of Collaboration in Comparative Study of Legislative Behavior," *American Behavioral Scientist*, IV (1961), 3–9.

62. Heinz Eulau is now conducting research on comparative local legislative behavior. See also Robert J. Huckshorn and Charles E. Young, "Study of Voting Splits on City Councils in Los Angeles County," *Western Political Quarterly*, XIII (1960), 479–97.

63. For example, Joseph P. Chamberlain, *Legislative Processes: National and State* (New York, 1936); and William J. Keefe and Morris S. Ogul, *The American Legislative Process: Congress and the States* (Englewood Cliffs, N.J., 1964). See also Samuel C. Patterson, "Legislative Leadership and Political Ideology," *Public Opinion Quarterly*, XXVII (1963), 399–410.

64. For example, K. C. Wheare, *Legislatures* (London, 1963); and George B. Galloway, *Congress and Parliament* (Washington, D.C., 1955).

65. See William H. Hunt, Wilder W. Crane, and John C. Wahlke, "Interviewing Political Elites in Cross-cultural Comparative Research," *American Journal of Sociology*, LXX (1964), 59–68; and Bruce M. Russett, "International Communication and Legislative Behavior: The Senate and the House of Commons," *Journal of Conflict Resolution*, VI (1962), 291–307.

66. See George B. Galloway, *History of the House of Representatives* (New York, 1961); and George H. Haynes, *The Senate of the United States* (Boston, 1938). The Inter-University Consortium for Political Research (Ann Arbor, Michigan) is beginning to retrieve congressional roll call, biographical, and constituency data which will eventually go back to the Continental Congress.

67. See Malcolm E. Jewell, "Comparative Research in State Legislative Politics" (Paper presented at a Conference on Research in Legislative Politics of the New York Legislative Internship Program, May 1, 1964); and the papers by Thomas R. Dye and Morris S. Ogul, published by the Pennsylvania State University Institute of Public Administration under the title *The Legislative Process in Congress and the States* (University Park, Pa., 1961).

68. John C. Wahlke and Heinz Eulau (eds.), *Legislative Behavior: A Reader in Theory and Research* (Glencoe, Ill., 1959), p. 355.

BIBLIOGRAPHY

Tʜɪs bibliography is not intended to be comprehensive, nor does it repeat all the references already listed in the footnotes. We have sought to select the published books and articles that are most likely to be of use to those who want to explore some aspects of legislative processes and behavior in greater depth. We have organized the bibliography according to the structure of this volume, and have provided brief descriptions of the longer or more important studies.

GENERAL

Few attempts have been made to include both national and state legislative bodies in a comprehensive study. One text that emphasizes the formal structure is Harvey Walker, *The Legislative Process* (New York, 1948). The most recent text, which also deals with the other components of the legislative system, is William J. Keefe and Morris S. Ogul, *The American Legislative Process: Congress and the States* (Englewood Cliffs, N.J., 1964). Two useful books of readings are Theodore J. Lowi, *Legislative Politics U.S.A.* (Boston, 1965), which is limited to Congress, and John C. Wahlke and Heinz Eulau, *Legislative Behavior* (Glencoe, Ill., 1959), which includes research at both the national and state levels.

Among the standard works on Congress are two by George B. Galloway, *The Legislative Process in Congress* (New York, 1953) and *History of the House of Representatives* (New York, 1961); the latter contains a wealth of historical information. Bertram M. Gross, in *The Legislative Struggle* (New York, 1953), analyzes the legislative process in terms of resolving group conflicts. A recent volume by Daniel M. Berman, *In Congress Assembled* (New York, 1964) emphasizes the formal organization and structure. Two volumes by Roland Young should be noted: *Congressional Politics in the Second World War* (New York, 1956) and *The American Congress* (New York, 1958); the latter includes a lengthy research guide and bibliography for students. A highly readable series of case studies by Stephen K. Bailey and Howard D. Samuel is found in *Congress at Work* (New York,

1952). A series of round-table talks at which congressmen discussed the operation of the House and their legislative roles is the source of a recent book by Charles L. Clapp, *The Congressman: His Work As He Sees It* (Washington, D.C., 1963). A two-volume study that provides historical perspective on the Senate is George H. Haynes, *The Senate of the United States* (Boston, 1938). Donald R. Matthews, in *U.S. Senators and Their World* (Chapel Hill, N.C., 1960), has combined statistical and interview data into a highly useful and imaginative analysis of the Senate. Two studies by knowledgeable journalists are lively, well-illustrated, but unsystematic: William S. White displays a point of view favorable to the Senate establishment in *Citadel* (New York, 1956); Neil MacNeil includes more historical background and factual detail in his study of the House, *Forge of Democracy* (New York, 1963). An excellent collection of essays reflecting the varied research skills of the contributors is available in a recent volume edited by Robert L. Peabody and Nelson W. Polsby, *New Perspectives on the House of Representatives* (Chicago, 1963).

A committee of the American Political Science Association, relying heavily on questionnaires sent to authorities in each state, studied state legislative practices and summarized its findings and recommendations in a volume edited by Belle Zeller, *American State Legislatures* (New York, 1954). State legislative politics are analyzed in a brief study by Malcolm E. Jewell, *The State Legislature* (New York, 1962). For a small but growing number of states there is a study of the legislature that is analytical and not merely descriptive and procedural. Among the best examples are: Hallie Farmer, *The Legislative Process in Alabama* (University, Ala., 1949); William Buchanan, *Legislative Partisanship: The Deviant Case of California* (Berkeley and Los Angeles, 1963); William C. Havard and Loren P. Beth, *The Politics of Mis-representation: Rural-Urban Conflict in the Florida Legislature* (Baton Rouge, La., 1962); Frank Sorauf, *Party and Representation: Legislative Politics in Pennsylvania* (New York, 1963); Gilbert Y. Steiner and Samuel K. Gove, *Legislative Politics in Illinois* (Urbana, Ill., 1960); and Duane Lockard, *New England State Politics* (Princeton, N.J., 1959).

Two of the most valuable sources of information on Congress are the publications of the *Congressional Quarterly*: its annual *Almanac* and its *Weekly Report*. These provide data on roll calls, the legislative histories of bills, and current information in great detail on the organizational structure and political controversies in Congress. Information about congressional districts can be found in the Bureau of the Census publication, *Congressional District Data Book*, and biographical information on congressmen can be found in the *Congressional Directory*. Comprehensive descriptive data on state legislatures can be found in a number of the publications of The Council of State Governments; see especially *The Book of the States*, issued biennially and containing many comparative tables on legislative organization. State "blue books" and manuals pertaining to legislative organization, rules, and elections vary widely in scope and detail. Their contents have been summarized by Charles Press and Oliver Williams in *State Manuals, Blue Books, and Election Results* (Berkeley, Calif., 1962).

There are a number of case studies concerning passage of legislation in

Congress. Among the most useful are: Stephen K. Bailey, *Congress Makes a Law* (New York, 1950); Daniel M. Berman, *A Bill Becomes a Law* (New York, 1962); Fred W. Riggs, *Pressures on Congress: A Study of the Repeal of Chinese Exclusion* (New York, 1950); and H. Douglas Price, "Race, Religion, and the Rules Committee: The Kennedy Aid-to-Education Bills," in Alan F. Westin (ed.), *The Uses of Power* (New York, 1962).

I. THE LEGISLATIVE SYSTEM

The only extensive investigation of American legislative systems is the four-state study by John C. Wahlke, Heinz Eulau, William Buchanan, and LeRoy C. Ferguson, *The Legislative System* (New York, 1962). Two works by David Easton deal with the problems of political systems analysis: *The Political System* (New York, 1953) and *A Framework for Political Analysis* (Englewood Cliffs, N.J., 1965). We owe much of our understanding of legislative roles to the work of David Truman, especially in *The Governmental Process* (New York, 1951). Students of political systems in this country have borrowed heavily from students of comparative politics, notably Gabriel A. Almond, "A Functional Approach to Comparative Politics," in G. A. Almond and J. S. Coleman (eds.), *The Politics of Developing Areas* (Princeton, N.J., 1960). Many of the concepts and interpretations of Talcott Parsons, e.g., *The Social System* (Glencoe, Ill., 1951), have been applied generally to American politics by William C. Mitchell, *The American Polity* (New York, 1962).

Other Sources

Birch, A. H., *Representative and Responsible Government* (London, 1964).

deGrazia, Alfred, *Public and Republic: Political Representation in America* (New York, 1951).

Fairlie, John A., "The Nature of Political Representation," *American Political Science Review*, XXXIV (1940), 236–48, 456–66.

Friedrich, Carl J., *Man and His Government* (New York, 1963).

Gilbert, Charles E., "Operative Doctrines of Representation," *American Political Science Review*, LVII (1963), 604–18.

Pitkin, Hanna, "Hobbes' Concept of Representation," *American Political Science Review*, LVIII (1964), 328–40.

Riker, William H., "The Senate and American Federalism," *American Political Science Review*, XLIX (1955), 452–69.

Sutton, Francis X., "Representation and the Nature of Political Systems," *Comparative Studies in Society and History*, II (1959), 1–10.

II. SELECTION OF LEGISLATORS

Among the best concise treatments of districting and apportionment are Andrew Hacker, *Congressional Districting* (Washington, D.C., 1963); Gordon E. Baker, *The Reapportionment Revolution* (New York, 1966); and Paul T. David and Ralph Eisenberg, *State Legislative Districting* (Chicago, 1962). A useful collection of readings edited by Howard D. Hamilton, *Legislative Apportionment: Key to Power* (New York, 1964), sets forth the major arguments and court decisions. A volume designed particularly for student research projects is Glendon Schubert, *Reapportionment* (New York, 1965). In Malcolm E. Jewell (ed.), *The Politics of Reapportionment* (New York, 1962), case studies are used to analyze the problem in terms of the political process. The judicial aspects of the apportionment controversy have been discussed frequently in the law journals, notably in a symposium in the *Yale Law Review*, LXXII (1962), 1–106. Brief state-by-state summaries have been compiled by the National Municipal League in its *Compendium on Legislative Apportionment*, which is revised periodically; the League's monthly *National Civic Review* reports regularly on apportionment developments in the states. The *Congressional Quarterly* periodically provides statistical tables and state-by-state summaries of congressional districting and legislative apportionment in its *Weekly Report*. A comprehensive measurement of the value of the vote in state legislatures as of 1961 is available in companion volumes by Paul T. David and Ralph Eisenberg, *Devaluation of the Urban and Suburban Vote*, 2 vols. (Charlottesville, Va., 1961–62).

Compilations of the congressional vote can be found in: Cortez A. M. Ewing, *Congressional Elections, 1896–1944* (Norman, Okla., 1947); the biennial volumes of *America Votes* (Washington, D. C.) since 1952; the *Congressional Directory*; and the *Congressional Quarterly Weekly Report*. Legislative election statistics are published in some states in manuals, in reports by the Secretary of State, or in publications by state universities—these contain historical data. There have been few published analyses of American legislative elections. Two studies that use survey research data are Angus Campbell and Homer C. Cooper, *Group Differences in Attitudes and Votes: A Study of the 1954 Congressional Election* (Ann Arbor, Mich., 1956); and William N. McPhee and William A. Glaser, *Public Opinion and Congressional Elections* (New York, 1962). Charles O. Jones has analyzed "The Role of the Campaign in Congressional Politics" in a chapter of Harmon Zeigler and Kent Jennings (eds.), *The Electoral Process* (Englewood Cliffs, N.J., 1966). The starting point for research in state legislative elections is V. O. Key, Jr., *American State Politics* (New York, 1956).

Biographical information on congressmen is available in volumes of the *Congressional Directory* and in the *Biographical Directory of the American Congress, 1774–1961* (House Doc. 442, 85th Cong., 2nd Sess.). Data for state legislators is found in state manuals as described by Press and Williams, *State Manuals, Blue Books, and Election Results*. Published studies of the characteristics of legislators are usually limited to a single legislature. Note particularly Donald R. Matthews, *The Social Background of Political Decision-makers* (New York, 1954), as well as his *U.S. Senators and Their World;* and David R. Derge, "The Lawyer as Decision-maker in the American State Legislature," *Journal of Politics*, XXI (1959), 408–33.

Other Sources

Baker, Gordon E., *The Politics of Reapportionment in Washington State* (New York, 1960).

Cox, Edward F., "Congressional District Party Strength and the 1960 Election," *Journal of Politics*, XXIV (1962), 277–302.

de Grazia, Alfred, *Apportionment and Representative Government* (New York, 1963).

Eulau, Heinz, and John D. Sprague, *Lawyers in Politics: A Study in Professional Convergence* (Indianapolis, 1964).

Gore, William J., and Robert L. Peabody, "The Functions of the Political Campaign: A Case Study," *Western Political Quarterly*, XI (1958), 55–70.

Havard, William C., and Loren P. Beth, *Representative Government and Reapportionment: A Case Study of Florida* (Gainesville, Fla., 1960).

Jones, Charles O., "Inter-party Competition for Congressional Seats," *Western Political Quarterly*, XVII (1964), 461–76.

Key, V. O., Jr., "The Direct Primary and Party Structure: A Study of State Legislative Nominations," *American Political Science Review*, XLVIII (1954), 1–26.

Klain, Maurice, "A New Look at the Constituencies: The Need for a Recount and a Reappraisal," *American Political Science Review*, XLIX (1955), 1105–19.

Lamb, Karl A., William J. Pierce, and John P. White, *Apportionment and Representative Institutions: The Michigan Experience* (Washington, D.C., 1963).

March, James G., "Party Legislative Representation as a Function of Election Results," *Public Opinion Quarterly*, XXI (1957–58), 521–42.

Page, Thomas, *Legislative Apportionment in Kansas* (Lawrence, Kan., 1952).

Press, Charles, "Presidential Coattails and Party Cohesion," *Midwest Journal of Political Science*, VII (1963), 320–35.

———, "Voting Statistics and Presidential Coattails," *American Political Science Review*, LII (1958), 1041–50.

Standing, William H., and James A. Robinson, "Inter-party Competition and Primary Contesting: The Case of Indiana," *American Political Science Review*, LII (1958), 1066–77.

Stokes, Donald E., and Warren E. Miller, "Party Government and the Salience of Congress," *Public Opinion Quarterly*, XXVI (1962), 531–46.

Walker, David B., "The Age Factor in the 1958 Congressional Elections," *Midwest Journal of Political Science*, IV (1960), 1–26.

Witmer, T. Richard, "The Aging of the House," *Political Science Quarterly*, LXXIX (1964), 526–41.

III. LEGISLATIVE ORGANIZATION AND PROCEDURE

Most of the works cited in the General section above give a substantial amount of attention to this topic. One additional book that emphasizes rules and procedures is Floyd M. Riddick, *The United States Congress: Organization and Procedure* (Manassas, Va., 1949). A valuable specialized study is Franklin L. Burdette, *Filibustering in the Senate* (Princeton, N.J., 1940). A classic work by Woodrow Wilson, first published in 1885, is *Congressional Government* (Cleveland, 1956). Party organizations in Congress have received little attention in depth; two exceptions are Hugh A. Bone, "An Introduction to the Senate Policy Committees," *American Political Science Review*, L (1956), 339–59, and Charles O. Jones, *Party and Policy-making: The House*

Republican Policy Committee (New Brunswick, N.J., 1964). Another void has been filled by James Robinson's concise study of *The House Rules Committee* (Indianapolis, 1963), and by several chapters in Peabody and Polsby, *New Perspectives on the House of Representatives.* The party organization of the U.S. House of Representatives has been described in further detail by Randall B. Ripley, "The Party Whip Organizations in the United States House of Representatives," *American Political Science Review,* LVIII (1964), 561–76. Biographies of congressional leaders usually dwell more on personalities than on the techniques of leadership; this is true of C. Dwight Dorough, *Mr. Sam* (New York, 1962), and William S. White, *The Taft Story* (New York, 1954). Studies of Lyndon Johnson more often discuss techniques of leadership; the best example is Ralph K. Huitt, "Democratic Party Leadership in the Senate," *American Political Science Review,* LV (1961), 333–44.

Several journal articles provide our best knowledge of congressional committee structure: George Goodwin, Jr., "The Seniority System in Congress," *American Political Science Review,* LIII (1959), 412–36, and "Subcommittees: The Miniature Legislatures of Congress," *American Political Science Review,* LVI (1962), 596–604; Nicholas A. Masters, "House Committee Assignments," *American Political Science Review,* LV (1961), 345–57; V. Stanley Vardys, "Select Committees of the House of Representatives," *Midwest Journal of Political Science,* VI (1962), 247–65. The most comprehensive study of congressional staffing now available is Kenneth Kofmehl, *Professional Staffs of Congress* (Lafayette, Ind., 1962). Of the several studies dealing with the legislative council movement in the states, the best analytical volume is by William J. Siffin, *The Legislative Council in the American States* (Bloomington, Ind., 1959).

Since 1959, Charles B. Brownson, a former congressman, has compiled and edited an annual volume on congressional staffs. The *Congressional Staff Directory* contains biographical material on key congressional staff personnel, as well as a great deal of detailed information on the personnel and organization of committee and member staffs.

Other Sources

Beck, Carl, *Contempt of Congress* (New Orleans, 1959).

Beth, Loren P., and William C. Havard, "Committee Stacking and Political Power in Florida," *Journal of Politics,* XXIII (1961), 57–83.

Breckenridge, Adam C., *One House for Two* (Washington, D.C., 1957).

Cochrane, James D., "Partisan Aspects of Congressional Committee Staffing," *Western Political Quarterly,* XVII (1964), 338–48.

Farnsworth, David N., *The Senate Committee on Foreign Relations* (Urbana, Ill., 1961).

Green, Harold P., and Alan Rosenthal, *Government of the Atom* (New York, 1963).

Jones, Charles O., "The Role of the Congressional Subcommittee," *Midwest Journal of Political Science,* VI (1962), 327–44.

Kampelman, Max M., "The Legislative Bureaucracy: Its Response to Political Change," *Journal of Politics,* XVI (1954), 539–50.

Lee, Eugene C., *The Presiding Officer and Rules Committee in Legislatures of the United States* (Berkeley, Calif., 1952).

Littlewood, Thomas B., *Bipartisan Coalition in Illinois* (New York, 1960).

Mann, Dean E., "The Legislative Committee System in Arizona," *Western Political Quarterly*, XIV (1961), 925-41.

Riker, William H., "The Paradox of Voting and Congressional Rules for Voting on Amendments," *American Political Science Review*, LII (1958), 349-66.

Rosenthal, Alan, *Toward Majority Rule in the United States Senate* (New York, 1962).

Shuman, Howard E., "Senate Rules and the Civil Rights Bill: A Case Study," *American Political Science Review*, LI (1957), 955-75.

Winslow, C. I., *State Legislative Committees: A Study in Procedure* (Baltimore, 1931).

IV. PARTICIPANTS IN THE LEGISLATIVE PROCESS

Lester W. Milbrath's book, *The Washington Lobbyists* (Chicago, 1963), is the first systematic study of the subject and is based upon intensive interviewing. The lobbying process is the central focus of David B. Truman, *The Governmental Process*, which remains a standard work. The results of an extensive survey of opinion formation and lobbying by business interests in connection with reciprocal trade legislation are analyzed in an outstanding study: Raymond Bauer, Ithiel Pool, and Lewis A. Dexter, *American Business and Public Policy* (New York, 1963).

The President's role as a legislative leader has seldom been studied as a separate topic, but it is covered at some length in several of the better studies of the Presidency. Richard E. Neustadt is concerned with the strategy of leadership in *Presidential Power* (New York, 1960). Two books that cover the cabinet and its legislative involvement are Stephen Horn, *The Cabinet and Congress* (New York, 1960); and Richard F. Fenno, Jr., *The President's Cabinet* (New York, 1959). Wilfred E. Binkley's treatment is historical in *President and Congress* (New York, 1962). Among the few studies of the state governor are two by Coleman B. Ransone, Jr., *The Office of Governor in the United States* (University, Ala., 1956), and *The Office of Governor in the South* (University, Ala., 1951).

Two recent publications describe the use of polls by congressmen to assess the opinions of their constituents: Carl F. Hawver, *The Congressman's Conception of His Role* (Washington, D.C., 1963); and Leonard A. Marascuilo and Harriett Amster, "Survey of 1961-1962 Congressional Polls," *Public Opinion Quarterly*, XXVIII (1964), 497-506.

Other Sources

Chamberlain, Lawrence H., *The President, Congress, and Legislation* (New York, 1946).

Cherington, Paul W., and Ralph L. Gillen, *The Business Representative in Washington* (Washington, D.C., 1962).

Eulau, Heinz, "Lobbyists: The Wasted Profession," *Public Opinion Quarterly*, XXVIII (1964), 27–38.

Freeman, J. Leiper, *The Political Process: Executive Bureau–Legislative Committee Relations* (Garden City, N. Y., 1955).

Garceau, Oliver, and Corinne Silverman, "A Pressure Group and the Pressured: A Case Report," *American Political Science Review*, XLVIII (1954), 672–691.

Jones, Charles O., "Representation in Congress: The Case of the House Agriculture Committee," *American Political Science Review*, LV (1961), 358–67.

Lane, Edgar, *Lobbying and the Law* (Berkeley and Los Angeles, 1964).

Latham, Earl, *The Group Basis of Politics: A Study of Basing Point Legislation* (Ithaca, N.Y., 1952).

Maas, Arthur, *Muddy Waters* (Cambridge, Mass., 1951).

Miller, Warren E., and Donald E. Stokes, "Constituency Influence in Congress," *American Political Science Review*, LVII (1963), 45–56.

Neustadt, Richard E., "Presidency and Legislation: Planning the President's Program," *American Political Science Review*, XLIX (1955), 980–1021.

———, "Presidency and Legislation: The Growth of Central Clearance," *American Political Science Review*, XLVIII (1954), 641–71.

Polsby, Nelson W., *Congress and the Presidency* (Englewood Cliffs, N.J., 1964).

Robbins, Robert R. (ed.), *State Government and Public Responsibility, 1961: The Role of the Governor of Massachusetts* (Medford, Mass., 1961).

V. THE LEGISLATURE AS A SOCIAL SYSTEM

Few attempts have been made heretofore to view the legislative body as a social system, by examining legislative norms and roles. The most definitive is the comparative analysis of legislative behavior in Ohio, Tennessee, New Jersey, and California presented in Wahlke, Eulau, Buchanan, and Ferguson, *The Legislative System*. Senate norms have been analyzed by Matthews in *U.S. Senators and Their World*, and the norms of the House Appropriations Committee by Richard F. Fenno, Jr., in "The House Appropriations Committee as a Political System: The Problem of Integration," *American Political Science Review*, LVI (1962), 310–24. Other studies that bear directly upon legislative norms and roles are those of Harris, Huitt, Dexter, MacRae, and Patterson.

Other Sources

Barber, James D., *The Lawmakers* (New Haven, Conn., 1965).

Dexter, Lewis A., "The Representative and His District," *Human Organization*, XVI (1957), 2–13.

Eulau, Heinz, "Bases of Authority in Legislative Bodies: A Comparative Analysis," *Administrative Science Quarterly*, VII (1962), 309–21.

———, John C. Wahlke, William Buchanan, and LeRoy C. Ferguson, "The Role of the Representative: Some Empirical Observations on the Theory of Edmund Burke," *American Political Science Review*, LIII (1959), 742–756.

Fiellin, Alan, "The Functions of Informal Groups in Legislative Institutions: A Case Study," *Journal of Politics*, XXIV (1962), 72–91.

Harris, Joseph P., "The Courtesy of the Senate," *Political Science Quarterly*, LXVII (1952), 36–63.

Huitt, Ralph K., "The Congressional Committee: A Case Study," *American Political Science Review*, XLVIII (1954), 340–65.

———, "The Morse Committee Assignment Controversy: A Study in Senate Norms," *American Political Science Review*, LI (1957), 313–29.

———, "The Outsider in the Senate: An Alternative Role," *American Political Science Review*, LV (1961), 566–75.

MacRae, Duncan, Jr., "The Role of the State Legislator in Massachusetts," *American Sociological Review*, XIX (1954), 185–94.

Patterson, Samuel C., "Patterns of Interpersonal Relations in a State Legislative Group: The Wisconsin Assembly," *Public Opinion Quarterly*, XXIII (1959), 101–09.

———, "The Role of the Deviant in the State Legislative System: The Wisconsin Assembly," *Western Political Quarterly*, XIV (1961), 460–72.

Silverman, Corinne, "The Legislators' View of the Legislative Process," *Public Opinion Quarterly*, XVIII (1954), 180–90.

Smith, T. V., *The Legislative Way of Life* (Chicago, 1940).

VI. THE LEGISLATURE IN ACTION

The major investigations of congressional voting behavior have been those of Turner, Truman, and MacRae. Using indices of party unity, cohesion, and likeness, Julius Turner correlated partisan and areal factors with roll call voting in *Party and Constituency: Pressures on Congress* (Baltimore, 1951). Concentrating on the 81st Congress, David B. Truman analyzed roll call clusters in *The Congressional Party* (New York, 1959); and Duncan MacRae, Jr., in *Dimensions of Congressional Voting* (Berkeley, Calif., 1958), submitted roll calls to cumulative scale analysis. A forthcoming study of the Survey Research Center of the University of Michigan correlated voting with data on constituent and congressional opinions. General studies of state legislative roll calls include: Malcolm E. Jewell, "Party Voting in American State Legislatures," *American Political Science Review*, XLIX (1955), 773–91, a comparative study of eight states; William J. Keefe, "Comparative Study of the Role of Political Parties in State Legislatures," *Western Political Quarterly*, IX (1956), 726–42; Thomas A. Flinn, "Party Responsibility in the States: Some Causal Factors," *American Political Science Review*, LVIII (1964), 60–71; and numerous studies of individual state legislatures.

We have some knowledge of the work of a few congressional committees. In *The House of Representatives and Foreign Affairs* (Pittsburgh, 1958), Holbert N. Carroll analyzes the House committees on foreign affairs and appropriations. *The Senate Committee on Foreign Relations* is a book by David N. Farnsworth. See also Malcolm E. Jewell, *Senatorial Politics and Foreign Policy*

(Lexington, Ky., 1962). Green and Rosenthal, in *Government of the Atom*, examine the work of the Joint Committee on Atomic Energy. The House Committee on Appropriations and the Senate Committee on Banking and Currency have been subjects of study by Richard Fenno and Ralph K. Huitt, respectively. Congressional revenue and credit committees have been analyzed by Huitt in "Congressional Organization and Operations in the Field of Money and Credit," in William Fellner et al., *Fiscal and Debt Management Policies* (Englewood Cliffs, N.J., 1963), pp. 399–495. Fenno has studied the committees on education, and some of his findings are in Frank J. Munger and Richard F. Fenno, Jr., *National Politics and Federal Aid to Education* (Syracuse, N.Y., 1962). The House Rules Committee has been investigated by Robinson (*The House Rules Committee*), and Peabody (in Polsby and Peabody, *New Perspectives on the House of Representatives*). Gilbert Y. Steiner provides a standard study of *The Congressional Conference Committee* (Urbana, Ill., 1951). A study of what has perhaps been the outstanding congressional investigating committee is that of Donald H. Riddle, *The Truman Committee: A Study in Congressional Responsibility* (New Brunswick, N.J., 1964). A general analysis of congressional oversight of the executive branch is Joseph Harris, *Congressional Control of Administration* (Washington, D.C., 1964). Harris has also examined the activities of the U.S. Senate in dealing with presidential nominations and treaties in *The Advice and Consent of the Senate* (Berkeley, Calif., 1954). Congressional fiscal control is the special focus of studies by Robert A. Wallace, *Congressional Control of Federal Spending* (Detroit, 1960); and Elias Huzar, *The Purse and the Sword* (Ithaca, N.Y., 1950).

Two excellent volumes deal specifically with the relationships in recent years between Congress and the federal courts: Walter F. Murphy, *Congress and the Court* (Chicago, 1962); and C. Herman Pritchett, *Congress Versus the Supreme Court* (Minneapolis, 1961).

From the large bibliography on foreign policy, we can cite a few studies that devote substantial attention to Congress. A standard work is Robert A. Dahl, *Congress and Foreign Policy* (New York, 1950). James A. Robinson, in *Congress and Foreign Policy-making* (Homewood, Ill., 1962), deals primarily with congressional initiative and legislative-executive liaison; this book contains an excellent bibliography. Cecil V. Crabb describes several cases of foreign policy making in *Bipartisan Foreign Policy—Myth or Reality?* (Evanston, Ill., 1957). Two studies of Congress include analysis of roll calls and the policy-making process: H. Bradford Westerfield, *Foreign Policy and Party Politics* (New Haven, Conn., 1955); and Charles O. Lerche, *The Uncertain South* (Chicago, 1964). The books by Jewell (*Senatorial Politics and Foreign Policy*) and Carroll (*The House of Representatives and Foreign Affairs*) are good companions. The best analytical case study is Bernard C. Cohen, *The Political Process and Foreign Policy: The Making of the Japanese Peace Settlement* (Princeton, N.J., 1957).

Other Sources

Derge, David R., "Metropolitan and Outstate Alignments in Illinois and

Missouri Legislative Delegations," *American Political Science Review,* LII (1958), 1051–65.

Dye, Thomas R., "A Comparison of Constituency Influences in the Upper and Lower Chambers of a State Legislature," *Western Political Quarterly,* XIV (1961), 473–80.

Francis, Wayne L., "Influence and Interaction in a State Legislative Body," *American Political Science Review,* LVI (1962), 953–60.

Froman, Lewis A., Jr., *Congressmen and Their Constituencies* (Chicago, 1963).

Gordon, Bernard K., "The Military Budget: Congressional Phase," *Journal of Politics,* XXIII (1961), 689–710.

Grassmuck, George L., *Sectional Biases in Congress on Foreign Policy* (Baltimore, 1951).

Havens, Murray G., *City Versus Farm?* (University, Ala., 1957).

Haviland, H. Field, Jr., "Foreign Aid and the Policy Process: 1957," *American Political Science Review,* LII (1958), 689–724.

Hilsman, Roger, "Congressional-Executive Relations and the Foreign Policy Consensus," *American Political Science Review,* LII (1958), 725–45.

Jewell, Malcolm E., "Evaluating the Decline of Southern Internationalism through Senatorial Roll Call Votes," *Journal of Politics,* XXI (1959), 624–46.

Karsch, Robert F., *The Standing Committees of the Missouri General Assembly* (Columbia, Mo., 1959).

Keefe, William J., "Parties, Partisanship, and Public Policy in the Pennsylvania Legislature," *American Political Science Review,* XLVIII (1954), 450–64.

MacRae, Duncan, Jr., "The Relation between Roll Call Votes and Constituencies in the Massachusetts House of Representatives," *American Political Science Review,* XLVI (1952), 1046–55.

Parsons, Malcolm B., "Quasi-partisan Conflict in a One-party Legislative System: The Florida Senate, 1947–1961," *American Political Science Review,* LVI (1962), 605–14.

Patterson, Samuel C., "Dimensions of Voting Behavior in a One-party State Legislature," *Public Opinion Quarterly,* XXVI (1962), 185–200.

Rieselbach, LeRoy N., "The Demography of the Congressional Vote on Foreign Aid, 1939–1958," *American Political Science Review,* LVIII (1964), 577–88.

Riker, William H., and Donald Niemi, "Stability of Coalitions on Roll Calls in the House of Representatives," *American Political Science Review,* LVI (1962), 58–65.

Scher, Seymour, "Conditions for Legislative Control," *Journal of Politics,* XXV (1963), 526–51.

Still, Rae F., *The Gilmer-Aikin Bills: A Study in the Legislative Process* (Austin, Tex., 1950).

Watson, Richard A., "The Tariff Revolution: A Study of Shifting Party Attitudes," *Journal of Politics,* XVIII (1956), 678–701.

VII. CONCLUSIONS

Congressional reformers have available to them a wide and elaborate literature. In the academic world, congressional reform is most identified with the work of James M. Burns, especially his *Congress on Trial* (New York, 1949) and *The Deadlock of Democracy* (Englewood Cliffs, N.J., 1963). Senator Joseph S. Clark has reiterated most of the contemporary arguments in *Congress: The Sapless Branch* (New York, 1964), and in a collection entitled *Congressional Reform: Problems and Prospects* (New York, 1964). Two recent conferences on Congress have produced useful volumes: Michael O'Leary (ed.), *Congressional Reorganization: Problems and Prospects* (Hanover, N.H., 1964); and David B. Truman (ed.), *The Congress and America's Future* (Englewood Cliffs, N.J., 1965).

Two essays that summarize legislative behavior research critically are Norman Meller, "Legislative Behavior Research," *Western Political Quarterly,* XIII (1960), 131–53; and John C. Wahlke, "Behavioral Analyses of Representative Bodies," in Austin Ranney (ed.), *Essays on the Behavioral Study of Politics* (Urbana, Ill., 1962). Some problems of comparative research on state legislative behavior are discussed in Wahlke et al., *The Legislative System.*

Other Sources

Anderson, Lee F., "Variability in the Unidimensionality of Legislative Voting," *Journal of Politics,* XXVI (1964), 568–85.

Andrain, Charles F., "A Scale Analysis of Senators' Attitudes toward Civil Rights," *Western Political Quarterly,* XVII (1964), 488–503.

Belknap, George M., "A Method for Analyzing Legislative Behavior," *Midwest Journal of Political Science,* II (1958), 377–402.

Coleman, James S., "Collective Decisions," *Sociological Inquiry,* XXXIV (1964), 166–81.

Eulau, Heinz, "Logics of Rationality in Unanimous Decision-making," in Carl J. Friedrich (ed.), *Rational Decision: Nomos VII* (New York, 1964), pp. 26–54.

Farris, Charles D., "A Method of Determining Ideological Groupings in the Congress," *Journal of Politics,* XX (1958), 308–38.

Grumm, John G., "A Factor Analysis of Legislative Behavior," *Midwest Journal of Political Science,* VII (1963), 336–56.

Harris, Chester W., "A Factor Analysis of Selected Senate Roll Calls, 80th Congress," *Educational and Psychological Measurement,* VIII (1948), 583–91.

Hunt, William H., Wilder W. Crane, Jr., and John C. Wahlke, "Interviewing Political Elites in Cross-cultural Comparative Research," *American Journal of Sociology,* LXX (1964), 59–68.

Price, H. Douglas, "Are Southern Democrats Different? An Application of Scale Analysis to Senate Voting Patterns," in Nelson W. Polsby, Robert A. Dentler, and Paul A. Smith (eds.), *Politics and Social Life* (Boston, 1963), pp. 740–56.

INDEX